N.º 6. OLD BOND STREET.

Bought of Love & Kelly,
Goldsmiths & Jewellers.

1808

London

Bo.t of Randall & Son
Wine & Brandy Merchants

N.B Bottles, Hampers &c to be paid for or returned.

£439. 6. 8

due on the above 50. 2. 4

£489. 9. 0

Sun Brewhouse.

ANN MATTAM,
AMBER, & TABLE BEER
BREWER,
ARRINGTON PLACE,
HYDE-PARK CORNER.
C. H. Reynell, Printer, No. 21,
Piccadilly, London.

March 5.th 18 19

Messrs. Hammersleys & C.º

Pay to Mr. Washington or Bearer

one hundred & fifty pounds

LORD BYRON
ACCOUNTS RENDERED

Also by Doris Langley Moore

THE LATE LORD BYRON

LORD BYRON
ACCOUNTS RENDERED

Doris Langley Moore

JOHN MURRAY

John Murray (Publishers) Ltd.,
50 Albemarle Street, London, W1X 4BD

Printed in Great Britain by
William Clowes & Sons Limited,
London, Beccles and Colchester

0 7195 3095 4

To my niece
Chloe Sayer

Contents

Appendices

Illustrations

* Reproduced by courtesy of the Trustees of the British Museum.

Introduction and Acknowledgments

To explain the nature of this book I must tell how it came to be written. About 1960, in one of my Byronic conversations with Mr John Murray at Albemarle Street, we were enumerating the many aspects of Byron's life which have had separate works devoted to them. His boyhood and adolescence, his travels, his politics, his friendships, his marriage; his career as poet, as playwright, as amorist, as knight-errant in Greece— we were surrounded by books on all these themes, and wondered if there could be others. 'No one', said Mr Murray, 'has yet written about the finances of Byron. We have a good deal of material here.' I remember mentioning that I had recently seen among the Murray manuscripts a bill for his clothes as a schoolboy, and that he seemed to have been very hard on them—which was hard on his mother. And there we left the topic.

I cannot recall the means by which I learned, some years later, that the papers of Byron's Italian secretary, Lega Zambelli, had been acquired by the British Museum and were now bound and accessible for study. My motive for going to look at them was a mild interest in Lega, of whom we had heard next to nothing until Iris Origo published *The Last Attachment* in which his role, though small, was memorable: and at first I merely investigated his life before he was drawn into Byron's orbit, and again after that unforgettable employer's death, and I found it remarkable and somewhat pathetic. It was not till after I had filled one or two note books with extracts from Lega's personal archives (summarized here in Chapter 7 and the Epilogue) that I really got down to reading his accounts—a shade forbidding to me at the beginning because of my total ignorance of bookkeeping, especially in Italian, the several currencies used, all obsolete, and the seeming dryness of the whole terrain.

But after a plodding day or two, there came a moment which reminded me of one in my childhood, when I had been gazing at views through a stereoscope not expecting them to differ in any way from views without that aid, and all of a sudden they sprang into three dimensions. Those payments for searching the coast from Leghorn to Lerici, those journeys with post-horses to places with names unfamiliar but not unheard of, the Bocca del Serchio, the Torre di Migliarino, the gratuities to sanitary officers, the wine and incense bought on the way to Viareggio—these items dotted here and there about the ledger in July and August 1822 were all occasioned by the quest for the bodies of Shelley and Williams and their obsequies! Those five extra beds hurriedly obtained on hire from 'the Jew De Montel'—why, that was the time of Leigh Hunt's arrival with six children whom Byron had not expected him to bring from England. (No wonder he gave Mrs Hunt a cool reception!) That letter to M. Beyle, which it cost four livres and ten soldi to post in May 1823, must have been the very one he wrote to the pseudonymous Stendhal to reproach him politely for his denigration of Walter Scott.

Besides the ledgers, thus turning out to be full of the most evocative information, there were notes, letters, and all manner of bills and receipts. Thanks to Lega's capacity for saving apparently trivial memoranda, we have Byron's domestic economy so minutely yet unconsciously reflected that there can scarcely be anything comparable in the annals of famous men. From the Zambelli Papers[1] we can learn what he paid his servants, what he spent on his table and his wine merchant, how he maintained his animals, what people he assisted, what clothes he ordered, and how much linen he sent to the wash. Similar records illumine, though with a greyer light, his life in Greece, and, equally, his death.

The fact that struck me most curiously was that no early biographer could have used more than a fraction of that information even if it had been available, because, until almost the present century, it was considered vulgar for anyone but a clerk or professional man to go into detail about money. Large sums could be touched upon—debts on an important scale, inheritances, dowries of rich brides, but not the cost of a dinner, a suit of clothes, a pound of wax candles. Reminiscences about Byron were written in abundance, but gentlemanly authors did not dwell on disbursements. (There were assuredly some ungentlemanly authors, but these were also among the most inexact.) Thomas Moore spoke a little more freely about money than other writers of the day, but he would not have gone out of his way to interview a courier or a household steward.

Now that the salaries of statesmen, the earnings of performers, the rents of landlords, the wages of workers, are a subject of discussion in every public medium, and a man's income is stated in print as readily as a woman's age, once equally proscribed, a chronicle of the ways and means of a poet whose modes of living were so vivid and so various can no longer seem as indelicate as our ancestors would have held it to be. So I thought again of Mr Murray's 'Financial Byron'. But I could not begin in Italy where he was, by contrast with his former difficulties, a fairly affluent

[1] Add. MSS 46871–46882.

man. I would have to trace out the principal stages by which he reached that liberation. Naturally, I made my way back to Albemarle Street.

And there, not a little gleeful over the *embarras de richesses* (and sometimes *de misères*) he heaped upon the desk where I had the good fortune to be reading, Mr Murray, now John Murray VI, brought cheque stubs, bank books, tradesmen's bills, leases, files of business letters, copies of Agreements and disagreements. As if these were not enough to keep me busy for years, I found, thanks to a clue given by my friend and fellow researcher, Leslie A. Marchand, the three tomes of Egerton Papers in the British Museum, which often supply the letters which are answered in the Murray MSS and vice versa.[1]

Still, I was bound to admit that, even if I were capable of writing it, a volume concerned with nothing but money matters would be for specialists only. Besides, I had an enormous number of exercise books and files of my own, the accumulation of many years, which it would be a pity to leave untouched. In my previous book, *The Late Lord Byron*, subtitled Posthumous Dramas, I said I had tried to give 'the portrait of a man as presented by the conduct of his friends, acquaintances, and enemies after his death'. Could I not contrive something on parallel lines, using a selection of that vast pecuniary documentation as the connecting thread, winding it in and out among the episodes of his life, and pausing to hang upon it particulars not generally known or necessarily skimmed over briefly by biographers with the whole tapestry to fill in?

Accounts Rendered—I lit upon this title, after working through several chapters with an unsatisfactory one, because it can be applied beyond the confines of finance to deeds for which a price is to be exacted, if not while a man lives then through his posthumous reputation. Byron performed many such deeds and most of them are linked up at some point with his financial story. There is little indeed in Byron's life or any other which is not linked up with some financial story.

I saw I should have to start with his father, who left his son nothing but old debts and the propensity to make new ones; I had the means of animating a little his hitherto rather static figure. And his other parent— that much under-estimated woman from whom he derived his compassion, his hot temper and, ultimately after many lessons, his desire to scrutinize his bills carefully and pay them regularly: it would be a satisfaction to tell something more than had yet been told of Mrs Byron. I would need to unravel, as far as lay in my power, the transactions with money-lenders, in whose complex webs the lordling was caught at eighteen like a foolish fly.

[1] Add. MSS 2611–2613.

Then—after the Grand Tour, financed by more debts and troubled by constant anxiety about running out of money—the high cost of being a man of fashion and the penalties of fame, with its corollary of begging letters from strangers and hard-luck stories from friends and the few he could call his family; the extravagances and generosities of his years as a sought-after bachelor, the rashness of his marriage to an heiress with no ready money; then exile, fresh scenes, fresh experiences felt with an edge not dulled, strangely, by expensive dissipation; self-realization as a poet despite outraged critics and, harder to defy, apprehensive friends and publisher; the realization too that his pen could and should provide revenue; domestication almost as an Italian; the hard-won pleasure of being solvent and business-like and knowing that he need never be humiliated again by duns, bailiffs, seizure of possessions; and, at last, the resolution actually to save, to grow rich, not only for the sister who was always on his conscience, but to have funds through which he might play, realistically, without heroics, some part in a cause worth helping.

From the process of dovetailing Zambelli Papers with the incomparable Murray collection, and especially Byron's later letters to Kinnaird and Hobhouse, we gain an insight into such perplexing tendencies as Byron's willingness to go to law rather than pay certain bills, and his insistence—almost startling in a nobleman of that time—upon settling others punctiliously every week; his habit of writing about money with miserly relish while perpetually giving charitable donations; his ability to combine a child's caprices with the paternalism which made employees older than himself claim that he had been a father to them.

If anybody had consulted Lega Zambelli, the accusation of avarice against Byron would never have been sustained or, at the worst, he would have been recognized as a man who, having had great kindness greatly abused, tries to build up defences. But although the archivist, who could have clarified so many obscure points and elaborated a hundred incidents recorded only in outline, lived in London from 1824 until his death in 1847, not a single writer during all those years seems to have taken the least notice of him. With what ease now could so confidential a secretary sell his intimate knowledge of both amatory and financial affairs to the Sunday papers!

When I had been engaged on my tale of profit and loss a couple of years (having begun, as authors always do, in the belief that it was going to be a much brisker and simpler task than it has turned out), an exasperating obstacle arose. British currency was decimalized and, as if its decline in purchasing power over the better part of two centuries did not pose problems enough, the very symbols in which the English accounts were kept changed their meaning. The shilling disappeared;

the penny at two hundred and forty to the pound had its nominal value much more than doubled, but was still worth less than the halfpenny, or even the farthing, of Byron's day—or for that matter, my own day. I can recall when, instead of giving a farthing in change, the nine-hundred-and-sixtieth part of a pound, drapers' shops presented a small packet of pins such as could not be bought for a 1970s' penny.

The efforts of translating all the sums I was dealing with into decimal terms scarcely seemed worth making when the result would still be a long way from an approximation to modern values, and in any case the foreign reckonings were all in money bearing even less relation to that in use today. The only method, I decided, was to give the reader occasional reminders and standards of comparison, and not attempt arithmetic beyond my capacity. Though money features largely in every chapter, I am hopeful that, thanks to my unhackneyed sources, much else will be found to engage attention.

I have not been able to follow a strict chronological order any more than in my earlier book, because some events happened concurrently or had lingering consequences, and others needed to be explained by reference to the past: but whatever is totally out of sequence and yet relevant is likely to be found in self-contained appendices placed at the end of the book. It would have been regrettable, for example, Byron having been so important to his servants and they to him, not to give indications of what kind of people they were and what happened to them. Again, since whatever excessive reticence early biographers observed, 'The Sexual Byron' has of late been prominent, I have felt bound to express my own opinion on theories about which I may reasonably claim to be entitled to one, permitted as I was to read and copy at will from Lady Byron's statements, her correspondence with her parents and her legal adviser, Dr Lushington, and a great horde of other documents the theorists have not seen, nor, so far as I am aware, tried to see.

I do not think I need apologize for a substantial appendix on the Hanson–Portsmouth Scandal because, though not involving Byron directly after 1814, it sheds strong light on the negligent but socially ambitious man in whose hands he drifted so near ruin—his solicitor. Likewise, I have allotted some space to the elegant and up-to-date furniture of Newstead Abbey, the inventory of which should dispel the time-honoured illusion that Byron's domestic quarters would have made a background to a Gothic romance. To be compelled to renounce all those fine things which had immensely increased his load of debt must have been nearly as painful as having to sell the Abbey itself.

For readers not already well acquainted with Byron biography, I have covered a certain amount of old ground, but with a constant endeavour to plant new facts upon it, and when I have resorted again to topics I myself have treated before, it is because fresh details have come to light; but I have allowed overlapping only when not to do so would be to assume more prior knowledge than it is fair to expect of an uncommitted reader.

For the privilege of being able to offer so much that is unfamiliar I am indebted primarily to Mr John Murray who placed every possible facility for research at my disposal and allowed me to use numerous documents not published, or only partially published, before; among them letters of Claire Clairmont, John Edleston, Nicolo Giraud, John Hanson, Richard Hoppner, the Hon. Augusta Leigh, 'old Joe Murray,' Robert Rushton, Susan Vaughan, and several others, not to speak of a selection from the account books of Mrs Byron and a great many personal bills of Byron himself, with such a quantity of miscellaneous material as my footnotes will show.

I must also thank others of that house who went out of their way to assist me, including Mr John Murray Jr, sometimes a fellow decipherer of handwritings. It has been a matter of pride to me that I have been acquainted with four generations of Murrays, beginning with Sir John (IV) who, long ago, kindly and courteously answered the request of a girl of nineteen recently come from South Africa, to let her see the Byron collection. I will not say, 'little did I dream' etc., because I believe I did have some faint premonition of the happy hours I should spend in that sanctuary.

Very happy too have been my days in the British Museum where the staff is always so obliging, and especially so Mr J. L. Wood, the Keeper of the Printed Books, and the Deputy Keeper Mr Howard Nixon and, between Printed Books and Manuscripts, Mr T. A. J. Burnett, Mr J. M. Griffin and Dr D. E. Rhodes. The only fault of the Students' Room is that closing time generally coincides with my lighting upon some magnetic manuscript. Mr Peter Fryer and Mr Cecil R. Woolfe were also among my literary consultants.

At the London Library Mr Douglas Matthews, the Deputy Librarian, and Miss J. Bailey have been unfailing in their ability to trace practically anything in or out of print. Very kind too have been the staff of the admirable library of the India Office, as well as that of the Italian Institute; nor must I forget the Assistant Librarian of the Department of Western MSS in the Bodleian at Oxford, Mrs Mary Clapinson.

Most ample thanks are due from me to the Nottingham Public Libraries, and to two of the Librarians now retired, Miss Violet Walker, an expert on Byron genealogy, and Miss Lucy Edwards who gave me, among a great deal else, the means of writing so literally about Newstead

Abbey. Mr David James, also of the Nottingham Central Library staff, accompanied me to the Abbey during its winter closure. Mr P. H. Shaw of the Vaughan Library at Harrow School promptly replied to one of my questioning letters.

In gathering information about John Hanson and Byron's legal affairs, I have troubled several distinguished people, beginning with the Rt Honourable Lord Simon of Glaisdale, formerly President of what was then the Probate, Divorce and Admiralty Division of the Royal Courts of Justice. Through him I was put in touch with the Law Society, which found what I was looking for, and with Master Ball, the Chief Chancery Master.

For my translations from the Italian of Zambelli, Ghigi, Byron himself, and others, I must not make anyone answerable but, on puzzling little usages, I have consulted with benefit and pleasure Dr Vera Cacciatore, M.B.E., Curator of the Keats–Shelley Memorial in Rome and a Byron scholar, Dr Adele Beghè, the Vice-Director, and Miss Itala Vivan, of the Italian Institute in London, Miss Milena Canonero, Mr Renato Capecchi, and Mr Michael Langley, a resident of Venice.

Mr George Bisbas was so good as to translate what Greek I needed and also enabled me to study the Goulandris Papers in which we find, damaged by fire but for the most part decipherable, numerous passages suppressed by Stanhope, 'the Typographical Colonel', showing him drawn by Trelawny into his unlikely alliance with that advanced liberal and avowed upholder of the free press, the brigand chieftain, Odysseus. I am indebted to the three Messrs Goulandris—John M., Leonidas and Alexander of that name—for having allowed me to make some use of these documents.

To fill in the financial background, I have had the advantage of reading Lord Kinnaird's copies of the Hon. Douglas Kinnaird's letters to Byron, an important complement to the other side of the correspondence. Without a friend of such integrity and capability Byron could never have amassed the money for his historic expedition to Greece. Mr R. R. Langham-Carter supplied my photograph of the original of Byron's bust by Lorenzo Bartolini, very superior to the all too well-known copy, with information as to how it came through the descendants of Charles Barry, the banker in Genoa, to the South African Public Library, whence Dr A. M. Lewin Robinson, the Director, sent permission for reproduction— together with a picture of the matching bust of Teresa Guiccioli done at the same time. (The sources of the other illustrations are named in the list of them.) Mr Langham-Carter also managed to unearth, in the annals of Cape Province, news of George Gordon Fletcher, second son of Byron's valet, and the little story of Charles Fairbridge and Byron's green jacket told by Mrs Phillida Simons.

With Mr Nigel Dennis, former owner of so many of the letters misquoted by Trelawny, I have been in enjoyable communication; while Mr Anthony Powell has told me much more than I had known before of the ill-advised and ill-advising Mrs Massingberd. It is an odd coincidence that two such eminent authors and critics as he and Mr Dennis should both have inherited letters directly concerning Byron.

On the question of the currencies which play so prominent a part in this book, I went to the Coins and Medals Department of the British Museum and very usefully saw Mr R. A. G. Carson, F.S.A. Mr J. G. Pollard of the Fitzwilliam Museum in Cambridge was equally helpful and also Mr M. H. Hendy, now at the Barber Institute in Birmingham. To have seen specimens of the coins handled by Byron and his household has made the subject a concrete one for me: but if I have committed errors, these experts are not responsible, not having seen my text.

How can I express my gratitude to Professor Leslie A. Marchand? He has done me every kind of favour, from lending me microfilm and photostats to accomplishing most unselfish acts of research while busy with his monumental work of editing Byron's letters by the exacting standards of modern scholarship. Whenever I refer in footnotes simply to 'Marchand', it may be taken that I mean the three-volume biography (for permission to quote from which I must thank Messrs Alfred A. Knopf Inc. in America and John Murray in England). When I write 'Marchand, *Letters*', I am alluding to one of the two first volumes of the complete edition now in preparation. At the time when my chapters were being typed, these books (*In my Hot Youth*, 1798 to 1810, and *Famous in my Time*, 1810 to 1812) had not been given names.

Where I have copied letters from original MSS, I have made acknowledgments, generally, on the pages where my quotations appear. The Lovelace Papers are the property of Byron's great-great-grandson, the Earl of Lytton, O.B.E., to whom I am much obliged. Lord Abinger is the owner of a great collection of documents relating to Mary Shelley and her entourage. Miss C. Draper, Literary Executor of the late Lady Wentworth, kindly permits me to use an extract from one of her letters to Sir John Murray.

Dr Roy Strong, when Director of the National Portrait Gallery, assisted me in connection with portraiture of Byron and his circle; Mr Michael Owen, Curator of the Roman Baths in Bath, informed me about the lodgings the schoolboy Byron occupied there, and Mr D. Cossart of the Wine Department at Christie's allowed me to consult him. Mrs Elma Dangerfield, O.B.E., and Mr Francis Lewis Randolph, of the Byron Societies in England and America respectively, sent me copies of documents that might be of service to me. There remains quite a long list of correspondents who, in the last dozen years, have written to me their ideas, some of them very interesting, but I think the moment has come when I must ask them to take my gratitude on trust and invite the reader to launch out on Chapter 1.

EDITORIAL NOTE

All numbered manuscripts given as sources in the footnotes are 'Additional MSS' in the British Museum unless otherwise identified. Folio numbers are not supplied where these collections are bound in straightforward chronological order.

When a footnote consists simply of an author's or editor's name, the reader is referred to the Bibliography at the end of this volume for the title of the work quoted. *LJ* denotes the seven volume edition of Byron's *Letters and Journals* edited by R. E. Prothero early in this century.

1

Jack Byron and the other Mrs Leigh

The 6th Lord Byron, christened George Gordon, was the fourth child born in wedlock to his father, but three of them had been by his first wife, and of those only one had survived, a daughter. The son by that marriage had drawn breath for no more than an hour.[1] Had it been he and not his second wife's boy who had outlived his father, he would have been brought up in grandeur like the girl, Augusta, moving from Lord Carlisle's Castle Howard to the Duke of Leeds's Kiveton Park, and then, in the season, to a variety of important town mansions in London: but the second Mrs Byron, born Catherine Gordon, could provide no such rich settings. She was hard put to it to maintain even simple respectability on the pittance her lawyers had managed to keep out of the hands of her prodigal husband. No one would have guessed, seeing her in lodgings in Aberdeen, making do with the minimum of domestic attendance, that she had been quite a notable heiress, was a lineal descendant of James I, and allied by blood to some of the noblest, if most turbulent, houses of Scotland.

Though too plump for her height, she had been a comely and a lively girl,[2] and could have done better with her fortune of above £23,000 than fall into the hands of a rake who everyone but herself could tell was only after the money. His former marriage, to a marchioness who would have been a duchess if she had not run off with him, and who was a peeress in her own right, had confirmed his habit of living beyond his means, for his wife had had £4,000 a year of her own, then a most splendid revenue; but that had ceased with her death, and there was nothing for a highly prepossessing spendthrift of good birth to do but look for another well-endowed wife. He found her in Bath at one of the Assemblies and married her there, to the distress of her relations, on an ill-omened day, May 13th 1785.

[1] Murray MS. Letter of Augusta Byron (afterwards Leigh) to John Hanson, 30 July 1805.
[2] Gordon, Pryse Lockhart.

She was perfectly devoted to him, incredibly magnanimous in the ruin he brought on her; nevertheless, they led a cat-and-dog life. Her very warm heart went with an equally warm temper and, for all her fine pedigree, she could be as loud and abusive as her namesake Kate the Curst. Being virtually deserted, despite a faint pretence of a parting by mutual consent, and soon after that widowed, her boundless affection was lavished on her son, whose face promised to be as handsome as his father's, and whose claims on her love were increased by a distortion of his right foot so serious that he was late in learning to walk.[1] Yet, even while she stinted herself of every comfort to seek remedies, she could not refrain when provoked—and his powers of provocation were beyond the ordinary—from calling him, once at least and perhaps more often, a lame brat.

He never forgave her—the feelings of rebellion and scorn that she inspired remained with him almost as long as she lived. But it may be that he had seized upon that primitive taunt as a stalking-horse, directing his conscience to a reason easier to admit than the real one. The fact seems to have been that he was ashamed of her, a state of affairs common enough in childhood and youth but exceedingly difficult to confess. She was not a presentable mother. She was corpulent, she had an ugly and awkward walk, she could not have been well-dressed for, besides her bad figure, she lacked the means to be. She had rows with schoolmasters, lawyers, and his guardian, and she was humiliatingly thrifty. She needed to be thrifty with her income of £150 a year, reduced to £135 when she raised a loan of £300, most of which had gone to her insatiable husband: but her money troubles would not have carried much weight with a little boy—a boy who knew from the age of six that he was to be a Lord, and who had possibly had it dinned into him more than was judicious. What else had the young widow in her decent but dull Aberdeen apartment to look forward to but the ennoblement of her son?

To be a peer in those days was to belong to a caste so privileged that it has no parallel in modern society. None but the enemies of revealed religion, an infamous crew, dared to deny that the social order had been ordained by God, and that the hereditary ruling class was his creation. The appalling goings-on in revolutionary France had only served to show how essential it was to uphold the system appointed by Divine Providence and administered, under guidance, by a divinely appointed

---

[1] Capt. Jack Byron wrote to his sister, Frances Leigh, on 19 Feb. 1791: 'For my son, I am happy to hear he is well, but as for walking 'tis impossible, as he is club footed.' George Gordon had been at least two and a half years old when his father had last seen him, and evidently still unable to walk.

monarch. The idea of 'blue blood' is said to have originated in Spain, where it was held that the veins of nobles had a more azure tint than those of plebeians, and although no one now took the phrase literally, still there was a vague notion that patrician lineage did in some mystical way infuse the vital fluid with a special quality so that those who possessed it, even at a rather far remove, were not quite as ordinary mortals. This belief has survived, very greatly diluted, till our own time, but without the mysticism which must have redeemed it, in many cases, from snobbery.

The prestige of English, Scottish, and Irish noblemen stood higher than that of all but a few foreigners, and not merely in their own estimation. For one thing, the French Revolution had left the House of Lords in no way shaken, but, rather, entrenched: for another, there was no devaluation of titles through over-production. In most foreign countries all the sons of—say—a Count were Counts and all his daughters Countesses, whereas British courtesy titles were much more restricted, and withheld altogether beyond the second generation. Thus Captain Jack Byron was the grandson of the 4th Lord Byron and nephew of the 5th, and son of Vice-Admiral the Hon. John Byron (jovially known as Foulweather Jack because of the way his ships had of running into trouble), but he and his younger brother had nothing but their rank in the army and navy respectively, and the recognition of their being 'well connected'—which would afford a tempting facility in obtaining credit.

One of the privileges a peer enjoyed was immunity from arrest for debt, but sons, grandsons, and nephews had no such exemption. Jack Byron had been seized in May 1786 and taken to the King's Bench Prison, and bailed out by his tailor, James Milne of Grosvenor Street, to the tune of £176. When years later the schoolboy Lord came to London, his clothes were always bought from Milne,[1] and the bills were paid, for Mrs Byron was very scrupulous.

That she told her son anything about the more sordid aspects of her husband's life is unlikely. Though she might rail at him when he misbehaved for being 'a true Byrrone', vehemently rolling the *r*, it would be the family's rashness and wilfulness she reproached him with, not dishonesty or vice. And indeed, though she knew 'Mad Jack' to be dissolute and headstrong, and blighted with what he acknowledged as 'my own Extravagance [for] which I often beat my Head against the wall',[2] the baser aspects of his character were either concealed from her or developed after their separation. If her son ultimately came to learn of them, they would account for a certain reckless fatalism in his own conduct; if not,

[1] Murray MSS.
[2] 21 Mar. 1788. Quoted by Maurois, *Byron*, 1930.

they form as strong and strange a case for an hereditary tendency as any geneticist is likely to encounter.

Nobody's curiosity seems to have been aroused by a remark of the leading Byron scholar of the period in a book privately printed by John Murray IV[1] for the Roxburghe Club in 1906, *Lord Byron and his Detractors*. It was intended as a counterblast to *Astarte*, that extraordinary production of Byron's grandson, the 2nd Earl of Lovelace, in which, attacking a succession of John Murrays with intemperate and entirely irrelevant abuse, portraying Augusta Leigh, Jack Byron's daughter by his first marriage, as a calculating villainess and Lady Byron—in the face of all the evidence he possessed—as one who had pursued a saintly 'Policy of Silence' to protect her, he provided the public with the first documentary support it had been offered of the incestuous relations of the poet with his half-sister; that is, if we except his secret book, *Lady Noel Byron and the Leighs*, printed in 1887 in an edition of only thirty-six copies, none of which, I believe, was circulated outside the author's family in his lifetime.

The passage to which I allude was by Rowland E. Prothero,[2] who had spent some years editing six volumes of Byron's *Letters and Journals*, a task which Lord Lovelace had originally undertaken to share, though, forgetful of extensive correspondence in the publisher's hands, he vigorously denied it.

> Lord Lovelace [Prothero wrote] has industriously raked from the muck heap a number of cases of such an attachment as that which he charges against his grandfather. But he has not done his scavenging fairly. He has suppressed the only case which is really pertinent. Byron was not the man to be outdone by his own father. His possession of certain letters, written by his father, Captain Byron, to his own sister, and his knowledge of their contents, would spur him on to boast . . . of a similar vice.

A statement to the same effect was made by an anonymous contributor to the volume, actually E. H. Pember, a legal expert who had been asked to weigh all the evidence from a judicial point of view, and who did so in that style of advocacy which is more useful to the prosecution than the defence.

No one came forward to demand an explanation of these striking utterances. The accusation of incest—even Byron's '*half* incest' as Lord Lovelace correctly called it—was considered inexpressibly dreadful: if it had to be made at all (and hardly anyone could see why it should), it was enough that it had been made against the poet and Augusta. The general

---

[1] Sir John Murray, K.C.V.O. (1851–1928), grandson of Byron's principal publisher.
[2] Rowland E. Prothero, M.V.O. (Lord Ernle, 1852–1937).

verdict was that it had been in extremely bad taste for a man to present a case against a distinguished grandfather for the sake of defending a grandmother whom nobody was attacking, and that there was no need to multiply such disclosures.

The irony was that the papers which had enabled Lord Lovelace to bring out a book which, however wildly written, was of much greater significance than the one of 1887, had chiefly been a gift to him from John Murray! *Lady Noel Byron and the Leighs* was only a compilation of letters showing what Lady Byron had suspected and confided to friends, what line she took with Augusta and Augusta with her, and how she embroiled herself with Augusta's daughter Medora whom she believed to be Byron's child, using the daughter against the mother as she had formerly used the sister against the brother. (Such was the opinion of her son-in-law.[1]) They supplied no proof. John Murray, knowing nothing of Lord Lovelace's desire to set up a sanctified image of his grandmother at the expense of his grandfather—an ambition of which he had never given the faintest hint—had unwittingly furnished him with exactly the material he required, the original MSS of Byron's letters to Augusta!

The story is a remarkable one and leads us to the other, hitherto untold, tale which will explain how Byron's father came to be implicated.

The beloved half-sister, Augusta, five years older than Byron, who, after his mother's death, was his nearest relation, had never been free from dire financial difficulties. Besides a husband addicted to the race-course and ne'er-do-well children, she had a strain of fecklessness inherited from her father and not modified by any of the down-to-earth realism the Gordons could always achieve in the last resort. Most of the large capital sum left by her half-brother was tied up for his wife's lifetime by the terms of the marriage settlement, a fact over which Lady Byron preferred to draw a veil when telling her friends of her ill usage—and, as it happened, she was to outlive Augusta by nine years.

Constantly dunned, Augusta had turned to Byron, who gave her or her husband a good deal of money, not expecting to get it back; and then, while he was resident in what she called 'that horrible *watery* city Venice',[2] she borrowed, very secretly, from his publisher, John Murray,[3]

---

[1] William King, 1st Earl of Lovelace (1805–1893), married the Hon. Ada Byron in 1835. He was then 8th Lord King, and was created Earl of Lovelace by Melbourne's Ministry in 1838. He had been a close friend of Lady Byron's and much in her confidence, but they fell out and were never on speaking terms after his wife's death in 1852. His opinion is given in a statement he made for Abraham Hayward in about 1870, now in possession of the Nottingham Central Library.

[2] Murray MS. 26 Mar. 1818.

[3] John Murray II (1778–1843), son of the 18th-century Scottish founder of the house.

and continued doing so after the poet's death. Full of expedients for repayment (which never worked), her letters make up a substantial and pathetic dossier, of which the following is a typical specimen:

> My dear Sir,
>
> It grieves me more than I can possibly express to ask you the favour I am about to do which is to lend me £10—& if possible tomorrow Morning— I know I owe you *this* sum and much more besides for Fletcher[1] & I can only say that a combination of no common troubles has hitherto prevented my returning it. . . .
>
> At the King's death £300 per annum *stopped* and now our pension![2] I need say no more or indeed I should rather say I have only that to offer in apology for my present request—which nothing but *most urgent* and *immediate* necessity wd induce me to make to *you*, who have been so kind.
>
> I am Dear Sir
>
>   Your very obliged
>   Augusta Leigh.[3]

After the death of John Murray II, begging letters to his son[4] became still more numerous: but it was not always an Albemarle Street charity, for a substantial quantity of important Byron manuscripts passed from her hands to his. On one occasion near the end of her harassed life, she received a large sum on the security of a sealed box of 'fifty or fifty-one letters' written to her by Byron. To have the money was, she said, a matter of life or death. 'It must be paid as soon as possible as regards *the* particular object mentioned to Mr Murray, of which Mr M. will feel the *vital* importance.'[5]

'The particular object' seems to have been to effect a new insurance on her life (there was a good deal of juggling in those days with life insurance policies) but it is difficult to be certain because of the confusing way in which she was accustomed to express herself, not letting her left hand know what her right hand was doing. Two of her three sons and two of her daughters had been deep in pecuniary troubles—they were all inveterate borrowers—and she herself must have been liable, from time to time, to arrest for debt. So many of her letters are undated that it

---

[1] She had undertaken to pay Byron's valet, Fletcher, £70 a year, but was unable to keep it up.

[2] Augusta had held the office of Woman of the Bedchamber to Queen Charlotte and continued to occupy apartments in St. James's Palace and receive the emoluments by grace and favour of King William IV, recently deceased. King George IV, when Regent, had granted her a pension though her husband, Col. Leigh, was in disgrace with him.

[3] Murray MS. 22 Dec. 1837. Lord Melbourne, Lady Byron's cousin, stopped the pension.

[4] John Murray III (1808–1892). Before succeeding to his father's publishing house, he wrote the very original continental travel Handbooks which preceded Baedeker.

[5] Murray MS. 28 Jan. 1850.

is seldom easy to identify the particular crisis she was staving off. As I make it out, the long-suffering publisher was lending her an amount of £225 which she wished him to bring up to £300, the price of the policy. She was prepared, she wrote, to waive any formal agreement. 'Mr Murray's *word she* regards as secure and sacred.'

She died the following year, and Lady Byron wrote, in 1854, to one of her many confidantes, Lady Wilmot Horton, that twenty-six money-lenders were laying claim to her estate.[1] Probate was not granted till 1856. Mr Murray was better than his word, and by a formal agreement made in 1864, he renounced £600 due to him by Augusta's heirs and, though he had never been repaid for his loan on the letters, handed over the box, still sealed, to her youngest daughter on the sole condition that its contents should not be published elsewhere.

That daughter, Amelia Marianne Leigh, known as Emily, had begun her life in high society, her mother being then a familiar figure at court and having for half-brothers and sister by maternal descent the Duke of Leeds, Lord Godolphin, and the Countess of Chichester, the three whom, as children, the Marchioness of Carmarthen had abandoned on eloping with Captain Jack. A kind of subscription was got up for Emily among the family, amounting at the utmost to £120 a year, towards which Lord Byron's widow, rich in her own right, contributed about £30, with a warning that it might be withdrawn at pleasure. Emily, thus in extreme poverty, was reduced to selling and pawning what relics of her celebrated uncle had not already been disposed of: so back came the sealed box to John Murray, who this time—in 1866—lent £50 on it.

When Emily Leigh died in 1876, her niece, Geraldine, daughter of her elder brother, George, made several efforts to get the box back, and Mr Murray was driven to mention not only an outstanding loan to Emily, but £600 advanced to Emily's mother. Quixotic to the end, however, in May 1886, he presented the contents to the poet's direct descendants, Lady Anne Blunt and Lord Wentworth, afterwards 2nd Earl of Lovelace.[2]

There were actually copies of many of these letters in existence, because Lady Byron had prevailed upon Augusta to let her see every communication she received from her brother after his departure from England and had, without Augusta's knowledge, transcribed each one

---

[1] *Lady Noel Byron*, 28 Dec. See Appendix 1, 'The Heirs to Byron's Fortune'.
[2] Lady Anne Blunt (1837–1917) married Wilfrid Scawen Blunt, the poet. Ralph, 2nd Earl of Lovelace (1839–1906), was the younger son of Byron's daughter, Ada. His elder brother, Lord Ockham, ran away from Lady Byron, who had brought Ada's three children up, and, dropping his titles, became a dockyard labourer under the name of Oakey. He died in 1862 and Ralph then succeeded to his Barony of Wentworth. It devolved several times through the female line.

into a small book: but of course Augusta's descendants had no idea of this, and copies would not have done for the revelations Lord Wentworth, all unknown to the donor of the originals, was contemplating, nor would it have been possible to publish from them without disclosing that his grandmother's sense of honour was peculiar.

There has been so immense a change in our point of view about nearly all sexual deviations that it does not now seem discreditable for Byron's grandson to have wished to prove his grandfather's and great-aunt's 'crime'—it was constantly called that, though not a crime in law when committed—but only that he used such tortuous methods of achieving his end and did so with such blind fanaticism. The Murrays' anxiety to protect the personal reputation of a poet closely associated with their house and a lady who had confided her many troubles intimately to two of them now appears prudish but was then deemed a very proper attitude. For some years, according to Lady Lovelace,[1] her husband felt restrained from publishing Byron's compromising letters by his sense of obligation for these and other gifts. He was fond, she wrote, of quoting a line of Bourget's, '*enchaîné comme je suis par les liens de la gratitude. . . .*'

By 1899 gratitude was so far forgotten that he had not only withdrawn from the editorial project with denunciations but endeavoured to stop John Murray IV from publishing any of Byron's letters to Augusta, including those which he had accepted from John Murray III! He had no legal control over the copyrights, these having passed to Lady Dorchester, surviving daughter of Byron's friend and executor, John Cam Hobhouse, but he strove by every means to get her on his side, concealing, naturally, his own intention to do exactly what she most disapproved. 'He dared not quarrel with Lady Dorchester,' wrote his wife in her book about him. 'Not only could she control all questions of publication, but she herself had inherited from her father Byron's intimate letters to Lady Melbourne. . . .'

Those letters made, of course, part of the proof Lord Lovelace had been building up over many years in support of his case, and Lady Dorchester had promised that those and all the rest of her great Byron treasure should be his when she died. Quite in the dark about the book he was engaged in, she had let him copy what she thought were some extracts from the now famous but then unknown Melbourne correspondence. The appearance of *Astarte* shocked and dismayed her so much that she asked for his copies to be returned.

Lady Lovelace, though in her husband's lifetime she had been most unhappy over his preoccupation of thirty years[2] with the 'miserable story', became, when he died, not less obsessed with it than he had been,

---

[1] In *Ralph Earl of Lovelace*, 1920.
[2] Such she states it to have been in a letter to Lady Dorchester, 31 Dec. 1909.

and she refused Lady Dorchester's request. Lady Dorchester persisted in her demand. Lady Lovelace rashly took legal advice and assumed a tone no offspring of Hobhouse was likely to tolerate. A correspondence of increasing asperity led to an exchange of telegrams when Lady Dorchester discovered that it was not mere excerpts but the Melbourne documents in their entirety which had been copied. The other then dispatched a registered packet which she said was all she could find.

To cut the lengthy and most intricate story short, Lady Dorchester made a new will, and in 1914 John Murray IV found himself the owner of her invaluable collection. Lady Lovelace wrote to Lady Dorchester's executors to say the papers *ought* not to have been left away from the family,[1] but since the only use the family had ever made of what it already possessed had been to assail (as it then seemed) its most illustrious member, and Lady Lovelace was of the opinion that nothing was 'likely to interest the public' in the unpublished part of Lady Dorchester's bequest except the Melbourne letters,[2] the moral claim was not very persuasive.

It gives some indication of how far Byron's descendants had become absorbed in a single aspect of his life that both Lord Lovelace and his niece, afterwards Lady Wentworth, had each secretly made another copy besides the incomplete one Lady Lovelace returned. Lady Wentworth showed me hers in her handwriting, and told me that, by notifying John Murray IV of her having it, and urging him not to bowdlerize the letters, she had prevented them from being expurgated when they were ultimately published.[3] I have since seen her communication, and it contained this admirable passage, which speculative biographers might well consider:

> As to what it is polite to publish in the interests of Byron's reputation, I can only say that the family now prefer the whole truth especially considering what has been written and that all over the Continent the 'mystery' is explained by a very much worse accusation even than the actual truth. . . . Giving to the world Byron's own words might do much to remove the blacker imputations thrown on him by those who in the absence of reasonable explanations have descended to the depths of depravity for a sufficient reason for the century of mystery and suppression and violent partisanship which have surrounded my unfortunate family. I have no fear to let Byron

---

[1] 31 July 1914.

[2] Undated letter to Lady Dorchester's executors.

[3] *Lord Byron's Correspondence*, 1922. It is true that letters other than those to Lady Melbourne in these two volumes were expurgated—they could not otherwise have been published at that date—but the omitted passages were restored by Quennell and Marchand respectively with the assent of John Murray V (Sir John Murray, K.C.V.O., D.S.O., 1884–1967) and John Murray VI.

stand or fall on his real merits. His genius is great enough to survive the truth.[1]

Taking a bird's eye view of the whole curious terrain, Byronians may think it fortunate that there were both Lovelace and Murray descendants, not to speak of Hobhouse's daughter. Without those factions, each protecting ardently what it held to be important—a matter about which they had such different estimates—we should not now have what must be among the most complete portraits of a many-sided man that exist in literature.

To return to Augusta Leigh's manuscripts, acquired by John Murray III; after his death in 1892, his son continued to enrich the Lovelace collection with many of them; and it is with the last of these precious packets that I am now concerned. It was sent to Lord Lovelace in 1899, the contents being thirty-three letters of Captain Jack Byron to his sister, who was also a Mrs Leigh and both the aunt and the mother-in-law of Augusta, marriages between first cousins being common and regarded as desirable. But the recipient, as I have explained, had grown hostile to the house of Murray, ostensibly on account of unexplained objections to the re-publication of almost any Byron correspondence before 1812, with specific mention of those harmless and indeed delightful productions of the poet's youth, the letters to his mother, to Miss Pigot, and to the Rev. Francis Hodgson! He neither thanked the donor nor returned the gift, but sent it unopened to Coutts's Bank; and it was not until 1907, a year after his death, that his widow unsealed it in the presence of his sister, Lady Anne, and promptly put it away again for another twenty years.

Rowland Prothero had thus made a natural error when he wrote as if Lord Lovelace knew those letters. Lady Lovelace understood their purport. That is very clear from her censorship when, in the late 1920s, she permitted some use of them to André Maurois for his biography of Byron. She had typewritten copies made for him of only eleven out of the thirty-three, withholding various passages and the last lines of one that might have set him thinking.

I have not time to say any more but that I love you—& can never cease to do otherwise [word torn by seal]. Do not make yourself too handsome as

---

[1] 8 July 1918. The Hon. Judith Lytton (1873–1957), 16th holder of the Wentworth peerage which descended to her by the death of Lord Lovelace's daughter in 1917. Being the daughter of Lady Anne and Wilfrid Scawen Blunt, she was Byron's great-granddaughter. She married the Hon. Neville Lytton, afterwards 3rd Earl of Lytton. She was famous as a breeder and historian of Arab horses. I found her remarkably unprejudiced in advanced age on Byron questions.

I am too mad already that you are my sister—all I ask is to love me as well as I do you.[1]

Maurois' quotations were adequate to show that 'Mad Jack' was dissipated and licentious, but not that his relations with his sister had set, in the spirit of black comedy, a pattern his son and daughter were to repeat as tragedy. Nor was the package disturbed again until I opened it in 1957 in circumstances I have described elsewhere.[2]

The Byrons prided themselves on their descent from the ancient nobility of France, and several of them had lived there. Jack Byron had been partly educated at a French Military Academy and, returning from the war in America, had stayed in Paris and at Chantilly with his two successive wives, the rich one and the impoverished one, so that when his sister, Frances, known as Fanny, who was parted from a husband she hated, furnished herself a house at Valenciennes, nothing was more natural than his seeking a refuge there. He had no possibility of remaining in England except as the inmate of a debtors' prison. His father, the redoubtable Admiral, had come to his rescue many times, but was provoked at last to declare in his will that, considering the sums already advanced, he could leave his elder son only £500. He died in 1786.

It was a legacy Jack Byron disposed of twice at least, binding himself to pay it to a French creditor, Perrigaux, but assigning it to the tailor who had freed him from the King's Bench and who had to meet other debts with the balance after his own £176 was repaid.

By September 1790, when Jack Byron finally left his second wife in Scotland, the many claims that were being pressed on him made him glad enough to see France again if only in provincial obscurity. Frances Leigh, separated from General Charles Leigh, was the eldest of the Admiral's several daughters, one of whom died two months after the poet's birth. The earliest letter, an isolated one, announces her demise to Frances with that formality in the use of titles and surnames which writers of period plays and novels so seldom reproduce.

My dear Fanny,
    I shou'd have answer'd your letter before, but I have not been well & I am now sorry to be oblig'd to tell you that poor Lady Wilmot is dead. Indeed I have been much affected, notwithstanding I have not seen her for some years—I am convinced that it must affect you. My Father & now my Sister dying within a few years really makes me reflect that it will [be] my turn soon, & I am quite depressed.

[1] Murray copies, 16 Feb. 1791.
[2] *The Great Byron Adventure*, four articles in the *Sunday Times*, 1959, produced in America as a pamphlet by the J. B. Lippincott Company.

Like so many others of his family, Lady Wilmot had been unhappily married.[1] Of her husband, he says: '. . . She never loved him, and only married to hinder herself from being a burthen on my Father — I am sure she is happy at present as she was a very good Woman & a good sister.'

He took occasion to tell Frances that a carriage such as she wanted him to buy for her in London would cost £80 to £100 and he thought that too dear.

> I wish it was in my power to get it you without asking any thing for it, I am sure I wou'd do it with the greatest pleasure, but I assure you my Income is but small, & what there is of it is settled on Mrs Byron, and the Child, therefore I am obliged to live in a narrow circle, which I need not have done, if those Rascals had not cheated me of a great deal by a Law suit I have in Edin[burgh] & I am obliged to pay the Jointure of a Grandmother of Mrs B. who is as tough as possible. . . .[2]

Such an attitude towards the family whose money he had been dispersing at so fast a rate was by no means unique when a married woman could own no property except what her lawyers might secure for her by a deed of settlement; but in the gross exaggeration of the amount of income allotted to his wife we recognize something worse than mere prodigality. It was in this letter, however, that he acknowledged his own weakness, adding, as if he had no volition, a fear that he might 'run again into Extravagance . . . by buying horses and perhaps hounds, in short I cannot answer for myself'. The most prudent thing, he said, would be to go to France, where he might live very well on his income. It had slipped his mind that, a few lines before, he had claimed that what income he had was settled on his wife and son.

It was not until about mid-September 1790 that he joined his sister in France, by which time he had squandered every penny of Gordon money he could lay his hands on. But Fanny Leigh, too, was an unscrupulous spendthrift, and when, by the death of their mother—who had been a close friend of Mrs Thrale—the business of legacies brought her to England, her brother at Valenciennes had to hold the fort against her creditors as well as his own.

Dependent entirely on her remittances, he writes mainly about money, but there is enough of bawdy gossip to make it plain that their

---

[1] She was Juliana Elizabeth. Her first husband was William, son of the 5th Lord Byron; her second, Sir Robert Wilmot, Bt. Their son was the Robert Wilmot Horton who was the friend and confidant of Lady Byron.

[2] 21 Mar. 1788. Part of this letter is missing. The context suggests that it may have contained an allusion to his unfortunate wife which his sister or his daughter, Augusta, destroyed.

life together had been one of total amorality. He had his mistresses, about whom he confided to her in the coarsest terms, and she her lovers, with whom he was friendly, but there was, or had been, between them some closer intimacy which his light conscience, and perhaps hers, could regard as an amusing escapade. His first letter in this series gives us the two keynotes, debt and ribaldry. [Spelling is left unchanged except where, according to his habit, he varies the orthography of names, in which case I have tried for consistency even if uncertain which version is correct. For clarity I have sometimes adjusted the punctuation.]

He begins by thanking her for a note—presumably a banknote—and three louis. At her request he has paid the Procureur, a kind of official attorney, 'as the Servant wanted the 12 livres & the other his 24 livres'.[1] It may be gathered that two menservants had sought legal aid to get arrears of wages.

> I have also paid my Taylor—& half the Baker's Bill and will pay the rest as far as it will go—to Henian the Notaire.[2] I have given three different drafts on Hammersley [a London banker] for one hundred pounds each, & I write to him that he must accept them, as the little you can get for me, you will put into his hands—& God knows I wish it was more as I never can forget your Sisterly Love & friendship to me, & I never can cease to Love so good a friend & Sister. . . .
>
> As for me the Schoners invited me to supper we had 3 bottles of Wine & Punch—all *drunk*, & le petit mari *farted* to such a degree by eating too much Sallad, that he was beastly—The chère Moitié made such love, that I am really in danger, how it will end I know not—I had a letter to day from the Maire of Rheims begging I wou'd assist him [by settling certain debts]. I sent him an answer, that I had *Labouré* too much with his wife before, & that he was un *Cocu*. . . .
>
> I sleep in your Room, & your little bird is [in] good health, & I take the whole care of him, as Josephine has been never sober—& Louis is not come back.

Josephine was a miserable servant who could not get her wages and consoled herself with drink. Louis, the remaining manservant, had accompanied his mistress part of the way to England.

> I was at the play last night, & since you are known to be gone Madame de Malteta has a mind to your Brother—but I hate people avec une *fesse* [a large posterior]. . . .
>
> Pray write as soon as you arrive, as not any thing in the world can make

---

[1] There were twenty livres to the gold louis.

[2] This Notary had written a letter empowering Mrs Leigh to collect her brother's legacy, left by their late mother, the Hon. Mrs John Byron (née Sophia Trevanion), under the terms of her marriage settlement.

me so happy—Mons. de Talusbrus is not arrived, as I inquired—I will scold him when I see him, do write & believe *Your* Ever Affec.

Brother & grateful Friend

J. Byron[1]

Talusbrus, nephew of a French general whose name I cannot trace in army records, was perhaps, as may be inferred from further allusions, Fanny's lover. A week later, Jack Byron wrote again:

My dear Fanny—

I am quite unhappy that I have not heard from you since you left Dover which last letter made me quite happy, I am convinced my Dear Fanny you are the only person I sincerely love. I am interrupted by Mon^r Renaud, who is this moment come, he is quite pale, & asks a number of questions— & I wish he was at the Devil. . . .

As for me here I am, & in love with whom, a new Actress who is come from Paris, she is beautiful & play'd last night in L'Epreuve Villageoise. . . .

Renaud was not a creditor, as his reactions might lead us to think, but an admirer of one Miss Hammerton, who was companion to Mrs Leigh, or perhaps *gouvernante* to her son Harry, and who had gone to England with her. There was a Byronic complication, because Jack Byron had also paid court to her and had asked his sister not to show her his gossip about the other women. 'I own', he wrote later, 'I am still attached to her, & I like her the more for being attached to you.'[2] The French actress had turned out to be a swiftly passing fancy.

As for Mad^{me} Schoner—she fairly told me when drunk that she liked me, & I really do not know what to do—However I hope she will be quiet till you come back. No duns appear as Fanny bites them all, & I am never at home. We are all well here, & Josephine in the best Order—as she gets no money & plenty of abuse, it is the only way to treat her. . . .[3]

By December 5th, still not hearing from Fanny, her brother was afraid some accident had happened to her. She had a box at the theatre which was paid for till February, and he sought distraction by going every night.

Every body inquires after you—& I am sure if a person is beloved you are. You know my tender heart. The woman who opens your Loge, said she shou'd never see any person so good to her as you was. I immediately gave her 3 Livres, & told her the *Byrons* were always so. Madame d'Arcourt [the manager's wife] continually asks after you, & the Man who receives

---

[1] 24 Nov. 1790.   [2] 25 Dec. 1790.

[3] 1 Dec. 1790. The biting Fanny was his dog, which he had named after his sister.

the Money at the door—says you promised him something from London, and begs you will bring him a steel Watch Chain—

Do write my dear Sister & continue to send the payment of those Drafts I sent, not any thing is to be paid till you come, & the Schoners are mad after you & continually praising you.

So far there is little that any vain and frivolous man might not write to a sister with whom he is on terms of raffish confidence, and whom he is disposed, from policy or genuine affection, to flatter rather grossly, but his letter of the following week cannot but convey the idea of a preoccupation somewhat abnormal in a fraternal relationship.

Valenciennes
Dec. 12th 1790

Mrs Leigh
No. 39 Brompton Row, Knightsbridge

My Dear Fanny,

I received your letter last night after coming from Madselle Marigny [a casual mistress] who I visit only to keep me from that Ennui that attends me, since you are gone, beleive me my Dearest Sister, there is no person I love so well as you, & that I wish you were here every minute. . . .

Mons Talusbrus is not come back, but you have received a letter from him I hope inclosed in mine, & I hope that he can excuse himself from *inattention &c.* As for me I have more upon my hands than I can do, as La Henry, who does the business well, is always after me, & I love to oblige her *Dames* now & then. As for La Marigny, she is as wide as a Church Door, & I really was resolved [not] to do it with her, because Renaud said that one must give her mony, & quoted the P[rince] de Ligne. Altho not so young nor so handsome as him, still the *Birons* are irresistable. You know that Fanny.

As for La *Henry* she told me that I did it so well, that she always *spent* twice every time. I know this will make you laugh, but she is the best piece I ever ——[1]

It may be asked whether a man would make such crude communications to a woman of whom he professed to be amorous, but where there is an obsessive physical vanity, he might think that to keep his prowess in her mind was more attractive than repellant, especially if there were on both sides the unusual sexual abandon these letters suggest. The next, at any rate, seems to me—as to Prothero, Pember, and John Murray IV— fairly conclusive. The writer speaks first of the arrival of Talusbrus, from whose servant he has had a message:

. . . I hope he will be able to excuse himself to me [for his inattention], as I am your Champion, for I declare I can find no Woman so handsome as

[1] All blanks are in the originals.

you. I have tried several, but when I do any thing *extraordinary* I always think of you. The Marigny slept with me two nights running but she is the worst piece I ever met with. . . .[1]

He transmitted a message from Renaud asking Fanny to bring him a seal from England 'with some Device that is very pretty'. Renaud was always with him because, he explained, 'I want a *Compagnon* or To[a]dy'. As he had no money at all, his last eighteen livres having been stolen out of his secrétaire by the unpaid servants, his only amusement was to drink the stock of wine—for which the bill was overdue—and go to the theatre, where he frequently annoyed the audience by making tipsy scenes. France was in the middle of a revolution, and his aristocratic airs were unpopular. When he pulled down the blind of Fanny's box, the people in the parterre resented it and wanted to interfere. 'I do not know how, I felt a little *Bold*, & it was after dinner—I only declared that the first person that offer'd to begin, was a *Jean foutre* & they left me quiet, & it still remains. Vive Les *Birons* after dinner. We were always so from the time of William the Conqueror.'

It is exactly as if the Byron we know, whom this irresponsible and vapid man fathered, had never developed beyond early adolescence. All the bravado, the misplaced pride, the indiscretion, of the rebellious Harrow boy are there. What is not there is the intelligence that would have made the Harrow boy incapable of writing such a sentence as: 'I hope you will be able to get me what little remains of my Mother.' But something of the poet is foreshadowed in the continuation—'& retain for yourself what ever you please, as I can never forget your kindness to me.'[2]

He was not heartless except to his wife. The plight of certain creditors disturbed him. He wrote more than once about some lace which Fanny was to sell in London on behalf of the Schoners who 'have not a farthing, & I have none to give them, they are very Civil & I hope you will be able to sell it, or send them a little Mony—if it is possible'. It was doubtless the elaborate kind of lace which, with the simplification of dress, had gone out of fashion, but England was not so far behind French modes that Englishmen and women were still buying ruffles. At any rate, no money came for it.

It was only a week since he had told his sister of his two nights with 'La Marigny' and now, after assuring her his amours were all finished, he inconsistently boasted of a new conquest:

I beleive I have had one third of Valenciennes, particularly a Girl, at l'Aigle Rouge, an Inn here, I happen'd to dine there one day when it

[1] 15 Dec. 1790.   [2] Ibid.

rained so hard—that I cou'd not come home, as there was no carriage to
be had & I step'd in there, & she immediately told me that she wou'd
give the World to live with you, if Josephine was going—upon which I
struck a bargain by saying I wou'd speak to you, as soon as you arrived, &
by that manner I got her—she is very handsome & very tall, & I am not
yet tired.[1]

The woman to whom one would tell of so mean a seduction could not
have been very fastidious. On Christmas Day he reported a yet more
squalid incident:

> Josephine drank yesterday fourteen Gills of Brandy to keep her Xmas—
> & she has been so insolent that I was obliged to kick her downstairs from
> your Room & she fell head foremost & is still at this moment in a state of
> Intoxication which I can hardly describe. [It was more probably concussion.]
> She broke open my Bureau & stole 18 Livres, which she glories in, & in
> short she is the D——t Bitch I ever saw. Louis is so insolent, that I was
> obliged to pull him by the nose, & he offer'd to fight me with a sword. . . .

Here he completely parts company with his son whose care for his
servants—though at times not without a measure of sternness—evoked
their lifelong affection, and who never lost his dignity with them. Threatened by Louis, Jack Byron began to learn the use of the sabre from a
Swedish chasseur. He contrived to give a drunken dinner or two in male
company, and to pay, though reluctantly, twelve sous a day for the lodging
of the chambermaid, who was now out of a place. 'She chuses to be very
fond of me—& I am tired of her—& I do not know what to do with her.
. . .' It was just three days since he had sent his letter to the contrary
effect.

> La Marigny & me are at daggers drawn. She says her Lovers—for she
> has five, have all left her—because I came. I do not beleive a word of it.
> As for La Henry she is an impudent Bitch—she played me such a trick.
> When I see you I will tell you.

La Marigny was obviously a courtesan on no very high level and La
Henry the keeper of a brothel. That Fanny had come to know them, or
even to know of them, under a code which fixed so wide a gulf between
ladies of quality and women of the town, demonstrates how different she
and her brother were from any of the well-bred couples in contemporary
novels.

> The Wine Merchant of Rheims [he continued], his Billet is échoué
> tomorrow the 26th, & I have no mony to pay him, however I hope he will be

[1] 22 Dec. 1790.

pacified. . . . I inclose a little of my hair. Pray send me some of yours. I will never part with it while I Breathe.

He also asked for newspapers, and thanked her for undertaking to have boots and shoes made for him, probably on his own last, in London. He desired shirts too, for which he had sent her his measurements, and two or three pairs of gloves. He added: 'Will you be so good as to send Miss Hammerton to Lady Holdernesse in Hertford St. & she will find there a Miss Bradshaw who is her maid, & inquire how my Daughter is— & her Address.'

The Hon. Augusta Mary Byron, aged six—'Honourable' because of her mother's peerage—was being decorously brought up by maternal relations, and as her grandmother had disowned her former son-in-law, it was only through the maid that any news could be ascertained. He seemed to care more for his daughter than his little son in Aberdeen, towards whom he gave no sign of anything but indifference; but his request for her address may have been because he did not want to lose touch with so rich a family.

Next day he sent another letter, an expensive business for Fanny as the recipient had to pay most of the postage. He had seen the notary, Henian, who had been recalcitrant, having guaranteed some of Mrs Leigh's bills, and not received the expected remittances: 'As for me I have done with him, & told him he was a *Cochon* to speak in such a Manner—he will not advance a farthing for Josephine, therefore, she must stay till she is paid.'

Besides her other debts, Fanny had gone off in a carriage for which Henian was liable, but Jack Byron was almost without the faculty of reasoning.

I will never speak to him any more, as he is a d—nd Rascal—therefore my dear Fanny, do not think of paying them. . . . Pray write immediately— I tell every body that I have bills from you but they are not due for some time, & I will not lose by the change, & they are content till now, but they begin to trouble me again—& this fellow has put me in such a passion.

The imaginary 'bills' with which he was staving off creditors were the equivalent of post-dated bankers' drafts, which could only be cashed in advance at a discount. He was not the man to sustain a position requiring coolness and diplomacy, and, ungratefully, he made enemies of those whom he should have been conciliating. Three days later he was writing again:

Henian has held such conversation about [your] taking the Carriage with you that I was obliged to call on him, & to tell him that if he was not satis- fied with your Conduct, that your Brother was not here to suffer a *Jean foutre* like him to speak in that manner—& . . . that I wou'd meet him with the Sabre when he wou'd. . . . It has made some noise in Valenciennes.[1]

Henian was forced to change his tone and become 'very civil' but the noise in Valenciennes was not friendly to the arrogant Englishman who called out '*Vive le roi!*' at the theatre when others were shouting '*Vive la Nation!*'

He had the occasional companionship of Miss Hammerton's admirer, Renaud, and Fanny's, Talusbrus, and the latter's uncle, whom he had met at the play, had invited a visit from him, but he had not been able to go. 'I have been very ill, & have been spitting Blood for these three days, but I hope I shall be better soon—it is owing to a Cold I have had for some time.'[2]

The cold remained with him. As early as 1788, he had mentioned his ill health and had wondered whether he would long outlive his father and sister, and we may guess, though he did not, that consumption had been undermining him for years, intensifying his reckless moods, his sensual appetites, his wild gaieties and glooms.

During the days of his confinement he had been pursuing one occupation that shows a distinct affinity between him and his son. He was looking after the pet animals and had trained a bird to fly out of the window and return to its cage. (Twenty-six years later, Byron was to write proudly to Hobhouse that his dog, Mutz, was 'learning to obey the word of command with a piece of bread upon his nose until permission is accorded to eat it'.)[3]

The need of a financial rescue was becoming constantly more acute:

> If it is possible you can raise mony for the little I have [his mother's legacy] do send it, to pay up what you owe. . . . Schoner has behaved like an Angel. The Wine Merchant will wait a week longer—for your pianoforte I will not sell it till you come, as you will lose, & it is a pity to sell it. It is so good an Instrument, every body says so.

Fanny had apparently sought aid from her younger sister, Sophia, who had not complied. Her means must have been very narrow and her knowledge of her brother assuredly sufficient to make her unwilling to risk them. He ascribed her refusal to meanness: 'You know mony is her *God*, & she is willing to make a Sacrifice to God, & I believe she would sell herself if possible, but les Marchandises sont bien rares.'

Sophia fulfilled this implicit prophecy. Lacking the attractiveness on which most Byrons piqued themselves, although in youth she had been pretty, she was to remain unmarried, and from one or two mocking

---

[1] 29 Dec. 1790.   [2] Ibid.   [3] 42093, Byron Papers. 19 Dec. 1816.

references in the youthful letters of her nephew, became a typical maiden aunt. She saw a good deal of Lady Byron at the time of 'the Separation', and was one of her confidantes.

On New Year's Day 1791 a letter arrived from Fanny enclosing one for Talusbrus, but nothing to relieve her brother's tormenting penury. He wrote next day in the pitiful tone he so often assumed with her, hoping she was not angry because he had asked for money.

> You have no Conception to what a pitch of Insolence the people are grown, every tradesman says you went to get your mony, & you might have raised some by this time . . . Really, the Schoners[1] are in the greatest distress, & never complain.

These too trusting friends had offered security for some of the furniture Fanny had bought, and *Gardes*, the equivalent of bailiffs, had come to collect payment. Schoner had just renewed his guarantee until March.

> If it is possible for you to raise some mony pray do. . . . I have not a Sous. but I do not mind that if you can silence these *bougres*. [As] for Josephine it is impossible for me to turn her away without paying her the whole of her wages. . . . Louis will not leave till he sees you—Therefore come as soon as you can—& if possible my Dear Sister, do send over to pay these Creatures—you know how they are, & notwithstanding what I say every body thinks you are gone.

He had not made his situation any easier by setting off a riot in the theatre, a riot which had been followed by a Knight of Malta being put into prison, and two officers, one of whom was Renaud, fighting a duel next morning in front of a large crowd. Both men had been wounded but Jack Byron thought it 'no more than the scratch of a pin'. There had also been the flight of the actor he had supported, who was compelled to take refuge for two nights in a granary dressed only in his stage costume—as a savage! He himself had appeared before the Mayor and Corporation, and maintained his right to applaud as he pleased, and they had politely asked him to remain indoors a few days. Louis had told him the mob was after him. And all because he didn't particularly want a Democratic play the audience had been calling for!

The wretched Josephine, who had been seriously ill, was weeping as she told her fortune by cards, which confirmed her fear that they would never have any money. He hoped Fanny would write to her:

---

[1] The name is written so illegibly and spelt in so many different ways that some doubt must persist that it always refers to the same persons; but it seems improbable that two married couples in Valenciennes, both in low water, would have made themselves answerable for Mrs Leigh's debts.

All my wish is to see you, & I am certain if that happens soon I care for nothing else—Pray get me a hat, round & Cocked à la Militaire, as I say here I am in the Service, so I am in the Militia & that is better than the Garde Nationale—Adieu do write directly & beleive me that I love you my tendrest Sister with the utmost affection.[1]

To be in the French Militia, which was an amateur army, was a strange destiny for a former British Guards Officer who had fought the Americans on their own soil, but he had gone on half-pay some years ago, and since then must have sold his commission.

A fortnight or so later, Fanny's draft on Hammersley's Bank, for which Henian had made himself responsible, had been dishonoured, and instead of the soft answer so manifestly called for, the notary had been treated to insults. In consequence he had enlightened the Schoners, whose friendship grew cool at last. It seems hardly believable that, with bills pressing on every hand, the incorrigible man had used some of the money he was borrowing to pay for Fanny's box at the theatre, although civil strife was keeping audiences away and he himself was not in fit health to go.

I assure you I have been very ill myself having kept my bed two days . . . It is continual Rain, & there is no stirring out. T[alusbrus] will write to you this Evening . . .

If you can send me some mony, pray do, as I am in debt & to persons I do not wish to owe. Remember that Henian has signed several Bills for you to be paid at the end of the Month, & if possible send him some Mony, or he will have cause to speak more than he has done . . .[2]

For four louis one could travel from Valenciennes to London, and he cajoled that amount from a Madame Tudoir, who loved Fanny, he said, to distraction, so as to send the manservant to give her a direct verbal report of their plight.

My Dearest Sister [he wrote on January 23rd],

By this time you will have seen Louis, & I hope you will not be angry with me for sending him—Your harpsichord is not sold, as the Man failed in paying for it, & it is here. The Indignity I have suffer'd in this Town is too much, as they are the d—— race that ever was—Schoner has taken the Harpsichord &c to himself—it is not his fault he is govern'd entirely by his wife — — —

As he reached this point in his letter, an irate one from Fanny was delivered. She had taken umbrage at his reiterated pleas for her to hasten the payment of his legacy from his mother, and had invited him to get

[1] 2 Jan. 1791.   [2] 19 Jan.

someone else to collect it. The emotional tone of his reply conveys an idea of his complete subjection to her:

> How can you hurt me so much. . . . I do not merit that, as you know it is all your own, & I am grateful to you even for my existence—without you I should be the most miserable person on the Earth. I have many faults, but to be in want of gratitude to you, I hope to God I shall never be—Keep this letter & show it to me always as it is my heart that speaks—For God's sake take the trifle & dispose of it as you like. I am certain you will never desert me & God has shown that tho' my *Parents* deserted me, I have still a Sister—who will protect me.[1]

He had at once forwarded an enclosure she had sent to Talusbrus, who was 'the best Creature existing', and he asked her to tell Miss Hammerton 'that I have wrote her some letters, & have yet no answer'.

This crossed with further reproaches from Fanny, and he thought some mischief-maker must have been at work. Between his oppressive poverty and his fear of estrangement from her, he was quite distraught.

> You do not know how much I have suffer'd in this d—ed Town—& much more so since you have wrote to Talusbrus—who mentions that you are angry with me, for what reason I know not. God knows, I love only you, & if ever we part I must be miserable—therefore my Dear Sister do not always listen to what they say.

Talusbrus had supplied eight louis to keep the wine merchant at bay. Against Henian Jack Byron had vented his rage with characteristic foolishness.

> I went with a person the other day & told him he was a foutu Polisson, & beg'd him to come out with me, & he refused it, & he is laughed by all the Town. . . . In short he is the greatest Coward existing—Pray do not forget to send me or bring the things you promised—I am really without a Shirt.[2]

No comfort came from Fanny either in material or spiritual shape. Instead, to her reproaches were added those of Miss Hammerton: 'She says in her letter that I have treated her very ill, in what I know not, that I have had all the women in Valenciennes, which is an infamous lie.'

In his usual inconsequential way, he had forgotten that he had claimed a few weeks before to have had half of them. Then, as if it would soothe the lady to whom he professed attachment, he went on:

> I have lived continually with one woman for some time past, which is the Hollandaise, who has quitted Monbar who cannot live. Her history is

[1] 23 Jan.   [2] 30 Jan.

very singular—as she is of a very considerable family in Holland, & is related to the Bentincks at the Hague. . . . As Miss H. seems determined we shall part, as much as I love you, I shou'd be sorry there should be any disagreements in your house relative to me & her, & I had rather return to my former misery, than to be the least burden to you.

The references to his owing his very existence to his sister, and a state of misery even greater than that in which he now found himself, promote speculation as to what deep trouble he may have been in before his flight to France. Perhaps he had seen the inside of more than one debtors' prison, or perhaps again the threat of a worse incarceration had hung over him.

In a state of tragi-comic confusion he continued:

Conscious of my own Innocence in regard to my conduct towards you I look forward, that you will find if I have erred it has not been intentionally.

I hope Louis is arrived, & that you will be so good as to let me have a little mony, as I am living here on absolutely nothing. . . . Write me sincerely if you wish me to be gone, as I cannot bear that you shou'd neglect me —& I will take my Resolution on receiving an answer to this—& to whom I am to leave your Birds & Fanny, who are all well—I am too unhappy to say more but I shall never cease to love you wherever I am, & that I can never forget your goodness to me. Adieu.

He scribbled a postscript: 'I forgot to tell you I have had my Picture drawn, if you wish to have it, I will leave it here.'[1]

Two days later he was obliged to defend his morals again, and did so with all his customary ineptitude.

I assure you that those who have mentioned to you, that I am with all the girls, forgot himself as my *Temperament* is quite otherwise, having enough to do with La Hollandaise whom the Devil cannot content, much more me . . . I am sorry that I have sent Louis since you do not like his coming, but what cou'd I do—every body upon my Back, & I have not had a sous in my pocket these 3 weeks. . . . It is as false as can be that I give mony to Women, on the Contrary, I have received from Marigny a very elegant present, & the only thing in return she will have, will be those Clasps. As for La Hollandaise, since I have known her I have never had a sous.

It was naive to expect that such excuses would appease either his sister or Miss Hammerton. This latter, he decided, was 'a very good girl' but only as a friend. He would keep her letter, which was 'curious', for Fanny's inspection—not a very honourable intention, any more than hers when she had shown Miss Hammerton his account of his gallantries.

She had written discouragingly about the business of his legacy, and

[1] 2 Feb. 1791.

he replied that it would be hard on him not to get the money, 'as I have bought several things that I wanted & must pay by the end of this Month'.

We cannot but be moved by a certain sympathy for a man so void of any capacity to disentangle himself from his difficulties, but it crumbles when we find him basely lying. 'What can be the Correspondence of Mrs Byron be [sic]? I hope not for mony, as she has had quite enough, & never would give me a farthing.'[1]

He is speaking of his wife, who had always been unable to refuse him anything, and who was obliged at that very time to sacrifice £15 a year from her tenuous income to pay the interest on the loan she had obtained chiefly for him. Mrs Byron's letter, about which Fanny had informed him, was one of the most pathetic ever written by that wronged woman. Though she had never met her sister-in-law, and plainly knew little of her character, she had humiliated herself to appeal to her:

> . . . Some time ago I wrote to Mr Byron telling him I had not a farthing in the world nor could I get any at present, and begging him to ask you to lend him thirty pounds or forty pounds to send to me, to which he returned for answer that he could not think of asking you as you had been so good to him but that he had wrote to a person that he hoped would send it to me. This was only to put me off, as I don't know a person in the world who would advance that sum for him but yourself & tho' it is all owing to the debts I became bound to pay for him & the extravagant way he would live when he was here which my income could not afford that I am in this situation, which all comes on me. I only say this to let you know what situation I am in & that me nor my child have not at present a farthing nor know where to get one . . . The reason I trouble you with this letter is to beg you will have the goodness to lend me thirty or forty pounds. I will pay you honestly in May next. I would not ask you if your mother had not been dead [i.e. if there had not been a legacy]. . . . I beg an answer as soon as possible.[2]

Fanny Leigh had sent news of this communication to her brother the day she received it, January 29th, but without mentioning the painful entreaty; otherwise he would not have enquired whether Mrs Byron was wanting money. As Fanny had not relieved his urgent needs in all these weeks, though most of the debts for which he was being dunned were her own, it would be too much to hope that she aided one who was a stranger to her; but at least she sent a friendly response, and Mrs Byron was able to write to her about her son, 'really a charming boy', and to try and enlist her aid in getting the surgeon in London, John Hunter, to have suitable footwear made for him. 'I am perfectly sure he would walk very well if he had a proper shoe.'[3]

---

[1] 4 Feb.   [2] 31037, Horton Papers. 21 Jan. 1791.   [3] Ibid. 8 May 1791.

Jack Byron was interested only in his daughter, and as a renewed and pressing request for her address followed immediately on the treacherous pretence that his wife had never given him 'a farthing', we may reasonably conjecture what notion was in his mind.

On February 8th, he had the dreadful news from Fanny that he had already signed away his share of his mother's estate, on which he had been counting implicitly to get him out of the trap. He could not see how it had happened, though he acknowledged he had put his signature to 'a paper at Deal . . . for the 500£' which a lawyer well known to the family had drawn up; but whoever was taking advantage of that must be 'the greatest Rascal on earth'—a title hitherto reserved for the French notary.

A week after that he reached a further milestone on his road to destruction. His clothes were seized at the instance of one Villette, a caterer who had supplied his dinners and suppers.

> I hope to God you will come soon—as it is impossible to stay here, without going to prison—I have not a farthing & [am] in debt to every body. As for Talusbrus he has lent me every farthing he has—& is the best creature breathing—
>
> God knows what I am to do—I never stir out & really have very little to eat or drink.[1]

He did not seem to grasp that, if he had assigned his £500, it was not in Fanny's power to collect it, and he went so far, in a later letter, as to say he would die in the King's Bench rather than forfeit it.

Fanny did at last remit £25 to him through Talusbrus, and he dealt it out among the grocer, the baker, and several creditors who were 'in absolute want'.

> For God's sake come as soon as possible as that rascal Louis has wrote [that] you owe six thousand pounds—& many other things—if I ever catch him I will break every bone he has.
>
> Talusbrus sup'd with me & he has staid till near 1 o'clock—drunk as a pig with Punch. Talk'd of you, & cannot live without you—I beg'd him to moderate his Ardour. . . .[2]

He himself was feeling 'used up', his perpetual cold still preying upon him, but that night he was going to the play. The Schoners and he had made friends again and they were proving benevolent, but within a few weeks the ardent Talusbrus was no longer to be counted on. He was 'dying for love' not of Fanny but a new actress, while the former companion, Renaud, was moving away with his regiment. The revelation by

---

[1] 16 Feb. 1791.   [2] 6 Mar.

Louis of Fanny's debts in England had effectually ruined any hopes of new credit in France, and the tradesmen whose bills were overdue were growing very sceptical about Monsieur Byron's reiterated promise of her imminent arrival with money.

> God knows what I shall do, if you are not here by the sixth of next month—as those Billets are payable at that time, & every body is so exasperated—that it is impossible to remain here—& indeed I know not what to do—
>
> I hope you will bring me a Coat as I have not one upon my Back—with some Linen—I have no credit & am obliged to borrow by little & little. If we have a war—with Russia I will try to do something—as I am tired of this idle Life. . . . Pray come. If the mony is good, you may easily borrow, as nothing is so easy.[1]

He must have regretted sending a servant to England who had so little cause to be loyal to him. Louis had made mischief between Fanny and M. Schoner, and she was disapproving of the friendship, which, since the desertion of Talusbrus, was the last that was left to him. But he and Schoner had been able, the day before his writing, to get drunk with two friars, 'very good sort of people', he assured her. 'Schoner could hardly walk.' Afterwards he had gone and picked a senseless quarrel with an actor named David, whom he had taunted with wearing false calves. 'There was the Devil to pay.'[2] His persistence in advertising indiscretions and follies that were sure to bring reproof upon his head has its very distinct echo in a voice he did not live to hear.

Fanny was altogether in a castigating frame of mind. In response to the news that her little bird, notwithstanding all his attentions, had died, she had accused him of carelessness, and he protested, 'Your bird was not trod to death, but died a natural death. I have got another as good. Fanny is well & my Canary birds are laying their Eggs like fury.'[3]

That was the last letter he was to write without the note of frantic distress, for his downhill career was gaining impetus. On April 9th, bailiffs inspected the contents of the house, and he had pawned every possession of his own at the Mont de Piété and had 'not a single thing left to sell'. Fanny's hairdresser had vainly tried to collect thirty livres from him, and Schoner was besieged by her creditors.

> I wou'd not pass a fortnight more so for the world—& if you do not come I will go to Mons as they cannot touch me there. . . . I do not know what you mean by your *Rencontres*, but I hope you will have the resolution to come here if possible—both for your sake & mine. . . .
>
> My dear Sister think of what I suffer. You have no Idea, I am really so

[1] 30 Mar. [2] 3 Apr. 1791. [3] Ibid.

alter'd that you will hardly know me. . . . I am never well, & drink so much Brandy & water—that I am never sober in order to drown care. Talusbrus is still in Love—& we seldom speak. I advise you to come directly as there are several Bills due, & Henian reports such things that I am ashamed to repeat.[1]

Three days more and the bailiffs were in full possession of her portable goods of value, and they had to lend him forks and spoons for his meals.

I dare not go out as every body points at me—& your Loge is let as they will not beleive you will come back. For God's sake come if possible, as it is impossible for me to remain here longer. The Man threatens to take the furniture away every minute, & I shall not have a bed to sleep on—no person will give me credit for a sous, & I live absolutely on mere Bread. I wish the Marquis was at the Devil as I am afraid I shall not see you for some time.

This is the first hint we have that not penury but a new love affair was keeping Fanny in London—unless his speaking of her 'Rencontres' in the previous letter has that significance. Perhaps her lover had been the means of her sending the £25 a month ago.

Talusbrus, from being 'the best creature breathing', had become in her brother's eyes 'a Scrub'. Unless Fanny could come and raise the siege he must somehow get away, or: 'A prison will be my Lodging . . . You perhaps think that the Laws were as before—I can assure [you] they are alter'd & exactly the same as the English.'

Josephine, who was still sharing his dreary lot, desired him to say that Fanny's watch, which had been pawned with many other objects—possibly to finance her journey to England—would be sold next week if the interest was left unpaid.[2]

Before this letter had completed its journey to London, another angry one came from Fanny, rebuking him for giving 'balls, etc': 'I can only answer that we had one Ball, the Mardi Gras—& there was nobody but the Servants of the house, with the Epicier & his family. . . . God knows what I have suffer'd, & I do not wish you to know it.'

So lowly a festivity for a man who had played host to the Maréchal Biron and the nobility of France when lording it with his first wife, gives us the measure of his *degringolade*. (That there were still resident servants in a house where the wages were unpaid and the food supply precarious must be as strange to some of us as the idea of literally going to the moon would have been to Jack Byron.)

The good-natured Schoner had pawned his silver buckles to keep his desperate friend going and was in danger of losing everything he possessed

[1] 10 Apr.   [2] 13 Apr.

when the bills he had guaranteed fell due. Fanny was told of this ('He is the best friend you have'), but nothing would mollify her. She had been annoyed, among other matters, at the word 'Rencontre'. The reply was abject:

> I meant nothing by it. You are certainly the mistress to act as you please. . . . I never meant to offend you, & when my Conduct is known, you will, I hope, think that I do not merit the letter you wrote, & whatever happens, you will always be dear to me & that I can never cease to Love you.[1]

Next he had to defend himself against the accusation of wasting money on actresses. He thought Miss Hammerton must have repeated some gossip she had heard from her many correspondents at Valenciennes: 'As for the Comediennes they have been the least of my Expenses—& God knows that they are poor for they all of them have left the Town without paying a farthing.'[2]

It must have been a sorry business to be a tradesman or an innkeeper in that region. The Revolution, little as many who lived through it recognized its existence, was reaching out to the provinces and changing for good or ill the normal order. The town had no present use for its demi-monde. La Henry, la Marigny, la Hollandaise, had departed. The theatre was 'all knocked up'. A well-bred wastrel who did not understand anything about liberty, equality, and fraternity, was *persona non grata*.

He toyed with different plans for making an exit from so cheerless a scene. Now he would enlist, if only as a non-commissioned officer, and now return to England to scrape money together somehow. And then he wondered if he could make his way to India, where his brother, George Anson Byron,[3] was a peculiarly low-spirited naval officer—to whom he had been owing money for years. But escape was cut off. The town gates had been closed against him by order of the magistrates.

> Beleive me that the predicament I am in is rather serious. Your Letters are short, & no ways comforting, as I have neither food nor cloaths to put on—
> Madame Schoner was so good as to say that you was a Lyar, & that you Lay in at Rheims which Josephine told her. I forgot Miss Josephine['s] Sex, & knocked her down & beat her so that she has kept her bed for these two days.[4]

The Frenchman, Amédée Pichot, who wrote an essay on Lord Byron's character and genius, clearly knew something when he spoke of Captain Byron's 'brutality' and his 'hardness and grossness', and the poet was

---

[1] 20 Apr.   [2] 24 Apr.
[3] His son and namesake became the 7th Lord Byron.   [4] 11 May 1791.

The Capricious Marchioness.   *The Boisterous Lover.*

Published by A. Hamilton Jun.r near S.t John's Gate Feb.1 1779.

Byron's father, Captain John Byron and his future wife, Augusta
Leigh's mother, the Marchioness of Carmarthen

Mrs Byron, the poet's mother, from the portrait by Thomas Stewardson

much mistaken in so emphatically denying these characteristics in his father.[1]

> You desire me to keep up my spirits [the despairing man went on, losing some of his humility]. How is it possible? when every person here denies me credit, & I live absolutely on mere nothing, wanting even beer, which is the cheapest article at present—as it is four sous to the pot.

Still Fanny left him to bear the whole brunt of the extravagances of both, and at last his deferential tone gave way to bitterness.

> Your letter dated the 10th I received on Friday—I am obliged to you for your consolation particularly as I am in the greatest distress, & cannot help thinking that you mean for me to remain here in Prison, as it must end in that. Poor Schoner keeps his bed, & Debuss the Tapissier [Fanny's upholsterer] has put the Gardes [in] & his things & goods are to be sold next week. . . . You must remember very well that Schoner signed a note for you payable in May—payable for 400 livres. . . . Every person is exasperated against you . . . I received from Henian an Assignat of 50 Livres—which is the same to me as 50 Sous—as it was all swallowed up the moment I received it by the Butcher & Baker &c. I have but one Coat to my Back, & that in rags—a Servant has robb'd me of 17 pairs of Silk Stockings—& when I cou'd prove the robbery the Judges wou'd not hear my witness, nor myself . . . Since you are gone all the Laws are changed. . . .
>
> I advise you to help Schoner if possible as he is not to blame & it is really hard for him, as he has been very kind of late to me but she is the D——st bitch that exists. . . . She says everywhere you have taken her lace & sold it for your own account.
>
> As for Miss Josephine she wishes me to pardon her—after the drubbing I gave her—but I never speak to her & she is Henian['s] spy. . . .

Though he remained so ill as to be confined to his room, he was thinking now of joining the French army even as a private: '. . . That is better than to remain in the despicable situation I am in. I am sorry to be so explicit, as I do not mean to offend you—but I wou'd rather be a Galley Slave than what I am at present—& suffer the indignity I do now —for I have neither Health nor Comfort.'[2]

This letter only made Fanny more angry. It was odd undoubtedly to hear that the writer had been robbed of seventeen pairs of silk stockings when he had only one ragged coat to his back, and she seems to have thought that some of his woes were fabrications.

> All I can say [he responded] is that when you arrive here, you will find that what I have suffer'd has not been exagerated—& that both you & me

---

[1] *LJ.* Letter to J. J. Coulmann, 12 July 1823.   [2] 15 May 1791.

have the greatest obligations to the General Talusbrus—for without him every thing wou'd have been sold in the publick place. When we meet I will explain every thing.[1]

The General, uncle of Fanny's former lover, was evidently fascinated as so many had been, by the attractive personality of the ex-Captain of Guards, who resumed his habit of going to the theatre nightly, and was guest to that gentleman in what had been Fanny's box, and this despite an effort by Henian to have his defaulting client forbidden the entrée. But at the end of May the box was let to another subscriber, so it would appear the General had moved on.

Mme Schoner had caused Fanny's clothes to be seized, but late in May, Fanny was able to send Schoner a remittance, and took the precaution of addressing it directly to him, which intensely annoyed her brother.

> . . . He has received your mony, but I have not a farthing & know not where to get a sous. You promised to send me some. He has kept the whole for himself, nor will he lend me a farthing. They are both so inveterate against you & me. . . .

Jack Byron's regard for his friends and relations hinged solely upon how readily they answered his incessant financial demands on them. Schoner, the boon companion who had pledged his shoe buckles to help him, had declined to pay the interest on Fanny's pawned silver, and was henceforth numbered with the enemy.

> I hope you do not intend to be godmother to Schoner's Child, as I have flatly refused my part of the Business . . . Today I am Godfather to a Son of one Smidt, a German, who teaches me the language & I have put you for Godmother, & he is very proud, & Madame Schoner is ready to burst with anger. It will cost you nothing.

It is a singular illustration of the magic that surrounded the gentry— or perhaps of the Byron charisma—that anyone should have wanted that bankrupt pair, in such bad odour with the tradesmen of the town, to stand sponsor to their child. There could have been no better hope of the godfather's capacity to promote the earthly prospects of the infant than its spiritual welfare. 'I have literally', he wrote on this occasion, 'but 3 pr of Stockings—& those full of holes—Shirts I have none, that can be called so.'

The sands were fast running out. Fanny sent nothing. He was neglected, sick, mistrusted, deprived of fellowship with any of his kind. He

---

[1] 25 May.

threatened that he would 'make the best shift I can—& take to my heels',[1] but he would have needed a disguise to pass beyond the town gates.

'It is useless in me to write my Situation', he lamented after some days, 'as you do not believe it', and he repeated with all the monotony of his limited vocabulary his dismal expostulation about not having 'a Sous to buy the common necessaries of Life'. How much he had depended on his appearance for his sense of well-being is to be judged by his more often complaining of being without clothes than nourishment. Yet his reputation for gallantry and patronage had not altogether evaporated.

> . . . Here is an english woman who plays on the Stage & is the first actress. She is married to an Actor who is the second, Bastalle. I do not know how but she has wrote to me, however I have not been to see her—nor will not till you come back—which I hope will be soon.[2]

He begged for two hundred livres to get him out of the straits he was in, 'every person refusing me credit'. Somehow he was managing to feed the bitch named Fanny, which was expecting a litter, and the birds were breeding too. 'I have already five young ones—that is all the good news.'

Before these poor little crumbs of self-consolation had reached the obdurate woman in London, she had sent him another of her remonstrating letters, to which he replied with the last he was destined to write to her.

Valenciennes—June the 8th 1791

My Dearest Sister

Your letter has made me too unhappy to say much, as you reproach me with *Ingratitude* which God knows I do not want towards you. If you knew my situation! You will forgive me when you know it.

I beg you will take what comes to me for yourself as it is your *due*. . . . I must try to shift for myself. As for the *friend* that told me you liv'd with the Marquis de [illegible name], the same who wrote you *word* of it was the same who informed me—

I received three Louis from Henian—which nothing but necessity cou'd make me take. I have not a shirt to my Back nor a Coat, as the one I had here is totally used.

You say every thing you do displeases me. I once more repeat that my situation is such, that if I utter'd any thing in my letters that has offended you, I am sorry for it, as my intention was never to cause the least uneasiness to you. For your own sake do not listen too much to those who write you all the news.

Adieu. Believe me Your Ever
Affecte Brother
J. Byron—

---

[1] Ibid.   [2] 5 June 1791.

On June 21st he dictated his will in French to two notaries, leaving Fanny as his executrix and sole beneficiary of the £400 he believed was recoverable from his father's and mother's estates, and charging his penniless son of three to pay his debts and funeral expenses. Six weeks later he was dead. He may have decided that the only solution for him, near starvation and almost in rags as we cannot doubt he was, and profoundly hurt by Fanny's defection, lay in a dose of poison, which could then have been procured from any pharmacist with no difficulty but that of paying for it; but Augusta Leigh believed his sister had been present at his deathbed,[1] and Mrs Byron wrote to her, 'You say he was sensible to the last.'[2] Fanny might of course have chosen to conceal an end so sombre and, in those days, criminal, as she must surely have concealed the seamy side of her own past glimpsed in these letters. On the other hand, he had long been in a deplorable state of health and may well have died from natural causes. Someone, seeing his extremity, may have sent her a message which finally brought her back to France.

On first reading this sequence, I was of the opinion that her nephew, Lord Byron, must have been acquainted with it and been drawn by a fatal impulse to trace, in his amatory life, the same path. That was the view formed by the authors of *Lord Byron and his Detractors*, except that they supposed he had 'boasted' of an act he did not commit—which, to our present way of thinking, would be worse than committing it, because it would have been wantonly involving an innocent party. I have now been obliged to reverse my conclusion as to his ever having set eyes on the correspondence at all.

It belonged not to him but to Augusta, probably coming to her through her husband, the elder Mrs Leigh's son, and it could hardly have been in her hands before the recipient's death, which did not take place till 1823, seven years after Augusta's last parting from Byron. Frances Leigh spent her latter years at Hythe in Kent in such good possession of her faculties that Augusta was writing to John Murray to borrow books for her. It is unthinkable that she would have allowed her son and daughter-in-law any opportunity of seeing letters with such gross allusions while she still retained control of them; odd enough indeed that she preserved them, but that may have been with a postponed intention to destroy them that was thwarted by forgetfulness and death.

That Jack Byron had loved her according to his cloudy lights, that his attitude to her was both sentimental and emotional, must, I think, impress itself on every reader; and she, selfish and giddy though she was,

---

[1] Undated letter of 1830 to John Hanson, the solicitor.
[2] Murray MS. 23 Aug. 1791. (See p. 49.)

must have been moved by some reciprocal feeling to have kept a souvenir so little likely to reflect well on her if discovered.

If Byron did not, by some remarkable accident, come across letters addressed to an aunt whom he scarcely seems to have met, neither need we suspect that he heard any rumour which would have fired his imagination with the idea of not being 'outdone by his own father'.[1] The 18th-century press was scurrilous, and had there been any scandal touching 'Mad Jack Byron's' conduct with his sister, quite capable of obliquely publishing it: but, though his adultery with Lady Carmarthen had been accorded full attention, no worse stories found their way into print. Fanny's household was in a part of northern France little frequented by her countrymen, and the curious obscure life she and her brother lived there was not witnessed by society gossips.

It would therefore appear that the poet and Augusta, in their much less culpable passion (for besides having only one parent in common, they had been brought up apart), were following a course to which they were, by inheritance of temperament, foredoomed.

At first it was Augusta who evinced a constant solicitude for a relative whom she had met so seldom that the occasions cannot be traced: and as she was reared among numerous young people—the Duke of Leeds, formerly Lord Carmarthen, having a family by his second wife as well as his first—this affection cannot be ascribed to the loneliness of an orphaned only child. All were warmly disposed to her—she speaks of their '*great* and *uniform*' kindness in a somewhat bridling letter to Mrs Byron,[2] who had evidently pictured her as neglected—and, beside their attentions, there were those of plentiful cousins, and particularly the dashing if thriftless young Hussar, George Leigh, whom she was to marry. Even during her long engagement to this man of fashion, a frequent companion of the Prince Regent, she was always deeply interested in the wayward adolescent at Harrow, who forgot her existence for months at a time.

Thus she writes from Kiveton, the Duke of Leeds's mansion at Worksop, to Hanson, Byron's solicitor, when she is getting on for twenty and Byron only fifteen:

> I take the liberty of troubling you with a few lines, being extremely anxious to hear from *you* some account of my Brother. . . . I can't prevail upon *him ever* to indulge me with a letter & his mother's are always short and *un*satisfactory about him . . . The very great interest I of course feel in all that concerns him will I trust plead my excuse for plaguing you with en-

[1] See p. 14.
[2] 25 Feb. 1802. All Augusta's letters here quoted are Murray MSS.

quiries. Be so good as not to mention to *Mrs B.* having heard from me on this subject.[1]

She intensely disliked 'Mrs B.' with whom, since infancy, she could only have been very slightly acquainted; but she had had adverse reports of her from Byron's reluctant guardian, Lord Carlisle. Some maternal instinct must have been aroused in Augusta by the criticisms she heard of young Byron's imprudent upbringing. At the Christmas season just past, he had attended Lady Riddell's masquerade in Bath dressed as a Turkish boy, and after the holiday she knew he had, for some time, refused to return to school. Augusta—most of whose children were to turn out incorrigible—was hoping he would be 'placed with some Clergyman till he is ready for Colledge [sic]'.

She saw him soon after this, for in June next year, asking Hanson to 'mention all you hear of my dear Brother', she remarked on how much she had been 'struck with his general improvement'. But though he had been 'a most delightful correspondent' while in Nottinghamshire, she could not get 'a single line from Harrow'.[2] He did in fact write to her intermittently, and in a charming and humorous strain, but it was generally to sketch out before her sympathetic eyes the bitter comedy of his quarrels with his mother. Whenever he lapsed into silence, she would anxiously question Hanson, the confidant of her benevolent plan to bring him and Lord Carlisle together without the interference of Mrs Byron.

In 1806 there was, however, an estrangement between them, in which Byron behaved with unusually prolonged sullenness. At the end of his first Cambridge term, before he turned eighteen, he addressed her, imploring 'the most inviolable Secrecy', to ask if she would stand as joint security with him—he being under age—for a loan of several hundred pounds from a money-lender.[3] She desired greatly to help him and at first seemed to acquiesce, but, not surprisingly, she hesitated and let the secret out to John Hanson and possibly Byron's guardian too. It was that, rather than her failure to support him in his foolish measure, which, presumably, offended him and lost her, for longer than a year, his friendship. He procured the money through the misguided connivance of his landlady, Mrs Massingberd, and ceased to communicate with Augusta.

This led to her writing a succession of letters to Hanson full of dismay and attempts at reconciliation. She met Hanson at her own request towards mid-February 1806, but addressed him again on the 21st:

I am afraid from your not having written to me since our interview that

[1] 17 June 1804.   [2] 13 Feb. 1803.   [3] Marchand, *Letters*. 27 Dec. 1805.

you have nothing of a favourable nature to communicate. I own I perfectly despair of my Brother's ever altering his tone towards me, for when one has put oneself very much in the wrong, it is very difficult to get right again —The only excuse I can make for troubling you again on this sad subject, is the wretchedness it has inflicted upon me—*time* serves rather to encrease than to remove it—and to have lost his affection & esteem appears to me a still more severe affliction than his death would have been.

This is an extraordinary degree of agitation for a socially successful girl, with an attractive suitor, to feel over an eighteen-year-old half-brother. On March 7th she expressed herself with annoyance we may suspect of arising from pique: 'I was much surprised and vexed to see my brother a week ago at ye play—as I think he *ought* to employ his time more profitably at Cambridge.'

On March 18th they were still at loggerheads, but she was glad to have a pretext for writing 'two lines' to him about an old family servant, Joe Murray, who was in want of a place. Byron would not have ignored this approach, protective to servants and ex-servants as he always was, but his reply, whatever it may have been, did not heal the breach. Within a month Augusta was again trying to organize, through Hanson, a meeting between the intractable youth and Lord Carlisle, with whom she was staying in Grosvenor Place. She feared from Hanson's silence that he had 'very unsatisfactory intelligence to communicate. I can't bear ye idea of ye *latter*. . . . Ld. C. seems very anxious to hear my Brother is a little more reasonable and I am sure you can imagine *my* feelings on the subject.'[1]

The following February (1807) she begged Hanson to call and see her: '*I* cannot forget I have a Brother or cease to feel anxiety about him & I know no other method of obtaining any intelligence.'[2]

At some date in July, the month before she married, she pleaded with Hanson despondently:

> Will you tell me if you think there is the slightest hope of his forgiving me—or the least possibility of my doing *any* thing in the world to obtain this forgiveness. I wd not torment you, but that I am sure you wish for a reconciliation between us and that I am *perfectly wretched* at his continuing angry—& you know there is not anything I wd not do to regain his good opinion & affection, which I trust I don't *quite deserve* to have lost—for that idea wd greatly augment my distress.
>
> I hear too that he looks ill & is grown quite thin in comparison to what he was—& I feel quite unhappy about him. . . .
>
> I did write him a line on his arrival to beg 10 minutes conversation with him—but have had no answer.

[1] 17 Apr. 1806.   [2] 1 Feb.

Hanson's mediation was successful, for on July 18th she wrote him a note thanking him for news which 'concerns my happiness so materially. God grant that yr *Predictions* may be verified & that I may see my Brother.' The fulfilment of those predictions was the greatest misfortune of Augusta's desolated life. We cannot say that, if she had never seen Byron again, it would have been a happy one. Her husband was a gambler and threatened with a court-martial for his shady handling of regimental funds as early as 1809,[1] and there would always have been troubles brought about by his debts, her fecklessness, and the headstrong follies of their children: but it is utterly improbable that she would have had to spend long years expiating cardinal sin and being used as an instrument to exalt the spiritual vanity of her sister-in-law: improbable indeed that Byron would have made so rash a marriage without his need to strive for 'redemption'.

I do not suggest that, when she longed to befriend the difficult, capricious, but disarmingly frank and amusing boy who loved her gaiety, she was aware for one moment of the sexual magnetism which was to turn him into an *homme fatal*: yet that must surely have played some unrecognized part in her insistent attachment to him; while on his side the attachment itself would gradually awaken kindred feeling, though of an immensely more complex kind. Augusta, with her mild temper, her beautiful manners, her easy adaptability, would have appealed to him merely by virtue of presenting a striking contrast to his mother. And then there was his belief that he was born under a compulsion to do dark deeds and violate the laws of society, yielding himself up—and sacrificing her—to a love which had 'something of the terrible in it', and afterwards to the hauntings of desperate self-punishing remorse.

The sight of his father's letters might have spared him all that. He could either have accepted his heredity with a shrug and renounced the heady sense of sin which had given his passion for Augusta its special quality, or even have felt discouraged from pursuing the passion. At all events he could scarcely have gone on idealizing his father.

---

[1] Murray MSS.

2

Mrs Byron and her Enfant Terrible

George Gordon Byron could have been little more than two and a half when he last saw his father, but he believed he could remember him and the rows with his mother before their parting in Aberdeen. Our recollections of early infancy are so tinged with what we subsequently learn that they are not altogether dependable, but Byron was adept at seizing and retaining impressions, and it may be that he did clearly recall the raised voices and his mother's angry tears. He was nevertheless always very tender to his father's memory, and could not bear her to 'rake up his ashes' in the spirit of foreboding—which indeed her son, when in his teens, seemed all too likely to justify.

Although a number of observations on his intelligence and vivacity written while he was still a child show that he was even then exceptionally prepossessing, there are many others that indicate he was also most difficult and hot-headed; and had he been born into an unprivileged class, might have found himself in scrapes that would have proved no laughing matter. The anecdotes of his juvenile years may have been coloured by later knowledge of his defiant character, but there are enough from good sources to leave no doubt that Mrs Byron's handsome little lame boy had been from early infancy 'an ill-deedie laddie', as one Highland critic of his behaviour put it, or 'the little deevil Geordie Byron' of several others.

We have stories of his striking Lady Abercromby in the face for recommending his mother to beat him, hitting someone with a switch for audibly mentioning that it was a pity about his leg, damaging a miller's wheel by putting sticks and other obstructions in it, dressing a pillow up in his clothes and throwing it out of the window, to give his mother, sitting near the window below, a fright. It was also told by his nurse as a sample of his boldness that, when he was taken to see *The Taming of the Shrew*, he listened in attentive silence to the performance until Petruchio contradicted Katherine with the line:

'Nay then, you lie—it is the blessed sun!'

whereupon he started up from his seat crying out loudly, 'But I say it is the *moon*, sir!' Sheer literal-mindedness, however inconvenient, was so typical of him throughout his life, that I cannot doubt the discredited May Gray's veracity in this instance. Mrs Byron, who was not deficient in humour, would have been amused at that, but her temper was unpredictable, and what would make her smile one day would annoy her on another.

It was a time when corporal punishment had the full approval of all but a handful of advanced educators, of whom she was not likely to have heard. She would suddenly inflict a hard and hasty slap on his face ('a box on the ear' in the current phrase), particularly when he bit his nails; but the cold-blooded canings most boys were subjected to, he was spared. Her temper gave itself vent mostly in shouting at him with the pungent invective of the North Briton: and although that may not have been edifying, it seems to have had no worse effect than to give him an unfair aversion from women who made scenes—unfair because he often provoked them.

On one occasion he was severely whipped, but not by her. When staying with the family of his solicitor, Hanson, during school holidays at the age of about twelve, the cook, whom he was in the habit of bothering, said or did something that enraged him, and he actually seized a gun from its place over the chimneypiece in the hall, aimed it at her and pulled the trigger. Her cap was peppered with shot. For this his host is said to have taken it upon himself to punish him with a horsewhip.[1] I think it very doubtful that Byron knew the gun was loaded, because, unless he had been able to plead with conviction that he had only meant to make a gesture, he would hardly have been invited to stay in that house again and again.

From infancy, then, he was an indocile, obstreperous boy and, having regard to the history of his ancestors, might have been so if his mother's demeanour had been that of Patient Griselda. Admittedly it was not, but the painful phase when everything she did and said was a nervous irritation to him only began after those alarming financial extravagances which filled her with dread lest he should follow the same courses as his father.

Who can doubt that he would have had more cause for shame in that reckless man, had he lived, than in the hot-tempered but staunch and honest mother whose sacrifice he never recognized? It is the tendency of children brought up by only one parent to form a rosy picture of the other whose weaknesses are not apparent to their view, and, for all her tantrums, Mrs Byron must have concealed her husband's worst defects,

---

[1] Prothero. This anecdote is not in the Hanson Narrative, and I should have thought it apocryphal if it had come from a less conscientious authority. Hanson does recall that Byron was troublesome to the cook. I am a little dubious about the horsewhip.

or Byron could not have cherished through life the image of a seductive improvident rake rather than a reprobate who would kick a woman downstairs. Augusta fully shared the idealized view, writing with disgust to John Hanson when Moore's biography came out:

> I am *greatly* vexed at *all* the details about my Father. I think to have said he was a wild extravagant young Man would have been *quite* sufficient as he died too early to have any influence on my Brother's character which his poor Mother's failings could not fail to have.[1]

And she took up her pen again to complain sarcastically of Moore's '*charitable* aspersions' and to say she had been searching day and night for a letter in her possession which would refute them. It was from Mrs Byron to her (Augusta's) mother-in-law after hearing of Captain Byron's death, and must have been her outburst of grief to Frances Leigh who had broken the news to her:

> . . . If I had known of his illness I would have come to him. . . . Necessity, not inclination, parted us, at least on my part, and I flatter myself it was the same with him; and notwithstanding all his foibles, for they deserve no worse name, I ever sincerely loved him. . . . I do not think I shall ever recover the severe shock I have received. . . . If only I had seen him before he died.[2]

Catherine Byron, poor, lonely, and twenty-six when widowed, had hoped for some intimacy with the sister of the man to whom she had been so inexpressibly indulgent, and in the letter above quoted, held out an eager hand: 'Believe me, my dear Madam, I have the greatest regard and affection for you, for the very kind part you have acted to poor Mr Byron and it is a great comfort to me that he was with so kind a friend at the time of his death.'

Mrs Leigh, however, had no desire for closer acquaintance with one of whom she had heard nothing but what was detrimental ('I defy you and all the Apostles to live with her two months', her brother had written to her)[3] and she let the correspondence peter out. Mrs Byron made fresh attempts:

> My dear Madam,
>   This is the third letter I have wrote to you since I heard from you nor can I think what can be the cause of your not writing. I should have supposed you would have wrote before now to have enquired about your Newphew

---

[1] Murray MS. 25 Jan. 1830. The so-called George Gordon Byron forged a version of this letter pretending Augusta had addressed it to himself.
[2] Murray MS. 23 Aug. 1791 (misprinted 1799 in *LJ*).
[3] 16 Feb. 1791.

[sic]. He is a fine Boy and very well and walks and runs as well as any other child.[1]

The reason why she was reopening a closed correspondence, and trying to acquit her little son of the blemish of lameness, was that she had learned by chance he had suddenly become heir to the barony. 'I hear Mrs Parker is dead[2] and that your Newphew Ld Byron's Grandson is dead but I have not been informed of it from any of the family. I shall be anxious till I receive a few lines informing me of your health. I have at last found out your direction.'

The fact that not a single one of her late husband's kith and kin had bothered to let her know that William John Byron, grandson of the 5th or 'Wicked' Lord, had been killed in battle at Calvi, leaving her son next in line of succession to the title and estates, gives some indication of their indifference to her. She and the boy living in the North of Scotland, whom none of them had ever set eyes on—unless in his cradle—must have seemed almost unreal to them.

A very few further letters were exchanged, and Mrs Byron asked Fanny if the 5th Lord were likely to give any financial aid with his heir's education. The reply could only be negative because he was an eccentric and misanthropic recluse with formidable pecuniary embarrassments.

Fanny's interest was centred on her brother's elder child, the socially more eligible Augusta Byron, and it was on her she bestowed her attentions. In the hope, we may imagine, of finding friends for her son in that station of life which he would one day enjoy, Mrs Byron had vainly humbled very high pride, and she was proportionately mortified by failure. She took a strong dislike to her unhelpful sister-in-law, which must have been reinforced when, her husband's futile will being translated and proved, it turned out that he had left nothing but debts to his son and £400 to his sister—and she could not be sure he had signed away his portion of his mother's marriage settlement as well as his father's legacy. She may even have come to know, eventually, how little that lady's character and pursuits had tended to influence Jack Byron beneficially. For at least one or two of these reasons, she took lasting umbrage when her stepdaughter, Augusta, became engaged to Frances Leigh's son.

During some period of her ill-fated marriage, and before her retreat to Aberdeen with her baby, she had looked after Augusta, then an infant, and nursed her through a serious illness, and as years went by she had made affectionate enquiries about her. There too she was rebuffed.

---

[1] 31037, Horton Papers. 23 Nov. 1794.

[2] Mrs Parker was Mrs Leigh's younger sister, wife of Vice-Admiral Christopher Parker, and the news of her death was less accurate than that concerning her nephew.

Augusta's maternal grandmother discouraged such overtures, as we may gather from Mrs Byron's blundering letter of condolence to Augusta when Lady Holderness died:

> As I wish to bury what is past *in oblivion* I shall avoid all reflections on a Person now no more, my opinion of yourself I have suspended for some years—the time is now arrived when I shall form a very *decided* one.
>
> I take up my pen however to console with you on the melancholy event that has happened, to offer you every consolation in my power, to assure you of the unalterable regard and friendship of myself and Son. . . .
>
> Your Brother is at Harrow School and if you wish to see him I have now no desire to keep you asunder.[1]

Clearly she had expressed such a desire when snubbed by Lady Holderness,[2] and that must have been after 1798 when she brought her ten-year-old son, now a peer, to England: while living nearly in the Highlands she would have had no occasion to keep them asunder.

Augusta's reply was apparently polite, and Mrs Byron, pathetically groping out for some link with the family to which she owed nothing but distresses, wrote again, evidently in a tactless and emotional style which put Augusta on the defensive on behalf of all her relations but particularly her aunt Fanny Leigh.

> It was by the desire of my Guardian as well as my own, that I *have* spent & *mean* to spend some part of the Year with my Aunt. I have felt perfectly happy with her, & as yet have discovered *none* of those failings which you seem to suppose in her, and you must excuse me Dear Madam, if I do my cousin Julia the justice to say that she has ever appeared to have that Love & regard for our Aunt which she so justly deserves from *all* her nephews and nieces.[3]

(Fanny was helping to bring up Julia and George Anson Byron, the children of her second brother, who had died in 1793, two years after the first.)[4]

If there was ever a meeting between Mrs Byron and Frances Leigh, I have not found the record of it. The criticism which drew Augusta's

---

[1] Pratt. 18 Oct. 1801.

[2] Lord Holderness, father of the Hon. Amelia D'Arcy, later Baroness Conyers and Mrs Jack Byron, had been Governor to the Prince of Wales and the numerous other sons of George III.

[3] Murray MS. 25 Feb. 1802, from Gogmagog Hill, one of the Duke of Leeds's seats.

[4] George Anson's son, of the same name, inherited the poet's title. He was, like his father and grandfather, a naval officer. He became a close confidant and partisan of Lady Byron's when she left her husband, and, from his shuddering shock when he learned from her of Augusta's frail morals, must have known very little about his and her Aunt Fanny.

spirited reply may not allude to specific incidents. Any woman, placed as Mrs Byron was, would have felt the bitterness of rejection. Her circle of acquaintance was most limited and she had little opportunity of extending it because her means were so narrow. It could not have been agreeable to her, a resolute Whig, to have to copy and dispatch a letter of appeal, composed for her by Hanson, to the Duke of Portland, Tory leader of the House of Lords:

> My Lord,
>
> Being a Stranger to your Grace, I feel much Embarrassment in presuming to address you upon a Subject of so much Delicacy, but the Knowledge I have of your Grace's Candour and Goodness and the Peculiarity of my own Situation prompt me to solicit your Grace's attention to what I am about to state.
>
> By the Death of the late Lord Byron that Title devolved upon my Son now 12 years of age and with it an estate not Exceeding £_____ a Year and that even in a most dilapidated Condition. My own Situation is simply this, upon my Marriage with the late Mr Byron he possessed my Fortune which was considerably more than £20,000, but unfortunately for myself and Son all that is left is £4,200—and to ye Int[erest] thereof I am entitled during my life subject to a Payment thereout of £60 a year to my aged Grand Mother, which reduces my income to £150 a year which is all I have to live upon and since ye Death of Mr Byron in 17__ to the Death of the late Lord Byron in May 1798, I have had to maintain my Son out of it.
>
> I am myself descended from an ancient & Noble family, namely Sir Wm. Gordon who _____. It has been mentioned to me that Persons in my Situation have been thought ye object of His Majesty's bounty. May I then indulge a hope that my Situation when represented to the throne _____.[1]

There the draft ends, blanks being left when Hanson was uncertain what she might correctly say or how she might wish to end. Lord Carlisle was approached by him to support the application. An uncle by marriage of Jack Byron, he had been desired in the latter's deathbed will to act as guardian to his two children, and had certainly done handsomely by Augusta, who spent much of her girlhood with him and her great-aunt, Lady Carlisle. To judge by Augusta's letters, he had every disposition to be paternal with Byron too, but his dislike of Mrs Byron overcame his good intentions.

The Duke's reply to his suppliant was prompt and gracious.

> . . . I must beg you to accept my thanks for the confidence you are pleased to repose in me, which I hope you will not have any reason to think you have

[1] Murray MS. 23 July 1799. Byron was actually eleven: Hanson was a year out, perhaps because the boy was so precocious.

misplaced, or that I am wanting in the Respect which I have always professed for both the Illustrious Families to which you have the honor to
belong.[1]

He seized the earliest opportunity of speaking to the King, and on
August 24th 1799, within a month of first hearing from her, was able
to inform her that Mr Pitt had been ordered to pay her £300 a year. He
ended by repeating with very little variation that he hoped she would
regard his assistance as a tribute to the 'great houses' with which she
was connected.

Nowadays it would seem most extraordinary for a Minister to award
a pension on the sole grounds of good birth, and it was not quite ordinary
then; the explanation may be that many years before, there had been a
complicated mortgage transaction which left the Duke owing £1,000 and
much interest to the Byron estate, and he might now be sure he would
not be pressed for it by the heir. (Nevertheless Mrs Byron, in November
1803, was asking Hanson, 'Has the Duke of Portland paid the 1000 £ and
the interest due to my Son?')[2]

The pension was immensely welcome, but like most pensions in
those unbusiness-like days, it was very irregularly paid; and even thus
enlarged, her income was still inadequate to all the demands on it. She
had arrived in England in 1798 with almost nothing in hand. Out of the
tiny capital acquired from selling up her furniture in Aberdeen—it
fetched without the linen and plate, £74. 17s. 7d.—she had to pay £35
in 'Expenses for bringing Lord Byron from Scotland', and £25 for
mourning clothes. It must have been a struggle for her, but to withhold the customary visible homage to death would have been most
indecorous.

'The late Lord's male servts' also had to wear mourning. Their black
cloth came to nearly £11, and as the late Lord himself had been reduced
to such penury by his various follies that there was hardly money to bury
him, the bill was sent to the heir's mother, who paid it.

Mrs Byron kept accounts until near her death. She was not a skilful
bookkeeper, she confusingly ran one financial year into another, and
many entries are undated; but it is possible to obtain from her little
notebooks[3] a rough idea of the careful but certainly not ungenerous
management by which her son's house and Nottinghamshire lands were
lifted from a state of extreme and quite deliberate depredation[4] to one
of comfort and promise of abundance.

---

[1] Ibid. 28 July 1799.   [2] Ibid. Hanson copies.   [3] Ibid.
[4] The 5th Lord had disapproved so violently of his son's marriage to Juliana Byron,
another of Frances Leigh's sisters (see note on p. 22), that he had tried to make the
inheritance worthless by reckless timber-cutting and other wastage. He had also dis-

Before we consider any details of her domestic economy, it is well to stress the futility of trying to establish systematic comparisons between the money of her day and of ours. Successive inflations, whether of the creeping or the galloping kind, have brought about such depreciation of currencies that their values bear only a distant relation to those prevailing before the financial débâcles of the present century. Seventy-four pounds and some odd shillings was a modest enough sum for the furniture of a peer's mother, but not less than the household goods of the average small family were then worth, secondhand, in Scotland.

Mrs Byron had lived on £135 a year and even less without debt, keeping a resident nurse for her child and assuredly employing someone of humbler grade to carry coals, lay fires, wash dishes, scour pots and pans, scrub floors, black-lead grates, empty slops, and perform all the other menial tasks which would have been universally deemed unfit for a gentlewoman. The whole income on which she supported three to four people would not today run to the wages of one daily help. At much the same period, Benjamin Constant found that, even as a foreigner, travelling on horseback in Scotland did not cost half a guinea a day, while his rent in London lodgings was half a guinea a week, and his food, eating out, three shillings a day, with three shillings more for all incidental expenses. One could dine at a London tavern for a shilling—five new pence.

But while most items, and especially labour, are becoming ever more costly, others, which were imports from distant lands—tea, exotic fruits, cane sugar, cotton, cashmere, and silk—have grown cheaper. Again, the value of money must be measured not only by its purchasing power but by what it is considered essential to purchase in the sphere where one's lot is cast. The luxury of one generation is the necessity of another. Mrs Byron did not have bills for electricity, central heating, telephone, television, running a car, and a dozen other amenities which anyone living in a big and remote country house would find it very hard to do without at the present time. She was certainly not the owner of a vacuum cleaner, a refrigerator, a washing machine, any appliance for heating water other than a kitchen stove, or even any taps and pipes from which water could be drawn. The absence of such contrivances made it all the more impossible to manage without the assistance of a number of servitors. Fortunately they were in plentiful supply, receiving rather less per annum (nominally) than their modern counterparts—when available—per week.

The salary of the old butler, Murray, who had been 'inherited' from the 5th Lord, was £10 a year, and, as he did not share the family table,

---

posed of entailed property illegally, leaving his heir with a dragging lawsuit on his hands.

Byron by Vincenzo Cammuccini, c 1817

Byron by Sanders, c 1812

John Hanson from an aquatint

he had a subsistence allowance of eight shillings a week. Many house-holders, including, later on, Byron himself, found it better policy to give additional 'board wages' and let the staff cater for themselves than to allow extravagant bills to be run up below stairs. Beer was liberally provided, tea not.

The gamekeeper, Hardstaff, related to several Hardstaffs who were tenants and to 'Lady Betty', once the old Lord's mistress, had a quarter's board wages amounting to £6. 14s. Most employees on country estates lived rent-free, being provided with cottages we should now think enviable. True, they were not equipped with water closets and bathrooms, but neither were the great houses.

May Gray, Byron's pious and untrustworthy nurse, had £9 a year and was maintained. She was sent back to Scotland in 1799 under a cloud. Sarah Watnell, paid at the rate of eight guineas a year, was perhaps the cook: country housemaids received less. From 1809, the wage of eight guineas was no longer paid to Sarah but to one Martha, who presumably performed the same duties.

Quick-tempered as she was, Mrs Byron could not have been unkind because her servants remained with her so long. From 1802 onwards, while the Newstead mansion was let (and that it proved tenantable is a testimony to her efforts, because she found it almost ruinous), she had what Thomas Moore calls a 'waiting woman' named Mrs Bye at twelve guineas a year, a salary higher than Murray's, whom she was obliged to dispense with temporarily. Mrs Bye was with her when she died in 1811. It was she who found Byron sitting in the dark by his mother's corpse, realizing at last what she had done and tried to do for him. ('I had but one friend, and she is gone.'[1])

Three different housemaids named Ann appear, besides a Betty and a Mary; Ann Hollis, Ann Coats, and Ann Smith. It is difficult to sort them out, but at least one, who received between £4. 10s. and £5 a year, kept her place a long while. Maids on low wages were often helped with gifts in kind. In 1808, Mrs Byron bought Ann a hat for eight shillings. Various other items of clothing entered from time to time may have been for under-servants.

Mealey, the steward and garden overseer, had nearly £100 a year and a house. His was a position of trust. Hanson sent him money for the wages of the several estate workers; but Mrs Byron made entries in the first few months which total to £37. 10s. 4d. given by her to Mealey for labourers 'at different times'. Possibly, though she did not pay for work on the domain, she was expected to settle for what was done in and about the house. Ryecroft, the plumber, had £12. 7s. 9d. from her, perhaps for

[1] Moore.

work on the leads of the roof. The sum of £2 in the same period for 'repairing Newstead House' seems incredibly small, but it may have been only for making two or three rooms habitable to begin with.

Soon after taking possession on her son's behalf, Mrs Byron bought garden tools for £1. 8s. 6d., forest seeds for £4. 5s., and garden seeds for £3. 7s. 5d. How much she spared for the garden after that we cannot tell because of her habit of making such entries as 'Pd different things', 'Paid sundry things', and 'Pd many things'. There had been little attention to the garden or woods in the latter years of the old Lord.

In 1801 there is an amount of £3. 8s. 10½d. for 'stone washing &c.' This may have been the cleaning of the façade in readiness for letting. The halfpenny is eloquent of the uselessness of trying to work out current monetary equivalents.

The 'Weekly Bills' are £2. 10s., £2. 15s. and sometimes a little more. That, I should suppose, covered the provisions apart from beer, of all who did not receive board wages, as well as the supply of candles, which would be tallow in the kitchen and servants' quarters and wax in the best rooms. Wax candles in the school room were, we know, the height of plutocratic luxury to Mrs Elton;[1] so Mrs Byron would not have had them in any very lavish quantity. When in lodgings her 'Weekly Bills' were more or less doubled. She would always have at least one servant of her own with her, as custom absolutely demanded.

She kept no carriage, a humiliating lack which her son was determined to remedy as soon as he could lay hands on the cash—or credit. A horse was indispensable. The first appearance of Byron's own personal servant in the accounts is a payment to 'Fletcher for Horse—£5'. That was early in 1804, and Byron, aged sixteen, had engaged the manservant who was to go with him through life, sometimes likened to Leporello but more often playing Sancho Panza to his Quixote. A farmer, he began his service as a groom, but was later turned into a valet.

Although much of the necessary outlay was administered not by Mrs Byron, but by Hanson, she did pay many of the taxes, which, owing to the war with France, were substantial. In 1799, half a year's tax on the Newstead residence was £14. 9s. 7d., still partly reckoned by the number of windows, which had caused many in large houses to be blocked up. A year's tax on the land was £47. Income tax had been introduced the previous year. On Mrs Byron's very small income it was £3. 16s. 3d., and on Byron's £85, his rents that year being £883. 11s. 6d. Any balance left from his heavily encumbered estate after its expenses were paid was put in trust for him, he being a Ward in Chancery. There were the Poor Rate and the Property Tax, a tax on male servants and armorial bearings,

[1] In Jane Austen's *Emma*.

and one on hair powder, which could not have brought in much because only footmen and old fogeys and gentlemen in full dress still wore it: and there were recurring unspecified taxes and stamp duties, trifling measured against those we are inured to, but troublesome enough, above all to those who disapproved of what was done with the money.

Mrs Byron paid her son's fees at Dr Glennie's Dulwich 'Academy', where he went at the age of eleven in 1799, and they were very high, £43. 5s. 6d. per half year, with a most ample allotment of clothes and pocket money. Her generosity in that respect was extravagant. She wanted, I surmise, to make up to him for having to go to his first boarding-school with a leg-iron—which instrument, Hobhouse wrote in the margin of Moore's biography, 'he wore with much impatience & one day threw it into a pond'. (But his ankle was still in a brace when he began at Harrow, and his treatments there made severe inroads on her means.)

He himself in one of his many fractious letters about her to Augusta was obliged to qualify his grumbling with: 'Not that I can complain of want of liberality, no, She always supplies me with as much money, as I can spend, and more than most boys hope for or desire.'[1] And again: 'I do not however wish to be separated from *her* entirely, but not to be so much with her as I hitherto have been, for I do believe she likes me, she manifests that in many instances, particularly with regard to money, which I never want, and have as much as I desire.'[2]

This rash munificence was made at the cost of great self-denial. She did not spend as much on clothes or any feminine pleasure or adornment as she gave the schoolboy for his amusements. Yet she was not turned thirty-six when Byron entered his teens, and, although he was quite as incapable of understanding it as his elders would have been at the time, had sexual needs and feelings which made it natural for her to wish for a second husband.

In 1830 Hobhouse wrote disapprovingly among his marginal comments on his friend's boyhood as described by Thomas Moore, 'Mrs Byron fell in love with a Frenchman whom she intended to marry & it was suspected that she designed to carry her son to France, a scheme that it required much vigilance to thwart'. He had gathered this information from Hanson in 1824. The original version is given in the notes he made after a talk with his fellow executor: 'She fell in love with a French dancing master at Brompton & laid a plan for carrying B. to France. The Frenchman called at Dulwich to take him away but the Master would not let him go.'[3]

[1] Marchand, *Letters*. 2 Nov. 1804.
[2] Ibid. 17 Nov. 1804.   [3] Hobhouse Journals. Notes headed 'Lord Byron'.

That sad little episode must have been the cause of her furious row with Lord Carlisle who, in October 1800, prompted by Hanson, forbade her customary access to his ward at weekends. 'I intreat your Lordship [the solicitor had written, at the instance of Dr Glennie] to excuse at present my assigning any reasons for this abrupt address but they materially involve the happiness & well doing of my little friend.'[1]

Though the little friend himself, aged twelve, would not have been told of it, Augusta, five years his senior and intimate with all Carlisle's family, may very well have founded her dislike of her stepmother on the indiscretion. The disgrace of an alliance with a French dancing-master would have been even worse than that of Mrs Thrale with an Italian singer. Brompton was not far from Sloane Terrace where Mrs Byron took lodgings for a time while her son was at Dulwich, but how and where she met the dancing-master, a Monsieur St Louis, is beyond conjecture.[2] Thirty-five would have been regarded as a ridiculous age for dancing lessons. It can only be said that Captain Jack Byron's dancing, learned in France, had been one of his many fascinations for her when they met in Bath, so she must have been fond of the art.

Since England was at war with France, it is somewhat implausible that she intended to elope to that country, placing her vital pension in jeopardy, and I suspect Dr Glennie of having greatly exaggerated the danger to Hanson. He was always most hostile to her, and the picture of a vulgar termagant that has come down to posterity through Moore's 'Life' was largely his contribution. The affair, whatever it may have been, could not have lasted long or it would surely have left traces elsewhere in Byron annals.

It seems not to have been until it was over that she treated herself to some little indulgences. In the Christmas holidays of 1800, which her son spent with the Hanson family, she made an entry, 'Pd. coaches for Plays &c &c—£3. 0. 7d.' and again 'Coach—14s. 6d.' and 'Plays—£1 2s. 6d.'. She was staying in Nottingham, which was visited by first-rate touring companies, and where she had several acquaintances who may have accompanied her to the theatre. It would have been out of the question for a woman to go alone. She was always a lover of the theatre, and attended an opera once that year for twelve shillings.

In 1801 she launched out twice into 'Cloaths'. The sums were £2. 1s. and £1. 7s. 5d. There were also purchases of shoes, amounting in all to £4. 2s. 1d. Then there was 'Perfumer—10s. 9d.' and even 'Hairdresser—5s.'. If these rare disbursements were dated, we should know whether they

---

[1] Murray MS. Hanson copies. 20 Oct.
[2] Ibid. I found his name, barely legible, among Hanson's notes giving the date of the meeting with Lord Carlisle.

were occasioned by her going to Brighton, as she did that year, or on her summer trip to Cheltenham, where she took Byron during the holidays.

In Brighton there was an amount of £1. 2s. for 'Bathers', so she must have placed herself in the hands of the stalwart women who plunged shrinking bodies into the sea from bathing machines. Lodging was exceedingly dear—£34. 1s., and there was £3. 18s. 3d. for someone who is simply called 'Servant', perhaps a temporary manservant hired to lend dignity. To be in so smart a place without one was not good style for a peer's mother.

Cheltenham was also very modern and fashionable, handsome squares and terraces being under construction. With Byron she went from there to Malvern, where the picturesque hills made a deeper impression on a boy just beginning to have poetical leanings. Two successive entries 'Paid at Malvern', £5. 17s. and £13, suggest that they were there some little time, as these figures are substantial enough to have covered board and lodging for two or three weeks.[1]

An item of 15s. for 'Coaches to Bath', is likely to relate to attending the baths either at Cheltenham or Malvern, both being watering places with mineral springs and medicinal bathing establishments. Such resorts were immensely frequented by the upper and upper middle classes in Georgian times. The Byrons patronized several of them.

While Newstead was let, Mrs Byron was homeless and unsettled. In February 1802 she re-visited Bath, once the scene of so much delusive felicity when she had triumphantly secured, as she thought, a husband to make other girls envious. She bought, not trinkets and souvenirs as when fresh from Scotland, a courted heiress, but shoes and gloves for £2. 4s. 6d. and a shawl for £1. 8s. 6d. A poor little purchase that must have been in the heyday of the sumptuous cashmeres not obtainable for less than £10 or £20, and often much more. But she had succumbed shortly before to the temptation of buying 'a desk & tea chest' at £6. 11s. I think these may have been her portable desk and travelling tea chest. Tea, though it had come down much in price—from twenty shillings a pound to about eight—was still a delicacy that one provided for oneself and kept in a locked caddy, spooning it out with the minimum of waste. (Byron took his own tea and sugar to Harrow.) She also spent a modest amount on wine—18s. 8d. at Cheltenham and as much as two guineas that season at Bath.

Sedan chairs had not ceased, there at least, to be a favourite mode of transport for the gentry, and Mrs Byron used them a good deal. The

---

[1] There is also an entry for 'Board—£5. 17s. 9d.' but whether at Cheltenham or Malvern is not evident.

chairmen could not have relished carrying the stout lady up the hill from the Pump Room or the Abbey to the Assembly Rooms, where there were cards, concerts, and dances, in surroundings rather too lofty and grandiose to be suitable for informal social intercourse. 'Chairs' were one of her main expenses. There was also, occasionally, the play. Wherever she went, she always subscribed to the circulating library.

Before Christmas 1802 her young son joined her at 16 Henrietta Street, a house that is still standing. He must have liked Bath very much as well as hating the ordeal of his first year at Harrow, for when the holidays were over, he positively refused to go back. Mrs Byron wrote to Hanson explaining why she had yielded to his will: 'I might force him to return, to be sure, but I know he would not remain, and I do not choose he should wander about the country as other boys have done that have been sent to school against their inclinations.'[1]

After Hanson had conveyed the straightforward yet not unsympathetic comments of his headmaster, Dr Drury, who commanded unvarying respect from Byron, he consented to be packed off (but not until February 15th, 1803) with £3. 1s. to pay for his journey, and permission to draw on the solicitor for £10 to spend at Harrow. One gown for £1. 11s. 6d. was all his mother had by way of clothes that season.

Her fees at 'the bath' came to £1. 13s. 2d. That may have been for Byron's swimming as well as her medicinal use of the facilities. There was the King's Bath, built in medieval times, large enough for real exercise. I do not remember that Byron gives any information as to exactly where he learned to swim—an accomplishment by no means to be taken for granted till our own century, but I fancy he must have begun young on what Moore calls 'his summer excursions up Dee-side', eagerly compensating with his muscular arms for the deficiency in his legs. The steamy mineral-loaded waters of the Spa were very different from the chill Highland river, but they must have had their attraction for a boy with a strong predilection for history. Walking, he was still, however reluctantly, obliged to wear an iron round his ankle, and in June that year (1803), he wrote from school asking Mrs Byron to have a new instrument ordered immediately for his leg, 'as I want one, rather'.

It is against the background of all the mortification he felt through having to struggle with pain and, worse, with the knowledge of physical inferiority, that his hot-headedness and determination to assert himself must be set. The friends who wrote about him after his death did him no service when, well-meaningly, they minimized the real cause he had for suffering, heightened as it was by the irony of his good looks. He had been

[1] Prothero. 19 Jan. 1803. Byron was at loggerheads with his tutor, the headmaster's son, Henry Drury, who afterwards became a much-liked friend.

used from infancy to hearing his beauty praised with a blunt, or an implied, qualification which seared him.

In the valuable account of Byron that Newton Hanson, the solicitor's younger son, wrote after his father's death,[1] there is the following passage about the first encounter of the Hanson children with the lordling who had already made a deep impression on their parents:

> My father and mother had somewhat piqued the curiosity of my elder brother & my sisters & myself, who were some of his age & myself 3 years younger, about Lord Byron. They had both spoken of him with admiration . . . I have a perfect recollection of the room and the way in which the great & little Dramatis Personae stood at the first moment after my father brought Byron among us. My mother, my eldest Brother Hargreaves, and two of my Sisters, one older one younger than myself, were alone present. My father brought Lord Byron into the room in his Hand—all eyes were upon him, but, as my father remained with him, he was not abashed. My 2nd Sister, who was then about 7, after examining Lord Byron from head to foot, during the pause after the 1st Introduction turning round exclaimed with the greatest gravity & Emphasis 'Well, he is a pretty Boy however'.

That 'however' must have told the sharp-witted, self-conscious eleven-year-old all too plainly that the parents had been tactfully preparing their family for the iron on his leg. And a day or two after, it was arranged, not very sensitively, that when he was brought into the presence of his important and fashionable guardian, the doctor who had been invited to pronounce upon his foot should be in attendance.[2] They had only been the briefest time in Lord Carlisle's splendid town house in Grosvenor Place, doubtless the grandest the child had entered until that day, when he turned to Hanson and said pressingly 'Let us go!' and appeared delighted to escape.

There was the trouble of his lameness and, from the time of his going to Harrow, the troubles of realizing that his fortune was inadequate to his rank. Mrs Byron strove, in her inept fashion, to console him with lavish pocket money, clothes from a London tailor, and moral support which he impatiently rejected: and as he rejected it, she grew irritable and unreasonable, her choleric temper bursting out in tirades of reproach.

The lonely woman stayed at Bath the best part of a year, always in the same Henrietta Street lodgings. In the Christmas holidays, 1802, she had written—twice—to the steward of Newstead asking that a basket of game should be sent in time for Lord Byron's fifteenth birthday,

[1] Murray MS. known as the Hanson Narrative. I have inserted some commas.
[2] Mid-July 1799. The doctor, Matthew Baillie, was brother to Joanna Baillie, the successful writer of moralizing plays, who was to become a confidante of Byron's wife.

January 22nd 1803. Mealey clearly disliked her for he wrote to Hanson saying he would wish to have *his* orders before doing so, although a little while before he had been complaining that all the game on the estate was going to poachers.[1] Hanson grudgingly answered that this time he might comply, 'but I fear we cannot without injuring the manor furnish any more this season'.[2] Yet Newstead was let to two maiden ladies who had no shooting, fishing or hunting rights!

Hanson's anxiety to restrict Mrs Byron to one basket of game may have been due to the fact that, the very day he replied to Mealey—taking his time as he always did—he had had an enquiry for the Abbey from Lord Grey de Ruthyn, a young sporting nobleman who would be sure to want a well-stocked manor. On the other hand, it may not have displeased him to assert his authority over his voluble client, who had no hesitation in letting him know candidly when she thought he was neglecting her son's affairs, as he very often did.

Newton Hanson speaks of his father's endeavours being 'much thwarted by Mrs Byron's singularity of conduct', and that it *was* singular, at least to superficial observation, is shown in many different ways. She was outspoken beyond anything society allows—a tendency she transmitted to her descendants—and had a way of being right in the wrong manner which made her no favourite with those who had to deal with her. We can read between the lines that Mealey, a confirmed grumbler at the best of times, was far from happy when he reported to Hanson that she had asked him to find a house for her locally, and not to stop looking until he succeeded. 'She mains [sic] to come to live in this Neighb[rhd] this spring', he announced apprehensively.[3]

He did not find a house for her but professed to be tired out with looking. She got one by herself at Southwell. It was called Burgage Manor, and she wrote to tell Hanson on May 30th 1803 that it had 'a Garden and grounds just as I could wish but I shall not go into it till July'.[4] She was then in lodgings in Park Row, Nottingham, after leaving Bath by some tortuous progress that made large expenses. First, there had been a trip to Bristol for £1. 17s. 6d., then another journey, a comparatively long one for £9. 13s. 9d., then yet another—£11. 11s. 10½d. with 'Pd at Inn &c—£5. 4s. 8d.' and also 'Pd Carriadge [sic] of things &c—£2. 11s.' This may be her return to Nottinghamshire, but soon after that there comes, inexplicably, twelve shillings for 'Journey to London', which is too little for transport between London and Nottingham, and in June still another journey, the costliest, £18. 0s. 9d., which is too much. It seems, however, that she made an excursion to Matlock

---

[1] Egerton 2612.   [2] Ibid. 12 Jan. 1803.
[3] Ibid. late Mar. 1803.   [4] Murray MS. Hanson copies.

in Derbyshire, another resort with thermal baths, before beginning the
move to Southwell, and the figure she entered must have included
inns.

The annual rent of Burgage Manor was alternately £23 and £24. 13s.,
a variation possibly depending on whether she or Mr Faulkner, the landlord, paid the taxes, which came to £2. 13s. a year. For the Newstead
mansion, now let to Lord Grey de Ruthyn, the rent was £50. This went,
not to her, but to the estate. She had only the advantage of being able to
live respectably with a smaller household than the Abbey required. Not
that the Southwell house was so very small by today's unspacious standards—it was for some years a Youth Hostel—but, compared with the
Abbey, it was a cottage.

Mrs Byron had partly to furnish it, because the Newstead furniture
was left at Lord Grey's disposal, and it was one of his undertakings that
he would purchase it at a valuation, giving the landlord the option of
buying it back when the tenancy ended. Having belonged to the old
Lord, born in 1722, and to his father before him, it must have seemed
dismally old-fashioned but its worth would now be inestimable, for the
old Lord, when a young one, had been in the habit of going to London
sales and buying anything that took his fancy regardless of cost, which
much reduced his fortune but would certainly have meant a fortune to his
successors had they foreseen how antiques would one day be valued.

The pictures were expressly excluded from Lord Grey's bargain, and,
as her son's property, Mrs Byron was entitled to have them in his home,
but the steward, in one of his many mischief-making letters to Hanson,
wrote:

> I take the liberty of informing you that Mrs Byron has sent for all the
> picktures that was at Newstead last week, what was in the house and what I
> had. She has got every one away from Newstead.[1]

They were mostly, I imagine, family portraits, for Byron writes to
Augusta of his mother 'pouring forth complaints . . . whilst in the background the portraits of my Great Grandfather and Grandmother, suspended in their frames, seem to look with an eye of pity on their *unfortunate descendant*. . . .'[2]

The Newstead furniture had not been left to Byron, but had been
acquired on his arrival with his mother so that the old mansion would not

---

[1] Egerton 2612. 10 Oct. 1803. Mealey was storing some things in his house.
[2] Pratt. 6 Aug. 1805. The Newstead Byrons were equally Augusta's ancestors, but
the possessive pronoun in the singular was used in speaking of near relations even to
other near relations, as may be seen in Jack Byron's references to 'my mother' and 'my
sister' when writing to Fanny Leigh. It would be interesting to know what has become
of these portraits.

be uninhabitable. There is a letter from Birch, Hanson's partner, to say he had induced a Mr Aisley, 'not without some difficulty', to agree that it might remain there if Mrs Byron would hire it at the rate of 6% and engage to give it up by Lady Day (March 25th), after which it was either to be sold on the premises or taken over by her at a price to be named by an assessor.[1] As there was no sale on the premises and no furniture for Newstead bought elsewhere, Mrs Byron having soon removed to lodgings, a transfer of ownership at a low figure was evidently effected.

She wanted household goods of her own choice at Burgage Manor in 1803 and purchased them. Apart from a number of things she retained on going back to Newstead six years later, the Southwell furniture fetched £200. 12s., so it must have been very presentable, taking into consideration the probable loss on it when secondhand. Her Civil List pension had been reduced, from the time when Byron went to Harrow, from £300 to £200, because the Chancery Court had decided that, to fit him for his station as an hereditary legislator, he was to have £500 a year from the revenue of his estate, which Hanson was supposed to be disburdening of its debts and entanglements. Mrs Byron received this allowance, but seems to have used little, if any, of it to equip the house, as most mothers making a home for a son would have done. There are sundry repayments to a Southwell banker named Wylde, from whom she borrowed more than once.

This was the period before she could have suspected the full extent of the rash and impassioned self-will, which, in conflict with her own fiery temper, were to drive her relationship with Byron upon the rocks; and, preparing what she believed would be a settled haven for her adored boy until he came of age, I fancy she must have enjoyed some of the happiest weeks she had known since the days of her courtship.

Byron, on the other hand, was already chafing, not only with normal adolescent resentment of control, but with the intense discomfort of being shamed by her Scotch accent (a faint trace of which was to make his own speech one of his most seductive attributes), her short stout figure, and her total lack of polish. That her bluntness was chiefly exhibited in his own interests made no difference. He was too young to know what his interests were and too headstrong at the present stage to care.

A hitherto unpublished incident supplies an example of how vulnerable she made herself to mockery even when she was acting in a

---

[1] Egerton 2612. 4 Sept. 1798. Robert Aisley was the executor of the 5th Lord, but in the self-same letter, Birch describes the death of one Mr *Ainslie* that very morning. It seems too much of a coincidence that he should have occasion to refer to two men of such similar names at the same time, so the spelling is probably a slip of the pen, and Birch had dealings with two Aisleys.

perfectly legitimate cause. On August 11th 1803 one of the Misses
Launder, who had come to Newstead Abbey as very temporary tenants,
addressed Hanson, in terms which curiously suggest that the writer
might have been sitting to Jane Austen for the character of one of the
Misses Steele, while at the same time the spelling is reminiscent of Mr
Samuel Weller, or perhaps his father:

> Sir,
>
> you vill be surprised at my troubling you vith a letter, but I have received
> such a very extraordinary one from Mrs Byron in vhich she mentions your
> name, and as neither my sister nor self, can possibly find out what she elludes
> to, I have taken the liberty to copy it for your perusal.
>
> She came to Newstead Abbey unexpectedly when ve vas from Home, at
> our return desir'd to have a Bed, staid a Couple of nights, and I can safely
> say met with every politeness and attention in my power to show her. Ve
> had a House full of Company to whom she behav'd vith the greatest Insolence
> and my friends certainly laughed at her Folly, but as for my sister further
> than joining in the Laughter she never said a vord about her either good or
> Ill-natured. As for her saying ve vas intruders at the time, she is greatly
> mistaken as ve vas then there by the consent and approbation of Lord Grey.
>
> Of course she vas the intruder as he vas the tenant of the place and could
> allow whoever he thought proper to be there. What she means by our dis-
> appointment, on your account, I shall be extremely obliged to you to explain
> as ve cannot understand it as ve met with no other disappointment, further
> than not having the pleasure of seeing you at the Abbey before we left it.
>
> My sister unites with me in best Compts.
>
> I remain, Sir,
Your obliged humble Servt
F. Launder.[1]

Now the fact is that these sneering ladies ought to have left Newstead
weeks before Mrs Byron's visit, that they were not there with Lord
Grey's approbation—very much the reverse—and that, although he was
paying the rent, he could not get possession, a state of affairs Mrs Byron
had shrewdly prophesied in her correspondence with Hanson. The lord
of the manor, away at school, has only an off-stage part in this comedy of
tenancies, but since it brings out the characters of three persons of importance in his story, his mother, his lawyer, and his principal tenant, a
brief version will be given.

When Mrs Byron bore down upon the Misses Launder, who, for all
their recommendation by Lord Grantley, belonged to some much
humbler walk of life, nearly seven months had passed since Lord Grey
had begun to negotiate. The condition on which they had been accepted
the previous November was that their tenancy should be only 'for a short

[1] Egerton 2611.

time while they sought something else'. They had, however, been formally given the option of a longer lease on the same terms as Lord Grey,
and had refused it. From the beginning they had made themselves as
tiresome as they could, ordering at the landlord's expense repairs and
improvements never contracted for, withholding the window tax and land
tax they were under obligation to pay, losing the inventory of furniture
belonging to the house, taking three weeks and more to answer letters
while the new tenant politely expostulated with the solicitor, and reject-
ing his request that they would house 'a puppy or two', while he was
waiting to move in, on the grounds that they needed the space for fatten-
ing pigs: and even after these had been killed, they had turned his gamekeeper away with the dogs.

> *The Ladies* appear much annoyed [Lord Grey had written as early as
> March 22nd] at the idea of quitting & anxious as I *always* have been to oblige
> these Angels of the Creation I am sorry to say in this instance I shall not be
> able to let them remain beyond the fixed period and I trust they will not
> again request it, for after the 25th inst. I shall be a perfect *Cain*.[1]

Next day he was again protesting:

> They appear to be greatly displeased with you for letting me Newstead &
> with me for taking [it]. I am persuaded you will so far as possible assist me
> & it really appears as if I shall want it.[2]

Hanson being of the most languid disposition, his assistance was so feeble
that we find Lord Grey writing to him again on June 9th:

> I have received an application from the Miss Launders to permit them
> to remain at Newstead some considerable time longer and I have this day
> returned an answer saying how much a compliance with their wishes would
> inconvenience me & in short explaining the impossibility of such a circum-
> stance taking place.

He pointed out that they could easily move to Nottingham while
waiting for the house they had taken to become vacant (several months
hence), whereas he had a numerous suite and nowhere for them to go.
He was additionally anxious because 'unheard of taxes' were going to be
imposed for carrying on the war and he wanted to reduce those on Newstead by blocking up windows and other retrenchments which could not
be begun except under his supervision: 'After so long a notice & so much
indulgence (for I cannot help nominating it such while I am actually
paying Rent for the *premises*) I do not think it candid or Right to urge
further consideration.'

[1] Egerton 2612. Misdated by the writer Mar. 23rd.   [2] Ibid. 23 Mar. 1803.

The Miss Launders, he went on, seemed to think him 'Sporting Mad' and only wanting Newstead on that account, but he desired a settled place of residence.[1]

On receiving Lord Grey's negative, Miss Launder, who had hoped to stay till the middle of August at the very earliest, called on Hanson to intercede: 'As ve cannot quit vithout the greatest inconvenience ve flatter ourselves he cannot be so unreasonable as to refuse', adding a typically unpleasant and irrelevant comment on Mrs Byron's opposition to the Tory candidate in a recent election: 'You vill be sorry to here [sic] that Mrs Byron has taken so active a part against him that ve heard the other day Mr Coke's Committee has it in contemplation to let her conduct be mentioned to the Government.'[2]

The only object of doing so mean a thing would have been to deprive Mrs Byron of her Civil List pension. Hanson had already heard several days before from Mealey: 'I am sorry to inform you that Mrs Byron is the whole talk of the Quallity of Nottingham and about it, for taking up with Burchs party [the Whigs] which they say there was not another Lady in the County did but hirself.'[3]

Political feeling ran so high in those days that the great Whig families would hardly recognize the Tories in social intercourse, and vice versa, and the mutual hostility descended in Montagu-and-Capulet fashion to retainers. Nottingham must have been a Tory stronghold—and both Mealey and the Launder sisters were as yet unaware that Lord Grey was a Whig.

Hanson received with equal inattention letters from Mealey complaining about the Misses Launder, letters from the Misses Launder complaining about Mealey, letters from all these parties indicating distaste for Mrs Byron (Mealey wrote with satisfaction that 'the Miss Launders and their visitors still more makes game of her',[4] and this was before the visit which occasioned their remarks about her insolence), and letters from Lord Grey begging Hanson to meet him at Newstead Abbey so that he could take possession. Hanson made various appointments to do so and broke them.

Such was the state of affairs when Mrs Byron, with her customary moral courage, had gone to Newstead in person and shown the Misses Launder that they and their houseful of company had no right to be there. Moreover she was successful in getting rid of them, though at some cost to her dignity. Here is the letter of which they complained:

Madam,
    As far as I could judge from appearances you seemed extremely civil to me when I was at Newstead, for which I thank you. I am however since

---

[1] Ibid.   [2] Ibid. 19 June.   [3] Ibid. 9 June.   [4] Ibid. 5 July.

inform'd that your sister has said several ill-natured things of me which I do not recollect, and if I did should hardly think it worth notice, as she can *know* nothing of me. There is a small mistake she has made, however, which I beg leave to rectify, it is this, she *and* her Visitors were intruders and not me, as you all ought to have left Newstead before I came there. Therefore if I gave any trouble you have only yourselves to blame, and any disappointment you have had concerning Mr Hanson you may impute to the same cause.

I am, Madam,

Your ob.^t Ser.^t

C. G. Byron[1]

In printing this from Miss Launder's copy I have not thought it necessary to reproduce the orthography, that being obviously the copyist's own, and she was almost certainly born within the sound of Bow Bells. With nothing to go on but her spelling and an air, in all her complaining, tale-bearing, and toadying, of being a little above herself, I picture her and her sister as retired tradeswomen, or perhaps the spinster daughters of a well-to-do tradesman or steward who had served Lord Grantley, a client of Hanson's. They disappear from the orbit of Byron's history as the more significant Lord Grey enters it, but not before giving and making a deal of trouble.

They had positively promised to be gone from Newstead by July 16th, Lord Grey having declared that was the latest date he could allow. He therefore asked Hanson to meet him there on the 17th so that he could be formally installed. Hanson having failed—without sending word—to turn up, they were able to hang on till the 24th, Mrs Byron presumably being an unwelcome guest in the meantime.[2] Then, instead of moving out finally and completely, as was expected, they had a quantity of their own furniture carried to what the disgusted Mealey names as 'the Abbey Room', and there it remained till November.

'The tradesmen', Mealey wrote, 'are much disapointed as they cannot get paid.'[3] These were the artisans who had put in two extra windows, a kitchen grate, and other matters which the Misses Launder had ordered despite a warning months before that it must be at their own expense or not at all. But by contriving to be about when the new tenant arrived, and to lend him a few household necessaries, they not only ingratiated themselves to the extent that he agreed to store their chattels and pay their bills, but artfully ensured that he should begin with a thoroughly bad opinion of Mealey.

---

[1] Egerton 2611. 6 Aug. 1803.

[2] Her letter to Miss Launder, above quoted, was written after their departure.

[3] Egerton 2612. 31 July.

Lord Grey, who was only twenty-three, was no match for two women whose capacity for exploitation was tireless, and, a couple of weeks after being given what Miss Launder called 'possession of the Abbey, and also the use of vhatever his lordship vas in vant of belonging to us till such time as he can procure them off his own',[1] he was writing, a little sheepishly, to Hanson:

> . . . I discharged the Miss Launders acct for windows as well as some other trifling jobs and which I did not feel myself bound to pay either in Equity or Honor after their having exceeded the time for giving one up possession but as I have found them very civil & obliging these trifling things were no consideration.

It was not, after all, to the Ladies that he turned out 'a perfect Cain' but to the steward, of whom he had their bad report. In allusion to the grievances they had been plying him with, he went on:

> I trust he will not be so imprudent as to make the attempt to annoy me in the same way. . . . My temper is not of that quiescent nature to submit to it. I do not mean in any degree to prejudice you against this man but Miss Launder informed me that they were obliged to write to you on his misconduct.

The young peer had shown his mettle without delay by dismissing the keeper whose charges, he said, were exorbitant (and whose house he wanted for his own keeper, Moore).

> The fact is whenever I find a Servant endeavouring to plunder his Master's pocket or in other words trying to discover how far he will admit of being duped I instantly dismiss him as an example to the other Servants.[2]

Assertions of this kind may be evidence of a cold, self-centred nature or, equally, the pose of a weak man striving to be a forceful one. In either case, they do not denote amiability. Owen Mealey who, so far as his correspondence shows, disliked everybody, tenants, workmen, employers and employees impartially, now added one more to the list of those about whom he could write in a disgruntled tone to the solicitor. Henceforward Lord Grey de Ruthyn shared with Mrs Byron his acute disfavour, and the more so because they were on very good terms with each other.

Whether Mrs Byron's bold request for a bed at Newstead Abbey had been the consequence of giving up her lodging in Nottingham a day or two before the Southwell house, twelve miles away, had turned out to be ready, or whether she had planned the move deliberately to relieve Lord Grey from being imposed on further by the tenacious sisters, she was then

[1] Ibid. 2 Aug.   [2] Ibid. 8 Aug.

or shortly afterwards on a most friendly footing with him, and he was franking her letters for her.[1] He had decided before arriving to be as hospitable as possible to his youthful landlord, telling Hanson as early as April 8th:

> If Lord Byron can make it convenient & agreeable to pass any of his time at Newstead I shall be most happy to receive him & to contribute to his amusements as far as lays in my power. You will have the goodness to hint this & I beg no ceremony may be used in any respect.

This courtesy towards a boy of fifteen coupled with much civility to herself made a great impression on Mrs Byron. She had at first been puzzled at not finding his name in the Peerage, but she must have been looking in an out-of-date edition, and she soon learned that, by royal licence granted in 1800, he had been allowed to inherit the very ancient barony going back to the 14th century, which was one of the titles of his maternal grandfather, the Earl of Sussex. The earldom had become extinct in 1799 with the last holder's lack of a male heir, but high rank of such antiquity was usually recognized by allowing a barony to descend through the female line.

Mrs Byron was not accustomed to being treated with much cordiality and it charmed her. No doubt she pictured her son finding in this engaging nobleman a most suitable companion; but any encounter the two may have had that summer could only have been fleeting. Byron did not arrive in Nottinghamshire for the holidays until July 27th and on about August 8th Grey went North to Harrogate, where the grouse-shooting season was beginning, and did not return till well on in October. There had been a plan that Byron should travel from London with Hanson and stay at Newstead on his way to his mother's, but Grey had written in the chaos of moving in:

> ... I am fearful Lord Byron if he goes with you must *adjourn to Mrs Clarkes* [of the neighbouring estate of Annesley] as we have literally but half a dozen plates, & knives & forks are *equally* scarce, not a bit of *plate* in the House & in short nothing but what these *good Ladies* have lent us.[2]

Byron did not on that occasion go to Mrs Clarke but to Burgage Manor. After having stayed a night or two at the Hansons, he had been given £6 for his expenses, and had come to Newark, a hundred and twenty-five miles from London, in a stage coach, doing the journey from there to Southwell in a post chaise.

---

[1] Letters with covers signed by a Member of either of the Houses of Parliament went free of the heavy delivery charges extant before the introduction of cheap postage.

[2] Egerton 2612. 24 July.

Mrs Byron must have looked forward eagerly to enjoying the lively schoolboy's company, no longer in lodgings, but settled in the principal house of a pleasant little country town, but Southwell, with its three thousand inhabitants, was too much of a backwater for a youth who longed to be out in the world, and domesticity with his mother was something he was beginning to find very irksome. From August 2nd, when he decided to lodge at Mealey's—much to the latter's annoyance—he spent most of his time away from the house, and contrived to become agonizingly enamoured of a girl two or three years older than himself, whom he could regard with a special thrill of Gothic romance because his great-uncle had killed hers in a highly irregular duel and subsequently been tried in the House of Lords for murder. This was Mary Chaworth, daughter of that Mrs Clarke mentioned by Lord Grey.

For the second time in a few months he refused to go back to Harrow, and his mother reported to Hanson without any of the facetiousness mature people usually assume in such communications that it was because he was 'distractedly in love'. He had not, she said, passed three weeks at home in the three months since his return.[1]

Evidently she had implored him to come to Southwell (he was now dividing his nights between the steward's house at Newstead and Annesley where he could feed upon his feverish longings); and the tone in which he replied, with its mixture of respectful candour, adamant self-will, and boyish nervousness of her displeasure, illustrates well what their relations were before they deteriorated on his side into sustained antagonism:

> . . . I *promise* you, upon my *honour* I will come over *tomorrow* in the *afternoon*, I was not wishing to resist your *Commands*, and really seriously intended, Coming over tomorrow, ever since I received your Last letter, you know as well as I do that it is not your Company I dislike, but the place you reside in. I know it is time to go to Harrow, It will make me *unhappy*, but I will *obey*; I only *desire*, *entreat*, this one day, and on my *honour* I will be over tomorrow, in the evening or afternoon. I am Sorry you disapprove my Companions, who however are the first the county affords, and my equals in most respects, but I will be permitted to Chuse for myself. I shall never interfere in yours and I desire you will not molest me in mine; if you Grant me this favour, and allow me this one day unmolested you will eternally oblige your
>
> unhappy Son Byron
>
> I shall attempt to offer no excuse as you do not desire one. I only entreat you as Governor, not as a Mother, to allow me this one day. Those I most Love live in this county, therefore in the name of Mercy I entreat this one day to take leave, and then I will Join you again at Southwell to prepare to go

[1] Murray MS. Hanson copies. 30 Oct. 1803.

to a place where —————— I will write no more it would only incense you, adieu, Tomorrow I come.[1]

He would not have broken so solemn a promise to return to her the following day, but some mistake in her conduct or some coquettish change in that of the girl—already engaged to be married—who was mildly toying with the schoolboy's infatuation, shattered his resolution to prepare for the new term at Harrow. Mrs Byron explained that she had done all in her power to make him go.

> If my son was of proper age and the lady *disengaged*, it is the last of all the connexions that I would wish to take place; it has given me much uneasiness. To prevent all trouble in future, I am determined he shall not come here again till Easter; therefore I beg you will find out some proper situation for him at the next Holydays. I don't care what I pay.[2]

The poor woman must have been driven to the limit of her endurance by his alternate raptures and miseries. Yet she found sufficient understanding to declare a week later: 'Byron is really *so unhappy* that I have agreed, much against my inclinations, to let him remain in this County till after the next Holydays.'[3]

He at last returned to Harrow in January 1804, having played truant for a term! He could not have been in the least aware how much further his mother was going in tolerance and sensitiveness than the average parent of that day, or indeed any day. To him she seemed only a clumsy obstacle between him and the pursuit of his 'Morning Star'. If he had been told that the time would come when Mary Chaworth would write him letter upon letter and he would not bother to spend a single hour with her, how incredulous he would have been!

When he came home at Easter, 1804, he complained merely of the dullness of Southwell, though he was happier there, had he but realized it, than he was often destined to be thereafter. He was a shade satirical about his mother in his letters to Augusta, but not more than any teenage boy having his fling at authority he hoped soon to shake off. Largely for his sake, I dare say, she took an active part in the social life of the small community. He writes of her going to an Assembly, and giving a party where he was to meet, for the first time, the 'Southwell belles', and, although the landlord, Mr Faulkner, had left a copious collection of books at their disposal, she joined the local Book Club. In the summer holidays, she even bespoke a play to be given by a professional touring company. 'Mrs and Lord Byron' appeared on the playbills of August 8th as joint patrons.

[1] Marchand, *Letters.* ? 15 Sept. 1803.
[2] 30 Oct.   [3] Murray MS. 7 Nov.

That vacation started off most auspiciously, and Mrs Byron wrote to Hanson: 'Never was a boy more improved in every respect; he is now truly amiable and I shall not know how to part with him.'[1] A misdated *cri de cœur* to Augusta, published by the editor of *Letters and Journals* as of August 18th 1804 (it was taken from a copy) gives the impression that, only five days after this, he was referring to his mother as his 'tor-mentor' whose '*diabolical* disposition . . . seems to increase with age and to acquire a new force with time', adding that 'the more I see of her the more my dislike augments', and that he was unable to conceal these feelings from her. 'In this society have I dragged out a weary fortnight.' He looks forward to his emancipation from maternal bondage, he writes, with more joy than a captive negro.[2]

The original of this letter was dated only August 18th by Byron, who had not left himself room to put the year. Someone else wrote '1805' on the cover, and over the five a four has mistakenly been superscribed. By August 18th 1804 he had passed not two weeks but nearly four in his mother's society, having arrived home in July, and moreover spent the time not disagreeably, constantly visiting and being visited by the con-genial Miss Pigot and her family, writing verses to her and others, sharing with his mother the sponsorship of the play, and flirting with the 'South-well belles'. If what he poured into Augusta's all too willing ear is set in its proper year, it will be seen to belong to a coherent sequence of com-plaints illustrating stage by stage the breakdown of his relations with his mother. Its premature introduction among his correspondence has thrown out of scale the whole unhappy domestic drama.[3]

Mrs Byron was by no means the stupid ignoramus depicted by biog-raphers drawing on the spiteful verbal portrait Dr Glennie provided for Thomas Moore. 'With an exterior far from prepossessing, an understand-ing where nature had not been bountiful, a mind almost wholly without cultivation, and the peculiarities of northern opinions, northern habits, and northern accent . . . ' such was Glennie's thumbnail sketch of her, which, coupled with Byron's letters to Augusta when he was at his most recalcitrant and the rumour published by a scurrilous paper that his mother was a drunkard, has formed the basis of many a denigration since. A countryman of Dr Glennie's, one of her first defenders,[4] has written that 'in his every line [he] declares himself the Anglicized Scottish snob'.

---

[1] Ibid. 13 Aug. 1804.

[2] Now Murray MS, but not when first published.

[3] It was in 1805 that he did not return till August and the span of a fortnight would have been correct. In Marchand's edition the error is set right.

[4] Symon, J. D.

Born less than sixty years after the Act of Union, immensely proud of her ancient Scottish lineage, Catherine Byron could not have felt the same fear of betraying her origin in her accent as a careful preceptor in an English school, nor had she been given much reason to believe that northern opinions and habits were inferior to English ones.

Her spelling was imperfect, but no worse than that of many another well-born lady. Her punctuation was odd but, uncorrected by editors, her son's was even odder. She was no grammarian but several of her apparent errors were good, if old-fashioned, usage at the time, such as 'I have wrote', or 'you was' when the pronoun is addressed to one person. I doubt if she would have been guilty of 'we was', like Miss Launder, and assuredly not, 've vas'. She read many books and newspapers and always took a wide-ranging interest in current affairs, and, though her letters were obviously composed impulsively and have no literary pretensions, she often expressed herself in very concise and apposite phrases. Thus as to letting Newstead: 'I hope Lord Grey will be a good tenant, but still it ought to be *put out of his power to be a bad one.*'[1] When her son was giving her and everyone concerned with him constant anxiety by his behaviour, she wrote to the lawyer: 'What is to be done with him when he leaves Harrow God only knows. He is a turbulent unruly boy that wants to be emancipated from all restraint, his Sentiments are however noble'[2]—a succinct and perspicacious verdict. And at a later date: 'I have as *high* an opinion of my son's abilities as any one can have, yet I am sensible that clever people are *not* always the most prudent in regard to money matters,'[3] and again, later still, 'His Heart is good, and his Talents are *great*, and I have no doubt of his being a *great* man. God grant that he may be a prudent and happy one also.'[4] These are not the words of a silly, vulgar woman.

Her nature was compassionate. When there was a risk that Lord Grey might dismiss an estate employee named Hibbert, she hurried off a letter to Hanson. 'The poor man will be deprived of Bread which would make me very unhappy. I wish you would settle the business.'[5] Again, in 1804, she was voicing similar uneasiness on account of a Newstead tenant, one Palethorpe, who was in prison for debt, and she urged Hanson to get him out.[6]

Her letters on financial matters, when she came to know the business of the estate, show such sound judgment that it is a pity she did not often succeed in moving the torpid solicitor to act as she—admittedly without

---

[1] Murray MS. Hanson copies. 17 Nov. 1803.
[2] Ibid. 12 May 1804.   [3] Egerton 2611. 23 Dec. 1807.
[4] Ibid. 5 Jan. 1809.   [5] Hanson copies. 1 July 1803.
[6] Ibid. 26 Apr.

much mincing of words—suggested. Her fear that Byron might make
some foolish bargain about the Rochdale estate when he came of age
prompted her to complain that those who had purchased part of it illegally from the late Lord might be protracting negotiations 'merely that
they might get him to agree to some compromise very much to his disadvantage before that period, it is impossible to say what a young man
may be *induced* to do that knows nothing of business more particularly
if he wants a little ready money'.[1] She was perfectly right. Byron, only
a few days before, had written to Hanson in favour of compromise.[2]
Largely through her nagging the lawsuit was pursued, however sluggish-
ly, and Byron in the slow course of time won it.[3]

Her failure as a mother was due as much to her virtues as to her defects and was the repetition of her failure in marriage. Even at the cost of
self-immolation, she could deny nothing either to her husband or her son,
and such magnanimity asks to be abused. Truth speaks in every line of
hers that survives, and courage never falters. Yet if she was dauntless
she was also pugnacious, while her truthfulness was carried to the verge
of embarrassing tactlessness. She suffered too from want of manner—but
not ignorance of polite forms. All her letters are in accordance with the
etiquette of the day, and if her appearance was vulgar, it could only have
been because it was not easy for an obese woman in neo-classical dress
to look refined. That she was deficient in sense is shown by her many acute
observations to be false. It was control that her spontaneous nature lacked.

It did nothing to soften the disrespect of her son that she had taken a
fancy to Lord Grey de Ruthyn which was expressed so visibly that the
baleful eye of Mealey could detect it, and his baleful pen convey news of
it to Hanson: 'He [Lord Grey] is very thick with Mrs Byron and Lord
Byron is displased at it[.] he [Grey] has been setting Mrs Byron against
me.' And: 'Mrs Byron and him is greater than ever[.] he has dined with
her several times sinc you left here, and whatever he says is right with
her. When he writes to her it is My dear Mrs Byron.'[4] If not 'very thick'
Lord Grey would, of course, have addressed her as 'Dear Madam'.

Most adolescents look on their mothers as elderly women, and when
thirty was universally deemed to be middle age, that attitude was more
pronounced than it is now. In Mrs Byron at thirty-nine, it seemed quite
ridiculous to be susceptible to a man fifteen years her junior, and Byron

[1] Egerton 2611. 5 Jan. 1809.

[2] Ibid. 17 Dec. 1808.

[3] The Rochdale estate comprised immensely productive quarries and coal mines.
Had it not been for the long and costly litigation, throughout which the seams were
worked and slate quarried to Byron's disadvantage, he would have been among the
richest instead of the poorest peers.

[4] Egerton 2612. 26 Mar. and 30 July 1804. The errors are not misprints.

had a double reason to be humiliated by it because he and Grey were not on speaking terms.

The acquaintance had opened out promisingly enough, when the latter returned from the North some weeks before Christmas, with Byron trying to emulate him in devotion to sport—for although Grey had disclaimed being 'sporting mad', it is very clear that he cared for little else. Mealey, who was still reluctantly harbouring the younger Lord, was soon able to dispatch one of his woeful reports to the solicitor; incidentally presenting a very un-Byronic picture of one who in later life greatly disliked shooting at live targets:

> Lord Byron is at Newstead with Lord Gray [sic] they goe out those moonlight nights and shuit pheasants as they sit at Roost. There is a great deal said about Lord Byron in this neighbourhood for staying away from school, and now being tutord by Lord Gray that kills all the game in the Country he has had 16 Hares in the House at one time he says he will turn the garden into a hare warren. . . .

Mealey never omitted to pass on any criticism that might disturb the recipient:

> Lord Byron says that his mother says that you ought to have taken the rents before now as he is loosing the Interest of his money by laying in the farmers hands so long and a great deal more that I can better explain to you when you come down. . . . I hope to God you will come down very soon to put things to rights here. The most of all me time has been taken up waiting of Lord Byron since the 1st of August. When I tell him that you will blame me not to attend to the work he says he [does not] Care that he must be waited on.[1]

Byron was apparently imitating the lofty style towards employees observed in his new friend—it is another unwonted touch—but Mealey, with his incessant grumbling, was very provoking. Mrs Byron wrote that he seemed 'always *stupid* with ale',[2] and there are numerous indications that, under a more energetic manager than Hanson, who had engaged him, he would hardly have been allowed to retain his post year after year, adding to its privileges.

The exact date when Byron broke off his intercourse with the sporting nobleman is not recorded. It could only have lasted a few weeks because in late January 1804 he went back at last to Harrow and did not return till March 22nd, and on March 26th he was writing to his sister:

> . . . Not being on terms of even intimacy with Lord Grey I avoid Newstead, and my resources of amusement are Books, and writing to my Augusta

---

[1] Ibid. 29 Dec. 1803.   [2] Egerton 2611. 12 May 1810.

. . . I am not reconciled to Lord Grey, *and I never will*. He was once my *Greatest Friend*, my reasons for ceasing that Friendship are such as I cannot explain, not even to you my Dear Sister, (although were they to be made known to any body, you would be the first,) but they will ever remain hidden in my own breast.—

They are Good ones however, for although I am *violent* I am not *capricious* in my attachments.—My mother disapproves of my quarrelling with him, but if she knew the cause (which she never will know), She would reproach me no more. He Has forfeited all *title to my esteem*, but I hold him in too much *contempt* ever to *hate him*.[1]

For Byron to keep a secret was always an effort—communication was his most ebullient gift, and it could not be suppressed for long—but at a time when a homosexual act between males was a capital crime, ladies were not supposed to know such practices existed, and it is quite likely that his remarks were as cryptic to Augusta as he meant them to be, and virtually certain that Mrs Byron was ignorant of her favourite's propensity. If her son had been unable at ten years old to tell her that his pious and trusted nurse had been getting into his bed and interfering with him sexually, he would not at sixteen have discussed what was then more shocking and embarrassing still.

That the hostility and scorn Lord Grey had evoked was the outcome of a homosexual advance is shown by a marginal comment of Hobhouse's on Moore's statement that an intimacy had 'sprung up between Byron and his noble tenant'. 'And a circumstance occurred', Hobhouse noted, 'during [this] intimacy which certainly had much effect on his future morals.'

It is odd to find Grey credited—or debited—with Byron's phase of cheerful abandonment, six years afterwards, to adventures with youths in the Near East, seeing that his reaction to the approaches had been horrified recoil; but perhaps in his account of this juvenile ordeal, he did not, considering his own deviations, lay much emphasis on the repugnance he had felt when obliged to resist a man eight years his senior.

We may be sure it was repugnance. He was still in love with Mary Chaworth. The strong sentimental attachments formed at Harrow had not yet developed. In any case, he was, in those green days of his youth, full of idealism; nor was he ever for that matter destined to be attracted to adult men otherwise than in friendship. He had been proud to find his company so welcome to one who was, by comparison, mature and sophisticated, but now the association was spoiled once and for all, and to add to the awkwardness of it, there was his mother, when he came home for the Easter holidays, making a complete fool of herself.

Lord Grey pretended nothing had happened, writing to Hanson:

[1] Marchand, *Letters*.

'I have learnt that Lord Byron is in Town. When you see him I beg you to say whenever he chuses to call I beg he will, sans ceremonie.'[1] Byron did not call. Grey tried to make it up through the intervention of Mrs Byron, whom he possibly cultivated with that end in view.

> . . . All our disputes have been lately heightened by my one with that object of my cordial deliberate detestation, Lord Grey de Ruthyn [Byron told Augusta, speaking of his mother]. She wishes me to explain my reasons for disliking him, which I will never do. . . . She also insists on my being reconciled to him, and once she let drop such an odd expression that I was half inclined to believe the Dowager was in love with him. But I hope not, for he is the most disagreeable person in my opinion that exists. He called once during my last vacation, she threatened, stormed, begged me to make it up, he himself loved me, and wished it, but my reason was so excellent that neither had effect, nor would I speak or stay in the same room, till he took his departure. No doubt this appears odd but was my reason known, which it never will be if I can help it, I should be justified in my conduct. Now if I am to be tormented with her and him in this style, I cannot submit to it.[2]

This letter is significant because it is the first in which he writes scathingly of his mother, as is shown by the following earlier passage from it: 'Now Augusta I am going to tell you a secret, perhaps I shall appear undutiful to you. . . . My mother has lately behaved in such an eccentric manner, that so far from feeling the affection of a Son, it is with difficulty I can restrain my dislike.'

It would have been absurd to open this topic as a fresh one, hitherto 'a secret', if Augusta had already had his much harsher letter so often quoted.[3] We thus see that Lord Grey played a part of more importance in the rift, and consequently in Byron's history, than has been recognized, and that Mrs Byron may indeed have become infatuated with him, setting off in her son a reaction of contemptuous disgust.

As she did not perceive, in spite of what must have been liberal indications, that the young man's interest in him was more than neighbourly, she may equally have mistaken the attentions a homosexual man will pay an older woman for feelings more flattering. With her highly strung nature and sexually frustrated past, this delusion might well cause her to behave 'in an eccentric manner', to exhibit various symptoms of emotional disturbance, and to resent the mysterious quarrel that lessened her freedom, when Byron was at home, to meet her supposed admirer.

> She is so very strenuous, and so tormenting in her entreaties and commands, with regard to my reconciliation, with that detestable Lord G. that

---

[1] Egerton 2612. 16 Apr. 1804.   [2] Marchand, *Letters*. 2 Nov. 1804.
[3] I.e. the one of 18 Aug. 1805, formerly misdated 1804. See p. 73.

I suppose she has a penchant for his Lordship [Byron told Augusta after receiving her ready letter of sympathy] but I am confident that he does not return it, for he rather dislikes her, than otherwise, at least as far as I can judge.[1]

He was probably right. When Grey's patience with Hanson's neglect of correspondence had run out, he reproached him sarcastically: 'It is extremely unpleasant to be obliged to write to you so often upon one subject . . . I should wish to know whether you have appointed Mrs Byron my lord Carlisle or the Lord Chancellor to reply to such letters of business.'[2]

Even in boyhood Byron had a peculiarly obsessing effect upon anyone who became involved with him, and Lord Grey went on alluding to him quite unnecessarily in his letters to the lawyer.

> You will excuse me in suggesting to you that altho' I should have felt much repugnance in being the instrument to Lord Byron's disadvantage in any way still I cannot on matters of business but feel excessively mortified in having failed to procure those replies which a common attention to business entitle [sic] me to expect.[3]

Byron, as a very young minor, had nothing to do with business or Hanson's inveterate slackness. (There never could have been a man who needed so many reminders to get him to reply to a letter, who was so slow in paying wages or any other moneys, or so nonchalant under the battery of his clients' protests. Remonstrances were liable to bring pleas of ill health, but if this excuse was true he must have lived a life of chronic invalidism, which was not the case.)

Complaining a few months later that a public road had been closed by Mealey and another man on the estate, Rushton, Grey wrote: 'Now, Sir, under the Shyness that exists between Lord Byron & myself, I should be sorry to urge anything which might be *construed* as an intention to obstruct his Plans, but I will assure you that I eye with jealousy any infringement of Public Rights.'[4]

Again Byron's name was gratuitously introduced. He was nowhere near the Abbey and not in control there. Hanson answered bafflingly:

> I am extremely sorry that any Shyness should exist between your Lordship and Lord Byron, the cause of which I never could learn. I had felt very comfortable in the idea that the most perfect cordiality would have prevailed and I yet hope it will when Lord Byron next visits Nottinghamshire. . . .[5]

[1] Marchand, *Letters*. 11 Nov. 1804.
[2] Egerton 2612. 25 Mar. 1805. Byron was one of the Lord Chancellor's wards. Grey has thus mentioned all his three guardians.
[3] Ibid. 28 Mar. 1805.   [4] Ibid. 16 July 1805.   [5] Ibid. 25 July.

He deferred looking into the question of the road. Grey retorted that, unless Mealey and Rushton had told him they were acting under Hanson's orders, he would have made the posts and rails crack—a specimen of his temper which may arouse a suspicion that he had offered some violence in his approaches to Byron.

> You will, be assured Sir [he continued] ever find me ready to meet your wishes at the expense of my private comfort where my Lord Byron's welfare is materially concerned, but you will excuse me if in future I do not strictly depend on the veracity of these presumptuous Heroes.[1]

His reiterated expressions of consideration for Byron bore no relation to his conduct. He was the worst of tenants. As fast as young trees were planted, so essential to the rehabilitation of the estate, the hares and rabbits he bred for shooting destroyed them. Because it provided cover for his game, he was enraged when undergrowth was cut down in the woods. He forced ponds to run dry, declaring, when Mealey protested, that he would not mind paying a thousand guineas for every fish he could get out of them. Mealey being at one time, for some reason, without a bed, he refused to keep a promise he had made to lend him one, and left him to sleep on the bare floor for ten nights. He suspected the steward of poaching, which was to him the worst crime in the calendar, and engaged a man to spy on him on the grounds that it was his wish 'to restore this manor to my Lord Byron more plentifully stocked with Game than it was on my taking possession of it'.[2]

There seems to have been a strain of cruelty in him which would have been repellant to Byron, and to Mrs Byron too if she had not been blind to it. '. . . I presume he goes on in the old way', Byron wrote to Hanson, 'quarrelling with the farmers, and stretching his *Judicial* powers . . . to the utmost, becoming a torment to himself, and a pest to all around him.'[3]

He was still telling tales on Mealey to Mrs Byron, according to Mealey's own account, in 1805, and still franking her letters as late as November 1807, but it was only through a messenger, because Byron was at Southwell during a great part of that year and the year before, so she could not be visited and did not go to Newstead. She had become so disillusioned that she was anxious for his departure and afraid lest he might overstay his five-year lease, writing to Hanson on the last day of 1807:

[1] Ibid. 28 July.

[2] Egerton 2612. 17 Jan. 1806. The various references to 'my Lord Byron' and 'my Lord Carlisle' have an ironical undertone.

[3] Marchand, *Letters*. 1 Dec. 1804. Grey had become a Justice of the Peace, with extensive powers to inflict punishment.

> I am glad Lord Grey de Ruthyn leaves Newstead at Midsummer . . .
> I may be mistaken but I believe there will be some difficulty in getting him
> out, and I know when the time arrives Byron will never rest till he is out,
> therefore you must take that business entirely on yourself as I would not
> have them meet on any account as they *hate* each other and I am sure they
> would quarrel which might end very seriously.
>
> I have not seen Newstead myself but I must inform you that almost every
> Person I meet informs me of the shameful state it is in, all the county talks
> of it and says it is quite a disgrace for any Person in the character of a
> *Gentleman* to keep a place in such a *Beastly* state (that was the expression
> that was used). The *new* windows in the long dining room have *disappeared*
> so I am told but all that must be looked after before his Lordship leaves the
> place.[1]

It can thus be seen that Byron retained his animosity to Lord Grey
with a stubbornness very unusual in one whose ill feeling was not often
of long duration, and on the other hand Mrs Byron did not retain her
penchant. It would not have lasted long after she learned how hollow
was his professed regard for her son's interests.

Grey was persistent in pretending ignorance of his offence. Byron,
being obliged to answer a letter of his about final arrangements when he
quitted Newstead, promised with some reserve to attend to his complaints
of Mealey, and continued with his usual frankness:

> I cannot conclude without adverting to circumstances, which though
> now long past, and indeed difficult for me to touch upon, have not yet ceased
> to be interesting.—Your Lordship must be perfectly aware of the very
> peculiar reasons that induced me to adopt a line of conduct, which however
> painful, and painful to me it certainly was, became unavoidable. ——
>
> On these I cannot enter at large, nor would the discussion be a pleasing
> one, while any further explanation is unnecessary. —— At the same time,
> though from these and other causes, much intercourse between us must
> entirely cease, I have still so grateful a recollection of many favours you
> have conferred upon me when a boy, that I shall always be happy, when we
> do meet, to meet as friends, and endeavour to forget we have been other-
> wise.[2]

At twenty, Byron could look back on his experience at fifteen as
'interesting' but still distasteful, and a sort of compunction drove his
ingenuous pen. Grey's reply was anything but ingenuous. He admitted
that he had written about Mealey with a temper 'somewhat ruffled'—
his temper was very frequently in that condition—and went on in seeming astonishment:

[1] Egerton 2611.
[2] 7 Aug. 1808. MS in Meyer Davis Collection, University of Pennsylvania Library.

With respect to that part of your letter which (?) recals to my recollection the days of our Youth, I can only say it will ever be the farthest from my wish to assume any character to Your Lordship but that of a friend, but as you seem to suppose me so well acquainted with the cause of your sudden secession from our former friendship I must beg leave to assure you that, much as I have (?) reviewed every circumstance and given to each its most full & weighty import, still I am now at a loss to account for it. We parted in 1804 the best of Friends, your letters were afterwards most affectionate, nay, I have even now a trifling pledge of your esteem which your mother gave me and therefore under all these counts you cannot wonder at my being somewhat surprised.

You say the break was painful to yourself, I need not say to you who know I have not the power to command my feelings when deeply wounded what my sensations were. . . .[1]

The absurdity of writing in one sentence that they had parted the best of friends and, in the next, that he had been deeply wounded by the break, must cause us to question the balance of his mind. His correspondence with Hanson shows that he had been fully conscious of the estrangement, while Byron's persistence in expressions of rejection to Hanson, to Augusta, to his mother, and to Grey himself militate strongly against the claim that he had sent affectionate letters to him. If his mother gave a 'pledge' of esteem, it was her own, not her son's.

Grey's part in the long succession of Byron dramas was a minor one, yet not to be overlooked because of the damage it did to Byron's relations with his mother.

Early in 1805 when he had just turned seventeen, she had to contemplate equipping him to go to College on leaving Harrow, and formed a most generous plan.

When he does go an additional allowance must be granted [i.e. by the Chancery Court] as I intend giving up the five hundred a year to him as I believe he cannot live upon less & before he goes it will take two hundred & fifty pounds to fit him for college, a hundred & fifty for Furniture Plate & linen, fifty for his Wardrobe, and he must have a Horse, I suppose which will be fifty more.

I am sorry I cannot make him a present of all these things, but I have

[1] Ibid. No date. Lord Grey married a yeoman farmer's daughter, Anna Maria Kelham, in 1809, and died the following year, aged thirty. In 1820 his widow took a second husband, the Hon. and Rev. William Eden, Rector of Bishopsbourne, Kent, and the couple became friends and close confidants of Lady Byron, and were instrumental in her disastrous interference in the life of Augusta Leigh's daughter, Medora, whom she supposed to be Byron's child. Widows who re-married were entitled to retain their former rank, if that was higher, and the Hon. Mrs Eden was confusingly known, till she died at eighty-three, as Lady Grey. Her first husband was succeeded by a daughter he had never known.

never been so fortunate as to procure any addition to my pension. . . . and I am determined not to run into debt.[1]

She had lived in comparative solvency while Byron's allowance as a Ward in Chancery was paid to her, out of which she defrayed all his expenses at Harrow and elsewhere and, with some of it, maintained a home for him; and now she proposed to transfer this £500 per annum entirely into his own keeping, leaving herself, unless Hanson could get some extra allowance for her, with only the £200 of her pension and her tiny revenue from Scotland. Byron in fact had what he admitted to be one of the best incomes in his College.

Her perpetual theme in writing to Hanson was that they must keep him from getting into debt, and to this end, she tried to ensure that he must 'have every thing found him that he can possibly want, even his Gown, that he may begin clear with his five hundred a year . . .'[2] Again, when he was preparing for his first term in residence at Trinity, Cambridge, she impressed on the lawyer that his apartments required renovation and new furniture. 'It is impossible for him to fit them up out of his allowance without beginning with and continuing in Debt which he wishes to avoid.'[3]

For all her reluctance, she was obliged to get into debt herself. The addition to her allowance was not forthcoming. I cannot find any trace of Hanson's ever having made a serious application for it, and he surpassed himself in his habit of ignoring her letters and keeping her in the dark about the figures that should have been made available to this intensely practical woman.

Her decision to place a clear £500 a year in the hands of Jack Byron's son, aged seventeen and a half, was, however, far from practical—an aberration due to the same fatal tendency which had made her sacrifice herself in married life. It could only lead to ridiculous profusion. Byron felt, he told Augusta, like 'a German Prince who coins his own Cash';[4] and in that spirit he gave his orders to tradesmen. So far from acknowledging any obligation to his mother, he insisted that the money was his own, refusing to see that, as long as he was under age, she might very well have doled it out to him as she thought fit and kept some back for the upkeep of the home. He assured his sister that his 'very handsome allowance' did not 'deprive her of a sixpence. . . . I shall be perfectly independent of her'.[5] He even persuaded himself that she was already in receipt of the extra allowance she had vainly asked for. But in the following January,

[1] Murray MS. 8 Feb. 1805.
[2] Ibid. Hanson copies. 25 June 1805.   [3] Ibid. 23 Sept.
[4] Marchand, *Letters.* 6 Nov. 1805.   [5] Ibid. 10 Aug. 1805.

when he was about to turn eighteen, she wrote in desperation: 'The Bills are coming in thick upon me to double the amount I expected; he went and ordered just what he pleased here at Nottingham and in London. . . . I am determined to have every thing clear within the year if possible.'[1]

It was not possible. Byron at Cambridge kept three horses instead of one, supported two menservants and expected his mother to provide for them when he went home, scattered money senselessly on dissipations, showed off with childish squandering, subscribing thirty guineas—ten times as much as was reasonable—towards a monument to Pitt, though politically of the opposite party,[2] purchasing a carriage and maddening his mother by insisting that it was for her convenience after she had refused to countenance it, and, at the age of eighteen, entering into a complicated and ignoble arrangement with money-lenders which was to embarrass him (and her) for years to come.

And all the time he was accusing her, in the thoughtless letters by which she has been judged, of meanness. 'I know Mrs Byron too well to imagine she would part with a sous', he asserted in a frenzy of indignation.[3] We cannot but painfully remember Jack Byron's graceless lament, 'She would never give me a farthing'.

If we consider the great disadvantages under which the incipient poet laboured, his heredity, the false man-of-the-world standards he had acquired both through his rank and his treasured image of a dashing and reckless father, the ups and downs of his childhood, and his strong temptation to recount his trials in the vivid and arresting manner which was his special gift, we find ourselves yielding him some indulgence. But what are we to think of Augusta's part in this correspondence?

She was five years older and should have exercised some restraint instead of encouraging him and even suggesting that he and his mother should be parted. Because of Byron's idealistic praises of her and our more recent recognition of her torments, entangled in a web of Lady Byron's contriving, biographers have tended to view her in a favourable light, but she does not come well out of an examination of her influence on her impressionable brother's youth. There is no trace of one sensitive or sympathetic feeling towards her harassed stepmother in all the archives.

Mrs Byron's temper at this period must have been like tinder, ignited by every spark. Byron accused her of using 'insulting epithets' and we cannot doubt it. He suggested that they were unrepeatable, and it is

[1] *LJ.* 11 Jan. 1806. The sum promised for furniture seems to have been about £100. He spent much more.

[2] He may have been compensating for his knowledge that Pitt had officially instituted Mrs Byron's quasi-charitable pension.

[3] Marchand, *Letters.* To Hanson, 4 Dec. 1805. Before this phase of sustained animosity he had acknowledged, in letters already quoted, her liberality.

likely enough that she had picked up some bad language from her husband, who may not have been more delicate with his wife than with his sister. But whatever she did or said, she could never be right with her son. When, for example, she had well-attested information that, while employed by her, a manservant who was now with Byron at Cambridge, had obtained money from a Nottingham tailor on false pretences, she wrote advising his discharge. He thought this was 'some caprice she had taken into her head', and, as usual, confided, quivering with reprehension, in Augusta: 'I sent back to the Epistle . . . a severe answer, which so nettled her Ladyship, that after reading it, she returned it in a Cover without *deigning* a Syllable in return.'[1]

She cannot have been less than deeply hurt to have done that; and it was a poor triumph for her when, ultimately, the valet had to be prosecuted for stealing a large quantity of Byron's clothes, as well as borrowing some money as if on his behalf, and was transported for seven years. (Byron tried in vain to get the King's Clemency for him.)[2]

But sad as it was for her to be rebuffed at every turn, it was infinitely more distressing to guess—only too correctly—that Byron had enmeshed himself in the most serious kind of debt. A letter couched in deliberately exasperating terms announced that he had happened 'to have a few hundreds in ready Cash' by him, and that he could hardly visit her while she kept no manservant because his own would be engaged about his horses.[3] It drew from her a cry of anguish we cannot hear unmoved:

> Where can he get Hundreds; has he got into the hands of Money *Lenders*, he has *no feeling, no Heart*. This I have long known he has behaved as ill as possible to me for years back, this bitter truth I can no longer conceal. It is wrung from me *by heart rending agony*. . . .
>
> He knows that I am doing every thing in my power to pay his Debts and he writes to me about hiring Servants and the last time he wrote to me was to desire me to send him £25. 0. 0. to pay his Harrow Bills which I would have done if I had had as much as he has—these hundreds. . . . God knows what is to be done with him. I much fear he is already ruined; at eighteen!—Great God I am distracted I can say no more.[4]

With the aid of an irresponsible landlady, he had indeed borrowed from rapacious money-lenders, and was enabled to defy his mother from a distance with a power of invective surpassing her own. She was driven again to give vent to her misery:

---

[1] Ibid. 6 Nov. 1805. Francis Boyce, known as Frank, was the valet, while Fletcher, who would not have been able to do a valet's work without some little training at it, was still a groom.

[2] Murray MS, quoted by Marchand.

[3] *LJ.* 26 Feb. 1806.　　　　[4] Murray MS. To Hanson, 4 Mar. 1806.

Dear Sir,

I will no longer submit to insults and abuse from a Boy. If it were possible to die of grief he would kill me.

I desire you not to pay any of his allowance till you see me or hear from me again. If he is *not* here in ten days from this date I come to London, he shall know he is not yet his own Master.

Yours sincerely,

C. G. Byron.[1]

Threats of cutting off his supplies were futile until his 'few hundreds in ready Cash' were exhausted, and his reply to the message when transmitted by the lawyer was utterly intransigent. But eventually that particular crisis of rebelliousness subsided, and the prodigal came home, impecunious, and was given a prodigal's traditional welcome. Mrs Byron became rather defensive with the man to whom she had, in her misery, unbosomed herself: 'My Son has been with me some time and is to remain till he returns to Cambridge in Oct.ʳ I am perfectly satisfied with his conduct indeed I have *no* reason to be otherwise.'[2]

So quickly was her wrath appeased. She tried to get £500 which Hanson had promised to lend him. 'The debt I shall take entirely upon myself . . . I will trust to my son's Honor to pay me.' Hanson had left three consecutive letters of hers unanswered and took no notice of this. She managed to rally a loan of £1,000 for Byron's aid, chiefly from his great-aunt by marriage, the Hon. Mrs George Byron, widow of one of the Admiral's brothers, and that lady's nieces, the Misses Parkyns, Byron's distant cousins, all living in Nottingham. It was on the security of a large fraction of her little capital in Scotland.

Hanson's handling of this matter was entirely unhelpful. He might have advised Mrs Byron against her foolhardy magnanimity, letting the young Lord, now nineteen, find his own way out of his self-imposed difficulties; or he might with no great effort have raised £1,000 without diminishing her income or compromising her property. After all, his client was the owner of extensive and valuable lands, the chief wealth of the early 19th century. As it was, he displayed complete indifference. The Hon. Mrs Byron's son, Captain John Byron, doubtless of the Royal Navy like so many of his kinsmen, wrote to him to say the money would be forthcoming if the security was absolutely sound, and asking Hanson's opinion.[3] Four weeks later he had received no reply. The same question was courteously repeated by Miss Parkyns, and ignored. Ultimately

[1] Ibid. 26 Mar. 1806.

[2] Egerton 2611. 25 July 1806. Misdated Oct. by her, evidently because she was throwing her mind forward towards Byron's intended return to Cambridge.

[3] Murray MS. 22 Feb. 1807.

Byron himself wrote, in accord with his mother for once, saying that both he and she were astonished that her letters, requiring an immediate answer, met with none.

That was on May 18th.[1] On June 11th he wrote again: 'In the first week of July I have *pledged* myself to pay upwards of £*350* to enable me to get rid of Cambridge for ever.' He asked Hanson to advance him £375, and added in the captious style of a spoiled youth, 'If the *ancient Gentlewoman* of Nottingham keeps her word, you shall certainly be repaid immediately, but in case of any demur on her part, as my Income passes through your hands solely, I cannot deprive you of your *right*, even if so inclined.'[2] Mrs Byron, pitifully concerned to keep her son from applying again to money-lenders, added a postscript promising that, if he could only have two quarters allowance advanced to him, £250, she would repay it herself in the event of his death.

She may have thought his death no unlikely contingency because, during his stay of nearly a year at Southwell, necessitated by his not having the means to meet expenses at Cambridge, he had used his retirement to do what was then most unusual. By rigorous abstinence and exercise, he had reduced his weight so substantially that he had turned himself from a portly young man into a slender one. With this his natural pallor was intensified, so that, to those who accepted the association, then normal, of abundant nourishment with health, he must have appeared to be almost in a decline.

The enhancement of his beauty thus achieved was to have a marked effect on his character and pursuits; and so did a second preoccupation, one which made him much more willing to forgo the convivialities of university life than he would have been without it. He was getting his verses into print and circulating them; first *Fugitive Pieces* (which were very fugitive indeed for he had all the edition except two copies destroyed when a friendly clergyman reproached him with some unseemly lines), then the revised edition called *Poems on Various Occasions*, finally one more extensive revision under the title *Hours of Idleness*. Byron's juvenile publications were a source of much pride to his mother, just as his oration on his last Harrow Speech Day had been, and as all his accomplishments were to be in the four years that remained to her. If being a poet occasioned expense, how trifling it was compared with the cost of being an undergraduate.

But suddenly, having renounced Cambridge for good, he decided to spend another year there. He had gone back in mid-June 1807, presumably with borrowed money (Mrs Byron had raised £200 from the Southwell banker, Wylde), and with his new looks and his new standing—

---

[1] Ibid. Hanson copies.   [2] Marchand, *Letters.*

the dignity of print—it was apparent that he might become a person of consequence there. It took him some days to realize it. On June 30th he was writing to Elizabeth Pigot to say he was quitting Cambridge for ever without regret as his old set had vanished; and on July 5th—so mercurial were his humours—he informed her that he would stay another year, 'as my Rooms, &c. &c. are finished in *great Style,* several old friends *come up* again, & many new acquaintances made'.[1]

There was also young Edleston, the object of his 'violent though pure passion', now recognized as having profoundly influenced his early years. The chorister whose singing had been an irresistible charm was leaving Cambridge, having taken a post 'in a mercantile house of considerable eminence in the Metropolis', Byron informed Elizabeth[2] with a pomposity rather touchingly framed to soften the unpalatable prospect of the beautiful, musical youth becoming a city clerk. And in the next letter:

> . . . I write with a *bottle* of *claret* in my *Head* & *tears* in my *eyes*, for I have just parted from 'my *Cornelian*' who spent the evening with me. . . Edleston & I have separated for the present, & my mind is a *Chaos* of *hope* & Sorrow . . . he has been my *almost constant* associate since October 1805, when I entered Trinity College; his *voice* first attracted my notice, his *countenance* fixed it, & his *manners* attached me to him for ever . . . I certainly *love* him more than any human being. . . .[3]

Byron was telling the truth of his feelings as they possessed him then, but though he may previously have seen a great deal of the choirboy (Edleston was only fifteen in 1805), his absences from the university had been so long that the constant association was not the intense affair that he makes it sound. I am inclined to doubt that the enthusiasm became crucial before this renewal of the friendship, when he found the fair-skinned blond youth with dark eyes 'grown considerably'. The carelessness with which, before the reunion, he left the cornelian heart Edleston had given him in Miss Pigot's desk,[4] not remembering whether he had lent or presented it to her, seems to contradict the idea of any overwhelmingly strong sentiment; but on his resuming his Cambridge life, his love blossomed again, and he was one day to discuss it with Lady Byron in terms which left her in no uncertainty that it had once been paramount.[5]

[1] Ibid.   [2] Ibid. 30 June.

[3] Ibid. 5 July 1807. The farewell dinner took place at The Hoop. Fourteen young gentlemen drank twenty-three bottles of wine and some cup. The bill, fifteen guineas, was promptly paid. Lovelace Papers.

[4] Pratt. Miss Pigot to Byron, 3 July 1807.

[5] His remembered allusions are in a Lovelace MS entitled 'Lord Byron and Literature'. It must have dawned on Lady Byron slowly that this mysterious person had been

He called the loved one Thyrza, telling his wife he had taken the name from Gessner's *Abel*, and it has long been understood that the poems to this being were inspired by Edleston's early death. To the extreme annoyance of Lord Lovelace, that was deduced as early as the 1890s by E. H. Coleridge when editing Byron's poetry. Lord Lovelace knew perfectly well of his grandfather's strayings from what were then the strictly ruled lines of the sexual norm, but he was determined to suppress a secret which, in the decade of the Wilde trials, would have been a degradation far more appalling than incest—and besides, he wanted only one scapegoat, Augusta Leigh. The unspoken reason, I conjecture, for his fury at John Murray's insistence on republishing the letters to Elizabeth Pigot was that, in the one from which I have just given an extract, Byron prophesied that he and Edleston would 'reside' together putting Lady Eleanor Butler and Miss Ponsonby[1] to the blush and outdoing David and Jonathan.

The very naïveté of this communication attests that the passion was 'pure', and so do many lines, published or rejected, in the Thyrza poems, and no Byron scholar has ever thought otherwise. When homosexual practice is regarded with odium, desires in that direction are generally— to use a word now quite out of fashion—sublimated. The effect of that sublimation may have heightened Byron's ardour while at the same time contributing to his feverish excesses with women. This is not to say that he was basically a homosexual engaged either in indulging his proclivity or striving to live it down—I entirely agree with Leslie Marchand in the belief that he was predominantly attracted by women[2]—but his sexual nature had many facets, and whenever he could adopt the rôle of patron and protector, he was likely to become emotionally involved.

What their relations were, how dignified, how free from anything approaching familiarity on either side, may be judged by a hitherto unpublished letter from Edleston to Byron after they had left Cambridge and ceased to meet. Edleston had written what Byron took to be an appeal for financial help. Byron at once offered it, and Edleston respectfully refused it.

3rd March 1809

My Lord,

    I had this day the honour to receive your Lordship's letter of yesterday's

---

a youth, not a girl, for her first remarks were written with female pronouns, which were crossed out and neutral ones substituted.

  [1] The celebrated 'Ladies of Llangollen' were still living together many years after their romantic elopement. Their intention had been to seek rural seclusion, but the faithful attachment of two well-born ladies was such a curiosity that they had numberless visitors. I am not aware that any aspersion was ever cast on their morals.

  [2] See Appendix 2, 'Byron's Sexual Ambivalence'.

date, and feel, most gratefully feel, the additional obligation which your Lordship generously offers to confer on me by pecuniary assistance to form some permanent means of subsistence; at the same time that I am incapable of describing my sensations on the occasion, I feel it my duty to explain the meaning of my former letter which has been entirely misunderstood by your Lordship; I had not the most distant intention of soliciting any pecuniary aid from your Lordship, in my present circumstances, my only wish being to be favored with your personal influence and patronage to assist me in obtaining employment in some respectable occupation, where my Services might meet with such remuneration as would maintain me without being burthensome to any one as I have no prospect, at the present, of any Business in which I could establish myself on my own account.

Should I ever hereafter be so fortunate as to meet with any opportunity of doing so, from the unexampled liberality of your Lordship towards me, I might be emboldened to look up to the favor of your support on such an occasion; but as that is at this time entirely beyond my hopes, I must beg leave again to acknowledge the deep and grateful sense I have of the honour conferred on me by your Lordship's parental kindness; of which I shall cherish an everlasting remembrance ——

At present I must beg leave to repeat that [it] is only the favor of your Lordship's *personal* Influence and Patronage which I humbly presumed in my last as well as now,—to request.[1]

The letter, written at Old South Sea House, Old Broad Street, ends with the formal flourish we should expect from its tone. Edleston, however musical, would pretty obviously have turned into a rather pompous and obsequious person, but the words 'parental kindness' from a youth of nineteen to a man of twenty-one are touching. Without Byron's aid, he became, for the short time he had still to live, a clerk at the Admiralty. We may wonder what proportion of the debts Byron accumulated at Cambridge was incurred in trying to provide for the beloved chorister.

Girls, too, were not to be had for nothing in those days, or if they had been, any gentleman would have thought it a disgrace not to pay for his pleasures when those who provided them had lost every claim to consideration but the financial one. And Byron had not yet attained a position when married women in the best society were available. He was also, in those last years of his teens, fond of being able to boast that he was 'fatigued with sitting up till four in the morning for these last two days at Hazard', or had just bought himself a bear.[2]

The consequence was that he could not produce the interest on the loans his mother had raised for him, and he was borrowing afresh. To

[1] Murray MS. Where Edleston has clearly written 'subsistence', Byron has corrected it to 'employment'.
[2] Marchand, *Letters*. To Elizabeth Pigot, 26 Oct. 1807.

run up debts while still a minor was a costly and intricate operation. One of Byron's ways of doing it was to undertake to pay annuities, when he came of age, to persons whose capital was secured by an insurance on his life effected by some other party at his expense. The premiums fell due relentlessly at moments of the greatest inconvenience.

His letters are a perfect object lesson on the distresses of incorrigible overspending, and would be boring in their reiterant demands, appeals, expostulations, if it were not for their candour and high spirits. Three days after his twentieth birthday, staying, not economically, at Dorant's Hotel in Albemarle Street, he sent an urgent request to Hanson for a loan of twenty pounds, and summed up his situation thus:

> . . . To Cambridge I cannot go without paying my Bills, and at present I could as soon compass the National Debt, in London I must not remain, nor shall I, when I can procure a trifle to take me out of it, home I have none . . .
>
> My Debts amount to three thousand three hundred to Jews, eight hundred to Mrs B[yron] of Nottingham, to Coachmaker and other Tradesmen, a thousand more, and these must be much increased before they can be lessened. Such is the prospect before me. . . .[1]

But what was the prospect before his mother, she who could so well remember the fatal road trodden by her husband? From her the saving graces of his warmth and humour were withheld. He shunned and despised her. 'Home I have none.'

All the time her unhappiness was aggravated by the futility of her attempts to goad Hanson into some activity that would reclaim the Lancashire property, which was yielding a large income to others. The lawsuit to recover the entailed estate had recently been won, but the litigants on the other side had appealed, and Byron's lawyer was contesting their plea with the utmost lassitude. Meanwhile, the portion which was not in dispute was being scandalously abused. Mrs Byron heard from a Rochdale man named Shaw that 'there were one hundred Colliers daily engaged in getting Coal, & double that number getting stone Flags and Slate'. Despairing of Hanson, she found an excuse to write to his partner, John Birch, who had actually taken the trouble at one time to go to Lancashire. Even to him her tone was somewhat of the bluntest:

> He [Shaw] says that the part of the Estate sold by the late Lord Byron is not *near* so valuable as what *never was* sold and what my Son has an undoubted right to, and if it had been properly managed Lord Byron ought to have had more than thirty thousand pounds saved out of that property by the time he came of age. *I will speak the truth*, why is my Son permitted to

[1] Egerton 2611. 25 Jan. 1808.

be thus *plundered* by you and Mr Hanson? Why don't you prevent it? What reparation can you make to him? . . .

A Lady who lives in this place whose father has an Estate near Rochdale just gives me *exactly* the same account, she says the *mismanagement* of Lord Byron's property there has long been the subject of conversation and astonishment to all the Noblemen and Gentlemen in the County of Lancashire, and that those who have the management of my Son's affairs are greatly censured and blamed for permitting a minor to be so plundered. . . .

I should ill fulfil my duty *either* as a Parent or a Guardian if I did allow it and rest assured I will not, he will be of age soon in eight months but that is too long a time to allow of his continuing to be *robbed* to such an amount. Therefore as you and Mr Hanson seem asleep I entreat you one or *both* to awake from your lethargy.[1]

Mrs Byron's total want of finesse or diplomacy in any shape was not calculated to endear her to the lawyers any more than to her son, who did not thank her for her endeavours. She wrote to him to convey the same views, hoping he would stimulate the men of business to some exertion. He showed the letter to Hanson, which was not what she could have intended because it contained the comment that Birch might be active but dared not interfere with his partner. The upshot was that she heard from both Hanson and Birch. The latter, while averring that their zeal to serve his Lordship was unflagging, and that they only desisted from further litigation because it would be ruinous to him (which turned out to be an error), admitted that Hanson had been 'much an invalid and from that cause could not give so much attendance at Rochdale as could have been wished', and, while he cautioned her against placing faith in her informant, he seemed to agree that she had some ground of complaint.[2]

But Hanson denounced Shaw as a liar motivated only by revenge because he had been dismissed from the post of 'sole and confidential Adviser to the very Persons who are resisting Lord Byron's claims', and also because Hanson had refused to appoint him as steward and had objected to some expenses he had charged.

> . . . If I had given credit to his Statements your son would have been involved in Suits which must have involved every farthing of his property and had he died under age it would have fallen upon you. . . .
>
> Mr Deardon and the other parties had obtained an Injunction to restrain the Verdicts we had obtained & nothing more could be done than to have an account kept of ye quantities of Coals gotten by them that we might be

[1] Egerton 2613. 23 May 1808.
[2] Ibid. 26 May. We can read between the lines of several of Birch's letters that he was embarrassed by his partner's negligence.

able to resort to them in case ye Court of Equity should confirm the Verdicts. This I ordered to be done and if I had gone down every *Month* to Rochdale it is all I could have done.[1]

Since the only representative Hanson had on the spot was one Richard Milne, a steward who was several years in arrears with payments due to the uncontested part of the estate, and who had more than once been bankrupt, the facilities for keeping track of the quantity of mining that was being done were, to say the least, feeble; the question of slate-quarrying was merely ignored; and Mrs Byron was supposed to be content with the explanation that Deardon, an opponent, had sworn the Collieries were not worth £100 a year.

She replied in one of her many astute, if too forthright letters, that— though Shaw might be a great rascal yet—

> . . . Rogues are often useful, and it is my opinion that he is the person on earth *most* likely to know the rich value of Lord Byron's property in Lancashire and this I believe for the *same* reason you give for doubting his veracity, namely, his having been employed by the same people now resisting Lord Byron's claims, and they having quarrelled with him (which was very unwise in them). . . . Who is more capable of giving accurate information concerning the situation of an army than a Deserter?

She was convinced that the chief appellant had perjured himself in gross under-estimation of the value of the collieries he was expensively trying to retain.

> Pray let me ask you if it is consistent with common sense to believe that Deardon and his partners would throw away thousands (which they have done) in the diffence of a property not worth a hundred a year? Improbable!!! For my part I never will swallow such inconsistent nonsense.[2]

Hanson had assured her he would go to Rochdale to look into all this in the first week of July, or probably sooner, and that he would make a point of calling on her at Southwell on his way. On July 4th, she asked when he was to take his journey, and on the 19th, addressing Birch once more, she became blunter than ever: 'I wrote to Mr Hanson some time ago desiring to know when he went to Rochdale, but have received no answer, as he seems to be a *sleeping* partner in the firm. I desire you will inform me when either you or Mr Hanson intend to go to that place.'[3]

A cross is scrawled on that note, and, in the writing of Hanson's son, Charles, the words 'What impudence. C.H.' There was more of the same to come.

---

[1] Ibid. Same date.   [2] Ibid. 29 May.   [3] Ibid.

Southwell
2d Oct.ʳ 1808

Sir,

It is now *four months* since you wrote to me that you or Mr Birch would certainly go down to Rochdale in a month!!! Why dont you go there? I suppose there is now *no* hopes of the law business being soon settled, therefore it is endless to wait for that. I hope your health is better.

I remain, Sir,

Your obed. Serᵗ

C. G. Byron[1]

Thus chivvied, Hanson went. But true to form, he had forgotten the payment of Byron's quarterly allowance with £75 extra he had agreed to advance to him; or rather, he had put the sum, £200, into a Nottingham bank, so Birch explained, and neither Birch nor Byron could get at it. An apology 'with the highest respect and regard' from the partner was no great consolation to one who was desperate for money by the end of every quarter, or much sooner.

But at least he was back at Newstead, and his mother need not picture him extravagantly dissipating at some Mayfair hotel, or flinging money to the winds among the gilded youth of Cambridge. Instead he was entertaining friends of a lively but intellectual cast, and writing the verses soon to become famous as *English Bards and Scotch Reviewers*. Mrs Byron was still at Southwell, kept at arm's length with an explicitness quite equal to her own.

. . . I shall live in my own manner, and as much alone as possible, when my rooms are ready, I shall be glad to see you, at present it would be improper, & uncomfortable to both parties.—You can hardly object to my rendering my mansion habitable, notwithstanding my departure for Persia in March (or May at farthest) since *you* will be the *tenant* till my return, and in case of any accident. . . . I have taken care you shall have the house & manor for *life*, besides a sufficient income.—So you see my improvements are not entirely selfish. . . .[2]

And a few weeks later:

When my rooms are finished I shall be happy to see you. . . . I am furnishing the house more for you than myself, and I shall establish you in it before I sail for India, which I expect to do in March, if nothing particularly obstructive occurs.[3]

The self-deceptions of youth are as cunning as those of age, and Byron may have told himself he had his mother's well-being in mind when order-

---

[1] Ibid.   [2] Marchand, *Letters.* 7 Oct. 1808.   [3] Ibid. 2 Nov. 1808.

ing costly equipment for his rooms, just as he had told himself that his carriage—still unpaid for—would be of service to *her* when it was nothing but an encumbrance. On the other hand, within the month he was writing to Augusta, 'Mrs Byron I have shaken off for two years, and I shall not resume her yoke in future. . . . I never can forgive that woman, or breathe in comfort under the same roof', and he said his heart had been 'bent, twisted, and trampled on'.[1] She must, poor tactless creature, have cancelled out, in his eyes, all her strivings, her sacrifices—if ever he recognized them as such—by accusations, remonstrances, and warnings of evil to come. But above all, I surmise, she had offended him by unbridled criticism of the friends he treasured and who seemed to her a thoroughly bad influence. (Augusta was one of them.)

Her satisfaction at being offered the privilege of taking residence at Newstead Abbey when he had celebrated his coming of age by travelling to some inconceivably distant country must have been very temperate. Happily, she did not yet know that 'making his mansion habitable' was not a matter of a few hundred pounds, but the beginning of a new spate of crippling debts, the brunt of which was to be borne by her.

It has been written, as an illustration of her violent temper, that she died in consequence of her rage on reading an upholsterer's bill. This bill, which brought bailiffs into the Abbey while Byron was enjoying his fruitful travels, was in no sense the cause of her death though it might well have been, for it was upwards of £1,500, a prodigious sum (and it was not all) for a young man to have spent on fitting up some rooms he hardly intended to occupy. But her health had started to fail before the time when he was making his delusively benevolent plans for her. Hanson, having at last gone to Lancashire, offered to visit her on the way back or to meet her at Newstead. She was obliged to explain that, though she would have been happy to receive him and Mrs Hanson, she was now not in a fit state to do so.

> I have been unwell almost a year but since the first of Sept[r] I have been very ill indeed and I do *not* expect ever to be better. I am quite unequal to come to Newstead, or even to talk of business if I was to meet you there or anywhere else. I am in a poor low way from many different causes.[2]

One of them must surely have been the studied coldness of the sole near relation left to her in the world. That he undertook to make provision for her in the event of his death could have been little consolation, and was merely ironical when she knew his income was mortgaged for years to come: 'My Son being now so nearly of age [she continued] I think

---

[1] Ibid. 30 Nov.   [2] Egerton 2611. 25 Nov.

you ought to inform him *exactly* of his situation in all respects and let him know the *best* and the *worst* of every thing.'

Did she tell Byron of her malady? And did he, if so, take it seriously, engrossed as he was with his entertaining friends, his writings, the gauntlet he was preparing to throw down to the *Edinburgh Review* and all the literary world, his new furnishings at the Abbey, his plans for what he would do when he had broken the shackles of his legal infancy? Or did she keep it to herself—the expectation of not recovering? She knew as well as anyone that he had 'shaken her off', and if she was not sensitive, nevertheless she had a great deal of pride; 'Scotch pride' Hanson's son called it, remembering her long afterwards.

3

The Holding of the Fort

It is very unlikely that Hanson obeyed Mrs Byron's request to tell her son 'the *best* and the *worst* of every thing'. There was little good to be told, and he was far too fond of keeping on cordial terms with a client whom he had always found captivating but mettlesome to submit him to any very severe lectures or prophecies. On one occasion when he had counselled prudence (it was while Byron was buying furniture for Cambridge), he had received such a stinging rebuke—though not without recognition of his frequent hospitality—that he had done an almost unheard of thing, replied without a day's delay!

> I never thought of acting as a Lawyer it being much more my habit to act as a Friend. I allow nothing to be set on the score of Hospitality. I have had a personal gratification in your Society which amply requites me for any little attentions. I have always felt a profound and most disinterested friendship for your Lordship and warm as I think your asperity has been it will not lessen the affection I feel for you. I am apt to be warm myself and can therefore make allowances for it in others. . . .[1]

After the gentlest remonstrances, he had subscribed himself his Lordship's 'most sincere and affectionate friend'. It was a flattering letter for an adolescent to receive, and Byron, who was never unmoved by generosity if graciously expressed, had written a penitent answer, which drew from Hanson a recognition of 'the Nobleness of your Disposition' and an admission that he had perhaps treated the young man's 'undisguised communications with too much of the sterile notions of a parent'. As for the real parent, at Southwell, Byron had given vent to his antagonism in a perfect tirade about her, and Hanson discreetly sympathized: he knew, he said, it must have been painful to be with her, but sagely added that,

> . . . great allowance must be made for the misfortune of Impetuousness of Temper, and your Heart is too well formed to forget that she is your

[1] Murray MS. 1 Dec. 1805.

Mother. . . . Indeed I have felt Uneasiness myself at the treatment I have
at times received from your Mother but it has grown into compassion &
there I am disposed to let it rest . . .

I would not have you entertain any uneasiness about your future
Supplies as you will ever find me more a friend than a Lawyer.[1]

This, and the dispatch of £50 forthwith, was little short of encouragement to the boy not yet eighteen to go on being irresponsible, and he took
full advantage of it, so much so that when the day came, as it inevitably
did, of his awakening to the inertia and carelessness with which his affairs
were being handled, a sense of obligation restrained him from doing what
it would have saved him an unending coil of money troubles to do—
namely, to put himself in the hands of a solicitor who was less affectionate
and more business-like.

John Hanson played so considerable a part in the poet's life and even
after his death—for by a will made before the eventual parting of their
ways, he became co-executor with Hobhouse—that it is a pity he has
tended to be crowded out from the numerous band of associates to whom
biographers have principally devoted their researches. He was by no
means a colourless man and certainly not a retiring one. He lived in style,
keeping, besides a residence in London, a fine mansion called Earl's
Court House at Old Brompton, which he had bought from the executors
of the rich and famous surgeon John Hunter. (It was here the Hanson
children first met Byron as a little boy.) In 1804 he sold this semi-rural
retreat—for such it then was—advantageously and acquired a genuine
country estate, Farleigh in Hampshire. Lackadaisical as he seemed, he
had much acumen in his own affairs.

His sons appear to have been obedient and attached, and his letters
suggest a genial personality, even while his inattention to his clients'
business verges on eccentricity. There is one anecdote which takes
eccentricity slightly beyond the verge, and as it affords a glimpse of Byron
at Harrow and I do not recollect having seen it in print, I will give it here.
It is a passage his third son, Newton, had intended to drop into the
memoir of Byron, which he began with a view to publication—the so-
called 'Hanson Narrative'. Newton had been taken by his father to a
Harrow Speech Day, his older brother, Hargreaves, being a fellow pupil
and contemporary of Byron's.

My father's costume I remember on that occasion was somewhat original. He wore a light pepper & salt Coat with plated buttons, a light summer
Waistcoat and nankeen shorts and gaiters; but the most curious thing was

[1] Ibid. 10 Dec.

his Hat. He had not long before launched a triangular kind of Judge's Hat the rim of which looped up at the sides & end by silk strung to Buttons.

It certainly was not common for Gentlemen or Solicitors however talented or eminent to wear this kind of [? headgear] but it was occasionally done by a few Geniuses, & the Article was perhaps a last lingering one in its way of the former Generation of the Grandisonian character.

On our arrival at Harrow we set out in search of Hargreaves & Byron but the latter was not at his Tutors, when three or four Lads, hearing my father enquire for Byron, set off at full speed to find him. They soon discovered him & laughing most heartily called out Hallo Byron, here is a Gentleman wants you and what *do* you think? Why, he has got *Drury's* Hat! They all quickly came up in a group enjoying the fun excessively, & I can still remember the arch look of Byron's eye first at the Hat, then at my father and the fun & merriment it caused him & all of us whilst during the day the Hat was perambulating the Highways and bye ways of Ida & back.[1]

Anyone who has ever known the hideous embarrassment of being visited at a boarding-school by an adult who excites the laughter of one's companions will realize that Byron and Hargreaves passed a pretty uncomfortable day, however merry the smaller Hanson may have thought it, and however archly Byron's look apologized to the lawyer for the bad manners of his reception.

Whether Hanson's almost pathological lassitude was a cloak for want of probity in his dealings it would take a member of his own profession, and one versed in procedures now obsolete, to discover, so complex were the matters he had to handle. But as the years passed, his reputation was tarnished by a scandal, and he was eventually pronounced by a judge (Sir John Nicholl) in the Court of Arches to have been guilty, with his family, of fraudulent conspiracy. This was in getting his elder daughter, Mary Ann, married to the rich but insane Earl of Portsmouth, towards whom he was literally in a position of trust, being his legal trustee. The case was among the longest ever to be heard in that Court; but as it did not attain its widest publicity till four years after Byron's death, it has never been accorded much more than a paragraph or a footnote in books about him. Byron was, however, involved in it and as we are concerned with Hanson's character, here it will be raised to the dignity of an appendix which is almost a chapter.[2]

Byron came of age on January 22nd 1809, and it was by no means the escape from bondage that he had longed for. He could contract debts, it is

---

[1] Murray MSS. The 'shorts' were probably knee breeches, still worn on all formal occasions (and a Speech Day was one) but not with gaiters, while a tricorne hat was not only immensely out of date—and this seems to have been a curious one—but out of the question with such informal materials as nankeen and pepper-and-salt cloth.

[2] See Appendix 3, 'The Hanson–Portsmouth Scandal'.

true, without roundabout procedures, but he was also personally liable for what he owed, and that was something in the region of £12,000.

There was feasting among the tenantry and servitors of the Abbey far beyond what he could afford, but nothing compared with the splendours provided by the 5th Lord for his ill-fated heir. Old Joe Murray, who had been the 5th Lord's butler, and was, said Hanson's son, 'a walking and living Legend of Newstead', told how then 'a vessel rigged and equipped was brought over land from one of our ports . . . that she had 21 guns & discharged them . . . the report being heard all over Nottingham and some of the adjoining counties . . . and open house was kept for many days'.[1] Byron was very proud of being Lord of so historic a manor and might have been glad enough to be master of equally impressive ceremonies, but embroilments of various kinds, particularly financial ones, decided him to remain absent.

Hanson wrote begging to give him a dinner at his Chancery Lane house, where they would drink his 'Health and long Life of Prosperity and Happiness' and enquiring how soon he would take his seat in the House of Lords. 'I would not for a Thousand Guineas be absent when you enter the walls you were born to sit within.'[2] Byron responded by appealing to him instead to represent him at Newstead Abbey, which he did. Hanson also sent diplomatic congratulations to Mrs Byron on the great event, so much more significant to a peer than a commoner. In her letter of thanks she wrote:

> I hope my son will *conduct* himself thro' life in a way to do honour to *both* the great families from whom he is descended and that he will be of *service* to his *country*. Of his talents there can be *no* doubt.
> My health makes it impossible that I can come to Newstead but I wish much to see you on many accounts if it was only for a few hours.[3]

She gave him directions how to get to her, still exiled at Southwell, and said she could provide beds for him and his son, but he did not go. For her, with her own son elsewhere and the worry about debts, which were merely augmented by the Newstead festivities, and her conviction that her life would not be long, it was a melancholy time. She was apprehensive that, unless 'coal mines turn to gold mines', the only road stretching before that brilliant but imprudent young man was the road to ruin—except, she added, if he were 'to mend his fortune in the *old* and usual way by marrying a Woman with two or three hundred thousand pounds'.[4]

[1] Murray MSS. Hanson Narrative.
[2] Egerton 2611. 14 Jan. 1809. Hanson was nevertheless absent on that occasion.
[3] Ibid., Folio 91. No date but obviously not far from 22 Jan.
[4] Ibid. 30 Jan.

It was a very old and usual way indeed for rank to be bartered for wealth through matrimony, and Mrs Byron was only a little blunter than most mothers of impecunious peers would have been in uttering this wish. 'Love matches is all *nonsense*',[1] she declared, more careless of her grammar than usual, in another letter. Her own infatuated marriage had given her the best of reasons for thinking so.

All the creditors who had expected their lordly customer to pay his bills when he reached his majority now began to claim their due, and by February 8th, less than three weeks after his birthday, he was telling Hanson that he was '*dunned* from Noon till Twilight' and had not £5 in his purse.

His taking his seat in the House of Lords, the Rubicon which had to be crossed before he could begin the career of oratory his friends were bent upon for him, was delayed by his being required to show proof of the lawful wedlock of his grandfather, the Admiral. I cannot but conjecture that with a more efficient solicitor this procedure would have been superfluous or at any rate much more expeditious. As Mrs Byron did not fail to point out, the legitimacy of Byron's descent had been proved already, before they could begin the lawsuit at Rochdale, and why had it to be done again? It was, she said, 'very *hard* and very *provoking*'.[2] It was also very costly. Hanson's bill for establishing the pedigree was near £158,[3] and that was a debt that did not wait for settlement.

Byron blamed his guardian, Lord Carlisle, for not sponsoring him, and to the Lord Chancellor, Eldon, when eventually he was able to take his seat on March 13th, he displayed marked coldness—an inauspicious start.

Probably his sullen humour was deepened by the irony of his situation—a nobleman, a legislator, owner of broad acres in the counties of Nottingham, Norfolk, and Lancashire, and yet besieged on every hand by sordid claimants to whom he had been able to put his future in pawn only because of those rare advantages. He was seized with a kind of panic, for some of his most pressing debts were debts of honour. At eighteen or nineteen, he had not been able to give legally valid security for borrowed money, but he had given his word.

It was a few days before his formal presentation in the Upper House that his mother made one more sacrificial gesture:

Dear Sir,
      I have had a very dismal letter from my son informing me that he is *ruined*, he wishes to borrow my money. This I shall be very ready to oblige him in on such security as you *approve*. As it is my *all* this is very necessary

---

[1] Ibid. 4 Mar.   [2] Ibid.   [3] Egerton 2613. Folio 42.

and I am sure he would not wish to have it on any other terms. It cannot be paid up however under *six* months notice. I wish he would take the debt of a thousand pounds that I have been security for on himself, and pay about eighty pounds he owes here. . . .[1]

The money he wanted her to lend him was very nearly all that remained of her fortune, £3,000 invested at five per-cent in Scotland, this interest being her sole income except the reduced pension. She desired him to use it to repay the three sums she had borrowed on his account two years before, which together made up £1,000. She was haunted by that liability, contracted, it will be remembered, to keep him out of the hands of money-lenders, and now apparently all but forgotten by him. Her pride was heavily committed to removing those obligations and she reverted to them often.

> Byron is now at Newstead [she wrote on April 9th] and talks of going Abroad on 6th May next, for God['s] sake see to get him to give security for the one thousand pounds I am bound for, two hundred and interest to Wylde & Co. Bankers, Southwell, three hundred pounds to Miss E. & F. Parkyns, and five hundred pounds to the Honble Mrs Geo. Byron. He must also leave funds to pay the interest.
>
> There is some Trades People at Nottingham that will be *completely* ruined if he does not pay them which I would not have happen for the whole World. He must really impower you & me to act for him when he is abroad, which he talks of doing, but he is so *unsteady* and *thoughtless* with the *best heart* in the World.[2]

Although his eagerness to travel had been expressed to her on several occasions, she seems only just to have realized that it was not nebulous but a fixed resolve which would not be thwarted. She had hoped that, being able now to take part in politics (in which she believed he would become 'a great speaker and a *celebrated* public Character'),[3] and having recently brought out a satire of distinction, he would be content to settle down to retrieving his affairs and fulfilling her ardent wish by marrying a woman of fortune.

The success of *English Bards and Scotch Reviewers*, published in mid-March 1809, was so eclipsed by the more brilliant éclat of *Childe Harold*'s reception three years later that it is not customary to think of it as a work which would have been memorable even if he had not become internationally famous. Nevertheless it made a stir and had some thousands of readers when the reading public was much smaller than in the present day (but, on the other hand, much more accustomed to relish

---

[1] Egerton 2611. 4 Mar. Three punctuation marks inserted.
[2] Ibid.   [3] Ibid. 30 Jan.

verse). Byron applied himself diligently to polishing and revising, but the passionate longing to see exotic lands which he had cherished since boyhood now towered over all other longings, and was intensified by the need to break out of the web of his own indiscretions.

To let his man of business cope with financial troubles, to escape from emotional ones by distance and change of scene—those prospects alone were sufficient to make him book a passage to Malta, the link between Western and Eastern Europe, before he had the means to go, and he urged Hanson again and again to supply him with cash either by mortgaging property or selling the Rochdale estate for anything he could get. Sometimes he became quite frantic in his importunity, hinting at an additional reason not to be named. When Hanson wrote saying it would be disastrous for him to go abroad while his affairs were in their present plight, he replied:

> If the consequences of my leaving England, were ten times as ruinous as you describe, I have no alternative, there are circumstances which render it absolutely indispensible [sic], and quit the country I must immediately. . . . I am pestered to death in country and town, and rather than submit to my present situation, I would abandon every thing, even had I not still stronger motives for urging my departure.[1]

In other letters too, a positive necessity of going abroad, beyond the unpleasantness of being beseiged by creditors, is recurringly insisted on. We might think he was merely trying to spur Hanson into some helpful activity if it were not that he adverted to the same theme when he was as far away as Albania.

> . . . I never will revisit England if I can avoid it, it is possible I may be obliged to do so lest it should be said I left it to avoid the consequences of my Satire, but I will soon satisfy any doubts on that head if necessary & quit it again, for it is no country for me.—Why I say this is best known to myself, you recollect my impatience to leave it, you also know what I then & still write that it was not to defraud my creditors, I believe you know me well enough to think no motive of personal fear of any kind would induce me to such a measure; it certainly was none of these considerations, but I never will be in England if I can avoid it, *why*—must remain a secret. . . .[2]

It is open to anyone to guess that Byron had arrived at the realization that violent passions could not always remain pure ones, and had fled from some particular temptation—or even towards a temptation. The

---

[1] Ibid. 16 Apr. 1809. One of the Newstead housemaids was pregnant by him, but he made no secret of that with Hanson who was requested to allow an income for her and the child. See p. 167.

[2] Ibid. 12 Nov. 1809.

scandal which had shattered William Beckford, for whose work he had an extravagant admiration, was one he could never risk in England. What was there a felony in the same category as murder—but judged on the whole to be worse—was in many countries no crime at all, and several remarks of Byron's in letters and verses show that he was shocked and fascinated by the idea of such strange freedom.

If he intended at setting out to indulge in a practice abhorred, it was thought, by nature, and thence invariably classified as 'unnatural', he was not very rational to choose as his companion a fundamentally quite conventional Englishman in the person of John Cam Hobhouse, possessively affectionate but unblinkingly critical and, even in youth, a shade intolerant. For all Byron's joking about the hyacinthine sailors at Falmouth,[1] when at last they waited for the tide, I should suppose that, though he meant to satisfy curiosity and to feel less uneasy about tendencies that must have troubled him profoundly, he had no conscious idea of turning homosexual.[2]

Meanwhile, as he fretted and expostulated, the plan to get his mother's capital from Scotland was hanging fire, because, as she said, 'if my son is abroad he cannot I suppose give security for it'.[3] She was more than ever justified in requiring security, as her astounded final postscript shows: 'He gave Lady Falkland five hundred pounds!!!'

Lady Falkland was the widow of one of the various naval men with whom Byron had contemplated sailing. He had died as the aftermath of a duel, which in its turn was the aftermath of a bibulous evening. Byron was godfather to one of his four children, and, hearing that the family was left in want, he had given, in the guise of a christening present, the actual amount Mrs Byron had stated. It was quixotic self-abnegation because the money would have relieved his own desperate needs. It was equally the abnegation of his creditors, one of whom was his harassed mother.

Such unrealistic generosities are not admirable, and Byron thoroughly deserved the ridiculous sequel. Lady Falkland concluded, when he grew famous, that he must be in love with her, and wrote letter after letter telling him she reciprocated his feelings. He drew back aghast, but she was persuaded this was only bashfulness. Her communications became more perfervid,[4] and finally he was obliged to ask his solicitor to hold her off.

When she was granted a pension of £500 a year—a most handsome

[1] Marchand. Letter of 22 June to C. S. Matthews.
[2] See Appendix 2, 'Byron's Sexual Ambivalence'.
[3] Egerton 2611. 9 Apr. 1809.
[4] Some of them will be found in *To Lord Byron*, Quennell and Paston.

one at the time—Mrs Byron thought she ought to pay back the sum accepted from Byron; but, of course, as she had not known his difficulties, she could not be expected to be troubled by them.

He, thus straitened, was doing everything he could to raise money by the ways open to a solicitor, but whether from policy or lethargy, Hanson was slow to move. Against the proposition that he should sell Newstead Abbey, Byron had set his face; otherwise he was prepared for any measure, even reviving the forlornest of hopes—that the Duke of Portland might be induced to pay the thousand pounds he had been owing so many years that the interest alone would have been a good round sum. Nothing came to hand from the interminable business of the Rochdale estate. His copyholds at Wymondham in Norfolk, part of the dowry of his great-uncle's wife,[1] were expected to realize several thousands, but there was some bother about the title deeds, and Hanson was the last man to cope speedily with that obstruction.

While Byron had been a Ward in Chancery, a certain amount of money had accumulated for him in the care of that Court, and, with the optimism of a layman, he had thought he would at least have that soon after coming of age. But he reckoned without 'the law's delays'—and Hanson's. The passage booked for April 22nd had to be cancelled, and he now resolved to sail in May. He parted with his mother at Newstead Abbey on April 23rd—for the last time if he had but known it—and came to London only to find another postponement unavoidable. After elaborate leave-taking from friends, it was sheer anti-climax to hang about London through May, and when, Hanson, casual as ever, took himself off to Basingstoke, Byron wrote with asperity untempered for once by humour:

Dear Sir,

Your quitting town has put me to the greatest inconvenience, it is really hard with some funds to be compelled to drink the dregs of the cup of Poverty in this manner.— I have not five pounds in my possession.— I do hope the money will be procured for I certainly must leave England on the fifth of June, & by every power that directs the lot of man, I will quit England if I have only cash to pay my passage.

I have long told you my determination, & beg leave once more to repeat that I cannot be detained any longer.—This is the *third* month, in which the money was to be paid from chancery. . . . In short I have made all my arrangements, and I do request that you will not treat me like a child, but assist me as my Friend, and as quickly as you decently can without putting yourself to inconvenience.[2]

[1] Copyholds were a form of land tenure, now obsolete, dependent on traditional manorial rights.

[2] Egerton 2611. 23 May 1809.

Hanson replied promptly enough with an assurance that he had done his best and an assumption that his partner, Birch, would have dealt with it all by now, but he dashed Byron's hopes of relief by reminding him that many payments were to be deducted from what he was to receive, among them legal expenses (chiefly his own), and he feared not above £700 would be left, a sum to be reduced still further by more charges to come.

> I am sorry your Lordship should think I treat you so insignificantly as you have expressed. I am certain you have not a more sincere Friend and one who is so little disposed to treat you with Disrespect or who regrets so much the Difficulties you have plunged yourself into.[1]

This was comparatively plain speaking, and most fully merited. At that very time, drinking 'the dregs of the cup of Poverty', the spoiled young man was buying books lavishly, having miniatures of his friends painted by the fashionable artist, George Sanders, and somehow contriving to pay a large sum for his own picture, which was to go to Newstead Abbey.

A mania of improvidence possessed him, and yet, so capriciously is the pattern of life woven, that hardly any of these follies failed, in the long run, to justify themselves. The travel books he purchased stimulated the alert, rewarding interest he was to take in the scenes he visited; Falconer's *Shipwreck* at one guinea was among the source materials for the vivid shipwreck passages in *Don Juan*; the portrait by Sanders, now in the Royal collection, has given posterity its best idea of Byron as a young romantic, and as the sole illustration of the first edition of Moore's biography, was an important visual contribution to the Romantic Movement; while the greatest extravagance of all, the mounting up of huge debts to go travelling, resulted in the writing of *Childe Harold* and the Oriental verse narratives which brought him unmeasured fame.

The miniatures of friends alone turned out a waste, for he burned two out of three of them in the presence of his wife, with, she noted bafflingly, 'a curious remark'.[2] Edleston's picture would surely have been one of them.

Birch was able to raise a loan from a Colonel Sawbridge, but the first instalment was only about £2,000, and the payment was retarded and, in any case, insufficient to meet the commitments pressing from every side: so Byron could not persist in his determination to leave England on June 5th. His impatience was mitigated to some extent, however, by preparing a revised edition of *English Bards*.

[1] Ibid. 25 May.
[2] Lovelace Papers. Minutes of her conversation with Lady Caroline Lamb, 27 Mar. 1816.

The discipline of his work was never long abandoned, but its success availed him nothing financially. Ever at his elbow at this period was his seedy middle-aged relative by marriage, Robert Charles Dallas, a minor novelist who had contrived to insinuate himself as literary adviser, and, before his young kinsman had turned twenty, to 'borrow' £200 of the money acquired from usurers, and who was later on to secure for himself the whole proceeds of *Childe Harold*, Cantos I and II, £600, and the £500 paid for *The Corsair*.

He was not the gayest of company, but Byron knew scarcely anyone who had had a book in print, and it is flattering to a beginner when a real author takes an intelligent line-by-line interest in his compositions.

Byron had one friend as improvident as himself, or yet more so. This was Scrope Berdmore Davies, about five years his senior, a wit and a Fellow of King's College, Cambridge, but also a compulsive gambler.[1] Though at least once he won more than £6,000 in an evening's play, it was not through a stroke of luck at the tables that he was able to produce, when all else had failed, a loan of upwards of £4,600, but by signing a bond to money-lenders, of whom we shall hear more. By this means, Byron was not only set free to go on his Grand Tour but had enough in hand to advance in his turn the considerable amount Hobhouse needed to accompany him.

They went to Falmouth to take their passage on the *Princess Elizabeth* late in June. Tides and winds conspired to keep the ship at anchor till July 2nd, but at any rate they were on board, and Byron was in such spirits that he wrote to his friend, Francis Hodgson, those spontaneous and lively verses which bring the experience of embarking in a sailing ship richly before the imagination even in the 20th century.

For all his mother knew he was already on the high seas in May, for he did not bother to communicate with her till June 22nd. It was from Hanson she heard in mid-June—and prematurely—that he had sailed. From the loneliness of Newstead Abbey, where she had been left in the very unenviable situation of chatelaine, she wrote:

Dear Sir,
  . . . On the 23rd of April *last* on his way to Town it was agreed between Lord Byron and myself that he was to take Mrs George Byron and the Miss Parkyns debt of eight hundred pounds *on himself*—that is to give *proper security* for the money before he left England and that he was to pay Wylde & Co the two hundred pounds with the *interest* due to them also *before* he left England. Indeed he *offered to leave the money with me* to pay Wylde

[1] 1783–1852. He was destined to die, like Brummell, evading his creditors on the other side of the Channel.

but that I would not *accept* of at that time as he said it would *take nearly* all the money he had about him. . . .

As to my own fortune he *insisted* that I would purchase an annuity with the three thousand pounds (which is all that is left) for my *own* life, he said he would have nothing to do with this money, as money transactions always made relations quarrel and he would not quarrel with me for twenty thousand pounds.

After all this I *own* I was much surprised to hear from you that my Son had gone abroad without *relieving* me from the *heavy* burden of this thousand pounds, indeed I had not an idea but that he would do as he promised. Do let me know what I am to do. I expect you will advise me both as a *friend* and a man of business. . . .

The *grief* I feel at my sons going abroad and the addition of his leaving his affairs in so unsettled a state and not taking the thousand pounds on himself, I think altogether it will kill me. Besides my income is so small that I shall be ruined if the thousand pounds is not paid up, and to add to all this bad health is expensive. . . .[1]

Why did Byron, 'with the *best heart* in the World', treat his mother so shockingly? The Marquess of Sligo, who travelled with him in Greece after Hobhouse had returned to England, told Thomas Moore that he seemed to have feelings towards her 'little short of aversion', and that it was to her 'false delicacy' at his birth that he owed his lameness—a great improbability though he may have believed it. He also said that she had 'never ceased to reproach and taunt him' with his deformity, and that a few days before their parting, she had prayed that he might prove 'as ill formed in mind' as he was in body.

I think we have a good deal of exaggeration here both by Byron and Lord Sligo—on the latter's part because everyone was prone to exaggerate Byron's utterances in order to convey the effect of them without the aid of his strong personality; on Byron's because he was, as we might now say, projecting on to his mother the guilt he himself must have been feeling, dwelling upon grievances that would excuse him.

Lady Byron records that he told her his mother had 'once' taunted him with his defect,[2] and as she could be dispassionate on this matter, I think her recollection has credibility. He always resented it, and very naturally so, but doubtless more in 1810, when he conversed with Sligo, than in 1815, when his mother was dead and his remembrance of her

---

[1] Egerton 2611. 17 June. Very slight adjustments have been made to punctuation.

[2] Lovelace Papers, 'Lord Byron and Literature'. In the same document she mentioned the distressing remark about his lameness by Mary Chaworth, which, Moore tells us, sent him darting wildly away from her house. It is evident that this embittering experience—which Hobhouse doubted—was no fantasy but an enduring memory.

more tranquil. And what Sligo reported about eighteen years after their discussions was, of course, written up by Moore.

In those last days together, Mrs Byron, distraught with anxiety and misery, may well have said many a harsh thing. To see Jack Byron's fecklessness continued in his son, to be reminded so sharply of the penury her adored husband had brought her to, must have driven her to hysteria: but they had parted in kindness, or she would not, inveterately truthful as she was, have written of Byron's declaration that he would not quarrel with her for twenty thousand pounds. He had guessed, we may imagine, that she would not take up his offer to strip himself of all his ready money for the payment of the banker, Wylde, but his promise to be responsible for that and the other debts she had so foolishly contracted for him was sincere enough when he made it. His various expectations, from Chancery, from the Norfolk property, the Lancashire property, the expected mortgages on Newstead, combined with the too sanguine confidence of youth, drew him into a labyrinth of commitments, fully believing that release was imminent. His mother's nagging seemed absurd and infuriating when he was to become solvent at any moment. And he felt he had conferred a favour on her by leaving her as mistress of Newstead Abbey with all its fresh wallpapers, curtains, and upholstery.

Mrs Byron knew that these fine things were unpaid for, and her object was to get them paid for if it meant living like a miser. There was a game-keeper who, besides his wage, got ten shillings a week for board. It was worrying. A female servant could be dispensed with during the summer, but not in winter when it would be '*full* employment' to maintain the rooms and keep the fires going. 'If that is not done the house is so damp that the furniture will be spoiled & the Paper fall off.'[1] Old Murray, that time-honoured burden, had been taken away by Byron together with young Rushton, a tenant's son, his page, but Mrs Byron was dreading his return because he was 'so *troublesome*'. She ended with three postscripts.

Lord Grey de Ruthyn had married a farmer's daughter, whereas one Smith Wright was engaged to a lady with a hundred thousand pounds. Who can doubt her thoughts were on her truant son for whom a great fortune would have come in so handy?

Then in her customary down-to-earth way she made a statement of her income.

Pension	£232	4
Deduct for tax	26	6
	£205	18

[1] Egerton 2611. 17 June.

Interest of three thousand pounds	£150	
Deduct for tax	15	
	£135	
	Total	£340 18

Received from Bowman according to		
Lord Byron's desire	£21	0
From Davy	£22	0

Out of the rent of these two tenants, £43, she paid £36 as interest to the Nottingham ladies on their loan, and some other matters. Her balance in hand was sixpence. If Byron would only give security for her £3,000 from Scotland (it could be done by a mortgage) she would lend him £2,000 and pay off at last what she had borrowed for him—leaving herself with nothing.

Two days after she wrote this, Byron was telling Hanson that, owing to delays in getting money—presumably the credit awaited from Scrope Davies—he had granted an annuity of £400 a year, more than his mother's whole income, to a Mr Thomas for an advance of cash.[1] Now he had so many commitments that, even with £6,000 to come from loans, his bills could not be met, and one presented by a bookseller was dishonoured by Hanson, much to his dismay, before he sailed. Literally unable to calculate, he was issuing daydream instructions from Falmouth about what to do with the *surplus* from the sale of Rochdale (still deep in litigation) after 'the liquidation of my debts of all descriptions'.[2]

His mother was pondering on the more immediate problem of how to run Newstead on practically nothing.

> Surely the *four constant* Labourers in the garden may be *dispensed* with, and also the *female Servant*, but more particularly the Labourers as it can *be no* advantage to Lord Byrons property to have the gardens kept in order as they *produce* nothing that *can sell.* You must be sensible that I am speaking *against* my own interest as it would be more *agreeable* to me to have them kept neat.
>
> I came here with a *fixed* determination not to put my Son to one Farthings expence. I and my servants are here it is true, but I maintain both them and myself, and I have a house rent and taxes going on at Southwell so I save nothing by being here nor do I desire it. I think no time ought to be lost in reducing *all* expences as much as possible.[3]

She wrote a rough reckoning of the present outgoings, from which we see that the female servant's maintenance and wages came to £30 a year,

---

[1] Ibid. 19 June. [2] Ibid. 25 June. [3] Ibid. 27 June.

while to feed Byron's 'wolf dog' cost £20. (The 'wolf dog' has come down to posterity as a wolf, for so it was credulously or facetiously described by Byron's friend Matthews in a letter,[1] while Byron himself supposed it to be half-wolf by maternal descent.) There was Mealey, the steward, paid by Hanson. He grew more disgruntled than ever when faced with being deprived of his labourers. By making mischief about the previous occupants of the building known as the Hut, which was the local tavern, he had managed to get their tenancy ended, though they were willing to pay a much-increased rent, and had settled there himself with his wife, running a prosperous business. He was therefore little disposed to attend to the Abbey garden.

Hanson wrote to Mrs Byron on July 4th agreeing that Newstead expenses must be curtailed, and saying he had ordered Mealey to dismiss three of the four gardeners. The gamekeeper was costing too much. If his standing wage was £39 a year, it was 'infinitely too high'; another gamekeeper could be found who would be satisfied with a guinea a week both for board and standing wages. Yes, the female servant could be dispensed with since Mrs Byron had servants of her own, and, as for 'old Joe Murray', at present with Byron, he should either be put on board wages at his return, or Mrs Byron should have an allowance for letting him share her servants' table.

Byron had with him a valet, a page, and a courier, and could not have needed a butler on his voyage. His only object in taking Murray, who was sent home from Gibraltar, was not to let the old man feel unwanted.[2]

Hanson was not very pleased that Mrs Byron had received the rent of two tenants and used it to pay interest due from Byron. The rents, he told her, were to be paid to him (Hanson) and were already appropriated for other purposes. Byron had never given him any instructions about repaying the Nottingham loans. He ended graciously, however: 'I am sure it is very kind in you to take charge of the Abbey for without it I dont know what would become of his Lordship's Property.'[3]

Byron, while his mother was cheeseparing on his behalf in the understaffed mansion, was writing to Hanson from Lisbon: 'I have been purchasing a few things of the Honble J. Ward, who as he is proceeding to England prefers a draft on London. You will pay him on demand thirty pounds sterling.'[4]

The irony of it was that Ward (afterwards Earl of Dudley) was remembering with amusement years later how he had cheated young Byron

[1] Moore. 22 May 1809. The dog was probably of an Alsatian type, supposed, even when I was young, to be of a wolf strain.
[2] See Appendix 4, 'Old Joe Murray.'   [3] Egerton 2611. 4 July.
[4] Ibid. 13 July.

over those purchases.[1] They were the English saddles on which Byron (and doubtless Hobhouse) rode several hundred miles through Portugal and Spain during the upheaval of the Peninsular War.

There never was a traveller who bore fatigue with better humour or entered so fully and vivaciously into the spirit of every occasion; and he recounted his adventures to his mother in some of his most memorable letters. Though he wanted to keep her at arm's length and addressed her formally as 'Dear Madam' or tepidly as 'Dear Mother'—rising only in two or three instances to 'My Dear Mother'—he was impelled to charm and entertain her because he could be sure of her responsiveness.

It has been said by myself and others that it is possible to divine the character of any of his regular correspondents by the varied styles in which he wrote to them. His love letters to the sententious Miss Milbanke are a world away in manner from those to the warm and unguarded Teresa Guiccioli. We can tell in half a dozen lines whether he is adapting his pen to the drawing-room and dinner-table sociability of Tom Moore, the much more serious 'committed' mind of Hobhouse, or the combined business-and-pleasure personality of John Murray. The denigrators of his mother never asked themselves whether such letters as he sent to her would or could have been composed for any recipient not intelligent, humour-loving, and of a very practical turn, in whose affection and loyalty he felt the most perfect confidence. Badly as he had often behaved to her, enraged though she had often been with him, at any sacrifice she identified his interests with her own.

She fought with him, and she fought for him, and now, seeing how Hanson was letting things drift, she took the great question of the Newstead rents in hand herself. The sole source of revenue from the estate, they had remained absurdly low and irregularly paid for years, and yet, owing to the war, any farmer worth his salt was sure of selling his produce at higher prices than ever before. '. . . Certainly malt, corn, cattle, wheat, &c &c &c is *treble* the price that they were at the time this Estate was valued', she told Hanson. Mealey was demanding that a stable be built for him at the Hut.

Pray does he pay an *advanced* rent? if he does not pay *more* than Mrs Bower did,[2] I see *no reasonable* cause why he should have any *superior* conveniences, the more particularly so as I believe, indeed *know* that the Hut is the *most*

---

[1] *Letters to 'Ivy'*, ed. Romilly.

[2] Mrs Bower, the former publican at the Hut, remarried in 1806, and Mealey had intrigued against her and her new husband, William Paling, to get the tavern for himself. Although Paling was recommended by Mrs Byron and Mary Chaworth's stepfather, Mr Clarke, with flattery of Hanson he succeeded. ('Sir, as you was always a gentleman of your word I hope you will stand my friend', etc. Egerton 2612. 1 Aug. 1806.)

profitable situation for making money as it now is, and I really don't see that Lord Byron has any money to *spare* for new buildings.

She urged Hanson to sell trees that had been felled. 'As wood is *dear* they never could be sold at a better time, and would *fetch* about seventy pounds.'[1]

Seventy pounds would have been a very substantial help—it would, for instance, have more than paid the gamekeeper's wages and board wages which were overdue and supposed to come from Hanson's funds—but if any order was given to sell the timber, there is no record of it. War, as always, was causing inflation, and Byron was as anxious as his mother that the rents, which had remained much the same since the 18th century, should be put up. But Hanson explained that this could not be done unless the tenants, instead of being subject to a year's or half-year's notice, were granted leases. Leaseholding farmers placed a landowner at a great disadvantage if he was obliged to sell, and Hanson was recommending, in the face of Byron's vigorous protests, that the Abbey be sold. It would be much easier and more remunerative for him to dispose of his client's embarrassments by means of one simple transaction yielding a large sum of money than to speed up the lagging affairs of Wymondham, Rochdale, and Chancery, and by proper management to improve the Newstead revenues.

From one port of call after another, Byron was writing to Hanson expressing his disappointment at not finding letters from him, requesting news of the arrival of the expected moneys, and, with continued optimism, giving instructions on how capital should be invested after provision had been made for meeting all debts.

> As to my affairs you must manage them as you best can, I have full confidence in your integrity, but expect & desire no favours, indeed I need not. —Whatever distress I may encounter, I will not sell Newstead, and whether further monies can be advanced or not, I expect at least a letter on the subject. . . .[2]

But, after a year and more, no letters from Hanson had arrived and certainly no remittances. Although, thanks to Scrope Davies, Byron had cash in hand and letters of credit, he was resolved to journey as far and for as long a period as his supplies would allow, and it was naturally disturbing for him to picture himself, an English Milord albeit one who could endure hardship, with an empty purse in Damascus or Kashmir (for India and Persia were among his goals on setting forth). Yet it never seems to have occurred to him to sit down with pencil and paper and

[1] Egerton 2611. 25 Aug. 1809.   [2] Ibid. 31 Aug.

balance what he could reasonably expect from his properties against what he owed.

Hanson remained supine, writing very seldom to Mrs Byron, who was troubled incessantly by the knowledge that the Nottingham bills for repairs and redecoration remained unpaid. Her August proposal for raising the rents drew no reply from him till October, when he said he would send a surveyor to re-value the estate, to which she eagerly assented; but it was very long before any surveyor came.

Byron, before leaving, had told her to disregard his need, and use her capital from Scotland to purchase an annuity, which would increase her income substantially but vanish at her decease, and Hanson now gave similar advice. But she firmly repudiated it. 'I again *repeat* I never will *deprive* Lord Byron of the three thousand pounds that remains by sinking the principal in an annuity for my life, and the money is very much at his service. . . .'[1]

It was well she made this stand because she had less than two years to live, and the gamble of an annuity would have been a decidedly losing one. Her first condition for parting with the capital was that the ladies in Nottingham and the Southwell banker should be repaid for their loans, and if she sounds a little too business-like in her insistence on security and interest for herself, it must be borne in mind that, in this selfsame letter, she was reminding the man in whose hands Byron had left all his affairs that Mr Wylde had never yet received even interest, let alone principal, for the £200 borrowed more than two years before. To pay for her son's luxuries she was living penuriously, and being penurious with others.

> Murray is in England & will soon be here & I am *sure* if he will be economical (which I am told he is) he can live on *much* less than could be allowed him for Board wages. A servant I left here for *three* weeks when I was at Southwell, only cost me *ten* shillings during that time, had I given her Board wages I could not have allowed her less than a Guinea.[2]

Of course this sort of thing, however honourable the motive, could not have made her lovable, and to seeming parsimony she added her ungovernable temper. Her rages must have been terrifying. We have an example in a letter she wrote to her neighbour at Annesley, the squire to whom Mary Chaworth was now very unhappily married.[3] She told Hanson he was assaulting Newstead tenants, breaking down fences, and generally playing havoc in his pursuit of foxes; which was doubtless true because he was of the fanatical sporting breed produced by excess of

---

[1] Ibid. 4 Oct. 1809. [2] Ibid.

[3] His name was Musters, but, being married to an heiress, he added Chaworth to it after the customary practice at the time.

leisure with inadequacy of intellect. Violent as he was himself reputed to
be, he must have been shaken by Mrs Byron's onslaught:

Sir,

   I must *insist* on your confining yourself to your own premises, or at least
not coming on Lord Byron's Manor to hunt and commit *trespasses*, which
you have been so *long* in the habit of doing that you now, I suppose, fancy
you have a right to do; but I am fully determined to convince you to the
contrary. Pray Sir, do you suppose that I will remain here and *tamely
submit* to every *insult* from you? If you think so you will find yourself
extremely mistaken.

   I cannot send out my Keeper but he must be abused by you on Lord
Byron's own Manor. You presume on his absence to *insult a Woman* and
assault an old Man; that is you insult his Mother, and injure the Property,
attack the Persons and threaten the lives of his Servants. In short, your language is unbecoming, and your behaviour totally unworthy a Gentleman . . .

   I will now take the trouble to inform you that Lord Byron's Tenants
shall be no longer annoyed by you with *impunity*, but that a *prosecution*
will be immediately instituted against you for *divers trespasses* and *one
assault*. You are surely not so ignorant as not to know that breaking down
fences and riding through fields of standing corn with your Hounds are
most *unjustifiable, arbitrary*, and *oppressive* acts, and will not be submitted
to in a *free country*, even if you was the first Man in it. I will not suffer my
Keeper to be abused or interrupted in the execution of his duty, and he has
my *positive* orders to use every possible means to destroy Foxes.

   Lord Grey de Ruthyn's poaching and these abundant, noxious Animals
have nearly deprived this once excellent Manor of game, and the woods on
this estate shall not continue as a *Depôt* for your vermin, and I'm *determined to extirpate* the breed here, and to suffer so great a nuisance no longer.
If the breed of Fox-hunters could be as easily got rid of, the benefit to society
in general would be great. . . .

                        I remain, Sir, &c &c,
                            C. G. Byron.[1]

   She wrote of this matter to Byron himself, adding after the list of
Chaworth's depredations, 'Take no notice. I will manage him better than
you have done', and saying she was having the offender '*indited*' at the
assizes for an *assault*', but of this we do not hear again. Perhaps he undertook not to repeat his trespasses.

   We may guess how such battles had embarrassed a youth going through
the stage of acute self-consciousness inevitable in the process of growing-
up; though, disapprove as he might, he sometimes behaved rather like

[1] Prothero. Late Sept. 1809.

her. But they could be very pleasant together. In writing to Hanson, she could not contain her delight at having just received a letter from Byron —the famous one in which he tells her of his flirtations with the Spanish ladies.[1] She began answering the same day (October 4th) in a tone responsive to his own, and we may take it to be their humorous style when they were not at odds. 'Dearest', she began, then crossed it out because he had only written 'Dear Mother' to her:

> Dear Byron,
> A thousand thanks for your *long* letter which amused me much. I see you are quite charmed with the Spanish Ladies. For Heavens sake have nothing to do with them. [Byron had spoken of possibly returning via Cadiz.] They make nothing of poisoning *both* Husbands & Lovers if they are *Jealous* of them or they offend them. The Italian Ladies *do the same.* Mind that my Lord, take care & not get into the *Harams* of the Turks for there the Men kill the lovers of their Women when they are Jealous, indeed I hear they make nothing of sacrificing both the Lady and her lover if they discover them.

Commenting on Lord Grey's marriage 'to a rustic', Byron had said in a postscript 'Well done! If I wed I will bring home a sultana, with half a score cities for a dowry, and reconcile you to an Ottoman daughter in law with a bushel of pearls not larger than ostrich eggs or smaller than Walnuts.' To which she answered: 'I will however agree to your marrying a *very pretty very sensible,* very rich Sultana, with half a Million to her fortune *not* less, and also a Bushel of Pearls & diamonds. No other is *worthy* of you nor will she be received by me.'

She went on to give him a compact account of public affairs in England —the rivalries in politics, a defeat of British arms at Walcheren in Holland ('a *dreadful* business, thousands of our Men & officers *died of illness,* not killed, and the expedition fitted out at an immense expense, & nothing got to make up for the loss of Men & Money'); the riots about the increased prices at Covent Garden's new theatre ('Catalani was engaged at five thousand pounds for the season, but was obliged to give it up, John Bull would not hear her sing'); a proposed jubilee to celebrate half a century of the reign of George III, longer than any for a thousand years; then the news about her feud with Chaworth followed by criticisms quoted from Pope and Goldsmith which she had read in a paper with approval because they indicated contempt for party politics.

'I am going this day to the gay Nottingham meeting,' she said in a rare allusion to her personal activities. '. . . I have been very ill but Dr

---

[1] 11 Aug. 1809. It appears in most selections of Byron's letters and is now correct in the Marchand text.

Marsden of Nottingham has been of great service to me.'[1] Nothing more of her health, nothing at all about her stringent economies, only some gossip of a non-personal kind picked up from newspapers, dropped in among which is: 'Tell Fletcher his wife & children are well. . . . Do dear Byron write to me often & wherever you go if you wish me to be happy, indeed not miserable.'

She was finishing the letter days later at Nottingham where she had been staying throughout 'the gay meeting', probably with her creditors, the Hon. Mrs Byron and the Misses Parkyns, for after signing 'Your truly affectionate Mother, C. G. Byron', she wrote '*All* this family desire their respects'. She concluded with 'Lord Rancliffe is a very ugly man, his wife not pretty'. Lord Rancliffe was a Parkyns and represented Nottingham in Parliament. The gay meeting was a Grand Musical Festival held for the benefit of the General Hospital, comprising, as she said, 'a ball, concerts & oratorios in St Mary's', which last were performed by many celebrated artists. Her sparing the money to attend must have been contingent on her having given up the Southwell house and receiving £200 for the sale of some of her furniture.[2] She had bills to settle there, but there was a balance in her favour.

It was the page, Rushton, home from Gibraltar, who had brought her son's precious letter, and she took him to Nottingham with her. '. . . He is as *handsome* & fine a Boy as I *ever* saw.'[3] The cost of posting this letter was three shillings and a penny, and the cost of receiving it several months afterwards no doubt much more.

There is, as far as my researches go, a lacuna in Mrs Byron's correspondence with Hanson until February 3rd 1810, when she dispatched a very urgent note to Chancery Lane with a message on the cover that it was to be opened by Mr Birch if Mr Hanson was absent. It told the solicitors that Brothers, the firm of upholsterers in Nottingham, had sent two bailiffs to the Abbey with 'a Paper', which she forwarded, asking what she could do about it: 'I *much fear* there will be more of this sort of proceedings from others. . . . I think it is *time* the Estate was valued.'[4]

The amount Byron owed for furbishing up the house—'more for you than for myself' as he had assured her[5]—was a tremendous addition to the load of his debts. He had spent £2,100 with Brothers alone and given him a note of hand, now overdue, for £1,600—an act of faith verging on fantasy. The bailiffs, she hurriedly wrote another letter to

[1] I presume it was Dr Marsden to whom she had paid five guineas for 'Medicle advise [sic] at Notts' in April that year. The journey by carriage was £1. 12s. 6d.
[2] Murray MSS. Her account book, entry of 1 Oct.
[3] Lovelace Papers. 4 to 9 Oct. 1809.
[4] Egerton 2611. 3 Feb. 1810.   [5] See p. 94.

say, had stuck a copy of the summons 'on the *outside* of the *Great Hall Door*'. Could she take it down?

> . . . It is extremely disagreeable to me as you may suppose. What am I to do in case of an *execution* in the House, concerning my *own* property, as I have a good *deal here*, Plate, linen, Wardrobe, and *some furniture* from my late House at Southwell &c &c &c.
>
> I would not answer for what may happen from others that Byron is in debt to, as you may be sure this business is *known* and will doubtless be the *talk* of the Country.[1]

It gives us the measure of this remarkable woman's devotion that, in writing to Byron the very day after the arrival of the bailiffs, she said not a word of the desperate trouble under which she was labouring through his extravagance, but addressed herself to giving him the assorted news, and in a manner that makes it topical for us even now:

> My dearest Byron,
>
> I will begin this letter by informing you what is going on in *our* World, tho' God knows when it may reach you. The French Emperor has *repudiated* his Wife, he informed the senate that he intends to marry again and have a family for the good of the French nation, and as he is but forty he hopes & expects to live long enough to educate them *in his own sentiments*. He made a speech, and Josephine made a speech, and both said they had long given over all hopes of having children, the divorce is by *mutual consent* at least so they said but many *doubt* that and I own I am one of that number. Bonaparte has put his late Wife off with many *fine* speeches and *high compliments*, and what is better than all has given her a large income, and Palaces in Town & Country. . . .
>
> Report has given Bonaparte as many Wives as would suffice for a Khan of Tartary, one of our Princesses and all, but nothing is *yet known* on the subject, it is also said he is to be crowned Emperor of the West. His late Wife is *allowed* to retain the title of Empress & Queen.

Besides taking an eager interest herself in public affairs, she was under the impression that she was supplying the want of newspapers, but his comment on these attempts was crushing: '. . . You fill your letters with things from the papers, as if English papers were not found all over the world, I have at this moment a dozen before me.'[2]

She did not neglect to pass on what she learned of his literary progress, always followed by her with detailed attention:

[1] 5 Feb. The word 'execution' in the sense of a distraint upon goods and chattels is now so obsolete that it may be as well to remind the reader of that meaning. 'The country' was often used where we should now say the locality.

[2] Marchand, *Letters*. 30 July 1810, from Patras.

Your 'E. Bards' are in the second edition. . . . Till your name was put
to the work many *wise* Folks were of opinion that it was not your writing
as they said you was not equal to it. 'Blundering' *Brougham* is returned
Member for the Borough of Camelford. . . .

To pass straight from the satire to Henry Brougham was either intuition
or a curious coincidence, because, although neither she nor Byron knew
it, Brougham was the perpetrator of the malicious anonymous attack in
the *Edinburgh Review* which had provoked Byron to add '*Scotch Reviewers*'
to the victims of his wit.

'I remembered the 22d of last month' Mrs Byron went on, alluding
to his twenty-second birthday. 'I never *can forget* it and the Farmers
drank your health. It is very odd that Mr Hobhouse left England without
informing his father, and he did not know where he was till lately.'
Hobhouse, in youth a most unpredictable man, had quarrelled with his
excellent father, which was the reason why he was travelling on borrowed
money.

Having begun her letter on February 4th, Mrs Byron went on with
it on the 9th, still not mentioning the debts and difficulties. She quoted
with pride some flattering couplets about her son which had appeared in
a new poem, *Pursuits of Fashion*. She noted also that the *Literary
Panorama* had printed a passage from the satire and was to review it
'again' next month. 'You seem to be a mighty reader of magazines',
he remarked when he got the letter at Constantinople four months later.
'Where do you pick up all this intelligence? quotations, &c &c?'[1]
There were no press-cutting agencies but somehow she kept *au
courant*.

Moore recorded with an air of surprise that a friend of his had told
him Mrs Byron had assembled all the notices of her son's early poems in a
bound volume, with marginal comments of her own which, he had heard,
were 'indicative of more sense and ability than, from her general character, we should be inclined to attribute to her'. If he had seen her letters
and known of the struggles in which she was perpetually engaged, he
might not have based his portrait of her on that of a hostile schoolmaster.
She wrote, as her son was to do, with an erratic construction but no want
of apt and energetic words. Her handwriting was strikingly like his. The
compact fashioning of her statements evolved into his own direct manner.
'A great mishap has befallen Miss Roushton [sic]. She is in the *family way*,
and John Bowman the *favoured swain refuses* to marry her. Robert
Roushton is gone to school.'

Miss Rushton was the daughter of a tenant, and sister to Robert

[1] Ibid. 28 June 1810.

Rushton, the page.[1] Byron, whose social views were those of the age in which he lived, replied, when at last he got the letter:

> It is my opinion that Mr Bowman ought to marry Miss Rushton, our first duty is not to do evil, but alas! that is impossible, our next is to repair it, if in our power, the girl is his equal, if she were his inferior a sum of money and provision for the child would be some, though a poor compensation, as it is, he should marry her. I will have no gay deceivers on my Estate, and I shall not allow my tenants a privilege I do not permit myself, viz—*that*, of debauching each other's daughters.—
>
> God knows, I have been guilty of many excesses, but as I have laid down a resolution to reform, and *lately* kept it, I expect this Lothario to follow the example, and begin by restoring the girl to society—or, by the Beard of my Father! he shall hear of it.[2]

Byron's ideas of a landlord's rights, though in feudal times he might have been able to enforce them, did not weigh with Bowman, who refused to marry.

Mrs Byron did not close her letter, started in February, for more than a month. It was no use posting until it was advertised that some vessel would sail, and she had been waiting in hope of hearing from him. On March 9th she was unable to stifle a cry of anxiety:

> Good God where are you? *No* letters by the Entrepenante that left Constantinople the 11th Janry *1810* and arrived in England the 23rd Febry. I hope & trust in God you are safe. *Neglect* no opportunity of writing if you have any regard for my peace. . . . God bless and protect you prays your truly affectionate and unhappy Mother—unhappy on your account.[3]

Meanwhile she had been trying to keep Brothers at bay, writing to Hanson her suspicion that his bill, which she had never been shown, would not bear inspection:

> I am greatly surprised that the amount should be *two thousand one hundred* pounds, which it is as the summons is for sixteen hundred pounds & if you have paid five hundred pounds, I think you ought to see that there is no imposition. Lord Byron had great part of his furniture from Cambridge, & Bannet of Nottingham furnished a great many things in this House, and I really don't see that Brothers bill can *fairly* amount to so much. . . .

Again she pressed for her capital in Scotland to be realized on some safe terms and used on Byron's behalf. She even calculated that something might be got from the publisher of the satire:

[1] Mrs Byron's spelling of the name indicates how it was pronounced in the Midlands.
[2] Marchand, *Letters*. 28 June 1810.
[3] Lovelace Papers.

English Bards is now in the *second edition*, and will be in the *third* next
month and when the third is sold that Book will have fetched seven hundred
& fifty pound, tho' that will not be *clear* but the Bookseller *will and ought*
to have a *good* deal of money to give you.[1]

What would her feelings have been if she had lived to know how far her
quixotic son was to go in his belief that authors with private means should
not receive money for their work?

She reminded Hanson that the surveyor was still awaited, and ended
by saying she had been much better, but was now ill again, 'as all this
trouble does me *no good*'. It could not have been lessened by a letter
shortly afterwards from the patient banker, Wylde, saying his firm
would be 'particularly obliged' for a remittance on Lord Byron's behalf.[2]
She sent it on to Hanson with the comment:

> Brothers has *sounded* the *war* [*w*]*hoop* and every one *takes* the alarm.
> Wylde has received no *interest* as yet, and I have promised him the interest
> *now* and the two hundred pounds in six months. Pray may I give him a draft
> on you for twenty pound?

Another appeal followed next day, February 28th:

> Sir,
>   For God sake let me have as *little trouble* in this business as possible for
> I am *teased* to *death* with one thing & another, answer the letter yourself
> for I know nothing of Laws either here or in Scotland.[3]

'This business' was the transfer of her money, the various complexities
attending it, and her anxiety not to lose the interest which formed so
large a proportion of her income. Since Hanson had done nothing, she had
taken direct action by writing to Scotland, but could not understand the
formalities to be completed.

Byron, convinced that his debts, or most of them, would by now have
been paid off from the funds he was counting on, wrote frequently either
to his mother or Hanson,[4] who was requested to convey his news to her,
but his letters took months to arrive, and by the time they did so, his
whole scene would have changed.

Considering that the fastest means of land transport was a horse, the

---

[1] Egerton 2611. 10 Feb. 1810. Byron let the publisher keep the considerable profits
of the satire, which went through four authorized editions and several unauthorized.
[2] Ibid. 27 Feb.   [3] Ibid.
[4] But three letters to his mother in *Letters & Journals* are forgeries, those dated
9 Apr., 1 July and 27 July 1810. Their first appearance was in *The Unpublished Letters
of Lord Byron* edited by H. S. Schultess-Young, 1872, a book which consists of letters
which had, in fact, been published interspersed with forgeries by 'George Gordon
Byron', the alias of the notorious de Gibler. It was suppressed by an injunction and is very
rare. If Prothero had been able to see Mrs Byron's side of the correspondence, he would
not have passed these spurious contributions, which contain several ineptitudes.

postal service at home was admirable: overseas mail on the other hand was slow and hazardous. Not till late April 1810 did Byron's letter of November 12th 1809 come to hand, the one from Albania, often reprinted, in which he told her of his visit to Ali Pasha and how that despot had sent her his respects, of his being nearly wrecked in a Turkish warship and lost for a time in the mountains, how he travelled (economically) with sixteen horses and six or seven men and how he had purchased three very magnificent Albanian costumes for fifty guineas each.

She replied in the fullness of her heart on May 11th:

A thousand thanks my *Dearest Dear* Son for your *long kind* and *entertaining* letter . . . Ali has done me much honor in sending me his respects and if ever you see him again you may give mine in return. I have *read an account* of him in some book.

I have written you *four* letters with *all* the English news *public* and *private* that I could *collect*. . . .[1] It is *lamentable* that we cannot hear from each other more regularly, pray let *no* opportunity *escape* of writing to me but I need not remind you of that as you seem very good in that respect, and I am sure I shall write always when I know where you are to be found. . . .

Not having yet had his rebuff about sending news which he could read in the papers, she proceeded to public affairs:

Your favorite Cadiz has been some time bombarded by the French, Napoleon has married Maria Louisa of Austria daughter to Francis, and there was the grandest fete given on the occasion that was ever seen or heard of in France before. He also gave fortunes to six thousand young girls who were married to soldiers last month, the same month with himself.

Without a single word about the worries she was daily contending with, she went on to describe Sir Francis Burdett's committal to the Tower for a libel on the House of Commons, when constables had broken open his doors to arrest him, sympathizers had rioted, and there had been injuries and deaths. (With her radical inclinations, she would have been pleased if she could have foreseen that Burdett was to become a friend and admirer of her son's.) 'Your "E. Bards"', she continued, 'is in the *third edition*, and I hear the universal opinion is that since the days of Pope nothing has equalled it.' She told him of the marriage of three heiresses, and lamented:

They will all be gone before you return. . . . As to myself I am not in very good health, sometimes ill, sometimes well, but I ever am
Your truly affectionate Mother
C. G. Byron.

P.S. I hear that the cause of Col Leigh's quarrel with the Prince is that he

[1] Byron had as yet received nothing from her when he wrote.

cheated him in selling a Horse for him, that is he *retained* for *himself* part of the purchase money.[1]

Colonel George Leigh, Augusta's husband, who had been in the intimate circle of the Prince Regent, fell into disgrace in June 1809 for having connived, during the past two years, at exhorbitant profits made by John Roberts, Paymaster to his Regiment, the 10th Hussars, out of the supply of military equipment, including soldiers' clothing, and for conniving likewise with the Paymaster in failing to credit the Regiment with the full allowances from the Government for postage, stationery, coals, candles, and veterinary and riding school accounts, as well as having made improper charges for non-commissioned officers' expenses, remount horses, coach hire, farriers' bills, etc., 'contrary to his duty as Commissioned Officer & to the breach of good order and discipline'.[2] He was threatened with a court-martial. His conduct in money matters was always shady, and it is likely enough that he did cheat the Prince in the way Mrs Byron stated, because there exists correspondence on behalf of the Commander-in-Chief, showing the Prince's desire that Colonel Leigh should not only quit the Regiment but also 'Newmarket and the turf'.[3] An anonymous letter signed 'Your anxious and real friend', says he has 'not a day, not an hour, to lose' in obeying the Prince's command to leave.[4]

For the reasons given in my second chapter, the Leigh family were no favourites with Mrs Byron, and she had disliked her son's youthful friendship with Augusta in the days when the latter was still Miss Byron. She could not suppose it would be revived after his attack on Lord Carlisle in his satire, because Augusta had lived with the Carlisles more than any other of her rich and noble relations. In her previous letter, Mrs Byron had written, 'Your Sister Mrs Leigh is I hear *much annoyed* at your *treating* my Lord Carlisle with so little ceremony',[5] to which he replied casually, '. . . I regret distressing Mrs Leigh, poor thing! I hope she is happy'.[6] It would have been well if Augusta had nursed her resentment, but, tragically for them both, her disposition was forgiving while her loyalties were always wavering.

Mrs Byron dispatched her letter to Hanson to be forwarded, and the following day, May 12th, wrote to him wearily to ask if he had as yet taken the steps required by Scotch law to get her money to England, pointing out that, if Byron could not give the needful security for it, being abroad, 'surely any other person would lend the same sum on Mortgage'. She reminded him, as she had *not* reminded Byron, that she

[1] Lovelace Papers.   [2] Murray MS.   [3] 31037 Horton Papers.
[4] Murray MS.   [5] The portion written on 9 Feb. 1810.
[6] Marchand, *Letters*. 28 June 1810.

had reduced every expense at Newstead, doing without the day labourer, and even finding homes with the tenant-farmers for two of Byron's dogs so that they might be kept for nothing. (The expensive wolf-dog was still retained.)

> *I can do nothing more*. The Bear poor Animal died *suddenly* about a fortnight ago.
>
> I much fear Bowman will have *sad confused* accounts and *also* Mealey who seems always *stupid* with ale. He has about ninety pounds of Lord Byron's money to account for, and God knows if he can give a proper account of it, but of this I am *positive* that they *both* shall. . . .

Hanson had sent her no aid whatever since Byron's departure. Now interest would soon be due on the Nottingham ladies' loans, and he had forbidden her to collect rents again from farmers to pay it as she had done in 1809. How reduced she was may be judged by her reminding him that she had given £2 out of that money to the 'female servant', Lucy Monks, whom she had sent home.

> I want forty eight pounds *immediately*, *twenty* to pay Wylde the interest of the two hundred pounds of which he has *not yet ever received* a farthing, ten pounds I have advanced to the Gamekeeper (or rather my *maid* has advanced it for I had not the money to give him) . . . As you must know well I can advance nothing out of my income. Mrs Geo. Byron & the Miss Parkyns's *must* be paid regularly, and I promised to pay Wylde his *interest* some time ago. The Gamekeeper poor Man has a *years wages* & board wages due to him, and his Wife *ready* to *lie in*, therefore it was impossible to refuse him, and I *borrowed* ten pounds of my maid to give him, as Mealey said he had *none* of Lord Byron's *money left* which makes me think *all is not right* there.
>
> I will be obliged to you to send a *full* and *particular* answer *immediately* to *all* the *contents* of this letter which is of *much importance* to me.[1]

While waiting, vainly, for a reply, she heard again from her son— a few lines from Smyrna dated March 19th. He told her he did not know whether he would travel to Persia or not. 'I shall stand in need of remittances whether I proceed or return.—I have written to him [Hanson] repeatedly that he may not plead ignorance of my situation for neglect.'[2] She wrote to the solicitor at once conveying the exact tenor of the letter, but he was in no hurry to respond.

Considering that she was noted for her violent temper, she had borne his cavalier treatment with exemplary patience, but it began to crack

---

[1] Egerton 2611.

[2] Marchand, *Letters*. This communication arriving on 19 May 1810 had been only two months en route, an unusual celerity.

when, by May 25th, she heard from Scotland that he had taken no steps at all about the withdrawal of her money.

> Sir,
>   I see by the inclosed letter that you *have just* done nothing in the business, but as I am *quite old* enough to take care of my *own* interest, I must inform you that unless you send me an answer *within one week* from this date I shall write to Mr Watson to desire that Sir James Grant may keep the money.
>   I must *insist* on an *immediate* answer. I should have thought the letter I wrote you lately *quite sufficient* to procure that as I suppose you have received my *three* letters *written* this month.[1]

She says any loss of interest that may occur in the transaction will be entirely his fault, and winds up pungently with: 'I hope Lord Byron has had remittances sent as it would not be *convenient* to starve in a strange country.'

Having waited eleven days, she took up her pen again, this time addressing Birch, saying she had sent four letters in three weeks without an acknowledgement and therefore supposed his partner must be ill. '. . . I wish to accommodate my dear Son if possible'[2]—that is, by getting her capital for him. Hanson at last vouchsafed an answer, and even enclosed £20 for the gamekeeper. Moreover, he had written as required to Edinburgh, but the Power of Attorney effective in England was useless north of the Border. He had sent to Scotland for the necessary Form which he could forward to his Lordship. He gave an explanation of his position which should have been offered months before:

> I think when you know of the various & daily Calls that are made by Lord Byron's Credrs. for Bills to the Amount of upwards of £10,000 and Ann[uitie]s daily accruing to ye Amount of between 2 and 3000 £ a year without any Funds to answer the tenth Part of them and his Lordship's continued Calls for Remittances you will allow that I am placed in a Situation of infinite Perplexity and I am sure if your £3000 is not forthcoming I dont see what can be done to appease the people.[3]

He was certainly in a very tight corner, but since he had never been in any hurry to get the £3,000 that would have gone some way to 'appeasing the people', that was where he deserved to be. He promised to pay Wylde's agent in London the interest due at Southwell, and he would deal with the ladies in Nottingham, and he informed her that he had deposited more than £3,000 at Hammersley's Bank for Byron since

---

[1] Egerton 2611. Hugh Watson was writer to the Signet of Edinburgh, a legal functionary, and Sir James Grant was the borrower who had been paying her 5% on her capital.
[2] Ibid. 4 June 1810.   [3] Ibid. 8 June.

his departure from England—but with typical slackness he had not bothered to observe the instructions as to how and where the longed-for remittances were to reach his client. And self-indulgent as Byron was, it is not to be imagined he would have been satisfied to have thousands of pounds lodged in his bank while his gamekeeper's wages were a year in arrear, and his mother obliged to borrow from her maid to keep the man's family from starving.

Having dealt with the irate Mrs Byron on June 8th, Hanson sought an éclaircissement with Byron on the 9th. He had written to him, he said, in October 1809 to Malta and in March 1810 to Patras. (But Byron had still had no letters from him more than fifteen months after leaving England.)

'. . . As money is the Burthen of your Song I now repeat in part what I sayd in my former Lies [sic] upon that Subject.' Out of £6,000 he had received for Byron from various sources, chiefly a further £4,000 lent by Colonel Sawbridge,

> £3000 was swallowed up with those Cursed Annuities & in answering some most lamentable Supplications of ye more deserving People. Wymondham we succeeded in selling for ye sum of £4400—but not a Shilling of ye money have I yet touched from a Hitch in the title which I have not been able to get over and I am sure I dont know when we shall. Rochdale I have not been able to get an offer for worth Attention so that at present I am without Funds to pay any more of the Cred[r]s and the Annuities which are coming round again.
>
> I have had Newstead Farms surveyed and valued and it is thought capable of being raised to about £1700 a year but to accomplish that a considerable sum of Money must be laid out in putting the Building into repair and affording greater conveniences and you must grant Leases, and I dont see how the former is to be done.[1]

He proceeded to urge the sale of Newstead, assuring Byron that it could clear all his debts and still leave him a sum the bare interest of which would be greater than anything he could get by keeping the estate going. After telling him he had no choice, he went on to say he had been arranging with Mrs Byron—as if he had initiated it—that her capital should be realized, but she was making a point of settling the debts she had contracted for her son with part of it. That it was her plain duty to pay those debts because she had faithfully promised to do so he seems not to have recognized. He had no intention of keeping *his* promise to pay the interest due on them, or he would not have added £300—'all that can possibly be spared from out of ye rents'—to the £1,000 he had caused to

---

[1] Ibid. Byron was much annoyed at the facetious and insouciant tone of this letter.

be dispatched abroad without first deducting the fraction of that sum which would have tided Mrs Byron over.

Byron himself was anxious about her resources, and had written to Hanson from Constantinople on May 23rd (though the letter had not yet come to hand): '. . . If Mrs Byron requires any supply, pray let her have it at my expense and at all events whatever becomes of me do not allow her to suffer any unpleasant privation.'[1]

On the same day as Hanson was pressing the sale of Newstead, Miss Fanny Parkyns was writing to Mrs Byron, 'I am sorry we shall not have the pleasure of seeing you as I think Dr Marsden might be of service'[2]— a remark which shows both that she had been invited to Nottingham and that she remained ill. It was a cordial letter with news about private and public events such as no one would have troubled to write to a stupid and sottish woman.

Her illness must have been severe because, in sending the game-keeper's receipt for the £20 to Hanson, she said despairingly:

> I would *struggle* with every *difficulty* to keep things *together* & God knows I have difficulties enough to struggle with besides bad health. I am hardly able to *sit* up to write this letter having a *low* fever.
>
> What does Brothers mean? by saying every thing is to be *sold up* here in a fortnight—that is in *about* a *week* from this *date*. Ease my mind on this subject. I never *drop a word* of my Son's affairs to any one and I hope you are equally careful. . . .
>
> P.S. If this letter is nonsense you must not be *surprised* as I hardly know what I am doing.[3]

As she never gives any description of her symptoms except feverishness we do not know what her disease was, but its long duration nullifies the myth of lethal rage over the upholsterer's bill—for which a writ had been posted up at the Abbey a year and a half before her death!

What had been done to prevent the unlucky Brothers from distraining months before is not explained in any correspondence I have seen, but on June 11th, when she wrote the letter just quoted, the house— now her sole home—was clearly in danger of losing its contents. By June 20th, nothing had changed. She was still ill, still worrying about Hanson's failure to get the Edinburgh money, and though Brothers's threat had not been carried out, it was still hanging over her head, and she wondered why Lord Rancliffe had owed him a bill for upwards of two years without having any writ served on him. (Possibly he had a better solicitor.)

[1] Ibid.   [2] Ibid. 9 June.   [3] Ibid.

Byron's complaints of Hanson's neglect renewed her apprehension of his finding himself on foreign soil without funds.

> This makes me [un]easy as if money is not sent, his spirit being *high*, God knows what must be the consequences.
> I hope you will let nothing be done against me, at least against Lord Byron. I have a slow fever. Grief I believe *does not kill.*

When Hanson broke his word about the interest for which she was liable, she settled it herself, and sent him, on the back of a polite plea from Wylde, who had said he would be 'peculiarly thankful' for a remittance, the account of her outlay, amounting, with the cost of messengers to Southwell and Nottingham, and £11 still required by the gamekeeper for wages, to just under £50, which she asked him to remit:

> . . . In one of your letters to me some *time since* you said that you . . . had written to Mr Wylde's Agent to call on you for his interest. If you have paid him let me *know* as it is not mentioned in his letter. . . . Send me an *immediate* answer.[1]

As she entered on September 6th a payment to Wylde of £100. 6s. on Byron's behalf, it would seem that Hanson must have been stirred to some activity. It cannot be denied that his position, with liabilities so much greater than present resources, was a hard one; but the more we look into his handling of affairs, the more evident it becomes that, in those days of amazingly long credit, he could have done much for the support of his client merely by dealing with letters punctually and not shuffling off so many claimants with silence.

In early September, Mrs Byron received Byron's letter written as far back as May 24th from Constantinople, with a complaint that he had as yet had nothing from Hanson 'but one remittance without any letter from that legal gentleman'.

> If you have occasion for any pecuniary supply, pray use my funds as far as they *go* without reserve, and lest this should not be enough, in my next to Mr H I will direct him to advance any sum you want, leaving to your discretion how much in the present state of my affairs you may think proper to require.[2]

Of course this was sent long before he heard of the stagnation of transactions at Wymondham and Rochdale, but his mother was as delighted as if relieved of all her difficulties: 'I am *obliged* to you for your kind offer of useing your fortune as my *own* but believe me I *never* shall apply it to my *own* use till you are in a better situation than you are at present.'

---

[1] Ibid. 26 Aug. 1810.   [2] Marchand, *Letters*.

Byron had asked her if she had yet received 'a picture of me in oil by Sanders in *Vigo Lane*'—the famous one of him standing on the shore with a small sailing boat and a boatboy in the background—which he had managed to pay for before leaving England. She had written to the painter three times asking for it, and, as late as September 9th 1810, begged Hanson to insist on its being sent to her.[1] She now gave utterance to her pleasure:

> I have received your Picture about three weeks ago, after a *great* deal of trouble. Saunders [sic] said he kept it to show as an honor and credit to him, the countenance is *angelic* and the finest I ever saw and it is very like. Miss Rumbold (Sir Sidney Smith's Daughter in law) fell quite in love with it they were all here.
>
> Murray is sometimes ill but as well as can be expected for a Man of his age, Fletcher's Wife & children are well. Robert Roushton is at School near Newark but when he is at home he is always welcome here, he is a favourite of mine. I believe he is a well disposed Boy. All his family seem very fond of him. He says he will tremble with joy when you return. If I *did* not like him I would notice him for *your* sake and at your *desire*.
>
> Bowman *will* not marry Miss Roushton, and what is worse he *allows his* child to become a burden on the Parish as there is only two shillings a week that he is obliged to pay for it and he will not give more. Old Roushton her Father has brought an action against him for seduction, how it will end I know not.
>
> I believe there was *no* rejoicing yesterday on the 50th anniversary of the Kings accession to the throne, on account of the Princess Amelias illness poor thing every day and every hour she is expected to breathe her last.
>
> Mrs Pigot says Mr Hobhouses Poems are absurd *vicious* nonsense, yours are of *course* captivating. I have read the book I think it is *well written*, and your share of it *beautiful*.

The book was the Miscellany got up by Hobhouse, with verses by Byron (signed L.B.), Hodgson, and others. Hobhouse's own contribution was very raffish and he was afterwards heartily ashamed of it. 'I like some of your additions to E. Bards. Lord Carlisle well deserves the note and the little word Amen at the end gives a good point.'

In the third edition of his satire Byron had introduced a footnote of nearly thirty lines beginning:

> It may be asked why I have censured the Earl of Carlisle, my guardian and relative, to whom I dedicated a volume of puerile poems a few years

[1] This conclusively proves the letter in which, on July 1st, Byron is supposed to express his satisfaction at hearing she has received the portrait, to be a forgery. It is a particularly clumsy one because a genuine letter of July 25th and another of Oct. 2nd ask whether she has yet had the picture, so he obviously could not have heard she was in possession of it at an earlier date.

ago. The guardianship was nominal . . . the relationship I cannot help, and am very sorry for it.

It ended with a shrewd but insolent quotation from Pope and the word Amen. Mrs Byron had not forgotten her bitter quarrel with Carlisle during Byron's early schooldays, while his dislike of her had been the origin of his unwillingness to perform the duties of guardian.

'I am glad you have not parted with all your English People', she went on, in allusion to his having kept Fletcher. 'I wish Hobhouse had remained with you.' She again made a reference—it was rather uncommon for feminine letter writers to do so—to the war going on over the Channel, and the expected battle that might 'decide the contest one way or another', but came back rapidly to a subject on which she was always wistful:

> All the great fortunes are married. I could name a dozen within the last eight months. Miss Long is yet left. She is just come of age. I fancy I think more about these Ladies than you do, but I hope you will come home and live in wealth and happiness in your *own* country. God grant that I may see that day. I am not well nor happy on account of your absence from England.

She gave him some Southwell news, and thanked him in a postscript for writing so often.[1] She had not mentioned a word about her acute money troubles; the letter was no sadder in tone than any mother's might be under the stress of an indefinite separation; yet only the day before she had informed Hanson that it had been necessary for her to raise £120 hurriedly to rescue one of Byron's neediest creditors. She had managed it by collecting the rents herself, despite Hanson's prohibition, from four of the most prosperous tenants—Davy, Hardstaff, Rushton, and Paling, each due to pay £30 last Michaelmas Day (September 29th).

> The poor man [one Farnsworth of Linby, a joiner] would have had all his goods sold or been put in Prison which would have been his utter ruin, and I have not that stoical indifference in my disposition to hear of such scenes without doing something for the relief of the Person if in my power particularly as my Son was the cause of it.

To forestall Hanson's objections, she quoted word for word the passage in Byron's letter in which he had asked her to make use of his funds— of which she said:

> I never shall avail myself further than to *pay myself*. . . .
> If I could have conveniently advanced the sum of money to Farnsworth at present I would have paid it myself, I would have rather borrowed or beg[g]ed the money than that the poor man should be ruined.

[1] Lovelace Papers. 26 Oct. 1810.

She reminded Hanson of the still outstanding thousand pounds, the fifty pounds paid by her in August as interest on that and the balance of the gamekeeper's wages, and proceeded with her Gordon turn of humour to tell him the tenants had been expecting their rents to be raised ever since Byron had come of age and it was a pity to disappoint them. Lord Rancliffe had raised the rents twice in five years, and Lord Chesterfield twice since the birth of his son, 'and the Boy is only four years of age!!!'[1]

Writing from Patras on October 2nd to reproach Hanson sternly with fifteen months of total silence, Byron was still in ignorance that the substantial sums of money he supposed his lawyer to be holding for him, from Norfolk if not Lancashire property sales, remained unrealized, so the calls he made on him are not so wildly irrational as first appears: but by the time he sent Fletcher back from Athens in early November, he knew his situation better. Nevertheless he entrusted the valet with a letter saying that he owed him £250 for wages and 'other accounts' which must be paid him as soon as possible. 'As he was brought up originally to farming if anything falls at Newstead which chances to suit, let him have the refusal.'[2]

That Byron really owed Fletcher so large a sum is not very probable. Thirty or forty pounds a year was then an exceedingly high wage for a manservant, nor, if Fletcher had disbursed large amounts from his own pocket, would he have failed to mention it when Hanson, as we might expect, all but ignored Byron's request. I conjecture that part of the £250, like the proposed offer of a farm at Newstead, was in the nature of a farewell gratuity, as Byron hoped to remain abroad. In the same style, he had given orders that Rushton's father was to have £25 a year for three years to send his son to school. It was the sort of thing that exasperated Mrs Byron intensely, though she thought well of both Rushton and Fletcher; and it made her more than ever determined that Byron should give security for her capital when at last it could be got. 'Otherwise I suppose I would be left in the lurch as I have been once already and neither receive principal nor interest', she told Hanson in the New Year as the dreary business dragged on and on, held up now until Fletcher arrived with documents for Scotland duly signed by Byron. She taxed the lawyer with broken pledges as to the payment of interest going back three years, and maintained in her dogged way that she was going to use the first £1,000 of her £3,000 in settling the debts contracted for Byron, plus any interest due to the lenders, and without renouncing the 5% she had been accustomed to get on the money.[3] A stranger might have thought her mean, but she was simply honest and reasonable, and, whatever she might

[1] Egerton 2611. 25 Oct.   [2] Ibid. Folio 213. 4 Nov. 1810.
[3] Ibid. 3 Jan. 1811.

threaten, she could no more hold out against her son than against her husband. Her firmness crumbled as she pleaded:

> I shall do what I *can* to *procure* the money but if the parties will not agree to give it, you *surely* will not let Lord Byron and me be *sold* out for the *paltry* sum of £1512. 2s. 0.[1] You surely can pay the money yourself and *secure* yourself by having a Mortgage on Newstead, or having security *on the effects* in the house. . . .

She enclosed a copy of Byron's letter to Robert Rushton's father of August 1809 telling him to deduct £25 annually from his rent to pay for the boy's education:

> I did not know any thing of this business till your letter made me inquire. It is a great pity my Son should *burden* himself with such *unnecessary* expenses till he can pay *all* his *lawful* debts. Old Rushton says he *neither wishes nor desires* Lord Byron to pay for his Son's schooling nor to be at any expense concerning him, and if I was in your place I *would not allow it.* Rushton can much better afford to be at the expense than my Son can. However they can settle that when he returns. . . .[2]

Serious illness increased her irritation. If only she could have got what was due to her, she said, she could have gone to London before now for medical advice. No one was better entitled to a measure, and a good measure, of self-pity, but she knew she was nagging, and her postscript is apologetic: '. . . I only desire the terms from my Son that I would get from a stranger.'

Alone in the shadowy old mansion during the long candlelit evenings, isolated by winter, by bad health, by straitened means, she brooded on Hanson's neglect and Byron's indifference to the obligations she had undertaken for his sake. She tackled Hanson again:

> I have been *extremely ill used* . . . by not receiving security before he left the country and also by not receiving the interest since that time [i.e. having paid it over to his creditors]. Pray how *can I go on* without it?

Is it to be wondered that it had become an obsession, when she had forfeited so much of her small income without one word of recognition from either her son or his man of business? And always she was under the threat of the seizure of the goods and chattels:

> I understand [she wrote pitifully] when there is an execution that every thing *on the premises is seized*, therefore I request to know in case the *worst* should happen what steps I am to take to *secure* or *recover* my own property, as I have furniture in this House &c &c &c. I shall expect an answer to

---

[1] Ibid. This was the exact balance of Brothers's bill.
[2] Rushton Senior nevertheless deducted the school fees from his rent.

this as it will save me the expense and trouble of consulting Lawyers and I shall know *how to act.*

Yet primarily she was thinking of Byron:

> At the same time I must inform you that my Son will be *extremely* hurt indeed if his effects are sold here. Indeed I do not think he will keep his senses if his books are sold, and it will be a thousand pities that so good a collection selected with such care and expense should be sold at all, and more particularly for almost nothing which they are sure to go at in this country.[1]

While she was thus agonized, Byron in Greece was preparing for further travels. He notified Hanson that, since Fletcher would have arrived by now with 'Mrs B's Scotch papers', funds could be sent to him to proceed with his journey whether the purchase money for Wymondham had been paid or not, and he wrote her a letter to the same effect with so little trace of gratitude that we are bound in fairness to remind ourselves he had heard nothing either from her or his solicitor to make him conscious of her sacrifices:

> Dear Mother,
> Being enabled by a firman from the Porte to proceed to Jerusalem & Ægypt, I shall visit the Pyramids & Palestine before I return.—You will be good enough to remind Mr Hanson of remittances & not allow him to leave me three thousand miles from England without cash or credit.[2]

Long before this reached Newstead, there was a crisis about the upholsterer's account which is somewhat inexplicable. Indeed the reasons for the continued postponement of his carrying out the execution, though Mrs Byron was always in fear of it, are not clear from any correspondence I have seen: but it would appear that to provide all that Byron—and possibly other extravagant customers—required, Brothers himself had been obliged to raise extensive credit. When she heard of his plight all her resentment dissolved and her compassion asserted itself.

It was the practice then to put one's signature to 'bills' rather as we might now, when short of money, tender a post-dated cheque which the recipient might or might not agree to cash. Such bills had been offered to Hanson—from what source I do not know[3]—for the purpose of settling with Brothers, and he had refused to honour them. Mrs Byron sat down and wrote, not to Hanson but to Mr France in his office, from whom she evidently thought she was more likely to get some attention:

[1] Ibid. 8 Jan. 1811.   [2] Ibid. Folio 226. 2 Feb.
[3] As a later letter shows, it was half of Mrs Byron's money from Scotland, still not collected, that was to be used to pay Brothers, so it seems likely that, on the strength of that, someone—possibly Mrs Byron herself—had signed the bills which Hanson was too cautious to accept.

Mr Bolton [the High Sheriff of Nottingham] informs me that if Mr Hanson had accepted the bills he would have saved a poor man, his Wife, and *eight* children from ruin, but that Brothers must either now go to Prison or be made a Bankrupt—perhaps both, and that all that has been done in this affair from the beginning throughout has been *solely* the acts of his creditors, therefore the man is not to blame as he gave up every thing to them. This is a very *disagreeable* business, as my Son will be represented as the cause of this man's ruin *whether it be true or not*.

Brothers's lawyer had actually had a bailiff installed at Newstead, but, because of some technical error in the proceedings, the High Sheriff had withdrawn him. He had, however, warned Mrs Byron that he himself would be out of office in a few days, and another Sheriff might not take the same view of the case.

Therefore I hope and expect Mr Hanson and you will be on the *alert* to prevent my being sold out. . . . As Mr Hanson has not accepted the bills they [the lawyers concerned] will *not believe* that there is any money to receive, at least *not soon*, otherwise they say he would have accepted them. This I know to be *false*, at the same time I am not surprised at their thinking so. . . .[1]

She wanted to know how these difficulties could be surmounted.

It seems quite noble in this harassed, lonely, and mortally sick woman that, in the midst of her continuing worries, she was able to reply entirely without reproaches and even with an air of high spirits to the letter Byron wrote her on February 2nd in which he emphatically stated his refusal to sell Newstead Abbey. It is the last communication he received from her while abroad, and I will give it in extenso. Her seal, a veined leaf, bears the apt motto, '*Je ne change qu'en mourant*'. He had addressed her again as 'Dear Madam', but she ignored it:

Nottingham 16th March 1811

Dearest Byron,

Your letter I have received. Fletcher is not yet come but he very properly had the letter put into the post Office. Before I say a word of your affairs I will mention some other things in case I should forget it. Earl Grey has been making the Lord Chancellor cry in the House!!! 'English Bards' is in the fourth edition. All the family desire to be *kindly* remembered to you, they have behaved *well* and given *no* trouble about their money.

I am glad you have *refused* to sell Newstead, *stick* to that, *stick* to it, but this I need not urge *knowing* your *firmness*, but Dearest Byron if you are unfortunate it will bring down my *gray hairs with sorrow* to the grave. I would *serve* you, I would *attend* you, and share my last farthing with you. I beg however that you will not remain abroad from any idea that you will

[1] Egerton 2611. 13 Feb. 1811.

disturb me at Newstead. I shall be *ready willing* and happy to give it up to you.

I did not know that a proposal had been made to you for selling Newstead tho' I could guess it as H——n said he had submitted a plan to you for settling your affairs, and his *wish* has been for you to sell Newstead ever since he *first* saw the place. I don't know for what reason, but one *there must be*. *France* [Hanson's employee—seemingly his surveyor] was down with me at Newstead a week, he says you are not yet ruined, or much *injured*, if you *take care* in *future* of what you are about. There are eleven miles *across* the country of your Rochdale property, all good Coals *underneath*, he values that property *clear* at a *hundred thousand pounds* after all your debts are paid. In short Newstead rents must be raised. Copt Mill recovered, your property in Lancashire is recovered, the Coal Pits must be worked, and you will recover some arrears and taxed costs.

When all this is done which will and must be, you will be rich again, the Estate that has been sold and my money will pay part of your debts. If you have a right to Rochdale you have a right to Copt Mill as it all comes to you under the same settlement. There has been a Person from Rochdale at Newstead lately, he says your *presence* is much wanted there, it would do much good to the People there and also to yourself as you (?) might get many thousand pounds by it, that is allowing People to build &c &c &c and you might make a good deal of your *Manorial* rights, this is what he says.

As to the Newstead rents I am sure they never would be raised was it not for me, nor would the farms have been worked but I will have the rents raised. Mr Neald says they can well *bear* it, and the Tenants have long expected it. As to H——n he may and I believe does wish you well, but I am neither satisfied with his activity or his diligence. At the same time you would make nothing by a change, things wont go right till you return yourself.

God bless you I wish you had kept one English-Man about your Person.
Your ever affectionate Mother
C. G. Byron

P.S. Neither the farms would have been *valued* nor the rents raised was it not for me. The rents are not raised but ought to have been so before now, but they shall soon—France says there are bits at Rochdale that you may sell to pay your debts without encroaching on the principal and it is all getting of more value daily.[1]

The imagination boggles at what she would have felt could she have known of the enormous wealth those eleven miles of Lancashire land were to yield—but not for her son, who was begging his solicitor to get rid of it.

On the other hand, he was so strongly resolved not to part with Newstead that he not only wrote to Hanson and his mother to that effect, but asked Hobhouse to make it trebly clear. Hobhouse accordingly passed on

---

[1] Lovelace Papers. The usual small adjustments of punctuation have been made.

this message—'he will not now or at any time sell his Newstead Estate, although he allows, and seems to feel very much the deficit of his ways and means even for present emergencies'.[1] Fletcher, whose spelling gave much amusement in the Byron circle, had sent Hobhouse a letter which he then quoted. *'"me Lord thinks of meaking a tower to Gerusalim."* . . . I do not think that his Lordship will make the said *tower*; and indeed I very much wonder that he should like staying so long amongst such uninformed uninforming barbarians as the Turks. I was sick of them long before I came to the resolution of leaving their country.'

Byron's interest in exotic peoples and scenes—but seldom in works of art except in so far as they recorded history—was by no means diminished after nearly two years of travel, but he had grown tired of perpetual uncertainty about 'remittances' and fear of being stranded, and the knowledge that he had left people in difficulties. He was in a poor state of health too, partly owing to recurrences of what we now recognize as severe malaria, and partly to 'balls, dinners, and amours without number',[2] one or other of these amours having 'clapped' him, as he told Hobhouse, Henry Drury, and probably all his other male friends.

He left Athens on April 22nd and arrived at Malta at the end of the month, finding to his embarrassment that the fascinating Mrs Spencer-Smith was all too faithfully awaiting him, a lady who had inspired him with 'an *everlasting* passion' on his way out, but with whom he now perforce had to come to 'the most diabolical of explanations'.[3] While he spent May on the island, parting with the Franco-Greek youth, Nicolo Giraud,[4] and trying to part with Constance, his mother at Newstead, ignorant even that he was coming home, was writing almost incoherent with misery to Hanson:

> Dear Sir
>
> I did not intend to say any thing as I had nothing to say but when enclosing this letter, Hutton the Bailiff and two of his men arrived from Nottingham. How is this? I thought this business would have been all *settled* as Fletcher brought the paper signed by Byron some time ago, at least I *suppose* so. I did not think you would let this come *on* me. . . . They say the things must be sold off immediately. . . .
>
> P.S. For God['s] sake do not let me live in this state. Something must be done immediately.[5]

Before Hanson could reply, she wrote again, this time to Mr France, saying that yet another bailiff was in the house—four counting Hutton—

---

[1] Egerton 2611. 23 Apr. 1811.   [2] Murray MS. To Hobhouse, 15 May.
[3] *Correspondence*. To Lady Melbourne, 19 Sept. 1812.
[4] See Appendix 2.   [5] Egerton 2611. 23 May 1811.

and the contents were to be sold at once unless, the Under Sheriff's Deputy being in London, *his* Deputy at Southwell would procure a delay, which she was about to plead for personally. Some deferment must have been granted her, because, many as were the calamities in wait for Byron on his return, finding his books and possessions gone was not among them.

In such harrowing circumstances we cannot find it other than natural in Mrs Byron to react angrily to Fletcher's claim for continuance of wages after leaving Byron's service. Beyond delivering 'the Scotch papers' in Chancery Lane, he had had nothing to do since the previous November, and here he was in May taking the attitude of one amazed and injured because, when he turned up at Newstead, there was no salaried employment for him. We may sympathize with his disappointment at not receiving £250 and a farm from Hanson, only £20 to go on with, but he was thoroughly aware of the acute shortage of money, so it was not very realistic to expect these benefactions to be promptly conferred, or to throw himself in their absence on the hands of his Lordship's distressed mother.

Fletcher was never very realistic: if he had been, he would not have returned to Greece, a country he viewed with much disfavour. He was a faithful and simple creature, singularly helpless all his life, and at times his inertia got thoroughly on Byron's nerves. More usually his naïveté promoted good-natured mirth; but a lengthy *cri de cœur* uttered while his master, unknown to him, was on the high seas, probably raised no mirth in Hanson:

> I told Mrs Byron that i had no objection to work in the Garding as it is in so Ruinous Condition but she was not a Greeable And as for my Money she was pretty Shure i should not Get it this six months if then——
>
> I think Mrs Byrons mode of Turning Servents a way is a new one, with out Either wages or warning, I never gave My Lord no reason to use me this way, and i know his honner will not let him do a Rong thing to injure a Servent.
>
> Sir I should be much Obliged if you will give me an order To Draw all or Part of my Money as i must be doing something And Nothing Can be Done with out money, I should be verry Glad to have your Approbation how to act in my verry Chritical Sittuation.
>
> Lord Byron Told me he thought that publick house at Rochdale might suite me if I liked it. But i shall be glad of it or any thing Else at either Rochdale or Newstead. . . .[1]

He went on to remark that additionally there were due to him travelling expenses of nearly £20, comprising coach fare from Portsmouth, baggage, and what he had borrowed from a passenger at Gibraltar. It goes without saying that Hanson did not reply, and we learn from a further letter that

[1] Egerton 2613. Folio 136. 30 May 1811.

Fletcher felt he was being pushed into selling '2 or three dwelling houses' at a loss.[1] He demanded £21 which Hobhouse had deposited for him, at the beginning of June, and this he succeeded in wresting from the solicitor on July 23rd.

Byron sailed from Malta on the frigate *Volage* on June 2nd, and wrote to his mother when he had been twenty-three days at sea. Owing to an unpropitious calm the ship only reached Portsmouth sixteen days later, and was then not allowed a berth on account of some movements of the Fleet. Letters were taken off on July 11th, but Byron kept this one till he disembarked at Sheerness on the 14th. His rather unconvincing excuse in a postscript was that she 'might be alarmed by the interval mentioned in the letter being longer than expected between our arrival in Port & my appearance at Newstead'. But his motive may really have been a natural desire to enjoy, without hurting her feelings, reunions with congenial companions before vanishing in the Midlands. Whatever the reason, it is unlikely that Mrs Byron had the pleasure of knowing her son was on his homeward journey until he was actually in London.

Nevertheless, he was coming with the resolution to behave better to her, telling her that he returned 'with much the same feelings which prevailed on my departure, viz. indifference; but within that apathy I certainly do not comprise yourself, as I will prove by every means in my power'. This was a comparatively warm declaration and, after more than two years without a sight of him, it must have cheered her very much. He asked her not to disturb herself on his account but to regard him simply as a visitor, and to bear in mind that he was on a completely vegetable diet, eating neither fish nor meat and drinking no wine, but requiring 'a powerful stock of potatoes, greens, & biscuit'.

He said that, by what he heard from Hanson, he had some apprehension of finding Newstead dismantled, but if Hanson thought he was going to be forced into selling, he would be baffled. He had bought her a shawl and some attar of roses. He also had in his luggage some four thousand

[1] Ibid. 12 July. These cottages were left him by his father, deceased in 1807 or 1808, and their value was ten pounds a year, so Byron stated in a letter to Hobhouse (16 Jan. 1808). As to Fletcher's return in advance of Byron, Hobhouse's much-quoted marginal comment that Moore had not 'the remotest grasp of the real reason which induced Lord B. to prefer having no Englishman immediately or constantly near him' in Greece was the product of his annoyance at Moore's rash observation that Hobhouse's own company had grown to be 'a chain and a burden'. Fletcher was with Byron more than three months after he began his escapades with the monastery '*ragazzi*' in Athens, and was sent back, as correspondence proves, because there was no quicker way of getting the signed 'Scotch papers', so urgently wanted, to Hanson. So far from wanting no Englishman near him, when he thought Fletcher was not pulling his weight, he tried to get a substitute from the Captain of the British ship on which he had travelled (29 May 1810).

lines of one kind and another generally destined to bring him renown, but these he did not mention to her. She was to miss *Childe Harold* and the presents.

He knew his affairs to be absolutely desperate, and told Hanson as he approached his native land that, after adjusting them as far as he could, he would try to procure recommendations to Lord Wellington or General Graham so that he could join one of the armies as a staff officer. (He was too lame, of course, for active service.) 'In the mean time I am compelled to draw on you for 20 or 30 pounds to enable me to proceed from Port & pay the custom house duties.'[1] His letter touched on many of his worries and obligations but particularly the account of the bookseller, Miller, to whom he had given the draft which Hanson had dishonoured, and he put his finger on the special weakness of his situation:

> However when I consider the sums I owe you professionally, I have nothing further to observe, I have made up my mind to bear the ills of Poverty. Two years travel has tolerably seasoned me to privations. ——
> I have one question which must be resolved, is Rochdale mine, or not? Can I not sell it? & why, if it will bring a sum to clear my debts is it not sold? Newstead is out of the Question, & I do assure you, that if any other person had made such a proposal, I should have looked on it as an Insult.

He reverted to Miller's bill, saying 'It shall be paid if I sell my watch, or strip myself of every sous to answer it. . . .' Altogether in three weeks he was to write on this topic to Hanson five times. It seems peculiar that Hanson had not been able to deal with a two-years overdue bill of £108. 7s. when Mrs Byron's 'Scotch papers' had been received, duly signed, months ago, when Wymondham copyholds were sold and only waiting at this stage for Byron's signature, when his own assessor had valued Rochdale at £100,000, and when his client had an income, however much less than it might have been, from Newstead. It was not as if any of the debts was actually being paid off: and we are driven to the conclusion suggested by Byron himself, writing to Hobhouse before his return, that he was deliberately manoeuvring the young man into a position where he would have to sell, 'partly I believe because he thinks it might serve me, and partly I suspect because some of his clients want to purchase it'.[2]

Byron made an effort, on reaching London, to reassure his creditors—Scrope Davies, who was needing his £4,600 very badly, Mrs Massingberd, the incredibly foolish ex-landlady who, to serve her own ends, had acted as go-between with money-lenders, and made herself liable with her daughter for large sums borrowed by a boy just turned eighteen, the Mr

Thomas, whose annuity of £400 had fallen into arrears, Miller's bookshop at 50 Albemarle Street, where one day Byron was to cut so much more creditable a figure, and doubtless others.

He paid a visit too to Hobhouse, who had made up his quarrel with his father, and was at Sittingbourne awaiting embarkation to Ireland, having obtained a captaincy in the Militia. He also passed a couple of days with Henry Drury at Harrow. It is very understandable that he should be eager to tell his adventures, unexpurgated, to old friends, Hobhouse in particular, who was engaged in a massive and interesting work, *A Journey through Albania and other Provinces of Turkey in Europe and Asia to Constantinople*, about which he desired to 'confabulate'. (Little foreseeing that they would play no negligible part in changing its status, Hobhouse and Byron regarded Greece as a Turkish Province.) But he could say truthfully to his mother that he was detained by business. 'It is with great reluctance that I remain in town.'[1]

Soon a new cause for delay was added—blazing and justified fury, much of it on her behalf. On July 24th, prompted by some report, he purchased an out of date copy of one of the scurrilous papers of the day, *The Scourge*. It contained an article by one Hewson Clarke, who had been at Emmanuel College, Cambridge, when Byron was at Trinity, and who had taken a violent dislike to him or his reputation—they never met—and especially to his college joke of keeping a pet bear 'to sit for a fellowship'. Clarke, who had gone down without a degree and become a journalist, had made various attacks in a magazine called *The Satirist*, in 1807 and 1808, and Byron had retorted in *English Bards* by some lines that were fairly well warranted:

> A would be satirist, a hired Buffoon,
> A monthly scribbler of some low Lampoon,
> Condemned to drudge, the meanest of the mean,
> And furbish falsehood for a magazine,
> Devotes to scandal his congenial mind;
> Himself a living libel on mankind.

After that, he had overstepped the mark in his hot-headed way by a postscript to his second edition with some witty but too sneering sarcasm about his low-bred adversary. Clarke took his revenge in March 1811 by the article in *The Scourge* suggesting that Byron had prepared a libel which he could circulate 'without the hazard of personal responsibility' having gone abroad. He held his own character up to admiration as that of one endowed with 'a temper unruffled by malignant passions, a mind superior to vicissitude', and said that compared with such gifts, 'the pride

[1] Ibid. 23 July.

of doubtful birth, and the temporary possession of Newstead Abbey are contemptible equivalents'. He went on to call Byron 'the illegitimate descendant of a murderer', one whose habit was 'to waste the property of others in vulgar debauchery . . . the son of a profligate father, and a mother whose days and nights are spent in a delirium of drunkenness'. He furthermore denounced him as 'a scribbler of doggerel and a bear-leader . . . hated for malignity of temper and repulsiveness of his manners, and shunned by every man who did not want to be considered a profligate without wit, and trifler without elegance'. He undertook, however, to refrain from exposing 'the infamy of his uncle, the indiscretions of his mother', or 'his personal follies and embarrassments' as long as the poet (or doggerel-writer) did not obtrude himself further on his attention.

Byron immediately took the steps necessary to prosecute for libels on his mother as well as himself, and the matter was put into the hands of the Attorney-General.

We must now pause to enquire whether there was any truth in the aspersions—not on Byron himself, these being so apparently based on burning animosity and some knowledge of his improvidence and dissipation, but the statement about Mrs Byron's perpetual 'delirium of drunkenness'. It is quite obvious from her astute if undiplomatic letters, her lively interest in books and journals, her practical attention to the details of running an estate, that the accusation was stretched to an extreme. At the same time, we must acknowledge that, if a woman in her forties, despoiled of fortune, widowed at twenty-six, disappointed in any sexual attachment she might have formed afterwards, living almost as a displaced person, severed from the country of her origin, unhappy in her relations with a son she injudiciously adored, left alone in the web of financial troubles woven by his imprudences—if such a woman had found in drink some relief from her anxieties and thwarted affections, it would not be in the least remarkable, but rather an occasion for intense sympathy.

It is within the bounds of possibility that she was sometimes intemperate. The principal evidence is Byron's letter to her of July 20th 1810:

> I trust you like Newstead and agree with your neighbours,—but you know *you* are a *vixen*, is not that a dutiful appellation?—Pray take care of my Books, and several boxes of papers in the hands of Joseph [Murray] and pray leave me a few bottles of Champagne to drink for I am very thirsty, but I do not insist on this last article without you like it.[1]

This certainly indicates that she was fond of champagne, but scarcely substantiates habitual drunkenness. Her meagre resources would not have

[1] Ibid.

permitted such indulgence; wine, when Britain was cut off from France and much of the Continent, was an expensive commodity. Two or three accounts for wine debited to Mrs Byron have been preserved, but they tell us little because she sometimes gave orders for Byron (e.g. 'Pray send Byron a Dozen of Wine to Harrow 6 Port 6 Sherry.'[1] This was at the time when she maintained him from her allowance). An unpaid wine bill of £12. 5s. 7d. for 1806 and another of 1807 for 'old port' and sherry, both at £2. 5s. a dozen, were obviously for Byron, as he settled them himself when he came of age: Mrs Byron never let her personal bills run on.

There is also a slightly later account from a Southwell supplier— seven bottles of rum and six of Hollands gin between August 1807 and February 1808; rum, thanks to the excise, as much as five shillings a bottle, gin six. Thirteen bottles in seven months, which included the Christmas season—that quantity would by no means have satisfied a heavy drinker. In contrast to the economical Southwell purchases, Byron himself in 1808 ordered wine for Cambridge and Newstead Abbey at a cost of £489. 9s., a bill which was much increased by the interest accruing on it when he failed to pay it. £215 of it was still due in 1813. He was of course laying down a cellar and entertaining convivial friends lavishly.

Under the nerve strain of her upsetting rows with him when he was an unwilling and turbulent occupant of Burgage Manor, Mrs Byron may have been tipsy once—or oftener, and that would have excited disgust in an intolerant boy, and accounted for his vehemence against her in his letters to Augusta: but the important fact is that, *while she was still alive*, he wrote to no less intimate a friend than Hobhouse,

> The 'Scourge' is in the hands of the Attorney General, the foolish fellow of an Editor instead of something like the shadow of truth, has run aground upon charges of 'Illegitimacy & Drunkenness['] against Mrs B. 'Descent from Murderers' & a variety of other phrases. . . .[2]

I doubt immensely that Byron, who talked so unreservedly, would have withheld a most material circumstance of his home life from a man who had been his travelling companion for a year, or indeed that he would have rushed headlong to law had he felt his position to be weak in the exceedingly sensitive area of his mother's conduct. More significant still, on his way to Newstead, he wrote to Dr Pigot, formerly of Southwell, who had known her for years, that the Editor of *The Scourge* would be tried for these different libels, and, as he was guilty of a 'very foolish and unfounded assertion', he would be 'prosecuted with the utmost rigour'.

---

[1] Murray MS. To Hanson, 28 June 1805.
[2] Marchand, *Letters*. 31 July 1811.

John Pigot had been in his confidence at the height of his youthful con-flicts, and it would have been absurd for him to take a lofty tone about his mother with one who had known she was a drunkard.[1]

(In the event, there was no prosecution, because Sir Vicary Gibbs, the Attorney General, considered that too much time had elapsed since the publication of the offensive article, and that Byron, having been provoca-tive himself, had better leave it contemptuously unnoticed. And soon he was engulfed in too many other distresses to care what an hysterical nonentity had written. His revenge was to be the fame of his doggerel.)

On July 30th, still lingering before his journey to Nottinghamshire, he wrote a proudly humble letter to the tenant of 50 Albemarle Street, not as yet John Murray, but William Miller, the son of the Thomas Miller whose unpaid bill was haunting him. William Miller had just rejected *Childe Harold*. His grounds were that it contained 'sceptical stanzas' and attacked Lord Elgin for plundering the marbles of the Acropolis. (Miller was Elgin's publisher.)

> Sir,
>   I am perfectly aware of the Justice of your remarks, & am convinced that if ever the poem is published, the same objections will be made in much stronger terms.—But . . . as is usual in similar cases having a predilec-tion for the worst passages I shall retain those parts though I cannot venture to defend them. . . .[2]

With a small degree of cutting and adjustment, it would surely have been easy for him to get the work published by Miller, but on a question of literary principle, it was not in him, even at twenty-three years old, to give way.

The following day, mortified by the thought of still owing money to the house where his poem had been refused, he called on Hanson and, not finding him at Chancery Lane, wrote him a note imploring him to settle the bill. 'I have used him so ill (God knows unintentionally) pray let him have the whole and speedily, & do not involve me in fresh dis-grace . . .'[3] He asked for a reply at once and did not get it, upon which he wrote again pressing for an answer. Whether he had one I do not know, but two days later, he was compelled to write yet more urgently. He had received the following express letter from an apothecary:

[1] Disraeli, in his novel *Venetia* (1837), introduces Mrs Byron as a ludicrous character, Mrs Cadurcis, who takes wine too freely; but he may have been basing his portrait on nothing more solid than the same rumour that had set the libeller going in the first place. It may very well have been through Byron's impulsive confidences to Augusta, confided again by her to members of the Carlisle family, and by them to others.

[2] Marchand, *Letters*. 30 July 1811.

[3] Egerton 2611. Folio 245. 31 July.

My Lord,

It is with concern I have to inform you that on my visit to Mrs Byron this Morning, I have found her *considerably* worse, so as to make me *most apprehensive* for the Event.— She is perfectly sensible and enquires after you—I am expecting Dr Marsden every minute from Nottingham.

I have the Honour to remain My Lord,

Your Lordship's obliged Servant

Benj. Hutchinson.[1]

Byron called at once on Hanson and found only Mrs Hanson at home, so he left a note:

Dear Sir,

Mrs Byron is in the greatest danger as Mrs Hanson who saw the letter can apprise you.—To enable me to leave town I have been under the necessity of drawing on you for *forty pounds*. The occasion must excuse me.

Yrs. very truly Byron[2]

So that day at last, August 2nd, he set off, but before he had reached the coaching inn at Newport Pagnell, less than halfway, a messenger confronted him with the news that his mother was dead.

Mrs Byron's illness was always treated as a very sudden one by early biographers, but now that so much of her correspondence is available, it must be clear that its onset had been slow and her premonitions well-founded. The lapse of time between Byron's setting foot on English earth and his arrival home must have seemed an age to her, and it is not, after all, surprising that she wondered to her maid, Mrs Bye, if she should be dead when he came. She was forty-six years old.

At first Byron took it calmly, relieved to hear she had met her end unconscious and without pain; relieved even, it may be, that her presence would embarrass him no longer. How would she have behaved if she had lived to learn that, in the midst of his ruinous predicament, he had just ordered a new carriage! There would be no more violent scenes about that sort of extravagance. As Hanson was coming to Newstead to make the legal arrangements following her death, he invited him to collect the vehicle from Baxter & Co. and travel in it—and we should not blame the lawyer if he had begged so incorrigible a client to take his business elsewhere.

To correct an announcement Hanson had drafted, evidently for the press, Byron wrote on August 4th, 'The *Earl* of Huntly & the Lady *Jean* Stewart daughter of James 1st of Scotland were the progenitors of Mrs Byron. . . . Every thing is doing that can be done plainly yet decently for

---

[1] Murray MS. 1 Aug. 1811. Received 2 Aug.   [2] Egerton 2611. Folio 247.

the interment.' He was not without compunction, and it must have made him feel less troubled by it to act with conventional decorum. He took a loyal but slightly theatrical posture:

> I trust that the decease of Mrs B. will not interrupt the prosecution of the Editor of the Magazine, less for the mere punishment of the rascal, than to set the question at rest, which with the ignorant & weak minded might leave a wrong impression.—I will have no stain on the Memory of my Mother. With a very large portion of foibles & irritability she was without a *Vice* (& in these days that is much) the laws of my country shall do her & me justice in the first instance, but if they were deficient, the laws of modern Honour should decide, cost what it may, Gold or blood, I will pursue to the last the cowardly calumniator of an absent man, & a defenseless woman ————
>
> The effects of the deceased are sealed & untouched . . . I understand her jewels & clothes are of considerable value.[1]

We look again at the words, incredulous. Jewels and clothes of considerable value! How can that be? Yet it was true, at least as to the jewels. There are among the Egerton Papers inventories of jewellery valued at substantially over a thousand pounds, a sum of which it is hard to give any idea in modern currency.[2] Diamond brooches, diamond bracelets, diamond earrings and necklaces, one with sixty-two collets, another with sixteen diamond links; a hoop of rubies, tassels and multiple necklaces of pearls, pearl bracelets, topazes, a parure of amethysts with a necklace of twenty-six collets and an amethyst stomacher: a diamond cross and a diamond feather, gold items, including a thimble, a fruit knife, a vinaigrette, a large gold and enamel bon-bon box, assorted fans, a tiara and ornaments of Siberian berry (? beryl) . . . these precious objects were, from the descriptions, almost all of the 18th century.

She could never have afforded to buy them herself, and if she had possessed them during the days when she was paying £15 a year on a loan of £300 for her husband, it is beyond belief that she could have kept them from his rapacious hands. The most likely source would seem to be inheritance from her paternal grandmother, born Margaret Duff, who died in 1801, fully enlightened as to the squandering that had gone on during the few years of the Byrons' married life, and well acquainted with the little boy, heir to a peerage, who used to visit her in her charming house at Banff. Descended from a rich banking family, only remotely tainted by the prodigal strain of the Gordons, she may well have been guarding the family jewels to hand down to the heiress she must have hoped he would grow up to marry: and his mother in her turn, with that same ambition

---

[1] Ibid.   [2] Ibid. Folio 253–258.

never far from her mind, cannily concealed the treasure, which otherwise would have been washed away without trace under the rolling tide of his debts.

That she thought a great deal about money cannot be disputed. The preoccupation had been forced on her from girlhood. But she had been willing to use her whole capital to pay her son's creditors, so it cannot be suspected that any selfish motive caused her to hold back the heirlooms she had so feared the bailiffs would find and seize.

The valuation done for Hanson cost £22. 10s. and Messrs Rundell & Bridge paid £1,130 cash down for the collection, credited to Byron's account on August 31st.[1] And when he did marry an heiress, he never gave her, as her mother afterwards complained, so much as an ordinary half-hoop engagement ring, only Mrs Byron's unlucky wedding ring which, having been bought by the impecunious Captain Jack, was of gold hardly thicker than wire.[2]

So, despite all secrecy and precaution, the treasure drifted away. Some of the proceeds filled the need of ready cash, and some must have been used to deal with very pressing creditors. For a few short months, there seems to have been no serious scrape. The bailiffs came to Newstead no more. The books remained for a while in the bookcases. For longer than two heroic years Mrs Byron had held the fort. Now, alone, she had raised the siege.

---

[1] Murray MS. Hanson's account for 1811. There is a letter from a Nottingham jeweller, Elizabeth Lingford, dated August 13th, giving a total of £983. 2s. 2d. and saying his Lordship would doubtless be perfectly satisfied. (Egerton 2611, Folio 252.) This may refer to a separate transaction dealt with by Byron direct a very few days after his mother's death, or may be merely an offer made in Nottingham which the London jeweller bettered.

[2] The wedding ring is still in family possession.

4

Entanglements and Disentanglements

The death at Newstead Abbey was almost eclipsed in Byron's mind by his grief over a fatal accident to the friend he deemed most talented, Charles Skinner Matthews, drowned in the Cam while Mrs Byron was still un-buried. It may have been his horror at this event that prevented his attendance at her obsequies. Funerals in those days were contrived to purge the emotions with awe and lugubrious drama. Byron only wished things to be done 'plainly and decently', but decency could not have been sustained without numberless yards of black bombazett and bombazine hangings in the church, black crepe for the pulpit and velvet for the pall, as many black scarves swathed round hats as there were mourners, not to speak of black cloaks, handkerchieves, ribands, and stockings, all provided by the undertaker, and tall staffs draped with crepe for the men called mutes whose curious profession it was to look solemn at funerals, and who never seemed to use the same scarf twice.

It was customary to present each mourner with a pair of black gloves, just as, at christenings, white gloves were distributed. There are thirty-five hatbands costing £29. 10s. 7d. on the undertaker's account, thirty-five ties for them at 17s. 6d. and thirty-five pairs of gloves at £3. 18s., as well as twenty-nine mourning cloaks and some black kid habits. The congregation in the church of Hucknall Torkard must have been largely the Newstead tenantry, and the servants. The undertaker's bill was nearly £200,[1] and of course the traditional refreshments would have been pro-vided, doubtless in the hall of the mansion on the party's return.

Byron saw only the departure of the hearse down the long drive, followed by its sable procession, but it had so adverse an effect on him that—little anticipating the immensely greater pomp with which he was to be taken to the same vault—he at once made a will directing that he should be buried beside his dog Boatswain in the Abbey garden without any ceremony whatever.

[1] Murray MS.

An extraordinary succession of fatalities, culminating in the news that the beloved chorister, Edleston, had died the previous May, while he was abroad, brought him almost to the verge of breakdown. 'Death has been lately so occupied with every thing that was mine', he wrote to Hobhouse, 'that the dissolution of the most remote connection is like taking a crown from a Miser's last Guinea'.[1]

Although it was well over two years since he had last seen Edleston, the blow made a tremendous impact. He produced the various lyrics 'To Thyrza' which were, as Moore percipiently said, 'the essence, the abstract spirit, as it were, of many griefs', forming 'one deep reservoir of mournful feelings'. Not only did Edleston and the other lost friends of his youth haunt his mind, but also, in his desolating retrospection, the unpossessed Mary Chaworth, married, living near by, and mother of 'The babe which ought to have been mine'.[2] He alluded in one letter after another to his lonely condition, and Hobhouse's absence with his regiment in Ireland must have been a severe privation; but there were times when he took a misanthropic delight in his solitude.

He could not change his mood by seeking the pleasures of London because he was waiting for Hanson to accompany him to Lancashire, and Newstead was more or less on the way, London just the contrary. On September 9th, he wrote to Augusta:

> My Rochdale affairs are understood to be settled as far as the Law can settle them, & indeed I am told that the most valuable part is that which was never disputed, but I have never reaped any advantage of them, & God knows if I ever shall. Mr H. my agent, is a good man & able, but the most dilatory in the world.—I expect him down on the 14th. . . .[3]

On the 25th he was telling Francis Hodgson that 'my ever-lasting agent puts off his coming like the accomplishment of a prophecy'. All unaware of the news about Edleston that was soon to arrive he remarked that he had begun to pluck up his spirits and gather his 'little sensual comforts together'.[4] These were the pretty housemaids engaged or re-engaged to replace his mother's plain ones. His tastes are indicated by his having forbidden them to wear caps or to cut their hair short, and given them permission to wear stays, 'but not too low before'.[5] He had also commanded them to dress in 'full uniform' every evening. Full uniform, white muslin, was more decolleté than the cottonprint of the morning.

---

[1] Murray MS. 13 Oct. 1811. [2] Lines dated 11 Oct.
[3] Marchand, *Letters*. [4] Ibid.
[5] The dresses of 1811 were extremely high-waisted and the only object of wearing stays, when not required to control serious embonpoint, was to emphasize the bosom by 'uplift'.

Meanwhile he was in correspondence about a matter which, though it was of great moment to him, he appeared to treat casually. With the prospect of pocketing whatever fees were paid for it, Robert Dallas had diligently applied himself to getting *Childe Harold* published, and had fixed on John Murray, the successor to his father, who had died in 1793, as what was then termed a bookseller, a man of peculiar acumen both in respect of authors and their works. Murray decided to publish the poem, but, like Miller, he was troubled by some matters in it. 'I hope your Lordship's goodness will induce you to obviate them,' he wrote very diplomatically, 'and, with them, perhaps, some religious feelings which may deprive me of some customers among the *Orthodox*'.[1]

He soon learned that, though his new poet was modest as to the merits of his work, when it came to altering it for the approval of the orthodox, he stood exceedingly firm.

> With regard to the political & metaphysical parts, I am afraid I can alter nothing . . . and as to my unlucky opinions on Subjects of more importance, I am too sincere in them for recantation . . . but if there are any alterations in the structure of the versification you would wish to be made, I will tag rhymes & turn Stanzas, as much as you please.[2]

Byron had a gift, hardly definable, which the publisher had at once recognized as the presage of a great career: we call it now 'star quality'. He had also the usually complementary endowment of 'star mentality', making him a difficult creature to handle. It is sometimes an egoistical assertiveness, the mere desire for dominance which will enable even a bad actor to hold the stage; and sometimes a kind of intuitively exercised authority, springing from the conviction of having a right to be entirely oneself. Murray became familiar with the gestures of that very high hand.

He had been warned, for example, that the young man did not want him to submit the manuscript to a critic they both respected enormously, William Gifford, because 'there is in such a proceeding, a kind of petition for praise, that neither my pride or—whatever you please to call it—will admit. . . . You will therefore retain the M.S. in your own care, or if it needs must be shown, send it to another.'[3] Three weeks later, Byron heard from Dallas that Gifford had nevertheless been shown the poem and he wrote one of his forceful letters, saying it had been 'most contrary' to his wishes:

> . . . I hardly conceived you would have so hastily thrust my productions into the hands of a Stranger, who could be as little pleased by receiving them, as

---

[1] *LJ.* 4 Sept.   [2] Marchand, *Letters.* 5 Sept.   [3] Ibid. 23 Aug.

their author is at their being offered . . . You have placed me in a very ridiculous situation, but it is past, & nothing more is to be said on the subject.[1]

He complained bitterly, however, to Dallas. His sensitiveness was
due to his having lauded Gifford in *English Bards* and feeling he might
be thought to have curried favour: he seems not to have been aware that,
being in Murray's employment as editor of the *Quarterly Review*,
Gifford was the obvious person to consult.

While yet he was unaccustomed to his author's oddities, Murray sent
him the proof of the work, requesting his opinion of the format, and
must have been surprised that, so far from poring over it with all the
delight of a youthful lover seeing an embodiment of his Muse, he asked
that it might be handed over to Dallas, '. . . who understands typographical arrangements much better than I can pretend to do. The Printer
may place the notes in his *own way*, or any *way*, so that they are out of
my way; I care nothing about types or margins'.[2]

Not only Byron's 'star mentality' but his lack of aesthetic feeling is
evident here—or perhaps he was overacting his casualness, because, although he spoke of quarto as 'a cursed unsaleable size',[3] when he did
examine the handsome pages, he mentioned with pride the 'good paper,
clear type, & vast margin'.[4]

Reaching his Lancashire estate at last, he was pleased to learn locally
that it might be made a source of substantial income.

> . . . The property there [he wrote to Hobhouse] if I work the mines myself
> will produce about 4000 pr.Ann.; but to do this I must lay out at least
> 10000£ in etceras, or if I chuse to *let* it without incurring such expenditure it
> will produce a rental of half the above sum, so we are to work the collieries
> ourselves of course.—
>
> Newstead is to be advanced immediately to 2100 pr.Ann. so that my
> income might be made about 6000£ pr.Ann.—But here comes at least
> 20000£ of Debt and I must mortgage for that & other expenses, so that
> altogether my situation is perplexing.[5]

Without the slightest knowledge of estate management, not troubling
to look at the collieries,[6] and in the hands of so supine an agent as Hanson,
to think of getting clear of debt and more than doubling his income was
building a castle in thinnest air. It had been his misfortune from early
youth always to have enough materials to tempt him to believe such
structures might prove solid.

---

[1] Ibid. 14 Sept.   [2] Ibid. 16 Sept.   [3] Ibid. To Hodgson, 13 Oct.
[4] Ibid. To Hobhouse, 17 Nov.   [5] Murray MS. 14 Oct.
[6] Byron, as he admitted in a letter to Hodgson (10 Oct.), 'never went within ken
of a coalpit'.

Hanson had for years been receiving letters from local persons of consequence telling him that Rochdale ought to have proper steward-ship and was capable of rewarding its owner, but he had gone on employ-ing the incompetent Richard Milne, with whom he was now in litigation. Mrs Byron's theory that he had from the first been determined on the sale of Newstead is very credible in the light of his apathy about any development whatever of the other property, which was considerably over twice the size of the Nottingham estate. What a relief to dispose of all the financial problems in one swoop, leaving his client without the dignity of manors to support his peerage but with a modest fixed income and the hope of marrying an heiress!

And the Newstead mansion was no longer old-fashioned and dilapida-ted as when Lord Grey de Ruthyn had inhabited it. Though the garden must have fallen into neglect, Byron had done up a good part of the house in a most handsome modern style and provided a quantity of the latest and choicest appointments. Besides the huge sum expended with the single firm of Brothers in Nottingham, there had been proportionate bills run up in Mansfield with at least three others, painters, joiners, and masons. Beginning before he came of age, he had spent, I estimate, not less than £4,000 on giving up-to-date elegance to a home he had no intention at the time of either selling or living in;[1] while, despite repeated appeals and commands to Hanson, the tenants were still paying pre-war rents.

We need not question Byron's perfect sincerity when he wrote to friends of his reluctance to raise the rents, but in the inflation of the war, all landlords had done so, and he had creditors who were in much more distress than his tenants, and had actually got into debt themselves to provide him with goods. He contracted liabilities not heartlessly, but heedlessly, partly no doubt because there was a history of insensate prodi-gality among his paternal ancestors, and partly, as I have suggested, because a rescue always appeared imminent.

Hanson, after all, did nothing to increase income, and Byron was driven to write to him very firmly:

Dear Sir,
    It is proper that the Newstead tenants should be made aware of the amount of the intended rental immediately, so pray, let the proportion of each be made out & sent down forthwith.[2]

Weeks later he remained uninformed as to what, if anything, had been going forward:

I have thrice written [he protested] without receiving any answer,

---

[1] See Appendix 5, 'The Newstead Furniture'.   [2] Egerton 2611. 18 Nov.

which I again request as the comfort of so many persons depends on our speedy determination. I presume that the new Rental has been sent to Notts, where I propose to proceed on Monday next.[1]

These two notes were written in London, where he had arrived by way of Cambridge and a visit to that intemperate and facetious don, Scrope Davies. He took lodgings in St. James's Street, and, after the four flattest months of his life, there was quite suddenly a brightening of the scene.

It began through a correspondence with Thomas Moore, a first-rate celebrity and a favourite in society. The story has necessarily been told in every biography—how Moore, not knowing Byron was abroad, sent him, in 1810, what amounted to a challenge on account of some very mild flippancies in *English Bards*, how Byron's Cambridge friend Hodgson sensibly kept back the letter, how in 1811 Moore re-stated his grievance, though in a remarkably conciliatory tone, and how the near-challenge became a subtle approach to the honour of his Lordship's acquaintance. Moore was able to add one more peer to the splendid collection his charm and dexterity had already acquired, and Byron, while fully retaining what Moore called 'his good sense, self-possession, and frankness', was delighted to meet a poet he had much admired and had formerly imitated and to be welcomed into a circle of established men of letters.

There is a famous anecdote, about the dinner Samuel Rogers gave to bring him and Moore together, in Rogers's *Table Talk* as remembered by Alexander Dyce. Byron, the story goes, would not partake of any of the food and wine proffered and, after asking for biscuits and soda water, which were not available, 'dined upon potatoes bruised down on his plate and drenched with vinegar'. Rogers added his own malicious and fictitious touch:

> Some days after, meeting Hobhouse, I said to him, 'How long will Lord Byron persevere in his present diet?' He replied, 'Just as long as you continue to notice it.' I did not then know, what I now know to be a fact,—that Byron after leaving my house, had gone to a Club in St James's Street and eaten a hearty meat-supper.

Hobhouse who was, as it happened, a stranger to Rogers was in Ireland in November 1811 when the dinner took place; nor did he return to London till late February 1812, by which time Rogers knew Byron well and had no occasion to enquire about his habits. Moore, a much better witness, tells us that Byron had 'contrived to make a rather hearty dinner' of the potatoes—so the second meal sounds improbable. Moreover, there is plentiful independent evidence that he was genuinely on an abstemious vegetarian diet.

[1] Ibid. 10 Dec.

In July, he had bought *A Treatise on Corpulence*[1] which may have sustained his belief in potatoes as a slimming diet. As will be seen when we come to his accounts for food several years later, he subsisted for weeks at a time on vegetables and biscuits or some equivalent which no modern dietician would countenance. Such fare was largely answerable, in my belief, for the very pale complexion, then regarded as a great refinement and enhancement of good looks, which may well have been a symptom of anaemia.

Moore has left an impression of their first meeting:

> What I chiefly remember to have remarked was the nobleness of his air, his beauty, the gentleness of his voice and manners, and—what was naturally not the least attraction—his marked kindness to myself. Being in mourning for his mother, the colour as well of his dress, as of his glossy, curling, and picturesque hair, gave more effect to the pure, spiritual paleness of his features, in the expression of which, when he spoke, there was a perpetual play of lively thought, though melancholy was their habitual character when in repose.

He was now on the way to real fame. His satire was about to go into its fifth edition; John Murray was taking his time about publishing *Childe Harold* but only the better to work up interest in it; influential Whigs had their eye on him as a likely recruit to their ranks; his extensive and unusual travels contributed to his glamour. It is a word that has been overworked but is not yet bereft of meaning. I have heard it described as 'the quality of appearing enviable'. This, for all his lame foot, Byron never lacked. Yet in the background there were numerous and sordid troubles, in particular those he shared with Mrs Massingberd.

*   *   *   *   *

It had been his mother who, little dreaming of the portentous consequences, had taken him, for part of the school holidays in 1800, to the house where Mrs Massingberd, assisted by a daughter, let lodgings of a superior class in Piccadilly. 'Board and lodging'—the phrase had not yet gathered the shabby-genteel associations which have hung about it in the present century. There were inns, but they harboured only the passing traveller; nobody except through *force majeure* stayed weeks or months at an inn. And there were hotels, but these resembled what we should now call service apartments: guests paid for their own candles and coals and such amenities as soap and writing paper, and, though food and attendance were obtainable when required, were generally waited on

---

[1] Murray MS. Ridgeway's bill. Mrs Byron's obesity must have kept the fear of growing fat constantly in his mind.

by their own servants. Most of the gentry, if away from home, still found accommodation in private houses, where such lettings provided a livelihood for a large number of widows, some of them well-connected. Mrs Massingberd was one of these.

Her husband had been a Post-Captain in the Navy. She herself was of a good county family; her father, Thomas Waterhouse, having been High Sheriff of Nottinghamshire in the 1780s. The 2nd Lord Byron had married one of her ancestors, which may explain her patronage by Mrs Byron. Her house must have been comfortable and also a suitable temporary abode for a youth who aspired to be fashionable, because he went back several times from choice.

On December 5th, 1805, still seventeen years old, he wrote from Trinity College that he would have occasion to pass a few weeks in town from the 18th and desired two rooms, one for himself and the other for his servant: no sitting-room would be needed. The servant was on board-wages, so only wanted lodging, but Byron himself would prefer living with the family[1]—that is, taking his meals at the *table d'hôte*, or *d'hôtesse*. This suggests that Mrs Massingberd and her daughter were agreeable company. 'Separate tables' were still in the far future.

He talked to them freely, telling them no doubt about his difficulties with his mother, of which they had already seen something, and about the lawsuit at Rochdale that he was sure to win, and the money accumulating in Chancery until he came of age, and his properties in Nottingham and Norfolk, and how badly he wanted a mere seven or eight hundred pounds. Mrs Massingberd could not produce any such sum because she herself was in debt, but she knew all the ways of raising money, and, though it was not through her that Byron had his first contact with 'the tribes of Israel'—for he recorded that he had answered the advertisement of one of them, a Mr King—it was she who helped him into the demoralizing trap from which he found no exit for many a year.

Mr King explained to him that, being a minor, he could not borrow money without the security of 'competent persons'. Byron then wrote to Augusta, as mentioned in my first chapter, proposing that she should guarantee the loan, no one else he knew being in a position to do so. Augusta failed him, so Mrs Massingberd, whose own guarantee was insufficient, got her adult daughter to join her in signing the bond. It was a transaction barely excusable in a silly boy who pictured himself taking possession of his fortune promptly and easily on his twenty-first birthday, and almost inexcusable on the part of an elderly woman who was not ignorant of the price to be exacted.

---

[1] Letter in the possession of Mr Anthony Powell.

In Byron's memorandum of five years later he says he became acquainted through Mr King with two other money-lenders, the third being a Mr Howard who interviewed him several times, once in Golden Square but more frequently in Piccadilly (i.e. at Mrs Massingberd's). Howard himself was uncomfortable about dealing with the youth. He told him:

> Ld B. was acting imprudently, stating that he made it a rule to advise young men against such proceedings. Ld B. recollects on *the day on which the money was paid* at Mrs M's house, *that he remained* in the next room, till the papers were signed, Mrs M. having stated that the parties wished him to be kept out of sight during the business *and wished to avoid even mentioning his name.* ——
>
> Mrs M. deducted the interest for two years & a half and 100£ for Howard's papers.[1]

The alacrity with which a large sum of interest was deducted before any of the money had passed further than Mrs Massingberd's hands was due to her needing it for her own use and treating it as a loan to herself. The £100 for the 'papers' must have been the fee for drawing up the agreement—how grossly excessive can only be estimated by more than ten-fold multiplication.

Needless to say, the arrangement was irresistibly tempting, although the interest and expenses were so exhorbitant that, after the deductions, a liability of £1,800 provided not more than £1,000 of ready money. Soon another loan was carried through, and six months after that another still was proposed, a bargain by which, at its best, Byron was to borrow £3,000 on condition of paying back £5,000 on his coming of age, now less than two years off. But it was even worse than that, for the £3,000 was all to be used relieving Mrs Massingberd of responsibility for the previous borrowing, thus freeing her own income on which her granddaughter had obtained a lien. (In return for capital furnished by relatives she had undertaken to pay them an annuity.)

Mrs Byron, isolated at Southwell, had nevertheless learned what was going on, and wrote urgently to Hanson:

Dear Sir,

Mrs M. is now trying to get my Son into another *Scrape*, that is to borrow more money. She is certainly a *Dupe* herself or *wishes to make* him one. I know her income has been seized for the payment of the Annuity & she wishes Ld B to allow her to borrow money to pay all off, which is to be procured on worse terms than the former Loan but upon these conditions, that he will have to pay nothing till he comes of age, that is to say she will

[1] Murray MS. 16 Jan. 1812. Written in the third person.

have nothing to pay for him, therefore she will enjoy the income for that period and then all will fall heavy on his Lordship. . . .

If *you* could take any steps to prevent it you would oblige me much. My name must not appear as I am supposed to know nothing of the transaction. Do not answer my letter but burn it. . . .

P.S. The people the last sum was borrowed from have wrote to her grand daughter to desire Mrs M[s] income may only be paid to them.[1]

The year before, as has been told, Mrs Byron herself had got into serious debt in the vain hope of saving him from doing so.

Nobody has ever been able completely to unravel Byron's financial dealings with Mrs Massingberd, but one unpublished letter of hers to him, out of several pressing the new loan on him—though with an air of begging him to decide for himself—might be illuminating to a chartered accountant who also had the gift of clairvoyance:

. . . With the three thousand pounds I propose to pay off both the Annuitys amounting to £3300. You know I have only money for the payment of the Annuitys for two years. Therefore it will be necessary to raise this time twelvemonth six hundred and fifty pounds for the purpose of paying them out of the twelve hundred that I had in Febr.ʸ and August. I shall have paid five hundred and a few pounds in Febry next.

Redemption if it was paid at that time would be £150 pounds more making six hundred and fifty pounds.

There would then remain near five hundred and fifty pounds which you would have.

Observe the money you have to pay to those people when you come of age.

The first money advanced	£1800
Second	£1500
Redemption	150
Two years annuity for the first	600
,, ,, ,, and a half for the second	475
Insurance	110
	£4635

By this statement your Lordship will find yourself a gainer. A gentleman (an Earl's son) together with his Mother are joined for the payment for ten thousand pounds, but taking the other five. He called upon me some time ago and was so perfectly satisfied with the reliance *I* had upon your Honor, that the only security he required was a letter from you assuring him you would pay the money when you came of age or six or twelve months after. When you have considered this affair you will let me have your answer.

[1] Ibid. 31 Jan. 1807.

It appears to me an advantageous offer, particularly as it relieves us from the difficulty of procuring the Six Hundred and Fifty pounds this time twelvemonth.
                    I have the Honour to remain with great respect and regard
                              Your Lordship's most faithful friend,
                                        E. H. Massingberd.[1]

With the most confusing effect, Mrs Massingberd seems to be using the word 'annuity' in two different senses—principal and interest. The loans already received together make 'annuities' of £3,300, while two years annuity on £1,800 is £600 (or interest at £300 per annum) and two and a half years on £1,500 is £475. But although we know from Byron's own careful statement to his lawyer that interest, under whatever name, for two and a half years had been taken by the go-between from the £1,800 before he was paid anything, he is to be debited with most of it all over again on coming of age! She admits to having had, herself, £1,200 in February and August, from which I infer that she not only helped herself to £750 from the £1,800, which was a February transaction —i.e. the two and a half years interest—but to £450 in August, the time of the second borrowing. The victim, having had less than £2,000, counting expenses and the premiums for insuring his life, was to pay back £4,635, but would somehow be 'a gainer' if he cleared off £3,300 immediately by a new loan of £3,000, which—so mad was the reckoning —would then leave him £550 in pocket because Mrs Massingberd would reimburse him part of what she owed him, and his debt on reaching majority would become £5,000 instead of £4,635!

Byron knew as little of arithmetic as any man who had spent years of his life at Latin and Greek verses, but even to him, just verging on nineteen as he then was, this hardly seemed feasible. Mrs Massingberd wrote again, varying the figures somewhat because, she said, the life insurance premium would go up every year. 'You know if this affair finishes before the 12th of next month you will have the remainder of the money I have in my hands.'

'I benefit nothing by the transaction', she assured him.[2] He replied doubtingly. She went off on a different tack, telling him that perhaps she hadn't properly comprehended the plan and so had not been able to explain its advantages to his Lordship:

I should not have mentioned it, and I am very sorry I did but here it ends. I shall never mention it again, only to observe it was no benefit to me and I am certain at the expiration of the time you will find I have disbursed the money left with me according to the agreement. . . .

[1] Ibid. 16 Jan. slight re-punctuation.   [2] Ibid. 23 Jan. 1807.

It is needless for me to say anything of your Lordship's superior judgment. You have long known my opinion on that head. I shall be truly concerned if you are offended with me. It may be an error in my head not in my heart . . .

I remitted the balance to your Lordship yesterday, and I am sorry to say that at the moment I cannot discharge Hughes bill. I have not twenty pounds in the world or I should have done so immediately. You know I have not the Perplexity of Riches.[1]

It has been thought that Byron was duly inveigled into the arrangement which, though of 'no benefit' to her, would have cleared her of liability and freed her tied-up income. Yet the deal must have fallen through, because she and her daughter remained liable, and when Byron listed his debts years later, there had been no liquidation of the principal of £3,300 which made up the two original loans, exclusive of all added charges.

Mrs Massingberd was too obsequious to let a disappointment about money come between her and a young nobleman, and she was able to oblige him again on a smaller scale the following year. He continued for a little while to frequent 16 Piccadilly and even to take disreputable girls there, one of whom the landlady did not view with favour judging by a somewhat sheepish note he wrote to her from Brighton on July 20th, 1808:

Dear Madam,
    I have parted with Miss Cameron, & I beg she may have her clothes & the trunk containing them.
                    Yours very truly,
                        Byron[2]

Miss Cameron was the young woman who had accompanied him to Brighton dressed, for discretion's sake, as a boy, and was passed off as a brother, Gordon. When Lady Perceval met them out riding, she admired the lad's horse, upon which she had this reply: 'Yes, it was gave me by my brother.' (Lady Perceval unwittingly increased Byron's load of debt by letting him have her opera box next season for forty guineas.)[3]

[1] Ibid. Hughes was a minor creditor whom the fraudulent valet, Frank Boyce, should have paid out of cash received, but did not.

[2] MS. in the possession of Mr Anthony Powell.

[3] Egerton 2613. Folio 41, entry of 20 Jan. 1809. Byron generally had a season ticket for the opera wherever he was. This may have been because attendance was a fashionable custom, but he had a much stronger feeling for music than he has been given credit for. Nathan, the composer, wrote: 'He was devotedly attached to music, and possessed much judgment in that science, but his natural timidity never allowed him to persevere in any practical attempt he made'.

Somehow it had come about that, by the time he reached his majority, Mrs Massingberd had made herself and her daughter responsible, through the money-lender Howard, for annuities to three persons who had advanced capital—for Howard, apparently, did not lend his own money. Naturally, she looked to Byron to pay this extortionate interest, and at twenty-one he was less happy about such obligations than he had been in his teens. In one of his letters to Hanson he called her 'the Beldam'.[1] To his mother she was 'that *vile* Woman'. She hoped Byron would pay back 'nothing but the sums actually received and lawful interest'.[2] Legally a minority debt could not carry interest of more than 5% and then only after the attainment of majority.

He did, however, endeavour to keep up the annuities, and had settled them for a whole year, no less than £530, a third of his Newstead revenue, in March 1809. But since, before going abroad, he had contracted large new debts for which, being no longer an infant in law, he was unquestionably liable, Hanson may be pardoned for showing indifference, in his absence, to Mrs Massingberd's claims.

On July 20th, 1810, Byron being in Greece, she sent the solicitor a letter from Howard notifying her that half-yearly payments to the three annuitants, Mr Kendall, Mr Jones, and Mr Woodward, totalling £265, were overdue and 'the parties' would not wait.[3] To say Hanson ignored that information is by now superfluous. On July 30th she wrote again to tell him that, if the annuitants were not paid, they would send 'an Execution' to her house. 'I am afraid', she said confidently, 'Lord Byron would be greatly hurt by my suffering on his account, at least if I can depend on his word and the several letters he wrote to me upon the Subject.'[4] Next day Hanson replied saying he had no funds in hand at the moment, and he hoped she would convince the annuitants that it was in their real interest to wait for payment. But, on August 9th 1810, she forwarded another and more threatening letter, as to which she said she could as soon discharge the national debt as pay the annuities herself and she trusted Hanson would prevent her being brought to 'disgrace and shame'.[5]

In some inscrutable way, Scrope Davies had been caught up as a guarantor in the coil of these transactions, and Hanson lost no time in apprizing him at King's College, Cambridge, of the risk that legal measures might be taken.[6] Scrope was by no means so insouciant as when he had lent Byron thousands of pounds, and he had already sent him a sharp letter saying that he (Scrope) was in danger of arrest day after day, and that if Hanson had not concealed the position, his friend would surely

[1] Egerton 2611. 2 May 1809.   [2] Ibid. 9 Apr. 1809.   [3] Egerton 2613.
[4] Ibid.   [5] Egerton 2611.   [6] Egerton 2613. 10 Aug. 1810.

have returned to England,[1] but Byron did not receive this till many months later, after April 30th, 1811, when he arrived at Malta on his journey home.

Hanson, beleaguered on all sides—compelled even to fob off the Colonel Sawbridge with whom his client had made a direct and binding engagement—could not, of course, pay the money-lender's annuitants, and while Byron was waiting for a ship at Malta, the creditor named Jones had Mrs Massingberd arrested with her daughter. She wrote in abject misery to say they were held at 'a spunging house', a place where debtors were detained at their own cost while given a little time to try to raise money before imprisonment. 'I am at a loss to know what steps I am to take to be released from so disgraceful a situation.' She again stated her conviction that Lord Byron would be hurt if he knew of it; she wanted to hear when he would be returning, and hoped that meanwhile the spunging house charges would be defrayed, 'as the Disgrace is sufficient without the Expense'.[2]

It does not appear that Hanson did anything to procure her release, because that was accomplished through a Mrs Atkyns, who was only able to give indemnity, not to pay the debt. The Massingberds therefore remained in deep trouble, and such was their plight when Byron at last returned. Unlike his father, he was not a quite unscrupulous squanderer. He had many qualms of conscience, but his sincere if absurdly sanguine belief that money owed to *him* would be paid when it was due encouraged him to indulge his extravagant tastes; and a high proportion of his expenditure was occasioned by the ardent generosity with which he responded to every appeal for aid. He had also as much susceptibility to being cheated as the most ingenuous youth who ever felt he had to live up to the title of Lord.

Mrs Massingberd herself had, in fact, written to him about the malpractices of his first valet, Frank Boyce, that there had never been one bill as to which he was not defrauded. 'It always appeared to me most extraordinary that a man of your Lordship's superior abilities (I speak what I think) should submit so long to be imposed upon by such a villain.'[3]

It is hard to tell from the fawning tone she always assumed with him whether she was very artful or, as his mother thought possible, something of a dupe herself. What are we to make of the letter she wrote on hearing of Mrs Byron's death?

I feel the concern natural for the loss of an Old Acquaintance, and also

---

[1] Ibid. 17 July 1810. The letter was postmarked at Malta on 15 Feb. 1811.
[2] Ibid. Folio 262. 16 May 1811.   [3] Murray MS. 27 Jan. 1807.

as the mother of your Lordship, as your behaviour to her according to my judgment, was truly filial, which is the consolation that alleviates the grief for the loss of a Parent.[1]

Could she have meant a word of what she was writing? He had sought sanctuary in her house after one of his most appalling quarrels with his mother, who had followed him there and whom he had at first absolutely refused to see, and after 'an obstinate engagement of some hours', he had forced her into a humiliated retreat—a scene that could not have escaped the landlady's attention. (He described to Hobhouse long afterwards how he had fled from Southwell in a chaise with four horses while his mother had pursued him with only two. Hobhouse remembered his reflection then, 'Poor woman!')[2]

Byron had written to Mrs Massingberd on his return to England assuring her of his best endeavours, but owing to his mother's death, the payment of 'the Scotch money', so long in coming, was subject to a further delay, and, in any case, wherever he turned there were creditors, so the Massingberd annuitants were still pressing their claims towards the end of that year. On November 1st, the self-same day on which he wrote to Thomas Moore, expressing in his most delightful manner his pleasure at the prospect of their meeting, he had a letter which must have made him profoundly uncomfortable.

> Since the unfortunate transaction last May [the arrest], together with the stoping [sic] my Annuity, I am not only deprived of *Bread*, but have for ever lost the friendship of every relation I have in the World, not one that would assist me with a Guinea. Your Lordship and Mrs Atkyns the lady who so generously released myself, and Daughter from our Confinement last May are the only friends I have in the world. To the latter I cannot apply, I confess I have too much Pride (if it can be so called) to ask relief from one who is only my superior in point of fortune, more particularly when I am under obligations that can never be forgot, Since had she not been bound for the Payment for which we were arrested we had suffered disgrace that would have Shocked your Lordship's feelings and been our ruin for ever, I mean going to Newgate as the County Jail. My Solicitor told me so, therefore can I after such an obligation impose upon her benevolence. . . .[?]
>
> The Owner of the House I now live in has twice demanded her rent, and much against my will I have made an excuse at the expense of my veracity. After this melancholy detail I hope your Lordship will have compassion upon us. The kind letter I had the honor to receive from you upon your arrival in England gave me hopes that you would not see me distressed without relieving me. Formerly I was frequently honor'd with letters from

---

[1] Ibid. undated. August 1811.
[2] Marginal note by Hobhouse in Moore's biography.

your Lordship, but the case is strangely altered, you will not now condescend to answer any that I write.

I am not conscious of ever being wanting in respect for nine years out [of] the Eleven since I first knew your Lordship and [of] the opinion I ever entertained of your honor my conduct gave sufficient proof, and I am also persuaded that I shall never have cause to alter my opinion.

She ended by saying that she knew well how he had relieved the distressed, but he could be assured there was none of them whose affection for him was greater than that of his most obedient humble servant.[1]

It was a situation to be ashamed of, having to take the pitiful reproaches of a woman who felt she had a moral claim on him—though she had not been disinterested. He sent the letter to Hanson, telling him something must be done: '. . . As to *her* annuities we can more easily manage (but I do not wish to commit my friend D[avie]s' name). Do pray contrive something.'[2] His not answering her letters directly was probably on the advice of Hanson who feared that, now he could lawfully do so, he would render himself liable for the debts.

On November 20th, when Byron was at the stage of becoming *persona gratissima* in the exquisite house of Sam Rogers, and was finding the company of Moore and other celebrities most congenial, came one more communication from the déclassée landlady, no longer taking aristocratic lodgers in Piccadilly but a lodger herself in a house where she was being dunned for rent. She had done herself the honour of calling on his Lordship to enquire after his health, and at the same time to say that she knew a gentleman in the country who could supply any sum of money he might want at 5%, and who was now in town. She had heard of this benevolent person 'quite accidental', and hoped his Lordship would not be offended. 'Nothing could grieve me so much as you are the only friend I have in the world.'[3]

Byron must have been under great duress to think of embroiling himself with any lender proposed by Mrs Massingberd, but a mortgage Hanson had thought he could arrange seemed to be falling through, and on December 7th there was a request from his bank, Hammersley's, that he would pay off his overdraft which they found 'particularly inconvenient' at that season, when books were balanced.[4] So he wrote that same day to Hanson:

[1] Egerton 2611.

[2] Ibid. Folio 261. 1 Nov. 1811. It should be explained that, not only were many more letters delivered by hand when servants were in plentiful supply, but the postal traffic in the capital was much more rapid than today. There were no pillar boxes, but postmen went through the principal streets ringing a bell and collecting letters, which, within the London area, were commonly received on the day of dispatch.

[3] Ibid.   [4] Ibid. Folio 274. Hanson paid the sum £267. 10s. 7d. on Dec. 12.

Dear Sir,

    We must come to the point. If your friend cannot furnish ye sum Mrs M's Norwich Gentleman will procure it in a fortnight. Pray let us determine. . . . I must leave town next week.

Yrs truly,

Byron[1]

He was going to Newstead, where he hoped Hanson would join him, to settle the business of the rents, still outstanding. He wrote again on the 13th stressing the need for a positive answer about the loan and saying if it was not forthcoming from Hanson's friend, he must take the securities on himself at all hazards.[2] Two days later, another frantic letter from Mrs Massingberd confirmed his resolution, and he requested the lawyer to arrange the matter with 'the Jews': 'There is nothing else left for it, I cannot allow people to go to Gaol on my account, it is better they should tear my property to pieces, than make me a Scoundrel. The remedy is desperate but so is the disease.' He left this note at Hanson's office where he had called in vain to see him, and he added a postscript: 'Cannot Mrs M. resist on legal grounds? do see & do something for the poor old Soul immediately.'[3]

    To round off here the painful Massingberd story—though its aftermath lasted most of Byron's remaining years—when that feckless woman died in October, 1812, she left her daughter a tangle of her own debts and her liability for the loans so rashly guaranteed. Dunned by the insatiable Howard, Miss Massingberd threw herself on Byron's good nature. She had been advised that her legal rights were nil. Indeed, by the chief creditor's particular wish, Byron's name appeared nowhere in the transactions: to Hanson's disgust, Howard would not even sign a receipt for any payment in which it was mentioned—'for reasons', as Hanson wrote, 'easily to be guessed at'.[4]

    Byron did not take advantage of Miss Massingberd's weak position but made very numerous payments to her both directly and through a Mr Fozard who applied to him on her behalf. In 1813 he sent £50 in answer to an appeal to assist with the medical expenses of her deceased mother, and early in 1814 he managed to produce £1,000 which enabled her to redeem 'those annuity deeds to which her name was affixed'. (Why no settlement ever succeeded in reducing the £3,300 principal could only be fathomed by a 19th-century money-lender.) Fozard promised that, this done, she had no further claim.[5] She wrote several letters acknowledging Byron's 'bountiful' behaviour towards her. The last in the file was

---

[1] Ibid. Folio 269.   [2] Ibid.   [3] Ibid. 15 Dec. 1811.
[4] Murray MS. 28 Dec. 1809.   [5] Ibid. 1 Mar.

on May 29th, 1815, when, after a preamble in which she admitted she was under numerous obligations to his Lordship and had agreed not to give him any further trouble, she 'humbly hoped in all humility'—anticipating Uriah Heep—that she would not be committing an infringement if she suggested that about twelve yards of unused lace bought by her mother abroad, might be purchased by Lady Byron.[1] Lady Byron, so recently married, doubtless had as many clothes as she needed, and liked the minimum of trimming on them, so it is not to be supposed that Byron reopened correspondence with one whose very name must have reminded him of the worst follies of his youth.

Miss Massingberd did not keep her promise to give him no further trouble. Years later, having misapplied the money that should have released her from creditors, she made renewed demands on Byron. He pointed out with displeasure that he had repaid more than the principal and whole legal interest on the sum she had helped to supply.[2] Some of the money-lenders' accounts were still outstanding in 1823, when he had the means to pay them off, but he had become obstinate, taking the line that the treatment he had received from the 'Israelites' had not been such as to encourage indulgence towards them, though he wished to be equitable.

Byron was not, for all these harsh allusions, an anti-Semite. Isaac Nathan, who set his *Hebrew Melodies* to music, wrote that he:

> . . . exhibited a peculiar feeling of commiseration towards the Jews. He was entirely free from the prevalent prejudices against that unhappy and oppressed race of men. On this subject he has frequently remarked, that he deemed the existence of the Jews, as a distinct race of men, the most wonderful instance of the ill effects of persecution. Had they been kindly, or even honestly, dealt with, in the early ages of the dispersion, they might, in his Lordship's opinion, have amalgamated with society, in the same manner as all other sects and parties have done.[3]

The inescapable fact was that, because they were not so amalgamated —and originally under very unpleasant compulsion—a rather conspicuous number of them had taken up the career of finance, either on the grand scale of Rothschild or Montefiore or in the grasping and ignoble way which earned their uncomplimentary nicknames from improvident young men like Byron.

*   *   *   *   *

To return to the close of 1811—the year which had seen his return from marvellously escapist voyages, the deaths of his mother and some

[1] Ibid.   [2] Murray MSS. 30 Dec. 1822 and 9 Apr. 1823.
[3] *Fugitive Pieces and Reminiscences of Lord Byron.*

of his most intimate friends, his preparations for his début as a romantic poet, and his first meetings with men of letters who were also men in fashion— he went at the Christmas season to Newstead in the hope that Hanson would soon be acting upon his repeated plea that the rents should be raised to a level more commensurate with current values.

Hanson did not arrive at the Abbey when expected, the new rents were not fixed, nor had 'the Scotch money' come to hand by January 1812. Byron wrote to say, 'The Creditors are extremely pressing, I mean those exclusive of the Annuities'.[1] This was after spending Christmas with his younger Harrow friend, William Harness, and his older Cambridge friend, Francis Hodgson,[2] all three deep in literary occupations, Byron correcting the final proof of *Childe Harold*, Harness reading divinity for his degree, and Hodgson getting out the *Monthly Review* he edited. Hodgson was not yet ordained, nor did his own mode of living at the time fit him to censure morals. He knew his host was making love to the pretty housemaid, Susan Vaughan, nicknamed Taffy because she was Welsh, but it was kept from young Harness towards whom Byron was always very paternal, and whose recollection of the visit was chiefly how they talked of poets and poetry and discussed religion, with Hodgson passionately trying to demolish Byron's scepticism.

> It was winter—dark, dreary weather—the snow upon the ground; and a straggling, gloomy, depressive, partially inhabited place the Abbey was. Those rooms, however, which had been fitted up for residence were so comfortably appointed, glowing with crimson hangings, and cheerful with capacious fires, that one soon lost the melancholy feeling of being domiciled in the wing of an extensive ruin. Many tales are related or fabled of the orgies which, in the poet's early youth, had made clamorous these ancient halls of the Byrons, I can only say that nothing in the shape of riot or excess occurred when I was there.[3]

It did not need anything in the shape of riot for Byron to creep up to the room Susan shared with another servant, Bessy, and also with little William and George Fletcher, the two sons of the valet, who was now back in his old employment.

Before industry and commerce had opened numerous non-menial

---

[1] Egerton 2611. 4 Jan. 1812.

[2] The Rev. William Harness (1790–1869), a future editor of Shakespeare, Ford, and Massinger, a scholar and a man described by Mary Russell Mitford as of 'varied accomplishments, admirable goodness and kindness' and 'all sorts of amusing peculiarities'. The Rev. Francis Hodgson (1781–1852), Fellow of King's College, a translator and satirist of distinction, endowed with very versatile talents; he became Provost of Eton in 1840.

[3] From the *Life of the Rev. Francis Hodgson*.

occupations to women without means, there were many domestic servants of superior intelligence and refined accomplishments. Richardson's
virtuous Pamela is the archetype; Susan seems to have aspired to be more
like Emma Lyon—or Hart—who began as a nursemaid and rose to be
Lady Hamilton. She could write fluently, if with small help from formal
education; she could report rustic dialogue humorously and acutely;
she could do fine needlework; and she had such a captivating way with
her master that, returning to London, he wrote to her three times on the
journey, beginning in Nottingham whence he sent her a handsome
locket with his hair in it.

Such was his infatuation that her fundamental coarseness seems to
have passed unnoticed among her reiterant assurances of impassioned
devotion:

> Believe me my dear Ld. Byron I have ever been a total stranger to
> *Love* untill now I thought when you were here it was impossible for any body
> to Love more than I did you but in truth I find an *increase* hourly I think of
> nothing nor any person but yourself and content myself a little with saying
> when alone *he loves me for sure* yes I love him sincerely and he loves me in
> return. . . .
>
> In yours from Newport Pagnell you mention the carriage box nearly
> falling I was very glad no accident happened on your account but I'm sure
> I should have laughed to see those two men [? the coachman and the valet]
> rolling in the dirt together don't be angry at my foolishness but I'm certain
> it would divert me more than anything. . . .
>
> I have so often kiss'd and cry'd ever since you left me every thing you
> where [sic] kind enough to give me. . . . My dearest friend you say you
> believe I love you that you have tried everything to win my heart, shall I
> tell you my heart was yours entirely long—long before you gave me any
> proof of your *Love*. In one of your books I found these two lines:
>
>> Many with bad designs will passions faign
>> Who know no love but sordid love of gain.
>
> that's not my love if you will believe me tis you I have placed my affections
> on not on your *welth* I dispise that but your person oh god I doat on it and
> yours I am entirely. . . .
>
> The *kiss* you gave me before you went remains on my lips. . . . I shall
> keep it sacred as you wish untill that happy moment arrives to restore them
> to each other again.[1]

Byron must have smiled at the girl's naïveté in crediting him with
'welth', but he was nearly incapable of conducting even the most
corporeal love affair without strong sentimental feeling. Raffish as he

---

[1] Murray MS. 15 Jan. 1812. Parts of these letters quoted are in *To Lord Byron*
(Quennell & Paston).

liked to sound, he needed to love and to luxuriate in being loved, and, far from treating the housemaid as one with whom he had merely exercised a kind of *droit de seigneur*, he gave himself up to the passion more naïvely in reality than she.

Unwisely, as it was to turn out, instead of confining herself to the endearments which delighted him, she could not resist a little mischief-making, for her conquest, not surprisingly, had turned her head, and she was putting on airs and graces with her fellow servants and seeking to excite her lover's sympathy by representing herself as persecuted.

> I am very distant with all in the house except Bessy for I cannot help seeing their frowns. *Lucy* in particular looks angry at me I observed it one day particularly—I asked her what was amiss knowing I'd done nothing to offend her forgetting how jealous she was. She answered me in a very unbecoming manner, but I took it from whence it came. I knew she was angry and still more ignorant poor thing.

For all this pretence of philosophy, Susan let it be known that she had shed many tears because Lucy had hurt her in a way that could not have happened had her 'dearest friend' been there. Lucy had actually been favoured by his Lordship first, and if she was jealous, so was Susan—though whether she was aware that less than three years ago, Lucy had borne a child by Byron is doubtful. She herself had evidently been in some anxiety, for she ended: 'The pain in my side still keeps bad but I have nothing *on my mind* now.'

Though letters usually took only two days or even less to reach London after being collected from the Hut near the Abbey gates, where the postman called, one of Susan's was delayed, and Byron wrote reproachfully and even suspiciously, while she replied with vehement protestations:

> . . . I can assure you my ever dear Friend that you are never out of my mind ten minutes together you are very cruel. . . . Pray, pray my dearest Friend dont be angry with me as Im not in fault.—Can I not perceive a coolness in this letter of yours that almost Breaks my heart oh god what can I do how Miserable I shall be untill I hear from you again. . . .
>
> You say my dear Ld. B. you must comfort yourself as well as you can I'm very much afraid you are going to *leave me* to do the same.
>
> How can I convince you my—Heart wanders no were but after you I wish I was with you heart self and *all* but I must content myself untill I can see you at Newstead. Oh Newstead I love it for the sake of its owner no tongue can tell how I Love you in short I think I love so much that Love will kill me.
>
> My eyes are very seldom dry and to night in particular I can scarsely see what I write. . . . It is quite impossible to write any more now I'm ready

to die God bless you my dearest dearest and only friend I have and the only one in the whole world I can sincerely love—I love my mother it is true but notwithstanding I must say I love you better or better than all the world besides.

Altho you say I am a true woman I'm perfectly aware of what you mean but even if you put me away from you tomorrow love you I shall for ever and if it please, my dearest Friend I am *yours*—& *yours only* untill you are tired or I die.[1]

Concluding that this must surely pacify him, she followed it next day by a light and pleasant letter 'to make you laugh'. She told him of the gamekeeper, Whitehead, and a labourer sitting at the fireside in deep silence when suddenly one of them, the labourer, broke out in 'the Nottingham talk'—very comical to Susan because she spoke as one who comes from the Welsh mountains:

'Nah Billy Whitehead these be sad times.' He answered with a sigh 'Nah indeed they bee. One dunnot know how to get on.'

'Well, say keeper Billy Whitehead, const thou inform me one thing?'

'Whye, I will if I can.'

'Then it is this. Doest thou know wither *Our me Lord* is gone up to that Lunnon to speech for the goode of the Nation or do thee think he [h]as a Pention out of the house? Why indeede I do not know for I cannot get round it at all—what the meaning of it is.'

'I cannot make out that,' says keeper. . . .

'Thou seest, Billy Whitehead, thee House of Lords and the House of *Peers* be so different, thou must know, that I dont know wether *our me Lord* as a Pention from the House, but, Billy Whitehead, doest thou think me Lord or any other *private gentleman* would go to that Lunnon spending maybe 20 pounds in the time he stays there? God bless us what a sin!'

Whitehead's speeche was as follows. 'I cannot make out what the *voating* means. I dont think they go a-*voating* any where beside only about Nottingham.'

'But I dunnot understand about it.'

'Hap, but I do,' says keeper, 'know all about it. Oh d—m their voating! D—m their voating! If they voat themselves to H—ll they will do no good to *our me Lord*. [He]'s got a *Chair* in the House and they cant get him out on't.'[2]

Byron loved women who made him laugh, and never put up for long with humourless ones. Whatever he had written to the lively Susan to follow his reproaches had fully restored her confidence, and next she

---

[1] Ibid. 18 Jan.

[2] Ibid. Almost all punctuation and paragraphing added. The omission indicated is because either the gamekeeper or Susan fell into a brief confusion. 'Hap' is possibly like the more northerly 'happen'—a sarcastic 'perhaps'.

dispatched a rather too wily letter in which, after declaring her still increasing love, she sought to consolidate her position by reminding him of certain details of their amour. She presented them as an example of the sharpness of little George Fletcher.

> You, of course, have not forgot the night you came up to our room, when I was in bed—the time you locked the door. You woked the boys and ask'd George if he knew you, and he told you he did, which he did indeed, so well that he has not let it slip his memory yet. He is up stairs with me now, and I have been asking him how he come to tell such storys . . . He looks very earnestly at me, and says he: Why, Susan, have you forgot Lord Byron coming to *bed to us*? So I asked him, what about that? Ah, says he, by G—d, if you have forgot it, I have not yet. Don't you remember, Susan, me Lord putting his hand so nicely over your *bosom*? . . . The D———l may have George Fletcher if he did not *kiss* you besides, and Bessy too.
>
> I could not help laughing at him. . . . I told him it was not Ld B. at all. Says he, you must not think to make me believe, Miss Susan, it was any body else, because I know there is no *Dowager Lord*, and D—n him if it was not a Lord that was with us.[1]

The Lord may have been amused at the child's racy turn of speech, but could not have felt very happy to have a scene that Fielding might have written so vividly recalled to him, and it was rash of Susan to follow this at once with insinuations about Lucy and the handsome young page, Rushton:

> I believe I mentioned in another letter how remarkable kind *Lucy* and *Robert* are they cant talk enough about you and me but they are under the necessity of going into—R['s] *Bedroom* so that they may not bee disturb'd in their conversation. It is nothing but Robert my *lad* and Lucy me *lass*. I know still further but you must excuse me saying, besides I should not wish my name to be brought into question about them they may please each other as I dont doubt but they do.

Other hints were dropped. Susan had begun to blunder. Byron wanted to hear how much she 'doated' on his person, not mean little things such as that his page had bought a bit of pork pie for Lucy without offering Susan any. Her interest in Rushton could not have been agreeable to him. When he received another letter written the same day telling him of her passion for him as if she were rebutting a very serious accusation, his suspicion must have been reawakened:

> Is there any occasion for me to assure my dearest friend in this letter how much I *love* Him. Surely you must deem me very very deceitfull and wicked beyond everything to immagine I should tell you so many false

[1] Ibid. 20 Jan.

tales. No I think you are not incapable of perceiving that I tell you no *Lies* I should be very sorry to try to make you believe I love you better than all the World besides if I did not. I do everything I can think of and say all I can to convince you I dont even like any but you.

Of her delayed letter she writes:

> I am very suspicious of *R*. He seems as if he was afraid and frightened every time I mention it. And besides there is so much wispering between Lucy and him that it makes me think they know something of it.

She harps on it and on how frankly she had avowed her love—'mentioned the locket and every thing'. The note of fervour becomes rather hysterical:

> Oh God how I hate all mankind but you My dearest friend your letters I read twenty times in the day if posoble I sleep on your last untill I get another. . . . Oh Lord Byron I love and doat on every thing that is yours. . . . Yes—yes, I am doatingly fond of you my dear friend . . . All I have I could not refuse could I see you I dream of you every night but cannot have a pleasant one I always fancy you are going to kill me. But how sure I am when I awake that you would not hurt me for Kingdoms. . . .

With this letter she sent neck-cloths she had embroidered for him with her own hair worked into the stitching. She had promised to make him a shirt, but the cambric Fletcher had bought 'would not do. 'Twas so very ordinary only fit for pocket handkerchiefs', and she asked that the finest French cambric might be got. She wanted the shirt to remind him of her—his poor friendless Taffy who, she said, was perfectly free from all sin 'except sinning in *Love*':

> Heaven knows its what never was practised by me, from what I have before told you untill I knew you. I dare say you will think I tell you wrong but if you disbelieve my word I have no other way whatever to let you know. Ah if all in this house had as little on their minds in respect to wickedness as I have they would sleep easy. . . .
>
> I know the greatest crime I ever was guilty of and that I never forget in my prayers night and morning to be forgiven that, as it is the real love I have for you makes me consent to everything you ask me. I know I have no power to deny you whatever you could desire me to do, I never shall be able to let you know the love I have for you unless you was to go abroad and take me. Then I'd show you my dear Ld Byron the dangers I'd expose myself to was there occation for you my dear and only friend I have in this world.[1]

She had shown a glimpse of her hand at last. Byron had been talking of going abroad again ever since his return. If she could get him to take

[1] Ibid. The second letter of 20 Jan.

her with him, what a change that would be from doing housework and sleeping in the servants' quarters! What might it not lead to?

It chanced that her birthday fell on the same day as his, January 22nd. She was turning twenty-one, he twenty-four, and she decided to celebrate by giving a party, for which she decorated a cosily furnished hall known as the stone parlour. Her description is radiant:

> But to tell you my ever dearest how very gay I made the room with hanging the Long Ivy carelessly all round the Parlour in drapings. It hung very pretty and very tasty done all about here said it was. The walls w[h]ere scarsely seen for green branches hanging loosely over them and the piller which stands in the middle was dress'd exactly like *Jack in the green*, with every green leaf and sprig I could find. I assure you it really looked very nice and gay. . . .

She had arranged a grand supper for the staff:

> . . . All the *pure virgins* was in white two in particular shining out to see which cut the dash in *gold chains*. Now laugh again, when I tell you how spitefully I look'd at Lucy's and she at mine.

Lucy had also enjoyed what was evidently a customary reward. They had all dressed in their best clothes to honour the day, and there was singing and dancing,

> . . . and three *virgins* had a reel, then it was supper time. The cloath was laid in great stile believe me. I had a spare rib of pork at the top an apple pie at the bottom a pork pie in the middle potatoes at one corner sellery at the other mince pies and custards at the other two corners. After that cheese and the cloth was removed a small table set round with *glasses* and *punch* we had forsooth. Mr Murry drank your health wishing you many happy returns of the day. Three cheers followed. In the next glass little T[affy] the same. . . .
>
> I did not tell you of a nice plum cake. We had more singing and dancing ended this grandure the company dispers'd and I find most pleasure in writing to you my dearest friend. . . . I love you my dearest I understand that perfectly.[1]

This was all very engaging, but it was to be her last carefree letter. In making sly aspersions against Rushton and Lucy, she had released a coiled spring. Byron was annoyed no doubt that Lucy, whom he had once got with child, should be ready to bestow herself on his page, annoyed that Rushton, whom he intended to promote to a stewardship, should seem capable of tampering with letters, and annoyed that Susan should complain or be given any occasion for complaint. Rushton could not have

[1] Ibid. Written in the small hours of Jan. 23.

participated in the birthday supper with the same enjoyment as the others because he had that evening received a rebuke from London, of which the purport was that Susan was not to be '*insulted* by any person over whom I have the smallest controul, or indeed by any one whatever, while I have the power to protect her'. He was urged to leave the women alone and attend to arithmetic, surveying, measuring, 'and making yourself acquainted with every particular relative to the *land* of Newstead, and you will *write* me *one letter every week*, that I may know how you go on'.[1]

Rushton, though only eighteen, was capable of defending himself and had the means of doing so. He conveyed as much, respectfully, by return of post:

> My Honor'd Lord,
> I received your Lordship's letter last night & I feel myself much hurt by your Lordship's stating my refusal to carry Susan's letter. I confess I did not offer to take the letter to the Hut but had she asked me I should not refuse that nor any other thing, the reason I did not offer to take it, there was one missing therefore I did not wish to put myself forward for fear I might be suspected of detaining it.
> Susan is the last *person* I should ever suspect could have lodged any Complaint against *me*, what her motive could be for it I know not, was I in the habit of making Complaints I could say a *good deal*. I hope I am not so remiss in my duty as not to acknowledge with the greatest gratitude every favour I have received from your Lordship's bountiful hands.
> It will ever be my study to oblige and serve so worthy a Master and a sincere Friend for God knows I have but few Friends at Newstead setting aside my own family. I will do the best in my power to instruct myself during your Lordship's absence.
> I remain Your Lordship's sincere and Dutiful Servant
> Robt. Rushton.[2]

Upon this hint, the youth was speedily commanded to disclose forthwith what relations there were between him and the housemaid.

> I have not been without some suspicion on the subject, and at your time of life, the blame could not attach to you. You will not *consult* any one as to your answer, but write to me immediately.[3]

Besides information, Rushton must have sent a letter of Susan's proving her infidelity.[4] Byron was appalled. In writing to Moore on January 29th, within a day of hearing this news, he put his mortifying discovery before any other topic, saying he was in 'a ludicrous state of

---

[1] Moore. 21 Jan.   [2] Murray MS. 23 Jan.   [3] Moore. 25 Jan.
[4] See Appendix 6, 'Byron and his Young Servants'.

tribulation'. Moore gives us the account in his own all too circumspect words and censors Byron's. But Byron took the precaution—very rare with him—of keeping a copy of what he wrote to Susan, which survives in the Lovelace Papers. It shows how wonderfully open and ingenuous he remained. Even at twenty-four, and with a fair experience of women, he was quite unable to dissemble:

> *8 St. James's Street,*
> *January 28th, 1812.*
>
> I write to bid you farewell, not to reproach you. The enclosed papers, *one in your own handwriting* will explain every thing. I will not deny that I have been attached to you, & I am now heartily ashamed of my weakness. —You may also enjoy the satisfaction of having deceived me most completely, & rendered me for the present sufficiently wretched. From the first I told you that the continuance of our connection depended on your own conduct.— All is over.—I have little to condemn on my own part, but credulity; you threw yourself in my way, I received you, loved you, till you became worthless, & now I part from you with some regret, & without resentment.—I wish you well, do not forget that your own misconduct has bereaved you of a friend, of whom nothing else could have deprived you. Do not attempt explanation, it is useless, I am *determined*, you cannot deny your handwriting; return to your relations, you shall be furnished with the means, but *him*, who now addresses you for the last time, you will never see again.—
>
>   Byron.
>
> God bless you!

What other young man, made to look ridiculous in the eyes of his household, would have thus admitted to having been deceived and rendered miserable? If Byron had been the man of the world he always tried to appear—at least with other men of the world—would he not have had the girl packed off without a word to salve her vanity? Packed off she was, but he did not pretend he had not been hurt. It was that generous candour that explains his fast hold on his friends.

Attacked with severe pain and illness on returning to his London quarters, and told (erroneously) he had stone in the kidney, he wrote to Hodgson, on February 16th:

> If the stone had got into my heart instead of my kidneys, it would have been all the better. The women are gone to their relations, after many attempts to explain what was already too clear. However, I have quite recovered *that* also, and only wonder at my folly in excepting my own strumpets from the general corruption—albeit a two months' weakness is better than ten years. I have one request to make, which is, never to mention a woman again in any letter to me, or even allude to the existence of the sex.[1]

---

[1] Moore.

If only he had been a little more subtle about women, he might have realized it was probably the sheer heady excitement of her situation that had caused Susan to behave so badly. Several short poems reflect his disillusionment and his various ways of trying to cope with it, and disclose how much more important it was to him than has generally been estimated. The first, as I judge it to be, seems not to have been reprinted since 1904:

> There is no more for me to hope,
>   There is no more for thee to fear—
> And if I give my sorrow scope
>   That sorrow thou shalt never hear.
>   Why did I hold thy love so dear?
>   Why shed for such a heart one tear?
>   Let deep and dreary silence be
>   My only memory of thee.
>
> When all are fled who flatter now
>   Save thoughts which will not flatter then,
> And thou recallst thy broken vow
>   To him who must not love again,
>   Each hour of now forgotten years
>   Thou, then, shalt number with thy tears,
>   And every drop of grief will be
>   A vain remembrancer of me.[1]

In Susan's first letter to him, on January 12th, she had quoted from some poem with the refrain:

> And my true faith can alter never,
> Tho' thou art gone perhaps for ever.

This naturally invited sarcasm, and from the poet's deeply ingrained literal-mindedness we learn that she had already lapsed before the birthday supper, because he had left Newstead on January 11th and he comments on her vaunted fidelity, 'Indeed it lasted for a week', and:

> Seven days & nights of single sorrow!
>   Too much for human constancy!
> A fortnight past—why, then tomorrow,
>   His turn is come to follow me.[2]

These light verses reveal the extraordinary mobility of his moods, for they are dated in the Lovelace fair copy 'January 1812' and so must have

[1] The verses appear in Vol. VII of *Poetry* from a fair copy in the Murray MSS, but the rough draft is in the Lovelace Papers with the drafts of the other Susan poems.
[2] In *Poetry* Vol. III from a Murray MS. This is taken from Byron's own copy in the Lovelace Papers.

been composed within a day or two at most of those gloomily vindictive ones in which he pictures her deserted and remorseful. Here he accepts his rebuff in good part:

> Adieu fair thing! without upbraiding
> I fain would take a decent leave.
> Thy beauty still survives unfading
> And undeceived may long deceive.

The allusion to her beauty is supported by a cancelled line in the stanzas previously quoted, 'Why read thy soul in that sweet face?' It may be assumed that she was an unusually prepossessing girl, and, following the example of his immediate predecessor at Newstead, who had lived with a servant and tried to leave her all he possessed,[1] Byron might have been well content with such a mistress if her own artfulness had not undone her.

He was to allow himself one relapse into bitterness, though with a humorous cynicism not found in the first outburst, and we may judge from these quatrains how far he was from thinking of himself as a man with a special power over women. But the fact is, he was a very provocative lover, frequently putting his mistresses on the defensive by playing upon jealousy. He had done that with Susan who, in one of her letters, asks whether he had yet met a pretty girl that he preferred to her. 'You once told me that it should bee so.'[2] Infidelity is often a form of insurance against being 'planted' by the other person, and Byron must have brought upon himself some of the 'betrayals' he is here lamenting:

ON THE SAME

> Again beguiled! again betrayed!
> In manhood as in youth
> The slave of every smiling maid
> That ever 'lied like truth'.

> Well, dearly was each lesson bought,
> The present as the past,
> What Love some twenty times has taught
> We needs must learn at last.

---

[1] Betty Hardstaff was the intended beneficiary under the 5th Lord Byron's will made in 1785. He refers to the bequest as a 'recompense for her long and faithful service'. This will was proved in 1798, but he had little that was not entailed upon the heir to the title. 'Lady Betty' was still alive in 1829, and in need of financial assistance. Augusta Leigh called her 'that dear old Woman', and was anxious but probably unable to help her. She alludes to 'Lady Betty's' son as her own 'reputed cousin'—i.e. begotten by the 5th Lord. (Correspondence in the Roe-Byron Collection, Newstead Abbey.)

[2] Murray MS. 20 Jan. 1812.

> In turn deceiving or deceived
>> The wayward Paphian roves,
> Beguiled by her we most believed,
>> Or leaving her who loves.
>
> Oh thou! for whom my heart must bleed,
>> From whom this anguish springs,
> Thy Love was genuine love indeed,
>> And showed it in his wings.
>
> And would'st thou not prolong thy stay,
>> Fair source of all my Sorrow?
> Oh, had thy Love outlived today—
>> My own had fled tomorrow.[1]

He did not publish this, and another was so poor that he left it in a state too rough for copying. In this last one, Susan's name is changed to Genevieve, to whom he bids adieu hoping that the next man she deceives will be less in earnest than he himself was; and, in asking for a farewell kiss, he tells her that smiles become her much better than treacherous tears.[2]

This was apparently his final attempt to express his sense of either grief or wry amusement at his treatment by one who was better fitted to be the soubrette in a comedy than 'a maker and unmaker of beds'.[3] The pang had been sharp, certainly much sharper than any he felt over her successor, Lady Caroline Lamb: even the obtuse Dallas noticed the strongly misanthropic feelings he had developed against women: but other business was pressing upon him—the awful debts, the impending publication, the renewal of recently formed London friendships, and above all, the preparation of his maiden speech, delivered on February 27th.

It was flattering to be in consultation about this with the great Whig, Lord Holland; flattering and a little embarrassing because that nobleman had been one of the victims of his satire; worse still, the reckless satirist had sneered at Lord Holland's formidable wife. Nevertheless, he— Holland—had the condescension (the word is Dallas's) to call on the young peer at his St. James's Street lodging.

> I happened to be there at the time [writes Dallas], and I thought it a curious event. Lord Byron evidently had an awkward feeling on the occasion, from a conscious recollection, which did not seem to be participated by his visitors. Lord Holland's age, experience, and other acquired distinctions, certainly, in point of form, demanded that the visit should have been

---

[1] Lovelace Papers. Byron's own fair copy, with slight adjustment of punctuation.
[2] Ibid.   [3] Byron's phrase to Hodgson. 25 Sept. 1811.

paid at his house. This I am confident Lord Byron at that time would not have done; though he was greatly pleased that the introduction took place. . . .[1]

Byron at once set about suppressing at his own expense the fifth edition of *English Bards and Scotch Reviewers,* which was nearly ready to appear. This turned out unpredictably very much to his advantage, because it was to have been accompanied by a new work, *Hints from Horace,* generally reckoned to be his least entertaining composition, which would surely have detracted from *Childe Harold's* triumph had it come out at anywhere near the same time.

Being Recorder of Nottingham, Lord Holland had a special interest in the riots around that area, where weavers, desperate for work, were going about in gangs breaking up the newly installed stocking-frames capable of replacing a large proportion of hand labour. Numerous troops had been sent to deal with the situation, and Lord Liverpool was introducing a Bill to the Lords under which frame-breaking was made punishable by death, and those whose machinery was broken were to be under legal compulsion to lay information. It speaks much for Byron's lively interest in public affairs that, even when he was so absorbed in private ones, he had found time to gather plentiful information about this uprising. He decided on this as the subject for his address.

Lord Holland had sent him a letter from a Nottingham resident seemingly intended for his guidance. Byron showed his independence—though modestly—in a courteous reply:

> . . . I have read it with attention, but do not think I shall venture to avail myself of its contents, as my view of the question differs in some measure from Mr Coldham's. . . . For my own part, I consider the manufacturers [factory hands] as a much injured body of men, sacrificed to ye views of certain individuals who have enriched themselves by those practices which have deprived the frame-workers of employment. For instance;— by the adoption of a certain kind of frame, 1 man performs ye work of 7—6 are thus thrown out of business . . . Surely, my Lord, however we may rejoice in any improvement in ye arts which may be beneficial to mankind, we must not allow mankind to be sacrificed to improvements in Mechanism. . . .
>
> The few words I shall venture to offer on Thursday will be founded upon these opinions formed from my own observation on ye spot . . .

With the deference free from sycophancy which gives his letters to distinguished seniors their peculiarly attractive quality, he added:

> I believe your Lordship does not coincide with me entirely on this subject, & most cheerfully & sincerely shall I submit to your superior

[1] *Recollections.*

judgment & experience, & take some other line of argument against ye bill, or be silent altogether. . . .[1]

Lord Holland with some misgiving left him to express his protest in his own way, and it was just as well because he had already written and rehearsed it. Everyone had prophesied he would be an orator—his mother, his Harrow headmaster, his solicitor, and several friends—and we cannot doubt when we read his elaborately wrought speech that he had some notion of making his mark in the sphere which to many was the goal of all ambition. A striking composition it is, humane, courageous, full of good sense yet not lacking the rhetoric then so much admired in oratory. The fact that he wrote it out in full does not mean that he read it. Having a remarkable memory, he had got it more or less by heart and used only a list of twenty-two numbered headings which form an excellent mnemonic.[2]

In a disarming beginning, he admitted having few acquaintances in that assembly '. . . a stranger, not only to this House in general, but to almost every individual whose attention I presume to solicit,' but later he made the most of his prestigious travels:

> I have traversed the seat of war in the Peninsula; I have been in some of the most oppressed provinces of Turkey; but never, under the most despotic of infidel governments, did I behold such squalid wretchedness as I have seen since my return in the very heart of a Christian country.

There were passages which must have made him seem little less than a firebrand:

> You call these men a mob, desperate, dangerous, and ignorant. . . . But even a mob may be better reduced to reason by a mixture of conciliation and firmness, than by additional irritation and redoubled penalties.
>
> Are we aware of our obligations to a *mob*? It is the mob that labour in your fields, and serve in your houses—that man your navy, and recruit your army —that have enabled you to defy all the world—and can also defy you, when neglect and calamity have driven them to despair. You may call the people a mob, but do not forget that a mob too often speaks the sentiments of the people.

The peroration was a *tour de force*, and rather too forceful to be acceptable to the Tory sponsors of the bill or even the Opposition which, though of more liberal sentiments, were very timid of radicalism.

---

[1] 51639. Holland House Papers. 25 Feb. 1812.

[2] Lovelace Papers. He used a similar but less carefully written prompting device for his next speech, in favour of Catholic Emancipation. Both sets of notes have wrappers in Lady Byron's writing certifying their origin.

But suppose it passed [the Bill], suppose one of these men, as I have seen them meagre with famine, sullen with despair, careless of a life which your Lordships are perhaps about to value at something less than the price of a stocking-frame; suppose this man surrounded by those children for whom he is unable to procure bread at the hazard of his existence, about to be torn for ever from a family which he lately supported in peaceful industry, and which it is not his fault that he can no longer so support; suppose this man—and there are ten thousand such from whom you may select your victims,— dragged into court to be tried for this new offence, by this new law,—still there are two things wanting to convict and condemn him, and these are, in my opinion, twelve butchers for a jury, and a Jefferies for a judge!

Byron's own impression was that his début had been a success, and as he never shrank from acknowledging failure, we may believe his elation was justified. Of his delivery, he himself says it was 'loud & fluent enough, perhaps a little theatrical'; and we may guess it had rather too much self-consciousness from his writing, 'I spoke very violent sentences with a sort of modest impudence'.[1] Dallas, in his *Recollections*, says that, when rehearsing the speech, 'he altered the natural tone of his voice, which was sweet and round, into a formal drawl, and he prepared his features for a part'. However, though Dallas ceased to be a toady when Byron dropped the practice of presenting him with valuable copyrights, and became retrospectively most critical, he admits that the address 'produced a considerable effect in the House of Lords, and he received many compliments from the Opposition Peers'.

What is surprising is that, just as there had been no one but Dallas to watch him take his seat in the Upper House three years before, so there was no one but Dallas—at least no one then known to him—to listen from the Visitors' Gallery to his first utterances there. Why Hobhouse, just back from Ireland, Hanson, Rogers, Moore and all the other old and new acquaintances were absent—that is a question I can only answer on the supposition that prior notice as to the exact day and time when Lord Liverpool would introduce the Bill may have been very short. Dallas was always at hand.

Another question about this famous speech may arise in the minds of readers who are observant of dates. Byron's Christmas visit to Nottinghamshire lasted just over three weeks. There is not the slightest reason to believe that, in snowy winter weather, writing, entertaining two guests, and wooing the housemaid, he made any sortie from the Abbey to investigate the privations of the unemployed weavers or to see their depredations on the new frames in the widely scattered premises where they were installed. We must conclude that he read the local papers

[1] Marchand, *Letters*. To Hodgson, 5 Mar. 1812.

attentively and brought his imagination and compassion to bear on the plight of the angry poor.

He never really had much contact with the labouring classes, nor, apart from some professional persons, including actors, painters and writers, with any class except his own and those who ministered to it— admittedly a numerous body. But he was profoundly interested, and his desire to understand the lives of an immense variety of people, from London pugilists to Mussulman soldiers, from a society hostess to an ancient Italian beggar woman, is so manifest as to cast doubt on his reputed egoism. He was selfish but not self-absorbed, nor did his selfishness preclude great generosity, and especially to ingrates.

The sanctimonious Dallas, reasonably successful as an author, knew him to be enmeshed by money-lenders and yet was willing to accept the total proceeds of his work, not to speak of having had a sizeable slice of what the money-lenders had provided. Byron may have indulged in high-flown notions about not taking payment for poetry, but it would not have been beyond the powers of a well-disposed older friend to persuade him to do justice to some of those creditors who were not 'of the tribes of Israel'. Dallas himself was certainly in debt—John Murray, who disliked him, was obliged once that year to release him from bailiffs without Byron's knowledge—but we may suspect he could have managed with something less than every penny of the fees for *Childe Harold* and, later on, *The Corsair*; or at least he need not have written in a grating and minatory tone demanding more such gifts when they were no longer accorded him.

The first presentation copy of *Childe Harold* appears to be the one Byron sent to Lord Holland on March 5th together with an unassuming letter in which he apologized gracefully for what he had uttered in 'boyish rashness' in his satire. The book had been announced for March 1st but was not yet on sale. From almost the hour when it was obtainable it had a sensational success, although only five hundred copies were originally printed. Not only did the population of Britain amount to less than a quarter of its present size (about 11,000,000 including Scotland) but that section of it which could read and purchase books was proportionately smaller still, while the book trade was kept at arm's length until the publisher organized a special sale for them; so that five hundred meant as much as, perhaps, five thousand today.

The retail price, with binding in boards only, was £1. 10s., while the total cost of the edition was little more than £260, plus £19. 13s. 6d. spent on advertising.[1] Reprinting began at once. In September 1812 John

---

[1] Murray Account Book.

Murray was writing 'the demand proceeds with undiminished vigour. I have now sold, within a few copies, 4,500 in less than six months',[1] which he said was unprecedented except in one instance—probably a work of Scott's. A few weeks later, he was even more triumphant, having just had his 'trade sale' when 878 copies of the fifth edition were ordered on one day.[2]

He had invested the £600 fee magnificently and was prepared next time to go still higher. (Scott said that when he received £1,000 for *Marmion,* it was a price 'that made men's hair stand on end'.)

To the Rt. Honble. Lord Byron   1813 Nov[r] 17 Wednesday Night
    6 Bennet Street
        St. James's
My Lord,
    I am very anxious that our business transactions should occur frequently and that they should be settled immediately. For short accounts are favourable to long friendships. I restore the Giaour to your Lordship entirely—and for it—the Bride of Abydos—and the miscellaneous poems intended to fill up the small edition—I beg leave to offer your Lordship the sum of One Thousand Guineas—and I shall be happy if your Lordship perceive that my estimation of your talents in my character of a man of business is not very much under my admiration of them as a man.
    I do most heartily accept [your] offer to me of your Lordship's portrait, as the most noble mark of friendship with which your Lordship could in any way honour me. I do assure your Lordship that I am truly proud of being distinguished [and] that it will be [my] anxious desire as your publisher and my endeavour to preserve through life the happiness of your Lordship's confidence.
                     I shall ever continue
                         Your Lordship's faithful Servant
                            John Murray.[3]

    Could any author of twenty-five years old ever have had a more flattering letter from a publisher? And his personal success was comparable. The fashionable world was then closely knit and, when literary and social attractiveness were combined in one author, the word spread swiftly. News of Byron's romantic attributes, from his ruined Abbey to his good looks, had been building up. His rank was, of course, contributory. '. . . In no class whatever is the advantage of being noble more felt and appreciated than among nobles themselves', wrote Moore—who knew

---

[1] Murray MS. Letter of 7 Sept. 1812.   [2] Ibid. 22 Oct. 1812.
[3] Murray Letter Book. The portrait Byron presented is the one by Thomas Phillips R.A. which still hangs above the fireplace where his Memoirs were burned. He paid a hundred guineas for it.

what he was talking about. 'The effect', he summed up, 'was accordingly electric;—his fame had not to wait for any of the ordinary gradations, but seemed to spring up, like the palace of a fairy tale, in a night.'

How Byron reacted to all this phenomenal acclaim is a matter of history—and, still more, of legend. Biographies, novels, films, television productions, plays, have told the story. I will not tell it again, at least not the side of it that inspires dramatic writers. And yet there was drama even in what could not appeal to a playwright.

At almost the same time that he became renowned, his mother's estate was at last wound up and yielded him about £4,500, while Hobhouse made peace with his father and was able to repay upwards of £1,300. Byron had urgent occasion for any funds that came his way, but he did not omit to send Mrs Massingberd £150. The cheque was dated March 5th, so the same messenger who carried his volume to the very grand library at Holland House may also have been taking relief to the unhappy ex-landlady at Brompton. On March 2nd and 24th, he was able to pay off £244. 10s. interest on the large loan from Scrope Davies,[1] who had been almost in despair a few months before about his friend's apparent neglect, and had written pleading with him to hurry on a deal for disposing of Rochdale:

> For God's sake do not inflict murder on one who has been guilty of kindness only towards you. Under my present anxiety existence is intolerable—I cannot sleep—and much fear madness. Mr Hanson says there is nothing to pay the interest of the annuities—why not tell me this? Write to me immediately or you shall hear of such things 'the day would quake to look on'.[2]

This was Scrope's mock-melodramatic way of being very much in earnest. He complained of having nothing at all to substantiate his claim should Byron die, so he must have signed his bond for the money with a light-hearted informality that could not be sustained when luck at the tables deserted him.

Two cheques with a total of nearly £140 went to Ross & Co. to settle debts incurred at Gibraltar, £20 of it being for the payment of servants. Byron did not need loans on his outward journey, being still in funds, so the borrowing must have been done hastily on the voyage home, when the ship touched at the Rock for water and fresh provisions. It will be remembered that, even so, he arrived without money to proceed from port!

---

[1] All cheque transactions are noted from bank books and stubs in the Murray MSS. I conclude that the payments to Scrope Davies were interest because the whole of the original loan was cleared on Mar. 28th 1814.

[2] Egerton 2611. Folio 291, undated.

Some old debts were settled or partly settled, but some were at all times curiously ignored. Much of his slackness may be ascribed to Hanson, whose management of most of Byron's financial affairs, both before he came of age and during his two years absence from England, was, as I have tried to show, lazy and inefficient. But Byron's continued extravagance must have created a vicious circle—Hanson negligent because his client was such a hopeless spendthrift, Byron a spendthrift because Hanson was so negligent. Something, however, is to be allowed for the climate of debt in which not only he but almost all members of the upper classes lived, from the Prince Regent and his ducal brothers downwards, a condition which inevitably spread out to the tradesmen who catered for them, the servants who waited on them, and the many who imitated them. And it must be recognized that 1812 was an extraordinary year which would have proved overwhelming to a much steadier young man than Byron.

Success did not go to his head in the sense of making him conceited about his work—that was never the case—or distant with intimate friends, such as Hodgson, to whom he was unboundedly generous, or Hobhouse, whom he eagerly drew into the circles where he now had entrée; but it did reduce his tolerance of clinging bores like Dallas, and it did give him an image it was impossible to live up to without considerable expense.

Dallas, whose endeavour to cash in on Byron's death as he had done on his talents during life I have related elsewhere, used him in his *Recollections* as a peg on which to hang his own moralizings and the tale, somewhat exaggerated, of his part in fostering the poet's career: but his account of how Byron yielded to society, after at first holding aloof, is doubtless true.

> Though flattery had now deeply inoculated him with its poison, he was at first unwilling to own its effects even to himself; and to me he declared that he did not relish society, and was resolved never to mix with it. He made no resistance, however, to invitations, and in a very short time he not only willingly obeyed the summons of fashion, but became a votary. One evening, seeing his carriage at the door in St. James's Street, I knocked, and found him at home. He was engaged to a party, but it was not time to go, and I sat nearly an hour with him. . . . He talked of the parties he had been at, and of those to which he was invited, and confessed an alteration in his mind; 'I own', said he, 'I begin to like them'.

Dallas was naturally shocked. The quarry he had hunted, gaining his acquaintance by flattering letters (he was the brother of a long-dead aunt by marriage whom Byron had never met) was escaping him to fall to the pursuit of ambitious hostesses—and enjoying it!

About this time Lord Byron began, I cannot say to be cool,—for cool to me he never was,—but I thought to neglect me; and I began to doubt whether I had most reason to be proud of, or to be mortified by, my connexion and correspondence with him.

The pain arising from the mortification in this change was little, compared to that which I felt in the disappointment of my hope, that his success would elevate his character, as well as raise his fame.

A great deal of the bitterness to be read between the lines, and often *in* the lines, of Dallas's sour and self-exalting book was due to his resentment with Byron for selling Newstead Abbey, which otherwise would have become the seat of his nephew, Captain George Anson Byron, who succeeded to the title, and whose character was perfectly suited to the taste of the pompous Pharisee who stated that, by writing *Don Juan*, the poet had alloyed 'his gold ore with the filthy dross of impure metal'.

It was in August 1812, the *annus mirabilis*, that Hanson got his way and, forced by difficulties, Byron, with immense reluctance, consented to put his ancestral home, so linked with his pride, on the market. It was offered by auction at Garroway's Coffee House. Dallas, of course, was there, and so was Hobhouse, who 'in a complete fever' raised the bidding to a hundred and thirteen thousand guineas, though he had only a trifle more than one guinea in the world.[1] But it was unavailing. Byron had fixed £120,000 as the lowest price he would take, and the property was bought in.

---

[1] Broughton, *Recollections*.

5

Steps towards Exile

Byron spent the best part of the next four years in London, with brief visits to resorts such as Cheltenham and Tunbridge Wells, and spells of work and social pleasure at country houses of the kind Felicia Hemans called The Stately Homes of England, putting a phrase into the language. Until his marriage he went occasionally to Newstead Abbey, but primarily he had become a Londoner, and a particularly urbane one, living first in St. James's Street, then at Bennet Street not far off, next at Albany in the most desirable of bachelor quarters, and finally and fatally among the splendours of the Duchess of Devonshire's house in Piccadilly Terrace, an extravagance for which his bride's aunt, Lady Melbourne, must be blamed, she having done their house-hunting, though it was Hobhouse who, at Byron's request, acted as intermediary.

The London of the Regency was immeasurably different from the vast conglomerate city we know today. Only about one-seventh of its present size—though it seemed immense then—it must have struck every traveller by its dedication to modern improvements. Very extensive parts of it were in the process of being laid out, according to harmonious and far-sighted town-planning, in streets, squares, and terraces designed by architects whose names are honoured to this day even while much of their work is destroyed or overshadowed by cheaply constructed tower blocks—Humphrey Repton, James and Decimus Burton, Sir John Soane, Sir Robert Smirke, the Wyatts, and John Nash. In the words of a contemporary enthusiast:

> Among the glories of this age, the historians will have to record the conversion of dirty alleys, dingy courts and squalid dens of misery and crime, almost under the walls of our royal palaces, into 'stately streets', to 'squares that court the breeze', to palaces and mansions, elegant private dwellings, to rich and costly shops, filled with the productions of every clime, to magnificent ware rooms, stowed with the ingenious and valuable manufactures of our artisans and mechanics, giving activity to commerce with all the

enviable results of national prosperity. Fields, that were in our times appropriated to pasturage, are now become gay and tasteful abodes of splendid opulence, and of the triumphs of the peaceful arts. . . .

Such works not only attract great and wealthy foreigners, but at the same time they increase commerce, create wealth, give employment to the labourer, the artisan and the artist; and make people love their native country. . . .[1]

Much was then razed to the ground that we may grieve not to have seen, but the Hogarthian lanes inhabited by poverty, drunkenness, and dirt, were opened out into wide roads with buildings of handsome symmetry. Those developments of the industrial revolution which ultimately replaced the old slums with new ones had not yet come about, and if we have reason to regret the open fields that were covered over with bricks and mortar, we must admit that never was such a transformation made more tactfully and gracefully.

The greatest single feature in the programme of public works, surpassing anything attempted in Britain until that time, was only embryonic in the year of *Childe Harold*, the changing of Mary-le-Bone Park, a marshy piece of agricultural land, into 'the Regent's Park', a spacious, beautifully landscaped garden surrounded by Nash's noble terraces. A fine canal designed by Le Notre ran about halfway round (a stretch of it has now been filled in to make a car and motor-coach park). It was part of a network of canals carrying freight all over England. The barges moved slowly, no faster than a horse pulling a tow rope could walk, but they were noiseless—except for the bargees' notorious language—and they kept heavy and dirty cargoes, such as coal, off the roads. For half-a-crown people of modest means could make a return journey from Paddington to the market town of Uxbridge sixteen miles away in a brightly painted barge where musicians played while a cold collation was served. 'This mode of travelling is the pleasantest imaginable,' says a guidebook[2] of 1813.

Byron's activities were mostly in the West End, but he must have observed the northerly building in progress, because to get to the Great North Road, on which he started his drives to Nottingham, he had to pass through the Regent's Park district to Camden Town and the almost rural suburbs of Hampstead and Highgate. He must also have seen the beginning of Nash's masterpiece, Regent Street, of which I saw the ending in 1922.

There was some primitive lighting by gas, but Byron ignores it describing London in *Don Juan* (Canto XI):

[1] James Elmes, *Metropolitan Improvements.*   [2] By Langley and Belch.

   The line of lights too, up to Charing Cross,
    Pall Mall, and so forth, have a coruscation
   Like gold as in comparison to dross,
    Matched with the Continent's illumination. . . .

A little guidebook of 1818, *City Scenes*, claims:

> Perhaps the streets of no city in the world are so well lighted as those of
> London, there being lamps on each side of the way, but a few yards distant
> from each other. It is said that a foreign ambassador happening to enter
> London in the evening, after the lamps were lighted, was so struck with the
> brilliancy of the scene, that he imagined the streets had been illuminated
> expressly in honour of his arrival.

This would apply only to fashionable thoroughfares, for the same
author mentions 'the link-boys, always on the watch, with their large
torches, at dark crossings and lanes, to light passengers through them.
They deserve the reward of a few halfpence, from those whom they assist'.
The outsides of houses glimmered with lantern-light. Within, there were
only candles in the major rooms. Lamp oil was too malodorous to be used
anywhere but in the stables and the backstairs quarters.

 What with the mud where there were no cobblestones, and the ordure
of a multitude of horses—eagerly collected for sale by scavengers—the
services of the crossing-sweeper were as welcome as those of the link-boy.
Working women, a numerous class, wore tall pattens to keep their feet
out of the dirt, but gentlewomen, who favoured kid or satin escarpines,
had to take care to alight from their conveyances close to the pavements.
Besides the link-boys and crossing-sweepers, there were children in every
stage of poverty, earning, begging, or stealing their bread—mendicants,
tumblers, singers, flower girls and match girls, little chimney sweeps
with blackened faces, news boys, post boys, and long files of 'charity
children', male and female, being herded to their various churches. If
religion enjoined charity, it also taught that nothing could happen on
earth except by the will of an all-knowing, all-seeing God, so even the
least callous were able to reconcile themselves to the sight of—

   The little beggar in the street
   Who wanders with his naked feet,
   And has not where to lay his head. . . .

convinced that there was a divine purpose in it. In the districts belonging
to the upper classes, parish beadles chased such unsightly ragamuffins out
of view.

 London was divided, as now, into the City of Westminster, which
contained all the fashionable world, and 'the City' itself—London City

where commerce flourished, where there were wharves, docks, ware-houses, and shipping, the Custom House, the markets of Billingsgate and Smithfield, the Rag Fair where out-of-date finery could be bought by the poor, the Inns of Court, several prisons, the Royal Exchange, the Bank of England, the East India House, major source of the nation's imported riches, and the sumptuous but dark Mansion House, residence of the Chief Magistrate, the Lord Mayor.

The classes who drew their income from inherited land, agricultural or comprising collieries and mines, looked down with the most blatant snobbery on those whose revenue was mercantile. They sneered at them in novels and fashion journals, and they kept them at arm's length socially—unless a city family had wealth so great that a daughter's dowry could purchase entrée to the *beau monde* and sometimes an aristocratic marriage. Such heiresses were called 'golden dollies', and there is probably one somewhere in the pedigree of every noble house which has retained its possessions. It might have been well for Byron if he had put himself in the way of meeting a few, for such unions often worked out to the satis-faction of both parties.

As it was, he seldom went to the City except to see his solicitor in Chancery Lane, and occasionally to dine with him and his family, and from the time of becoming acquainted with John Murray in 1811, to visit Fleet Street. (The firm did not move to Albemarle Street till September 1812.) Several times he went to see Leigh Hunt in the Surrey Prison, Horsemonger Lane, taking with him gifts of books which he carried under his arm instead of letting his footman bring them in as etiquette preferred, and little dreaming that one day this kindness would be interpreted as cunning flattery—'for he could see very well that I had more value for lords than I supposed'. Hunt was equally far from realizing that a man—a Lord—who had been presented to the Prince Regent and found him exceedingly gracious, needed moral courage to call on one who was in gaol for libelling him.

Whether because of the Prince's unpopularity or his own ingratiating manners, or both, Hunt had succeeded in getting uniquely favourable treatment from the prison authorities—a private room decorated to his own taste and arranged with his furniture, books and ornaments, a little garden with flowers and trellises, his family to live with him, and a succession of visitors till ten at night. What was especially gratifying to him was that he was spared a noise which, for the first few weeks, had disturbed him, the clanking of the chains of the less privileged felons, the sound of which, as he explained in his autobiography, 'wore upon my spirits in a manner to which my state of health allowed me reasonably to object'. He might have considered that it wore upon the spirits of the fettered prisoners even more, but that thought did not occur to him—only such reflections as: 'Doubtless the good hours and simple fare of the prison contributed to make the blood of the inmates run better, particularly those who were forced to take exercise.' He meant on the treadmill.

There was a hangover of brutality from the 18th century, yet it was not a brutal age but one of great aspirations towards humane ideals; and we may read hundreds of letters of Byron and his friends without finding one sentence to upset the most squeamish. Indeed, it is *they* who might be aghast at what we can stomach in the 20th century. One death in a duel then created a greater sensation than twenty in a bomb outrage today. The wars on the Continent were horrible, but, except for taxation and high prices, the civilian in Britain was little engaged. So free from rabid nationalism were the members of educated society that it was possible to admire openly, however misguidedly, the arch-enemy Napoleon without being interned or ostracized. For those who were ready to pay the necessary lip service to the Divine Will that appointed everything in the universe for the ultimate benefit of the Supreme Being's supreme creation, Man, the world was about as comfortable as it has ever been—more comfortable, naturally, for the rich than the poor, but when and where is that not so?

For the Londoner it was a much lovelier world than we have known. The countryside all round was several miles nearer, and there was more of it to enjoy, with not nearly so many disfigurements. Watermen, whose pride was the neatness of their little boats, plied up and down the Thames, and on festive occasions there were aquatic processions and bands of music playing in gilded barges. In the streets there was none but equine traffic, and many splendid vehicles and horses could be seen as well as some sorry ones. Pleasure gardens and tea gardens abounded, and those at Vauxhall on the river at Lambeth, lighted by fifteen thousand variegated lamps, were both popular and fashionable. On all fine summer evenings, the entertainments concluded with a grand display of fireworks.

Cold weather brought a gloomy change. Almost every chimney of every house, shop, office would be belching smoke, creating grime and fog such as we are beginning to forget. That is one of the things Byron recalled most vividly about London—

> The Sun went down, the smoke rose up, as from
>   A half-unquenched volcano . . .
>
> A mighty mass of brick, and smoke, and shipping,
>   Dirty and dusky . . .[1]

---

[1] *Don Juan.* Canto XI, Stanzas LXXXI and LXXXII.

There was ceaseless noise too, not only the clatter of horses' hoofs and steel-trimmed wheels on cobblestones, but the handbells of town crier, postman, dustman, pieman, muffin man, and the raucous cries of street vendors making a din that began early in the morning with the milk-woman's yodelled 'Milk below, maids!', the pathetic wail of the climbing boy's 'Sw-e-e-p! Sw-e-e-p!', the watercress girl's 'Buy my water cresses!' (for some reason it was pronounced 'creeses'), the weariful 'Knives to grind! Scissors to grind! Razors to grind!' of the man with the whetstone. Besides the London cries, the watchman's voice intoned the hours from darkness to dawn, stifled sometimes by the crude pranks by drunken roisterers.

The criminal element was dangerous, though the rate of serious crime was lower than now. Pickpockets abounded, but it was unusual for a lady or a gentleman to meet with violence in cities. Once out of town, footpads and highwaymen were dreaded. The incident of Don Juan's being com-pelled to shoot a highwayman, one of four who set on him, is done with a kind of humorous sympathy for both parties, and a zest for underworld slang for which credit is given in a footnote to 'my old friend and corporeal pastor and master, John Jackson, Esq., Professor of Pugilism'.[1] Jackson was a man admired on every hand for what Moore called 'the correctness of his conduct', but among the boxers who frequented the rooms where he taught his art and supervised bouts, there would have been opportunity for becoming familiar with the language of 'the select mobility and their patrons'.

Byron was assiduous in the study of boxing, shooting and fencing, partly because he would naturally wish to master those physical accom-plishments which, like swimming and horsemanship, could be practised despite his handicap, and partly because they were sporting activities of a man-about-town, and this was an aspect of his life that he had cultivated from early youth. It has seemed to some critics unworthy of a poet to care about the world of fashion, but his genius derived its sustenance from the variety of his experiences and all the contrasts they provided, which gives *Don Juan* its flashing interplay of poetical and mundane images.

He wanted, I think, in the beginning, when he first cut a dash at Harrow and Cambridge, to become the sort of man he believed his father had been, and this in some measure because he was so hostile to his mother. To dress regardless of expense, to keep more horses than he

---

[1] *Don Juan*, Canto XI. 'Gentleman' Jackson (1769–1845) was England's champion boxer for several years, fighting with bare fists. After his retirement from the ring in 1803 he taught pugilism. His beautiful physique had not declined when Byron knew him.

needed, to be capable of fighting duels, to have raffish adventures, to drink deep and play deep and get deep into debt, to move in a circle of men with the same devil-may-care attitudes as his own—these were the ambitions which had filled his mother with apprehension and voluble reproach and made his behaviour to her still more defiant. Fortunately, he had a much better brain than his father's, could not help reading extensively, had a turn for writing, gambled for the sake of living up to the pattern he had set himself but without any genuine taste for it, and made friends at Cambridge with young men who could be dissipated but had on the whole a serious and scholarly bent.

Being intellectual, however, could not make him economical. A certain degree of display was required of him. Noble undergraduates had gold tassels on their mortarboards instead of black ones,[1] and for public occasions, elaborately decorated gowns to distinguish them from commoners. The deference every class was so ready to pay to rank had to be earned by outward and unmistakable signs of it. If Byron had been born a few decades earlier, it would have been proper for him to wear superb embroideries, costly lace, jewelled buckles. As it was, noblesse was expected to oblige with at least the vicarious show which was provided by servitors.[2]

He did not wait to become a celebrity before launching into large expenses on his own behalf, beginning as soon as he came down from Newstead in January 1812 by ordering: 'An Extra Spfine [superfine] Corbo Pelisse full trimmed with braid, & Sleeves body & Skirt lined with Silk £18. Rich Sable Fur collar cuffs & trimming £8. 4s.'

£26. 4s. for one garment was a tremendous extravagance. It gives us, I feel pretty sure, a near date for the two Sanders miniatures, one of which is often reproduced—the earliest of the open-collar portraits that were to mislead future generations into believing Byron did not wear the neck-cloth or cravat of ordinary male attire. One of these pictures was published in *Astarte* as by a 'Painter Unknown' and Byron's age was given as twenty: Lord Lovelace's widow repeated that mistake, but I believe it to be one of the likenesses about which Byron corresponded with John Murray in October, 1812, saying he had '*a very strong objection*' to an engraving of it which Murray wanted to use as the frontispiece of his new work (*The Giaour*), and that he would not be easy till he heard the proofs were destroyed, and again, insisting he would compensate for the damage, and yet again, when he was assured the plate had been destroyed: '. . . It was unlike the picture; & besides upon the whole, the frontispiece

---

[1] Called tufts, hence the word 'tuft-hunter'.
[2] See Appendix 7, 'The Byron Liveries'.

of an author's visage is but a paltry exhibition . . . I am sure Sanders would not have *survived* the engraving'.[1]

When we sit for a portrait we usually choose to be dressed in the most recent thing we regard as pleasing, and in the two miniatures by Sanders Byron is wearing a velvet pelisse—'Corbo'—with a border of long-haired fur, sable by its colour. On these grounds, I ascribe them to one of the winter months of 1812, when he had turned twenty-four.

He actually went to the expense of having a second extra superfine pelisse enriched with sable, made at the same cost, in September, but it was brown which the one in Sanders's portraits is not. With a profusion that almost passes belief, he treated himself to yet a third, described exactly like the first—Corbo, sable and all—on February 2nd 1813, but of course this could not have been the one engraved in 1812. It would be no easy feat to wear out winter pelisses at such a rate, and I can only conjecture that Byron's sales resistance was low. The long credit tailors were expected to give was taken into consideration in their prices.

He spent nearly £900 with this firm alone from January 1812 to September, 1813, and he still owed more than £100 to Green & Ibberson in Nottingham, and was proportionately indebted for footwear, headgear, linen,[2] and jewellery, not to speak of swords and pistols. And yet in everyday life, he was discreetly, not showily, dressed, as many commentators noticed.

> He wore his nails very short, and was very particular about his teeth and his linen, but not otherwise remarkable in his toilette. From his portraits it has been supposed that he wore no cravat, but went with his neck open—which was not the case. He used to wear a small cravat with the collar turned down; but always sat for his likeness without one.

So wrote an anonymous contributor to the *Literary Gazette* in May 1828, with accuracy except as to the last point. There are portraits which show him with his neck as completely covered as that of any other Regency gentleman.

John Murray III said he remembered Byron as a man who limped badly and wore his collar open; but he was about seven when he had last seen him and, brought up as he was on famous Byron paintings, engrav-

---

[1] Marchand *Letters*. 12, 17, and 23 Oct. A very astute publisher would hardly have wished to use as a frontispiece a likeness, done four years before, which no longer resembled his prize poet. Lord Lovelace made more than one mistake in his captions to pictures, the most serious being his guess (for such it was, as I heard from Lady Wentworth) that Augusta was the subject of a miniature which, on costume evidence, cannot possibly represent her, but may conceivably be one of her daughters, Georgiana or Medora, both of whom were taken up for a time by Lady Byron who owned the picture. It is constantly reprinted as Augusta.

[2] See Appendix 8, 'A Young Gentleman's Linen'.

ings and drawings, I fancy those images had worked their way into his imagination. A child would be quicker to notice the limp than the clothes.

At all times portrait painters have directed attention to the features deemed to be aesthetically desirable in their period, and Byron had a fine throat, a great merit in an epoch of smooth neo-classical sculpture. There had long been a tradition of depicting sitters in whatever was held to be 'artistic dress', often out and out fancy dress, and the poet's good looks offered an irresistible temptation to garb him in picturesque draperies which were largely fictitious. There were, it is true, the luxurious pelisses but, when not in the artist's studio, he would seldom have been seen in those unless out of doors, custom demanding that one should hand one's outdoor things to a footman before entering a reception room, the sole exception to this rule being the *chapeau bras*.

Byron himself certainly had a taste for the picturesque, had worn a scarlet and gold uniform when being presented to dignitaries abroad, and bought Albanian dresses, laden with gold, in one of which he was to sit to Phillips: but as a frequenter of drawing-rooms his opportunities for indulging in colour and lavishness were limited. What with the aftermath of the French Revolution and the reign of George Brummell, clothes that proclaimed wealth and high position ostentatiously were stigmatized as vulgar. Yet since those who belong to a privileged order like to let the fact be known somehow or other, the new simplicity was merely a more restrained way of suggesting one's membership of the enviable leisured class. The principle of non-utility was strictly applied. Breeches or panta-loons that would show up the least speck of dirt, gloves in the palest tints of kid guaranteed to be soiled in one wearing, immaculate linen—these were delicate signs of being able to defy down-to-earth requirements. Ruffles at the wrists were out, but one could indicate that one did no useful work by sleeves so long that they half-covered the hands and neck-cloths so high and starched that they made free movement of the head a little difficult.

Waistcoats might be more overtly distinctive. Byron, however, was satisfied with fine white quilted ones, for which he had an enthusiasm which caused him to buy them in surprising quantities—six on March 23rd and six again on April 7th, and yet a dozen more on June 20th, 1812—£31 4s. in all. They would at first have been a form of half-mourning after he came out of full mourning for his mother; but he was wearing black coats long after colour had become admissible again, and continued to acquire white waistcoats, always quilted. Their effect must have been soberly striking, but to have upwards of twenty-four at one time was rather excessive.

As for trousers, he favoured nankeen or white jean which would have been washed each time they were worn; nevertheless orders of half a dozen, and even a dozen and sometimes two dozen pairs at once, seem to border on eccentricity.

His addiction to black is a little unexpected because its use was generally confined to the clerical and legal professions. The explanation I hazard is that he had learned during his period of mourning how well it set off that 'pure spiritual paleness' of his. The fair skin that often goes with auburn hair was possibly one of his many Scottish inheritances. It may also have owed something, as I suggested in the previous chapter, to anaemia through deficient diet. A light complexion was valued very much both in women and men. Songs and sonnets traditionally comparing white skin to lilies or snow were addressed to women, but men too regarded anything resembling sun-tan as coarse and plebeian. Byron's pallor was remarked upon again and again, and always as an attraction. Jane Porter, the novelist, described it as 'a moonlight paleness'. Though his hair was so dark as to be sometimes mistaken for black, he had the odd advantage of a very fair beard so that he never looked blue-shaven.

From time to time he grew a small moustache which, being blonde, was out of keeping and disliked by all commentators. Phillips may have darkened it a little in the Albanian portrait, or even taken artist's licence to add it, since a clean-shaven face with Oriental dress would have looked effeminate.

Although he ordered a brown sable-trimmed pelisse on coming out of mourning, he went back to *corbeau* (blue-black) the following February 1813, and superfine black coats were a recurring item in his wardrobe. Here he played his part in setting a fashion that proved all too durable. Men were still wearing such colours as blue, mulberry and dark green, and cream silk waistcoats with minute polychrome embroidery. Byron's black and white made a great effect and, for full dress, it became 'the thing' and ultimately the only thing.

Another mode he rapidly advanced was the adoption of wide trousers as a socially acceptable garment. Knee breeches, though gradually going out, were still *de rigueur* for formal dress, and a very few pairs figure on his London tailor's bills; but the lameness to which he was so acutely sensitive made him unwilling to be seen in them. He covered his legs with gaiters whenever possible, ordering them in large numbers.[1] Even before

[1] The late Sir Denis Browne, F.R.C.S., an eminent orthopaedic surgeon, made a close study of Byron's lameness, and I heard him lecture on it. He considered it was due to dysplasia, which would cause the affected leg to be much thinner than the other. Gaiters may have been used either to mask that defect or because they partially concealed the feet. Full dress would be disliked whether one leg was thinner or the lameness were only of the foot, because it called for light shoes or pumps. When there was

the Cossack officers appeared with their Emperor in 1814, using ampler trousers than Englishmen had yet seen, Byron's were cut wide at the ankles. It is one of the details picked up by caricaturists for the prints in which they assailed him when his wife returned to her parents. The style was imitated abroad. England's influence in setting male fashion had been well established in the 18th century, and Byron, in any case, was very soon a European figure. If any credit is to be attached to getting rid of breeches and also of tight stocking pantaloons, some of it must go to him.

In 1812, he prepared for one occasion when full formal dress was inescapable, and black, at that date, out of the question. This was a levée to be held at Carlton House. He had been presented to the Prince Regent at a party given in June—Lady Caroline Lamb claimed, not very convincingly, to have performed the introduction[1]—and the Prince had been so agreeable and so pleasing in his conversation that Byron decided to pay his respects at Court. He therefore had delivered to him on July 1st a superfine olive green coat lined through with white silk and adorned with '25 Elegantly Cut & Highly Polished Steel buttons', 'a very rich Embroidered Court dress Waistcoat', a pair of 'rich black silk breeches', and a 'rich steel dress sword' with a chain and silk sword belt. All this richness cost approximately £52, and to add to the outlay there must have been buckled shoes and a cocked hat. He also had a hairdresser to powder his hair—still requisite for Court attendance.

With his unerring instinct for turning up whenever something noteworthy was going forward, Dallas dropped in that morning, found Byron dressed to go, and formed the opinion that hair powder 'by no means suited his countenance'. His countenance may have been rather grim. The levée had been suddenly put off, and he had not heard of the postponement till he was in full regalia. He could have gone to the next levée but, says Dallas, 'it was the first and the last time he was ever so dressed, at least for a British Court'. He had been somewhat embarrassed, we may suppose, to have contemplated appearing in such a Tory circle as the Court then was—embarrassed not only because his Whig friends would be disapproving, but because two stanzas attacking the Prince's turncoat politics, which had been published anonymously in the *Morning*

---

any choice, Byron invariably wore boots. His insistence on being married by special licence in a drawing-room instead of going to his bride's parish church may well be attributable to the fact that he would have had to wear knee breeches for the ceremony.

[1] 36461. Hobhouse Papers. Dallas says: 'His Royal Highness sent a gentleman to him', and it is certainly unlikely that he would have been presented by a lady unless she were the hostess. It was not Caroline's party, but Miss Johnson's. This lady was probably the daughter of Col. John Johnson, who had been Groom of the Bedchamber to the Prince before his Regency.

Post as recently as March, were actually from his pen.[1] Had he only attended the levée on that first impulse, his history might have been different. The Regent, as Byron himself admitted, had the most perfect manners and knew exactly when and how to be gracious. Having experienced that graciousness a second time, Byron might never have been ungracious enough to re-publish the verses in 1814 and insist on owning to them—a futile act of bravado which was his first explicit challenge to the code of high society. It brought a storm about him, and to no particular purpose or effect.

Truly there was something in him at this stage that bent his steps towards fatality. For a man who had regarded his destiny as bound up with his Abbey, so that he and it would stand or fall together, it is almost inexplicable, except on such an assumption, that he had continued to augment the load of debt that inevitably forced him to sell it. He burned the financial candle at both ends, prodigal in expenditure to assist needy friends and even strangers as well as to indulge his taste for dandyism.

His temptations must furnish him with some excuse. Noblemen were credited, correctly as a rule, with being rich, and he, being famous too, received many begging letters, to which he remained vulnerable as long as he lived. He was amusing and good-looking and in demand, and to have rejected all occasions for going into the company that sought him would have needed superhuman self-abnegation. Their habits were beyond his means—the tipping of retinues of servants alone was a heavy toll—but their appeal was not merely a snobbish one for their numbers included wits, beauties, the gifted and the learned. Yet his agonizingly divided nature made him long to be elsewhere even while he was storing up pleasurable impressions of the people he met, the entertainments he shared with them. Or perhaps the creative energy, that made him so ebullient, wrought him up by a kind of pressure to feverish bouts of restlessness such as afflicted another similarly disturbed and disturbing genius whenever he was hammering out the lines of a work to be written. 'I sit down between whiles to think of a new story', Charles Dickens told John Forster, 'and, as it begins to grow, such a torment of desire to be anywhere but where I am; and to be going I don't know where, I don't know why, takes hold of me, that it is like being *driven away*'.[2]

Byron repeatedly found himself in that same mood. He had meditated going abroad again ever since coming home, but he could not do so without having fresh funds in hand, and since the visit to Rochdale with Hanson

---

[1] The lines beginning 'Weep, daughter of a royal line'.
[2] Quoted by Forster without date. Written between *David Copperfield* and *Bleak House*.

in 1811 had proved abortive, Newstead would positively have to go. As I told at the end of my last chapter, it had been bought in at the auction in August 1812, the highest genuine bid being ninety-five thousand guineas. He must have been both relieved and disappointed; but a fortnight afterwards a solicitor named Claughton entered into a private treaty with Hanson, his offer being £140,000, which was £20,000 more than Byron had named as an acceptable minimum. For this sum, however, he was to have 'all the Household Goods and Furniture of him the said Lord Byron in the Mansion house and offices (save and except the Plate Linen Glass Books Fire Arms Swords Sabres Pictures Wines and Liquors of all sorts which the said Lord Byron reserves to himself)'.[1] Afterwards Claughton objected to having the linen and glass and such equipment removed, and said he had only intended the books and pictures to be reserved but, as he was under contract, he offered reluctantly to pay for the essential domestic items rather than be obliged to replace them.[2]

By October two deposits of £5,000 each had been credited to Byron's account and enabled him to release Scrope Davies from a liability contracted on his behalf. There had been a lot of borrowing from Peter to pay Paul, and Scrope had somehow become indebted for no less than £1,500 to Agar Ellis who required it back. He must have looked forward confidently now to the repayment of Byron's main debt to him, the several thousand pounds which had largely financed Childe Harold's pilgrimage. But £10,000, though helpful, did not go the whole way. Besides the numberless other claimants, there was Hanson who sent in a preliminary bill for £1,500 which could not be withheld, and there was always the interest on the so-called 'Jew debts' and the loan from Colonel Sawbridge.

At Newstead, in uncertainty as to their future, the tenant farmers were at sixes and sevens. They had been warned by Hanson not to increase their crops, which would have to be purchased at a valuation, but they were all hoping to have the chance of keeping their farms when those became the property of the new landlord. Claughton's taking possession seemed so imminent that Hanson wrote to Mealey on October 23rd to say the keeper had better be instructed to find new homes for Lord Byron's dogs immediately and to sell the mule, 'a very fine one', for as much as could be got.[3] Mealey replied that Fletcher's wife had heard his Lordship wanted the mule to go to Mr Claughton.[4]

Mealey from now on had a number of very real troubles to grumble at. He must have been worried about whether he would be able to keep the Hut, that he had schemed so hard to get, and if he was to lose his post

---

[1] Murray MSS. Draft dated 17 Aug. 1812.   [2] Ibid. 26 Aug.
[3] Egerton 2613.   [4] Ibid. 11 Nov.

as steward after all these years. The tenants in their unsettled state would not do as he directed, and Claughton, though presumed to be responsible for the maintenance of the estate, was not paying any labourers nor supplying the means of preventing it from running to seed. Six months after the signing of the contract, Hanson was receiving increasingly anxious letters warning him that the farmers were committing every irregularity: '. . . There is scarcely any land at Newstead that will bring spring corn but what is ploughed up'.[1] Mr Claughton made no communication, but had sent two of his pointers the previous year to be looked after. Mealey desired guidance but got none. Hanson had met his match for elusiveness and procrastination, and could not bring Claughton to the point—the vital point of producing the balance due, £70,000, allowing for £60,000 to remain on mortgage.

Meanwhile, the effect on such a spendthrift as Byron, of having money in hand and depending on a great deal more to come, may easily be guessed. As early as January 1813 Hanson, who could be astute when it required no great exertion, had warned him that Claughton was making excuses to shuffle out of his bargain:

> My dear Lord,
>
> I assure you I would have written to your Lordship if I had had any thing worth your hearing to communicate. I have had a correspondence with Mr Claughton who is very stubborn in refusing to pay any more of the Deposit until we furnish him with the Information called for by his Counsel on the title. I am fully prepared to solve their doubts, but I am satisfied with your Counsel's opinion that no more papers ought to be handed over until he has performed that part of his contract. . . . I am persuaded he has not got the money or he never would have allowed himself to be placed in so awkward a Situation. . . . Any loss resulting from it must fall upon himself. He talks of coming to Town but I dont think he will come until he has got the money.
>
> However if he does not move we must[,] and our best mode of proceeding will be to bring an action against him to enforce the payment of the remaining part of the Deposit (£15,000) which he covenanted to pay this Xmas [i.e. the Christmas of 1812].[2]

Despite his painful experience of litigation, with the Rochdale lawsuit still dragging on, Byron optimistically ran up more debts, one of which was a huge bill with Love & Kelty, the Royal Appointment jewellers, to whom he already owed more than £650. Some of the items he purchased were for women—or a woman. 'A suit of very fine Aquamarines' and '6 pink Topaz ornaments' for a hundred guineas on February 12th 1813,

---

[1] Ibid. 30 Mar. 1813.   [2] Murray MS. 5 Jan.

and a chrysolite and diamond brooch for sixty the same day—the recipient of these jewels could hardly have been other than Lady Oxford, Caroline Lamb's successor. A few days before he had paid Lord Oxford the rent, fifty guineas, for Kinsham Court, a dower house about five miles from Eywood, the Oxfords' country home, where he had been conducting what remains the most obscure in detail of his major love affairs, twice as long in duration as his affair with Caroline. The Countess was forty, advanced middle age in those times, but she had retained her beauty and seductiveness.[1] She had enjoyed a classical education, and was what would later have been called an aesthete. Byron had a notion of going abroad with her and her very tolerant husband, but the rapturous phase of the amour was over by the time they departed, in June, and he lingered behind drifting into new attachments.

Under the threat of a lawsuit, and standing to lose what he had already paid up, Claughton managed to raise the £15,000 in two instalments that summer, and from July 1813 Byron began to occupy himself in earnest with preparations for a second grand tour. He did not know where he was going or with whom. Both the Marquess of Sligo, who had joined forces with him for a while in Greece after Hobhouse's return to England, and Hobhouse himself, had laid projects before him; but, wherever he went, he was resolved to do it in style.

At Love & Kelty's he bought seven gold snuff boxes for three hundred guineas, and seven less costly ones, of gold and semi-precious materials for a further two hundred. These were to serve as presents for any grandees who might afford him hospitality. A 'Gold & Enameld Musical Box with figures sett with Pearls &c' for a hundred guineas must have been meant for the highest potentate he was likely to meet. A gold watch for thirty guineas and a gold watch-key for five were also intended for presentation, as may have been a toothpick case for the modest price of £3. 12s. 6d., though later that year he bought a gold one 'richly chased' for thirty-six guineas, containing four gold toothpicks at a guinea each, which sounds more fit for his purpose. Two rings, one emerald and one turquoise, for twenty-two guineas were among the 'gewgaws for such of the Pagan women as may be inclined to give us trinkets in exchange'.[2] A silver mount for his own cane, a morocco case, an afterthought of three more snuff-boxes at fifty guineas, evidently for regaling minor dignitaries, brought his jeweller's bill by August up to nearly a thousand pounds.

July 14th was one of his busiest shopping days. He bought himself

---

[1] Lady Oxford was an intimate friend of Caroline of Brunswick, the Regent's discarded consort, and in all probability it was through her that Byron made the Princess's acquaintance and burned his boats at Court.

[2] *Correspondence.* To Lady Melbourne, 18 Aug. 1813.

some new luggage at Wells & Lambe, 'Copying Machine Makers to his Royal Highness the Duke of Cumberland'. In these times of air-light suitcases, it strikes us oddly that his dressing-case was mahogany lined with velvet, fitted with silver boxes, and having a leather cover. His new portable writing desk, which had a secret drawer, was also of that heavy wood. Having ordered a pocket-book to be engraved with his coronet and an 'old English' B, he had spent—on credit—£46. 4s.

The scarlet uniform he had worn on his first voyages—it was that of an aide-de-camp—was apparently an admissible dress as no one questioned it even among those members of the diplomatic corps who had criticized his demeanour at Constantinople. Indeed its impact on the Pashas was all he could have desired—or rather more. He had decided to have this cleaned and furbished up with new cuffs and collar and coatskirt ornaments but, not to be parsimonious, he also put in hand a superfine scarlet staff uniform trimmed with rows of gold twist buttons, fifty-eight in number—embroidering the buttonholes cost £15. 19s.—twenty-five yards of gold lacing, a scarlet sash for seven guineas, a pair of 'Very rich Gold Epaulettes' for £33. 1s. 6d. and a great many extras and accessories. At the same time, he took delivery of a 'Tartan Jacket handsomely braided' and fastened with olivettes (olive-shaped buttons), and two pairs of tartan trousers with matching gaiters. From the swordsmith, Richard Johnston in St. James's Square, he acquired all sorts of additional embellishments in the shape of gold bullion knots, embroidered belts, crimson cords, gilt gorgets—every item, naturally, 'very rich'. There are a number of plainer accoutrements which must have been for his suite; he had an Indian sabre and four swords incised with his coronet and cypher, and purchased three black belts with leather knots, as well as his own gold-mounted ones, suggesting that these attendants were to be armed.

While his travel plans were still vaguest of the vague, and he did not know whether he was going to Moscow with Hobhouse or the Mediterranean with the Oxfords, he had written to Lady Melbourne of 'hiring doctors, painters, and two or three stray Greeks' as well as a Mameluke from Napoleon's guard. 'These I am measuring for uniforms, shoes, and inexpressibles without number.'[1] The 'inexpressibles' appear on his tailor's bill on March 9th—sixty pairs of nankeen or white jean trousers and two pairs of 'cassimere pantaloon overalls'—the last being, we may assume, for his own use. The imprudence of his allowing himself to be 'quite overwhelmed with preparations of all sorts' when, until the Newstead transaction was completed, he literally had no means to go, shows a boyishness at once preposterous and touching.

On July 15th he went to Bryant's Military Warehouse at Ludgate Hill

[1] *Correspondence.* 18 Mar. 1813.

and really got down to business, buying equipment for camping out, whenever it might be required, in a gentlemanly manner. His bill includes a fitted basket canteen, a camp table and two chairs, two four-post patent bedsteads with mattresses and mosquito nets, pillows, blankets, and counterpanes—these, with covers and straps, cost £42. 10s.—and three patent bedsteads complete, but with no mention of mosquito nets, for £57. 5s., perhaps 'Wellington beds', of which this firm claimed to be the sole inventors. Purchased next were a pair of canteens partly furnished with 'silver articles' and a second pair described as 'elegant' and 'compleat with Plated & Prince's Metal Ware'. Like the less expensive beds, those may have been for his suite; he himself travelled with silver cutlery.

The second patent four-poster was for the use of whatever companion he might have, as also was one of the two choice military saddles at £25 from the same supplier. Three good saddles for servants cost £34. 15s. 6d.

For £65. 12s. eight 'large solid leather trunks' were provided, while two carpet bags cost three guineas. A nest of camp kettles with a stove, leather buckets for horses, leather pails, water vessels, quantities of small brass plates to be affixed to the baggage as labels, matting to wrap up the more fragile items, a hammock to sleep in when at sea (it must have been a good one for it cost ten guineas) . . . having made these acquisitions he emerged with nearly £400 more added to his debts.

He was already in possession of three first-rate waterproof cloaks for riding, one of which was lined with velvet and fastened with 'treble gilt hooks and eyes', and had a small circular cape that could form a hood. For these he owed £25. 1s. to 'William Pulford, Supplier of Cloaks by Appointment to Their Royal Highnesses the Prince Regent, & the Dukes of York and Gloucester'.

Colonel Stanhope was to write that, in the Greek War, 'he was soldier mad', but this was much less true of his last days than his youth. He seemed to be excitedly anticipating a quasi-military campaign and, before July was over, went to two different gunsmiths, buying rifles, pistols, of which he already had a number, powder flasks, carbines, ramrods, bullet moulds, cartridges, balls, gunpowder and a magazine for storing it— setting himself, or his creditors, back approximately £200—while in June he had sent Manton of shooting gallery fame a cheque for £56. 10s. which must have covered the price of one additional pair of pistols if not more.[1]

On July 24th he visited a firm which made what were then called Philosophical Instruments at the sign of *The Golden Spectacles* in Sackville Street. There he gave orders for six portable 3 feet telescopes, the

[1] E.g. a pistol with an ornamental magazine in a lined case cost just under £30; a pair of steel-mounted pistols twenty guineas.

same number of sliding gilt 'astromatic operas', which I take to be similar to opera glasses but with a longer range, two silver hunting spring compasses and, on approval, an elaborate sextant in a mahogany case and a thermometer. If the last two items were kept, there was £77 or so to pay. Most of the things were designed to enrich the splendid array of gifts he was to carry to foreign hosts.

It may be wondered why, with plentiful cash at two banks, Hoare's and Hammersley's, he went on amassing debts. The fact is that his commitments, generosities, and self-indulgences made short work of the money. No sooner had the last instalments come to hand than Hanson, having had £1,500 out of the previous one, borrowed £2,840 to pay the deposit on a property he desired in Essex.[1] Over £600 went in four instalments to Mr Love of Love & Kelty. Yet he was still owing £1,079 15s. to the firm at the end of the year.[2] He bestowed, as a loan, £1,240 on Francis Hodgson, now Reverend, to enable him to marry Henry Drury's sister, adding two further amounts the following year. (When Byron died, Hodgson meanly denied all remembrance of these benefactions.)[3] He frequently gave sums of £20 and £25 to his cousin, George Anson Byron, Dallas's nephew, who was to prove wholly disloyal to him at the time of the Separation: he paid Dallas £50 over and above the copyright fees to help in equipping his son for the army. He lent two amounts of £500 each to James Wedderburn Webster who never made the slightest attempt to repay. And to assist Augusta, who had begun to confide her ever-pressing necessities to him, he presented her feckless husband, whom he despised, with £1,000. £800 went to the further relief of Scrope Davies. To Ridgeway's bookshop in Piccadilly he paid a bill of over £133, to Sheldrake, who made his surgical boots, £42 and to Thomas Phillips fifty guineas towards the price of the portrait he later presented to John Murray. Cheques to Fletcher for above £1,200 may have covered domestic

[1] Murray MS. Byron to Hobhouse, 24 Feb. 1815. Hanson promised to repay in a month and did not. It was eventually deducted from his immense bill.

[2] He settled it in full in 1814, but not before receiving a severe admonitory letter saying 'the common interest *exceeds* any profit that can be gained on the articles sold your L.ship' (Murray MS., 19 May 1814). But see p. 218 Chapter 6 for Byron's discovery that at least one of his gold snuff boxes was only silver gilt.

[3] When Hanson had Hodgson's letter to this effect, he wrote to his co-executor, Hobhouse: 'I hope he has really lost his Memory for the Salvation of his Honesty. O Tempora, O Mores Ecclesiae. He certainly never discharged the Debt and it is impossible he can have forgotten so formidable a Transaction.' (Murray MS, 30 Aug. 1824.) On a remonstrance from Hobhouse, Hodgson expressed his regret and promised an explanation. It turned out to be to the effect that the money had been a gift, but Byron stated in a letter to Hobhouse (26 Jan. 1815) that he had 'lent rather more than £1,600 to Hodgson' and moreover he complained that a firm promise to pay something back in six weeks had been kept 'with the usual punctuality—viz: not at all'.

bills, minor necessaries of the wardrobe, and living expenses. These comprised a sizeable stable account, although he had been obliged to sacrifice, temporarily, his horses and groom the year before. The biggest outlay of all was £3,000 for circular notes to take on his foreign expedition, and two purchases of doubloons for just under £300.

It will be seen that his new wealth was rapidly melting away, and now there was a grinding anxiety—when was Claughton going to complete the Newstead contract? He had sent furniture to the Abbey and it was still stored there, but Byron was now more apprehensive than Hanson that the deal on which he had been counting would fall through.

On August 21st 1813, nearly a year after negotiations had begun, Mealey was writing to Hanson to say the gamekeeper didn't know what game to kill and what to preserve, or where to send any, or whether it would be right to let the Rev. 'Hennery' Byron come a-shooting as he wished on September 1st. Mealey's salary had been paid by Claughton up to last February, but as he had no instructions, he was uncertain what authority he could consult as to goings-on he disapproved of. Young Rushton and his wife had taken possession of the rooms in the Abbey recently occupied by Mrs Fletcher. 'I durst not say any thing to them about it.'[1] Rushton was still receiving wages from his Lordship prior to going into Webster's employment, so it was a decidedly confused situation. 'Newstead lands will be found in a bad way in another year', Mealey prophesied, but Hanson would not be moved.

Mr Claughton was going through with his purchase of the estate, he replied. 'I imagine he will very soon be at Newstead and I request you will give him every assistance you can.'[2] All the gamekeeper must do was to keep people off the manor. He evaded, in his typical way, saying explicitly that the Rev. Henry was to be refused; his client had still not paid back the large amount borrowed for him years before from that gentleman's mother, the Hon. Mrs Byron of Nottingham.

Claughton did turn up, but not till October, when he commanded Mealey to cut and thin the plantations, 'the same as he ordered last year which I do not like to do without your orders or begin on them before I hear from you. Lord Byron has been at Newstead one night and has ordered me to inform you that Mr Claughton has forced the wine cellar door opend and took what wine he wanted . . .'[3] Byron had intended to present Claughton with the contents of the cellar on handing over, but this really was insupportable.

It seems extraordinary that Hanson was allowing things to go from bad to worse, recently planted trees cut down, game neglected, rents

---

[1] Egerton 2613, Folio 186.
[2] Ibid. Hanson's copy on verso, 28 Aug. 1813.   [3] Ibid. 12 Oct.

unpaid because the tenants, growing more and more demoralized, were taking advantage of the lacuna in landlordship; and it is not to be wondered at that Byron's patience wore very thin. His longing to go abroad became as frantic as it had been when he had been obliged to wait from month to month after his coming of age. Sometimes he thought of provoking Claughton to a duel, sometimes he urged Hanson to raise some money for him by selling Rochdale for any price at all, were it only a few thousands, and from time to time he expressed, as urgently as if he were flying for his life, his determination to leave the country, come what might.

> . . . Do not trifle with me, for I am in very solid serious earnest, and if utter ruin *were*, or *is*, before me—on the one hand—and wealth at home on the other—I have made my choice, and go I will.[1]

I do not think sufficient weight has ever been given to the effect, on a man who suffered from a sort of spiritual claustrophobia, of being caged in, as it transpired, for years by dependence on two unbusiness-like business men. His prolonged suspense as to the real extent of his resources gave to everything he did a feeling of transience, of unreality, so that he meandered into situations from which he thought he could escape—hectic love affairs, proposals of marriage which were nothing but half-hearted gropings towards stability, and the passion for Augusta that began, I should suppose, merely as a fascinating experiment with sin.

By 1814, while he became engulfed in a moral and financial quagmire—for Augusta was immeasurably the most expensive of his attachments[2]—Claughton had reduced the administration of Newstead to chaos; but having put down a fortune, he had no intention of retreating while he could hold off Hanson and, being himself a lawyer, he knew all the ways of doing so. Byron's letters on this subject, not being amusing or about famous people, are excluded from popular selections and so are little known, but they are numerous and graphic in their portrayal of his distress and his increasing recognition of Hanson's ineptitude.

There was a crisis in July when Claughton, having said first that he would withdraw, asked if Byron would meet him with legal advisers for discussion. Hanson senior was out of town, and Byron was obliged to deal with his son, to whom he wrote:

[1] Marchand Letters. 3 June 1813.

[2] She had something near £3,000 from him in 1813 and 1814. Murray MS, Byron to Hobhouse (26 Jan. 1815) explaining what had happened to Claughton's deposit. On 15 November 1814, when his marriage was imminent, he wrote to Augusta asking her how much George Leigh owed: 'I shall be able to make some arrangement for him —or at all events you and the children shall be properly taken care of. What I do for him might be seized.' Horton Papers, 31037.

Dear Charles,

I called just now with some expectation of hearing further of Mr Claughton and your conference with him. Whatever is done, must be done *now*. I cannot wait till your father's return, and have lost too much by delay already. Pray have the goodness to tell me if you have seen him, and what will be the conditions, supposing me disposed to relieve him and take back the property.

I must once more represent to *you* the necessity of some actual *conclusion*. For years and years, I have been sinking gradually deeper and deeper. I do not mean to exonerate myself; my own extravagance has doubtless been the principal cause, but at the same time I must add that *delay*,—never ending, still beginning delay,—has materially contributed to assist my own imprudence in adding to my involvements. . . .

Let me hear something of Mr Claughton, whom I am willing to meet any where, or any how, and come to something decisive, one way or the other.

Yours ever truly,
Byron.[1]

Charles did nothing, and Byron wrote again on July 15th to the effect that he found it 'a little extraordinary' that, at a time of such importance to one of his clients, Hanson senior had not only failed to see Claughton, but failed even to answer the letter his son must, by now, have addressed to him. He said he himself would meet Claughton, however unwillingly, the next day and requested Charles to fix an appointment and to be present. Hanson was apparently staying with his daughter, whose recent elevation by marriage to the Earl of Portsmouth seems to have exhausted his diligence. Byron did not see Claughton but heard from Hanson on July 17th on lines that may be guessed from his prompt answer:—

Whatever arrangements Mr C. may mean to make, I trust they will be *speedy*. When he talks of *sacrifices*, he forgets the confusion into which the non-performance of his engagements plunges my affairs . . . If he can complete his purchase in proper time, and method,—very well; if not, I humbly conceive, in law and equity, that the loss ought not to fall upon the person who is ready to fulfil *his engagements*.

'Do Pray', he begged, 'give a serious glance at my concerns, and don't let me be *fooled* any longer.'[2]

[1] *LJ*. 11 July 1814.
[2] Ibid. On 1 Feb. 1814 Byron had written to Hanson saying, 'By all I hear, *Leigh*, and not Claughton is the *real* purchaser. If so he is well able to adhere to the contract. . . . He is of age and has ample funds. . . .' (LJ) Certainly £140,000 was a huge and unlikely sum for a professional man to undertake to spend except with a client in view; but to the best of my knowledge Mr Leigh was never involved further, so either he relented of the bargain made for him, or Byron's conjecture was mistaken. Chandos Leigh, a landed gentleman of large means born in 1791 (for whom a peerage was created in

Two days later he called vainly on his still absent solicitor to say that if Claughton would forfeit £25,000 or even £20,000, he would take back the estate.

> So much am I convinced that he is a man of neither property nor credit. He has never *once* kept his word since the sale was concluded, and, at all events, I will do any thing to be rid of him . . . *You* will cling and cling to the fallacious hope of the fulfilment, already shewn to be so, till I am ruined entirely. . . . Pray think of Rochdale; it is the delay which drives me mad. I declare to God, I would rather have but ten thousand pounds clear and out of debt, than drag on the cursed existence of expectation, and disappointment, which I have endured for these last 6 years, for 6 months longer, though a million came at the end of them.[1]

Claughton was induced by Hanson—his one stroke of efficiency—to agree to forfeit £25,000, and Byron then urged him to consider 'something immediate' as to the letting of the estate and settling the rents. 'In short we must turn over a new leaf and since the property is still to be mine, at all events it shall not be as it has been.'[2] But still the wretched business dragged on. A few weeks later, Claughton, unable to face the loss, endeavoured to revive the transaction.

This must have been in the first week of September 1814, for, on the 2nd, in one of the letters by which, in her tortuous and ambiguous way, she was striving to draw from him a renewed proposal, Miss Milbanke expressed surprise at learning he was staying at Newstead Abbey, having heard he had sold it, and he replied on the 7th:

> Newstead is mine again—for the present—Mr. Cn. after many delays in completion—relinquished his purchase—I am sorry for it—he has lost a considerable sum in forfeiture by his temporary inability or imprudence—but he has evinced a desire to resume or renew his contract with greater punctuality—& in justice to him—though against the advice of lawyers—and the regrets of relations—I shall not hesitate to give him an opportunity of making good his agreement—but I shall expect—indeed I will not endure such trifling in future.[3]

Shortly afterwards, Byron, in very sensible terms, suggested to Hanson that Claughton should be given until November at the latest to

---

1839), had just come of age in 1812 when the offer for Newstead was made. Perhaps it was on his behalf. He was a poet and is said to have acquired a portrait of Byron by Phillips painted in 1813. This seems to indicate a particular interest.

[1] Ibid. 19 July 1814.   [2] Ibid. 3 Aug.

[3] Lovelace Papers. The lawyers who advised Byron not to continue negotiating with Claughton do not seem to have been the Hansons, judging by his letter of July 19th reproaching Hanson senior with clinging to 'the fallacious hope of fulfilment'.

find the money and repeated the gist of his remarks just quoted: 'I think it but fair to give him such an opportunity in consideration of the sacrifice he has made'. Claughton had excused himself for his procrastinations by hinting that the other side—Hanson's side—had been slow to produce the needful title deeds, and Byron, in a tolerant mood, commented: '. . . You know a man is loth to blame *himself* in all cases, and as he has paid so round a sum, you can't expect him to be in the best of humours.'[1]

The catastrophic marriage to which he now committed himself may be called the nearly direct outcome of Claughton's speculation. Had the purchase price of the estate been paid when legally due, he would have fulfilled the ardent longing to go abroad for which he had made such concrete provisions; had it not again been offered, the odds are that he would not have thought himself eligible for Miss Milbanke, to whom he proposed two days before sending to Hanson the letter last quoted. As it was, the delaying tactics caused much friction before and after the wedding. Annabella's doting parents—and never was the adjective more aptly bestowed—took umbrage on her behalf at the lingering processes of the marriage settlement, held up by the interminable Newstead negotiations, while he, besides the annoyance of vainly pressing his solicitor to expedite them, had daily vexations from an ancestral home over which he no longer wielded any authority.

Rents were withheld and tenants averred that Claughton had chosen to take part of the settlement—to which he had no right—in the form of manure for the land! William Hibbert, a farmer who happened to be a part-time tax collector, claimed to have paid his half-year in the form of taxes that were due for his Lordship's male servants, carriage, and armorial bearings; and it turned out that these sums, £36. 16s., had already been disbursed in London.[2]

While Byron was on his honeymoon, Mealey wrote to him to say that one Whiteman (or Wightman) was cutting a waggon road to his farm through a plantation and destroying thriving trees to do so:

> and to no porpose for i am afraid he will never be able to pay his rent He says Mr Claughton promised him he should have a road there i hope your Lordship will pleas to give orders to put A stop to these proceedings.[3]

And to the torpid Hanson, on March 25th 1815, when the property had been tottering on the verge of passing into Claughton's hands for two and a half years:

> As to Newstead God knows what will be the end of it for the land and fences is going to rack and ruin every day and nobody durst speak a word.

[1] *LJ.* 11 Sept.   [2] Egerton 2613. Various dates in Aug. and Nov. 1814.
[3] Ibid. 27 Jan. 1815.

All the new tenants Claughton has took on say the estate is still his but be aware [beware] of the *rent this lady day* or else you will have as much or more trouble to get the rents than ever you had for Hibbert cannot get the taxes of them.[1]

He implored Hanson to give some definite orders and let them know who was their master. 'I hope Lord Byron', he ventured, chastened. Hanson tardily sent demands for rent to the tenants Claughton had established in the place of those who had lived at Newstead for generations but they did not pay, and meanwhile Mealey wrote, 'Mr Clauton's stock is adoing a deal of injury to the farm.'[2]

To Byron in mid-May he sent a note of what little he had collected: 'When the rest of them will pay I cannot say for they are all promises. I blive there is not as much ready money among them as would pay one man's Rent.'[3]

Soon after that Whiteman, whom Claughton had installed, had bailiffs in for £200 of debt over and above his rent. Hanson sent too late an authority to distrain on his property. Mealey reiterated his plea that Hanson would come to Newstead. That was on June 29th, but he did not go till September.

The large sums which Claughton had been prevailed upon to disgorge created a complex situation, but it would certainly seem that a more energetic agent could have taken firmer measures. Byron's main source of income having thus been cut off while his wife's dowry was so tied up as to provide her only with a small amount over her pin money, he was beset with worries, which were in no way mitigated by the recognition—which he never shirked—of his own contribution to them.

At the Duchess of Devonshire's great Piccadilly mansion where he, like his tenants, could not pay the rent, the news that he had married an heiress caused him to be dunned as never before, and his bride was too busy analysing and pondering over both his wildest and his lightest utterances to sympathize with the genuine distress this humiliation inflicted on him—a distress to which she was always quite insensitive. Soon after the wedding, her mother had inherited the large fortune of Lord Wentworth which would eventually come to her; so, although her father was in debt and unable to produce ready money, she had the sense of security natural to those who have never personally known difficulties. That is to say, material security; of any other kind, Byron swiftly denuded her.

Sometimes he drowned his anxieties in brandy; sometimes he gave vent to them by playing upon her easily shocked susceptibilities, thus

---

[1] Ibid., Folio 208.   [2] 1 May 1815.   [3] Ibid. 19 May.

setting up a vicious circle of guilt and consequent ill humour, ill humour and consequent guilt. He was miserable and in bad health, partly through his own intemperance, and, almost worst of all, unproductive—though only by comparison. The works from his pen in 1815 were *Parisina, The Siege of Corinth* and the *Hebrew Melodies,* those lyrics on biblical themes, set to music by Isaac Nathan, which he may have undertaken originally in the hope of achieving the conformity and respectability Miss Milbanke's friends might desire in her fiancé, the first-fruits, as E. H. Coleridge put it, of 'a seemlier muse'.

Nothing he had looked for from matrimony had come to pass; nor could it, even if he had not been an impossible husband. His wife was the least cosy of women. She had always been waited on—that was to be expected—but her want of any interest in domesticity went far beyond what was normal in a girl of her station. Her letters throughout her life show an indifference towards clothes, surroundings, hospitality—except when she could patronize—and the numerous little feminine hobbies of the day which could not have been exceeded by a nun in some austere order; and the fact that, for most of her brief married life, she was pregnant, and Byron too troubled to be considerate, intensified their neurotic effect upon each other.

He had renounced the bachelor comforts of his chambers at Albany, the dinners sent in by a caterer and eaten while he went on composing in a happy fever of concentration, the more convivial dinners in lively company at one of his clubs, the luxury of believing he could be at will a romantic traveller in distant lands or a young peer about town. And his beautiful, beloved Abbey had virtually passed out of his hands. Claughton's deposit had made it a kind of no man's land. Hobhouse had warned him— not that he needed it—that Hanson was bungling the whole affair and, very soon after his wedding, they had been corresponding as to what could be done to retrieve the situation. 'I am lost in wonder & obligation' Byron had written from his father-in-law's house on the Durham coast 'at your good nature in taking so much trouble with Spooney & my damnable concerns. . . . N. must be sold, without delay, and even at a loss *out of debt* must be my first object, and the sooner the better.'[1]

To get him out of debt was an appeal he had made to Hanson passionately and repeatedly, but of course, as he admitted, 'duns—necessities— luxuries—fooleries—jewelleries—"whores & fidlers"' had made the task prodigiously difficult. He did not mention his generosities: perhaps he classed those with his fooleries, for they amounted to folly. A few months before, he had given a hundred and fifty guineas to a petitioner from the

---

[1] Murray MS. 26 Jan. 1815. Spooney was Byron's nickname for Hanson—a variation of spoony—silly.

literary underworld named Thomas Ashe who had published bogus letters from the Princess of Wales to her daughter Charlotte, and his only explanation was that no one else was likely to oblige such a charlatan.[1] And in October 1814 a perfect stranger, Miss Eliza Francis, who sought his subscription for a volume of poems she hoped to publish, was amazed when, in the midst of a polite conversation, he handed her, not a payment for one or two copies, but what turned out to be a cheque for £50. It must be admitted that he seems to have been attracted to her, and she was dazzled by him—though he did not take advantage of it—and that it was at the time when he had some renewed expectation of Claughton's final settlement.[2]

When it fell through again, although Hanson was still his solicitor, he asked Hobhouse to get counsel's opinion as to what ought to be done.[3] Within a week of that, however, he wrote saying that Claughton, according to Hanson, was seriously about to complete. Hobhouse had told him something derogatory of Hanson, on which he remarked that he was truly sorry to hear such things and a little sorry for himself. He had furnished the money to release himself from the mortgage of £6,000 held by Colonel Sawbridge, which had to be done before Newstead could finally change hands.

> . . . If possible see H. & it may be as *well* to *hint* about the instalments being paid to *me*. . . . To return to my Ipecacuanha [he wrote in a postscript]— I suppose Clau. wont be such a fool as to pay Hanson till I have signed the new contract—preparatory—& in that case of course I will lay my digits upon the cash in person, the trustees for Lady B. are only concerned for her settlement of £60,000, which will be received on mortgage of the estate, & the rest of course to me, & I propose to pay all debts . . .[4]

On February 17th 1815 he told Hobhouse, '*I* am disposed to give up, and not hold out with Clau:', the underlined pronoun suggesting that Hanson, a letter from whom he enclosed, was of the contrary opinion.

---

[1] So far from realizing that any sacrifice was being made for him, Ashe accused Byron of neglect for not coming to his aid instantaneously. His fraudulent work was called *The Spirit of 'The Book'*. Byron settled with John Murray for this charity on 23 and 27 May 1814. By request of the adventurer himself, the money was first advanced at the rate of £10 a month, but after several instalments, he asked for a lump sum to go to Australia, and got it. Whether he went I do not know.

[2] Byron's cheque to Eliza Francis is dated 25 Oct. 1814. She kept a record of their encounters of which I give some brief extracts in Appendix 9, it being an unique first hand account of his gallantry when he was behaving well—or only misbehaving a little.

[3] Murray MS. 5 Feb. 1815.

[4] Ibid. 11 Feb. I am not clear how Byron obtained the £6,000 unless it was the part of Lady Byron's dowry of £20,000 which her father had been able to raise. The whole dowry was settled upon her issue (Ada) and remained mostly unpaid at Byron's death.

But he asked Hobhouse then, and again next day, to try and see the man and Hanson too. Hobhouse had evidently expressed grave misgivings, and Byron wrote, 'Tremble, if *you* tremble what must I? I must be a little Earthquake.'[1]

From now on, Hobhouse and their mutual friend, Kinnaird, became more and more active on his behalf and Hanson less and less so, his negligence about answering even the most pressing letters having grown incorrigible.

When Byron said that he was driven mad by delay, he was speaking almost literally. Under the strain of uncertainty affecting his circumstances so profoundly, his conduct approached the insanity his wife suspected in him: and it was paralleled by the crazy confusion at Newstead. Hanson wrote feebly to tenants saying Lord Byron was 'very much surprised' at their objection to paying rent, but those who replied had baffling excuses. Farmer Walker wouldn't pay a shilling, Mealey assured him, until Claughton had settled a large bill for improvements he had made on the farm. He had been served with a warrant for distraint and meant to turn rough, he added apprehensively.[2] Old Joe Murray and the sole housemaid left didn't know what to do because Paling, whom Claughton had put in possession of the mansion, wouldn't allow them anything for expenses.[3] Paling was the man whom Mealey had deprived of the Hut, and it must have been most satisfying to him to lord it over the hapless steward, and torment for the steward to see him and his family doing as they pleased in the great house: 'Whiteman has had the bailiffs in three times since you was at Newstead and i am afraid will have them again without Mr Claughton helps him'.[4]

Whiteman was especially unfortunate because, before moving to Nottinghamshire, he had sold his own property to none other than Claughton himself, and had not been paid for it. He went to Lancashire where the defaulter resided to try and get some part of what was due to him, but came back, Mealey declared, 'without one shilling', and had to sell his sheep.[5] One of the Hardstaffs, whose family had held tenancies since the 18th century, was sufficiently solvent to acquire a farm elsewhere; but Walker did a moonlight flit, taking his horses, waggons, and furniture with him, after first managing to sell his hay. He had left the premises in 'a most dissilate state; the farm lays in waste'.[6] If only Mr Hanson would come and settle the question—*who was now the landlord?*

While this nerve-racking state of things continued month after month, Byron had no alternative but to pay a skeleton staff to keep the place from utter disintegration or, in the case of old Murray, to prevent destitution.

---

[1] Ibid. 18 Feb.   [2] Egerton 2613. 3 Oct. 1815.   [3] Ibid. 5 Nov.
[4] Ibid. 8 Jan. 1816.   [5] Ibid. 8 Feb. 1816.   [6] Ibid. 8 Feb. and 4 Mar. 1816.

Murray had nine shillings a week board wages, and two maids at first were given the same, but at some time before the end of 1815, one of them, Mary Pearson, received two pounds for her coach fare to London; only Susan Child remained and she at her wits' end what to do when Paling, by Claughton's orders, moved in.[1] William Whitehead, formerly the gamekeeper, had the comparatively high wage of eighteen shillings a week, and his brother fifteen, many weeks on end for harvesting and other agricultural work, and there was another man too, Samuel Turner, receiving between fifteen and eighteen shillings, who assisted them.[2] The keeper had ten shillings a week—and Byron believed he was selling the game for his own profit. (From the time of his 1814 visit, the last he was to pay, he had wanted Hanson to get rid of him, and also of the ineffectual Mealey,[3] whom Kinnaird described later as 'the old drunken Steward',[4] but Hanson found it convenient to deal with those he could leave to muddle on in their own way.)

The tug-of-war between Byron's employees and Claughton's, upon such questions as who was entitled to the game, incessantly produced little dramas. Claughton, whose payments up to date amounted to £28,000, would not positively retract and could not go forward. But in June that year Byron broke out of the trance-like abstractedness of his marriage to attempt a decisive step. A Mr Bolton from Mansfield, who seems to have been a valuer and agent, took up temporary residence with instructions to dispose of the property. He did not succeed, and two or three months later, Byron grew wrathful on hearing that Mealey had put difficulties in his way by giving enquirers adverse reports. Mealey was such an inveterate grumbler that we cannot imagine him doing otherwise, but he hastened in letters both to Hanson and Byron to rebut an accusation that put his already dubious future in peril. There is a certain pathos in his impassioned denial, so gropingly accomplished:

> My Lord
>   I hope your Lordship will excuse me for addressing these few lines as Captain Byron was pleased to tell me that your Lordship has been informed By Mr boultain that I had under valued your Lordship's Estate at Newstead. My Lord such a word never come out of my mouth. i should be adambed rouge and a villian if Ever i offered to do the like when i have got my bread, so Many years—my Lord i blive Mr Boultain was displaised As Mr Ward would not except of his service to shew the Estate. . . . And as to the other three Gentlemen from Basford that come to view the estate the[y] will

[1] Murray MS. 27 Oct. 1815.   [2] Ibid. 8 Dec. 1815, and other dates.
[3] *LJ.* 3 Aug. 1814.
[4] Kinnaird copies. 16 Oct. 1821. In that letter Kinnaird said he had learned at Rochdale that Hanson had shamefully neglected Byron's interests.

testify that there was nothing mentioned any more than that some of the formers [sic] had ploughed to[o] wide which isaid they did. As to what motive Mr Boultain can have in informing your Lordship such a thing iam at a loss to know as it can soon be proved to the contrary.[1]

Whether Byron was convinced or not, within a few days he had another serious annoyance. He discovered, perhaps through reading the auction sale catalogue of the contents of his house, that his cellar was substantially depleted. Claughton had already raided it, as may be remembered, two years before, but the lock had been replaced and the old butler alone had the key. Suspicion therefore fell on him, and Byron reproached him in a manner which drew from him a most pained letter repudiating the idea that he could have committed such a breach of trust. 'After all these many long years of honest and faithfull servitude I should think myself base beyond every thing.' What had happened was that he had been prevailed upon to open the cellar door for Mr Bolton, who had seemed most offended by his reluctance, and had said that if he was not allowed to take what wines he wanted, he would send to Mansfield for his own and charge them to Lord Byron's account. Murray, thinking how expensive that would be for his Lordship, had given in. Bolton had lived at the Abbey exactly a month, and during that time had drunk or entertained his guests with fifty bottles of port and Madeira and ten of different sweet wines, besides two of brandy and two of rum which he had debited to Byron's account at the Hut.

Murray confessed that he himself, having been ill, had taken two bottles of port and, with Rushton, five or six of porter. He had no words to say how sincerely he begged pardon for Bolton's depredations.[2]

It seems likely that, since Bolton stayed so long, his engagement had comprised making the inventory for the London auctioneers,[3] but by October, when this correspondence took place, the sale had been suddenly cancelled. The vacillating Claughton had insisted that he would definitely take possession, and old Murray's letter conveyed the news that Paling, on Claughton's behalf, had ordered Mealey to give up the keys to him.

The decision to stop the sale was exceedingly rash, and according to Mealey, caused much local annoyance.[4] The household effects of the famous Lord Byron could not have failed to fetch a sum which would have relieved him at least of his most urgent difficulties, and nothing

---

[1] Ibid. 13 Oct. 1815. The Captain Byron who passed Byron's complaint on to Mealey may have been either one of the sons of the Hon. Mrs Byron of Nottingham, who would have been in a position to know local affairs, or else Captain George Anson Byron, R.N. who sometimes went shooting at Newstead.

[2] Ibid. 27 Oct.   [3] See Appendix 5.

[4] Egerton 2613, Folio 224. 22 Oct.

would have been lost as far as Claughton was concerned, since he could not after all produce the balance due. Newstead, relapsed into the almost ruinous state in which Mrs Byron and her little son had found it eighteen years before, became more and more unlikely to attract an affluent purchaser, while the complex business of the legal separation of Byron from his wife in the spring of 1816 gave Hanson all the excuse he needed for letting the rest of his client's affairs slide.

The break-up of the marriage has probably had more space devoted to it in print than any comparable domestic event in English history, and it would be superfluous to trace here the dismal steps by which it was accomplished. The union had been a folly of vanity on both sides—on his wife's because, in her self-complacency, she had pictured herself, as various letters and papers plainly show, reforming and remoulding the celebrated and sought-after young poet, and was possibly not without some happy consciousness of scoring off her distasteful cousin-in-law, Caroline Lamb: on his, because it seemed amusing for him, a rake, to carry off the most strait-laced girl he had ever met, the Princess of Parallelograms.

Financial harassments from beginning to end had preyed on his mind and given her a sense of injury which grew upon her as she came to believe that, among his other villainies, he had married her for money. Here, as so often, she had misjudged; if the attractions of an heiress had been paramount he could have done much better.

In his own blunt summing-up six years after he had last seen her, when her mother, Lady Noel (formerly Milbanke), died and he asked Kinnaird to appoint Sir Francis Burdett as one of the arbitrators of the estate:

> The principal points for the consideration of my referee, besides those more technical ones . . . are—*firstly*—the large Settlement (Sixty thousand pounds, i.e. ten thousand more than I was advised to make upon the Miss Milbanke) made by me upon this female; *secondly* the comparative smallness of her then fortune (twenty thousand pounds, and *that* never paid) when surely as a young man with an old title—of a fortune independent enough at that time, (as Newstead would have made me, had the then purchaser kept to his bargain) with some name and fame in the world I might have pretended to no worse a match than Miss Milbanke anywhere, and in England to a much better whether you take into the balance fortune, person, or connection. Thirdly, my leaving both her father, Sir Ralph, and her Uncle Lord Wentworth (notwithstanding that I was again strongly advised to the Contrary) perfectly free to leave their property as they liked, instead of requiring the previous settlement upon her, thereby showing (what was true) that I did not wed her for her expectations. . . .
>
> . . . . I have been made a victim of this woman's family and have been absolutely ruined in reputation, and anything but a gainer in fortune by the

'Old Joe Murray', from a portrait by T. Barker, commisioned by Byron at Newstead Abbey

Cost of publication of *Childe Harold* cantos I and II, 1812, from John Murray's ledger match hitherto. I certainly did by no means marry her for her fortune, but if, after having undergone what I have 'Fortune' (like Honour) comes unlooked for I feel by no means disposed to abandon my just *claim* to my just share, at the same time neither desiring nor requiring more than is fair and honourable.[1]

It must be borne in mind that this was written many years before the Married Women's Property Act, and when matrimony was quite commonly a sort of pecuniary transaction, and a bride's dowry all but advertised in the press. Byron was bitter when he thought of the scandals and mortifications he had suffered as the result of a marriage in every sense unprofitable, and one he had brought upon himself through an absurd impulse. Miss Milbanke having drawn him into correspondence by pretending she was in love with someone else, his proposal, after months of indulging in what he supposed was a Platonic pen-friendship, had been made with so little expectation of being accepted that he had written to Hobhouse eagerly inviting him, with details of preparations, to go 'direct and directly' to Italy with him—unless, he said, a circumstance happened which was as unlikely as Joanna Southcote's 'establishing herself as the real Mrs Trinity'.[2] That circumstance was of course Miss Milbanke's consent.

When, after a year of lacerating incompatibility, the débâcle came, he suffered from it at first far worse than she. The glare of adverse publicity was focussed, naturally, upon the more conspicuous and ostensibly dramatic figure. He fell, as idols fall, with shattering impact, while she was sustained by a belief in her own unswerving rectitude, to which she often alluded, and the over-brimming sympathy of all the friends and relations to whom she confided, among them several of Byron's—his cousin and heir, his maiden aunt[3] and his sister, whom she used in a manner which now strikes us as so cruelly artful.

But Augusta too could be very artful, and, having a remarkable gift for running with the hare and hunting with the hounds, got from Byron, during the months of his most crucial struggles with his wife and his creditors, no less than £720 in four payments, in addition to the thousands already mentioned.[4] Although a cheque stub was discreetly marked 'Mrs Leigh for home expenses', it was certainly not *his* home that was in question. Lady Byron's retrospective conclusion was that the motive of Augusta's 'crime' was money, and she may well have been right.

---

[1] Murray MS. 19 Feb. 1822.
[2] Ibid. 13 Sept. 1814. Hobhouse endorsed the letter to the effect that, one or two posts later, he had another to say his friend was going to be married.
[3] Jack Byron's sister Sophia who, he thought, made money her God. See p. 29.
[4] Murray MSS cheques of 20 Dec. 1815 and 21 Feb., 4 Mar. and 11 Apr. 1816.

In the end, Lady Byron proved the more grievously hurt. He had resilience, she almost none. He was self-critical and, in acknowledging 'the nightmare of my own delinquencies', could in some measure purge them. She was self-admiring, and contemplated with ever-renewed amazement the transcendent injustice of her ill usage, feeling more and more virtuous, more and more wronged, as the years went by. He was able to distil from his experiences new materials, new ideas about life, and an enlargement of his range as a poet which could never have been achieved while he was a spoiled young lion of English society. To him, though he was sometimes homesick, exile meant freedom—freedom to write in genuine defiance of convention, freedom from the hypocrisies of party politics and the religion of keeping up appearances, and ultimately freedom, even, from that dreadful burden he had laid upon his own back and borne every hour since the age of eighteen, his Old Man of the Sea—debt.

6

From Debt to Credit

Byron left London on April 23rd 1816. Prodigal to the last, he had bought himself a splendid new carriage requiring four to six horses. It was modelled on one made for Napoleon and cost £500. On the 24th, while he was at Dover with Hobhouse and Scrope Davies who had come to see him off—staying at an inn where ladies dressed themselves as chambermaids to catch a glimpse of him—Fletcher reported that everything he owned at 13 Piccadilly Terrace had been seized. It was the culmination of an extensive series of visits paid by bailiffs to that unlucky house, and Hobhouse was so afraid creditors would descend upon the superb vehicle that he immediately had it taken on board the ship, though rough weather made sailing impossible till next day.[1]

Accompanied by Fletcher, Rushton and a Swiss courier, Berger, Byron went by a leisurely route to Switzerland, gathering material which he used to great advantage in a continuation of *Childe Harold*. With him also was a private physician, John William Polidori, who had been paid in advance £30, probably a quarter's salary,[2] and was maintained as a gentleman-companion after the 18th-century fashion.

In Switzerland a young poet proved more congenial, Percy Bysshe Shelley, who was there with his future wife, Mary Godwin, an intelligent and pretty blonde, not yet nineteen, and her less attractive and still younger step-sister—the 'odd-headed girl'—who had so pressingly sought and won an encounter with Byron in London, Claire Clairmont. Polidori was a literary aspirant by no means disposed to play second fiddle to Shelley. Everyone without exception found him tiresome, and Byron parted with him before going to Italy in October with Hobhouse.

Though slow to realize it, he had put England behind him irrevocably. If only because it is natural to value what we have been deprived of, he

---

[1] Hobhouse, *Journals*. Berg Collection, New York Public Library.
[2] Murray MS cheque 17 Apr. Within two or three days of the sailing date, Polidori had further cheques for £202, I do not know for what purpose as the courier would normally have held the cash for travelling expenses.

had sought reconciliation with his wife; but his tentative overtures through Mme de Stael had been rebuffed. Lady Byron had told too many sympathizing friends of his depravity to be able to climb down now, and besides, Henry Brougham, who detested him, was one of her legal advisers, and he got wind of Mme de Stael's amiable intention and took care to circumvent it.[1] After this, Byron's attitude changed. In Switzerland he had been comparatively discreet, resenting and trying to contradict damaging rumours—undoubtedly circulated, if not set going, by Brougham who was at Geneva—but when he perceived how little chance there was of his ever living down the opprobrium that had been generated about his name, he became first indifferent, then defiant.

In Venice, where he arrived on November 10th 1816, he settled down to a comfortable love affair with his landlord's wife in the Frezzeria, Marianna Segati, whom he described to Kinnaird as 'a very pretty woman—so much so as to obtain the approbation of the not easily approving H[obhouse] who is in general rather tardy in his applause . . .'. She was furthermore 'a mighty & admirable singer'.[2] He had meant, he said, to give up gallivanting, but the *'besoin d'aimer'* had come back upon his heart and, after all, there was nothing like it. On no occasion did he ever profess that the rash Claire Clairmont, awaiting his child under Shelley's protection in England, had revived or fulfilled any *besoin d'aimer*.

His affair with Marianna has not formed any very solid portion of the numberless books in which he figures because, unlike his more notorious liaisons, it left almost no aftermath: but excepting his attachment to Teresa Guiccioli, it was the longest amatory relationship of his life. It lasted, though not without some infidelity, from November 1816 until February 1818, and for at least the first six months or so gave him an active kind of contentment which he imparted eagerly to his friends. He was so much in love with this girl of twenty-one that he had her painted by a miniaturist and took the portrait to be mounted in the lid of one of the gold snuff boxes he had bought originally for Eastern potentates— only to find that the London jeweller had cheated him: the box was silver-gilt. He wrote wrathfully to John Murray, to whom he entrusted every kind of likely and unlikely commission, requesting him to tell Mr Love of Love & Kelty 'with due ferocity' of his displeasure and insistence on restitution.[3] Being cheated was an occupational hazard of young Lords

[1] How Brougham conducted himself in this matter is told in *The Late Lord Byron*. My theory is that his hostility began with his being that very 'Scotch Reviewer' who had, in omniscient style, predicted a career of nullity for Byron, and his having his prophecy so soon and ludicrously falsified. He was obliged to keep his authorship of the silly review secret till his old age.

[2] 42093. Byron Papers 27 Nov. 1816. [3] Moore. 25 Feb. and 2 Apr. 1817.

who liked to be lordly, but at twenty-nine, after a world of financial worries, he was beginning to take exception to it.

Yet he was spending as lavishly as ever on his pleasures. That was inevitable with such a mercenary mistress. Moore tells a story of her being given 'a handsome set of diamonds' by Byron, which she secretly sold. The purchaser, a jeweller, offered them, unknowingly, to none other than Byron himself who bought them back and presented them again to the same recipient—with comments. This anecdote has the shapeliness that is rather incompatible as a rule with literal truth, but it is certain that Hobhouse noted in his diary, when the affair had been going some ten months, that Byron had spent about £500 on her,[1] and that was a substantial amount of money in Venice, one of the least expensive cities of Europe.

But in Marianna's favour it should be noted that Teresa Guiccioli, who must have formed her impressions wholly or largely through Byron himself, took a very favourable view of her influence, going so far as to say that it had nourished his genius. She excuses the adultery on the grounds that Signor Segati hardly seemed to exist (he had, in fact, a mistress of his own), and describes Marianna as charming and pretty, though superficial. She balances Byron's Venetian nights against his days at the Armenian Monastery and the respect he felt for the dedicated lives of the monks. Discussing the end of that amour, he had told her that he was incapable of really loving any woman who was ill-bred or ignorant; and Marianna's letters, in Teresa's otherwise generous judgment, did give only too much evidence of an 'intellectual and social lacuna'.[2] Of course, Teresa's lover was taking a line that would please her, well-bred and well-read as she was, and proud of her familiarity with great literature; but it is very likely that, as he gained a deeper knowledge of the Italian language, he grew more sensitive to Marianna's limitations.

The *relazione*, as he called it, was, in the most direct sense, far from profitless because it was on hearing from Marianna's husband an amusing piece of gossip, about a Venetian couple restored to each other after the man had long been thought lost at sea, that he wrote *Beppo* which was the *ballon d'essai* for *Don Juan*. By a happy coincidence Lord Kinnaird, who was in Venice at that time, read him Hookham Frere's *Whistlecraft*, asking him if he did not consider it 'a very clever and a very difficult performance'. Byron replied that it was very clever but not very difficult, and in two days he composed *Beppo*.[3]

---

[1] 6 Sept. 1817, quoted by Marchand.

[2] *La Vie*. Marianna's letters to Byron, which he evidently kept, do not seem to have survived.

[3] Murray MS. This interesting note on the genesis of *Don Juan* is from Hobhouse's

It must have been for the sake of the privacy he could hardly enjoy under Marianna's roof that eventually he took the sort of retreat known then as a casino at Santa Maria Zobenigo, keeping rendezvous there with the women who would supplant her. Of these the principal was a baker's peasant wife, Margarita Cogni—'La Fornarina'. When in love with Marianna, he had likened her in her beauty to an antelope: Margarita he characterized as a tigress, 'a fine animal but quite untameable'.

Teresa is not nearly so kind to Margarita as to Marianna. She writes of her as an example of Byron's charity and tolerance. There she was in error, though it was certainly almost as a mendicant that this uninhibited illiterate first approached him. In his own words, he and Hobhouse were:

> sauntering on horseback along the Brenta one evening, when, amongst a group of peasants, we remarked two girls as the prettiest we had seen for some time. About this period, there had been great distress in the country, and I had a little relieved some of the people. Generosity makes a great figure at very little cost in Venetian livres, and mine had probably been exaggerated—as an Englishman's. Whether they remarked us looking at them or no, I know not; but one of them called out to me in Venetian, 'Why do not you, who relieve others, think of us also?'

He answered her, 'My dear, you are too beautiful and young to need aid from me', to which she rejoined that if he saw where she lived and what she ate, he wouldn't say so. They were half jesting on that occasion but: 'A few evenings after, we met with these two girls again, and they addressed us more seriously assuring us of the truth of their statement. They were cousins; Margarita married, the other single.'

Still doubting, Byron proposed an appointment with them for next day. Hobhouse had taken a fancy to the cousin but, being unmarried, she could not enjoy Margarita's freedom, and he made his advances in vain— 'for here no woman will do anything under adultery'.

> . . . Mine made some bother—at the propositions, and wished to consider of them. I told her, 'if you really are in want, I will relieve you without any conditions whatever, and you may make love with me or no just as you please—*that* shall make no difference; but if you are not in absolute necessity, this is naturally a rendezvous, and I presumed that you understood this when you made the appointment.' She said that she had no objection to make love with me, as she was married, and all married women did it: but that her husband (a baker) was somewhat ferocious, and would do her a mischief. In short, in a few evenings we arranged our affairs, and for two years, in the course of which I had more women that I can count or recount, she was the

account of Stendhal's fictions about Byron, in particular his claim that a Contessina N. had lent a collection of MSS. works of Buratti to be read to Byron in Milan.

only one who preserved over me an ascendancy which was often disputed, and never impaired.[1]

Moore, quoting this letter, made the 'two years' a 'long space of time' perhaps because he had noticed the statement was inexact. Hobhouse did not join Byron in his summer villa on the Brenta until July 31st 1817 and August 5th, according to his journal, was the day they 'made assignations'. Marianna was still his mistress and it was not till more than a year later that Margarita became, despite his protests, an inmate of the Venetian palazzo to which he had moved. 'She has been here this month' he wrote to Augusta on September 21st 1818. 'I had known her (and fifty others) more than a year, but did not anticipate this escapade, which was the fault of her booby husband's treatment . . .'[2] She was ejected, after much knife-brandishing and hysteria, a few weeks later—having first acquired, Byron told John Murray, 'a sufficient provision for herself and her mother &c'. The duration of the episode was short, and how intermittent may be gathered from his own chronicles of his debaucheries, in one of which he names 'the Fornaretta' casually in a list of women, 'some noble some middling—some low—& all whores'.[3]

Except when his variable moods are involved, Byron is a most reliable witness, but while he refrains from trifling with literal facts, so that even to err about a period of time is very rare with him, he is inclined to dramatize characters and situations. Margarita, the handsome amazon, unable to read or write, knocking down those who got in her way, standing on the marble steps of the Palazzo Mocenigo in a storm with her hair streaming and 'lightning flashing round her head', proud and ungovernable—here was a splendid subject for his Caravaggio style, and as he knew it was his publisher's habit to read parts of his letters to favoured callers at Albemarle Street, I think he dressed up the portrait a little. By his own account in that very description, the poor young woman actually longed to discard her picturesque peasant garb and bought herself smart clothes, which he burned, tried to learn reading, and was readily employed as his housekeeper, economizing rigorously on his behalf—none of which suggests the noble female savage.

Arsène Houssaye, Director of the *Comédie Française*, in his *Voyage à Venise* (1850), says he met Margarita Cogni there, and that she had become an oyster seller, apparently at some kind of stall or buffet, and that as long as she talked about Byron, he and his friend went on eating oysters. It is significant that, though she was frank enough about their relations, she only claimed to have spent six weeks under Byron's roof.

[1] Quennell. To John Murray, 1 Aug. 1819.
[2] Quennell.   [3] Murray MS. To Hobhouse and Kinnaird, 19 Jan. 1819.

Her violence and the daily complaints of the servants she provoked would not have permitted her reign to endure much longer, and Byron in fact wrote on November 16th 1819, 'I have not for now a year touched or disbursed, a sixpence to any harlotry',[1] indicating that the date of Margarita's congé was about November 1818, if not a little earlier.

Intrigues with women whom he could dismiss as 'all whores' had done nothing to lighten the burden of debt left behind for Hobhouse, Kinnaird and Hanson to cope with. His income was bigger because pressing need had compelled him to accept in person Murray's liberal payments for his productions, but his outlay on philandering adventures kept pace with it.

> In two years [he wrote to James Webster] I have spent about *five* thousand pounds, and I need not have spent a *third* of this, had it not been that I have a passion for women which is expensive in its variety everywhere, but less so in Venice than in other cities. . . . more than half was laid out in the Sex;—to be sure I have had plenty for the money, that's certain—I think at least two hundred of one sort or another—perhaps more, for I have not lately kept the recount.[2]

Such crude boasting was obviously uttered in a spirit of bravado and was a kind of reaffirmation to himself that he had burned his boats, for sometimes he hankered after his English friends with their more temperate way of life, and then he had to tell himself—and them—how he hated England and was enjoying himself riotously where he was. There was an element too of feeling revenged on his unyielding wife—an absurd childishness because the gossip her friends assiduously brought her only increased the measure of her self-justification.

Venice, as seems better known than any other fact about Byron, was the scene of his most reckless profligacy, injurious to his health and appearance, destructive to his already damaged reputation, shameful to his conscience, yet, as no one but himself recognized at the time, immensely stimulating to his poetic faculties. During the two and a half years he spent there, besides a number of minor but not negligible poems, he finished *Manfred*, writing the third act twice, and composed Canto 4 of *Childe Harold*, *Mazeppa* and two complete Cantos of *Don Juan*—a tremendous performance.

The reception of much of that output by his publisher and friends was lacking in enthusiasm, and *Don Juan* caused absolute consternation. Even those among them who were able to appreciate its merits as literature were worried about it as a display of moral turpitude. The comic approach to human frailty seemed particularly offensive, and the cynical realism

---

[1] Ibid.   [2] 8 Sept. 1818, quoted by Marchand.

even worse. *The Corsair* with his 'thousand crimes' had been acceptable in every drawing-room because he bore as much correspondence to life as the actors who brandished knives and pistols in theatrical prints. There were no unreal characters in *Don Juan* and so it was outlawed—almost literally. Murray who, notwithstanding his disapproval of Byron's changed style, had paid a high fee for the first cantos, succeeded in getting an injunction against infringement of his copyright in 1819, but the following year it was dissolved by the Lord Chancellor Eldon on the grounds that a poem of so much levity and licentiousness did not deserve the protection of the law. (The curious result was that renewed piracies hugely increased circulation.)

Shelley was one of the few who recognized the quality of that work, but he could not see that a mode of life which horrified him had contributed to it. Moore, who himself had written poetry once deemed improper, could acknowledge that the life had produced the epic, but, while praising, he dexterously apologized for it. 'Never did pages more faithfully, and, in many respects, more lamentably, reflect every variety of feeling, and whim, and passion, that, like the wrack of autumn, swept across the author's mind in writing them.' And he called them 'the most powerful and, in many respects, painful display of the versatility of genius that has ever been left for succeeding ages to wonder at and deplore'.

It fell, fifty-odd years later, to one of the most moralistic of Victorians to explain how a writer of intense creativity who, however headstrong and self-willed, was always alive to the necessity of work, could shape a masterpiece out of what would have been ruin to most others:

> It is remarkable that this indulgence of the senses neither clouded nor weakened the intellect of the man, who had formerly been encouraged in abstinence by the mental clearness and activity which it afforded him. On the contrary, inconsiderate observers might have inferred from the development and fecundity of his genius throughout this period of moral declension that his mind was fortified and quickened by the excesses of his body. . . . To account for this expansion of Byron's faculties under conditions that might have been expected to dwarf and blight them, readers must remember that he was precisely at the age when genius hastens to maturity; that he had for years been gathering the wealth of thought and feeling, which he now poured upon his readers with brilliant prodigality; and that by stimulating his combativeness the circumstances under which he revealed his full mental magnitude, and spoke, now to the world's amazement and now to its delight, from the depths of his soul's anguish and daring, were conducive to intellectual energy in proportion as they were destructive of his happiness and hurtful to his nature.[1]

[1] Jeaffreson, *The Real Lord Byron.*

A group of Byron's friends, with Hobhouse as their spokesman, had united in urging him not to publish the unseemly work. He was shaken by their appeal, and went through several reactions to it, at first seeming acquiescent but insisting that fifty copies must be privately printed at his own expense and distributed as he should direct, next building up an elaborate pretence that he wanted the money a publisher would pay, the loss of which would break his heart. He grew peremptory:

> I name no sum from Murray—but you may suppose that I shall greatly admire the largest possible. Don't answer me with any more damned preachments from Hobhouse, about public opinion—I never flattered that, and I never will. . . .[1]

He would not change a word, he said, for either publisher or public, which was hardly the attitude of a man whose main object was cash. In the end Murray brought out the offending cantos, but without his imprimatur—which Byron did not readily forgive. He was kept some time in doubt as to their success, the object being to discourage him from continuing in this vein although the sales were brisk.

By now Byron was within sight, though distantly, of the end of his material difficulties, because towards the close of 1817 a most desirable purchaser for Newstead Abbey had come forward in the shape of a former Harrow schoolfellow, Thomas Wildman, a rich and respectable young lieutenant-colonel who happened to be Byron's great admirer. The purchase price was much lower than Claughton's—£94,500—but the years that had passed, since the first abortive sale, had by no means improved the property and in fact the tenants, under the weak and careless administration of Hanson, had practically ceased to pay rent. Byron was very well pleased with the offer—he would have been glad to settle for £80,000—and Wildman intended no delay in completion; but it was requisite that the contract should be signed by both parties, and the solicitor had become an all but immovable procrastinator.

Byron had suggested that a clerk should bring the papers to Venice, but Hanson drove him to fury by proposing instead that his Lordship should come to Geneva. Vainly, in letter after letter, each taking weeks to reach London, he pointed out that, apart from the inconvenience, the journey of a clerk from Geneva to Venice would cost much less than his own transport in the opposite direction. The months passed by and when, in September 1818 Hanson, having reached Geneva himself, wrote explicitly refusing to go further, and hinting that the transaction might thus fall through, Byron dispatched several remonstrances the terms of which may be sampled here:

[1] Murray MS. To Kinnaird, 6 Mar. 1819.

Spooney writes that he will not advance beyond Geneva. I have answered that he may return—for I would not cross to meet him were it only to Fusina or Maestri. . . . Pray tell him on his return from his fool's (or rogue's) errand, and that I would see him and all Chancery Lane in Hell before I would cross a Canal for them—what, am I to be made the Polichinello of an Attorneo at thirty years of age? he may be damned—*they* may be damned.

I have written to Douglas Kinnaird, & beg you to assist him with advice in a Committee upon this tedious mountebank's eternal dawdling.[1]

Byron won this battle, but when Hanson turned up in Venice with the documents on November 11th, just six weeks after the dispatch of his client's irate protest, instead of magnesia, tooth powder and the other English commodities John Murray had arranged for him to bring, together with eagerly awaited books, his cargo consisted of nothing more than a kaleidoscope and some corn rubbers![2] 'Only think, he has left everything,' Byron groaned, 'everything except his legal papers.' And he urged Hobhouse to send a courier to Italy at a cost of up to £300 with the missing items. 'Never mind expense nor weight. I must have books & Magnesia—particularly "Tales of my Lordlord."'[3]

This fantastic command, coming from a man who had been complaining for months because his funds in Venice were running out, and who still had large debts in England, was sensibly ignored. It is an evidence of the eccentricity in money matters which now becomes more and more apparent in his letters. He had always been a spendthrift, and so openhanded that few of the strangers and near strangers who accepted his largesse could have been aware of the strain they were putting on his resources. How could Coleridge, getting an immediate cheque for £100 when Sotheby wrote a begging letter on his behalf, suppose that his benefactor was under siege from bailiffs?[4] How could the playwright, Charles Maturin, suspect, when a cheque for £50 was enclosed for him as an encouragement to go on writing, that the apparently casual sender was himself in serious financial straits?[5]

Such instances might be multiplied from evidence, but there are many

[1] Ibid. To Hobhouse, 30 Sept. 1818.

[2] Byron's frequent need of corn rubbers reminds us what men of fashion endured when, for many years, there had been a vogue for pointed or chisel-toed footwear, often too tight-fitting as it was thought a sign of refinement in both sexes to have small feet. His lameness must also have caused special stresses.

[3] Murray MS. 11 Nov. 1818. *Tales of my Landlord* was the title given to each series of novels by Walter Scott, five in number up to 1816.

[4] The cheque is dated 12 Feb. 1816 (Murray MS.). It was Byron who used his influence to have Coleridge's tragedy *Remorse* staged and to get a volume of his poetry published by Murray.

[5] Cheque of 30 Dec. 1815. Byron was instrumental in promoting the representation of *Bertram* at the Drury Lane theatre.

more than are known because, while the deposit on Newstead lasted, he drew—generally through Fletcher—big sums of cash, some of which certainly went into the pockets of suppliants who never seem to have gone empty away. But when he had lived abroad two or three years, he came to recognize how often he had been duped, how quixotic had been his conduct in respect of his literary earnings, and how little deserving were most of those who had sponged on him. He then began to set a value on money, at first so that he could purchase an abundance of the pleasures of a voluptuary, which, as he reached what he deemed to be middle age, thirty, he felt he could not devour too avidly. His self-indulgence became for a while febrile, not only in sexual matters, but, as we have seen, in the gratification of any whim, such as acute impatience to read the latest novels of Scott. An extremist by temperament, he grew as eager to charge the highest fees for his work as before he had been indifferent or even determined not to be paid at all.

'I hope you are not dreaming', he wrote to Hobhouse when he was awaiting a large amount for recent publications, 'of any plan for Murray's money—except spending, life is too precarious to buy annuities & I want the whole directly!'[1]

That was the first stage of his recoil from the kind of self-abnegating generosity by which, instead of taking any fee for the lyrics set to music as *Hebrew Melodies*, he had insisted, hard-pressed by creditors though he was, on making the composer a present of £50.[2] He was still a lavish giver—Hoppner, the British Consul at Venice, stated that 'he was ever ready to assist the distressed and . . . most unostentatious in his charities'[3]; but he had outgrown his high-flown notions of benefiting others regardless of their deserts or of the cost to himself. He had come to a resolve, or at least he said so, that what he called his 'brain money' should be devoted to his bodily enjoyments. 'I shall not live long—and for that Reason I must live while I can. . . . Recollect—I care for nothing but monies.'[4]

Money, and how he loved it, became his theme in numerous letters, constantly quoted by those who are more inclined to observe his words than his deeds; but in reading these declarations it is fair to make allowance for his chameleon-like changes of mood, expressed with such astounding lack of reserve, the vein of facetiousness he expected his intimates to understand, and certain turns of phrase that he adopted as catchwords—equivalent among his friends to family jokes. It must also be borne in mind that as his ties with England were severed one after another, he worried lest he should find himself without resources in a foreign country;

[1] 42093 Byron Papers, 15 or 16 June 1818, one of many letters of the same tenor.
[2] Nathan, *Fugitive Pieces*.   [3] Moore.
[4] Murray MS. To Kinnaird and Hobhouse, 19 Jan. 1819.

and, when there were delays in the dispatch of remittances, he would start a sort of half-serious nagging.

Then, as he tired of libertinism, came his idea that if only he could accumulate enough to make him independent, he might buy a new lease of life in some remote and unspoiled part of the world where slanders and controversies and fame and infamy would concern him no longer. South America figured largely in his escapist dreams. He thought of taking his little daughter Allegra, whom Claire had handed over to him, to Venezuela and having a settled life, a home and the citizenship of what he pictured as an incomparably free and enlightened country. But it will be found that the dates of his letters asking Hobhouse or Kinnaird to advise about such possibilities coincide with crises in the very serious and demanding love affair which, in 1819, brought to an end his career as a dedicated profligate.

Teresa Guiccioli has not, on the whole, been a favourite with biographers. In her own time she was subjected by all who were interested in Byron to a critical inspection of her physical attributes and defects, but moral condemnation was mild because the situation of an old man rash enough to have married a young bride was the jest of so many operas and comedies that sympathy was more likely to lie with the wife than with a husband asking to be made ridiculous. The Victorians took another view. They were much less outraged by *Don Juan* than their forefathers—time had tested it and made it a classic—but on the other hand they were much more censorious of adulterous females. Extenuating circumstances were disregarded; and Teresa was especially to be condemned because she survived till 1873 and, instead of sinking into poverty and disgrace after the approved pattern for mistresses, had the effrontery to marry a very rich marquis and to publish a book about her famous lover.

Shelley, who had been so shocked by Byron's Venetian dissipations, found him after Teresa's advent 'in every respect an altered man'[1] and in various letters praised the reform she had effected, but Jeaffreson, the biographer last quoted, who brought out two substantial volumes on Byron in 1883, could only contrast her disgustedly with an English gentlewoman. In one respect she did bear a strong resemblance to an English gentlewoman—indeed to his sister. She entreated him not to continue *Don Juan* and, for a while, he obeyed her. But as she had also brought to an end the course of degrading promiscuity which, if persisted in, might have resulted at last in his not being able to write anything at all, literature is still in her debt. In justice to her it should be said that she could read only a French prose translation and was disturbed rather by

[1] To Peacock, ? 10 Aug. 1821.

the rabid rage the poem was provoking, and his depressions when he received letters from England, than by the work itself.

Teresa's detractors from Leigh Hunt onwards seem to have taken pleasure in the idea that she was not really loved by the man for whom she risked and, in the course of time, had to sacrifice means, position, security, and even pride. I would suggest that the deeper layers of evidence reveal an absorbing attachment which lasted, in its active phase, about as long as most masculine attachments do before they subside into prosaic familiarity—two or three years, possibly longer. Assuredly Byron does not come well out of our scrutiny of the affair in its early stages, a roué of thirty-one describing to his friends his conquest of a girl not out of her teens, yet appearing to criticize *her* for want of discretion; rising to the bait when gossiping male acquaintances try to make mischief about her; deliberately looking round for prospects of infidelity.

The explanation of all this is plain enough with the documentation now available.[1] It was the defensiveness of a very vulnerable man who could hardly believe in his own good fortune when, after the coarse and wanton excesses of his recent career, and the havoc they had wrought in him, he succeeded in winning, in an almost public triumph, a lovely young countess, refined and yet voluptuous, appealingly sentimental yet notably high-spirited and moving in society where none of his Italian partners hitherto had been admissible. The first letter in which he mentions her to Hobhouse, written at four in the morning, gives us, sometimes with subtle undertones, the effect she had made on him.

> . . . It is Passion week, & rather dull. I am dull too, for I have fallen in love with a Romagnola Countess from Ravenna—who is nineteen years old & has a Count of fifty—whom she seems disposed to qualify, the first year of marriage being just over.
>
> I knew her a little last year at her starting, but they always wait a year—at least generally. I met her first at the Albrizzi's—and this Spring at the Benzona's—and I have hopes, Sir,—hopes, but she wants me to come to Ravenna, & then to Bologna—now this would be all very well for certainties, but for mere hopes, if She should plant me, and I should make a 'fiasco' never could I shew my face on the Piazza. It is nothing that Money can do—for the Conte is awfully rich—& would be so even in England—but he is fifty and odd—has had two wives & children before this his third—(a pretty fair-haired Girl, last year out of a Convent—now making her second tour of the Venetian Conversazioni . . .)

'If she should plant me!' He was already fearful of that shaming possibility before he had possessed her, already wondering if, following her

---

[1] Much of it is published in Iris Origo's book, *The Last Attachment*.

to Ravenna on the strength of 'mere hopes', he was to be defeated—he who had been entering into his Don Juan rôle as he had once in London drawing-rooms affected the lonely gloom of Childe Harold. He pretended, rather to himself, I fancy, than to Hobhouse, that he could view her with detachment: 'She is pretty but has no tact . . .' She had called him 'mio Byron' so audibly that there had been staring and whispering. Can we not detect, beneath the disapproval, how flattered he had been by that? 'What shall I do?' he ended more honestly. 'I am in love—and tired of promiscuous Concubinage—& have now an opportunity of Settling for life.'[1]

That was how he saw it from the beginning—a contrast to the transient relations with women who, even if not common prostitutes, could be bought by money and could claim nothing more. Then he succeeded in taking her to his casino and becoming her lover. It was not difficult; much practice had made him a virtuoso, and she was yielding, for her husband was nearer sixty than fifty and Byron, however he might have declined in the eyes of those who had seen him in his former glory, had remained eminently attractive. Her surrender did not cause the reaction usually experienced by Byron and other rakes after satisfying desire. He became more involved.

'She is as fair as Sunrise—and warm as Noon', he told Kinnaird with his customary inexcusable licence in communicativeness. 'We had but ten days to manage all our little matters in beginning middle and end, & we managed them . . .' He went on with his pretence, ironical in the circumstances, that her indiscretions were quite embarrassing to himself and her husband, but finished once again with candour: 'I am damnably in love, but they are gone—gone, for many months—and nothing but Hope keeps me alive *seriously*.'[2]

Of course Hobhouse wrote and warned him to break off so dangerous a liaison, and of course he disregarded the warning and went to Ravenna, though not without delay and indecision; and, after vicissitudes such as reduced him at times to a very low state of mind, he stayed there.

It is one of the most striking facts about Byron—and perhaps it applies to any celebrity who is also a fascinating personality—that he inspired in numbers of his friends a quite inordinate possessiveness. I have tried to show in *The Late Lord Byron* that long-standing jealousy of Moore was Hobhouse's prime (though completely unrecognized) motive for bringing about the destruction of those Memoirs which Moore had received as a gift from Byron's hand. The same sort of jealousy, related to the renown and social distinction of the poet, actuated two of his

---

[1] Murray MS. 6 Apr. 1819.   [2] Ibid. 24 Apr

Venetian acquaintances in an unscrupulous effort to break up his love affair and so end his sojourn in Ravenna. One of these was the Consul, Richard Hoppner, whose Swiss wife had, for a handsome fee, taken charge for a while of Byron's little daughter by Claire Clairmont. Hoppner has come down to posterity for his famous scandal-mongering about Shelley. Alexander Scott, an intimate of Hoppner's, was a Scot whose common ground with Byron was that he was a first-rate swimmer, and who made himself useful in as many ways as he thought would ingratiate him. Hoppner had never met the Countess, Scott only at one or two conversazioni, but they knew hers was the sole influence which had removed the most interesting member of their circle, and they belaboured him with letters hinting at reasons why the association with her would prove disastrous.

Only a few days after Byron's arrival in Ravenna, Hoppner had taken up his pen to plant a barb that would go on rankling. In a style at once deferential and somewhat over-familiar, he managed by a sidelong approach to tell his Lordship that he was bringing trouble upon himself.

> It is a thousand pities for your sake as well as my own, that . . . if I tell you something for your own advantage, which immediately concerns another person, you directly acquaint that third person whence you received the information, & then what was intended for your good alone becomes a means of making me hated by others.
>
> Though I burn to tell you my secret I dare not, while I know it will cease to be one the moment it passes my pen or my lips. . . . By the time you return I will endeavour to find out a means of letting you into the significance of all this without your suspecting that the explanation comes from me, by which you will be benefited, & my conscience at ease without risk to my person.[1]

Byron seems, rather creditably, to have withstood the temptation he must have felt to learn the secret from the man who burned to tell it, and merely sent instructions to Venice about dispatching his horses and carriage and disposing of his casino, stating to Hoppner that the duration of his stay at Ravenna would depend entirely upon his 'Dama'.[2] Neither did he take much notice of a later suggestion that he might meet with 'a blow in the dark' from a stiletto wielded on behalf of the Count, although he himself believed something of the kind might happen; and at last Hoppner was constrained without encouragement to disburden himself of his malice by an odious letter, informing the lover, as from reliable sources, that his mistress had entangled him in her nets merely from

---

[1] Murray MS. 16 June 1819.   [2] *LJ.* 20 June.

Bust of Teresa Guiccioli by Lorenzo Bartolini, 1822

Bust of Byron by Lorenzo Bartolini, 1822

vanity, and when she thought herself sure of him, would leave him in the lurch and make a boast of it.[1]

> Again beguiled! Again betrayed!
> In manhood as in youth!

For all the long train of women with whom he might fairly consider himself to have been victorious, supposing sexual love to be a kind of warfare, those words written when a servant girl had deceived him, were still apt for feelings resting on such a sense of insecurity as his. He was too enraged to answer Hoppner direct, and too alarmed to ignore the interference, and he lashed out in a letter to Scott in which, while condemning Hoppner for his expressions of 'bile—*gratis* and *unasked*', he retorted upon the unfortunate Teresa: '. . . All I know is that *she* sought me—and that I have *had her*—*there and here and everywhere*—so that if there is any fool-making on the occasion I humbly suspect [? suggest] that two can play at that'.

But while taking this contemptuous and, it must be acknowledged, contemptible tone, he had the grace to admit that he loved her, though he would be cured by 'the least change or trick on her part', and he requested:

> As you are much more in the way of hearing the *real truth or lie* than H[oppner] perhaps you will tell me to what Gossip he alludes. . . . Pray answer by return of post—lest I should be off again.

He was absolutely distracted by his mistrust, and put a postscript almost as long as the letter, the gist of which was:

> You should give me notice in time, that I may be the first to throw up the Cards . . . Give me but a proof or a good *tight suspicious confirmation* and I will rejoin you directly, and we will village at the Mira—there is a bribe for you.[2]

In his final outburst he is as pathetic as an Othello beset by two Iagos:

> You will think me a damned fool—but when she was supposed in danger —I was really and truly on the point of poisoning myself—and I have got the drug still in my drawer.

His frantic jealousy would not let him rest, and he was impelled to translate for her parts of Hoppner's letter, and then he had the satisfaction of hearing her volunteer to declare to Scott in her own words that the alleged rumours were false. With touching humility she wrote to this

---

[1] Pierpont Morgan Library. 9 July 1819, quoted by Origo.
[2] Ibid. 12 July. La Mira was Byron's retreat on the Brenta.

near-stranger that time would prove her constancy. 'What a wretch I should consider myself if I feared that, one day, so great a man would blush to have loved me! But I am as sure of myself as I am of seeing the Sun again tomorrow.'[1]

Byron seldom hesitated to bring into confrontation people who had spoken ill of one another or, as in this instance, to confront the speaker of ill with the person calumniated. It was undiplomatic, indeed gravely embarrassing, but at times it cleared the air, and in Greece it was to turn out a useful method of dealing with faction and intrigue. Hoppner had shown he was aware of this habit; to Alexander Scott it was a surprise, and when he had Teresa's astounding vindication, he wrote Byron a somewhat nervous protest:

> ... I must not let slip an opportunity of teasing you—Tis a generally received maxim that a man ought never to repeat to a woman the things he may have heard said of her, for in many cases it may be a cause of feud—of much mischief, and in no case can good come of it. You translated part of H's letter to the G——. Surely those were no pleasant things. I think I have you there! Departing from your own principles at the very moment you were angry with H. for so doing.[2]

That he was taking his courage in both hands to write in such terms is shown by his beginning cautiously 'My dear Lord' instead of his previous very informal 'My dear Byron'. However, though timorous, he continued his machinations to separate the lovers, now striking raffish and jocular notes, now anticipating Byron's dislike of 'observations from officcious freinds' [sic].

When the Hoppners had left for Switzerland in July, they had placed the little girl, Allegra, whom neither of them really cared for, with an Italian family named Gelini, where there were four daughters who were all delighted with her; and Scott, though he did not see her himself, could send reports which gave him a pretext for correspondence with her father. But Byron desired to have the child with him in Bologna, where he had now followed Teresa, whose elderly husband had obliged her to go there with him, in the hope no doubt of ending the liaison. Scott took occasion to explain that Allegra's journey had been delayed because there was no governess to travel with her.

> Observe [he wrote fatuously] no embargo has been laid upon yr Daughter, though one studying her comfort might safely have laid such embargo. The delay in her setting out is solely owing to the want of a Gouvernante—
> May I now be permitted to tell you what I think on the subject—
> Allegra once in the hands of your Dama (you will not keep her at a hotel)

---

[1] Ibid. 23 July. Origo's translation.   [2] Murray MS. 27 July.

will be a hostage for your future conduct and if she should be there put in a convent it will be no easy matter to get her out again. Has the Count any male children? Has he asked you what *Dote* you mean to give her—You see I think myself a knowing man & your L[ordshi]p will think I am a fool— but what I am sorry for is, that your sending for Allegra is a sign that you do not think of soon returning to Venise [sic].[1]

To suggest to anyone so intransigent as Byron that an embargo might be laid on his having his child brought to him was tantamount to fixing his decision, and the insinuation that the Countess wanted her as a hostage and the Count as a well-dowered bride in fifteen years or so for any son he might happen to have, could not have helped Scott to gain his objective. Byron must have hoped the youthful Teresa would find some amusement in the companionship of the little girl, not yet three, and he himself felt much more affection for her than has been recognized by those who interpret his flippant utterances solemnly. There were potentially other motives which have never occurred to his critics. He had been told explicitly by the Hoppners that the climate of Venice was very bad for the child—they had proposed sending her to Switzerland—and he may well have considered that he now had a favourable chance of getting her into a cooler and healthier place, and at the same time releasing them from any obligation they might feel to offer her a home with them again.[2] Besides being angry with Hoppner (as, with his usual candour, he duly told him), he cannot have been quite insensitive to their dislike of the infant, because, though his contribution to their very modest household budget must have been a useful one, they were so eager to get her into some other family. '. . . In Venice she costs you upwards of £50 a year at present', Hoppner had written. 'In Switzerland you will be able to place her comfortably for much less . . . I know that this is no considera- tion to you: but I am scrupulous in the performance of my duty . . .'[3]

Byron did not want the child to be taken to another country. It is even conceivable that he remembered his promise to Claire to have her with him. He replied urgently to Scott, sending a special messenger for whom he had to get a passport from the police. A woman must at once be engaged to accompany an ex-clerk at the Consulate whom he employed as accountant and factotum, Richard Edgecombe; and they were to bring Allegra to Bologna forthwith:

[1] Ibid. 18 Aug.

[2] 'I always think', Mrs Hoppner had written to Mary Shelley [6 Jan. 1819], 'it is very unfortunate that Miss Clairmont requires this child to live in Venice, where the climate is injurious in every way to the little one's health'. Quoted in French in Grylls's *Mary Shelley*.

[3] Murray MS. 1 July.

I wish to see my child—and have her with *me*—now that Hoppner is no longer in Venice—and her being with me will not prevent my return [he put in as a conciliating touch] . . . I send this by express that Allegra may set out without loss of time—you can surely find a proper woman to accompany her.[1]

There was another man in Venice besides Edgecombe who attended professionally to Byron's affairs, H. Dorville, Vice-Consul, acting as Consul during Hoppner's absence. Dorville assisted with the task of dismantling the little casino where so many scenes, romantic or highly unedifying, had been played, and of keeping habitable the Palazzo Mocenigo and the villa; and he also watched over Allegra, to whom he seems to have been most kind and paternal. Before hearing that she had been sent for, he described her present situation to Byron:

> Dear little Allegra is very happy among her new acquaintances, I can assure you not forgotten by me. I commonly visit her 3 or 4 times a week & am generally a welcome visitor taking her some sweets &c. She was left in the Casa Gelini by Mrs Hoppner as Mrs Marten hesitated taking her on account of the Coff [sic] she was then afflicted with, since Mrs H's departure Mrs Gordon sent for her,[2] but my feelings would not let her be removed, she had formed an attachment for the young females in the same house, as also they have for her, & being in Venice I had an opportunity of looking after her myself which affords me no small pleasure for she is a dear little child.
>
> The Governante that was with her at Hoppner's is gone & at present she has none, not requiring any in the situation she is now, for several young females are in the house who are much attached & take every care of her possible.[3]

I quote this hitherto unpublished letter because it is so plainly in a style no one would adopt with a neglectful and indifferent father. A second one apologizes for not having obeyed Byron's orders immediately. Apart from the question of the missing nurse, Dorville feared the reason his Lordship had sent for Allegra was that he might have been under the impression she was not well looked after. She had now been dispatched with Mr Edgecombe and 'a female'—Byron had for some reason placed a veto on Edgecombe's wife—and they had been cautioned by Dorville 'to *take every care* of your Daughter & attend to her Comfort & pleasure on the Journey'. He had furnished Edgecombe with forty sequins which, he said, was much more than they would need.[4]

On the same day Alexander Scott, who was conveying as many worries

[1] Pierpont Morgan Library. 22 Aug. 1819, quoted by Origo.
[2] Mrs Marten was the wife of the Danish Consul who had arranged to take Allegra, but did not. I do not know the identity of Mrs Gordon.
[3] Murray MS. 13 Aug.   [4] Ibid. 26 Aug.

by post as he could, wrote: '*From* Venice you can hardly expect *news*. For
Venice, the best news will be your Lp's return. Is it true that the Society
in Bologna is as *charming* as report would have it [?]'.[1]

Scott seems to have been obsessed with a longing to destroy the liaison
even after he himself had left Venice. In December when Byron, back
at the Palazzo Mocenigo, was preparing to go to England with Allegra, it
was rumoured that he wished to 'plant' the Countess and could only save
face for her by leaving the country; and Scott wrote most unpleasantly
to the effect that, as long as she had been persuaded 'to go home quietly',
there was no need for Byron to put himself to the inconvenience of
travelling in winter. 'Do pray sham sick for a couple of months, and then
the weather will be milder.' He hoped his letters did not annoy or impor-
tune the recipient.[2] It is pretty certain that they did, because by this time
Byron was not only more deeply enamoured of Teresa than ever, but he
had attained sufficient confidence in her to have discarded those weapons
with which he had cruelly and crassly armed himself so that he might
strike before receiving a blow.

It was impossible for him to desist entirely from the facetiousness his
friends expected of him, and therefore we shall still find in his letters
some gentle ridicule of his mistress as well as of his own situation in the
rôle of *cavalier servente*, but there are also simpler expressions of devotion
than he ever bestowed on any other woman—his love for Augusta not
having been simple at all. He spoke of Teresa to Kinnaird as 'my Sovereign'
and of his relations with her as 'my pleasure, my pride, and my passion'.[3]
Telling Hobhouse he must leave Italy because there had been a dénoue-
ment in which the Count had demanded that she should choose between
husband and lover, he said:

> The lady was for leaving him—and eloping or separating—and so should
> I, had I been twenty instead of thirty and one years of age—for I loved her,
> but I knew the event would for her be irreparable, and that all her family—
> her sisters particularly and father would be plunged into despair for the
> reputation of the rest of the girls—and prevailed on her with great difficulty
> to return to Ravenna with her husband, who promised forgetfulness if she
> would give me up.

He had assured the Count, after ten days of what must have been
agonizing scenes, that he would disturb his family no longer but remove
himself beyond the Alps. 'Italy will be now to me insupportable.' And he
stated his emotions on the occasion without pride or disguise:

> She agreed to go back with him—but *I* feel so wretched and low, and
> lonely, that I will leave the country—reluctantly indeed, but I will do it,

---

[1] Ibid.   [2] Ibid. 18 Dec.   [3] Ibid. 16 Nov.

for otherwise, if I formed a new *liaison* she would cut the figure of a woman *planted*—and I never will willingly hurt her self-love. . . .

I will say no more, except that it has been as bitter a cut up for me, as that of leaving England.[1]

Although he did decently want to save face for Teresa, his leaving her had been by no means to gratify any wish of his own but far otherwise.

In the event, he did not go to England. Before he had dispatched the letter just quoted, in which he had said, 'I mean to plod through the Tyrol with my little "shild" Allegrina',[2] the infant had gone down with a severe fever, and he took up his pen the following day to say, 'I will not & can not go without her'. He himself had been very ill with this tertian, as he called it: he had contracted it on his first travels and, by its recurrences through his life, it seems to have been malaria. Now four others of his household had also been infected. Venice was plagued with mosquitoes and no one as yet knew they carried the disease.

Two weeks later he was in touch with Kinnaird to inform him that he had postponed his intention of returning: 'Neither the season nor length of the Journey would have suited my daughter's health after her illness'.[3]

Doubtless he availed himself readily enough of the excuse for remaining in the country 'where dwelt the lady of his love', celebrated in verses as lyrical as any he ever wrote (though acknowledged jovially by the ribald Kinnaird with appreciation of his ode to a lady on a *pot de chambre!*)[4] But he revealed in many ways that he was attentive to Allegra and concerned for her. Just as he was almost incapable of refraining from discussion of the topics that were particularly significant to him, so he rarely wasted words on those that were not. It is curious how much his letters have been quoted without the inclusion of those passages which show he had the normal feelings of a father.

After a period of tormented indecision—and while Teresa too was ill with misery—suddenly, with the entire preparations for his voyage complete and while waiting in his outdoor clothes, even to gloves and cane, to set off, he resolved instead to turn again to Ravenna. Perhaps to

[1] Ibid. 20 Nov.

[2] The reason for Byron's frequent references to each of his daughters as 'my shild' would appear to be his remembrance of a line from a play as pronounced with deliberate or unconscious distortion: 'Ah Coquin, vare is my shild?' He put the phrase in inverted commas when mentioning to Hobhouse his wish to have Allegra brought to him. (42095, 3 Mar. 1818.) I have not identified the piece. He quotes very often from plays.

[3] Murray MS. 2 Jan. 1820.

[4] Kinnaird copies. 16 May 1826, alluding to the *Stanzas to the Po*, which Byron had sent him on 14 Apr. 'Damn your quibble', Byron wrote, retorting to Kinnaird's joke (1 June).

some extent he was actuated by his realization that in England he now had nowhere to go.

> I have nobody to receive me but my sister; and I must conform to my circumstances and live accordingly—that is meanly in London, & difficultly, on that which affords splendour and ease in Italy.[1]

But his longing to see Teresa was once more paramount.

> I do not mean to stay at Venice, I shall go again to Ravenna—anything better than England, it is better to be with a woman whom I love at the risk of assassination, than in a country where I neither like nor am liked . . .[2]

So he threw in his lot with this young girl and became her recognized cavalier or gentleman-in-waiting in an historic but provincial little city, occupied apartments in the palazzo of her inscrutable husband, was an accepted favourite with her initially disapproving family, resumed his routine of writing or talking through long hours of the night (for love-making had to be managed while the Count took his siesta), joined a secret society for the liberation of Italy from Austrian domination, was involved in the Count's belated appeals to the Pope to redress his conjugal wrongs, and was watched and reported on incessantly by the secret police. And when, after nearly two years, Teresa's patriotic father, Count Ruggiero Gamba, was exiled from Romagna, taking her with him, Byron loyally if loiteringly followed them to Tuscany; and on their further exile from Tuscany, he uprooted himself again, though it was a process he hated, and domiciled himself with them in Genoa.

Of course he sometimes felt the strain; of course he had notions of becoming his own man again, for who that feels himself bound, by whatever silken bonds, does not sometimes make a bid to be free? Yet on the whole he was well content and wrote a quantity of letters saying so. He summed it up for Augusta towards the end of 1821: '. . . Without being so *furiously* in love as at first, I am more attached to her than I thought it possible to be to any woman after three years . . . and have not the least wish nor prospect of separation from her'.[3]

His rippling verses beginning, 'Could love for ever run like a river', have been cited frequently as a revelation of waning regard for his mistress.

> Wait not, fond lover,
> Till years are over,
> And then recover
>   As from a dream!

[1] Murray MS. To Kinnaird, 16 Nov. 1819. If he had known it, even his sister, utterly subjugated by his wife, would not have been able to receive him.
[2] Ibid. 10 Dec. 1819.   [3] Lovelace, *Astarte*. 5 Oct.

The poem was first published by the malicious Lady Blessington after a supposed conversation in which he tells her that liaisons 'not cemented by marriage must produce unhappiness', with the innuendo that he was confiding to her his desire to escape from his exigent countess. Actually the manuscript, which belonged to Teresa herself, is dated 1st December 1819, and the verses were written while he was in profound gloom having, as he believed, parted from her and being about to make that parting final by his journey to England. They are an attempt at plucking up spirits which echoes a hundred ostensibly light-hearted songs and epigrams exhorting us to accept the inevitable flight of love.

There are nearly a hundred and fifty letters from Byron to Teresa which range in feeling from green-eyed infatuation to a husband-like taking-for-granted, and must, or ought to, dispel any idea that the part she played in his life was less than a vital one. If, even while facing their separation with the admission that he was 'wretched and low and lonely', he could contemplate forming a new liaison in the future, it was not want of tenderness but because he would not let sentiment blind him to the realities of human nature. Later on he was to say 'This is a finisher', and to think it impossible he could live with another woman.[1]

They never did in fact live together in the sense of sharing bed and board as married couples do. She was obliged by papal decree to reside with her father, but although, despite this, there were periods when they were under the same roof, the large houses they occupied enabled them to have separate suites of apartments and staffs of servants. Byron never cared for dining with women, and the irregular hours he kept, through his method of working, made him no fit partner for a fully domesticated relationship.

He suffered many an hour of nostalgia, was often hurt by the long silences of his friends, the consciousness of being out of touch with much that was vivid, pungent, notable in London life; but, apart from his preoccupation with Teresa and with Italy, he knew, as we have seen, that by the standards of the British peerage the income which afforded him 'splendour and ease' abroad would be a very narrow one in London. Thanks to the dexterity with which Kinnaird was handling his financial resources, he was not only being gradually relieved of liabilities but was furnished with more money than he had ever yet enjoyed. Kinnaird acted as his literary agent as well as his banker and drove hard bargains with Murray, a task which became progressively more difficult as Murray grew rather to dread than to welcome those manuscripts, once so fashionably romantic, now so full of every kind of subversiveness—even, his solicitor warned him, blasphemy.

[1] *Astarte.* 15 Oct. 1821.

It was Kinnaird who dealt with the horde of creditors, paying interest on long-standing tradesmen's bills which Byron sometimes flinched from settling in a manner that seems, at this distance of time, capricious. At first, he had urged that the purchase price of Newstead, minus the very large proportion (more than two-thirds) which went to secure his wife's jointure, should be used to free him from his millstone of debt; but he became less eager when he realized how little would be left after meeting various necessary expenses.

While Rochdale remained unsold and still subject to litigation, his capital was £84,000 tied up in Government stock with a very low yield and, in his opinion, dangerously invested, for he was sure a new revolution was brewing. Kinnaird agreed that he might do much better by taking the money out of 'the Funds' and buying one or two first-rate mortgages, and he wrote to Hanson pointing out that the proceeds of the whole sum were only about £2,400 per annum, whereas if the stock were sold at a nominal loss of £6,000 and reinvested in an Irish mortgage at 6%, there would be an increase of £1,000 a year. His Lordship ought to fix his attention on income since it was improbable that he would ever have the principal, tied up as it was for Lady Byron and her daughter.[1] Notwithstanding the strongest pressure from Byron, nothing came of this proposal. Hanson wanted £30,000 of the money for his son-in-law, Lord Portsmouth—or, more accurately (that nobleman being insane), for his daughter, Mary Ann, soon to be deprived of her title of countess—while Kinnaird favoured a mortgage for Lord Blessington who was borrowing on his valuable Dublin property to pay for extravagant diversions with his 'most gorgeous' lady. Consent had to be obtained from the trustees of Lady Byron before any deal involving settled property could be transacted and, after much delay and irritation, they opposed it on the grounds that the Trust Deed excluded it.

Byron by now was anxious, for reasons I have touched upon, to have cash at his own disposal, and he often protested humorously against Kinnaird's allotment of large sums for debts:

> . . . As to my parting at this present with a thousand guineas—I wonder if you take me for an Atheist to make me so unChristian a proposition. It is true that I have reduced my expenses in *that* line [harlotry in Venice], but I have had others to encounter. On getting to dry land, I have had to furnish my house, for here you find only walls, *no furnished* apartments—it is not the Custom.

He added, in a rare allusion to his charities, which were very considerable in Ravenna: 'Besides . . . whenever I find a poor man suffering for his

[1] Kinnaird copies. 2 May 1820.

opinions, and there are many such in this country, I always let him have a shilling out of a guinea.'[1]

And later that same year: '. . . Though I have a very decent sum of monies in hand, yet I love Monies, & like to have more always. I have no dislike to any thing so much as to paying anybody.'[2] And again: 'As to the debts, the interest of them may be kept down but as for the principal, I can't disgorge for the present.'[3]

Kinnaird's patience must have been tried by his having to leave some of the bills outstanding—for instance, the luxurious Napoleonic carriage made by Baxter in 1816 was still unpaid for in 1823,[4] and 'the tribes of Israel' were still collecting interest which must have left them with few regrets about their investment; but there was one account that Kinnaird himself recommended his client not to meet without the fullest enquiry, and this was the staggering amount charged by Hanson and his son, Charles, for their legal services, in all £13,600. Their bill was rendered with scarcely any attempt at itemization and, apparently, in complete forgetfulness on Hanson's part that Byron had lent him nearly £3,000 which he had never paid back.[5]

Kinnaird's situation in handling so immense a debt was difficult because it covered a period when he himself had not been conversant with his friend's monetary concerns, and Byron had been in the habit, first from necessity and afterwards from carelessness and want of application, of leaving such matters to be looked after by others. Things had come to a pass now where he saw the folly of his former ways and even reproached Kinnaird for not treating Hanson with sufficient firmness. Kinnaird, however, lacked neither energy nor dedication, and he wrote many sharp letters to the Hansons demanding explanations of why they had improperly detained sums paid to them for Byron's credit; why, again, a well-informed man of business should not be engaged to look after the Rochdale property instead of Hanson's son, who was now the manager and confessed he knew nothing about it, and what justification this same son had for charging upwards of £150 for his trouble in connection with the Blessington mortgage when, if he had merely read over the Trust Deed, he would have known in advance that the transaction must prove abortive.

Hanson had so arranged matters, by what was no better than sharp practice, that Rochdale was his security;[6] and perhaps that was the reason

---

[1] Murray MS. 23 Mar. 1821.   [2] Ibid. 16 Nov. 1821.
[3] Ibid. 4 Dec. 1821.
[4] It was sold the following year, after Byron's death, for less than a tenth of its purchase price of £500.
[5] See p. 202.
[6] In *Correspondence* will be found the letter of 9 Dec. 1818, in which Byron protested to Kinnaird that he had not known, when signing legal parchments of several

why, contrary to the usual *laisser faire* of his methods, he had recently met every successful appeal about the contested part of that estate with a prompt counter-appeal—at Byron's expense of course—although repeatedly implored by Byron to settle for anything he could get. He refused to subtract a single guinea of his huge fees and had, in fact, proposed that Byron should make a composition with his other creditors— i.e. induce them to accept less than he admittedly owed—rather than dock anything he (Hanson) considered due to him.[1] Yet it was quite impossible to break finally with him, both because of the Rochdale imbroglio and of his being a trustee for the marriage settlement as well as other involvements.

Byron had learned in a hard school the truth of a recommendation daringly made by Hoppner in a letter about the depredations of Richard Edgecombe, the clerk already mentioned, who had been entrusted with his domestic accounts in Venice:

> I hope his successor, whoever he is, may prove less troublesome to you than he has done, but until you can make up your mind to look a little after your own affairs, it will be difficult for you to find a steward who will not take advantage of you.[2]

Byron could not quite bring himself to look after his own affairs. The habit of delegating them to others was too ingrained. There had been from childhood the complaisant solicitor, then the money-lenders' go-betweens, and the valets, coachmen, estate stewards who simply ran up bills for what they needed, or said they needed. On his travels, a courier or dragoman had hired horses and paid for accommodation. His terms for the publication of major early works had been negotiated by the self-seeking Dallas. Intermediaries of all kinds had spared him from ever having to get down to what, at Rochdale, they called brass tacks. When it was borne in upon him at last that he had been the victim of innumerable great and small impositions, he over-reacted in his typical manner, and determined to make known his love of money and his resolution never to be cheated again.

He could not very well go about making petty disbursements from his own hand—except of course to mendicants—for the opinion held by Edmund Burke in the 18th century still generally prevailed: 'No gentleman can give his time and attention to such details as are necessary to minute economy'. But he could now afford to have a household

---

kinds for Hanson, chiefly in connection with the sale of Newstead, that there had been substitution of a vital document.
[1] Broughton, *Recollections*. 28 Dec. 1818.   [2] Murray MS. 30 Oct. 1819.

steward—a *segretario*—to organize the servants and pay their wages, to correspond with tradesmen, dispense charities, scrutinize the bills and keep accounts systematically, proper accounts that he could and would himself inspect once a week. He had the very person available—Lega Zambelli, until now a steward of Count Guicciolis.

Lega had been deputed to keep watch on Teresa under the pretext of getting apartments ready for her when she had travelled from Bologna to Venice for the purpose, she had assured the Count, of consulting the famous Dr Aglietti, taking advantage of a seat in Byron's carriage. She had ended her journey at Byron's palazzo, not her husband's, and had gone with him after that to his villa at La Mira; and instead of espionage, Lega had connived at the socially perilous escapade. Less romantically, he had, by request, examined Edgecombe's accounts and found out their discrepancies. Thus recommending himself in more ways than one, he passed from the old patrician's service to the younger one's.

The situation was bizarre, for, when Byron came back to Ravenna, the Count, either from rashness or from cunning, invited him to become the tenant of the *piano nobile* in the Palazzo Guiccioli, while he himself retained the ground floor with his wife. But in some months Teresa left him, throwing herself upon the protection of her father and the Pope (the Count, having courted trouble, had become decidedly unpleasant on getting it); Byron continued stubbornly to occupy his rented part of the palazzo, on hostile terms with his landlord and spied upon both by the secret police and his landlord's contingent of servants. Lega adapted himself to this peculiar state of affairs with uncommon discretion. He had been obliged to adapt himself indeed to many vicissitudes, having been in his time a priest, an advocate, a tax collector, a cataloguer of great master-pieces, a sort of town clerk and a number of other things before it strangely fell to his lot to become the financial historian, down to the most minute particulars, of a famous poet's last years.

'. . . Lega, (my *Secretary*, an Italianism for steward or chief servant) . . .' Thus he was introduced into the journal Byron briefly kept in Ravenna,[1] but as he became more and more conversant with his master's affairs, Lega acted as a secretary in the English sense, much of the Italian correspondence being left to him—not very wisely as it turned out. But as to the accounts, he kept them beautifully.[2] He handled money, both small sums and large, with scrupulous exactitude, unflagging in reckoning

---

[1] 9 Jan. 1821.

[2] Harold Nicolson based his statement in *Byron, the Last Journey* (1924) that 'Lega did the accounts and he did them very badly' on jottings among Greek bills and receipts, and unfortunately other good writers have taken their cue from him. He never saw the actual account books, which were still in the hands of Lega's great-granddaughter.

the last soldo. His determination to watch over his patron's interests became almost the object of his life. The trouble was that he was inclined to overdo it.

The zeal which was his most marked characteristic, and which is the word that recurs again and again in his testimonials, not only made him officious and a little ridiculous, but gave a misleading impression of the person he was accustomed to allude to as Il Nobile Lord. Not that the Noble Lord himself did not contribute lavishly to that impression, nor that Lega's care for money was without its influence on him, or his own pleasure in possessing money without its influence on Lega. Yet if we set Byron's reputation for avarice against his actual expenditure, we find that the letters in which he boasted of loving lucre have little relation to what he did with it when he began to have it in comparative abundance.

Before considering Lega's much maligned bookkeeping, it will be as well to consider Lega himself because, though by far the least known of Byron's entourage in Italy and Greece, he was by no means the least important.

7

The Secretary and his Money Boxes

Lega's customary signature was Antonio Lega Zambelli, but his grand-daughter, Clelia, an ardent and romantic genealogist, tells us his full name was Antonio Tommaso dei Zambelli della Lega di Varnello, and that he had been reduced to poverty through the political turmoil of his youth and had lost an ancestral castle, Varnello by name, which had been owned by the Zambelli family since the 13th century. No castles find mention in his own annals, but he did have property which he sold or let injudiciously, in particular a benefice at Lugo farmed out to one Paolo Silvagni, from whom he was unable to collect his dues with any regularity.

He was born at Brisighella in the province of Ravenna late in 1770, and thus was nearly nineteen years older than Byron; that is, getting on for forty-nine when, before the end of 1819, he exchanged his service with the eccentric Italian Count for that of the still more eccentric English Milord. He had been bred for the Church on account of the living at Lugo, bequeathed to him by an uncle, and it has been assumed that he was ordained and was afterwards unfrocked. Byron certainly jokes about 'this priest'. He could not, however, have been active in Holy Orders for a great many years, because no letter addressed to him, though he preserved a large number, gives him any sacerdotal title; and moreover from 1800 onwards Citizen Zambelli was employed in various departments of the anti-papal Government of the Cisalpine Republic, and later, when Italy became a kingdom under Napoleon, in further purely secular offices.

There is an extremely illegible document dated at Faenza, December 11th 1800, in which someone has underlined with a red pencil the words *espulsione della Chiesa* (expulsion from the Church); but on being deciphered it turns out to be an invitation to Lega to give his opinion about the conduct of a certain Citizen Giovanni Battista (?) Maretta who had apparently chased someone bodily out of *a* church, and as the writer was presiding over an enquiry into the matter, and had heard contradictory accounts of it, he asked for Lega's own version of the 'expulsion' so

that he might do justice.[1] This request is on Liberty-and-Equality paper
with a dramatic engraving of the assassination of Julius Caesar—an event
highly approved by the revolutionary party—and clearly has no connection at all with the Vatican.

The suppression of religious orders, beginning in 1796, deprived many
of the clergy of their livelihood, but Lega, whether formerly priest or
layman, had thrown in his lot enthusiastically with the anti-clericals, and
successively filled several official posts from superior clerkships to Collector for the Agency of National Welfare (taxes), Assistant to the Police
Commissioner at Forlì, Cancelliere, equivalent to Chief Officer of Justice
charged with preparing cases to go before the court, member of the
Commission drafting men for military service, officer appointed to
investigate the property owned by the Church in the Department of the
Rubicon, Protocollista—that is, keeper of Registers and Records, and
Delegate from the Commission of Public Health with the duty of disin-
fecting the Lazaretto during an epidemic (aromatic vinegar was the sole
means suggested) and power to make a *cordon sanitaire*, a business calling
for forceful and decisive measures.

He must have displayed some skill in organizing because, with the
metamorphosis of the Republic into a Monarchy in 1805, he was entrusted
with a portentous commission—to collect and make ready for dispatch all
those pictures belonging to religious bodies which, by decree of the Vice-
roy, were to be sent to the capital for the establishment of a national
gallery.[2] Furthermore, Lega and his coadjutor, one Federico Mortorelli,
were to identify the said pictures, some of which 'by tacit concession,
provisional custody, or disposition of local authority' were on view in
churches and public buildings; and they were to persuade those concerned
to submit with a good grace and provide all required information. Another document, giving directions for packing, demanded exact descriptions of each painting with particulars of the artists. It is surprising that
such momentous work was not put in the hands of experts—unless
Mortorelli was one—but as expropriation was going on all over Italy,
there may not have been enough to go round.

The Republican Police Commission was superseded by a Monarchist
body, and Lega was engaged in settling some problems of its dissolution.
That led to his being invited to become Municipal Secretary to the Com-
mune of Forlimpopoli. He was able to combine this office with actually
defending accused persons in criminal trials at Forlì, which, according to
a judge who gave him a testimonial, he did with great advantage to

[1] 46871 Folio 9.
[2] The Brera in Milan. It was stocked with pictures which were spoils from the
suppressed churches and monasteries.

his clients. Indeed, in every situation his zeal, ability, and fitness for a position of trust had commended themselves.

When a new regional Tribunal of Justice was established, he applied for, and eventually got, the post of Usher, which closely resembled that of a Clerk to the Court in Britain. His grand-daughter credits him with being a Doctor of Law, but I doubt whether this was so. Though he and his correspondents were sticklers for form, he was never addressed as *Dottore*. The number and strange variety of the jobs he did within a short space of time, although he was a steady and a diligent man, eloquently convey the abnormal stresses that prevailed, allowing many formalities to be waived, but casting an uncertainty over the outcome of all efforts at advancement.

Lega was now at the end of his fourteen years of bureaucratic service. In aspiring to become an officer of the Tribunal at Forlì, he had imagined he could keep his position as Municipal Secretary to the much smaller town of Forlimpopoli, merely putting in a deputy to carry out his duties, a common practice at the period. With the collapse of Napoleon's empire, the Tribunal was abolished or reconstituted, and in 1814 Lega sought to resume his previous occupation. The deputy, Antonio Masserini, then claimed that his engagement had been permanent. Lega insisted that he had never resigned. The Mayor as Chief Magistrate supported him and gave Masserini a month's notice. The new Provisional Government, that of His Majesty the Emperor of Austria, intervened and ruled that neither of the men held the office, and that another Municipal Secretary must be appointed. Lega's polite but vigorous protest failed, and the correspondence took an acrimonious turn when he was unable to secure the fees he considered due to him, which were little enough, for minor Government employees were most inadequately paid. In 1815 and 1816 he was striving, often with quite pathetic desperation, to get money from various debtors. Private lending was a very customary practice where facilities for borrowing from banks were scanty. The rate of interest was usually one per cent per month, a fair source of income if it were dependable, but such loans frequently proved a bad investment to Lega, while the property he had inherited at Lugo was a source of trouble for many years on end. For one who had pledged himself whole-heartedly to the banished French conqueror, there was little hope of finding employment under the Austrian régime, and so he was thrown back entirely on such private means as he could scrape together.

Presumably it was this endeavour which took him to Venice in 1815, because there too he had some property—several houses, one of them a palazzo on the Grand Canal adjacent to the Austrian Governor's, if his grand-daughter was not misled by family pride. His association with

Count Guiccioli, a landowner with widespread interests both in Venice and Romagna, may have begun through one of his business dealings. In April 1817 he mentions that an agent of the Count would be undertaking a negotiation on his behalf, and in July he dispatched to the Palazzo Guiccioli in Ravenna, not yet the habitation of Byron, a cook and a valet: from which it may be inferred that he had by now become a factotum, though as yet only in a very occasional way.

Since his coming to Venice, Lega's life had taken an exciting and emotional turn, an odd contrast to that of the circumspect local government official earnestly collecting testimonials. He was now the delighted father of a child by a woman with whom he was passionately in love, and more than ever anxious to get money because he was determined to support her and the baby, Aspasia Maria Paolo Adriana, baptized in the Church of Santa Maria del Carmine on March 10th 1817, the future custodian of his hoarded records.

Aspasia was born within a few weeks of Byron's Allegra. It was her mother, Francesca Silvestrini, Lega's adored Fanny, who was the go-between in the affair between Byron and the Countess Guiccioli, helping the young lovers to deceive an unsympathetic husband nearly as old as his wife's still living grandfather.

Whether Lega had ever technically been unfrocked or not, he kept no evidence to show. There were many priests who, through the upheavals of revolution and war, willingly or unwillingly renounced their ministry—La Mésangère, for instance, who took to running an admirable fashion paper in Paris. But it is very strange that, though Lega had been remote from the Church since 1799 at the latest, except by helping to deprive it of treasures, the watchful clergy of his native province seem not to have known it. The Archbishop of Ravenna wrote to the Secretary of State in Rome complaining that the priest had 'abandoned his ecclesiastical robes, giving himself up to an entirely secular life'.[1] If unfrocked what else could have been expected of him? And since Count Guiccioli, though of Liberal inclinations, had not quarrelled with the Church—the title was in fact Papal—it is unlikely that he would have had as his chief servant a cleric who had positively been cast out. I would hazard a theory that Lega in his youth did take Holy Orders, that when Napoleon invaded Italy, supposedly to establish Liberty, Equality, and Fraternity, he was idealistic or politic enough to be on the side of the victor and, in the ensuing revolution, was able to adopt a secular life and pursue a secular career without his defection bringing upon him any anathema, so that when the Church resumed its former power, he was still deemed to be a priest, though a bad one.

[1] Origo. 5 Feb. 1820.

The system of espionage by which information about potentially subversive characters was passed from State to State was far from dependable. Lega was not merely unpriestly: he was perpetually risking imprisonment by membership of the secret society to which his new patron also belonged, the Carbonari. Its aims and undertakings—set forth in French in a document of Lega's less cryptic than it was meant to be[1]— were of the most exaltedly ethical kind, its rituals proportionately solemn, but it was all on too large and abstract a plane to be of much use in furthering its main object of freeing Italy from foreign tyranny, and it is not to be wondered at that Byron with his inveterate realism became disillusioned.

Little as it would appear from the generally facetious remarks scattered through his early letters to Teresa (not published till 1949), the substantial danger Lega was willing to undergo for a cause dear to both must have won the respect of his fellow conspirator. Still, there was something about him that was inherently comic—fussy and meticulous as he was, obsequious in a grandiloquent style, at times officious and at other times timorous; and with it all of an amorous propensity. His mistress too—for so Byron regarded her—the genial and venial confidante, was another figure of comedy. Byron never realized that Lega felt the deepest devotion to Fanny, looked on her as his wife, and handed over to her what were for him large sums of money. He would have feared in those first days with Il Nobile Lord to touch off his easy mockery.

When, in 1820, she bore him another child, a son, Byron in a somewhat tasteless letter to Teresa[2] speaks of an intention to send it to the foundling hospital and of his advice to Lega to send the girl too; but this was probably one of those flippancies in which he all too often indulged, the more readily in this case because he had taken an aversion to the mother. The boy may have gone to the foundling hospital, though it seems altogether improbable in view of Lega's strong paternal feelings and his praise for Fanny as 'the best of mothers', or he may have been among the sad majority of babies of every class who died in infancy. At any rate, I can trace no future reference to him, whereas a most fond solicitude for Aspasia is attested in dozens of letters.

Fanny Silvestrini fared no better than go-betweens usually do when their ministrations become superfluous. Byron had rewarded her with an ample gift of money. Later on she hinted that more might be forthcoming, and he ungratefully called her a procuress.[3] The aspersion need not be taken literally. She had been on intimate terms with Teresa, a convent-bred girl of very proper family, before her marriage and, assuredly not

[1] 46878 Folio 142. [2] Origo. 26 July 1820. [3] Ibid. 25 Oct. 1820.

for any scandalous reason, was a kind of protégée of the Countess Gritti, member of a great Venetian house, who in numerous letters bears witness to her affection and care for Aspasia. If only half her granddaughter's particulars about her are correct, Fanny herself was of more than respectable background and ancestry. But her effusive and obtrusive personality grated on Byron's nerves and he told Lega to keep her away from him. Lega's position was a hard one because he was anxious to stand well with the Noble Lord but could not bear to break with Fanny, and it indicates either adroitness or slyness in him that he never did break with her but that she seems to have troubled Byron no more.

Lega was a very supple person—supple and yet persistent; nevertheless he seems to have been fundamentally an honest man. His explanations of financial matters are often not easy to follow, and his way of disposing of them was at times misguided; as a business man he had no gifts whatever; but he was loyal and conscientious in what he deemed to be the cause of his employer. A dishonest man would have been under considerable temptation because, for all the normal outlay of the household, including rent and wages, cash was used, and Lega was in charge of sums which were pretty large in England and immense in Italy— several thousand crowns at a time, equal to nearly as many pounds in England.[1] Big robberies were rare in houses which were never empty of servants, but theft and pilfering were common enough. With responsibility for what was to him substantial wealth, Lega developed, or perhaps he had always had, an air of excessive precaution.

Nor need we doubt that a reformed spendthrift, whose difficulties had been brought about in great measure by his own rash liberality, enjoyed his accountant's assiduity in husbanding all those very tangible symbols of good credit (elegant too in themselves)—the Venetian *zecchini* which were in English the fabled sequins of the *Arabian Nights* and likewise the ducats of Shylock, *fiorini* or florins with a lily motif delicately embossed, broad *scudi* with their ancient heraldry, handsome silver medallions called *colonnati* because they bore two columns representing the pillars of Hercules, once thought to be the bounds of the world.

Byron's aesthetic perceptions were limited, apart from the beauties of nature, but he had numerous very good snuff-boxes, some gold chains, rings, seals and other jewellery, and could appreciate the craft of the goldsmith and silversmith. The treasure derived an additional lustre from the thought that fortune would mean freedom to begin the new life he recurringly dreamed of, in Spain perhaps or in one of the far Americas.

'I am collecting gradually a lot of *modern* gold coins', he told Kinnaird

---

[1] Byron informed Kinnaird that twelve hundred crowns went about as far as a thousand pounds. (Quennell. 20 July 1820.)

in 1821,[1] 'Napoleons &c (with the *real* Emperor on them) which are scarce. Now what will they fetch in England if sent there by & by [?]'. Those who have never acquired any object in the hope that it might increase in value are entitled to regard this as a symptom of avarice; but whether spent or hoarded, money had an intrinsic charm which has been lacking since gold ceased to be currency. To jingle gold in one's pocket must have been very different from fingering slips of paper in a notecase. Gold was a pleasing substance in itself and had associations hallowed by antiquity; and it conveyed a sense of power that is hard to imagine in a society inured to taxation on a scale then absolutely inconceivable. A man could heap up guineas or Napoleons or louis d'or and count them, enjoying their solidity, their glitter, secure in the knowledge that no one had the right to intrude on his privacy by demanding how many of them he owned, claiming a share of them, or placing restrictions on where he might take them. One did not need to be a miser to relish the possession of money, especially if one had intimately known what came of squandering it.

Byron lived in Italy free of income tax and supplied with sterling, the world's major currency, to an extent which enabled him to appear a rich man. Every Briton who could afford to travel was supposed to be rich, much as Americans were a few decades ago, before the 'package tour' with its stress on economy dissolved that illusion. A good deal was expected of an English Milord, and prices were liable to go up as soon as he appeared, which naturally stimulated a complementary alertness against being imposed upon. That was where Lega came in, unsparing of himself and of any tradesman who tried to take advantage.

His was not the easiest of tasks because, wherever his patron settled, the currency was different. The chief unit for everyday transactions was always some piece with the status of an English crown, but divisible into smaller denominations that changed according to locality. In one state it was called a scudo, in another a francescone, in yet another a tallero. There was also the colonnato, a Spanish dollar but acceptable everywhere. (During the shortage of silver arising from the Napoleonic Wars, Spanish dollars stamped with a miniature head of George III had passed as coin of the realm even in England.)

The Tuscan crown, or francescone, chief unit of Byron's accounts in Pisa, was worth ten pauls, and the paul worth eight crazie; whereas when he moved to the Duchy of Genoa, though there were crowns—scudi—all but important expenses had to be worked out in Genoese livres, each livre equal to twenty soldi, each soldo equal to twelve denari. When, to anticipate, Lega went with Byron to the Greek islands and to Greece, he had to

[1] Murray MS. 16 Nov.

reckon again in currencies wholly new to him. Besides these complexities, there were the fifty-pound notes from Ransome's Bank to be negotiated, loss or gain on exchange to be considered, and loans to be recovered where possible.

Byron lent a friend 224 francesconi, probably in autumn 1821, and Lega noted in January 1822 that this gentleman, Signor Shelly, would settle at the end of the current week. On January 29th he did settle, but may not have been pleased to have his attention called to the debt, and the phrase Lega used (*esatti dal Sigr. Shelley*) suggests that he had done so.[1] In January and February 1822 Shelley had nine fifty-pound notes from Byron through Lega, and on March 6th two more, £550 in all; but the bulk of this money must have been for Leigh Hunt, who was far from honest about his obligations to Byron. The latter told Kinnaird in February: 'My only extra expense . . . is a loan to Leigh Hunt of two hundred and fifty pounds and fifty pounds worth of furniture I have bought for him.'[2] The purchase of the furniture may have been undertaken by Shelley who possibly also made a down payment for Byron on the *Bolivar*, then being built at Leghorn with his own ill-starred yacht.

Once having engaged a steward, Byron gave him the care of all his resources except those in the hands of bankers, and empowered him to manage as seemed best to him, only insisting on seeing a weekly reckoning. 'He was the most munificent man I ever knew, but he had a very proper dislike of being cheated', John Cam Hobhouse wrote when asked whether Leigh Hunt's remarks about Byron's avarice were true.[3] Certain it is that he grew very suspicious of being cheated and that often enough he had good reason to be. Lega was so much more suspicious still that, even when repaying little sums his Lordship had borrowed from Fletcher or Tita, the ex-gondolier, he would make his entries in this form:

> To Fletcher for the amounts he says he gave Milord
> To Tita for what he says he gave a poor man by
>   order of Milord

With the closest application, I have never been able to learn whether Lega was inclined to ascribe to his employer views and wishes which fitted

[1] 46876 Folio 4. Perhaps this money was for Emilia Viviani who, five days before her wedding (8 Sept. 1821), had written to Shelley asking, on behalf of a friend, for a sum so considerable that he thought he might require Byron's help in providing it.

[2] Murray MS. 23 Feb. 1822. The second 'and fifty' has been omitted by error in *Correspondence*, making it appear that the sum advanced was £200. I do not know why Shelley told Hunt that Byron had paid him the £250 'in Italian bills' (2 Mar. 1822). The numbers of the English banknotes he received are all recorded by Lega.

[3] Murray MS., from the answers to a questionnaire by John Bowring about Leigh Hunt's virulent attack on Byron. They are given more fully in *The Late Lord Byron*.

his own convenience. Yet Byron had undeniably become very meticulous, and early in their association had written to him angrily, 'You know the system in my household is to have receipts even for the very smallest things—so that I know what I pay and what I have to pay'.[1] A large sum was involved in this instance, and the person from whom Byron had vainly sought a receipt through Lega was the Count Guiccioli, whom he distrusted.

To those who believed they or their friends should have a bigger share of Byron's money, it was inevitable that the secretary appeared niggardly, if not dishonest. Trelawny wrote of him as 'a thorough miser [who] coiled himself on the money chest like a viper'. Anyone who has had the opportunity of learning what desperate demands for Byron's funds were made almost daily in Greece, or what pressure Trelawny himself tried to exert to get money for his hero, the covetous Odysseus, will scarcely wonder at Lega's vigilance.

There is a passage in a letter of Byron's to Leigh Hunt which might mislead readers to whom his 'scherzo' style is unfamiliar:

> For whatever money you want apply to Lega—I never have any about me—in pocket for I love it in a casket, but not in a purse. Pray do not deem this out of the way—for when I have occasion for a sixpence I send after it to him—and he is [a] damned rascal.[2]

The last words are merely a kind of percussion, the utterance of an inapposite swear word to cover an irritation of which the real cause must be suppressed—and the real cause was Hunt himself with his nerve-racking family, his touchiness, the cultivated helplessness by which he was accustomed to exploit his friends, and worst of all, the painful archness of his written requests for money.

Seeing that Lega was still the cashier when Byron went to Greece, we cannot doubt that Hamilton Browne, a good witness, represents the latter's genuine opinion:

> [He] sometimes spoke in unqualified praise of the extremely careful and penurious character of Lega, his Maestro di Casa. The man, he said, guarded his treasure like the Dragon watching the golden fruit in the garden of the Hesperides, and viewed his monies with the same self-satisfaction as if they were his own property, grumbling and murmuring at making the

---

[1] 46878 Folio 7. About Feb. 1820. In Italian. A rare example of an undated letter by Byron. The occasion was his contribution towards the engagement of a great singer for the opera at Ravenna, Mme Pasta. He had paid half his promised four hundred crowns, and refused to give the other half until Guiccioli acknowledged what he had already received.

[2] 15 Sept. 1822. Letter in the Berg Collection, New York, quoted by Marchand.

most trivial disbursement on Lord Byron's own order, and sleeping on the boxes of specie, yet was strictly honest.[1]

This is entirely compatible with all that is revealed by Lega's correspondence. Mary Shelley might write, after seeing him in London, that he looked 'a most preposterous rogue' but apart from her general tendency to make sour and disagreeable remarks, she was under the influence of Leigh Hunt, who had resented the secretary's being in a position to 'dole out' cash to him 'like so many disgraces'.

Byron himself also had cash doled out by Lega, for his remark about never having any about him is almost literally true. And how Hunt, eagerly accepting another eighty crowns, must have seized on that piece of self-denigration about loving money in a casket, and stored it up and regretted not being able, because its purport would have belied his tale of grievances, to publish the letter!

That Lega was no rascal is manifest in his being entrusted with the coffers in which Byron was gleefully accumulating gold and silver. Here is a list made in Pisa in 1822:

> Moneys and gold pieces of various sorts belonging to the Noble Lord Byron...
>
>   4 gold Napoleon doubloons of 40 francs each
> 13 ordinary Napoleons of 20 francs
>   8 different gold coins
> 95 Gold Louis
> 40 ordinary Napoleons of 20 francs
>   4 Napoleon doubloons of 40 francs
>   1 Gold Medaglia of 10 Roman sequins representing Pope Alessandro VII [The medaglia was an antique coin]
> 58 ordinary Napoleons of 20 francs
> 24 Gold Louis
>   5 Genovine [Genoese pieces, probably gold]
>   7 Rusponi [new sequins]
> 322 Napoleons of 20 francs
> 66 Napoleons of 40 francs
> 33 Napoleons of 20 francs paid by Dunn [Byron's Leghorn banker] on the 24th April 1822[2]

The loose way in which the hoard is catalogued indicates that it was added to on different dates as Byron continued to increase this delectable

---

[1] Article in *Blackwood's Magazine*. Jan. 1834. It may be noted that while Browne, quoting Byron, pictures Lega as the dragon which, in classic lore, was coiled about a tree, Trelawny, twenty-four years later, likens him to a viper coiled about a money-chest. He seldom says anything in his *Recollections* which is not an echo of some previous writer, except when inventing. To Hamilton Browne he was particularly indebted.

[2] 46873 Folio 185.

property. Regrettably enough—for who that has seen specimens of that coinage would not be glad to collect it?—he was obliged to renounce his hobby when he left Pisa for Genoa, realizing that it was dangerous to carry such a quantity of cash with him. (Napoleons were still good tender, valued more than the local currencies, which were unwelcome except in the States of their origin, and expensive to change.) The banker Webb in Leghorn credited Byron's account with £630 for his gold.[1] It would now be worth a fortune.

He felt an evident pride, after having left England in a condition of frightening insolvency with bailiffs dividing his chattels, at being in such good credit—hardly any debts left except to his solicitor. In his own words: 'I suppose you will laugh at all my pecuniary plans, but (having known the miseries of embarrassment) it is natural to try to provide against their recurrence.'[2]

As usual he was excessive, telling Kinnaird reiterantly about all the economies he was effecting, praising his surprised friend and banker for being so very 'oracular & sensible and of the world'.

> In short, Doug, the longer I live the more I perceive that Money (honestly come by) is the Philosopher's Stone, and therefore do thou be my man of trust & fidelity, and look after the same, my avarice, or cupidity, is *not* selfish, for my table dont cost four shillings a day, and except houses and helping all kinds of patriots (I have long given up *costly* harlotry) I have no violent expenses, but I want to get a sum together to go amongst the Greeks or Americans and do some good. . . .[3]

Judged by his acts, as he asked to be judged, he was telling the unvarnished truth. He wished to throw himself into some noble cause, but meantime he did not live as penuriously, either in respect to his own or others' comfort, as his often quoted letters would have us believe.

---

[1] Murray MS. 27 Oct. 1822.   [2] Ibid.   [3] 12 Sept. 1822.

8

The Household at Pisa

We begin the housekeeping accounts with the big ledger in which Lega made his first entry at Pisa on New Year's Day, 1822.[1] Byron had been domiciled in that city since about November 1st the previous year, having taken the Casa Lanfranchi, a very large and handsome old house on the Lung'Arno, found for him by Shelley. Teresa Guiccioli, accompanying her father and two of her brothers into exile from Romagna, had preceded him by several weeks, and with Mary Shelley's help had made the palazzo habitable. The Shelleys were looking forward eagerly to his arrival, having settled in Pisa themselves some little while before.

I must pause here to deal with a circumstance which has remained unnoticed by a remarkable number of biographers—not surprisingly as far as Shelley is concerned because so many of them were hostile to Byron, but a strange lapse in Byron's defenders. I refer to what is known as the Hoppner Scandal, which I will outline in an appendix for the benefit of those who are unacquainted with the story,[2] merely mentioning now that it first formed the theme of an attack on Byron in 1883,[3] a time when the sacrosanct Shelley of Victorian hagiology had been endowed with legendary features altogether Christ-like, and not to be assailed with impunity: above all not to be assailed with such devastating aspersions as his begetting an extra-marital child. The baseness of which Byron stood accused was that, having been asked to forward to Mrs Hoppner an impassioned refutation by Mary Shelley of the scandal, Byron despicably suppressed it rather than admit to Hoppner that he had repeated a tale told him in confidence a year before. Mary's letter of 1821 was found among the papers which had passed into the hands of his executor, Hobhouse, and which belonged after Hobhouse's death to his daughter, Lady Dorchester, and the conclusion at once drawn by Shelley idolators, who

---

[1] 46876   [2] See Appendix 10, 'Hoppner's Garbled Revelation'.
[3] By J. A. Froude in *The Nineteenth Century*.

in those days were invariably Byron detractors, was that it had been withheld from the intended recipient.

It is not generally known—in fact I think it is not known at all—that the whole *canard* was started by Byron's eccentric grandson, Lord Lovelace, who was admitted to Lady Dorchester's collection without the least awareness on her part that he was searching like a detective, not for material that would assist John Murray IV in his projected thirteen-volume edition of *Poetry* and *Letters and Journals*, but for evidence that would convict his grandfather of incest. A true descendant of his grandmother, he managed, as I related in my first chapter, to do a great amount of stealthy copying; and, just as Lady Byron, when she learned that a would-be blackmailer had taken extracts from Lady Caroline Lamb's indiscreet diary, sat down and wrote, not to the diarist but to one who would convey it to William Lamb, her husband,[1] so did Lord Lovelace, when he found that letter to Mrs Hoppner with its seals broken, immediately send the news where it could do most damage—to Lady Shelley.

Byron's cowardly concealment of the letter having been presumed more times than can be counted, Sir John Murray, who had become its owner on Lady Dorchester's death, told, in editing *Lord Byron's Correspondence* (1922), how it had the remains of two distinct seals on it, suggesting that it had been sent to Mrs Hoppner and returned in another cover, a tiny fragment of which still adhered to the original paper. It had not been sealed at all when handed to Byron—that is clear from a letter of Shelley's to his wife. But Sir John's explanation had little effect on those who had persuaded themselves that to vilify Byron was somehow to glorify Shelley.

Professor Leslie Marchand, in his three-volume biography of Byron (1957), indicated some features of Byron's character, such as his notable courage and outspokenness, which made it very unlikely that, for fear of Hoppner's disapproval—which he had repeatedly flouted—he would let his friend lie under a grievous aspersion; but it was left to me to lay stress on a point Sir John Murray did not ignore but glanced over without emphasis and which seems to me a conclusive rebuttal comprised in half a dozen words—Byron chose to go to Pisa!

How is it credible that, if he had secretly retained a letter of the utmost importance to both Shelley and his wife, he would have decided afterwards to live at close quarters with them, seeing Shelley almost every day and letting his mistress form an equal intimacy with Mary? Would he not have studiously avoided the Shelleys' company lest they should ask how Mrs Hoppner had responded to Mary's agonized protest? Would *they* have been content to remain month after month without that

[1] This incident of 1826 has its place in Chapter VII of *The Late Lord Byron*.

information? Having practised such a treachery, would not Byron have destroyed the evidence instead of leaving it among his papers and discussing it with Teresa who, in her still not fully published book—written, it must be remembered, many years before Byron had been accused—refers explicitly to the scandal?

Teresa states that Byron had repeated it to Shelley so that the latter might refute it, and that it produced between Shelley and his wife 'a touching correspondence'. That correspondence can only have been Mary's loyal response to Shelley when both were deeply affected by Hoppner's ill report. I find it wholly unbelievable that Teresa, who met Mary literally scores of times in Pisa, never once exchanged a word with her about the trouble they had both had through Hoppner's taste for scandal, and had he come into their conversation at all, there surely would have been some kind of *éclaircissement*.

And why should Byron be so uncharacteristically afraid of admitting to Hoppner that he had broken a confidence (not solicited on his side) seeing that Hoppner had already reproached him in the plainest terms with his inability to keep a secret? 'I know it will cease to be one the moment it passes my pen or my lips.'[1] Though Byron might certainly want to send an explanatory comment of his own with Mary's letter, he had no reputation in the confidence-keeping line to live up to with Hoppner.

It has been adduced as bearing out the suppression theory that no recognition was exchanged between Mary and Isabelle Hoppner when they came upon each other at Florence years later. To anyone not bent on making a case against Byron, it would appear obvious that Mary was resentful and Mrs Hoppner ill at ease, as well she might be. It can no longer be supposed that Mary's defence of her husband had only to be seen by the Hoppners for them to be convinced: we have known since Newman Ivey White's biography of Shelley was published in 1947 that, however distorted the scandalous report may have been, it was not a fabrication but based on something concrete, if misunderstood. In Appendix 10 I offer a new interpretation of why that famous letter was found among Byron's possessions.

Having an absolutely clear conscience in regard to Shelley, whom he had described to Kinnaird as '*truth* itself and *honour* itself, notwithstanding his out-of-the-way notions about religion',[2] Byron had no hesitation in

---

[1] 16 June 1819, quoted in Chapter 6.

[2] Murray MS. 2 June 1821. Byron had heard from Shelley some time previously that Murray had told Thomas Mitchell (translator of Aristophanes) that he had gained little or nothing, except credit, by being Byron's publisher, and that Byron was not what he seemed but an avaricious man—from which we learn that, truthful and honourable as he might be, Shelley himself was not above passing on mischievous gossip.

adopting his suggestion of a residence in Pisa and for the first time in years was constantly in the company of Englishmen, chiefly those introduced by Shelley.

Once installed, he gave dinner parties, hired some land for shooting practice and became the centre of a circle in which the only Italians, except for an occasional passing visitor, were members of the Gamba family. He could afford to live as he pleased because of the artificially high purchasing power of his income from England; but the literal translation of his foreign expenditure into pounds and pence can be of no use, nor would the reckoning in American dollars and cents be much more helpful, having regard to the instability of modern money. Dollars were then a rather outlandish specie very unfamiliar in Europe, but always bearing a constant ratio to the pound, so that dictionaries were able to state, in edition after edition, that one pound sterling was about $4·86, just as the lira was equivalent to a franc—which, as every tourist knows, is no longer a reliable calculation.

The most practical plan for gauging the cost of living for Byron, who was no longer prodigal but, on the other hand, not at all parsimonious, is to treat the currency as self-contained, and to give some varied examples of what it would buy. His Pisa accounts run unbroken for nearly ten months and exhibit the financial side of many events which have made their mark in biography, and which receive new light and shade from the prosaic figures in the secretary's ledger or his correspondence with Byron's Italian banker. It also happens very conveniently that, while there, the servants kept their own table out of their wages and that, with the exception of certain items, all the catering was for himself and his guests. We can thus look more closely at his domestic habits than when—as at Genoa or in Greece—he was directly maintaining his entourage.

The Tuscan crown, generally called a francescone, was divided, as I have already mentioned, into pauls and crazie; eight crazie to the paul, ten pauls to the crown. Here is a list which gives some notion of its local value:

RENT, LIGHTING, HEATING	Tuscan Crowns	Pauls	Crazie
4 months rent for a large palazzo on the river	140		
4 months rent for extra stables in an annexe	9		
About 4 months street lighting [paid by each individual householder]	31		
18 sacks of coal and their delivery from Leghorn by barge	3	1	4
Oil for house and stable lamps for a week	1	6	6
Tallow candles for a week		3	4
Wax candles by weight 1 lb.		5	
Ten fine wax candles (of a large size)	1	7	4

	Crowns	Pauls	Crazie
ITEMS OF HOUSEHOLD EQUIPMENT			
A billiard table with all accessories	66	2	
6 lampstands for the billiard room and some additional work	7		
A bidet with cabinet back	1	9	
A chamber pot		1	2
A cherrywood bedstead with canopy [these two items were probably for the use of the Hunt family]	2	5	
Large tablecloth with 13 napkins	3		
PROVISIONS, WINE AND CIGARS			
71 bottles of fine claret with Customs Duty and delivery from Leghorn	61	6	5
A bottle of Vermouth		2	2
6 dozen oysters	1	8	
1 lb. of olives			6
2 lobsters		3	
2 cockerels		4	
400 small doughnut-shaped bread rolls		3	
6 sorbets from the café		3	
50 cigars	2	4	
PERSONAL EQUIPMENT (for Milord)			
A pair of leather gloves		3	
A cap with a peak [perhaps the one he wears in the silhouette by Mrs Hunt]		6	
A whalebone riding-whip silver mounted	1		
A hat 'mounted with brown'	3	7	
Another hat, not described	3		
Gold mount for a seal	7	8	
A pair of pistols	24		
(For servants)			
A pair of dragoon's boots with spurs for the courier	8		
2 striped nankeen jackets for the grooms	7		
SHOOTING EXPENSES			
Lead balls at 1 paul per 7 lbs., powder, cartridge paper for rifles	3	2	4
The gunsmith for cleaning pistols every day for a week [i.e. at 4 crazie a day]		3	4
TRAVEL			
His Lordship posting with 9 horses from Pisa to Montenero, with tips to stablemen and postilions	20	6	
The same journey made with two horses by the secretary	2	5	
MEDICAL EXPENSES			
Visit of Professor Vaccà, the leading doctor in Pisa, to Fletcher	6		
Visit of Professor Vaccà to the courier	2		
Present from his Lordship to Vaccà on leaving Pisa, for professional attendance generally	50		

MAINTENANCE OF ANIMALS OTHER THAN HORSES	Crowns	Pauls	Crazie
The pets, consisting in Pisa of 2 monkeys, 2 to 3 dogs, and a few birds, 3 of which were geese, were in general provided for more liberally than their master. In an average week they cost:	2	6	
[Byron's subsistence, exclusive of wine and bread, was sometimes little more than half of this.]			
Clipping the coats of the dogs	1		
MAINTENANCE OF 9 HORSES			
Their upkeep is difficult to calculate because large amounts of hay, corn, bran, oatmeal, beans, and honey would be bought for them at one time. Roughly, their feeding stuffs per week cost:	15		
Making six horseshoes	1	1	

Having seen that sixty-six crowns would buy a billiard table with all appurtenances except lamps; that a pair of chickens did not cost even half a crown, and that a gunsmith cleaned pistols every day for what would have been in English or American money a couple of pennies (no doubt the chasseur took them to his premises and collected them), we may now consider the wages of Byron's servants in a fair perspective.

There is a tendency to quote the cost of services as if money had an absolute instead of a relative value, and many a writer has aroused sympathy for the ill-used domestics of past epochs by giving figures which, in real terms, had as much purchasing power as those of today—a fact proved by the savings that the thrifty ones were able to accumulate. Naturally, wants were fewer because many things now deemed essential to comfort on every social level were then prohibitive luxuries or not even invented, while, in upper class households, outside entertainments could easily be dispensed with, since the numerous members of the staff formed a kind of club, and company was never wanting.

Byron in Pisa had a full-time staff of eight and a part-time gardener for the courtyard and garden. Although Lega was head of the 'family'— for such it was always called by the Italians—Fletcher received higher pay, having a special allowance for his provisions which Lega did not get. His salary was a little over two hundred and forty Tuscan crowns a year, with nearly four crowns a week for his board, and that usually surpassed Byron's expenditure on his personal table; but his wine and spirits were on a separate account whereas Fletcher would have had to pay for his own.

How handsome Fletcher's wages were may be understood by comparing them with the forty pounds per annum which was considered a liberal rate in England; as well as by the substantial savings he had invested with the banker Ghigi—some twelve hundred crowns at this time. He was, of course, supplied with lodging, light, heat, washing, and certain perquisites, and, seeing that the local wines cost little more than a crown per dozen bottles and plain food and fruit was remarkably cheap, he could seldom have needed to spend his whole allowance on '*cibarie*'. Lega always carefully differentiates between the sustenance of gentlemen, ordinary men, and animals. Gentlemen were nourished by *vittuarie* (victuals), the staff with *cibarie* (food), while the animals had their *mantenimento* (maintenance).

Fletcher's salary was at this time paid half-yearly. The cost of wages per month works out as follows:—

	Crowns	Pauls	Crazie
Fletcher, the valet, with his extra allowance for board at 3 crowns 9 pauls per week, approximately	36		
Giovanni Battista Falcieri (Tita), formerly Byron's private gondolier in Venice, now his *cacciatore*— literally a huntsman but in practice something between a page and a footman	13	0	2
Gaetano Forestieri, the cook	13	0	2
Vincenzo Papi, the coachman	20	8	3
Giuseppe Strauss, the courier	15	6	2
Giovanni Manuzzi and Giovanni Vecchi two middle-aged grooms at 8 crowns 4 pauls a month plus an allowance of 10 crazie a day each for one pound of meat and a bottle of wine, approximately	18	6	
The part-time gardener	1	5	
Lega Zambelli, secretary and steward	22	0	1

Not counting tips, there is thus an amount of about a hundred and forty crowns a month for service, augmented by expenses incurred when any of the staff travelled on their employer's behalf or fell ill—in which case he paid for their medical care—the cost of their liveries, and sometimes other disbursements.

It may seem surprising that Tita, a trusted servant of nearly four years standing, should have received less than the courier, who was a newcomer. His duties, however, were less exacting, and he was only twenty-four. It is also possible that the large sum (twelve hundred livres) which Byron had paid to his father to buy him out of conscription, might have been taken into consideration, though I think it unlikely. Byron spared no expense to aid him when he was unjustly arrested and exiled after what is known as the Pisa affray.

From the time of his settling in Italy in a dwelling of his own, all the work of his household had been done by men, but three of the staff had wives in Ravenna, and when they missed them, Lega arranged with Pellegrino Ghigi to have them brought to Pisa, one of the numerous tasks entrusted to that versatile banker. It was a troublesome business as they had to have passports, and a costly one even if performed, as Byron (or Lega) requested, with maximum economy. The wives of the cook and the coachman agreed to leave their homes, though they were reluctant to make the journey in winter and it was delayed some weeks; but Signora Capelloni refused, and that seems to be why Agabito Capelloni, the courier until that date (January 1822), departed and made way for Giuseppe Strauss.

Like most of Byron's affairs from the time when Lega began to handle them, this minor transaction led to annoyances. Lega wrote to Ghigi complaining that the two women had only been taken as far as Bologna and then been put into another conveyance for the rest of the journey, nor had they been given meals or fires to warm themselves as promised in the quoted charge of forty crowns.[1] The carrier admitted making them change at Bologna, but claimed that one of his horses was unfit. Their meals had been provided, he said, but not—he admitted—the stipulated fires at the inns in Bologna and Faenza. The women still affirmed there had been no food for them. The carrier came to Ghigi, accompanied by his employer, and produced a receipt for thirty-two crowns supposed to have been paid to the driver who had taken over, protesting that he had done his own part at a loss. Ghigi was sceptical, but he was an amiable rather than a strong-minded man, and often hesitant and ineffectual—as he was to prove in the much graver matter of Allegra's illness and its aftermath.

There were two unfortunate complications. Lega was a close friend of Ghigi's and therefore they could never be altogether businesslike. He was also, like so many others, extremely possessive about Il Nobile Lord and not disposed to encourage him to have direct dealings with anyone; and though of course that would hardly have been expected when it was a case of enquiring into refreshments for the wives of servitors, it makes for uncertainty as to whether it was Byron's wish that some tradesmen and artisans should reduce their bills or whether Lega, with the zeal which had so often won praises, was showing how thoroughly he earned his salary.

'You know his system', he wrote to Ghigi in an appreciative echo of his employer's words, 'of always having his accounts perfectly in order at the end of every week, and why it is necessary to conform to this laudable old custom.'[2] But men of rank usually expected long credit and were charged accordingly, and Lega's week-by-week calculations were a

---

[1] The two men made a small contribution from their pay towards this, deducted in convenient instalments.

[2] 46873 Folio 65. 17 Feb. 1822.

bother to Ghigi, who was being asked to rearrange some financial matters to suit them. He replied somewhat ironically about Milord's laudable custom.

Of how shopkeepers, bootmakers, carpenters were dealt with in pre-Lega days there is little evidence except that Byron was capricious, and would sometimes rebound sharply against imposition and sometimes tolerate it. He may or may not have been personally responsible for reducing the price of boots for the courier from more than ten crowns to eight, or the fees of the carpenter from nearly twelve and a half to ten. Both of them continued to welcome custom from the same quarter, and Tita had a new pair of boots a week or two later, so it is clear no one was dissatisfied. The pharmacist must assuredly have sent a very excessive bill because he permitted Lega to reduce it to twelve crowns from more than twenty. The withholding of any part of a payment, however, was rare, and uncommonly prompt settlement must have made up in the eyes of most tradesmen for the likelihood of careful scrutiny. The same suppliers appear repeatedly in the accounts.

Byron's applications to Lega for pocket money were frequent and variable. Taking an eventful month of the Pisa sojourn, we find:

			Crowns	Pauls	Crazie
March	1st	Given to Milord	1		
	2nd	,, ,, ,, [an unusually large amount]	10		
	2nd	To Fletcher for what he says he lent Milord	5		
	6th	Given to Milord		6	5
	7th	,, ,, ,,	10		
	9th	,, ,, ,,	4		
	12th	,, ,, ,,	4		
	14th	,, ,, ,,	2	4	
	15th	,, ,, ,,	4		
	17th	,, ,, ,,	3		
	18th	,, ,, ,,	4		
	21st	,, ,, ,,		3	
	22nd	,, ,, ,,	4	5	
	23rd	Repayments to Fletcher for loans to Milord the previous week	1	5	
	24th	Given to Milord	6		
	25th	,, ,, ,,	3		
	27th	,, ,, ,,	2	5	
	28th	,, ,, ,, 5 louis d'or and 4 francesconi	25		
	31st	Given to Milord	5		
		Total	95	8	5

The exceptional sum on the 28th may have been intended to meet contingencies arising from the 'affray' which had taken place on the 24th.

It will be discussed in the next chapter. In February, Byron's pocket money, supplied by Lega, Fletcher, and Tita, had been only nineteen crowns, unless he had some balance of a hundred given him in one lump sum on January 12th; but as that forms part of a separate entry, it is likely to have been for a special purpose, perhaps the settlement for 'some English household comforts' he had bought in Leghorn before Christmas, saying he had been a stranger to them for six years.[1] Without that outlay his January dole was eleven crowns.

Most of the money must have gone on shooting expenses. Medwin says his favourite target was a five-paul piece, and that, when he hit it, he would give another to the farmer who owned the ground used as a pistol range, keeping the damaged coin. His being a good shot might thus account for a fair number of crowns every month. Shooting deep dents in silver coins is, I should say, a wasteful rather than a miserly practice.

Going back to the ledger for March, we have the following recorded charities:

			Crowns	Pauls	Crazie
March	1st	To a poor old lame woman			4
	2nd	To two Franciscan nuns	1		
	4th	To a poor old man			4
	5th	To a Greek, Spiridione d'Antonio, by way of assistance [*sussidio*—it is Lega's customary word for entering gifts to persons not, theoretically, in the habit of making appeals]	6		
		Charity to four people, three old men and a lame woman		2	
	8th	To a poor old man			4
	10th	The courier's petty expenses and charity in the country by order of Milord	2		
	11th	To ten poor men [presumably a passing group of mendicants]		1	2
		To a poor lame woman			6
	17th	The courier's charitable expenses, which include a tip to someone holding the horses	1	7	4
	23rd	Borrowed from Fletcher for charity to a poor man	1		
	27th	Given to the poor		8	5
	28th	Given in two separate donations to the poor	2	6	5
	29th	To a poor lame man who spoke the English language		5	
	31st	Borrowed from Fletcher to give to a poor boy		1	1

[1] Murray MS. To Kinnaird, 18 Dec. 1821.

	Crowns	Pauls	Crazie
March 31st To the Capucine monks three pauls a week until mid-March when the amount was raised to four and a half pauls	1	5	
	17	9	3

We need not suppose this list is complete. It shows simply what was given by Byron's direction but not from his purse; and as his Pisa routine precluded any activities of the man-about-town, it is reasonable to conclude that, after the shooting, his own expenditure was chiefly on little gifts of money to children, of which several instances are known, casual tipping, and largesse to beggars who approached when his servants were not at hand. There were great numbers of mendicants in Pisa and some, who knew his habits, waylaid him on his rides. When ten crazie would buy a pound of meat and a bottle of wine, donations of three or four were at least sufficient for a loaf of bread.

Tips were on a more lordly scale. A servant of Captain Hay's twice in a week received a crown for bringing gifts, one of them a wild boar which the Captain had shot.[1] Someone had to be engaged to skin and cut it up, and Byron sent half of it to the Shelleys, where it was the main dish at a dinner. Later, the same servant brought a present which may have been more welcome; it was a dog, and the man was tipped four crowns two pauls, perhaps more than it would have cost to buy the animal.[2] When Byron lost his brooch—which contained some of Augusta Leigh's hair— Tita had a crown for finding it.[3]

The 'subsidies' must have given the grudging Lega some afflicting moments. It was all very well to produce five pauls for a hairdresser named Bechi who was in straits,[4] but the decayed gentry and nobility were a costlier nuisance. On April 8th, Mancinforte, Marquis of Ancona and Knight of Malta, was regaled with eight crowns, and on the 22nd, twenty (nearly a month's salary for Lega) were handed to one Giovanni Battista Masotti for the purpose of assisting him, in what capacity we do not know. On May 12th, Mary Shelley's Greek teacher came to Teresa's brother to collect his fee which Signor Shelley had forgotten to pay him, and Lega, 'by order of Milord', had to provide him with ten crowns.[5] In July came Brancaleone Mainero from Genoa (his identity obscure) receiving two crowns; and in October, he or a Cavaliere of the same surname had twelve, while September 12th brought a lady, the Marchesa di San Giuliano, who took away no fewer than thirty.

[1] 19 Jan. Hay figures in Lega's accounts as Hee.
[2] 24 Mar. Monkeys cost six crowns each.   [3] 7 Feb.   [4] 17 Feb.
[5] Shelley requested this favour of Byron in his letter of May 3rd, the one in which he told of Claire's grief at Allegra's death.

By comparison, benefactions of one crown to such people as 'the widow of an unfortunate bricklayer' were trifling, but a really competent miser, like John Elwes or the sculptor Nollekins, would have managed to turn a deaf ear to distressing stories about bricklayers and noblemen alike.

Then there were the modest amounts spent on matters that pleased his Catholic household . . . two crowns to the Prior of San Matteo for coming to bless the house, three pauls towards bell-ringing for the souls in Purgatory,[1] a crown a time plus carriage fare for the priest who drove out to Montenero to say Mass, a crown for the Madonna of Montenero, two crowns for the Madonna del Carmine when her procession passed the house.[2] Such tributes from an unbeliever may be counted among charities.

Partly no doubt they were a satisfaction to Teresa and her family—to whom, in fact, there were many little kindnesses, though, after all he had spent on women in Venice before meeting her, he was so proud of her disinterested love that he liked to have it demonstrated. But he did, in Pisa, pay the expenses of her carriage, enabling her to send her own coachman back to Ravenna, with his fare and passport supplied by Lega and several crowns to help him on his way, and he was always very careful that her brother, Pietro, was fully and promptly refunded for any outlay incurred through their association.

During their last weeks in Pisa, Teresa was without means because her husband had successfully appealed to the Pope against paying her an allowance, and she borrowed from Byron to the extent of nearly ninety crowns. It would be interesting to know whether he let her pay him back, and we would hope he did not, but most frustratingly the accounts for the next few months are incomplete. She was decidedly averse from accepting money or even costly presents—at any rate, after the early days of their passion when she had not the heart to resist the significant offering of a ring for which he is said to have paid three hundred and fifty scudi.[3] She had also let him acquire a pianoforte for her, but had amazed him by returning his gift of a diamond brooch as too valuable. For many months before he went to Greece, she was visited every day by an English teacher at a very high fee always debited to Byron. This, however, is in another ledger, and was in another mood.

Among his minor gifts to her there may have been a coral *cornetto* taken to a jeweller to be fitted with a gold clasp, and for which he later had a little case made[4]—possibly so that she should not lose it as she had lost the ring.

We could scarcely have a better example of the tendency to believe

---

[1] 7 Apr. and 22 May.   [2] 21 July.   [3] Origo.
[4] 16 and 19 Jan. and 7 Feb. It was, we may assume, a little horn-shaped brooch or pendant.

what a man says about himself instead of observing what he does than the criticisms of Byron's parsimony by those who were the recipients of his lavish hospitality at the Pisa dinner parties which, for a short time, were held almost weekly. The hard-up Medwin, not above taking an odd crown at the hands of the valet,[1] who disliked him intensely, was early in the field with the tale of avarice, but admitted the unstinted plenty provided for guests. Trelawny, who did much better out of Byron than could be known until accounts became available, attended those parties yet represents the host as one who never paid for anything if Shelley was there to spare his pocket. Shelley, who borrowed from Byron both for himself and his friend Leigh Hunt, contributed to the impression of a vastly rich man hoarding his money, but, on his own disgruntled showing, the guests were encouraged to make 'vats of claret' of themselves, which, however regrettable, does not indicate want of generosity, for the claret was of the best.

The dinners began the month after Byron settled at the Casa Lanfranchi, but surviving correspondence and accounts for that period are mostly concerned with clearing up at Ravenna. We know only that there was a party on December 17th and one on Christmas Day, described by Shelley's friend, Edward Williams, as 'a splendid feast'. Besides himself, Captain Hay was present, with Shelley and Teresa's father and younger brother, Count Pietro. But the first dinner party we see through the accountant's eyes was on January 2nd 1822. The dates and figures from then onwards are as follows:—

	Crowns	Pauls	Crazie
Dinner for a company of six exclusive of wines and cigars	10	9	5
Coffee afterwards [it is always entered separately and must have been a luxury]		2	6
Bill for hiring plate, candelabra, and copperware for the kitchen	1	4	
Extra help, with food and wine. [The staff also had the remains of the meal]		5	3
Total	13	1	6

That the staff, the *servitù*, had the '*avanzi della tavola*'—which must have been substantial judging by the sole menu preserved—is always mentioned in the accounts; but it is not clear whether Lega means the whole staff or the extra helpers. Medwin says Byron ordered the remains to be given away 'lest the servants should envy him every mouthful he eats'. Giving the food away would have been more likely to promote than prevent envy.

[1] 9 Mar., the day Medwin left Pisa.

		Crowns	Pauls	Crazie
Jan. 9th	Dinner as before	11	3	3
	Coffee, extra help, staff refreshments, hiring tableware, etc.	2	0	7
	Total	13	4	2

This amount may be compared with Byron's personal consumption of 'victuals' that week; apart from bread it was one crown, six pauls, four crazie.

		Crowns	Pauls	Crazie
Jan. 16th	Dinner for eight	14	4	4
	The usual additional expenses	1	9	
	Total	16	3	4
	Byron's own table for the week	1	9	
	Food for the pet animals for the week	2	5	3
	Food for the horses for the week	15	8	2

The party on the 16th was attended by Bartolini, the sculptor, by Williams and Shelley again, and by a Captain Scott, as well as Trelawny, who had just been introduced, and was to claim that he always quitted his host's gloomy halls with relief, but failed to explain why he kept going there. Medwin and Williams at least admitted to enjoying themselves, and Captain Hay must have done so because he sent so many presents. Another appreciative guest was the Count Pietro Gamba. No women were invited.

		Crowns	Pauls	Crazie
Jan. 24th	Dinner for eight	13	0	2
	Additional expenses as before with provision of two washbasins for the kitchen	1	8	3
	Total	14	8	5

On this occasion a man from Dunn's, the English merchant at Leghorn, was tipped a crown for 'specially' bringing a smoking set to Pisa. It must have been required for the dinner party. Subsequently smoking expenses became frequent. The Oriental style of pipe seems to have been favoured.

That was the last of the dinners as a regular event. Perhaps Byron was seeing the same guests too often, for most of them dropped in on him constantly, besides shooting with him daily. And after February 15th, when he heard of the death of his mother-in-law, entertaining would have been improper for the first fortnight or so.

He had not pretended to be other than grateful for the prospect of Lady Noel's demise which, by virtue of a marriage settlement highly advantageous to his wife when it was made, might now bring him a great increase of income; but some show of mourning was required by etiquette. A defiance of that strict convention by one who had already defied so many might have created prejudice, and the inheritance was subject to arbitration.

He bought two pairs of black gloves, one of silk, one leather, and had crape veils put round the hats of all his 'family' of eight at a total cost, gloves included, of not quite eight crowns. This, the very least that was acceptable, is what Medwin, with typical extravagance, called 'deep mourning'. A black scarf on the hat was simply equivalent to a black arm-band in more recent times, and servants were expected to be identified with their masters in the semblance of either grief or rejoicing.

Byron was requested by Kinnaird to add the name of Noel immediately to his own,[1] and that too was represented as a wilful affectation by those unfamiliar with the system of inheritance by which so many double names have descended. Among his kinsmen and acquaintances were Wilmot Horton, Duff Gordon, Lockhart Gordon, Leveson Gower, Chaworth Musters, and the very grand heiress, Margaret Mercer Elphinstone, all so named through the conjunction of estates. Even his wife did not take any exception to what was so obviously an expected procedure.

After a six weeks lapse, on March 8th, there was dinner for a company of six. Medwin writes of it as a farewell party for him, and there is no reason to doubt him. There is no reason to doubt Fletcher either, who was most anxious to publish in the press the falsity of Medwin's claim to have noted down 'The Conversations of Lord Byron . . . during a Residence with his Lordship at Pisa in the years 1821 and 1822'—which of course had never taken place.[2] The work enraged everyone connected with Byron and inspired Fletcher to write one of his inimitable letters to the Hon. Augusta Leigh:

> Honᵈ Madam,
>   I hope you will pardon me for this Intrusion of this letter but I feel So very much hurt at the infamous Manner In which My ever to be Lomented Lord and Master's Memorey his *Insulted* By such a Mean Despicable Low Villan has This *Medwin* whom my Lord has so Repeatedly Sent From his Door and Moreover Said if he Calls a Thousand times I will never see him If I see him it shall be when I ride but no time else and then never alone

---

[1] Kinnaird copies. The signature, Noel Byron, seems first to appear in Byron's reply to Kinnaird, 17 Feb. 1822, and in brackets above it, 'Since it must be so'.

[2] Medwin's defence was that his publishers had added the sub-title without his knowledge, but it is ridiculously improbable that an author who corrected proofs was not allowed to see how his book was titled until it came out. It is the subject of a chapter in *The Late Lord Byron*.

And he wishes to make the world believe he was on the Most Intimate Terms Possable with My Lord, which is all false and I hope will be Soon proved so, Mr Hobhouse his not in town or I would have Spoken to him about it, But I have seen Mr Murray and Mr Rogers whom both says I ought to Contridict has far has I can statements which which [sic] I feel it my Duty to do, For his Trash of a Book his all false Except some few words which he picked up from Mrs Shelley which she now seems verry Sorry for and his quite out of Humour with him. Of all the falshoods this seems to beat every thing. Pray Madam Oblige me by letting me know how to act For I would not willingly act in any thing without your Aprobation. But this passes every thing I ever saw when my Lord has said to me 20 times I will not see him and send him to the —— where I think he Deserves sending in good Truth . . .

    I cannot rest Night or Day till Something his done to Contridict it.

Byron, in the first flush of mixing with Englishmen after his comparative isolation in Ravenna, had indulged freely in reminiscence, as he easily did with anybody (it was his charm and his most incorrigible weakness), but in a few weeks Medwin had become as big a bore at the Casa Lanfranchi as he was at the Tre Palazzi, where Mary Shelley dreaded his presence; and, as a player who has been giving a dreary performance may receive, on making his exit, applause which is really only a manifestation of relief, so Medwin would have had a gracious farewell from Byron.

'I am often with him', he proudly declared, 'from the time he gets up till two or three in the morning.' Yet he knew that Byron wrote late at night, and even that he would turn to his work as soon as his persistent visitor had left. '. . . After sitting up so late he must require rest; but he produces, the next morning, proofs that he has not been idle. Sometimes, when I call, I find him at his desk, but he either talks as he writes, or lays down his pen to play at billiards . . .'

There is an obtuseness here that makes us understand why Medwin was ultimately denied admission until his departure from Pisa was assured. It may have been he who unconsciously brought the banquets to an end—except for the valedictory one. This was somewhat less lavish than usual, though that was not necessarily deliberate.

		Crowns	Pauls	Crazie
Mar. 8th	Dinner for six	9	6	4
	Additional expenses as before	1	7	6
	Total	11	4	2

Byron had a hangover next morning because the 'symposium . . . closed with a midnight of more Brantwein and water than agrees with me'.[1]

[1] Murray MS. To Hobhouse, 9 Mar. 1822.

After that, there were no more dinners except on three successive evenings in April when Sam Rogers and his travelling companion were house guests, and then Shelley and Trelawny were invited. The 'weekly' functions so often alluded to as if they had been a thoroughly established feature of the Pisa scene are thus sifted down to four in January 1822 and two in December 1821. Mary Shelley, who was given to exaggeration, wrote in a letter to Mrs Gisborne on December 20th 1821, 'My Lord is now living very sociably giving dinners to his male acquaintance and writing divinely', but this cannot be other than an expansive allusion to the party of three days before and the one to be held on Christmas Day. Williams's journal, the most literal source we have for the daily activities of the Pisa circle, records seventeen meetings with Byron, generally through morning calls or shooting practice, before the first reference to dining (December 17th). Mary's tone would not have been so pleasant if the all-male gatherings which sent Shelley home with his nerves 'shaken to pieces' by late hours and the wine-drinking of his fellow guests[1] had been going on for long.

Byron had arrived at the beginning of November, but even allowing for Teresa's ministrations in advance with Mary, it must have taken some time for his eight waggon-loads of furniture from Ravenna to be arranged in the new house. There was then an acute shortage of the kind of equipment required for entertaining. Tablecloths and napkins had to be bought—one set specially made, another sent from Leghorn. The kitchen was so ill provided that carpenter's work and purchases of the most ordinary utensils were going on for many weeks after the move, and, though a particular effort might be made for the Christmas season, nothing much in the way of organized hospitality seems to have been going on before.

The menu of one of the famous dinners survives through the accident of having had a letter by Lega copied on the back of it. There were, as was customary, two main courses and a dessert, each course consisting of several different dishes all served at once and laid on the table in a formal pattern, centre, sides, and corners. It was not until much later that one dish at a time with its appropriate accompaniments was handed round by waiters. The *à la Russe* style had been introduced by an Ambassador to France in Napoleon's time, but was only accepted gradually. Under the old system still prevailing, soup, fish, poultry, and vegetables were set down together before the guests, who selected what they pleased from

[1] Letter to Horace Smith, 25 Jan. 1822, the day after the last of the dinners as a regular function. We may wonder whether Byron perceived Shelley's lack of conviviality and, what with this and Medwin's dullness, decided to abandon the parties forthwith.

the assortment displayed, their plates being changed at need by the attendants.

On the removal of the first course, another, equal in size and variety, was brought in—to all intents and purposes a second meal—and the appetite was tempted to revive. There was now a set piece on which the cook lavished his artistry by making a composition of heaped-up viands. The diners helped themselves and each other to the minor items, but it had become *de rigueur* for the host or hostess or both to do any carving that was necessary. Guests 'took wine' with one another from decanters they circulated amongst themselves, offering private toasts and sentiments and also joining in general ones at the end of the repast. It was all no doubt much cosier than receiving everything at the hands of waiters. The two great defects from the modern point of view were that many of the dishes must have become half-cold standing on the table and that the quantity was overwhelming; but the taste for very hot food is probably of fairly recent cultivation, and profusion was an accepted convention of hospitality.

In Britain there would have been a third course with sweet puddings, pies, trifles and jellies, before the removal of the cloth for fruit and nuts; but in Italy the dessert itself was—mercifully—the third *portata*. Byron, who, when alone, sat down to most meagre fare, served his guests luxuries. The letter copied on the back of the single sketched-out menu that exists is dated February 4th 1822, but the dinner is likely to have been the one of January 2nd as *cotechino* is a New Year's dish. A few short words and ends of words are missing. Two or three others defy modern translation.

First Course
Thick dark vegetable soup, or herb soup *à la santé*
Fried sweetbreads, or a cream cheese dish
Codeghino [usually spelt cotechino] *col Salgravi*
[Boiled and sliced salami of pork served hot with lentils. Salgravi may be the name of a sauce]
Another friture, spinach, or a dish of ham
Boiled capons, and beef garnished with (?) potatoes [end of word missing]
A fish stew

Second Course
A *granita* of veal garnished with (?) [the word is missing]
Two roast capons with sauce
Roast game—woodcocks
Baked fish—whichever is suitable
A fricassee of poultry in gravy [i.e. *in umido*]
Another stew of *latticini tiratti* [sic]

Third Course—Dessert
Fruit—blanched almonds, plain almonds served with other desserts of various
kinds, pears, *seleni*, oranges, and roast (?) chestnuts[1]

It is wonderful that Gaetano Forestieri, unassisted even by his wife,
who did not arrive till the weekly dinners were over, managed to cook
and dish up such a meal as this. The amounts of a little over a crown a
time paid to Nicolai Andrea for the use of tableware, candelabra, and
cooking vessels, could not have extended to the provision of hired scullions
at whatever low rate of pay, and Lega allots nothing to extra labour
beyond the four or five pauls which included refreshments in the kitchen.
Tita helped to serve and Fletcher must have done so too, and the others
of the household may have given some aid behind the scenes, but the
cook's job with a very limited range of utensils was still an unenviable
one.

When not called on to entertain, however, nothing could have been
easier, because Byron followed a régime of distressing inadequacy.
Medwin states that his dinners cost five pauls a day—three and a half
crowns a week—and that he asked a lady of his acquaintance to examine
the bills in case he was being overcharged. The fact is that, during the
time when Medwin was in Pisa, half a crown was actually very much
more than the usual day-to-day expenditure on catering for Byron, and if
he asked any lady whether he was being overcharged, it must have been
in a jesting vein to enjoy her surprise at his abstinence. No one but a very
humourless person could have believed that a man who gave sumptuous
dinners for guests, and kept nine horses, three dogs, two monkeys, and a
number of birds, all notably well nourished, reduced himself to almost
beggarly fare for fear of spending too much!

His anxiety was lest he should gain weight, and this was not merely
because it caused his looks to deteriorate, but because he had, as Leigh
Hunt wrote—with evident satisfaction—'a real and even a sore lameness',
and when he grew heavy it became more painful for him to walk.
Nothing was known about diet scientifically, and Byron's principal
specifics were vinegar and purgative pills, both of which recur again and
again in the accounts. He would soak potatoes or biscuits in vinegar and
eat little else for days on end. These biscuits, which appear regularly in
the housekeeping bills as *ciambelletti biscottati*, were, so far as I can

[1] 46873 Folio 58. I have left *latticini tirati* in the second course untranslated because
the Italians I have consulted are not in accord as to what dish it could be in this context.
The *granita di vitello* (veal) is also controversial. One adviser thinks it may be a mould
or aspic, another says veal served in garlic, parsley and lemon sauce. *Seleni* may be an
obsolete name for a pale-coloured type of apple. It must be remembered that this is
simply a kitchen jotting.

ascertain, very small ring-shaped rolls, like crisp doughnuts, but un-sweetened, of which no fewer than four hundred were supplied every week.

It is quite incredible that any person, in whatever state of ignorance about nutrition, could have eaten upwards of fifty doughnuts a day. I therefore think these were among the few items of food of which the whole household partook. Olive oil was one of them and vinegar another, for we see 'Vinegar for the use of Milord', and simply 'Vinegar', two or three jars at a time. The servants may have been entitled to bread and certain ingredients for dressing salads, which were a staple commodity. When Byron left Pisa to go to Montenero, the quantity of rolls was reduced to half. After he settled in Genoa, they are mentioned no more.

The crown or two a week that went on victuals other than *ciambelletti* must have covered his consumption of green tea and the raw egg with which, if Medwin is right, he broke his fast—usually standing, Teresa tells us. Occasionally there is an extraordinary indulgence—a Stilton cheese,[1] nine ounces of truffles,[2] several dozen oysters, sometimes shared with guests, but often taken in solitude—unless one of the Gambas enjoyed a snack with him. On March 31st, Fletcher was repaid three crowns for ten dozen oysters, and it passes belief they were all consumed by one man, however immoderate his partiality.

That wine or gin could add anything to his weight he had not the least notion. It is impossible to estimate how much he drank because a good deal of what he ordered from Leghorn was shared with guests, not only at the dinner parties but during the late night conversations, and indeed whenever hospitality was called for. Tea and coffee were offered only in the evening after dinner; morning callers—if treated in the English tradition—would be given sherry, port, or Madeira, or in summer a glass of white wine.

Byron liked hock and soda water. Little boxes of soda were often among the steward's purchases, but what method was used for the aera-tion of water I do not know. His favourite drink at table was claret, and he is on record as saying, 'I hate anonymous wine'.[3] Claret at nearly a crown a bottle was one of his extravagances. Bearing in mind that three crowns would have bought a large damask tablecloth and a bakers' dozen of handmade napkins, we must conclude that avarice would hardly run to a taste for French wine in Italy. He rationed himself to one pint a day except when entertaining. No native vintage appears at all in the Pisa ledger. There had been some at Ravenna, but it was left behind to be sold by Ghigi who, with difficulty, got nine scudi for three barrels. The

---

[1] 46876. 16 Mar.   [2] 17 Mar.   [3] Account by James Forrester, R.N.

money was spent on an old woman to whom Byron still made an allowance.

Approximately two hundred and fifty bottles of foreign wines were supplied between January 1st and October 6th 1822, when the accounts in Tuscan currency were closed. Even allowing for some stock in the cellar when the New Year began, that is not a heavy consumption for a household where British visitors called frequently. It works out at less than a bottle a day. Twelve additional bottles were delivered in Byron's absence 'for the guests'.[1]

These guests are in the ledger as 'two American gentlemen lodged in the house at Pisa'. Wax candles were bought for them on June 16th. Byron at the time was in a rented villa at Montenero. The only American acquainted with him whom I can fit into the month of June is W. E. West, who painted his portrait, not very brilliantly, at what he calls 'the Villa Rossa'. It was a red house more generally known as the Villa Dupuy. West mentions 'my friend who had made me acquainted with him' and who was a compatriot, and indicates that the friend was present at one or more of the sittings, so he was perhaps the other American who enjoyed the wine and wax candles at the Casa Lanfranchi soon after.

Byron, who loved to listen to Americans talk—but vainly tried to make West say 'I guess'—must have invited them for dinner after the Montenero sittings, because there is a general increase in the catering bills for the first fortnight of June as well as a small dinner party on the 9th. West says: 'We always dined alone', but his memory was faulty; and assuredly it strayed when it made him think he had stayed a few days *with* Byron at Pisa instead of merely in his house.[2] The latter was unquestionably elsewhere from May 18th to July 2nd, and had no house guests on his return but the sufficiently numerous Hunts, who had just arrived from England.

(It is a revealing fact that, when dates are carefully scrutinized, so many who left recollections of Byron turn out to have exaggerated the amount of time spent with him, the worst deceivers—or self-deceivers—being Medwin, Trelawny, Stendhal, and Lady Blessington.)

What wines were in the cellar can be gathered from the following unfinished order by Fletcher:

[1] 18 June.

[2] Article in the *New Monthly Magazine*, 1826. It was written up from an interview which may account for several inaccuracies, such as that the portrait was done at Montenero in August, when in fact Byron was not there. West was an eye witness of the scene when there was a brawl among the servants and Count Pietro was slightly wounded in trying to separate them. This took place shortly before Leigh Hunt's arrival but on the same day, probably June 29th; so if, as I believe, West was one of the two American guests at Pisa, he must have returned to Montenero before he left Italy.

Sir, Please to send My Lord 6 Best Cut Glass Decanters and 6 labels for each bottle. In the following manner, first I mean to say 6 on the whole not has I have mistated 6 for each Ingravin on Ivory W.[hite] Whine Madearia Claret, Champagne, Grave[1]

The sixth wine is not named. Fletcher's spelling may have given out, or he may have paused to wonder whether champagne would really require a decanter or whether 'W. Whine' was adequate for hock, and left the task of ordering to the secretary, the Leghorn merchant being bilingual. A single bottle of 'Sottern' was got for one occasion, but the spelling was Lega's.

Gin figures largely in Byron annals but not so much as one would expect on his accounts. It had to be obtained from Leghorn, and a dozen bottles are entered on February 16th, another dozen on March 18th, and yet another dozen on July 16th. The order was not renewed till August 29th, when tea accompanied the purchase and the Duty and cost of transport show that the number of bottles was less—possibly half a dozen. There were two bottles only on September 21st. An express was sent to Leghorn the following day for eight bottles, but whether of gin, wine, or any other beverage is not stated. Taking the quantity from February up to the date when the supply ran out in August as six bottles a month, that is not a drunkard's ration, though it may have been of greater strength than now and, combined with the pint of claret, was more than enough to undo the effect of dieting. It is difficult to believe, even when he himself tries to persuade us, that such works as *Don Juan* and *The Vision of Judgement* were composed in a befuddled state.

Leigh Hunt, who would not voluntarily have omitted a single blemish he could discover and magnify, actually allowed that Byron 'was not often nor immoderately' in his cups; but that admission was made, we may suspect, because he had just said that his host was 'by far the pleasantest when he had got wine in his head', thus turning his sobriety into one more defect. Barry, the banker at Genoa, told Hobhouse that Byron did not care to drink alone,[2] which confirms that he was not the sole consumer of the gin punch to which he was partial. After his removal to Genoa, more gin and less wine were ordered. Brandy is scarcely found on the accounts until the departure for Greece. Twelve bottles of beer were sent from Leghorn on April 25th.

Many men have owed their amatory successes to tête-à-tête suppers served by candlelight or lamplight at tables garnished with flowers and

[1] 46873. 4 Dec. 1821.

[2] Hobhouse Journals. 6 Oct. 1826. Medwin says he drank gin under the impression that it was good for 'a nephritic complaint'. The belief that it conferred some benefit on the kidneys was current early in the present century.

laden with delicacies, but Byron's aversion from women of substantial appetite (Lady Byron had one), or even any obvious need of food, debarred him from intimacies based on eating. He had come to manhood in a day when the fashionable beauty, draped with airy muslin, aimed at attaining the lightness and grace of a nymph, and some traces of the taste he had then acquired lingered, though he did not like thin women—and Teresa was not one. If he seldom sat down with her to a solid meal, he did not mind seeing her eat sorbets or drink lemonade. In hot weather he had both sent from a café, and ice was delivered frequently at considerable expense. For the first few days after the return from Montenero, ice and lemon water cost nearly four crowns, in the second week of July five crowns four pauls; and in the third just under six and a half crowns, an astonishing outlay set against the small amounts commonly allotted to nourishment.

In August from four to seven sorbets a day were brought from the Caffe del'Amicizia, and sometimes coffees as well. Leigh Hunt, in spite of himself, painted a charming picture of Byron and Teresa in the garden, Byron in his nankeen jacket and peaked cap jesting or singing snatches of Rossini, whose compositions Hunt despised, Teresa with her pretty smile and long blonde hair (Titian red-gold, not yellow as Hunt tells us),[1] the garden with its little orange trees and green, well-tended shrubs, and the blue sky over it.

By Papal decree Teresa was not supposed to be living with Byron and, until the sojourn at Montenero, she and Count Ruggiero Gamba, and two of her brothers, Vincenzo and Pietro, had been housed further along the Arno in a quite separate dwelling, where Byron had habitually visited her in the evenings. But by the time of the Hunts' arrival, discretion had been relaxed. She had gone to the Villa Dupuy with Byron, travelling apart, it is true, and accompanied by members of her family; and now, though with an appearance of Gamba chaperonage, she was at his palazzo. Hunt speaks of her descending to the garden in the mornings after completing her toilette, and of two or three chairs then being brought out to them—ordinary house chairs, for there were as yet no portable garden seats. Teresa would sit listening to her lover talking in a language she did not understand to a man she did not like, and it may have been then that she first formed her resolve to learn English.

For her it was by no means a cheerful time though she put a good face on it. She had struck up a friendship with Jane Williams and Mary Shelley, who spoke Italian, but they had gone months ago to a villa at

---

[1] There is a lock of it in the Murray Collection. As an example of Hunt's insincerity, in one paragraph he says Teresa's fashion of wearing her hair was 'as if it streamed in disorder', while a few pages later he speaks of her 'sleek tresses'.

Lerici. There had been Allegra's death, which she had had the pain of breaking to Byron, with possibly some feeling of guilt too for not having wanted the intrusions of the child in the life she had looked forward to in Pisa. Her husband had withdrawn her alimony. Her father's liberal political views, not to speak of the connection with Byron, placed him and her brothers in jeopardy. And Byron himself was restless, sometimes wondering whether he might not aid the Greeks now that they seemed disposed to break their Turkish shackles.

He had never had any such durable liaison before, and while his affection had gained in depth and sympathy, she could not but perceive it was no longer so all-absorbing as to prevent his having plans that might exclude her. With her uncommon inborn sagacity in matters of love, which had enabled her to hold that difficult man more than three years, she was not old enough at twenty-two to appreciate the subtle compliment of being taken for granted. After her happiness in Ravenna, where he had fitted himself so endearingly into the world she knew, to see her *cavalier servente*, her prize, among his countrymen must have given her some sense of deprivation.

Byron too, though enjoying the convivialities, the stimulating talks with Shelley, and the unabated vitality in writing, had not been without anxieties. The year 1822 was fruitful of the misunderstandings and annoyances which arose from the lapse of three weeks, more or less, before he could receive any letter from England. His sales were as good as ever, but piracies reduced the benefit to Murray, whose increasing nervousness about handling work which was publicly condemned for obscenity and blasphemy resulted in a discouraging attitude that eroded their once eminently successful association. Perhaps the worst discouragement of all had been a letter from Kinnaird saying that he heard, 'and pretty generally too', that Byron was publishing too much: the supply must be adjusted to the demand, and it would be better to have one or two failures than let the public get a fixed idea about over-production.[1] It is rather difficult to see how having failures would prevent a celebrity's reputation from declining, but Kinnaird and Hobhouse were both so fond of him and so proud of his fame that they lived in constant apprehension of its being tarnished. If Byron's admiring friends had had their way *Don Juan* would never have seen the light.

As to his enemies, they were for ever attacking, and an onslaught by the Poet Laureate, Southey, in a spirit of malignance hardly warranted even by Byron's onslaught on him,[2] induced such fury that Kinnaird had to suppress a letter of challenge. He had been uneasy too about having

---

[1] Kinnaird copies. 16 Oct. 1821.   [2] *Don Juan*, Canto III.

committed himself, under the influence of Shelley, to founding a periodical in partnership with Leigh Hunt, who came out to join him for the purpose, and against whom several close friends warned him.

Such were a few of his worries from England. In Tuscany he was being harassed by the authorities, who from the first had suspected him of harbouring subversive designs and who, after the enraging incident when one of Byron's servants had seriously wounded a dragoon, had something, as they thought, to go upon. There had been an obstinate struggle between himself and Claire Clairmont over the upbringing of their child, and it had ended most disastrously with his being blamed for little Allegra's death. His expensive schooner, the indiscreetly named *Bolivar*, gave much more trouble than pleasure: and Shelley's smaller craft, the *Don Juan*, built at the same time, was to take both Shelley and the likeable young Edward Williams to their deaths. Grief for Shelley apart—though he keenly felt it—that tragedy was to bring many nagging irritations in its wake; for it happened just when Leigh Hunt at last arrived, with a wife and six children and a seventh in prospect, and turned out, quite without warning, to have no other means of support than Byron.

So, by one of the contrasts life affords all too abundantly, the period of the ices in the garden coincides with the weeks when Shelley's death was making its impact in many different ways on all those in Italy whose lives were linked with his. Before we come to that calamity, taking a slightly new aspect as it does from the steward's ledger, we shall see what glimmerings those pages and Lega Zambelli's letters shed upon certain other events which have only been touched upon.

9

Finances of the Pisa Affray

The story of the clash of horsemen at Pisa has been told many times and most fully in C. L. Cline's valuable book, *Byron, Shelley and their Pisan Circle*. I will go briskly over the same ground because the steward's accounts enable me to give new down-to-earth details of its troublesome aftermath.

In the early evening of March 24th 1822 the riding party, returning from shooting practice, consisted of Byron, Shelley, Pietro Gamba, Trelawny, and the Captain Hay who had sent Byron the wild boar and, that very day, a dog. Byron's courier, Giuseppe Strauss, was in the rear. Mary Shelley and Teresa Guiccioli were taking a drive some little distance before them on the same road, with Byron's coachmen on the box of Teresa's carriage. Less than half a mile from the eastern gate of the old city, the men were joined by John Taaffe, a cultured Irishman who was writing a commentary on Dante which Byron was pressing the reluctant Murray to publish. It was a matter of general agreement in the 'Pisan circle' that Taaffe's horsemanship, albeit a subject of pride to him, was not good.

As they rode on, engaged in animated conversation, another horseman, coming from behind, suddenly pushed between Taaffe and a ditch running beside the road, making Taaffe's horse rear up and plunge against Byron's and frightening those of the other riders. Resentfully, Taaffe exclaimed, 'Have you ever seen the like of that?' and Byron spurred his horse to catch up with the unmannerly stranger, followed at once by Shelley and Trelawny. Taaffe, unable for some moments to control his own mettlesome animal, dropped his hat and, when it was retrieved, fell to brushing it very carefully until the others were out of sight. Mary and Teresa were alarmed when all their party rode past them in a little whirl-wind of dust.

The creator of the disturbance, a sergeant-major of dragoons named Masi, realizing he was being pursued, at length slowed down, and Shelley, who was beside him first, asked him to explain his behaviour. The reply was offensive enough to make Shelley think he was drunk. All the others except Taaffe having come up, Byron likewise demanded an explanation and received a similar style of answer, the soldier having his hand on his sword.

Byron then committed a mistake that was to turn out prodigiously embarrassing to a literary nobleman versed in tales of chivalry and knightly etiquette. Misled by the dragoon's fine uniform and epaulettes into thinking him a commissioned officer—technically a gentleman—he presented a visiting card and challenged him. The response was bellicose rather than gentlemanly, and the situation was not helped by confusion as to exactly what had happened, the complainant Taaffe being still behind, and Trelawny not understanding Italian.

Someone—Williams's diary identifies him as Pietro—struck the dragoon in the chest with a riding-whip, calling him '*Ignorante*', whereupon the angry man, who had not the presence of mind to tell these other angry men that he was late for the roll call, shouted to the guards at the town gate, now only a few yards away, 'Arrest them! Arrest them!' at the same time using a volley of abusive language. Byron defiantly pushed through the gate while the guards seized their guns and bayonets, and Pietro went after him.

Trelawny, Shelley, Hay and the courier, reacting less quickly, were caught in a scuffle in which Shelley, trying to aid Trelawny, who was being beaten about the thighs with the soldiers' swords, was knocked off his horse and hit so violently with the hilt of Masi's sabre that he fell to the ground unconscious. Hay in turn strove to get between Shelley and Masi, but received a stroke with the naked sword which, though partly deflected, slashed through his hat, bruised his face, and severely cut his nose. Masi, who was a doughty fighter if a wild one, next thrust his sabre at the courier with such force that afterwards the injury brought on a haemorrhage of the lungs.

All this was witnessed by the terrified ladies in the carriage, but it had fallen too far behind for them to hear the altercation or have the slightest inkling of what had caused it. Byron meanwhile was speeding down the Lung'Arno to invoke the law.

Evidence, where a number of rapid incidents have taken place simultaneously, is never without points of conflict, but the deposition made the following day and signed by Byron, Hay, Shelley, and Trelawny is unlikely to have contained any misstatement of demonstrable fact. It was first published by Medwin in a free translation which omitted, without indication, several important details—such as that Shelley had gone to Trelawny's aid and Hay to Shelley's—and added to the names of

the signatories that of Pietro Gamba, who was not one of them.[1] This
statement affirms that:

> The noble Lord, reaching his house, gave orders to his secretary that he
> should go at once to inform the police; then, not seeing his companions, he
> turned again towards the gate, and on the way met the Hussar,[2] who rode
> up to him saying 'Are you satisfied?' [In Masi's own version, 'Are you content
> now that I have beaten you all?'] The noble Lord, as he knew nothing of the
> affray which had taken place at the gate, answered him, 'I am not satisfied—
> tell me your name!' The man replied 'Masi, Sergeant-Major.' A servant of
> Milord's came out at that moment from the Palazzo, and seized the bridle
> of the sergeant's horse.

This was Byron's fierce-looking bearded *chasseur*, Tita, who had
rushed up bearing two sabres. Byron, when sending Lega for the police,
had also had a sword-stick brought to him, which, when he encountered
Masi again, he had half-drawn to show that he was armed. Masi caught
his hand to check him, and for some paces they rode together with an
ironical semblance of clasping hands. Some onlookers imagined they were
shaking hands to signify the end of the quarrel, and Byron too fancied the
gesture might be a pledge of peace. When Tita snatched the soldier's
bridle, Byron told him to let go, and as he did so, Masi rode off at full
speed, daunted at last.

It was a Sunday so there was a crowd of bystanders, many of whom had
collected round the house when Byron returned to it again, followed by
the remnant of the shooting party, Trelawny and Shelley supporting
Hay, who, having lost much blood, was only able to make his way very
feebly. Shelley had been sick and was also in a shaken state; but at any
rate no one had been arrested. Just before their entrance, the carriage
with the agitated women had drawn up at the palazzo, and Teresa's
footman, who had been standing behind according to custom, lowered
the steps. Gaetano, the cook, let them into the house, Tita having gone
out with the sabres. Teresa ran upstairs in an hysterical state, which could
not have been calmed by the sight of the blood-stained Hay when he
came in with his dishevelled companions. Mary Shelley, who had been
in tears, soothed her, and Byron sent for a surgeon, and ordered water and
vinegar, which was considered disinfectant, for washing Hay's wound.

Taaffe still lingered behind, having reached the town gate just after
the fracas was over and while Masi was sheathing his sword. He claimed
in his deposition to have remonstrated sternly with the dragoon, reproached him in front of numerous onlookers for drawing his sabre against

---

[1] It was undoubtedly Byron's wish not to involve him in an affair which might, and
did, have serious consequence for his family, including Teresa.

[2] They did not distinguish between an hussar and a dragoon.

unarmed gentlemen, and called on the guards to make a report: but the impression, on which all the group were in accord, was that he had kept well away from a scene which he himself had started by his cry of indignation. When it transpired that, in his eagerness not to be implicated, he denied that being nearly thrown from his horse by a boorish rider had given him any offence, a distinct coolness arose between him and the others.

It was not until an hour or two after their return that, from one quarter and another, they learned the dragoon had been wounded and was in the hospital of Santa Chiara. Daylight had gone when he passed the Casa Lanfranchi after his second confrontation with Byron, and what with the darkness and the ever-increasing concourse of people, it was easy to miss the sight of him swaying in the saddle, his shako tumbling from his head. Byron, as he hurried the others into the house, was surprised (he said in evidence) to see the shako fall but had no notion that the man himself was hurt. Nevertheless, he had been stabbed and, after staggering a few steps into a café, was carried away in a deplorable condition. Various stories were told, rumours were immediately circulated surpassing in their extravagance even those Byron was accustomed to, but one thing seemed certain—Masi's assailant had emerged from the palazzo with some long instrument like a pitchfork or lance and struck him as he tried to gallop away.

Byron's situation had now become a most unpleasant one. He was well aware that police spies in the pay of the Austrian-dominated Government watched and resented him, though he could not have known that he was depicted in the reports of the indefatigable informer Luigi Torelli as an assassin surrounded by a dangerous gang. As for the Gamba family, their political embroilments had already made it difficult for them to get even a temporary permit to reside in Tuscany, and it was quickly given out that Pietro had horsewhipped one of the local military. If Taaffe persisted in disclaiming any provocation, Byron and his friends would appear to have committed an act of sheer aggression.

Byron's recent works had raised such an outcry against him in the British press that the thought of giving them wherewithal for new denunciations was infuriating, while to find that he had proposed a duel to a man whose rank did not qualify him for it was as humiliating to him as if he had been Don Quixote. At his request, Shelley and Pietro Gamba, accompanied by the unlucky Hay, whose wound was still untreated by any surgeon, went to the Governor's palace to make a report to the Adjutant. The Governor was Niccolò Viviani, father of the beautiful Emilia who had formerly enthralled Shelley. He was—perhaps diplomatically—indisposed, as they were apprised before they set out, Taaffe having called and told his own story to the Adjutant very speedily. (Byron himself may have felt that, unless he was sure the Governor would receive him, he ought not to call personally.)

'All again return mutually recriminated and recriminating', Williams wrote in his diary that night, adding at ten o'clock, 'How the attack ought to have been conducted is now agitating—all appear to me to be wrong'. Although he had not been present at the brawl, his next entry, March 25th, records: 'At 7 this morning an officer from the Police called here demanding my name—country—Profession—and requesting to have an account of my actions between the hours of 6 & 8 yesterday . . . 12 o'clock. S[helley] calls. The wounded dragoon much worse. Hear that the Soldiers are confined to their barracks, but they swear to be revenged on some of us.'

Feeling against the English naturally ran high, and it took courage for them to go out for their usual ride in the afternoon. Even Shelley, who, though not the 'lean and feeble' creature Hobhouse considered him, was inclined to pacifism, agreed with Trelawny that they should be armed. Pistols were worn, swordsticks were carried, and they passed through a tense crowd concealing the discomfort each must inwardly have felt.

Taaffe had hopefully sent news that the soldier's wound was slight after all, but before they went out, they were informed that he was not expected to live, and as to the manner in which he had come by his injury, the tales grew more and more outrageous. Byron and his friends, jointly and severally, prepared statements; but Taaffe played so back-sliding a part throughout that, much to the approbation of the others, Jane Williams nicknamed him False-Taaffe. Probably the key to his equivocal attitude lay in 'the custom of Milord to . . . laugh at the jumps that my horse often made, and at the consequences (such as getting into the ditch) which sometimes resulted'—a rather pathetic passage in the deposition Byron ultimately wrested from him.[1] And a very unhelpful document it turned out to be.

The eminent surgeon Vaccà had been concerned with the case from the start, having attended the courier Giuseppe the same day that he received Masi's ferocious blow in the chest, which rendered him unfit for duty for some weeks. Where Vaccà had gone before or after that visit is not clear,[2] but he had not been available when sent for to deal with Teresa's unnerving hysteria which had developed into a fit of convulsions: and a Dr Foscarini had been fetched instead, who applied the age-old panacea of letting blood. Thenceforward both he and Vaccà treated

---

[1] Quoted by Cline.   [2] Possibly, as Cline suggests, to see Masi in hospital.

Masi in hospital at Byron's expense, Vaccà taking a pessimistic view of the patient's chances and the nature of his wound, which he thought had been made by a long and murderous stiletto.

The police had to make arrests, and began with Byron's courier, but let him go on evidence that he had not been near the spot where the weapon had done its mischief. Next day, they took up the coachman, Vincenzo Papi, and the chasseur, Tita; and he, as if his immense black beard had not been prejudicial enough, made a very bad impression by coming to the examination armed with a pair of pistols and an outsize stiletto. The coachman, after a night in custody, was allowed to go, since the story that he had driven the countess's carriage to the stables and remained there at work until summoned again was corroborated by the grooms, Vecchi and Manuzzi.[1] Tita was still held in prison, rather because the public wanted reprisals than because there was any evidence against him. And now Teresa's footman, Antonio Malucelli, was seized, and his confused testimony provided an excuse for holding him.

After Masi had belied expectations and recovered, the wrath of the citizens died away, but the authorities were determined to make full use of their opportunity for harassing Byron and the Gambas, so Tita and Antonio were kept incarcerated.

Byron wrote letter after letter to the British *Chargé d'Affaires* at Florence, E. J. Dawkins, hoping he would use his influence to see justice done. He complained of the rigour with which the servants were treated in jail—'I cannot contemplate the probable duration of the detention in the harshest confinement of two innocent men—without great uneasiness on their account . . . they have not had fair play granted them.'[2] He devoted hours to circulating his friends in England with statements that would arm them against misrepresentation in the newspapers, and he engaged a lawyer on Dawkins's advice both to look after the interests of the imprisoned Tita and Antonio and with an intention of eventually prosecuting Masi, a step that might contribute to getting the two servants out of jail.

If he harboured some vindictiveness, it was largely, I fancy, because he felt he had been made to look foolish, not only by his hot impulsive pursuit of the man and the challenge that was contrary to a code he believed in, and by Taaffe's virtual repudiation, but by his frustrated attempts to protect those who called themselves his 'family'. Selfish as he was capable of being about many things, Teresa was able to say with incontrovertible truth that his 'indulgence towards his servants became,

---

[1] The spelling of their names differs somewhat from that given by Cline. I took it from their passport. 46878 Folio 2. They themselves were probably illiterate.

[2] Letter to Hay, 12 Apr., quoted by Cline.

at the least mishap that befel them, an almost paternal solicitude, and one might add that it extended to all their distresses, and particularly those to which his service had given cause or occasion'.[1]

The cost of the affair must also have been an annoyance, though it was not nearly so great as the spy, Torelli, imagined when he composed his secret report, getting the facts all out of focus as he invariably did. It has been commonly believed that Byron paid bribes on all sides—Torelli estimated three thousand crowns—for the prisoners' freedom. Had he done so it would have been pardonable, but such measures could hardly have been taken without the payments showing somewhere, under whatever disguise, in his accounts—which we shall now investigate.

To begin with, we have the fee immediately paid to Vaccà, Professor of Surgery at the ancient and famous university of Pisa, for visiting the injured courier, two crowns. Eight pauls and five crazie were given to the poor on Byron's orders three days later, but there was nothing in the least out of the ordinary about that, and it affords little support to Torelli's statement that 'contrary to his custom, he distributed alms in front of his palace in order to conciliate public opinion'.[2] Lega's entry makes it clear that this sum of less than one crown was not 'distributed' in person by Byron. To perform so trivial a gesture 'in front of his palace' would have been ridiculous.

On March 27th, the first staffetta (express letter) was sent to Dawkins in Florence. It cost five crowns, and two post office employees were tipped a half-crown. Several more staffettas followed, the correspondence with Florence being continued as fast as horses could carry it, and there were some smaller payments for receiving communications in return, reaching a total of about fifty-five crowns in all—a troublesome expense but a perfectly open one. Numerous letters were also sent to London and elsewhere, but which of those was occasioned solely by the skirmish cannot be determined.

One Pietro Gabrielli had a crown on March 28th for acting as coachman while Vincenzo was under interrogation, and the same day the steward handed Byron twenty-five crowns in gold and silver. It was admittedly much more than he habitually carried, but if he risked bribing anyone with it, which I find somewhat incredible at a time when he was seeking intervention by a British diplomat, he achieved no advantage, because the servants continued in harsh custody after their innocence was proved. Part of the money may eventually have found its way to Tita, who was able to give 'a feast' to his fellow inmates of the prison when he was, briefly, let out of solitary confinement; but that was not till weeks later.

[1] *La Vie.*   [2] *LJ.* Vol. VI.

Throughout April we find a sequence of curious entries: 'Given to Milord in crazie.' That is to say, he took to receiving some of his pocket money in the very smallest change, fifty or a hundred crazie at a time, which certainly suggests that he was scattering coins to beggars whenever he went out. This may have been the basis of the tale of alms bestowed to win favour; but he did not begin the practice till Masi was out of danger and public excitement had cooled, and he kept it up a good while after the matter had been disposed of—in a way far from satisfactory to himself. Nor, if conciliation was his purpose, was largesse to the destitute likely to have much effect since they had no power to serve him.

On April 16th, Lega sent the surgeon Foscarini his fee for looking after the wounded sergeant-major, a substantial one of forty crowns. Vaccà was not paid until Byron finally left Pisa in September. What proportion of the fifty crowns then given was for attendance on Masi in hospital is not shown in the accounts. The sum may also have covered his (erroneous) diagnosis of Mrs Leigh Hunt's illness. Apart from agonizing sunburn through swimming, Byron himself seems to have needed no medical care in Pisa, while, for visits to his staff, the fee was in ready cash.

A fine of thirty-six crowns seven pauls and four crazie 'to free Tita from punishment and detention for carrying arms' was settled by Lega on the 17th: but Byron then learned with disgust that he was not freed, only allowed for one day to mix with the other prisoners and returned to his solitary cell. A fresh protest was at once dispatched to the Legation in Florence. Little could be done from that quarter for one who was not a British national, but Byron may have thought that being deprived of the man he called 'my best servant' was a line that could be effectually pursued, and Dawkins was in touch with the Florentine lawyer who was about to go to Pisa on his recommendation.

On April 26th, the Examining Magistrate and his writer waited on Byron, as a courtesy, at his house instead of sending for him, and were regaled with coffee at the trifling outlay of one paul one crazia, and even that was probably begrudged—charmingly, according to Torelli, as he received them—because he had learned a few days before that the police had sentenced Tita to be exiled. It was a sheer act of persecution, for, once acquitted of wounding the soldier and fined for carrying arms, there was nothing to charge him with. The object was to provoke Byron, as he rightly suspected and subsequent events proved.

The lawyer, Collini, counselled that Tita should appeal against the decree in Florence, the headquarters of the Buon Governo, as the all-powerful police department oddly insisted on calling itself. He was granted a fortnight's grace to go there but was refused a safe conduct by the Pisan Governor, Viviani. Byron paid for his journey—six crowns three pauls—

though it took place under a military escort of two and he was lodged in jail on arrival. There he was spitefully required to shave off the beard he was so proud of, and by which he was known as Il Barbone. During the whole of this discreditable episode, the young man—greatly liked both by the Shelleys and Byron—remained in a state of pitiful bewilderment, scarcely believing what was happening to him.

Meanwhile Byron, to make sure of his being befriended, had sent Pietro in advance to Florence, reimbursing him forty-seven crowns six pauls four crazie for his expenses; and Tita was paid one month in arrear— the time he had spent in prison—and one in advance, twenty-six crowns two crazie. He was taken to the frontier whence he travelled to Lerici, where the Shelleys had arranged with Byron to receive him at their summer retreat if his appeal failed.

On May 17th Lega parted with a single crown 'to the Notary Fini in connection with the action at law of Sergeant Masi', and on the 24th he settled a swingeing bill from the Advocate Collini, whose advice was scarcely worth the two hundred crowns he required; but Byron bore it philosophically, writing to Dawkins, who had been apologetic about it: 'You are perhaps a little too hard on the premature demand of our Man of law—if you had had as much to do with law and lawyers as I have (which I hope you never will), you would perhaps be more inclined to marvel at his modesty.'[1]

By this time his angry pride was subsiding except when it was revived from time to time by new inconveniences. He was about to move to the villa at Montenero, and after a change of scene he seldom retained more than a fitful interest in what he had left behind. He lived acutely and emotionally in the present, and he cast nostalgic glances at the past—but only when it had receded to a distant perspective.

Masi recovered and lived to give a much falsified version of his exploit, becoming not a little vainglorious of the notoriety it had brought him. Amongst the details he related to a French writer, Poujoulat, sixteen years later,[2] were that he had refused to see an English surgeon sent to him by Byron and had scornfully returned a hundred gold louis from the same source. That would have been an enormous sum to a Tuscan soldier, four hundred crowns, and I cannot conceive that Byron, seething with indignation against the man and determined to prosecute him, would have offered what must inevitably have been interpreted as an atonement. As for the English surgeon, a Dr John Todd had in fact been sent to examine him and duly did so.

[1] Letter of 17 May, quoted by Cline. Byron was thinking of the Hansons' monstrous bill.
[2] Quoted in *LJ*. Vol. VI.

Giuseppe Strauss remained very ill, suffering repeated haemorrhages. Lega writes of his being attended for three weeks while at Montenero by an English doctor who was unsparing in his attentions, going constantly from Leghorn to see him, and charging only thirty crowns when he was cured.[1] This must have been the same one who visited Masi. He was readily paid by Byron, and, we may assume, from his own purse or by his banker, as there is no ledger entry. A temporary courier was needed at one stage, getting six pauls three crowns for his work as deputy.

At the end of June it was decreed that Giuseppe should follow Tita into banishment. At least in the meantime he had been free, but Teresa's servant, Antonio, though guiltless, received the same sentence after three months of imprisonment without trial.

Torelli thought that only bribes could have brought about their discharge, but had Byron spent thousands of crowns on getting the men released, he might assuredly have done a little better than stand helplessly by while they were deported, all innocent as he knew them to be. He had learned at the beginning that Masi's assailant was the coachman, Vincenzo, who had rushed at the soldier with a pitchfork under the impression that he had made an attack on Byron and was running away.[2] Byron had not seen or sanctioned the onslaught but he could not betray his would-be defender, and both he and the others who were in the secret connived at some deceptions, including, if Teresa's account in old age is reliable, sufficient disguise to render identification difficult. The grooms had naturally supported their colleague's story.

The consciousness, for weeks on end, that the wrong men were being held on suspicion must have dismayed everyone concerned, but there is not a single sum recorded by Lega which could have been used to bribe even the most temptation-prone officer of justice. The ledger mounts up washing bills, repairs of clothes and boots, shoeing and feeding of horses, getting parcels of books through the Customs, buying candles, writing paper, paper for the privy, a collar for the monkey, coals, firewood, supplies of oysters, scores of household things, but none of sufficient price to cover an illicit disbursement of more than a few crowns.

After the Advocate Collini, the largest payment was a draft on Florence for a hundred crowns given to Signor Gaetano Balatresi;[3] but this was the supplier of imported goods who sent Byron claret and German lottery tickets, and he had been the recipient of nearly as much the month before the imbroglio. A bribe would hardly have changed hands in the

---

[1] 46873 Folio 157.

[2] Letter of Mary Shelley, 6 Apr. quoted by Marchand. She does not name Vincenzo, but Teresa does so in *La Vie*.

[3] On 18 April.

form of a bank draft through the secretary. Byron could of course have got money from a Leghorn banker, Webb or Henry Dunn, without Lega's intervention, but the simple fact seems to be that the Justices were disposed to behave with the utmost correctness, if only because the police had it in their power to deport all who were not Tuscans whenever they pleased, and that suited their purpose better than prison sentences since it was one step nearer to getting rid of the Gambas and the man who was certain to accompany or follow them, as he had done when they were obliged to leave Ravenna. So correct were they indeed that they refunded in full the fine paid on behalf of Tita.

It is a pity to lose the attractive image of the poet buying liberty, however dearly, for his devoted servants, but had he done so—and to the tune of three thousand crowns or anything approaching it—some clue better than the conjecture of a spy for the Austrian police, a spy who never got anything right, would have been revealed, we might suppose, by now.

Counting all the matters I have mentioned, fees to doctors and lawyers, express postage, payments to employees who could not perform their normal services, passports and journeys for those who were banished, I estimate the Pisa affray cost Byron some five hundred crowns, a large sum but the expenditure in nervous energy and anger was beyond calculation, and we shall see that the repercussions were deplorable.

The Pisa sojourn which Byron had begun in a spirit of foreboding— for he had settled down happily in Ravenna and was most reluctant to leave—had not been without its signal pleasures. He had enjoyed the palazzo and the legends attached to it; he had enjoyed the companionable rides and the shooting parties and his own dexterity, and being able to entertain and to gossip about England, and having money at his disposal with expectation of more. He must have taken some delight in ordering a fine schooner and looking forward to adventurous voyages, reviving the happiness he had always felt at sea. Even the furious rage about Southey had proved stimulating to his comic muse; and Teresa had lifted her ban on *Don Juan* so that he had been reunited with a hero beside whom his Conrads and Laras now seemed a mere imposition on public taste.

But after the wretched affray all sorts of things went wrong, and one of them so grievously and cruelly that no one was ever able to talk to him about it, and it remains the only episode of his life about which he, the least reticent, the most rashly communicative of beings, never sought to make himself comprehensible.

10

The Beginning and the End of Allegrina

1. THE BEGINNING

The tale of Byron's brief liaison with the romance-hungry girl who changed her name from Jane to Clara, from Clara to Clare, and from Clare to Claire Clairmont, has been told very often—much oftener than if her connection with the Shelleys had not given her a reflected importance. But for that, it is doubtful whether her life would have ever become entangled with Byron's at all, because it may be presumed without extravagance that it was her stepsister's success in captivating a young poet who was not only a charming person but perceptibly a member of the upper classes, that set off her determination to win a poet of her own, and one of lordly rank.

That her reckless, persistent advances were made at a time when he was in the depths of bitterness at the collapse of his marriage and the accompanying public opprobrium, and thus could be persuaded to take without consideration what was so pressingly offered, was an immense misfortune for her, and the more so because her disposition, as may be judged from the overwhelming evidence of diaries, letters, and conduct, was singularly deficient in resilience and in genuine independence of spirit.

She was brought up in a set of beliefs about which none of the family she lived with seems to have been sincere. William Godwin, apostle of free love and social equality, was outraged when Shelley eloped with his daughter, Mary, but soothed by his making an honest woman of her, and delighted with her prospect of becoming a baronet's lady.[1] Mary, having

---

[1] Godwin's typical letter of condolence to her on Shelley's death says: 'I looked on you as one of the daughters of prosperity, elevated in rank & fortune; & I thought it criminal to intrude on you for ever the sorrows of an unfortunate old man & a beggar. You are now fallen to my own level . . .' Though he thought it criminal, he had intruded his (financial) sorrows on the young couple until even Shelley's generosity could endure no more, and we cannot doubt why he was 'impatient to hear' what his daughter might have inherited. Letter of 6 Aug. 1822 quoted by Jones.

tried free love in practice, ultimately became so circumspect that she shunned contact with old friends whose reputation might cast a shadow on hers. Claire lived in as much terror of the discovery of her past as if she had never heard of her stepfather's first wife, Mary Wollstonecraft, the pioneer of Women's Rights, and never absorbed the gospel of the 'Otaheite philosophers'. She erased Allegra's very name from her journals,[1] and yet to have had a child by Byron would have been a distinction rather than a dereliction in that epoch if she had carried it off with the right kind of bravura.

Partly, of course, her fear was due to her having at times to earn her living as a governess, and partly to an acute sense of injury which could be nurtured and kept alive by cultivating apprehensions even where the likelihood of exposure was remote, but largely it was a simple class distinction. Bringing illegitimate children into the world caused only mild scandal in the section of society where there was no trouble about providing for them. They were received without demur in quite straitlaced circles. The Byron wedding ceremony had been performed by the Rev. Thomas Noel, an illegitimate son of Lord Wentworth, the bride's uncle. Henry Luttrell went everywhere and met everyone because his father, Lord Carhampton, had produced the means for him to do so. Children of married mothers but known or believed to be the fruits of adultery were never rejected if rank was grand enough. It was not expected that those born altogether out of wedlock should be accorded high office or marry into the best families—that would have been resented—but sons could go into the Church, the Army, or the East India Company, and for daughters with dowries presentable middle class husbands were not hard to find.

It was far otherwise where no such advantage was obtainable. Claire, herself of illegitimate birth,[2] had spent her impressionable years in lively and intellectual company, but undoubtedly aware of her stepfather's chronic shortage of money, so public and perpetual that all sorts of literary men had responded to appeals to keep him out of a debtors' prison; while her mother ran a small business publishing books for children, and dealt with customers in the shop, which was regarded as demeaning. Claire had not, either financially or socially, that inner sense of security which is an essential requirement for those who rebel against conventional codes, and which enabled Shelley to be almost uncompromising—but seldom unmannerly—in his defiance of them.

Claire was decidedly unmannerly. The tactlessness of her letters to Byron when she thought she loved him makes us flinch with vicarious

---

[1] Now published in full, edited by Marion Kingston Stocking.
[2] Stocking, Introduction.

embarrassment; the vulgarity of her remarks about him when she knew she hated him manifests a trait he must have recognized and disliked at an early stage in their relations. However talented the members of the Godwin household may have been, the young girl who ran away with Shelley and Mary, and became a tormenting burden to one and sometimes both of them, does not appear in her adolescent writings as a person of good breeding. There are passages of her diary which are crudely common. Of a fellow traveller on their first rough and dangerous voyage she wrote: 'Molehill was very sick indeed—& made me almost be washed away with laughing at him—Every one of the Passengers was sick except myself.'[1] Even at sixteen, laughing at a man being violently sea-sick suggests a coarseness of grain that is unattractive. At twenty-two, signs of unfeminine callousness are actively displeasing.

> Monday Sept. 25th [at Leghorn, 1820] . . . I see a beggar sitting at his post yawning with *ennui*—another crawling on all fours politely saluting a young washerwoman a bundle on her head & bare footed. . . . Further I met . . . numerous old women ugly hag-ridden beldams rich in nothing but deformities . . . violins squeaking & women singing—Life every where but like to the life which is engendered by putrefaction creeping crawling worms. . . .[2]

That style of comment must always have alienated Byron who, rude as he might be about fellow poets or his mother-in-law, felt an individual compassion for beggars and had poor old crones as pensioners. Her allusions to his lameness after he had rejected her are of a crass kind of spitefulness. She apostrophizes him several times as Don Juan:

> The deformity of your mind surpasses all that can be imagined of monstrous, but in your birth Nature had set her warning mark on you, unheeding that, by my own blindness, have I fallen.[3]

And he is imagined seeing himself:

> Stamped with a mark of Nature in my birth from which disgrace I can never escape. . . . As black vapours hover over their parent marsh and are imbued with hereditary pestilence, so does my being waiting ever upon me, inherit deformity informing myself and man, and the pure air of the hideous soul it interprets.[4]

The obsessional loathing is often gross, as in the verbal 'caricatures' she sketches as if offering themes to Gillray:

> Another [caricature] to be called Lord Byron's receipt for writing pathetic poetry. He sitting drinking spirits, playing with his white mustachios. His

---

[1] Ashley 394. 11 Sept. 1814.   [2] Ibid. 2819 (3).
[3] Ibid. 12 Dec. 1820.   [4] Ibid. 17 Dec. 1820.

mistress, the Fornara opposite him Drinking coffee. Fumes coming from her mouth over which is written garlich [sic]; these curling direct themselves towards his English footman who is just entering the room & he is knocked backwards.

Lord B. is writing he says, Imprimis to be a great pathetic poet. Ist Prepare a small colony, then dispatch the mother by worrying & cruelty to her grave afterwards to neglect & ill treat the children—to have as many & as dirty mistresses as can be found; from their embraces to catch horrible diseases, thus a tolerable quantity of discontent & remorse being prepared to give it vent on paper, & to remember particularly to rail against learned women. This is my infallible receipt by which I have made so much money.[1]

I give these quite minor examples of Claire's tastelessness—many pages could be filled with them—to account for her rapidly becoming unbearable to Byron. The painful story has so often been set down without any attempt to consider it from another point of view than that of Claire, of whom it must be said, without the least want of sympathy for her self-deluding youth and the agony of her dashed aspirations, that even if she had not had the imprudence to force herself on Byron's attention and the ill luck to secure some ungracious measure of it, she never could have been happy.

Her character was formed so that Shelley could write, when she was sixteen, of his despair at 'Jane's insensibility & incapacity for the slightest degree of friendship'.[2] She had suffered through morbid self-pity from childhood, and represented herself as ill-done by in whatever circumstances she found herself. Though her reasons for being grateful to the Shelleys were numberless and she looked upon herself as entitled to share whatever they possessed, she had succeeded, before ever meeting Byron, in giving her stepfather the impression that while with Mary and Shelley she was entirely sunk in 'melancholy and despondency; leading a life of solitude and retirement and indolence, completely disregarded and neglected by her friends, meeting them only at meal times'.[3]

The fact was exactly contrary. Shelley, for all his original exasperation, found much that was congenial in having so ardent a disciple, her views and tastes on abstract topics being wholly formed by him, and on many a night when Mary, pregnant and often in poor health, was obliged to go early to bed, Shelley would be downstairs talking into the small hours with Claire, and on many a day when Mary was kept at home, Claire was

[1] Ibid. 8 Nov. 1820. 'The Fornara' is better known as La Fornarina. Her ascendancy must have come as a shock to Claire, who prided herself on her intellect and could not imagine the attractions of an amusing illiterate.

[2] 14 Oct. 1814.

[3] Maria Gisborne's Journal. 9 July 1820. Godwin was reporting to Mrs Gisborne what Claire had told him years before.

his companion on long walks and excursions, until Mary yearned for her absence.

Byron wrote to Augusta Leigh that he was never attracted nor pretended attachment to her, and Claire's letters to him show that he was speaking the truth. They abound in reminders of his breaking appointments, keeping her waiting in his hall, and saying 'Now pray go', 'Now will you go?' He is 'out of town' when she calls, and he bids her 'write short'. She often implores him to see her if only for an instant. 'You rather dislike me', she admits, and 'You do not feel even interest for me', she writes after the physical union was consummated.[1] Never was there a collection of love letters so totally without evidence of mutuality. Only in one of those manic phases of illusion which afflict very young people in love could she have kept up her plainly unwelcome advances.

A mistaken conjecture that a famous poem dated March 28th was written in 1816, because that was the year of its publication, has given rise to a belief that it must have been addressed to Claire, who is thus provided with some justification for imagining her feelings to be reciprocated.

> There be none of beauty's daughters
> With a magic like thee;
> And like music on the waters
> Is thy sweet voice to me.

Claire sang, but there is no iota of evidence that Byron ever heard her do so on or before March 28th. He was deep in the legal business of his separation and the turmoil of making ready to leave England. His poetry reflects the intensity of his preoccupation with his wife, his sister, and the woman whose influence on his wife he knew to be baneful, Mrs Clermont (with whom Claire in later life mendaciously claimed kinship). He finished the first draft of his furious verses, 'Born in the garret, to the kitchen bred', a hundred and four lines of burning indignation, on March 29th, and nothing could be more unlikely than that, the preceding day, he was writing a serene lyric to one whom, on her own showing, he found most wearful, with such a sentiment as:

> . . . The spirit bows before thee,
> To listen and adore thee.

That is his earlier style, and it would seem to have been addressed to John Edleston.[2] His allusions to the young chorister's beautiful singing are frequent.

---

[1] All Murray MSS. The earlier letters are undated. The last quoted is 6 May 1816.
[2] Leslie Marchand was the first to call attention to this probability.

No one who had dispassionately read Claire's letters to a man who from first to last was obviously trying to evade her could harbour any notion of his pouring out his enchantment at the joy of hearing her voice while,

> The waves lie still and gleaming,
> And the lulled winds seem dreaming

Only extracts from her correspondence have generally been published, because *in extenso* it is sadly boring. Nevertheless, one or two examples should be given without abridgement, merely to illustrate the want of any quality which, at that stage of her life, could engage Byron's recalcitrant affection; and it was to that stage of her life that his knowledge of her was confined. He became acquainted with her in the third or fourth week in March and parted from her finally in August 1816. She was then eighteen.

Even he, accustomed as he was to receiving absurd letters from young women, had never had one so little likely to attract him as her first:

An utter stranger takes the liberty of addressing you. It is earnestly requested that for one moment you pardon the intrusion, & laying aside every remembrance of who and what you are, listen with a friendly ear. A moment of passion, or an impulse of pride often destroys our own happiness & that of others. If in this case your refusal shall not affect yourself, yet you are not aware how much it may injure another. It is not charity I demand, for of that I stand in no need. I imply by that you should think kindly and gently of this letter, that if I seem impertinent you should pardon it for a while, and that you should wait patiently till I am emboldened by you to disclose myself.

I tremble with fear at the fate of this letter. I cannot blame [you] if it shall be received by you as an impudent misfortune. There are cases where virtue may stoop to assume the guise of folly; it is for the piercing eye of genius to discover her disguise, do you then give me credit for something better than this letter may seem to portend. Mine is a delicate case, my feet are on the edge of a precipice. Hope flying on forward wings beckons me to follow her & rather than resign this cherished creature, I jump though at the peril of my Life.

It may seem a strange assertion, but it is not the less true that I place my happiness in your hands. I wish to give you a suspicion without at first disclosing myself, because it would be a cruel addition to all I otherwise endure to become an object of your contempt & the ridicule of others.

If you feel your indignation rising, if you feel tempted to read no more or to cast with levity into the fire, what has been written by me with so much fearful inquietude, check your hand. My folly may be great but the Creator ought not to destroy his creature. If you shall condescend to answer the following question you will at least be rewarded by the gratitude I shall feel.

If a woman whose reputation has yet remained unstained, if without either guardian or husband to control she should throw herself upon your mercy, if with a beating heart she should confess the love she has borne you many years, if she should secure to you secresy & safety, if she should return your kindness with fond affection & unbounded devotion could you betray her or would you be silent as the grave?

I am not given to many words. Either you will or you will not. Do not decide hastily, & yet I must entreat your answer without delay, not only because I hate to be tortured by suspense, but because my departure a short way out of town is unavoidable & I would know your reply ere I go. Address me, as E. Trefusis, 21 Noley Place Mary le Bonne.[1]

Byron ignored this silly overture, but shortly afterwards a quite brisk note arrived, the handwriting unrecognizable, signed 'G.C.B.' It said that a lady desired to communicate with him 'on business of peculiar importance' and asked to be admitted 'alone and with the utmost privacy' at seven that evening. If that was not possible, he was to name his own appointment. The rhetorical style of 'E. Trefusis' appeared nowhere in these few lines, delivered by hand while she waited for an answer on a Sunday morning, either March 18th or 25th.[2] To him it must have seemed that the writer had something of consequence to tell him relating to his widely publicized separation from his wife and the rumours that were working to his detriment.

He wrote curtly to say he was not aware of any importance which could be attached to an interview with him, but would be at home at the hour mentioned: and he took a copy of this reply—a rare precaution and one which shows he did not envisage just another case of infatuation.

He must have felt some irritation, to say the least, when the stranger turned out to have nothing more important on her mind than herself, her ambitions, her life story, which she recounted in detail, and her idea of achieving independence by going on the stage—but without, as she told him in her next letter, 'the intolerable & disgusting drudgery of provincial theatres before commencing on the boards of a metropolis'. It was a characteristic naïveté, and one which would not have been pleasing to a man who was a member of the Committee of Management of the Drury Lane theatre.

---

[1] Murray MS. In *LJ* 'remembrance' is misread as 'circumstance' and there are one or two other variations. Her writing at this period takes much deciphering. According to the practice of the time, Prothero revised punctuation and disregarded ampersands etc.

[2] Augusta Leigh did not leave his house until Friday Mar. 16th, and nothing that happened was likely to have gone on while she was there. Since Claire's attempts to see him followed one another thick and fast, there was time for their relations to have developed in a month or less to what they were when he left England on April 25th.

Having failed to establish the rapport she had hoped for at their meeting and called on him twice in vain, she now acknowledged that 'the kindest favour I can confer on you is to make my letter short & my demands slight, since you are overwhelmed with affairs & cares'. But that was a favour she did not confer. Instead she lectured him, as all unseductive women did:

> My style is harsh and my sentiments ungracious. . . . Remember how many live & die, blamed & despised, whose meed should have been praise. How many whose aspects are forbidding, who are incapable of any earthly affection, hide within themselves the warmest feelings. It is not the sparkling cup which should tempt you but the silent & capacious bowl.[1]

The taciturnity implied here, and vaunted in her first letter ('I am not given to many words'), must have seemed a comic self-deception in the wordiest correspondent he had ever had. He tried to pass her on to Douglas Kinnaird, who was also on the Drury Lane Committee. She wrote at greater length than ever saying she was considering his proffered introduction, and the theatre presented 'an easy method' of becoming independent; but she would not apply to Mr Kinnaird without his (Byron's) approval of her changing her name for she could not appear under her own. She made as much as she could of this—to him—quite uninteresting problem.

To set as many snares for his notice as possible she had either sent or brought him on her visit Shelley's new work, *Alastor*, and she expressed pleasure at his approbation.

> Do you know from the fear I entertain of your believing me mad, I endeavour to write as short & laconic sentences as I can, which must needs give my letter a strange appearance. I am so afraid you think me intruding & troublesome.

He did indeed think so, and could not have changed his opinion when she went on to inform him she was now 'wavering between the adoption of a literary life or a theatrical career'. Shelley used frequently to express appreciation of her literary talents, but then 'his affection might blind him'. She wanted Byron to advise her about a half-written novel of hers, yet imagined that, as he rather disliked her, he might be prejudiced.

After much more tediousness of this kind and a discussion of her own foibles, she asked pardon for all her 'tiresome explanations', and demanded a speedy answer, ending affectedly with: 'Pray speak ill of me. I had almost said I should be pleased with it.'[2]

That letter was delivered on a Thursday, and I hazard that it was the

[1] Murray MS. Undated.   [2] Ibid.

same week as the Sunday on which she had met him, because every communication strikes the note of frantic impatience and pressure. Her two abortive calls on him, when his servants had told her—untruthfully—that he was out of town, may have been made on Monday and Tuesday. Her request for advice about going on the stage followed immediately. Byron, if he answered a letter at all, generally did it punctually, and he would have lost no time in referring her to Kinnaird. There were then posts every hour, and she might easily have received on Wednesday evening or Thursday morning the lines, doubtless not very numerous, to which she sent her pitifully long-winded reply. The very next day she was writing to him again: 'I sent you yesterday a long letter but your answer is not yet arrived . . . I entreat you to return me an answer by my messenger.'[1]

This too he ignored, but, bent with all the concentration of a head-strong child on forcing some reaction from him, she addressed him once more: 'There is little in your lordship's stern silence to embolden me to lay before you my production. But however I may be wrong.'

She sent it all the same and in a rough, uncorrected state, admonishing him: 'A jeweller you know prefers the unpolished stone'. She then gave him an extensive outline of her theme, which was autobiographical and about 'a character committing every violence against received opinion', knowing 'no other guide than herself or the impulses arising from herself', who nevertheless was highly amiable, 'full of noble affections & sympathies', with a sweetness of nature which would ensure the reader's tolerance of errors which otherwise would 'infallibly disgust & terrify'. It was clearly conceived as propaganda for Shelley's system of ethics. She requested him to glance over the manuscript as soon as possible, and to make his comments long and explicit.

Byron read the MS or part of it and held out no encouragement whatever: but in some way, because she had become almost inescapable, she managed to see him again and perhaps to arouse some physical response in him, and presently she was sending him another clamorous letter:

> You bid me write short to you & I have much to say. You also bade me believe that it was a fancy which made me cherish an attachment for you. It cannot be a fancy since you have been for the last year the object upon which every solitary moment led me to muse.
>
> I do not expect you to love me; I am not worthy of your love. I feel you are superior—yet much to my surprize, more to my happiness, you betrayed passions I had believed no longer alive in your bosom. Shall I also have to ruefully experience the want of happiness shall I reject it when it is offered[?]

[1] Ibid.

I may appear to you imprudent, vicious; my opinions detestable my theory depraved, but one thing at least time shall show you that I love you gently & with affection, that I am incapable of any thing approaching to the feeling of revenge or malice; I do assure you, your future will shall be mine & every thing you shall do or say, I shall not question.

Have you then any objection to the following plan? On Thursday Evening we may go out of town together by some stage or mail about the distance of 10 or 12 miles. There we shall be free & unknown; we can return early the following morning. I have arranged every thing here so that the slightest suspicion may not be excited. Pray do so with your people.

Will you admit me for two moments to settle with you *where*? Indeed I will not stay an instant after you tell me to go. Only so much may be said & done in a short time by an interview which writing cannot effect. Do what you will, or go where you will, refuse to see me & behave unkindly, I shall never forget you. I shall ever remember the gentleness of your manners & the wild originality of your countenance. Having been once seen you are not to be forgotten. Perhaps this is the last time I shall ever address you. Once more then let me assure you that I am not ungrateful. In all things have you acted most honourably, & I am only provoked that the awkwardness of my manner & something like timidity has hitherto prevented my expressing it to you personally.

Clara Clairmont[1]

In a postscript revealing what Byron—or almost any other man of his time—would have considered an entire want of self-respect, she added, 'Will you admit me now as I wait in Hamilton Place for your answer?' Hamilton Place was a sector of Park Lane at the back of his house. If there was anything Byron disliked it was being importuned by a woman, and especially the sort of woman who could be found waiting to hear from him in the street, where ladies were hardly to be seen without an escort. He had the hunter's love of exercising skill in the chase. He was stimulated by obstacles, uncertainties, and, provided they were not carried too far, coquetries.

He could be roused easily enough to the transient male sensuality which women, with their more emotional commitment, have always found it hard to understand: yet even here he behaved with some scruple, for, later on, in expressing her grief at his failure to write to her, she added: 'I know what you will say. "There now I told you it would be so. I advised you not. I did every thing I could to hinder you & now you complain of me."'[2] What can this mean except that he had given way, literally protesting, to her solicitations?

Claire did not belong to any of the types that appealed to him. She was neither gay nor beautiful nor endowed with social graces. The one

[1] Ibid.   [2] Ibid. 6 Oct. 1816.

mildly interesting thing about her was that she was the stepdaughter of William Godwin. It was but two or three months since he had asked John Murray to assist Godwin by handing over to him six hundred pounds out of a thousand and fifty offered for two poems of his own, and to divide the rest between Coleridge and Maturin.[1] He had only seen Godwin once, and he himself was in very great financial difficulties, but Murray's unwillingness to make that payment brought them near to a quarrel. (Perhaps it was because the intended benefaction was not forthcoming that Godwin formed the opinion that Byron was 'a very ugly man',[2] a verdict not endorsed by any contemporary.)

It is possible that Byron was barely aware of Shelley's existence before Claire spoke of him, although Shelley had sent him years before a copy of *Queen Mab* with a letter detailing at full length all the accusations he had heard brought against his (Byron's) character, and handsomely offering, if the charges were not true, to make his acquaintance.[3] Regrettably, that communication has not survived. Byron received so many letters and volumes from literary aspirants that he may not have read Shelley's youthful work before Claire drew his attention to it. What she told him of Shelley and Mary and their doctrine of free love must have startled and somewhat shocked him. His views of sexual morals were those of a libertine who broke the code, not a propagandist for reforming it.

As she was out to make herself arresting by every daring device, she probably gave him some notion of how willing Shelley had been to share Mary with his great friend, Jefferson Hogg, and how there had been a *ménage à trois*, if not *à quatre*, the previous year with Shelley inviting Hogg to enjoy 'our common treasure' and 'this participated pleasure', and Mary making, with what now seems to us desperate playfulness, an attempt to enter into the spirit of those progressive and idealistic ways of thinking.[4]

Claire would have known all about it because she was with them at the time, and Shelley was not being secretive but an eager proselytizer for breaking down all the artificial restrictions of society—or rather, all except those particular ones which were now and then defied by Byron. He was so well known for it that Benjamin Haydon, who had met him several times, remembered with lingering animosity how he had heard Shelley 'hold forth to Mrs [Leigh] Hunt & other women present . . . on the wickedness and absurdity of *Chastity*'. Hunt himself had on that occasion enraged Haydon by saying 'he would not mind any young man, if he were agreeable, *sleeping with his wife!*' But while Haydon did not

---

[1] *LJ*. Letters of Jan. 1816.   [2] Maria Gisborne's Journal. 9 July 1820.
[3] Moore, Chapter XXVII.   [4] Scott, *New Shelley Letters*.

then or later attempt to conceal his disgust at an 'attempt to shake the established principles of sexual intercourse', he conceded more than Shelley's admirers were to do for the next hundred years and longer: 'Shelley courageously adopted & acted on his own principles—Hunt defended them, without having energy to practise them & was content with a smuggering fondle.'[1]

Byron had never had the smallest reason to suppose himself the seducer of a virgin, for Claire had assuredly told him that she and Shelley had put their theories into practice, though she disclaimed still doing so. More-over, she made a brave if unconvincing promise to share Byron's favours with Mary, whom she had brought one night to meet him at his house:

> ... You will I suppose wish to see Mary who talks & looks at you with admiration: you will I dare say fall in love with her; she is very handsome & very amiable & you will no doubt be blest in your attachment: nothing can afford me such pleasure as to see you happy in any of your attachments. If it should be so I will redouble my attentions to please her. I will do every thing she tells me whether it be good or bad for I would not stand low in the affections of the person so beyond blest as to be loved by you.[2]

This is palpably insincere, but the fact that such an enticement could be offered, if only in self-tormenting jealousy, attests what idea of Shelley's circle she must have given to Byron.

His own man-of-the-world attitude, raffish about women but friendly and considerate towards Shelley when he had come to know him, is well shown by his remarks to Douglas Kinnaird when Claire had become pregnant—and it gives us the measure of the change in our outlook that this passage was suppressed without indication when the letter was published in *Lord Byron's Correspondence* (1922):

> You tell me Shelley's wife has drowned herself, the devil she has—do you mean his *wife* or his Mistress? Mary Godwin?—I hope not the last. I am very sorry to hear of any thing which can plague poor Shelley—besides I feel uneasy about another of his *menage*. You know—& I believe saw once that odd-headed girl—who introduced herself to me shortly before I left England, but you do not know that I found her with Shelley & her sister at Geneva;— I never loved nor pretended to love her—but a man is a man—& if a girl of eighteen comes prancing to you at all hours—there is but one way—the suite of all this is that she was with *child*—& returned to England to assist in peopling that desolate island.—Whether this impregnation took place before I left England or since I do not know—the (carnal) connection had

---

[1] Marginal notes by Haydon in his copy of Medwin's *Conversations of Lord Byron*, Roe–Byron Collection at Newstead Abbey.
[2] Murray MS. 6 May 1816.

commenced previously to my setting out—but by or about this time she is about to produce—

> The next question is[,] is the brat *mine?* I have reasons to think so—for I know as much as one can know such a thing—that she had *not lived* with S[helley] during the time of our acquaintance—& that she had a good deal of that same with me—[1]

In the light of facts and letters concealed, falsified, or undiscovered until well into the present century, this is surely most clear evidence that he was aware there had been relations between the 'odd-headed girl' and Shelley before his own meeting with her.

Despite the ungallant style, which often strikes a jarring note in Byron's letters about women, and our knowledge of his trying to escape her presence in Switzerland, there is little hint here of the depth of repugnance which, in a few months, was to bring about his refusal to take Claire's child unless he were released from any obligation to see the mother. That he reached so implacable a decision, from which he could never be moved, was due, I suspect, to the almost unbelievable fulsomeness with which she continued to send him perfervid love letters when he had done everything in human power to deter her. Some of them, forwarded from Switzerland, did not arrive till months later, and at the most inopportune time, when he was enjoying his first carefree affair for years with Marianna Segati, the sort of woman who delighted him—good-looking, amoral, physically yielding but not clinging.

He was contrasting Marianna with Claire when he wrote to Kinnaird from Venice of his satisfaction at having 'a handsome woman who is not a bore—and who does not annoy me by looking like a fool & setting up for a sage'.[2] 'Looking like a fool' may have signified his dislike of Claire's dress which was eccentric and at times slovenly. 'Setting up for a sage' is appropriate to many sententious comments in her journals which are hardly likely to have been absent from her conversation.

Byron at twenty-eight had only the most limited experience of girls in their teens and all the uneasy showing off, the little fatuities, which are touching to detached onlookers but exasperating where there is some unwanted involvement. The girls he had known at Southwell in his Harrow days were silly enough—always excepting the pleasantly rational Elizabeth Pigot—but then he had been only a schoolboy going through the equivalent stages himself, and they had no tiresome intellectual pretensions such as provoked him, in Claire's case, 'to rail against learned women'. Mary Chaworth, the idol of his adolescence, was two or three

---

[1] 42093. Byron Papers 20 Jan. 1817. The child had actually been born on 12 Jan. but Byron did not receive the letter announcing it till May.

[2] Ibid. 27 Nov. 1816.

years his senior and, if only in comparison with himself, poised and self-sufficient.

Claire's gaucheries found no understanding in him but rather, we may suppose, heightened his disgust at his own weakness in letting himself be drawn into such a relationship. It was complicated too by his having struck up a friendship with Shelley, who, apart from her varied claims on him as a proselyte, felt a special responsibility for Claire because he had so audaciously encouraged her to leave her home at sixteen. Byron had warned her to expect nothing of him: he had made his reluctance to her following him to Switzerland so manifest that she had been reduced to pleading with him not to go without at least giving her his address. He had urged her not on any account to come alone; and she had readily promised, fairly safe in the knowledge that Shelley and Mary, unsettled as they were and eager admirers of Byron, could be prevailed upon to accompany her. And it worked out that, though at first he had given them a cool reception, Shelley's company had almost reconciled him to an otherwise vexatious situation.

She had written to him from Paris on her way to meet him, as she hoped, at Geneva, assuring him she had no passions. 'I had ten times rather be your male companion than your mistress.' This is not a captivating approach from a woman to a man she is pursuing, and to whom she is incessantly offering herself in febrile terms. It could not have deceived Byron, but it has deceived some biographers, who have apparently forgotten how few of us there are, male or female, who never threw dust in our own eyes when calm comradeship seemed more likely to gain us possession of an elusive object than frankly acknowledged desire. Byron was not likely to credit the denial of passion when, although he took no notice of her being in Geneva, she wrote reproaching him both with cruelty and 'marked indifference', and then proposed that he should go up that evening to the top landing of her hotel where she would be waiting to take him, unseen, to her room.

He may or may not have gone to that assignation. It was not his style any more than letting a girl abduct him in a stage coach (that was an invitation he had not accepted), but if not then, soon afterwards he succumbed again to pressing demands, and for a few weeks their relations, made tolerable by the presence each day of Shelley and Mary, were resumed on the same footing as in England—that is to say, without pretence of attachment on his side. Of all young women, Claire was the least fitted to comprehend what he tried to make so plain. In the rarefied ambience of the Shelley circle, a sexual union was exalted into some glorious fusion of beings. Shelley was not the unvirile platonist of the legend once assiduously fostered, but neither had he anything in common with Byron's robust worldliness. No warning from him would help her to realize that a man might yield to a physical siege without a vestige of sentiment.

Claire's intensity took her further every day towards the total defeat of her ends, and the news that she was pregnant must have been received with dismay. Such consequences had to be borne, however, by both parties if luck was not on their side, and Byron's immediate anxiety was for her to be out of the way by the time his friends, Hobhouse and Scrope Davies, came to stay with him. He spoke 'decisively' to Shelley about the unwelcomeness of her visits to Diodati, his villa, and at last, on July 16th, she wrote: 'We go I believe in two days—are you satisfied[?]'[1] Her absence lasted only about four weeks while touring in Switzerland with the Shelley party, but when they returned, Byron, though undertaking to look after the child, remained adamant in keeping her at arm's length. On August 29th she set out for England under the care of Shelley and Mary—whose sacrifices for her she invariably took for granted.

Nothing would stop her writing at immense length to Byron, who, up to that time, could not have behaved so heartlessly as some accounts imply, because she admits his 'gentleness' and patience with her and her own tendency to be 'wretched': but as letter followed letter, each more maladroit than the other, he hardened towards her and ended by becoming unmoved and immovable.

Profuse with the warmest terms of endearment, she gave again and again extravagant pledges of devotion, sometimes taxing him with not appreciating the boundless wealth and eternal durability of her affection; sometimes persuaded that his coldness was due to his doubts of her sincerity, imagining him saying to himself: 'She is a little trifling soul who does not love any one thing two moments together.'[2] She enquired with such inveterate and imploring reiteration about his health that we may guess he had often used it as an excuse for avoiding her company. She dropped into arch prattle, calling the expected child 'itte babe' and herself 'little me'. All her editors have spared her by omitting these particular ineptitudes, but I am trying to account for Byron's conduct, which cannot be faithfully done by suppressing those traits he was most likely to find uncongenial.

Declaring she would die with pleasure to procure him one single moment's happiness,[3] she could not refrain from little touches she must

---

[1] Several authors have published this letter, or extracts from it, with the date changed to 26 Aug., supposing it to have been sent on the verge of going back to England; but 16 July is quite unmistakable in the MS and, as Marchand indicates, the occasion was the Swiss tour, beginning at Chamounix.

[2] All Murray MSS. 6 Oct. 1816.   [3] 17 Nov. 1816.

have known would irritate—criticisms of the 'mean spirited paltry soul' of John Murray[1] (who had praised Shelley's poetry without publishing it); of Douglas Kinnaird, whom Shelley had seen and disapproved of as 'a man of the world', which she repeated to Byron with the gratuitous information that, besides that, she thought him ugly.[2] She spoke scornfully of Hobhouse, whose cynicism she deemed a cover for 'his conscious unworthiness'.[3]

She regretted that in the French Revolution they had not succeeded in passing a law for 'the extinction of all women after the age of forty . . . there would be an end of these old Beldams'.[4] The allusion was specifically to Mrs Hervey, who had fainted—or nearly—when Byron was announced at Mme de Stael's, but as that lady was considerably above forty, we may wonder if the gibe was due to retrospective jealousy of Lady Oxford, Byron's maturest former love, whose beauty he continued to laud. (Mrs Hervey had better reason for fainting than has been recognized. Her half-brother, William Beckford, had left England under a cloud of scandal as dark as Byron's, and the parallel may have struck her with shock and guilt, for she had been busy reviving him.)

As it was almost impossible to know Byron without being aware that he was an enthusiast for any work by 'the author of *Waverley*', Claire, with self-control, might have withheld the trifling news that she had been reading *The Antiquary* and finding it 'stupid'.[5] Some perversity of temperament which she never outgrew drove her to try and make an effect by childish provocations; and to provoke must have been the sole motive of writing: 'Kinnaird says you told him I was an Atheist and a Murderer',[6] an absurdity which has been taken seriously by more than one author and editor. Claire's apologists ought to know, but seemingly do not, that both for business reasons and out of his long-standing friendship, Kinnaird kept all Byron's letters, as well as copies of his replies, and there is not a word in them about Claire worse than I have quoted; nor is it credible that, in their one interview about a literary contract, he would have passed on this remarkable statement to Shelley, the only channel through which Claire, then living in seclusion at Bath, could have heard it. Her object was surely to say something—no matter what—that would tease a response out of Byron.

The breaking of his undertaking to write to her—whether it was a formal promise or something more vague which she construed as such—is

---

[1] 12 Sept. 1816.
[2] 29 Sept. 1816. Byron had probably told her Kinnaird was handsome, which was the general opinion.
[3] 12 Jan. 1818.   [4] 29 Sept.
[5] 12 Sept. 1816.   [6] 29 Sept.

to his discredit; but since the burden of her ever-renewed appeals was that he would write *affectionately*, his position was not an easy one. How could he answer her repeated pleadings? 'Be kind to me in your letters,' coupled with 'There is nothing in the world I love or care about but yourself'.[1] Or, 'Take care of your health, you dearest love & write me a consoling kind letter . . .'[2] Or again, 'I do feel a little angry that you should make me so very wretched for want of sacrificing a little time to tell me how you are & that you care a little for me'.[3]

There she was, pitiable girl whom he had so often tried to talk out of her obsession, pregnant, low-spirited, and begging for evidence that he cared for her. It would be too callous at such a time to remind her that he had never professed to care for her; yet to offer false reassurances would mislead her even more cruelly. And he was quite astute enough to gather that wounded *amour propre* was giving her much more anguish than love.

> My dearest darling Albé pray won't you write to me. . . . I would do anything, suffer any pain or degradation so I might be so very happy as to receive a letter from you. . . . Do you know dearest I do not like to be the object of pity & nothing makes me so angry as when M. & S. tell me not to expect to hear from you. They seem to know well enough how little you care for me & their hateful remarks are the most cruel of all! How proud I should be of a letter to disappoint their impertinent conjectures. Now I have told you all my dearest Albè & I hope you won't be angry. How proud how happy I should be to receive any mark of your affection and care for me.[4]

These pathetic passages reveal the extent of her humiliation at being unable to hide from her closest and kindest friends that she was not loved by her famous poet—a fact that, with their greater sensitiveness, they must have known by now at least as well as she did.

People who put themselves in a position to be humiliated are commonly much more resentful when this happens than if they had never set their pride at risk. True pride turns, after a fall, to self-examination, but when Byron proved obdurate Claire did not, then or later, acknowledge any folly in her own behaviour except that she had been blind to his deformed foot!

---

[1] Undated, about 31 Aug. 1816.   [2] 29 Sept.   [3] 6 Oct. 1816.
[4] Begun on 27 Oct., continued on 15 Nov. 1816. Byron's nickname, Albé, came into use at the same time as the 'i' in Claire, and I believe both may be ascribed to their having recently read a French novel, *Claire d'Albe* by Sophie Cottin, and her wishing to link her name to one which might stand for his. She often wrote Albe without an accent or with acute or *grave* accent indiscriminately. The usual explanations—that it stands for Albaneser, because Byron jokingly imitated an Albanian song, or else L.B., —seem far-fetched. He never signed 'Albé', and discouraged Claire from calling her child Alba.

Heart-rending though her communications about giving up her child may be, it is well to remember that this was done entirely by her own desire and in an expressed belief that he might prove an indifferent father.

> I cannot but see that if you have but little care to prevent any of my sufferings the chance is very small in favour of the affection you may show to the poor little Child. This above all makes me the most miserable of human Beings.

With such apprehensions, why did she contemplate parting with the baby? Byron would have acted at least as well as other men of his class who expected to pay from a distance for an indiscretion, and Claire, provided with means to bring up the child, and having completely uncensorious friends in her confidence, would have been better off than most unmarried mothers. The answer always accepted has been that they thought Byron able to offer brilliant social advantages outside their reach, and that is what Claire herself certainly told him in one of her letters. It is a rather surprising belief for three persons with backs deliberately turned upon social advantages to hold—and concerning an infant of sex as yet unknown, whose father, however eminent, was the centre of resounding scandals and in voluntary but unavoidable exile.

If we look again at Claire's long outpouring last quoted (Oct. 6th), we may find a more convincing reason for so odd a decision:

> ... I could take care of my Child myself & would but the idea of those poor little helpless things wanting the cares of a father & being deserted & becoming unhappy perhaps as myself makes me cry from hour to hour. . . . Indeed my dearest dear Albé if you will write me a little letter to say how you are, how all you love are, & above all if you will say you sometimes think of me without anger & that you will love and take care of the Child I will be as happy as possible. But if you do not dear indeed I shall cry myself ill every day.

Like many another infatuated girl, Claire believed she could keep some hold on a retreating lover by the bond of a child, and much more so if that child were under his roof, so that, having access to it, she would have access to him. But as one impassioned remonstrance followed another, Byron merely became more fixed in his resolve to set his face against that. The expression of her misgivings did not bring from him the comfort she had striven on page after page to extract, but only a letter to Shelley which caused her to excuse herself humbly:

> You seemed to think I entertained doubts of your intentions: indeed I never did. I cannot wonder you are suspicious; we all know how dreadfully

you have suffered. For the future best and dearest I will be quite content with what you choose.[1]

She meant, what he chose in regard to the child. There was no other subject about which he could write to Shelley of her entertaining doubts of his intentions. Buoying herself up, it may be, with some youthful daydream of winning his love when he met her with the infant in her arms, she thus gave it, before its birth, unreservedly into the hands of a man of dissolute habits who had not sent her one line, and whose probable negligence she had foreseen and continued to foresee.

Byron was not indifferent to the prospect of having the child with him, as letters quoted in my sixth chapter show, but on account of his irregular life in Venice and the complications of the long journey, he lingered over the arrangements. Claire would not let a nurse accompany the little girl, christened Allegra, to Italy, which is natural enough. It would have been still more natural if, with the torturing apprehensions she professed, she had refused to let it go at all.

Writing to Hobhouse a letter in which he mentioned that he had been 'clapt' by a gentlewoman ('to be sure it was *gratis*'), he went on to propose that when Hanson sent a clerk to Venice with legal documents in spring, the infant could then be brought, of course with an attendant. 'I wish you would settle it that way with Shelley—who has written to me frequently upon it. . . .'[2] He did not foresee that Hanson would not arrive until November 1818.

Claire meanwhile had written him a tremendous letter in which she unrestrainedly pulled out all the maternal stops—and several others. Addressing him, after eighteen months' silence on his part, as 'My dearest friend', she said it was her little darling's first birthday so she could not do better than write to him. She gave an elaborate description of Allegra's features, with poetical touches—'eyes of a dazzling blue[3] more like the waters of the lake of Geneva under a summer sky than any thing else I ever saw, rosy projecting lips & a little square chin dented in the middle exactly like your own'. She sent a lock of Allegra's hair, dwelt with a feint of impartiality on faults ('She can neither walk nor speak but whenever she dislikes any thing she calls out upon papa'), then went into raptures which had a very uncomfortable undertone:

[1] 19 Nov. 1816, added to letter begun on 27 Oct. Byron's suffering in this context may be a reference to his loss of Ada, soon to be made a Ward in Chancery, which he felt as an acute insult and privation. He was deeply sympathetic to Shelley for having been refused custody of his children, though in the circumstances in which he deserted his pregnant wife, that no longer seems an unjust decision.

[2] 42093, Byron Papers 23 Feb. 1818.

[3] This appears as 'daytime blue' in all the printed versions I have seen, and without the comparison that follows.

My dear friend how I envy you. You will have a little darling to crawl to your knees and pull you till you take her up—then she will sit in the crook of your arm & you will give her raisins out of your own plate & a little drop of wine from your own glass & she will think herself a little Queen in Creation. When she shall be older she will run about your house like a lapwing; If you are miserable her light and careless voice will make you happy, but there is one delight above all others: if it shall please you, you may delight yourself in contemplating a creature growing under your own hands as it were. You may look at her and think 'This is my work.'

Having painted an idealized picture of fatherhood quite outside Byron's experience—drawn, perhaps, from watching Shelley with his little William—Claire proceeded with some disingenuous flatteries of Byron's qualities in the rôle of protector:

How kind & gentle you are to Children! How good-tempered and considerate towards your servants, how accomodating even to your dogs! And all this because you are sole master and lord; because there is no disputing your power you become merciful & just: but let some one more on a par with yourself enter the room you begin to suspect & be cautious & are consequently very often cruel. I hope therefore that I shall at least be happy enough to see you fond of the darling.

This uneasy approach must have strengthened his determination that she should not see him at all: and the tone of mounting hysteria in which she went on, while it must have aroused pity, could only alienate sympathy.

What a beautiful sight it is to see a child leaning against a parent & turning up their wondering eyes in astonishment at the extraordinary thing it is seeing. . . .

How careless you were of every feeling when you proposed to send her in care of a nurse. Do you think I would trust her with such a person. She is all my treasure—the little creature occupies all my thoughts, all my time & my feelings. When I hold her in my arms I think to myself—there is nothing else in the world that is of you or belongs to you—you are truly a stranger to every one else: without this little being you would hold no relation with any single human being.

You might as well have asked a miser to trust his gold for a sea voyage in a leaky vessel. Besides various and ceaseless misgivings that I entertain of you suppose that in yielding her to your care I yield her to neglect and coldness. Then am I assured that such will not be the case?

She would have been more than human if she had not wanted to disburden herself of some of the rancour her failure with him had engendered; but the tactlessness of informing him that she felt so much mistrust when she was nevertheless bent on handing the child over to him must have added to all the other annoyances of her minatory style. She herself realized its inconsistency.

> True it is as I have before written that I have observed generosity in your disposition towards defenceless creatures but at the same time on so important a point I feel tremors of doubt & uncertainty. I so fear she will be unhappy I am so anxious to be cautious to do nothing hastily—& to consider and examine all things[.] Poor little angel! In your great house left perhaps to servants while you are drowning sense & feeling in wine & striving all you can to ruin the natural goodness of your nature who will be there to watch her[?]
> She is peculiarly delicate—her indigestions are frequent & dangerous if neglected—a moment might take from me all I hold dear—a moment might create for me memories long & dread too terrible even in this instants conception.

Had it only come sooner, such a letter might have shown Byron the hopelessness of taking on a responsibility he could never fulfil to Claire's exacting standard, and by causing him to insist on some other arrange-ment—which she could hardly have refused if he had firmly stated his incapacity to change the character she so freely criticized—it might have altered the destiny of everyone concerned. But she was already on her way.

> Do not think me selfish [she went on]. Whatever I may be to others with her I cannot be so. My affections are few & therefore strong—the extreme solitude in which I live [i.e. with the Shelleys and their children] has concentrated them to one point and that point is my lovely child. I study her pleasure all day long—she is so fond of me that I hold her in my arms till I am nearly falling on purpose to delight her.
> We sleep together and if you knew the extreme happiness I feel when she nestles closer to me, when in listening to our regular breathing together I could tear my flesh in twenty thousand different directions to ensure her good and when I fear for her residing with you it is not the dread I have to commence the long series of painful anxiety I know I shall have to endure it is lest I should behold her sickly and wasted with improper management lest I should live to hear that *you* neglected her.
> My dearest friend if all this [? reaches you] while your feelings are good & gentle then have I done you an irreparable wrong in thus suspecting you & most sincerely am I grieved for I well remember my own silent though bitter burnings when you would often half in jest accuse me of thoughts & actions which I detested. I cannot pardon those who attribute to me rude & indelicate feelings; or who believe, because I have unloosed myself from the trammels of custom or opinion that I do not possess within myself a severer monitor than either of these; who do not behold in the height & loftiness of my hopes the security I pledge of my purity & innocence.

Transported by this self-portrait, she dropped into a metrical form:

> I have loved it is true but what then?
> Have you suffered through me or my love?

(In a previous letter she had apologized for all the trouble she had given him, and thanked him for his forbearance.)

> ... Find me another human being who has borne unkindness & injustice with the patience & gentleness I have? I have a child and show me a better & more attentive fond mother. When affection & tenderness, when sacrifice & generosity shall be demonstrated as odious then may I be classed among selfish and detestable beings but not before.

She came at last to her real grievance:

> This long *tirade* as you will call it has been drawn from me by my hearing repeated some expressions of your's concerning me which mark an utter want of discrimination in you, if you really thought as you spoke which I do not believe.

Claire's illusion that she was a frequent victim of slanders was an aspect of her self-importance which led to her becoming an extremely quarrelsome person. Byron was by no means so proud of the liaison as to bandy her name about. When he had occasion to mention her to the closest of his old associates, Kinnaird and Hobhouse, he did so with what was, for him, discretion. To Augusta Leigh, he never gave her name. As it is the highest degree unlikely that anything could have reached her through one of these, she was, we may guess, enraged at something repeated to her, no doubt under provocation, by Shelley or Mary.

> ... Alone I study Plutarch's lives wherein I find nothing but excitements to virtue & abstinence: with Mary & Shelley the scene changes but from the contemplation of the virtues of the dead to those of the living. I have no Hobhouse by my side to dispirit me with easy & impudent declarations of 'the villany of all mankind'. . . . I have faults. I am timid from vanity; my temper is inconstant and *volage*. I do not like our Mary sail my steady course like a ship under a gentle and favourable wind. But at thirty I shall be better and every year I hope to gain in value.

She now told him in glowing terms of the publication of Mary's *Frankenstein*—'a most wonderful performance full of genius'—(which Byron in fact admired very much), but she spoiled the pleasure of this good news by launching into another tirade, this time on feminism:

> ... Whatever private feelings I may have at not being able to do so well myself yet all yields when I consider that she is a woman & will prove in time an ornament to us & an argument in our favour. How I delight in a

lovely woman of strong and cultivated intellect. How I delight to hear all the intracacies [sic] of mind & argument hanging on her lips! If she were my mortal enemy, if she had even injured my darling I would serve her with fidelity and fervently advocate her as doing good to the whole.

When I read of Epicharsis the slave in Tacitus & of Hypatia of Alexandria in Gibbon, I shriek with joy & cry Vittoria! Vittoria![1]

We may leave Claire victoriously shrieking. For Byron there was more to come. I have quoted only part of the letter, yet a larger amount than will be found elsewhere. My object has been to show the inveterate obtuseness with which she insisted on identifying the child with herself, indeed obtuseness of every kind.

It was the Shelleys, ever restless and not sorry for an excuse to see Italy, who took Claire over the Alps accompanied by three children all doomed to early death. On April 24th 1818 Byron wrote to Hobhouse:

Shelley has got to Milan with the bastard & it's mother—but won't send the shild—I have sent a messenger for the child—but I can't leave my quarters & have 'sworn an oath'.[2]

He had vowed that he would never meet Claire again, and he never did; but despite his typical levity in speaking of 'the bastard'—which he dropped when Allegra became a real person to him—he had every intention of being a benevolent father, of having her well educated and furnished with a handsome dowry; and if he came to lay some stress on his wish that she should practise a religion and be one day a married woman, it must be admitted he had seen the very seamy side of life as lived by 'a character committing every violence against received opinion'.

2. THE END

No child whose span of years was as little as five and a quarter has been the subject of so much biographical writing as Allegra. She figures in the annals, separate or united, of Shelley, Mary, Claire, and Byron, and has had two short works devoted to herself.[3] On the whole Byron cuts a poor figure in these various accounts. He refuses, inhumanly, to accept Allegra unless she is yielded up entirely by her mother; he takes the child into a household where he is pursuing a course of immorality; he then lets her share the nursery of the British Consul's wife, Mrs Hoppner, a straitlaced Swiss who finds her unsympathetic; he goes to Ravenna after his mistress, the Countess Guiccioli, who, according to Claire, has her put in a convent because she is jealous of her, having tried and failed to have

[1] Murray MS. 12 Jan. 1818.   [2] 42093. Byron Papers.
[3] *La Figlia di Lord Byron* by Emilio Biondi and *Allegra* by Iris Origo.

a child by Byron herself. The convent is described to Claire as a gloomy place where children of low birth are half frozen in winter and undernourished all the year round. She represents the nuns as a mendicant order. When he leaves Ravenna, Byron disregards Shelley's appeals and lets Allegra remain immured. She becomes ill and he does not bother to go to her. She dies, and he refuses to pay the embalmer's fee!

The case is black but some extenuating circumstances have already been indicated. He had not wanted the affair, had sought to avoid it, but when a child resulted from it, he behaved as if he had been the seducer and promised paternal care: and though the mother had told him she entertained 'various and ceaseless misgivings' about the way he would keep that promise, he had not withdrawn it but only protected himself from intolerable scenes by stipulating, not a total severance of the mother from the child (in autumn 1818 he lent the Shelleys a house at Este where Claire had Allegra with her), but her total severance from *him*. Mrs Hoppner had made a most favourable impression on Claire, and it was better for an infant of three to be with her than in the unhomely and unsuitable atmosphere of the Palazzo Mocenigo.

That the Countess Guiccioli had suggested the convent at Bagnacavallo is true, but not for the ridiculous reason given—it would have been socially and financially disastrous for her to have an extra-marital child[1]— but partly because the political situation made her family's residence in Romagna, and consequently Byron's, precarious, and partly because Allegra, in any case, did not spend long in the Palazzo Guiccioli, where it would have obviously been improper to keep her, but lodged in a villa some miles from Ravenna. One of the servants who looked after her there had a habit of lying and another brought out Allegra's tendency to mockery. At four years old, encouraged by these, she sang popular Italian songs, no doubt in that vulgar manner children pick up which, while amusing to outsiders, gives concern to guardians.

We may grant that Teresa, who recounts these matters in the reminiscences she wrote in old age,[2] idealized somewhat the motives which had actuated her in youth, and that she may simply have not wanted another woman's child to add to the already sufficient complexity of her life: but we must also ask ourselves, having regard to the frenetic

---

[1] Claire invented a piece of dialogue for her which I translate from the Italian in which, fifty years later, she wrote it: 'We have tried our utmost, but we have no children and it is a heavy cross for Milord and me, especially when I think that this young Englishwoman of good birth has given him a baby.' She is supposed to have heard this from the friend, Mr Tighe, who gave her the false information about the convent, but how Mr Tighe heard it she does not explain. That Teresa would have classified Claire among the well-born is not a convincing touch.

[2] *La Vie.*

statements in Claire's journals and letters, whether there was any course Byron could have taken with Allegra which would not have excited strenuous objections.

The Capucine Convent of San Giovanni answered in no way to her report. The children were not those of small tradespeople—though an egalitarian should not have looked down on those—but from the best families in the district. The school was new, founded in 1818, with modern equipment, and the fees were high—seventy scudi per half-year —and Allegra was well fitted out for all her needs. The nuns were by no means strict disciplinarians. Teresa, herself convent-bred, could not see it as a cruel fate to be brought up like the most favoured of her compatriots, and Byron could not see it as a cruel fate to be brought up like Teresa.

Claire's vitriolic letter of protest against the Convent must surely have been framed to make his hackles rise, for it could have no other effect. Its argument was that all Italian women, by reason of having been bred in convents, were utterly despicable—an opinion aimed at the Italian countess. 'They are bad wives, most unnatural mothers; licentious and ignorant, they are the dishonour and unhappiness of society.' After proliferating objections in far too many words, she proposed to place the child in an English boarding-school at her own expense, which meant at Shelley's expense as Byron very well knew, and accused him of using Allegra as an instrument of his hatred against her (Claire). She even turned his arrangement to pay extra fees into an aggravation of her grievance: '. . . If it is a place suited to Allegra why need you pay a double pension to ensure her proper treatment and attention[?]'[1] Since she claimed, untruthfully, to have Mrs Hoppner as her adviser, Byron sent the letter to Hoppner with indignant comments. He believed that, while accusing him of heartlessness, she had abandoned a child in the Foundling Hospital of Naples.

Various friends and acquaintances of his went to visit Allegra in the convent, including Teresa's Gamba grandparents, who at first had been very wary of Byron, but were softened by hearing that his natural daughter was to be a Catholic. He has been condemned for leaving her unvisited himself and Shelley praised for doing the reverse; but earnestly as Shelley wanted to play a benevolent part, and do whatever Claire would approve when she came to know of it, he himself did not hurry to Bagnacavallo. He had arrived at Ravenna as Byron's guest on August 6th 1821, and, usually omitted without indication from his letter of the 11th to Mary, is this passage: 'I have not yet seen Allegra—indeed today I suffer

[1] *LJ.* Vol. V, Appendix 1, 21 Mar. 1821.

so much from the pain in my side—brought on I believe by this accursed water—that I do not feel myself equal to a ride of 24 miles.'[1]

He went to the Convent on or about August 14th (there is some confusion in the dating of his letters), much nearer the end of his stay than the beginning. If Byron seems infinitely more remiss in never going at all, he is being judged by the standards of the 20th century, but the age of tender consciences towards children was then hardly begun. School terms were much longer, fathers in the upper classes more remote, in the lower, more violent. Boys were subjected to an amount of corporal punishment we now think horrible, nor were little girls spared harsh slapping and knuckle-rapping. The high death rate had no effect in modifying these severities because the birth rate kept pace with it. Not very long had passed since Rousseau, whom both Byron and Shelley revered, had confessed to putting five of his own children in the Foundling Hospital, year by year as they were born. Infant life was cheap.

Notwithstanding that unhappy fact, many parents dearly treasured their children, and amongst those Shelley must decidedly be numbered, while Byron—though he had said the silly things young bachelors are liable to say about their sympathy with Herod—had a most marked paternalistic bent. That he did not drive the few miles to Bagnacavallo to see how Allegrina, as he called her, was going on was perhaps because he felt self-conscious about facing the Reverend Mother and the Sisters as an illicit father, for he knew that, however discreetly received, he would not be less an object of curiosity there than anywhere else.

Teresa takes the responsibility for having urged him to let Allegra remain where she was when, the Gamba family being exiled, Byron left Ravenna for Pisa: 'Why do you want to bring the little one out of the convent [she had written]? Would it not be better to leave her in the place of safety where she now is?'[2]

She also mentions that the Shelleys had approved of his arrangements, and certainly from their letters Byron had little reason to think otherwise. In a verbal portrait chiefly devoted to extolling Shelley at Byron's expense, Leigh Hunt wrote that he was sometimes guilty of 'condescending, though for the kindest of purposes, to a little double dealing'.[3] This tendency is especially noticeable in his relations with Byron. He was, of course, in a most delicate position between Claire, who was deeply in his confidence, and the poet whose work he respected enormously and

---

[1] He was naturally counting the distance both ways. MS Bodleian Library, Oxford.
[2] *La Vie.* Presumably about Sept. 1821. Hobhouse returned to Teresa all her numerous letters to Byron, and she apparently destroyed most of them; but wherever I have been able to check anything quoted by her, I have found it materially dependable.
[3] *Lord Byron and Some of His Contemporaries.*

whose friendship he considered a privilege, whatever he felt of disappro-
bation and, at times, inevitable envy of success. ('If I esteemed thee less,
envy would kill', was one of his lines in a tentative sonnet.)

While Shelley practised diplomacy, Mary defended the Convent plan
openly, pointing out that Bagnacavallo was a much healthier place than
Venice[1] and terrible were the condemnations of her that Claire recorded:

> Would to God she could perish without one note or remembrance, so the
> brightness of his [Shelley's] name might not be darkened by the corruption
> she sheds upon it. . . .
> What should one say of a Woman who should go . . . and gaze upon the
> spectacle of a Child led to the scaffold—one would turn from her with
> horror—yet she did so, she looked coolly on, rejoiced in the comfortable place
> she had got in the show, and . . . never winced once during the exhibition
> and after all was over, went up and claimed acquaintance with the exe-
> cutioner and shook hands with him. I never saw her afterwards without
> feeling as if the sickening crawling motions of a Deathworm had replaced
> the usual flow of my Blood in my veins.[2]

Little dreaming that he would be likened to an executioner for placing
his daughter in a well-recommended boarding-school, Byron was writing,
talking, riding, shooting in Pisa, and corresponding with his men of
business in England on the arbitration respecting his late mother-in-law's
estate.

He had left the banker, Pellegrino Ghigi, in charge of whatever he
had not been able to bring from Ravenna—most of the animals (the list
of them does not quite tally with the menagerie described by Shelley in a
famous letter), his local charities, the few money matters outstanding, and
such of Allegrina's requirements as the nuns might communicate. Ghigi
would write to Lega on these and other tasks he had all too obligingly
shouldered, and Lega would consult Byron and reply with instructions
which usually left a considerable amount to Ghigi's discretion.

His banking house must have been on a modest scale, and as I have
said elsewhere, he was too amiable and too intimate a friend of Lega's, to
practise strictly business-like methods. No business-like agent would have
undertaken to look after a number of animals without specifying any
charge for their maintenance, or encumbered himself with taking
inventories of an awkward lot of things left behind, or replacing broken
glass of Byron's landlord, Count Guiccioli, or selling his client's wine and
disposing of the proceeds to buy bed-linen and shoes for an aged beggar
woman, or forwarding an appeal from 'the poor old man of the pine wood',

---

[1] Letter of early Feb. 1822.
[2] Grylls, quoting passages Claire meant for incorporation in her Memoirs.

or getting an extra blanket for Madamigella—who was Allegrina.[1] But in Ghigi's small pond, the noble Lord was a very big fish, and besides, Byron had a remarkable fascination for bankers. One after another they went out of their way to do him unlikely services.

The animals were particularly tiresome. With a sort of comic opera humour, Ghigi complained repeatedly of the nuisances they caused in loosely versified letters, the jests of which veiled real exasperation. The two monkeys were in the habit of biting him, a badger had died on his hands, there was a crow with only half a beak, a small mongrel dog, a goat which had gone lame since Byron's departure through breaking a shoulder blade, and several birds.[2] By February in 1822, the male monkey had become very ill and Ghigi had had to pour wine down its throat and wrap it up in warm cloths, renewing them till nightfall; and during this crisis the female monkey had been frantic. If Milord would relieve him of the responsibility, it would be a kindness.[3] But whether through slackness on Lega's part or want of imagination on Byron's, it was several weeks before Ghigi was invited to find someone he could trust and send the animals at his lordship's expense[4]—and that proved beyond his power.

On April 3rd, Lega received a letter written on March 26th—it took several days for the mail to reach Pisa—saying that the Abbess or Reverend Mother, Sister Fabbri, had bought Allegrina six pairs of thread stockings, six linen chemises, two linen petticoats, eight white hand-kerchiefs, a straw hat, one coloured and one white cambric dress, a length of black velvet ribbon, a comb, muslin veiling for covering cushions (pin-cushions perhaps: a word is torn by the seal), pins, needles, and assorted sewing threads. The clothes were doubtless renewals of the spring wardrobe. Like other children of the time, and women too, she wore few warm garments, but had shawls for cold weather.

On April 17th, Lega had another letter, written by the banker in Ravenna on the 13th. It began with some discussion of his financial affairs, which Ghigi handled for him, and went on to say that Allegrina, who had recovered some months before from a bout of feverishness, had in the last few days been troubled by a recurrence, though the Reverend

---

[1] 46873, numerous letters.

[2] Writing to Peacock on 10(?) Aug. 1821, Shelley had listed the animals as 'ten horses, eight enormous dogs, three monkeys, five cats, an eagle, a crow, and a falcon . . . five peacocks, two guinea hens, and an Egyptian crane'. There were then eight horses and three dogs one of which was the small mongrel (Byron took one monkey and two dogs to Pisa, where he acquired one more of each). No cats or peacocks are mentioned by Ghigi, and no badger or goat by Shelley. He wrote half in fantasy, likening Byron's domain to that of Circe.

[3] 46873. 19 Feb. 1822.

[4] Ibid. 15 Apr. The crippled goat was to be put out to grass.

Mother told him the fevers were 'light and slow'. However, she had taken care to send for Dr Rasi (a Ravenna physician instead of the one at Bagnacavallo), who had seen Allegrina before and knew her constitution, and he was going to the Convent again that morning. In the evening, Ghigi would have word from him. If it had not been a busy day, he would have gone himself. After another reference to the business matter, he asked to be remembered to the noble Lord, and ended with a phrase equivalent to 'not to worry'.

Since, in the earlier paragraphs, about a debtor of Lega's, Ghigi had said he was writing 'in confidence and friendship', Lega could not hand the letter to his employer, and how he conveyed its news, whether in a serious or a reassuring manner, we do not know. On that very day, Byron had learned with rage that his guiltless servant, Tita, had not been set free as expected on payment of his fine. He was deeply engaged in trying to get him and the other innocent man, Teresa's footman, out of prison. The question of their release or exile was not a triviality because, apart from their hardships, it would be a clue to the future of the Gambas. If there had been any untoward development at the Convent, a staffetta, travelling much more rapidly than the ordinary post, would surely have arrived before a letter which had been four days en route. So must Byron, so might even the most dedicated of parents, have concluded.

On the 19th, two further letters arrived, neither sent by express. One was from the Abbess to Lega. It notified him with regret that Madamigella had had 'a little inflammation' which had threatened this lovable child, and that the greatest care was being lavished on her. Briefly—and most illegibly—she conveyed the impression that the danger was past, but that she was not omitting any of the steps proper to be taken where there had been cause of anxiety.

Ghigi for his part had not been in haste to follow up his news of the 13th, on which day Dr Rasi had found Allegrina with a slow but continuous fever. As it had attacked her chest, he had thought it well to consult Dr Berardi, the Convent doctor, and they decided she should be bled—that perilous remedy which so mysteriously commanded the faith of the medical profession for many centuries. She had shown a sudden improvement. Still, Dr Rasi had stayed all Saturday and left orders should further bleeding be called for. Every day the Sisters were keeping Ghigi informed by express letters of the child's condition, and tomorrow he would be going in person to see her. He would continue to send word by ordinary post, but if things took a bad turn, which he was reluctant to believe, then by express. He wanted his lordship to know of all the nuns' untiring efforts and his own watchfulness.

These communications would have been more disquieting in Pisa but for the fact that they did come by the ordinary post, and an express had been unmistakably promised if there were any need of urgency. Byron had just received Samuel Rogers and his travelling companion as house guests. By long-standing arrangement, they were to be with him two or three days and he was giving them a dinner party tonight with Shelley and Trelawny. Rogers, though charitable in deed, had so caustic a tongue that Byron may not have cared to speak of Allegra in front of him; but I find it hard to believe that he never mentioned her illness to Shelley, who was especially fond of her. He was seeing him every day, and it would have been quite unnatural for one so spontaneous to suppress the information—unless he restrained himself because Shelley had already lost, through illness, the two children who had come from England with him; but that kind of sensibility was, I think, rather foreign to Byron.

If Shelley was told, he did not urge his friend to leave his guests and hurry to Bagnacavallo. Byron's note to him after imparting the tidings of Allegrina's death make that very clear. It would have been out of all reason to say that he was not conscious of having anything to reproach himself with in his conduct, although in such moments 'we are apt to think this or that might have been done',[1] if he had actually rejected a suggestion by Shelley that he should go immediately to the sick child. (Not that going immediately was as easily done as said. No one could pass from one Italian state to another without an official permit, as Shelley had learned to his cost when Mary had been held up at a frontier with their dying infant, Clara.)

Two additional letters about the course of the illness have been published, dated when they were written, April 20th and 21st but without any indication that they did not reach Pisa till the 24th, two days after the announcement of Allegra's death.[2] That alone was sent by staffetta, arriving on the 22nd, and outstripping Sister Fabbri's report that the illness had become dangerous, and that all the sorrowful nuns were praying for her recovery. Any humane father would have striven to get to Romagna on that signal if it had not come too late. A bulletin from the faithful but amazingly over-confident Ghigi, written under the delusion that, though the child had been very ill, there was a good prospect of recovery, must have been harrowing to read by those who knew her to be dead. But perhaps Byron did not read it, for Lega took it upon himself to withhold anything that might add to his distress. It is a thousand pities that, from first to last, hardly anything was communicated direct to Byron. Every-

---

[1] *LJ.* 23 Apr. 1822.

[2] Iris Origo gives her source as copies in the public library of Forlì. Possibly only the postmarks giving the date of dispatch were recorded. The date of receipt in Pisa, also postmarked on the originals, must have been omitted.

thing even when personally addressed to him was filtered through a well-meaning but sometimes misjudging go-between.

Allegra's end had come less than twenty-four hours after Ghigi had parted from her in an optimistic frame of mind. The Sisters, he said, were in the utmost affliction and himself confused with problems, the first of which was whether the father would want the body to be embalmed. He asked Lega to find a suitable moment for breaking the news.

It was Teresa who did so, and her too romantic account of Byron's sublime expression but apparently perfunctory grief as mistranslated or, rather, falsified by Moore, has done nothing to disarm those who have felt he showed little sign of more than superficial feeling.[1] What Lega wrote to Ghigi very early on the first morning after receiving the belated staffetta strikes a different note. It was futile, he said, to try and convey the profound and inexpressible sorrow with which his lordship had heard of the loss of his most delightful of daughters. He was in a state of shock, and inconsolable: 'You cannot imagine the sadness and the desolation that reign in our house after such a calamity. I cannot yet rid myself of the contraction of my heart that I felt on opening your letter.'[2]

Lega authorized Ghigi to pay the doctors and contingent expenses and to have everything appropriate done with propriety and convenience. Allegrina had been the playmate of his own little daughter, Aspasia, whom he adored, and even the poor expectation of life of every young child had not prepared him for such a loss. When the overdue letter containing the account of what had turned out to be her last day arrived, telling how Ghigi had found her lying on a little bed in a big room, three doctors with her, and the nuns surrounding her begging to help, and she, poor infant, after two more blood-lettings, asking Ghigi to bring her some of her favourite cheese, Lega was quite overcome.

> Allow me at this time not to dwell on the matter [he wrote] because my heart is utterly oppressed by the intense love I had for the most dear and graceful creature I have ever known, as well as by the painful duty that obliged me to share in the appalling announcement to the most feeling of fathers.

He asked Ghigi to be kind enough to make arrangements with Henry Dunn, the banker and merchant of Leghorn, for shipping the body to London:

> Milord is still in the utmost affliction and inconsolable at his loss. He approves of all you have done and sanctions the expenses incurred and to be incurred. He is most grateful for your care and interest on his behalf.

[1] Moore actually added to what Teresa wrote him the sentence about Byron's sublimity and superiority in grief.
[2] 23 Apr. 1822. All these letters are in 46873.

He ended by suggesting that Ghigi himself might accompany the coffin to Leghorn and then come to Pisa to see his Lordship. When all allowance had been made for Latin eloquence, it seems evident that, unless Lega was an out-and-out liar, Byron was grief-stricken at his child's death. Indeed he himself wrote to Lord Holland in a letter not published till 1950: 'Her death, I confess, chilled my blood with horror. It was perhaps the most lively sorrow I have ever felt.'[1] If he told Teresa that they must speak of it no more, it was doubtless as much to spare her feelings as his own, since there must have been a temptation to blame her for her unfortunate advice. Had he been the hardest hearted of men, he must still have suffered tortures of embarrassment, remembering how he had disregarded Claire's protests and how she would be able to reproach him.

And now began that multiplicity of lugubrious preparations which the disposal of the dead involves, made much more complex by Byron's impulsive and sentimental decision to have the child buried in the church at Harrow which he had attended in his boyhood. This, whether he knew it or not, necessitated embalming the body before it was encased in lead; but Ghigi's equally impulsive decision to have that done was taken on his own initiative before hearing anything from Pisa—or rather, I suspect, on the initiative of a surgeon, Enrico Marmani, who had been called in to see the child on her deathbed, and who had his eye firmly on the main chance.

We do not know how much Byron saw of the ensuing correspondence. Lega suppressed completely a letter of condolence from the Reverend Mother which he judged would too deeply 'wound his heart', and which was besides in a 'distasteful' style, calling Allegra an incomparable gift from heaven which heaven had taken back because the earth was unworthy to possess it. He asked Ghigi to send her a few lines to explain the father's profound sorrow and excessive sensitiveness. Because his Lordship did not want his distress increased, he had also opened and decided not to show a letter addressed to him direct by Ghigi, but he had orders to convey again much gratitude and to repeat his promise to pay the expenses Ghigi was incurring.

(It is strange to find after this a request for some truffles, a delicacy his employer particularly liked. On the other hand to offer creature comfort in time of misery is neither an unusual nor a reprehensible custom.)

As so much was being withheld from Byron, he probably had little notion how many dismal tasks, absolutely unsuited to an essentially humorous temperament, his Ravenna banker was performing. The lead coffin was enclosed in an oak one, the organs and heart were placed in two

[1] Quennell. 11 May 1822.

lead vases and these in an oak casket. Having seen to that, Ghigi had to get permission from the Cardinal Legate and the Bishops of all the dioceses through which the funeral carriage must pass as well as the priests of all the parishes whose boundaries it must cross so that they might see it escorted to the next boundary. At least so the Legate of Ravenna had told him, but the Legate of Ferrara assured him it was quite needless, and he had no idea where to turn for advice. Then the Bishop of Faenza had to be asked for assent to the removal of a corpse from Bagnacavallo, and there had been a tremendous business about sealing the caskets, an affair which required the sanction of the Governor, the head of the Cathedral Chapter and other officials, and all the certifications had to be in triplicate and authenticated by a notary. Instructions about passing through the Customs also had to be taken, and he had sent an express to the Tuscan frontier to make sure of those.

He could not come himself but he had arranged an escort consisting of a priest who was his brother-in-law, Don Fabiani, and one Signor Girolamo Baldini, who knew the route, and he had hired a carriage for sixty-five scudi for the return journey, not counting meals. He would tell Lega about all the other expenses when the list was complete. He did not care to mention them to the noble Lord. Marmani would expect a high fee for the embalming; it was usually done only for great people.

That Ghigi should hesitate before sending staffettas was understandable, because from Ravenna to Pisa they cost sixteen scudi a time, but he had carried economy too far when dispatching news of Allegra's illness, and now he repeated his mistake so that this letter, written on April 30th, which should obviously have preceded his brother-in-law and friend to Pisa, only arrived on May 8th, four days after they did! Moreover, the letter they brought from Ghigi to Byron was the very one that Lega was to suppress with the comments I have quoted. Byron has been censured for not receiving these two emissaries, but as no information whatever relating to them had been seen by him, neither the letter they carried nor the one meant to apprise Lega of their coming, it is not astonishing that the welcome they had looked forward to was limited to a talk with the secretary.[1]

If Ghigi himself had been able to accept Byron's invitation and take to Pisa his first-hand report of Allegrina, saddening as it would have been, we need not suppose there would have been any failure of hospitality, but to meet two perfect strangers, who had completed their mission as

---

[1] A note to Lega from Ghigi (Folio 99 in this series), hastily written overnight before Fabiani and Baldini set off at dawn, was delivered personally by them; but its contents, plaintively summarizing his difficulties and his apprehension about what Marmani might charge, show that it was not meant to be read by Byron.

far as he knew when they had left the coffin in the keeping of Mr Dunn at Leghorn, this was what he may not have realized was expected of him. As it afterwards transpired that they were counting on a handsome 'gratification' for their trouble, they went back to Ravenna doubly disappointed.

But Byron had an additional reason that day, May 4th, for not attending an uncomfortable interview. It was the one which brought an express from Lerici. Claire, who had been in Pisa without Byron's knowledge when he had the news of their child's death, left for Spezia with Jane and Edward Williams on April 23rd, before any of them had heard it. When they returned two days later, the Shelleys decided she ought not to be told while in Byron's vicinity, and, with Mary and Trelawny, she was hurried back to Spezia on April 26th, still in ignorance. How she guessed it from the others' manner when she came into a room where they were talking, in the small house they had rented for the summer at Lerici, has been told in numerous biographies. She took it better than they had hoped. Allegra had, after all, only been with her during the first quarter of her brief life and, though Claire had indulged in day-dreams of getting her out of the convent by means of a forged letter, if the whole tenor of her conduct is viewed with detached consideration, it may be thought she had been more eager to score off Byron than to repossess a little daughter whom she had no prospect of supporting except with the straitened means of Shelley, deep in debt as he was. 'The death of her child seems to have restored her to tranquillity', wrote Shelley.[1] But before she settled into that calm she gave vent to her emotions in one terrible letter.

That it is still in existence is unlikely, because Byron sent it reproachfully to Shelley, and it was the sort of document a friend destroys. Shelley replied to Byron apologetically, saying he and Mary would not have allowed such a letter to be sent if they had suspected its contents.[2] I do not think it is a very far-fetched conjecture that she had taunted Byron with deformity of body as of mind, the theme which had already been so obsessive to her before Allegra's death, as may be seen by the quotations from her journal given earlier; and that she did so in the blackest words she could contrive, having a power of invective that was not negligible. Her friend Lady Mount Cashell, who within a few months foolishly appealed to Byron to settle a small annuity on Claire, admitted that 'the furious letter' might have been a stumbling block, and she seems to have had a good idea of its nature.[3]

---

[1] 18 June, to John Gisborne. He repeated this to other correspondents.
[2] 9 May.   [3] 14 Jan. 1823, letter to Mary Shelley, quoted by Stocking.

To have his lameness added to his sins was a cruelty that would have filled him with lingering bitterness and certainly put him out of the humour to practise such social courtesies as Ghigi had intended.

We now reached one of those sinister passes where no one was able to put a foot right. Ghigi had conferred many obligations upon Byron which were too readily forgotten when his own omission had to be faced —that he had not attempted the least enquiry into what Marmani would charge for the embalming of the child's body, a matter about which he began to feel exceedingly nervous as, time after time, the surgeon informed him how difficult was the process, how immense the skill needed to accomplish it. The druggist's bill for spices and other preservatives had been nearly eighty scudi, which the banker had paid without question, and that too was an indiscretion. But Lega had also been in the wrong, assuring him many times that all expenses would be met, without any indication that there must be some control over them—and so experienced a man might have known that advantage is taken of those who do not like to seem conscious of money on mournful occasions.

Lega could not, however, have anticipated anything so extreme as Marmani's behaviour. While others had been quick—almost indecently so—to send Ghigi their bills, Marmani bided his time, then suddenly, on May 24th, wrote protesting at the delay in giving him his reward. He indicated in no uncertain terms that it should be adapted to the importance of the thing done and the rank of the person for whom it was done. Lord Byron was said to be rich and generous, and perhaps the lowest demand one could make without offending him would be two hundred gold louis. He knew nothing of what an ordinary embalmer might ask. He was not an ordinary embalmer but a surgeon, and he threw himself totally on the generosity of His Excellency Lord Byron.[1]

Two hundred gold louis was eight hundred Roman scudi, a sum for which one could easily have bought a fine carriage and horses. Ghigi was staggered. Bad as his fears had been, this was far beyond them. He sent a letter to Lega and begged his advice, 'because, to speak straight forwardly, it seems to me a mad pretension, or rather, the maddest'. He had written to Marmani saying he had not had the courage to send so large a claim in case it was thought there was connivance between them. 'I have told various people of his letter and everyone marvels at his strange demand. Let me know what I should do',[2] he begged.

Byron and his household had gone to the Villa Dupuy at Montenero, and there was some delay before Lega could reply. 'Nothing more strange, nor more excessive, nor more ill-judged, than the preposterous claim of

---

[1] 46873. 24 May.   [2] Ibid. 25 May.

the Signor Surgeon Marmani. Before mentioning it to Milord, I should wish you to find out how much the embalming of Cardinal Malvasia cost.' When he had as many details as could be got about that, and not before, he would decide what to do. He himself, curiously enough, had heard from Marmani's son, a student in Pisa, who had written—unaware that his father had done so—saying Marmani Senior was considering five hundred scudi a proper fee, which made the demand for eight hundred still more scandalous.[1]

Much as Byron liked his rank to be recognized, anything in the nature of an extortionate tax on it provoked him to stubborn resistance. 'I will submit to no exorbitant charge nor imposition', he had written to Hoppner on a comparatively minor matter.[2] Having more money tends to confirm rather than diminish such a resolution, especially when there is a steward like Lega to reinforce it. When it turned out from Ghigi's own investigations that the surgeon Urbini who had embalmed the Cardinal Malvasia had been content with a fee of fifty scudi and eighteen more for expenses and was willing to testify to that effect,[3] he flung to the winds the conventional delicacies of a sorrowing parent and started to look narrowly at all the accounts, so far as Ghigi could be induced to render them.

The upshot was that, after much correspondence, with increasing consternation on Ghigi's side, Lega was writing on July 22nd and 24th that the noble Lord was prepared to pay Dr Rasi the fees he would get for treating any patient without distinction, plus allowances for his journeys to the Convent within the customary limits, and not the forty scudi, at ten for each visit, that he was requiring. An English doctor had attended the courier for three weeks, unsparing in his attentions, and, having restored him to health, had asked no more than fifteen, including his journeys. Dr Rasi was invited to use that figure as his guide. A reasonable financial acknowledgement could be made to the two persons who had accompanied the coffin to Leghorn. As for Marmani, a gentleman from Florence had provided the example of a little girl of seven recently embalmed by a surgeon who had been fully satisfied with a fee of ten louis—forty scudi.

Furthermore, his Lordship had been advised by skilled medical men that the druggist's prices for embalming materials had been much augmented. The expenses incurred with Ghigi's assent, not counting the admittedly fantastic sum asked by Marmani, were getting on for three hundred Roman scudi, and the noble Lord would not honour his promise to pay where there had been any gross over-charge.

[1] Ibid. 3 June. The letter from Marmani's son is dated 29 May.
[2] *LJ.* 20 July 1820.   [3] 46873. 10 June, received 14 June.

This was astonishingly unfair to Ghigi, who may have stressed the celebrated Milord's rank unnecessarily, thereby ensuring in his simplicity that every item would go up, but who could with justice plead that no one had warned him of the scrutiny to which the figures would be subjected. His situation was most unenviable because those whom he had paid or who were claiming payments were his friends and acquaintances in Ravenna, people he constantly met, and who, he complained, were now regarding him as an imbecile.[1]

If we could be sure Byron had had before him copies of all the letters Lega had exchanged with Ghigi before the grasping Marmani had tried to cash in, we could not refrain from blaming him for a peculiar want of scruple: nor is he fully acquitted when we know that much had been withheld from him, because that was by his own wish, and people who delegate authority are answerable for the mistakes of those to whom they transfer it. Nevertheless, it was odd for a banker, while pressing for the settlement of his bill for disbursements, not to send any itemized accounts of them for three months!

Marmani's greed had, in everyone's eyes, overreached itself. To have indulged it would have been mere feebleness. He wrote blustering letters demanding his rights, declaring that services of such high importance as his merited prompt payment, that his fee was not an extravagant one for 'His Excellency Lord Byron, a Grandee of Europe' to pay, and he would not tolerate any tardiness about it. He crazily compared his embalming of this little illegitimate child in an obscure convent with that of Lord Cowper, a great dignitary, which a surgeon had performed at vast expense in Florence, a radiant memory of his student days there.[2] He got his son to write to the British Minister, requesting him to agree that a fee of five hundred scudi was modest, and when there was no reply, he himself took pen in hand and informed the doubtless wondering Lord Burghersh that if, after all his labours on 'the unparalleled Madamigella Allegrina'—as if she were some famous diva—his bill were not settled, he would have recourse to the law, the delicacy of a Grandee of Europe being compromised. The Minister could ask all the universities in Italy, including Pisa, where a Royal Prince of Saxony had been embalmed—though not by him—if a hundred gold louis (he had lowered his sights) was not a fair amount for a rich man, a Lord, a peer of England, to accord him. The Minister remained diplomatically mute.[3]

If Marmani had been able to carry out his threat, he might have had a

---

[1] Ibid. 27 July.

[2] Ibid. Enclosed with letters of Ghigi dated 10, 15 and 29 June.

[3] Ibid. The Minister's wife, Lady Burghersh, had taken an unauthorized copy of Byron's Memoirs. Unhappily, she was persuaded by Moore to burn it.

humiliating shock. In a similar case, discovered by Ghigi, where there had been a lawsuit, the court had awarded only eighty-two scudi to the embalmer, though the subject had been a man, and for little Allegrina probably half that sum would have been judged reasonable. Local sympathy would have been with Byron who had established a reputation for magnanimity, while the surgeon's cupidity had caused many murmurs of disapproval in Ravenna; but unluckily it was only Ghigi who could be sued, since he alone had engaged Marmani's services.

Byron, as was his temperament, over-reacted. He instructed Lega to affirm that thirty scudi would be enough for the surgeon, and fourteen for the druggist. Dr Rasi, who was calling constantly on Ghigi for his fee, was not to be paid till he had reduced it to twenty. The nuns, who had sent a bill for just on thirty-five scudi, must be reminded that, while he had the highest respect for them, they had received seventy in March for the half-year's fees, and the child had died in April, so they had something in hand to meet whatever her illness had cost the convent.

Ghigi's growing resentment was not assuaged by hearing that his own personal expenses would be met in full without being subjected to any examination.[1] Seeing that he was still saddled with Byron's animals, which it had lately been suggested he should sell though they were not at all an attractive assortment, and that his personal service had gone far beyond what any client could expect of a business agent, Lega's conciliatory remarks about Byron's complete confidence in his probity did little to pacify him. Acrimony and sarcasm began to enter into his protests. What is surprising is that Byron—or Lega—did not adopt at once his reasonable suggestion that, if they were to continue arguing about the three hundred scudi, they might at least, while doing so, pay for the items not in dispute.[2]

That Byron often acted irrationally and even, on occasion, with the callousness of a very spoiled young man, no one could convincingly deny; but usually he was not without a high pride which would have prevented his laying himself open to the criticism of his obliging, if too complaisant, banker.

His obstinacy seems to have been the product of several factors. First, I would put Claire's 'furious letter' with whatever accusations and insults it had contained. He had tried to behave well, had sent her a miniature of Allegra with a lock of her hair, and messages intended to be of comfort; and now she had revived all his aversion, so that his genuine grief became tinged with some of the displeasure he had felt when he had seen a fleeting resemblance between the mother and the daughter. A shade had been thrown over Allegra's memory.

[1] Ibid. 7 Aug.   [2] Ibid. In a letter enclosing the belated accounts, 31 July.

Then, as all the funeral arrangements had turned out so complex and so grim, he had become impatient with his mistake in not having her laid peacefully in earth where she had died, and the sordid opportunism of Marmani had revolted him. When he was angry, it had always been his habit to lay about him indiscriminately. In early July came Shelley's death, a major calamity and one which left him with several problems on his hands, amongst which Shelley's friend and his own petulant enemy, Leigh Hunt, was the most oppressive. The hostility of the secret police to the Gambas, resulting in their having to leave Tuscany as they had had to leave Romagna—and ostensibly as the outcome of a brawl between one of his servants and theirs—necessitated yet one more uprooting;[1] while among less grave but still substantial annoyances there were the large bills to meet for the *Bolivar*, almost unused, a long delay in his receiving anything from the Noel revenue, although the arbitrators had awarded him half, and the fact that Count Guiccioli had succeeded in withdrawing Teresa's income.

That 1822 was perhaps, apart from the year of his marriage, the unluckiest of his life does not excuse his inconsiderateness but it may go some way towards explaining it. And Lega's part as intermediary had not been well played.

But now it was Ghigi's turn to put himself in the wrong. He too had been hoping for a 'gratification' and at last told Lega so bluntly—'*ogni fatica merita premio*'[2]—and once again he was put off with a promise that every just debt would be honoured. Yet no money was sent. He held, as has been stated, investments of Lega's, and in an unguarded moment, some weeks before Allegra's death, Lega had told him in writing that if he had not adequate funds to meet some outlay for Milord, he could for the time being use what he had in hand for him (Lega).[3] As the situation between the two deteriorated, largely because of their timidity in dealing with Byron, Ghigi determined to reimburse himself with Lega's money and also hold on to what Fletcher had invested with him.

The consequences of this extraordinary proceeding were that, so far from hastening to Lega's rescue by a settlement with Ghigi, Byron became quite intransigent—his invariable response when he felt there was any attempt to corner him. He advised Lega to go to court, and signed a letter stating that everything his secretary had done had been with his

---

[1] Until the relevant documents from Pisan archives and other sources were assembled by Cline, this domestic fracas at Montenero, in which Byron's pugnacious coachman, Papi, had again used violence, was believed to be the cause of their second banishment, but it is now known that a decision had already been made not to renew their permits. They were, of course, unaware of that.

[2] 31 Aug.   [3] 2 Mar.

approbation.[1] The affair was put in the hands of an advocate named Fava; and so ended the very warm friendship that had existed between the banker and the steward. The law moved no faster in Italy than in England: departure for Greece slowed it down still further, and the case remained outstanding when Byron died. It came before the Tribunal in the spring of 1825, and ultimately Lega and Fletcher were refunded, and Ghigi was compelled to repay with interest the sum he had sequestered. He was reimbursed for his actual expenditure by the executors, for whom Lega had written several précis of the transactions. Hanson found Lega and his importunities most vexatious.

What Hobhouse thought of it all his journals do not record. Lega, with capital to start a macaroni factory in mind, was so very insistent in his eagerness for money that the executors may have concluded there had been a little sharp practice, but that a few hundred scudi were not worth bothering about when there were those great lists of Byron's payments for the maintenance of Suliots and pretended Suliots, for supporting the Artillery Corps of Missolonghi, for the repatriation of numerous Turkish women and prisoners, for subsidies to Greek families in distress, and the daily provisions of a sizeable suite.

Nor do we know how and when Marmani was compensated; nor what happened to Allegra's clothes and little possessions, of which Ghigi had sent an inventory which elicited from Byron no instructions. The animals were sold, even the unfortunate goat. Count Guiccioli, a most unpredictable man, bought one of the monkeys which had formerly been an unwelcome resident in his house. Ghigi had frequently been asked to send a bill for keeping them, but did not do so till after Byron's death, when it was duly settled.

Whatever labyrinth of emotions may have made Byron's conduct so refractory in the matter of Allegra's posthumous expenses, he was perfectly compliant as to those incurred for her funeral in England. These were dealt with by John Murray, that much-tried publisher who had been asked to oblige his poet in many different ways in their association of eleven years, but surely no service had been required of him so bizarre as to receive the mortal remains of a child and perform the offices necessary for disposing of them.

Byron's future references to Allegra, though sparse, show that he felt a deep sense of deprivation, which was accentuated by the news that, on sanctimonious grounds, she had been denied sepulture in a church. On receiving paragraphs from England to the effect that he had tastelessly wished his illegitimate child to have a tomb opposite a pew occupied by Lady Byron, he wrote in one of his letters to Augusta:

[1] Copy in Lega's hand with Byron's signature.

There has been . . . a stupid story in the papers about the funeral of my poor little natural baby—which I directed to be as private as possible, & they say that she was to be buried and epitaphed opposite Lady B's pew——now—firstly—God help me! I did not know Lady B. had ever been in Harrow Church and should have thought it the very last place she would have chosen,—and 2. my *real* instructions are in a letter to Murray of last summer —and the simplest possible as well as the inscription.——But it has been my lot through life to be *never pardoned and almost always misunderstood*— . . . The story of this Child's burial is the epitome or miniature of the Story of my life. My regard for her—& my attachment for the spot where she is buried—made me wish that she should be buried *where*—though I never was *happy*—I was once less miserable as a boy—in thinking that I should be buried—and you see how they have distorted this as they do every thing into some story about Lady B.—of whom Heaven knows—I have thought much less than perhaps I should have done for these last four or five years.[1]

The epitome and miniature of his life was also in some measure that of his death, which in this same letter he foresaw, saying he had no reason to believe his time would be long, never having felt well since the summer. Between his end and Allegra's there were many features in common. Both died of a fever, both were subjected to repeated blood-letting which reduced their chance of survival, and both were posthumously victims of large claims by medical attendants. (Even the Greek doctor, Vaya, sent the executors a bill for putting in an appearance at Byron's deathbed.) Both too were rejected where a resting place had been sought. Westminster Abbey refused interment to Byron and Allegra was not allowed beyond the porch of Harrow Church.

The accounts for the materials used in embalming them are to be found in the Zambelli Papers,[2] lists of names which are still seen on the decorated jars of old chemists' shops—myrrh, aloes, camphor, cinnamon, frankincense, gum storax, mastic, nutmeg, alum, sulphur, cloves, aromatic herbs. Only Allegrina had attar of roses and oil of lavender; but then, the pharmacist's bill had been nearly twice as much as for her father. It must have been a double frustration for Marmani that nobody had looked at his handiwork.

---

[1] Murray copies. 12 Dec. 1822. The inscription was to have been 'I shall go to her, but she shall not return to me'. 2nd *Samuel*, XII, 23.

[2] 46874 Folio 37 and 46873 Folio 157.

11

Rites and Wrongs

Although Shelley's rarefied notions about human perfectability and his active proselytizing against religion struck Byron as odd and far-fetched, he was always generous in praise of him, and quite pathetically ignorant of Shelley's bouts of animosity towards himself. Shelley's denigrations of Byron have often been quoted as if they had permanent validity and without the self-contradictory utterances made on other occasions. While Byron was a man of moods, but with a fundamental steadiness in his friendships which made them durable, Shelley suffered violent oscillations of opinion.

At first he marvelled at his good fortune in having persuaded Byron to come to Pisa. 'Who would have imagined it!' Byron was, after all, a brother poet whom he full-heartedly admired and a first-rate celebrity whose status it would have been an affectation to pretend to ignore. He suggested to Mary that Byron's presence in Pisa would contribute to 'security and protection'. (He had, throughout his short life, what we now call a persecution complex, always seeing himself as harassed and pursued by enemies.)

> . . . Lord Byron has certainly a great regard for us—the regard of such a man is worth—*some* of the tribute we must pay to the base passions of humanity in any intercourse with those within its circle—he is better worth it than those on whom we bestow it from mere custom.[1]

The qualification here was probably a recognition of his having said, a few lines earlier, that Byron was 'not a man to keep a secret, good or bad', and, illogically, that he had made himself a pander and accomplice to slander because he *had* kept the secret in question a year.

Shelley's attitude to Byron was ambivalent from the first. When highly gratified to find himself on an intimate footing with him in Switzerland, he had made such comments in his letters as '. . . he is a slave to the vilest and most vulgar prejudices and as mad as the winds'.[2]

[1] 16 Aug. 1821.   [2] To Peacock, 17 July 1816.

So it was natural that the pleasure he took in his brilliant friend's company should have diminished in the course of months at Pisa. 'The demon of mistrust & of pride lurks between two persons in our situation, poisoning the freedom of their intercourse. . . .' Thus he had written to his wife during his 1821 visit to Ravenna when there had been much less time to develop grievances. 'I think the fault is not on my side, nor is it likely, I being the weaker.'[1] Byron's references to Shelley do not convey the slightest awareness of anything poisoning the freedom of their intercourse, whereas it is evident that 'the demon of mistrust and pride' was very prone to rear his head in an ultra-sensitive young man who keenly felt the world's neglect of his genius and its misunderstanding of his benevolent aspirations.

In Pisa he complained, according to Medwin, that 'the magnetism of Byron', 'the Byronic energy', was hostile to his own powers, and he certainly communicated, however unwittingly, to his friends the idea that they would be brightening his fame if they cast shadows on Byron's. Byron being richer, more eminent, and older than most of the company he kept, it was to be expected that, once the novelty of his hospitality had worn off, the little contingent would begin to rebel against his dominance; and his total rejection of Claire, his seeming indifference to Allegra, heightened their resentment. He remained oblivious to it. Nothing is clearer from hundreds of letters to him still existing than that, behind the affability so many people remarked on with surprise, there was an intimidating character, and Shelley, by far the most dauntless of the group, was tactful with him to the point of duplicity.

Moore notes in his Memoirs (May 14th 1822) that Rogers told him Byron treated 'his companion Shelley very cavalierly'—a view he must have formed when he was a house guest of Byron for two or three days in April just before the news arrived of Allegra's death.[2] Rogers's style of reporting was generally acidulous, and Moore would have been glad enough at the time to hear anything that portended estrangement from Shelley, being one of those friends of Byron who thought he was unwise to have such an associate, and who had written warning him against it.

To excuse himself to Claire for his shooting, dining, riding and talking

[1] 10 Aug. 1821.

[2] There was entertaining on three successive days at the Casa Lanfranchi, specified by Lega as dinners 'for company'. They took place on Apr. 19th, 20th and 21st, the first of their kind since early March. The staffetta announcing Allegra's death came on the 22nd. Byron must have sent it at once to Shelley, to whom he wrote next day that the blow had been 'stunning and unexpected', so long having elapsed since he had heard of her amelioration. 'There is nothing to prevent your coming tomorrow, but perhaps today and yester-evening, it was better not to have met.' This indicates that Shelley had offered to come to him at once, and supports Lega's statements to the effect that Byron was inconsolable and not to be approached. (See p. 331.)

with the object of her loathing, Shelley wrote that he was trying to lull him into security until circumstances might call him to England, and was really only wanting 'to put an end to his detested intimacy',[1] but he continued to frequent Byron's palazzo, and was in fact at this very time promoting with eagerness the journey of Leigh Hunt, his great friend, from England to launch a venture wholly dependent on Byron's money. While he gave one explanation to Claire for consorting with the enemy, he offered another to Hunt; namely, that he was concerned to do what Hunt had asked—'to keep him in heart with the project till your arrival'.[2] '. . . Lord Byron has made me bitterly feel the inferiority which the world has presumed to place between us', he continued in a later complaining letter,[3] thus thoughtlessly ensuring that Hunt would be on the defensive about his own status from the beginning.

It is inconceivable that Byron, whose remarks on Shelley are so different in their tone and import, was conscious in any way of inflicting feelings of inferiority but no doubt he grew restive under sermons about the necessity of overthrowing the whole 'system of society' to which Shelley treated all his friends, not to speak of his very vocal objections alike to worldly habits and Christian beliefs. If he had any influence over Lord Byron, he assured Horace Smith, he would 'employ it to eradicate from his great mind the delusions of Christianity, which, in spite of his reason, seem perpetually to recur . . . '[4] Shelley was quite unable to refrain from giving utterance to his opinions on these topics, and may have occasioned irritation the cause of which he misinterpreted.

Amelia Curran's painting of Shelley, almost all there was to go upon, served to increase the mists of illusion through which his character came to be regarded. Not a work of much strength to begin with, it was reproduced a hundred times, emasculated by so many copyists and engravers that sometimes it seems the picture of a dainty young girl. Much verbal portraiture has been equally false, as we may learn from the straightforward and rewarding process of reading his letters. But there is one word-picture which is little known, having been buried many years in Teresa Guiccioli's French manuscript, *La Vie de Lord Byron en Italie*. It has the merit of giving a vivid idea of Shelley and confirming the esteem in which he was held by Byron—for Teresa, who wrote of Trelawny as a liar and of Leigh Hunt as an ingrate and calumniator, would not have dwelt affectionately on Byron's enjoyment of Shelley's company unless she had pleasant memories of him. Notwithstanding her flowery style in describing the intellectual banquet of their conversation, which ranged,

[1] 20 Mar. 1822.   [2] 2 Mar. 1822.   [3] 10 Apr.
[4] 11 Apr., eight days before he met Rogers at Byron's table.

with wide divergencies of outlook, over 'all the great problems of human existence', she draws Shelley himself with an objective pen.

He was not, she says, a man like any other but a combination of physical contrasts and harmonies without parallel:

> God had made him such, and the bizarre circumstances of his life had contributed. It was said that in his adolescence he was good-looking—but now he was no longer so. His features were delicate but not regular—except for his mouth which however was not good when he laughed, and was a little spoiled by his teeth, the shape of which was not in keeping with his refinement. His skin which, one could see, must have been fine,—either from exposure to rough weather or by reason of his health, was covered with freckles. The hair growing on an extremely small head was chestnut-coloured and thick but not well-groomed—and had already been invaded by some premature silver threads.
>
> He was very tall, but so bent that he seemed of ordinary stature, and although very slight in his whole person, his bones and joints were prominent and even coarse. And yet all these elements opposed to beauty formed an exceedingly sympathetic being—and one must stress the word Being, for truly Shelley appeared rather a Spirit than a man. He was also extraordinary in his garb, for he normally wore a jacket like a young college boy's, never any gloves nor polish on his boots—and yet among a thousand he would always have seemed the most finished of gentlemen. [Teresa wrote *gentlemans*.]
>
> His voice was shrill—even strident, and nevertheless it was modulated by the drift of his thoughts with a grace, a gentleness, a delicacy that went to the heart. Sir Walter Scott said that Byron's beauty was a thing to dream about, as if he would have called it almost supernatural, and such it was. But one might say the same of Shelley from another point of view, for perhaps never did anyone ever see a man so deficient in beauty who still could produce an impression of it. . . . It was the fire, the enthusiasm, of his Intelligence that transformed his features.

It is interesting and convincing that, while Leigh Hunt in his Autobiography (1850) said Shelley's face, despite a weak profile, had from a front view 'a certain seraphical character that would have suited John the Baptist', Teresa, who would not have borrowed anything from that book, if she read it, recalled that his expression was like that of the saintly, ascetic heads in the pictures of Italian primitive painters.

Presenting her subject thus favourably, she saw with clarity nevertheless that Shelley's worship of liberty was an abstraction, that he was Utopian and, as she said, out of touch with the human realities, and therefore caused more harm than he cured: '. . . Shelley for all his goodness was not tolerant towards those who did not think as he did, or who annoyed him. He mocked them pitilessly and did not spare them contemptuous epithets'.

Teresa's sketch has been abundantly verified by evidences she had no chance of seeing, largely suppressed as they were by pious biographers, a widow who brought up her infant son to make an idol of him and, ultimately, a daughter-in-law dedicated to serving at his shrine.

Shelley, intermittently detesting Byron, maintained cordial terms with him and, at their last meeting, on July 7th 1822, borrowed £50 from him. The following day he was drowned with his friend, the young naval officer, Edward Williams, who in Teresa's recollection was 'amiable, polite, and charming'. It was a profound shock to Byron. Without the least notion that Shelley had recently called him 'the nucleus of all that is hateful and tiresome' in society,[1] he sent his publisher and friends those eulogies that have so often been quoted.

Edward John Trelawny now steps into the limelight assiduously generated by himself. From the moment Shelley set sail in the *Don Juan* (never known in contemporary annals as the *Ariel*), fatally bound for Lerici after welcoming Leigh Hunt to Italy, Trelawny by his own account was the principal witness or protagonist of every event. He was what Mrs Thrale called 'one of those large, loose talkers that scarce mean to be believed', and it must have been a joyful surprise to him that, in their gratitude to the man who had given them exactly the Shelley they wanted, Victorian readers placed implicit confidence in him, even when he contradicted himself grossly, invented conversations with people he did not know, and played the swashbuckling hero in every scene his imagination built up.

Something of the reverence he inspired in his role of the old buccaneer who had 'elevated Shelley' (in his own phrase) and constantly snubbed Byron (on his own showing) went on glimmering about him until modern times. Whether or not the mystical tenderness he once inspired still exists, it is now proved beyond dispute that he added a forged passage to a letter from Commander Roberts and most significantly altered the real text.[2] But, long before that discovery, sufficient was known of his fabrications and extravagances to make it remarkable that his testimony,

[1] To Gisborne, 18 June.

[2] The original (sold at Sotheby's on 17 Dec. 1963) shows that Roberts, writing on 18 Sept. 1822, actually said Shelley's boat had been swamped by heavy seas. Trelawny's sensational mind preferred to represent it as having been run down by Italian feluccas for the sake of the bag of money on board. He began to circulate this as Roberts's opinion as early as the following month, even telling Mary so and adding 'a most bitter pang' to her grief. (Jones: Letter to Jane Williams, 15 Oct. 1822.) He published an altered version of Roberts's letter (*Times*, 27 Dec. 1875, reprinted from the *Athenaeum*) to support a tale that an old sailor had made a death-bed confession of the murder to a priest still living at Spezia: and he reproduced this concoction again in his *Records of Shelley, Byron, and the Author* together with other garblings intended to heighten his importance.

unless supported strongly from other sources, continued to be accepted. The unwillingness to discredit one who claimed to have admired Shelley when he was 'a forlorn outcast'[1] resulted in a most unscholarly flinching from investigation. It is an astonishing fact that he could even claim to have deserted from the navy after thrashing an unjust superior officer without a single one of his biographers and editors taking the precaution of seriously researching his quite innocuous naval career.[2]

Liars, once we know them as such, soon grow tedious, and I would not introduce Trelawny into these pages at all (having done so pretty adequately in my earlier volume), if it were not that the Zambelli Papers reveal more of Byron's conduct from the night of his hearing of Shelley's disappearance than we have hitherto been allowed to learn, Trelawny having taken the centre of the stage like an actor who wants to keep all the good lines for himself. So hypnotic was his effect on his audience that no one, quoting his picturesque dialogue with 'my Genoese mate' as he watches the oncoming storm that was to engulf the *Don Juan,* seems to have wondered how an Italian sailor acquired such a command of English, or conversely, how a man who spoke no Italian could have memorized that very idiomatic weather report.

Trelawny not only had no Italian, but no Genoese mate either. The boat was Byron's *Bolivar,* classed by Trelawny himself as a 'small yacht' and 'a little schooner', and the hired crew consisted of a boy, two English-men named Frost and Beeze, and, irregularly, an Italian named Gaetano who was not the mate but a *marangone*—that is, diver, joiner or handy-man. Lega's accounts show that he was employed on carpenter's work, domestic as well as nautical, and as he also calls him a *legnaiuolo* he was more a joiner than a diver.

(There is the complication of another Gaetano in the ledger— Forestieri, the redoubtable but untrustworthy cook. On June 30th he received three pauls for a carriage to take his luggage from Montenero to Leghorn. That was the day after the fracas between him and the coach-man when a knife was drawn, Count Pietro slightly wounded in trying to separate the combatants, and the police called in. Leigh Hunt turned up while calm was being restored. Gaetano, dismissed, wrote to Count Guiccioli complaining about the insufferable way the Countess and her brother were taking over the management of 'Milordo's house',[3] but

---

[1] Letter in the *Athenaeum,* 3 Aug. 1878. 'Fearing to be forgotten', as Teresa shrewdly put it, whenever that seemed likely he broke into public utterances, waiting however for the deaths of those who could contradict him.

[2] This was accomplished at last by Lady Anne Hill with every sympathy for one whose childhood had been extremely brutalizing. The results were published in the *Keats–Shelley Journal* (America), 1956.

[3] Origo, Chapter VII. Letter of 30 June.

though he had a passport procured for him immediately so that he could go back to Ravenna[1] and was temporarily relieved of his duties, he remained in Byron's service nearly three months longer, furnishing the old count with secret reports that helped to release him from paying alimony to Teresa. Byron made a feint of getting rid of the coachman, who had already brought such affliction on the Pisa household by nearly killing a dragoon: but this violent man rejoined his master in Genoa and we find, not without astonishment, that among the domestic suite on the Greek expedition, the aggressive but faithful Vincenzo Papi was included.)[2]

Leslie Marchand has shown that Trelawny composed at least ten narratives of events connected with the death of Shelley and Williams, not counting references in letters, and that there are disparities in them which become greater with time, so that the earliest ones are the least elaborated and 'nearer to the truth than what Trelawny wrote from memory in his later years when all the other English witnesses were dead and when Shelley's reputation was growing and Byron's diminishing'.[3] I do not propose to offer here any close analysis of the self-important assertions of one whose 'autobiography' has been described as 'in essence a boy's dream of heroic and romantic adventure',[4] and whose private conduct was such that Shelley's biographer, White, though giving him much more credence than he deserved, felt obliged to acknowledge 'a recognizable strain of ruffianism' in him, but there are items in the Pisa ledger which make some reassessments desirable. I will preface them with a few paragraphs explaining how Byron came to be concerned.

On the day after the servants' brawl—which gave the authorities a pretext for once more uprooting the Gambas—Fletcher had handed his Lordship just under three crowns to pay for a boat to go out to the *Bolivar* and to provide a repast for the sailors. Trelawny was on board, having met Leigh Hunt on June 28th at Byron's request and brought him to Leghorn from the harbour of Genoa. Hunt is vague about dates, but concurrent events fix his arrival at Montenero as the 29th and his departure, after staying the night, as the 30th, Byron driving to Leghorn with him—we may reasonably assume from Lega's entry—and taking him on board the schooner again. It must have been an unpleasant surprise to learn that Hunt had brought six children with him. I say a surprise because Lega, returning to Pisa in advance of Byron, had immediately to hire five beds, besides buying an extra one later that month.[5]

---

[1] 2 July. All Pisa and Montenero entries for 1822 are in 46876 unless otherwise stated.
[2] E.g. 46877 Folii 129 and 168 where he is named. He did not go as far as Missolonghi.
[3] *Keats–Shelley Memorial Bulletin*, 1952.
[4] Hill, *Keats–Shelley Journal*, 1956.   [5] Entries of 1 and 28 July.

Hunt put up at a Leghorn hotel with his family, and Shelley came from his temporary summer residence near Lerici to see him, and they spent a day or two there, during which Shelley told him—we have Hunt's word for it—some unpleasant things about his future host,[1] and also, as we learn in a more roundabout way, enough about his own married life to make Hunt feel aggrieved with Mary. She, in a dark cloud of depression and foreboding after a serious miscarriage, was with Jane Williams at their ill-chosen retreat. She wrote Hunt a letter imploring him not to let any persuasion of Shelley's induce him to come there, and expressing a wish that she could break her chains and leave that dungeon.[2]

Hunt and Shelley went to Pisa where the former was then installed in Byron's palazzo, much less appreciative than Mary had expected him to be, and Shelley left for Leghorn, where Williams was awaiting him, very eager to be home. They embarked for Lerici on July 8th, Shelley first changing the £50 borrowed from Byron into crowns—about two hundred and twenty,[3] and spending some of it on provisions for their lonely sea-shore house. Byron, while at his banker's, arranged to send another two hundred crowns to Moore for the relief of the Irish poor, entrusting it to the Rev. Thomas Hall, a British chaplain at Leghorn.

The story of the *Don Juan*'s non-arrival at Lerici, of the agonizing anxiety of Mary and Jane, and their setting forth themselves, after days of suspense, to find out what had befallen the *Don Juan*, their coming to Pisa with post-horses and being received kindly and feelingly by Byron and Teresa near the midnight of the 12th after Hunt had gone to bed—this is one of the most familiar tales of literary history. Mary drove with Jane to Leghorn in the small hours of the 13th, and after a brief attempt to rest, they found Commander Roberts[4] at another inn. It was he who confessed to them his apprehensions and how, standing first on the mole, then on a tower, he had watched the gathering storm swallow up the little boat. Trelawny does not figure in Mary's famous letter describing the calamity[5] until he accompanies her back to Lerici where he stayed with the two unhappy women until the evening of the 18th; but in his own accounts he is ubiquitous, 'patrolling the coast with the coast-guard, stimulating them to keep a good look-out by the promise of reward', etc.

---

[1] E.g. 'I have had bitter reasons . . . to regret the loss of my beloved friend, who, between ourselves, only remained on terms with Lord B. latterly, in order to do me service.' (Hunt to his brother, John Hunt, 26 Dec. 1822.)

[2] Jones, 30 June.

[3] Williams had changed £100 in Nov. 1821 for just under 450 crowns. The rate had not diminished in 1822.

[4] Trelawny's friend, Daniel Roberts R.N., also a notable braggart, promoted himself from Commander to Captain—except when writing annually to the Admiralty for extension of his leave.

[5] To Mrs Gisborne, 15 Aug. 1822.

The patrolling was actually done by Roberts, to whom Byron wrote on July 14th, 'Your opinion has taken from me the slender hope to which I still cling [clung]. I need hardly say that the Bolivar is quite at your disposition . . .'[1]

Byron himself was very active. On the 13th, the morning after Mary's midnight visit, he sent an express to Dunn, the banker and merchant in Leghorn, and next day we find these entries by Lega:

		Crowns	Pauls	Crazie
July 14th	To Gius[eppe] Carlesi of Leghorn who on instruction from Dunn searched the seashore to obtain news of Sig^r Shelley and Villiams [sic]	2		
	To the carrier Dom[eni]co Bini for a light carriage to Sarzana with Dom.co Saviozzi, sent to Lerici with the above object	6		3
	To the said Saviozzi for his fee	2		
16th	To Matteo Giuntini for going express to Leghorn where he had to spend the night		6	
17th	[Milord] Posting with 4 horses to the Bocca del Arno with tips to postilions and stablemen	6	4	

We know that the mouth of the Arno, like that of the Serchio, was explored. On the 18th the messenger Giuntini was again sent express to Leghorn, and I conclude the purpose was to keep in touch with Roberts on the *Bolivar*. One of them must have suggested a meeting at Serchio.

		Crowns	Pauls	Crazie
July 18th	[Milord] Posting with 4 horses to the Foce del Serchio, with tips as before	9	2	
	To Dom.co Saviozzi for acting as guide to the coachman		5	
	Dinner [at an inn] with guests	5	9	4
	To Giovacchino [acting coachman] for his expenses at Serchio and elsewhere	1	5	4
	Refreshment of horses and stable expenses	4	5	5

The guests at the dinner were Leigh Hunt and Roberts, as we may note from a letter Hunt wrote to Trelawny at Lerici, the cost of posting which Lega reimbursed. It is dated the evening of the 17th which is, I think, an error. Apart from the several entries in the ledger, there is a reference by Hunt to a body 'lately' washed ashore and buried at Serchio. If the 17th were right, it would have been that very day, for it was then that Williams's corpse was found.

The week's accounts for housekeeping at Pisa were much larger than usual, comprising fourteen crowns four pauls for meals 'with company'. No normal entertaining was going on, so the guests must have been the companions of the search.

[1] Quoted by Marchand in his notes to the article in the *Keats–Shelley Bulletin*.

On July 22nd Byron made the return journey to Bagni di Pisa, five or six miles from home.

	Crowns	Pauls
Posting with 4 horses	4	7
Coachman's expenses and dinner at an inn	5	4

I tentatively assume that this had some connection with the quest, but Shelley's body, and that of Charles Vivian, the unfortunate boy who was drowned with him, whose death did not evoke one word of recorded sympathy from anyone, had already been found at different sites near Viareggio, and Mary, with Jane, had just returned in uttermost misery to Pisa. Perhaps Byron, like Roberts, was now endeavouring to trace the missing boat. His correspondence for this period is scanty and, for the most part, concerned with worry about the absence of expected remittances from England. Though Shelley had irresponsibly informed the impecunious Hunt that the death of Lady Noel had made Byron rich, 'a still richer man',[1] not a penny had yet come from her estate, nor even his normal income. Kinnaird had dispatched it by a route which made him complain of 'your Circular or Circuitous notes'.[2] He was having trouble too with his Montenero landlord, Dupuy, who had fallaciously guaranteed a good water supply at the villa, and was suing him for breaking his lease. (It was perhaps because of the necessity of using salt water instead of fresh for his daily bath, regarded by Hunt as a sybaritic effeminacy, that he conceived a fancy for it, and had it brought in casks to his palazzo. The recurring payments for this luxury are a constant feature of his Pisa bills after the return from Montenero on July 2nd.)

Expenses which can be attributed directly to the loss of the *Don Juan* now cease until August 7th, when we find:

	Crowns
To Mateucci, Sergeant Commandant of the Fort of Migliarino by way of gratuity for service rendered and to be rendered	1

The Fort of Migliarino was near the place where Williams's corpse had been cast up nearly three weeks before, horrendously disfigured and corrupted. It had at once been interrred in an adjacent field where it could and should have been decently left. The gratuity to an officer at the Fort with specific mention of the service to be rendered might suggest that Byron was there, about nine miles from Pisa, but there is nothing else at all in the ledger to indicate that this was so, only that he went there on August 15th for the cremation. Trelawny, in some statements, gives the impression that he made the identification dramatically in the presence of

[1] 17 Feb. 1822.   [2] Murray MS. 31 Aug.

Byron, but identity had to be established before permission for the cremation was granted.

I think Trelawny saw the body very soon after its discovery, and that
he may have tipped the officer a crown which he reclaimed later on from
Lega, Byron being the recognized paymaster for the search operations,
and also in the habit of paying minor expenses for Trelawny—e.g. six
pauls for his return journey in a carriage when he visited Montenero on
June 19th and anything it cost him to live on the *Bolivar*. I bring what
may seem an extremely petty matter to the reader's attention because
Trelawny was the man who wrote, to the long detriment of Byron's
reputation:

> In all the transactions between Shelley and Byron in which expenses had
> occurred, the former, as was his custom, had paid all, the latter promising to
> repay; but as no one ever repaid Shelley, Byron did not see the necessity of
> setting the example.[1]

Byron never allowed Shelley to be out of pocket through him on any
occasion. The statement that he left Mary Shelley 'destitute' after her
husband's death, with which Trelawny immediately followed the one
quoted above, is also malicious nonsense.

Shelley's body, recovered on July 18th, was, like Williams's and the
boy's, revoltingly mutilated. Trelawny identified it before the sanitary
authorities of Lucca had it buried in strong quick-lime.[2] The boy, lucky in
having no friends desirous of tampering with his remains, was interred
near the spot on which a wave had washed him—that is, according to
more than one of Trelawny's narratives; whereas, in an official letter he
himself eventually published, the body is said to have been burnt at once
on the shore.[3]

Who it was that proposed to disinter the others we can only guess. The
original purpose was to give Christian burial in the English cemetery at
Leghorn to two men, one of whom was a most ardent anti-Christian and
the other almost certainly a sharer of his views—it being very difficult to
live at close quarters with Shelley and not share his views. The idealization
of the 'pagan rites' which actually took place has obscured the first intention, and the fact that Trelawny, through the Rev. Thomas Hall, went so
far as to order full-sized walnut coffins appears to be little known. Hall,

---

[1] *Recollections*. This passage was omitted from the book when it was republished as
Records.

[2] Biagi.

[3] *Records*. Letters reproduced in that volume must be read with caution, for, whenever the originals turn up, they are found to have been freely edited, even altered. It is
rather remarkable that the boy's body was burned when Shelley's, subject to the same
laws in the same Duchy, was put in quick-lime.

however, wrote a statement with his bill to the effect that Edward Trelawny, Esquire, 'an intimate friend of the deceased' (i.e. Shelley), had made the necessary preparations for the re-interment:

> But in consequence of subsequent orders, most unexpectedly arriving from Florence [the seat of the Tuscan Government], countermanding the former, —all they had done—was now no longer of any use, for the purposes for which they were intended,—& consequently new arrangements were to be made, in order to effect what the Government had finally consented to,— viz—the burning of the bodies—on the ground where they had been buried, —to the no small prejudice of the Heirs of the deceased.—This declaration, the underwritten deems it necessary to make for the justification of himself —as well as his Colleague,—for the amount of the several following accounts, notwithstanding every exertion they could make for their diminution.[1]

Trelawny paid the bill on behalf of the heirs, four hundred and thirteen Tuscan livres; but this sum included the iron grid for the cremation, sixty livres, and the boxes for the ashes, described as walnut covered with black silk velvet, and two copper plates which were engraved for them. In English money this was about £17, from which we may gather some perception of what an economy it was to live—or die—in Italy.

Trelawny took charge of all the obsequies and did it with tremendous gusto. Even Guido Biagi, an Italian who, in the 1890s, investigated and published much of the official correspondence, and who accepted Trelawny at his own valuation, was obliged to admit that he 'rather seems to enjoy describing the lugubrious scene', and he might have held that opinion more strongly if he had seen how many times he did describe it, dwelling even till advanced old age on the macabre details—and changing them at will.

That Trelawny had a schoolboy's taste for the ghoulish and the gruesome could not be denied by anyone who had read his *Adventures of a Younger Son*; and the two cremations completely organized by him satisfied that craving to play the leading role which resulted even in such artful falsifications as his publishing a letter from Roberts to Mary Shelley with a pretence that it had been addressed to him—'Dear T'.[2]

At the time of the wreck Mary was greatly under his influence, for it had fallen to him to break the news to her, and this he had done with exemplary tact. It may have been at his prompting that her request for disinterment was made. She herself, as we can judge from the turn of her talents and her successful plea to be allowed to look at Byron's body after it had been in spirits for months, was by no means shrinkingly sensitive,

---

[1] Peck, Vol. II, 405–406.

[2] *Records.* It was to tell her the *Don Juan* had been salvaged. The original was sold at Sotheby's with other dishonestly edited letters. (See p. 336.)

but we may doubt if she would have consented to have her husband's corpse dug up had she known what pitiful remnants were left of it. Anticipating criticism, Trelawny said, in what may be his first written account, that the graves were so shallow the sea would have reclaimed the dead, and also that an officer had warned him half-wild dogs would devour them at night.[1] So far from really supposing such violations likely, the quarantine authorities had at first refused permission to remove Williams, while weeks passed between the burial of Shelley in July and his exhumation on August 16th without anything of the kind having happened. Dogs do not devour quick-lime.

Mary liked the idea of the pagan rites. Of Jane Williams's feelings we have little knowledge. She faded from the picture as Shelley's growing fame so heightened the value of anything relating to him that Trelawny began to transfer features of the Williams ceremony to that of Shelley. As for Byron, he probably thought that the quarantine laws positively required the unburying. 'Neither Mrs Shelley, Byron, nor Leigh Hunt, knew anything but what I told them', Trelawny boasted years later,[2] and in this instance he was doubtless writing the truth.

We return to the dispassionate commentary of the ledger:

		Crowns	Pauls
August 15th	Journey posting with 4 horses to the Torre di Migliarino with tips to stablemen and postilions	10	2

That was the day of Williams's cremation. There is no allusion to any refreshment, but Byron had twelve crowns in cash given to him before leaving, so he could have paid for anything they felt able to eat.

		Crowns	Pauls
August 16th	To the Sanitary Officer of Leghorn Antonio Gori for assistance at the exhumation of the late Capt. Villiams	2	
	To the Sergeant Commandant of the Torre di Migliarino for services rendered with his guards at the said operation	3	

These sums were gratuities. There is in the Shelley collection at the Bodleian Library a bill from the Health Office of Leghorn for the journey of the Guardia di Sanità to Spezia and their hire for five days. The amount, like that of the Rev. Thomas Hall, is given in Tuscan livres, £62. 13. 4. (i.e. sixty-two livres, thirteen soldi and 4 denari, about

[1] Document in the *Keats–Shelley Memorial*, Rome, Narrative 1 in Marchand's numbering.
[2] *Records*, p. 242.

thirteen crowns).[1] By some arrangement the Livornese guard may have been present at both ceremonies, though Shelley was cremated in the Duchy of Lucca. This seems to be borne out by the period of hire being so long and by Byron's tipping being done the next day, when he was at Viareggio, the same officers apparently being in attendance.

Byron had gone back to Pisa with Hunt on the 15th, after swimming and suffering severely from nausea. Williams's ashes were committed to his care in the box Trelawny had ordered, but I fancy he would have sent them at the earliest opportunity to Henry Dunn, who had taken charge of Allegra's coffin on its way to England. At any rate, the usual messenger, Giuntini, went to Dunn next morning, and Williams's ashes were dispatched to England when Shelley's were taken by Trelawny to Rome.

		Pauls	Crazie
August 16th	A bottle of wine from Florence to take with Milord to Viareggio	2	1
	To the pharmacy *del Serpente* for 2 lbs of incense	8	

We can hardly doubt that these purchases were the wine and frankincense thrown on the pyre. It is an oddity in its way that the pharmacy was called the Serpent, one of Byron's nicknames for Shelley.

	Crowns	Pauls	Crazie
Posting with 4 horses, return journey to the Torretta with tips	9	7	
The carriage with 3 horses from the Torretta to Viareggio, and from Viareggio to the Torretta, with tips	13		
To the coachman for his expenses yesterday at Migliarino	3	7	4
To the same for expenses today at Viareggio	5	3	

The topography of this second journey I confess I find somewhat baffling. There was a place called Torretta (or equally La Torretta), but it was a number of miles south of Leghorn whereas Viareggio is to the north. If they went there first, that might explain why they arrived there with four horses and left with three, a horse having been sold that same day. On the other hand, why should Byron go a long distance out of his way, prolonging the sad drive for hours, to sell a horse for as little as twenty-nine and a half crowns? And would Hunt have missed such a fine

---

[1] Leaf 534–5. The sign for livres was the same as for pounds, which makes for confusion, but Italians avoided it by writing *sterlina* when British money was meant. Trelawny states in one of his narratives (No. 3) that all who had assisted were paid and discharged on the same day, but that may be as accurate as the date he has assigned to the proceedings, Aug. 13th, which is two days before they took place.

opportunity of expatiating on his niggardly and cynical behaviour? The simplest explanation is that the Torretta in question was one of the turrets along that coast-line—there were many—which had been fixed upon as the landmark for the coachman, driving from Pisa by an overland route, via Lucca. There was no direct coastal route. Trelawny had spent the night at Viareggio and went by boat to the spot where Shelley was buried, which it took some time to locate.

Leigh Hunt was understandably incapable of watching his most generous friend being incinerated, and he remained in the carriage, but within view of the horrible spectacle when he dared look. Byron too, he says, 'kept studiously aloof, and was not in sight while the melancholy proceedings took place'.[1] Byron confirms this:

> Ld Byron was not present at the burning of Mr Shelley's body—some delay having taken place in the exhumation. Ld B. took the opportunity of bathing in the interim and having swum to the Schooner which lay in the offing the operation was finished before his return.

This was written at the end of the one narrative of Trelawny's which he was certainly shown—a version meant for publication by Leigh Hunt and genuinely prepared within a few days of the events.[2] It avoids specific mention of whether Byron was present or not present, merely stating 'Lord Byron wished the skull to be preserved', and this was transmuted thirty-six years later into a resolution on Trelawny's part to save it from being profaned by use as a drinking cup![3] Having seen Williams's body reduced to a single bone (the jawbone, which Trelawny pocketed), Byron might well express a hope that Shelley's skull, so recently the seat of an extraordinary brain, would remain intact, but this was clearly before the exhumation, since he says he went swimming while that was delayed, and it cannot be imagined that, on a document he knew was to be given to Hunt, he would write a declaration the other would instantly recognize as false.

Afterwards, when Trelawny's claim to distinction rested on his much-advertised familiarity with two great poets, he could not bear to admit that such a celebrity was absent from such a celebration, and he had Byron observing the scene 'silent and thoughtful'.

---

[1] *Lord Byron*, 2nd Edition.

[2] 39168. Narratives numbered 5 and 6 by Marchand; No. 5 relating to Williams, No. 6, a continuation, to Shelley. Trelawny's hope of having his account printed in *The Liberal* was not realized. Mary, when she read it, may have objected to the grim details (though much less painful than in other versions) or possibly dreaded publicity that might annoy Sir Timothy Shelley. A few years later Hunt used an abridgement of it in his book.

[3] *Recollections*.

Byron's swim to the *Bolivar* resulted in sunstroke and excruciating pain which left a prolonged aftermath of ill health. In two letters which do not touch on the death of Williams and Shelley at all,[1] he gives the duration of the swim as three hours in blazing heat. To Moore he wrote:

> . . . The consequence has been a feverish attack, and my whole skin's coming off, after going through the process of one large continuous blister, raised by the sun and sea together. I have suffered much pain, not being able to lie on my back or even side; for my shoulders and arms were equally St. Bartholomewed. But it is over—and I have got a new skin, and am as glossy as a snake in its new suit.[2]

In this letter he did allude to the cremations, but calmly and distantly, and I think he makes no further reference to them. My impression is that, haunted by the sight of the drowned and defaced Williams, he suddenly felt he could not see Shelley in the same plight, and was unwilling to admit what would have seemed weakness to his admirer; for, however sneering Trelawny might be about Byron in retrospective jealousy, an admirer at this period he most eagerly made himself out to be.

Before taking leave, for the moment, of the fancy-dress Pirate whose legends have so muddied the sources of biography, I would call attention to a remark of Shelley's which is missing from every published eulogium of his 'intimate friend'. We know that Shelley himself barely mentioned him in his letters—I believe the only two conspicuous references to him are his telling Leigh Hunt he would be met on his arrival by 'a Mr Trelawny, a wild but kind-hearted sea-man', and his writing to Gisborne a doubt as to how long 'the fiery spirit of our Pirate will accommodate itself to the caprice of the Poet' (i.e. on the *Bolivar*). In that same letter, on June 18th three weeks before his death, complaining to his correspondent about the lack of congenial company, Shelley made an exception of the Williamses, who were then at Lerici. Jane's taste for music and 'elegant form and motion' compensated for her not having 'literary refinement', and Williams was 'the most amiable of companions'. He went on: 'I have a boat here which was originally intended to belong equally to Williams, Trelawny, and myself, but the wish to escape from the third person induced me to become the sole proprietor.'[3] That third person could only have been Trelawny.

In the first of the many books which were to 'elevate Shelley' at the expense of Byron, Leigh Hunt tells how, on a drive 'worthy of a German ballad', they returned to Pisa putting on 'a monstrous aspect of mirth', and how having dined little and drunk too much they had hastened

---

[1] Murray MSS, to Kinnaird, 20 Aug. and to Hobhouse, 2 Sept. 1822.
[2] 27 Aug. 1822.   [3] Jones. The passage is suppressed by Ingpen.

away from the site of their ordeal 'singing, shouting, and laughing'. It has always been assumed that this wild hysteria was after the second cremation, Shelley's; but if Hunt's reminiscence is read carefully, it will be noticed that it followed on '*one* of our visits to the sea-shore', and that must have been the first. Apart from the careful vagueness of the phrasing, Hunt being well aware that the reader would find it more interesting to associate the grotesque ride with Shelley's obsequies than Williams's, there is his remark, 'What the coachman thought of us God knows; but he helped to make up a ghastly trio'. It was a trio after the visit to Migliarino, but a quartette when they left Viareggio, because, as we discover from one of his entries, Lega was there:

	Pauls	Crazie
Expenses of Lega on the journey to Viareggio and Lucca	8	4

That sum would have amply covered his refreshments, but could not have come anywhere near paying his fare in a separate vehicle, so he must have been taken and brought back in Byron's carriage. It would have been his business, naturally, to sell the horse, which may have been unharnessed at the Torretta and delivered by him to the purchaser, one Cavaliere Roncioni.[1] It is in the ledger as 'the Spanish horse'.

A week or so before, Byron had sold two better horses to Henry Dunn for a hundred and eighty crowns, and a stableboy had disposed of two monkeys for twelve.[2] The reduction of the stable which it cost him so much to keep up was his most rigorous economy. The monkeys—not the same two that he had left in Ravenna—may have changed hands because they were troublesome, especially with Hunt's children on the premises, or else in preparation for the impending removal from Tuscany, which now occupies a large amount of space in the ledger, and was a necessity he very much regretted.

With this ahead of him, he was working himself up into a state of real nervousness about money. In some measure it was due to the exasperation most people feel when they learn how much red tape has to be unwound before they can take possession of an inheritance. Byron's apportioned share of his late mother-in-law's revenue was long in coming, and his bad relations with his wife and her lawyers made him suspect deliberate obstructiveness. This drove him to fury, because so much of his capital was under their control through the marriage settlement. He must also have been worried by his realization that a family of eight, not to speak of a

---

[1] Why Byron was paying for hired horses if using his own is a question I shall not attempt to answer, ignorant as I am of the mysteries of the Italian posting system.
[2] 46876 Folio 34.

baby yet unborn, were helplessly and resentfully dependent on him. Trifling in comparison but still disturbing was Teresa's deprivation of any income whatever. He had also to contemplate the decline of his literary earnings, not through decrease of sales but the cheap pirated editions which reduced Murray's profits and, as a result, what he could afford to pay for new works.

He wrote Kinnaird several pressing letters about his anxieties, and their plain statements of his financial position show how ludicrously the unworldly Shelleys had exaggerated what they called 'his enormous fortune'. In a summary just before he left Pisa, he reminded Kinnaird that he still had debts in England to pay off, the principal creditors being the Hansons:

Now to meet these, let us see. Besides your late Credit of 2000 in *advance* (which I do not mean to touch unless in some emergency) I have still £1700 in your former Circulars, and 1200 in ditto lately received—in all 2900 £,— also in the bonds of Messrs. Webb of Leghorn 630 £ sterling (3530 in all between you) and about three or four hundred pounds cash in the house, total about £4000—more or less. Now supposing me to spend a thousand pounds between this and J[anuar]y 1823, in removing to Genoa, which is expensive as comprizing furniture and a complete establishment, there would still be a surplus of 3000 remaining to begin the year withal. This would have been still greater, but I was foolish enough to build a slight Schooner which *was* to have cost £300, but did eventually cost nearly £800, her expences since amount monthly to about *60 dollars*—i.e. 720 dollars per annum, say about £180 sterling pr annum including men's wages and sundries.

I have however sold *three* horses, and keep of course that number less in my stable, having still six, three carriage and three saddle. Then I lent Leigh Hunt 250 last winter, bought him 50 pounds worth of furniture, have advanced him about 50 more, and lent Shelley fifty, besides buying his furniture since his decease, in all—say—about five hundred pounds more or less. This with one or two unexpected expences of about one hundred more, make in all about fourteen or fifteen hundred pounds, which *would* have been added to the *3000* of present surplus at the end of this year, had I not been imprudent.

I could not help assisting Hunt, who is a good man, and is left taken all aback by Shelley's demise.[1]

Byron had bought Shelley's furniture, and that of Jane Williams too, to help them through their difficulties, and he knew the loan to Shelley would never be repaid because he has asked Mary to keep the ninety-odd crowns that were left of it, salvaged with the boat, offering as well to be

[1] Murray MS. 26 Sept. 1822. He later estimated the schooner at £1,000.

her banker till her affairs were cleared up.[1] (He had put the matter in Hunt's hands, which was about the worst thing he could do, for Hunt, unknown to him, was borrowing from her.)

With their fantastic ideas of his wealth, any cautiousness about expenditure seemed to members of the Shelley circle contemptible meanness. Shelley himself from early youth had lived and assisted his friends mainly by reckless borrowing on terms even more ruinous than those Byron had consented to at eighteen. While radically disapproving of inherited wealth, he had made disastrous use of his expectations from the entailed estate of his father, and until the latter should die, his own consisted of nothing but debts, the major part of which were the consequence of his approaches to two authors much older than himself, both of whom he had informed, before meeting them, that he was the son of a man of property. William Godwin and Leigh Hunt had known exactly how to welcome that kind of admirer.

Mary's intense grief was heightened by her being stranded in a foreign country, but before she was worked upon by Leigh Hunt to reject Byron's offers, she wrote many times to him and others of his kindness to her, and after his death she asked herself in her journal if she could ever forget his 'attention and consolations' to her during her deepest misery[2]— though she had so far forgotten them during his life as to label him for posterity a man of 'unconquerable avarice'.[3] She may have been unaware that a donation of £25 from Byron had gone to the assistance of her father, Godwin.[4]

It is not possible except in a few instances to separate Byron's financial help to Mary from his own domestic expenses at the time of his reluctant move to Genoa in the wake of the Gamba family, because even Lega could not work out what proportion of the sums paid to packers, carters, boatmen and bargemen for the transport of immense loads of household goods was for the Hunts and Mary and what was Milord's. The Shelley and Williams furniture could not have filled any real need of Byron's for he had brought several waggonloads of his own from Ravenna and had purchased more in Pisa: but Jane required ready money to go to England, and Mary to live in Italy while he tried, as executor, to persuade Sir Timothy Shelley to make some provision for her and her son; and he lost no time in getting an appraisal, which was done on August 25th.

---

[1] *LJ.* 6 Oct. The boat was found towards mid-September. Roberts wrote to Mary on 14 Sept., 'I shall see Ld Byron and arrange for paying the expences of getting her up'. Trelawny falsified this correspondence almost beyond recognition.

[2] Jones, *Journal.* 15 May 1824.

[3] Jones, *Letters.* To Jane Williams, 23 July 1823. The estrangement between Byron and Mary Shelley is the subject of Chapter XII in *The Late Lord Byron*.

[4] Murray MS. 24 Oct. 1822.

On September 7th and 8th, Lega's principal entries were:

	Crowns	Pauls
To Signor Dunn for the expenses of the Bolivar	227	
To the widow Shelley for furniture sold as receipt[1]	221	4
To the widow Williams for the same	148	4

The *Bolivar* had been used chiefly by Trelawny, who saved his pocket whenever he could by living on the boat. (This was stated by Teresa, with evident veracity, when she had read what he published in 1858 of Byron's avarice.)[2] Byron seems scarcely to have gone on board except the day he took Hunt back from Montenero and on two previous occasions, June 19th and 26th, when he was accompanied by Count Pietro. He must have intended to make much more use of the vessel, having had six tablecloths and a set of napkins supplied for it by Dunn in time for his second visit, and a code of signals devised which included the message, 'I have those on board that it would not be pleasant for you to join',[3] showing that close communication with the *Don Juan* had been planned; but of course the Shelley catastrophe took all the promise of pleasure out of that costly toy.

Biographers have generally tended to echo Trelawny's scornful tone about Byron's slowness and difficulty in uprooting himself from any place where he had settled. Having a retinue of servants, horses and other animals, a houseful of furniture, a great quantity of responsibilities, and a compulsion, no matter what changes he made in his environment, to keep hold of the thread of his creative work, he naturally found it more of an effort to move house than a footloose wanderer without serious attachments. The departure from Pisa moreover was complicated by Hunt's insistence on going too with all his family.

Important letters from Byron were suppressed, as I have shown in my previous work, when Thornton Hunt edited his father's correspondence for publication, but Byron kept the replies which prove that he had strongly advised the Hunts against coming to Genoa, and had offered to pay for their return to England. Contrary to Hunt's highly disingenuous account of setting up the *Liberal*, which he ascribes to Byron's initiative, representing him as 'mainly influenced by the expectation of profit', expecting 'very large returns', and thinking 'he should get both money and fame', he was perfectly aware that Byron's notion of starting a periodical had originally been conceived with Thomas Moore in mind, that Shelley had seized on it as a way of bringing his friend to Italy and procuring him financial assistance, and that Byron had become hesitant at

[1] See Appendix 11, 'The Shelley Furniture'.   [2] *La Vie.*
[3] Item in Sotheby's Catalogue, 17 Dec. 1963.

an early stage. He could scarcely have forgotten that Shelley had professed to be maintaining good relations with Byron only for the purpose of 'keeping him in heart'.

Hunt's assertion that a poet of European reputation had hoped to enhance his fame by publicly launching on a venture with him is yet more absurd than his alleged belief in the magazine as a means of enrichment. Byron had every reason to know the association was regarded as a shocking comedown for him: and Hunt had every reason to know that Byron would not be getting any profits. He wrote to his brother soon after the issue of the first number: 'Lord B. by the bye said to me the other day that he did not mean to call upon us for his money for the Liberal, till we had realized a good deal.' The miser who was financing the paper had added in that conversation 'that it would be advisable to get as many good writers as possible, & pay them handsomely'.[1]

The *Liberal* did make profits, which Hunt duly retained—and how hurriedly he slipped that fact past the reader after lingering over Byron's mercenary motives! ('I shall only mention . . . that I unexpectedly turned out to be in the receipt of the whole profits of proprietorship.')

But the success was far from brilliant though the first issue contained one of Byron's most brilliant works *The Vision of Judgment*—which swiftly brought a prosecution for sedition on Hunt's brother as publisher. From the first Byron had needed bringing to the sticking point, and the disapproval of his friends, his dislike of Mrs Hunt—who had always, Hunt tells us, disliked *him*—the depressing circumstances surrounding the whole undertaking, made it most weariful to him to contemplate having that family on his hands as long as he remained in Italy: but there they were plainly resolved to be, as Hunt demonstrates answering a letter in which Byron must have said that they ought to have stayed in the milder climate of Pisa or been repatriated:

> With regard to my coming to Genoa, it was a most unwilling journey on my part, but my wife herself urged me to take it, and I concluded that it would be less frightful to her to go into a worse climate, which was still Italian, than remain in a place where we should have none to help us, & could not possibly reckon upon anything but the most alarming anxieties; for I sometimes feared, even as it was, that my health would not stand out much more writing, yet this, of course, was the only resource on which I could reckon after Shelley's loss: and I came to Genoa, purely that the Liberal might go on.
> Of all the pecuniary kindnesses which you have done me, I have a particular account, except with regard to the expenses of that journey. (I

[1] Pierpont Morgan Library. 26 Dec. 1822, quoted by Marshall. 'I tell him I am not a good man of business', Hunt remarked in his Skimpole manner in the same letter. He was advising John Hunt for the sake of form to send accounts.

think for instance I can say without even referring to my books that during my abode under your wing I received altogether about seventy pounds, *including* the very unwilling expenses I was obliged to go to in the inn where you wished me to wait, before departing to Genoa!) An account of the expenses to Genoa I should be much gratified if you would tell Lega to give me, having asked for it at the time in vain.

I thank you therefore for the renewal of your offer about England, but I have only a choice of evils, & Italy is at all events a good deal wholesomer & cheaper for me.[1]

An account of the expenses would gratify him! The occasions when Hunt paid anything he owed to anyone must be rare indeed, nor do I suppose Byron would have been so fatuous as to have a bill prepared for him. Had he done so we can imagine what Hunt would have made of it when he cashed in on all his grievances. But if one had been seriously required, Lega would have been ready with it.

I have spoken of the ledger as 'dispassionate' but there are one or two instances in which it discloses Lega's feelings. In Hunt's case, he wrote against each entry in darker ink a conspicuous cross. Whether he had learned enough English by 1828 to read Hunt's onslaught on the patron whom he (Lega) described as his 'tutelary spirit' and 'the most celebrated and respectable man of the century',[2] or whether Fletcher, who spoke a kind of pidgin Italian, gave him some account of it, or whether again, he had resented the Hunt ménage while the six children were still practising their parents' doctrine of untamed naturalness in the Casa Lanfranchi, we sense those baleful crosses as a denunciation. And here they are, signalizing with precision all but the amounts that did not go through Lega's hand—namely, whatever Byron paid from his pocket or through his bankers, or bestowed on Hunt by way of copyrights and renounced fees:

			Crowns	*Pauls*	*Crazie*
July					
1	X	To the Jew de Montel for hire of 5 beds for a month	15		
27	X	Given to Signor Hunt by order of Milord	20		
Aug.	X	„ „ „ „ „	80		
Undated	X	To the Jew de Montel for 5 beds used by Signor Hunt for the month of August	15		

[1] Murray MS. July 1823. His repeated refusal to return to England, all expenses paid, was conceivably so that he might gather from the *Liberal* enough money to keep him out of a debtors' prison on arrival. He had left many creditors behind.

[2] 46874. To Barff, 21 Apr. 1824. *Rispettabile* might, perhaps, be better translated as 'worthy of respect'.

			Crowns	Pauls	Crazie
Sept.					
6	X	To Fletcher for collecting a letter for Hunt		2	2
11	X	Given to Signor Hunt by order of Milord	40		
15	X	,, ,, ,, ,, ,,	20		
17	X	Collecting letters from the post for Hunt [Mrs] Shelley [Mrs] Williams and Clermont [sic]		6	4
18	X	Given to Signor Hunt by order of Milord	80		
20	X	Collecting Gazettes and a letter for Hunt		2	3
29	X	To the glazier Mattei for repairing and replacing broken glass and windows in the house	3	0	4

This last item was presumably damage done by Hunt's children. There was also paintwork or wallpaper to be dealt with. 'Can anything be more absurd', Mrs Hunt had written in her diary two days before, 'than a peer of the realm—and a *poet* making a fuss about three or four children disfiguring the walls of a few rooms.'[1] Mr Hunt, she said, was much annoyed by his complaining of it.

The family must have been requested to spend the last night or two at a local inn so that the furniture could be packed and the damage to the ground floor made good. Quantities of stuff had been dispatched throughout the month; and a carrier had delivered on the 25th a specially made basket for his Lordship's three geese, the ones he had been nurturing for a Michaelmas feast, but had decided instead to keep as pets.

The cortège went off in two parties, travelling sometimes by water and sometimes by land. Byron was attended by his courier, his valet, and the men concerned with horses, and soon he had his chasseur too, for Tita joined him delightedly when they reached the Duchy of Lucca, to which territory his sentence of exile did not extend. The Hunts proceeded separately, with Lega, holding the purse strings, following the same route.

			Crowns	Pauls	Crazie
Sept.					
27		Bread grapes and wine for the Hunt family at Pietra Santa[2]		3	
28	X	The Inn at Massa for tea and supper yesterday evening, staying the night, breakfast, roast fowl with fruit and bread to eat en route, and fodder for the horses	9		

[1] 23 Sept. 1822, quoted by Origo.

[2] I give entries not marked with a cross only when Hunt's name appears in them or when they duplicate Byron's. A number of expenses of the removal would have been incurred in any case, and others again must have been increased by the eight extra travellers but cannot be separated.

Sept.			Crowns	Pauls	Crazie
28		Fee for entering the Duchy of Lucca and a tip at the Customs	1	4	
		Tips for the chambermaid, stable-men etc.	1		
		Guides crossing the river Massa with the Hunt party		6	
	X	To the two Dutchmen of Pisa, car-riage and relay of horses as far as Lerici with tips	18		
30	X	To the innkeeper of the Croce di Malta for Saturday evening, yester-day and this morning for the Hunt family and two horses with tips, as per account	23		
		Beans and hay for the horses[1]	3	7	4

The parties met at Lerici, where Byron was held up four days by illness, which he told Kinnaird nearly a month later was 'a violent attack of bile and rheumatism & constipation &c &c, but [I] recovered, all but a cough, which has somewhat thinned me'.[2] From the time of his acute affliction of sunburn which must have kept him in pain and fever for some days, he lost weight and went on losing it after the curious assortment of symptoms which overcame him at Lerici until, when Lady Blessington met him six months later, she found him 'extremely thin, indeed so much so that his figure has quite a boyish air'.[3] Though he spoke of being recovered, he was never again a healthy man. Hunt, preoccupied with his own health as he was to a most neurotic extent—though he was to live to be two months short of seventy-five—was incapable of making the slightest allowance for Byron's.

Having travelled post with eight horses, Byron arrived at Lerici before the Hunts' more unwieldy group, but, owing to his illness, they left at about the same time, Hunt first visiting Shelley's recent abode with Trelawny, who was bringing the *Bolivar*. Lega came overland with a stableboy on horseback, the carriages being dispatched by water, and had a most unpleasant ride. After seeking a guide and other assistance, he reached an inn at Borghetto 'exhausted by a disastrous journey', and his horse had to be re-shod. It takes an effort of imagination now to conjure up roads that were often mere ruts in the precipitous hillsides and miles on end without landmarks. The Hunt family, however, went from Lerici to Sestri in a felucca.

Sept.			Crowns	Pauls	Crazie
30	X	Porterage and transport to and from the inn to board the felucca with the Hunt luggage		5	4

[1] Byron's own stable expenses are a distinct weekly item.
[2] Murray MS. 7 Oct. 1822.   [3] Blessington, *Conversations*.

Oct.			Crowns	Pauls	Crazie
3	X	Carriage to take the Hunt family from the marina to the inn [at Sestri]		3	
4	X	The innkeeper at Sestri providing for Lega and horses for 3 days, supper and breakfast for the Hunt family [after staying the night]	13	2	
	X	Refreshments for the Hunt family and horses at the inn on the road	1	8	5
	X	Carriage for the Hunt family from Sestri to Genoa including tip to the coachman	15		
5	X	To the skipper Poggi for taking the Hunt family from Lerici to Sestri with the landau [Three carriages and part of the household form a separate entry]	20	0	6
27		Given to Signor Hunt	100		

The last item was, of course, the 'cool hundred' of Byron's crowns which Hunt demanded with a kind of airy insolence, adding that he would soon be coming upon him for more.

It will be seen that the journey, which he took because he was determined to be near someone who would support him but towards whom he felt intense animosity, was not a trifling matter, and that, apart from several hundred pounds supplied to him before his coming to Italy or by the proceeds of Byron's works, he had had about five hundred crowns in cash or kind from Lega, who perhaps did 'dole it out' to him rather grudgingly, that sum being nearly double his annual salary. Both Byron and Shelley wrote in different contexts that a crown was worth about four times as much in Italy as the nominal equivalent in England, and Lega saw money through Italian eyes.

Hunt did not fail to 'come upon' Byron for more, but the additional payment was not made through Lega. It was wanted, Hunt explained, for paying Mrs Shelley back 'some crowns' he had borrowed from her, 'it being my intention (which you will be kind enough not to let her know) to avoid, if possible, putting her to any expense at any time, this being the very least I can do in return for all Shelley did for me'.[1] Here was a truly Hunt-like way of saying that Byron was to give him the money to pay Mary back without making her aware where it came from.

Shelley had been by no means ignorant of his friend's parasitic tendencies, having helped him repeatedly and incurred, with Hunt's full knowledge, crippling debts to do so. Hunt had arrived, he wrote to Mary, 'with no other remnant of his £400 than a debt of 60 crowns'. The

[1] Murray MS. 24 Oct. 1822.

absence of comment here is itself a comment. Byron, for all Shelley's adverse tone throughout this letter, seems to have repaid the debt, for, touching on the trying situation in one of his financial discussions with Kinnaird, he mentions having settled a bill for Hunt at Leghorn.[1]

On the day of his communication to Mary, Shelley received from Lega ten crowns. If this had any connection with the exiled servants, Tita and Antonio, we should expect Lega to mention the purpose following his custom, and I think it more probable that Shelley, who was very short of cash himself, needed it for hospitality at Leghorn to the entirely penniless family he had imported. It is also noteworthy that only 'ninety odd crowns' out of the £50 he had borrowed were salvaged from the boat. (About four hundred crowns in all were found below the deck, but the greater part belonged to Williams who had also drawn cash at Leghorn.)

I doubt exceedingly that Shelley had spent a hundred crowns and more on provisions in those pre-refrigeration days. It is open to conjecture at any rate that part of the £50 was handed over to Hunt, to postpone as long as possible his next application to Byron, which Shelley anticipated with embarrassment, being so largely answerable for his becoming Byron's guest. Otherwise we cannot fathom how Hunt, arriving with nothing, lasted out till July 27th, when he had his first contribution from Lega's strongbox.

'Mrs Williams Claire & I live all together we have one purse & joined in misery we are for the present joined in life.'[2] So Mary told Maria Gisborne when she had been a widow seven weeks. It was generous of her to put it so, for Claire as usual was merely a dismal burden upon her. She had been supported by Shelley's bounty—and perhaps some scruples he had reason to feel about her—from the age of sixteen, and now she drew on the slender resources of Mary, who wrote to her on September 15th: 'I wish when I was in Pisa that you had said that you should be short of money & I would have left you more—but you seemed to think 150 francesconi plenty. . . .'[3]

This was an answer to a letter Mary had received from her expressing her utterly self-absorbed dejection at the prospect of going to her brother in Vienna. When we remember that it was addressed to a grief-stricken young woman who had lost an adored husband, three out of her four children by him, and every happy prospect in life, we may understand Byron's aversion better even than by reading the dossier of Claire's vehement communications to him.

To me there seems nothing under the sun but misery, misery . . . I am to begin my journey to Vienna on Monday. . . . Imagine all the lonely inns, the

[1] Ibid. 23 Dec.   [2] Jones, c. 27 Aug. 1822.   [3] Ibid.

weary long miles if I do. Observe whatever befalls in life, the heaviest part, the very dregs of misfortune, fall on me.

> Alone, alone, all, all alone,
> Upon a wide, wide sea,
> And Christ would take no mercy
> Upon my soul in agony.

. . . If I should write you scolding letters you will excuse them, knowing that with the Psalmist 'Out of the bitterness of my mouth have I spoken.'[1]

Though Mary's attitude to Byron was, like Shelley's, vacillating, they seem to have had a mutual understanding about Claire's selfish disposition, because, in an allusion to something Mary wrote to Byron about an offer by Claire, he replied, 'As to "sharing Mrs Godwin's small estate"—I rather suspect that [it] is your own which she means'.[2] Mrs Godwin was still very much alive and her estate was less than nil, whereas Shelley had left Claire £12,000. She could not possess it until his father's death, but they were all optimistically convinced that Sir Timothy was a fragile old gentleman instead of a hale and hearty one who was to live till 1844, keeping Claire in a state of tormented anxiety. After the death in 1826 of Shelley's elder son, Charles, born of his first marriage, the baronetcy and entailed fortune—or what Shelley's post obit bonds had left of it— would descend, on Sir Timothy's demise, to Mary's Percy, and if *he* were to die, Claire's only hope of independence would vanish with him. When she thought him exposed to any risk she wrote letters barely concealing the reason for her solicitude. Meanwhile, Mary's means being insufficient, Claire had to maintain herself at last.

She has been praised for her courage in becoming a governess and going as far as Russia in that capacity. Hundreds of Englishwomen were governesses in the remotest parts of Europe, and few, I fancy, could have been so submerged in self-pity: 'I am always unhappy for I can enjoy nothing—for I am always surrounded by common people and their incessant squabblings frighten[s] away every happy thought and every sublime meditation.' She calls herself: 'the wretched wanderer who is condemned to live with such tasteless animals. My whole heart turns to gall. . . . I can only compare myself to some unfortunate miscreant pursued by a shouting rabble. I wish I could paint the hate and disgust these people inspire me with.'[3]

Yet she was not stranded among barbarians, but in a circle which

[1] Clarke, probably 11 Sept. 1822. The verses are misquoted from *The Rime of the Ancient Mariner*.
[2] Bodleian Library, fol. 526, 10 Sept. 1822.
[3] Stocking, *Journal.* 2 May 1825.

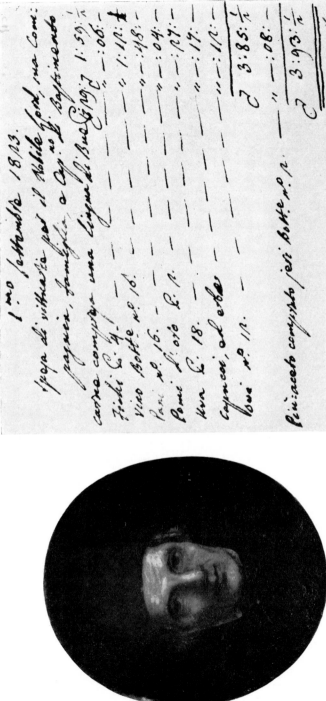

Account for one day's catering for Byron and his suite in Zambelli's manuscript, 1823

Lega Zambelli from a miniature which belonged to his daughter

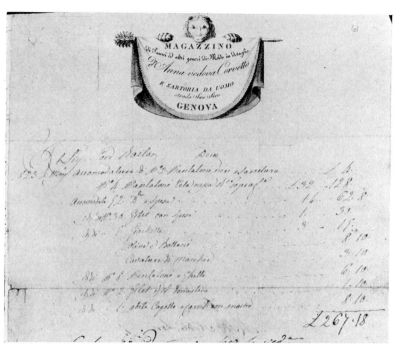

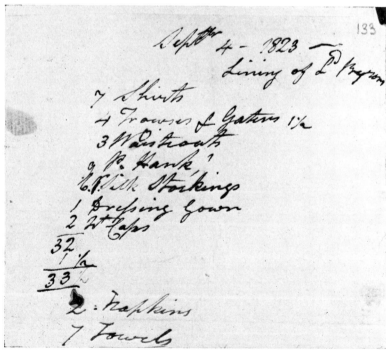

Bill for clothing on Byron's departure for Greece, Genoa,
14 July 1823

Laundry bill for Byron in Fletcher's manuscript, Cephalonia,
4 September 1823

contained well-educated and polite acquaintances of her own nationality—
some of them governesses it is true—and an admiring, intellectual
German, Gambs, who shared the tastes she derived from Shelley. What
Mary suffered through Shelley's curious attachment to this jealous,
irritable, and demanding incubus is expressed in a rash outpouring to
Trelawny, who had pretended to be in love with both, and was typically
treacherous to both:

> Claire always harps upon my desertion of her—as if I could desert one
> I never clung to—we were never friends.
> Now, I would not go to Paradise, with her for a companion—she
> poisoned my life when young—that is over now—but as we never loved
> each other, why these eternal complaints to me and of me. I respect her now
> much—& pity her deeply—but years ago my idea of Heaven was a world
> without Claire—of course these feelings are altered—but she has still the
> faculty of making me more uncomfortable than any human being—a
> faculty she, unconsciously perhaps, never fails to exert whenever I see
> her . . .[1]

The human condition is never static, but unfortunately for the judg-
ments of posterity, when cataclysmic events happen it is as if a film were
suddenly stopped in the midst of projection and all the actors stand poised
making their dramatic gestures, which thus receive an artificial effect of
perpetuity. Shelley dies after being reunited with Hunt in everlasting
friendship—with Byron as the common enemy. Mary is the tragic wife
turning in her need to the noble-hearted Trelawny, Claire the wronged
victim eternally paying the price of one youthful indiscretion.

But let the reel go on turning again, and we shall find that nothing
about these characters is permanent after all except the fact that one of
them is dead and another soon to follow. Claire becomes a cantankerous
and mendacious old woman, much disliked for her pretentiousness,
quarrelling with everyone, trying after Mary's death to sell Shelley's
letters to Shelley's son, who loathes her; the noble Trelawny turns into an
equally cantankerous and even more mendacious old man, the vindictive
public and private disparager of Mary. She for her part lives long enough
to find him envious, dirty, and disagreeable, 'destroyed by being nothing',
while Byron she looks back upon as 'generous, openhanded and kind'.[2]
Hunt, having profited much from writing about Byron with malice unparalleled, grows penitent, or at all events sees a chance of profiting again,
and re-introduces most of what he has said before, but wearing a guise of
magnanimously admitting his former want of magnanimity. He, the

[1] 14 May 1836, quoted from Sotheby's catalogue 17 Dec. 1963.
[2] Murray MS. To John Murray, 26 Jan. 1830.

radical and republican journalist, vitriolic in polemics, mellows down into a supplier of adulatory verses in the *Morning Chronicle* hailing the birthdays of Queen Victoria and the births of her royal infants, and is granted a civil pension. He also draws a useful annuity from Mary, who looks upon him contemptuously now, with an undeluded eye.

Such are a few of the developments unfolded among those whose years were not cut short. Who can doubt that Shelley, if he had lived, would have been equally subject to change, and that Claire might have followed Elizabeth Hitchener and Eliza Westbrook into the outer darkness where Brown Demons dwell, and Hunt, like Godwin, been recognized as an opportunist who had basely taken advantage of a gullible and ambitious young man?

12

Domestic Economy at Genoa

Genoa was foreign territory requiring passports and permits. Two frontiers had to be crossed with all the luggage, huge boatloads of it, passed by customs officers. The removal was a painful upheaval which had unsettled Byron and his household for weeks. As early as September 2nd he had written to Hobhouse, who was about to visit him, that his furniture was being packed and he had not a table or chair and scarcely a stool to sit on, and when he left Pisa on the 27th, he was already weary and dispirited, and perhaps sickening for whatever disorder it was that detained him at Lerici and left him debilitated for a long while afterwards. Hobhouse had come and gone, urging him to break the damaging connection with the Hunts. The scandals that had gathered about his name had been on the grand scale, but now the hostile press treated him as one who was keeping company with the second-rate, and the worst of it was, that company had turned out neither amusing nor grateful.

He really could not help working—it was a necessity to him: the main source of all his pleasures was communication, and he was sure he had never communicated in a wittier or wiser style than now: but here were his friends advising him not to write so much, and his publisher Murray resenting the Hunt alliance, yet not showing the encouragement that might have helped him to escape from it. So even the material benefits of his fame were failing him. A kind of panic possessed him as he wrote his letters to Kinnaird about the Hansons' incredible bills (for which they still could not be induced to render a detailed statement), the distresses of his new publisher, John Hunt, who paid no advances nor, ultimately, any arrears either, the revived claims of Mrs Massingberd's daughter and the delays in receiving any proceeds of the Noel estate.

It worried him very much that his share of his wife's inheritance was contingent upon her survival because she was reputed to be on the verge of the grave, subsisting only on a milk diet (her addiction to mutton chops was a family joke, but ever since the separation her admiring circle had regarded her as an invalid); and he repeatedly asked Kinnaird to see that her life was insured for a large amount.

He became preoccupied with money to an extent that gave some justification to those who murmured amongst themselves about his avarice, though they were all persons who in one way or another had drawn some benefit from his liberality. His friends, who knew his moods and eccentricities, smiled over his assurances that he was 'keeping a sharp look-out on candle ends',[1] and waited for his next outbreak of profusion. He was not wholly jesting, for he decided soon after being installed in his new enormous home, the Villa Saluzzo, that he would relieve Lega of the bookkeeping and do it himself. He had so little knowledge of arithmetic that he asked Kinnaird to send him a ready reckoner, telling him: 'I cast up my household accounts, & settle them daily myself, and you cannot imagine the difference.'[2]

It is possible that the servants who had direct dealings with tradesmen had been in receipt of some small rake-off—that was a very ancient custom—and Byron may not have become suspicious of the extent of it until he went over all the disbursements of recent weeks for moving his carriages, livestock, goods and staff. If there was any row, it probably arose from his discovery, not made till October, that Lega had given no less than thirty crowns to the cook, Gaetano Forestieri, to return with his wife to Ravenna after his long-deferred dismissal following the fight with the coachman. A departing groom had been content with only eight crowns for the same journey. By now Byron had almost certainly learned that Forestieri was in Guiccioli's pay, and he was so annoyed that he deducted twelve crowns from the steward's salary. Lega was naturally aghast at this, but found his patron adamant. Nevertheless, according to a statement he was to make to the executors,[3] the noble Lord, some little time afterwards, admitted that Lega had not been wholly in the wrong and, while he would not restore the twelve crowns, said he would make it up to him in some other way, but never did so.

The executors reimbursed him, though sceptical about that and some of his other several claims. Lega, trying to get capital for starting up his macaroni factory (a plan about which the executors knew nothing), was tiresomely importunate. I cannot picture him, from his correspondence, as a man who would let his employer get away month after month with an absolutely unfair deduction, and I think there must have been something dubious in his transaction with Gaetano—they had both worked for the old Count—which caused Byron, in his extreme way, to say he would distribute his own money for the future. At any rate, though Lega still

[1] Murray MS. 27 Oct. 1822.
[2] Ibid. 16 Dec. misdated 19th in *Correspondence*.   [3] 46878 Folio 105.

dealt with the weekly catering, the full-scale ledger is blank from October 27th 1822—exactly the date on which Byron first informed the amazed Kinnaird that he was paying all bills personally—and, unless some Zambelli Papers have been lost, it was not resumed till April 14th 1823. The Genoa housekeeping is therefore not as consistently documented as that of Pisa and Montenero.

The currency changed to the Genoese livre, or lira,[1] often called a franc in the reckonings because Genoa had recently been a French outpost and the values were equal. The rate of exchange stood at upwards of thirty to the pound sterling in the 1820s, so anyone with English money to spend enjoyed an even greater advantage than elsewhere. The use of the pound sign for a unit worth little more than eight English pence is at first puzzling, and as it has led several Shelley biographers and editors into error, I shall avoid it. Eightpence in Genoa had a purchasing power of two or three shillings in Britain, and that again would have bought ten to twelve times more than in the year before our decimalization in 1971.[2]

Byron paid £24 per annum for the Villa Saluzzo with a courtyard, a garden, and more than forty rooms, and everything else was proportionate. With that as our basis, we may glance at some items in the ledger before, in autumn 1822, he relieved Lega of keeping it, and from spring 1823 when he decided that watching candle ends was a diminishing satisfaction and reinstated his accountant.

Having reduced the number of his horses from nine to six, and shortly afterwards to four, he had one groom less, and Giuseppe Strauss, the courier who had been hurt in the Pisa affray, was also given his travelling expenses and returned home. Whether for convenience, because they were living in a suburb, or economy, the staff, consisting of Fletcher, Tita, Lega, and Giovacchino (the coachman who at Montenero had temporarily taken Papi's place) now had their meals provided for them, and a charge was made upon their wages of fourteen livres a week each. The remaining Romagnole groom continued to have his allowance for a pound of meat and a bottle of wine a day. Seventy livres a week were given to Lega to cater for the rest, including his Lordship. Who now did the cooking I have failed to discover; perhaps someone from the Gamba-Guiccioli household, which shared the establishment. It was not an arrangement Lega cared for.

---

[1] I am using the term *livre* because *lira* cannot now convey any notion at all of what the coin then meant. The words both of course stand for libra, a pound.

[2] I take this estimate from Vol. III of Gerald Reitlinger's book, *The Economics of Taste*, finding it fully verified by the prices of commodities advertised in magazines and tradesmen's lists.

There were some extras for Milord, paid for separately, chiefly his own special vinegar, the sugar and lemons now constantly at hand to make lemonade for him, his tea, and, above all, his asparagus. From April 1823 asparagus was bought almost daily at from two to four livres a time until it went out of season. That sum would have purchased a good deal in Italy, so we may take it that he had a marked fondness for it. Oddly enough, there does not seem to be any consumption of butter compatible with such a penchant. Dairy products other than cheese never appear much in the lists. Byron was partial to truffles, a very expensive delicacy at three livres five soldi for six ounces, but they could seldom be got for him. Otherwise his diet was plain and nearly vegetarian.

There were no more *ciambellette* (tiny doughnuts) but there were *biscottini*, which he may have soaked in vinegar as he had formerly done with potatoes. He was no longer in need of losing weight, but the use of vinegar had become a habit, like the destructive practice of taking strong purgative pills, still occurring repeatedly in the cash book. This too, with frequent doses of aperient salts, had begun as a slimming aid but seemingly persisted as a need. His chemists' bills indeed were always very big, but that may have been because he was inclined to dose his household. I do not mean he went among them like Mrs Squeers administering brimstone and treacle, but he was ready, whenever there were feverish symptoms, with such remedies as Peruvian bark, now known as quinine, while potash water and magnesia were in liberal supply. It would take a medical historian to interpret the uses of most of the contents of his medicine chest.

He had great faith in the health-giving properties of honey, and large quantities of it were bought at all times to make a mash for his horses. In Greece he provided honey for two sick stableboys.[1] For pain there were only soporifics, chiefly alcohol or laudanum, with their uncomfortable aftermath; for disinfectants little but vinegar or wine. 'A flask of wine to wash Medoro, bitten by Moretto',[2] 'Wine for treating the sailor's wound',[3] 'Wine for washing the English dog',—these items figure in the later accounts making us wonder what little incidents gave rise to them. The English dog was a new character and destined to be an important one. He makes his appearance in the ledger at the beginning of May 1823, when Byron received him as a present from a young naval lieutenant, Edward Le Mesurier, gratefully promising to take care of him and never to part with him for any consideration.[4] Lyon, named after an earlier

[1] 46877. 24 Jan. 1824.

[2] 46876. 25 May 1822. Moretto was a bulldog, Medoro the dog presented by Captain Hay on the day of the Pisa affray.

[3] Ibid. 24 Aug.

[4] 46877 and *LJ*. 5 May 1823. Lyon—or Lion—received his injury on 11 May. Perhaps the other dogs were jealous of the newcomer.

favourite, was actually an outsize Newfoundland. He remained in the closest companionship with his master till the latter's death, and accompanied his body to England.

Of table wine Byron, since his illness, had taken very little, that is unless he drank some of the *vin ordinaire* supplied for the staff at one livre per large flask, which is unlikely because his taste, when he indulged it, was still for first-rate claret. Even his gin, bought in earthenware bottles at four livres each, averaged only about one bottle every five or six days—though to be sure the bottles are described as large. The *limonata serale*, as Lega called his evening drink, was possibly gin punch made with lemons. He was, however, very temperate at this time, finding that every excess brought disagreeable consequences.

The complacent James Wedderburn Webster, who was so universally disliked that his *entrée* to intelligent society is as inexplicable as the knighthood which had just been conferred on him, had written some little while before, 'I hear you are strangely alter'd, what I don't credit— grown stupendously corpulent'.[1] And it must have been gratifying when this old acquaintance turned up in Genoa—still owing him £1,000 borrowed nine years before—to be found as thin as he had been in his youth.

One of the first things he did on settling in Genoa was to engage a tailor, who was paid five louis[2] for work that seems to have been alterations, as there are no corresponding bills for materials. The ostentatious Lady Blessington recorded, as her first impression, that, although his whole appearance was 'remarkably gentleman-like'—as opposed, presumably, to poet-like—his coat was much too large for him, and his clothes looked years old and 'purchased ready-made', so badly did they fit him. This was in April 1823, just before he had a second tailor working for him seventy-six days on end preparing his wardrobe for Greece. What she does not say is that the Blessingtons had called on him unexpectedly and inopportunely, when he may well have been wearing one of the outfits he was about to discard. His youthful extravagance had naturally subsided, but certain particularities remained to the end of his life—an abundant supply of very fine linen being the most notable. 'He invariably paid the most scrupulous attention to cleanliness [wrote Hamilton Browne], and had a certain fastidiousness in his dress, strongly savouring of dandyism, of which he was far from disapproving; at least, he infinitely preferred it to a slovenly disregard of dress.'

Compared with Lady Blessington's lover, Alfred D'Orsay,[3] who got

---

[1] Murray MS. No date, c. 1819.

[2] 46786. 13 Oct. 1822. In livres, just under 119.

[3] The diaries of Henry Edward Fox, who was thoroughly familiar with the *ménage*, completely nullify Michael Sadleir's theory (in *Blessington–D'Orsay*, 1933) that D'Orsay

through three fortunes, including hers, largely by his expenditure on personal display, Byron's appearance in 1823 was doubtless modest, but he never lost his aptitude for cutting a figure whenever he was minded to; and Lady Blessington's writings are so often an attempt to demonstrate her superiority in compensation for her not being received in society, that we may ascribe some of her more belittling opinions to the various kinds of pique from which she suffered, and, of course, to her skill as a journalist, writing with the 'slant' magazine readers have always enjoyed. The 'Conversations' first came out as a series in the *New Monthly*.

Byron was not above having his old clothes repaired, an economy D'Orsay would hardly have cared about. It cost one and a half livres to recover a collar with black silk, the same price as a tablet of superfine transparent soap.[1] Ready-made clothes were unthinkable except for gloves, hats, and accessories. He bought a straw hat in Genoa for eight livres.[2] We must adjust our idea of the Byronic 'image' to picture him wearing it. Less Byronic still, there was a silk umbrella, described as old when repaired in Pisa for three pauls;[3] but I think that must have been for his chasseur to hold over him as he entered or left his carriage on wet days: umbrellas were for pedestrians.

On account of the weakness of his ankle, he always wore boots. He had a pair of *coturni* made in Genoa for twenty livres by one Luigi Giacchiere, and he must have been delighted with them because he ordered two more pairs from the same maker, and yet again two pairs ten days later, and still more—three pairs of waxed cloth boots at nine livres a pair—before going to Greece, besides repairs to existing footwear.[4] His right foot required a special kind of sole added inside, and so he went with an ample reserve. Polish was a fairly costly item at two and a half livres a bottle. A pair of gloves was only six.

Throughout his last weeks in Italy, Byron was renewing his wardrobe. From the widow Corvetto, who supplied all sorts of men's wear, and whose billheads suggest a shop that was worth seeing, he ordered among other

---

was asexual, Lady Blessington anti-sexual, and their relations platonic. Lord Blessington Fox called 'a drivelling drunkard', whom she had persuaded to marry her. D'Orsay made an arranged marriage with Blessington's daughter for her fortune, which he squandered, and, though often unfaithful, he continued to keep house with Lady Blessington during her widowhood.

[1] 46877. 15 Apr. and 15 May 1823.

[2] Ibid. 12 June. It was perhaps the Leghorn chip straw mentioned by Hamilton Browne.

[3] 46876. 30 May 1822.

[4] 46877. 30 May 11 June, 21 June and 9 July 1823. The cothurnus at this date seems to have been a laced-up boot, as several pairs of laces were furnished. Waxed cloth was the nearest approach to waterproof. The pantaloons were fastened over the boot beneath the instep with little straps.

things, four pairs of superfine cloth pantaloons at thirty-two livres each, and had many repairs done to his own and his servants' garments. Her bill was just under two hundred and sixty livres,[1] while a jobbing tailor, Battista Devoto, was paid just over three hundred. Devoto charged two livres a day extra for working at the villa 'for the greater convenience of Milord'.[2]

His work included making a tartan *pastrano*—the kind of long cloak that can be spread out over the crupper of one's horse—lined with fine imperial serge and trimmed with bronze braid. Materials, even to sewing threads and linings, were listed apart from workmanship, but there is no invoice for Byron's tartan, a Stewart, which he may have had by him some years. D'Orsay did a drawing of him in a tartan jacket with a sort of fringe round the collar. Ten years before, he had shown a partiality to Scottish dress by having with his two pairs of plaid trews and matching gaiters, an elaborate jacket worthy of young Lochinvar.[3] For his Scoto-Italian *pastrano* there were buttons and pockets covered with something called white devil skin. Double and triple rows of buttons with fancy buttonholes were the trimming *par excellence* for men's clothes in the 1820s and especially for jackets made *à la militaire*, which Byron naturally favoured when preparing for Greece. Cords, braids, and untranslatable kinds of haberdashery, were used for his froggings and borders.

Fresh bread was bought for 'thoroughly cleaning' a blue cloth cloak, and white wine for washing new nankeen for a jacket. (Nankeen itself was perfectly washable so this small item is slightly mysterious.) Byron had a merino cloak—probably the one in which he wrapped himself to sleep on deck when he gave up to Fletcher, who was afflicted with a chill, the only mattress on board the vessel that took them to Missolonghi.[4]

One of Devoto's many varied tasks was to mend some mothholes in his Lordship's uniform. Unless I am in error, this must have been the very aide-de-camp dress of scarlet cloth which he had ordered from his London tailor when planning, abortively, to set out on new travels in 1813. With its resplendent epaulettes and gold lace, he could never have had any occasion at all to wear it, and there had been three or four years when it would not have fitted him; but now that he had regained his youthful measurements, it could come in useful at last. It may have been the suit in which he disembarked at Missolonghi, a red uniform according

---

[1] 46877 Folio 9 and 46878 Folio 61.   [2] Ibid. Folio 116.
[3] Murray MS. The 1813 bill of John & Thomas Edwards. In 1822 the visit of George IV to Edinburgh had created a vogue for clan tartans even on the Continent, but Byron's enthusiasm for Scotland as romanticized by Scott did not need that stimulus. He wore Stewart by reason of his maternal descent from James I.
[4] Murray MS. Letter from Count Pietro Gamba to Hobhouse, 11 Aug. 1824.

to Gamba. In the five trunkfuls of clothes he took to Greece, however, there were at least four uniforms, eight pairs of gold or silver epaulettes, and innumerable swordknots and other soldierly ornaments.[1] These, with a large amount of headgear, must have been supplied by military tailors and hatters and paid for from his bank account, as they do not appear in the Zambelli Papers.

Among the last invoices for his Genoa purchases is one for eighteen handkerchiefs, two silk velvet cravats, and six of cotton velvet.[2] Immaculate starched neckcloths were gradually giving place to less uncomfortable ways of announcing exclusiveness. In D'Orsay's drawing Byron is wearing a wide black stock—and black stocks had been anathema to Brummell. The young D'Orsay was to bring in very different fashions from those restrained ones Brummell had favoured—though at twenty-one the 'Parisian Paladin', as Byron called him, was not yet a full-blown dandy.

His letters to Byron are deferential, as indeed are Lady Blessington's, and for that matter almost anyone's except those of brash acquaintances and genuinely intimate friends, for no man outside the circles of princes was more accustomed to be addressed in adulatory strains. The patronizing air with which Lady Blessington was to write and talk about him in the years to come are nowhere hinted at in her many flattering approaches to him during the two months spent courting his society.

Although he several times refused her invitations, his going at all into the company of this handsome, exuberant, and notorious woman was naturally disturbing to Teresa, whose life had become more and more enclosed since the days when she had paraded her cavalier before the assemblies of Ravenna. She was even now only twenty-three and, apart from the factor of jealousy, might have wished to participate in the lavish entertainments which were Lady Blessington's speciality. Her social position as Byron's mistress was a sacrificial one and besides this there was the language difficulty. She resolved to conquer it, and began to take regular English lessons, one of the few ways in which she put her lover to any expense. The teacher charged a high fee, eight livres a lesson six days a week.[3] Byron never lived to hear her speak English, but by the time she came to London in 1832, an object of intense curiosity, and was taken up in gushing but two-faced friendship by none other than Lady Blessington, she not only spoke and wrote adequately, with the sort of mistakes that lend an attractive piquancy, but had the doubtful pleasure of reading all the books and magazine articles that came out about Byron.

It was during the Blessingtons' stay in Genoa that Byron started on the preliminaries of his Greek venture. At first he had contemplated

[1] Inventory of 31 July 1824, quoted by Marchand.
[2] 46878. 12 July, Folio 61, 1823.   [3] 46877, numerous entries.

making use of the *Bolivar*, laid up some months at the Arsenal as one of his economies. Commander Roberts who, having built the schooner, practically regarded her as his own, had nevertheless been doing her up at Byron's expense, and was half disposed to sail her to Greece—in which case, the expedition might have had a second disaffected and disloyal member to go hunting with Trelawny.[1] But a day or two before leaving Genoa, Lord Blessington visited the boat unaccompanied by Byron, and was seized with a 'headstrong wish' to acquire her.[2] He got her, nearly new as she was, for four hundred guineas, less than half her cost. Byron, notwithstanding his eagerness to amass a sum of money substantial enough to be of real service in Greece, wanted to hand the *Bolivar* over in a condition that would do him credit, and paid one Agostino Gunino a hundred and forty-four livres for some re-gilding and a dyer, Brindarsi, sixteen livres for re-tinting the covers of her ten silk cushions.[3]

At about the same time, he was finding that the four horses to which he had reduced his stable were not enough for his needs, and the question arose of his buying one of Lady Blessington's. In *The Idler in Italy* she represents him as beating her down over the price, eighty guineas, though he had 'begged and entreated' her to sell the horse; but, like many others who published reminiscences—Hunt, Trelawny, Galt, Harriette Wilson—she did not realize that posterity would be able to read the letters he received as well as those he wrote. These in no wise support her tale of pressure brought to bear on her to obtain a favourite animal at a low price but rather indicate some little pressure on him to buy a second one! I have told in another work how Byron paid at once for the horse, while his banker, despite many efforts, was unable to get Blessington to pay for the *Bolivar*, and how, when after much delay he appeared to settle for it, his draft was dishonoured. Byron died long before a settlement was made—if ever it was. Lady Blessington's credibility as a witness may be judged by her needlessly recounting both transactions, quite inexactly and in such a way as to cast a slur of meanness on Byron.

The horse she sold is called Mameluke in *The Idler in Italy*. No such name figures in the ledger or in any letter I have seen; but on May 31st there is an entry to the effect that the coachman of 'the Noble Lord Blasinton' was given twenty-eight livres twelve soldi by order of the other Noble Lord.[4] This seems to be a tip and some incidental expense in connection with delivering the horse, which henceforward appears as '*il*

---

[1] On the prospect of going at Byron's expense to Greece, Roberts wrote to Trelawny, 'I am much of your taste for a Gun or two and something that has *leggs* in case of a chase!' (Sotheby's catalogue, 17 Dec. 1963, letter of 5 June 1823). Trelawny's proud triumph in Greece was to go woodcock shooting with the defector, Odysseus (see p. 389).

[2] *LJ.* 9 Apr. 1824. To his Genoese banker, Barry.

[3] 46873. 8 and 16 June, and 46877. 26 June.   [4] 46877.

cavallo Normando', and that seemingly was its name. Like 'the English dog' it received special treatment.

Lyon, perhaps because of his great size, was allowed nearly as much food as the other two dogs put together, and theirs cost ten soldi a day—three and a half livres a week. They were all well fed, Byron's attachment to his dogs being notable—and attributed by his wife to their not having reasoning power to condemn his wickedness.[1] In Genoa he also had cats which were nourished with fish, rabbits feeding on green stuff, and a supply of grain for his doves and his famous geese, which walked unmolested in and out of the house. And it is characteristic that, when he set sail, taking live poultry on board for eating, as was the custom before cold storage, he left the three pet geese behind with his puzzled banker, who had arranged to live in the villa till his return.

If we can rely implicitly on Lega's honesty, the servants had less reason to be satisfied with their diet than the animals. The seventy livres a week allotted to him for the whole 'family's' catering, exclusive of wine, had proved inadequate, he told the executors, and he had paid, during the nine months the arrangement lasted, three hundred and thirty-two livres out of his own pocket.[2] Without casting any reflection on Lega in a general way, I find too much evidence of his dogged persistence in demanding any money that was due to him, even when it had been politically dangerous to do so, to believe that he helped to maintain the household unrefunded; nor is it likely that so niggardly an employer would have been able to get his employees to accompany him on an adventure full of risk. My conclusion is that, desperately disappointed at the absence of legacies to the staff in Byron's will, Lega stretched every conceivable claim, and some inconceivable ones, as far as they would go, not only because of his prospective macaroni business, but because he could not forgive the executors and 'the mother of the heirs', as he called Augusta, for placing him on the same footing as 'the valet Fletcher', an indignity he felt bitterly and about which, little dreaming what the future was to hold, he protested in several letters, even addressing one to Lady Byron.[3]

During all the period when Byron was seemingly so penurious, his charities continued, not quite on the same scale as in Pisa, but to an extent not negligible—and we are aware only of those that went through the steward's hand, and hardly ever of what he gave out of his own purse or

---

[1] She wrote an undated observation soon after leaving him, 'Reason why some tyrannical characters have been fond of animals—& humane to them—because they had *no exercise of reason*, and could not condemn the wickedness of their master.' She thought the same motive actuated Byron's love of children until they could pass judgment on his conduct. (Lovelace Papers.)

[2] 46878 Folii 112 to 114 and 106.   [3] Ibid. Folio 100.

sent through his banker. Even Lady Blessington, though she slyly deni-
grates everything about him, from his horsemanship to his taste in
furniture, was impelled to admit: 'He bestows charity on every mendicant who asks it; and his manner of giving is gentle and kind . . . many
recount their affairs, as if they were sure of his sympathy.'

'To two unfortunate German travellers to buy themselves shoes, 12
livres',[1] 'Aid to a poor woman, 4 livres', a weekly allowance to the local
monks of one or two livres, numberless soldi distributed by the coachman,
the occasional 'subsidy' to a superior applicant down on his luck, these
entries in the ledger negate the accusation of avarice, a word Byron
used in the sense of cupidity, the desire to gain money, not a resolve to
hold on to it. How sincere and steady his generosity could be is shown by
entries such as the following: 'To Count Ruggiero [Gamba] for various
payments by his father of the pension for the two past months, March to
April, of the nonagenarian, M. Montanari of Ravenna . . . 52 livres.'[2]

The nonagenarian?—I was baffled by that word until I remembered
the woman with whom he had recorded an interview in his Ravenna
Journal:

January 26, 1821.

Returning [from a ride] on the bridge near the mill, met an old woman.
I asked her age—she said '*Tre croci*.' I asked my groom (though myself a
decent Italian) what the devil *her* three crosses meant. He said, ninety years,
and that she had five years more to boot!! I repeated the same three times—
not to mistake—ninety-five years!!!—and she was yet rather active—*heard*
my question, for she answered it—*saw* me, for she advanced towards me;
and did not appear at all decrepit, though certainly touched with years.
Told her to come tomorrow, and will examine her myself. . . .

January 29.

Yesterday, the woman of ninety-five years of age was with me. She said
her eldest son (if now alive) would have been seventy. She is thin—short,
but active—hears, and sees, and talks incessantly. Several teeth left—all in
the lower jaw, and single front teeth. She is very deeply wrinkled, and has a
sort of scattered grey beard over her chin, at least as long as my mousta-
chios. . . . Gave her a louis—ordered her a new suit of clothes, and put her
upon a weekly pension. Till now, she had worked at gathering wood and
pine-nuts in the forest—pretty work at ninety-five years old! . . . Her name
is Maria Montanari.[3]

A strange pair they must have made—he handsome, not unconscious
of being beloved, sought after, noble; she nearly three times his age,

---

[1] 46877. 21 May 1823. They had come from Greece. Byron assisted them substantially with money.
[2] Ibid. 24 May.   [3] Moore.

reckoning years in crosses, gathering wood for a living like an old witch
in a fairy tale. He did not forget the pension. At first, on leaving Ravenna,
he had paid it through Ghigi, but now that there was the unpleasantness
about the affair of Allegra's embalming and the steward's sequestered
money, which was the subject of a lawsuit brought by Lega against his
former friend, the responsibility had been transferred to Teresa's grandfather, still in Ravenna.

Byron had a lawsuit of his own going. It was against a tailor named
Bottaro, and he was spending hundreds of livres on writs and advocates'
fees. What the nature of the case was I am unable to fathom, but a bill
for a hundred and eighty livres from a Dr Punti for a judicial deposition
in this action was one of the last accounts to be paid before he went to
Greece,[1] having urged Kinnaird repeatedly to place every financial
resource at his disposal so that he need not stint the cause, and carrying
'ten thousand Spanish dollars in ready money, and bills of exchange for
forty thousand more', with 'chests of medicine sufficient for a thousand
men for a year'.[2] He was indeed a singular person—or perhaps I should
say, a plural person.

---

[1] 46877. 9 July.   [2] Gamba.

13

Down to Deeper Earth

Though he saw the prospect before him with the minimum of self-deception and indulged in no heroics, once his mind was made up Byron, assisted by his enthusiastic friend, Count Pietro Gamba, threw himself tirelessly into his preparations; and how complex they were can only be known from the plethora of documents they engendered. It would be of little interest to the general reader to enumerate all the purchases that were made, the stocking up of edibles for men and animals, the work of locksmiths on strong boxes, keys and bolts, the toolmakers' supplies of pincers, saws and files, the blacksmith's provision of nails, rasps and veterinary instruments, the stationer's order for paper, ink, pens and sealing wax, the making of shirts, the needles, buttons, scissors and sewing requisites, the shoeing of horses, the washing of dogs, the laundering of linen for the whole suite, the embarkation of livestock, the loading of goods, the banking arrangements, the settling of bills, the filling of cash boxes—all going on to the last hour.

The ship was the brig *Hercules,* for which Byron paid £115 sterling—that being one month's hire commencing on June 30th 1823, and three hundred and eight livres extra for fitting up a cabin,[1] for it appears there was little or nothing in the way of passenger accommodation. Besides the Captain, John Scott, there was a crew of seven, all Scots or Englishmen if we may include the mate whose name in Lega's accounts is Deves, which I take to be Davis. (Lega writes of the ship's two pilots but, from the context, I think he meant first and second mate.)

Lega's papers show that Teresa's brother was perfectly accurate when he stated, briefly and modestly in his book, *Lord Byron's Last Journey to Greece,* that he undertook the preliminaries of the voyage. Long after Pietro's death on Greek soil, still engaged in the cause, Trelawny wrote a book of his own in the only cause he could ever be trusted to support—that of magnifying his importance—and we might suppose from it that,

---

[1] 46878 Folio 54. Receipt dated 11 July.

if not nominally the leader of the expedition, he nevertheless got what he wanted done, perpetually berating and urging the slow, shuffling, ineffectual poet whose status he generously raised by the gift of a jacket and a negro!

'. . . In our voyage from Italy, Byron persuaded me to let him have my black servant, as, in the East, it is a mark of dignity to have a negro in your establishment.' Being somewhat suspicious of the various means by which Trelawny conferred dignity on Byron, I kept a sharp look-out for the coloured groom in the accounts, but barely recognized him at first under the name Bengemara Luigi, especially as there was another Luigi in the party, the servant of Pietro. Lega also had a rather confusing habit of calling him *Il Moro*, and I was slow to recall that the word then meant a black man. However, *Il Moro* and the second Luigi coalesced at last into Benjamin Lewis, the American aged twenty-six who addressed Byron as 'Massa' after the fashion of slaves in the Southern States—and probably had been one. It transpired that he had been engaged by Byron at a wage of eight crowns a month to date from the start of the voyage —receiving twenty crowns in all before sailing—ten and a half from Pietro and the rest from Lega.[1]

Trelawny did employ this young man for a very short time, but changed him in Genoa for an Italian named Croci. He wrote to Roberts from Florence to say the negro had 'a smattering of French and Italian', understood horses and cooking, and was 'a willing but not a very bright fellow. He will go anywhere and do anything he can, nevertheless if you think the other more desirable I will change . . .'[2]

Evidently Roberts advised his friend to take 'the other'. Croci figures as Trelawny's servant in the accounts from the beginning of the venture, but remained in Byron's entourage as cook when his first master, in his own words, 'determined to be off'. In the same paragraph in which he has Byron persuading him to hand over 'my negro', we may read: 'He likewise coveted a green embroidered military jacket of mine; which, as it was too small for me, I gave him; so I added considerably to his dignity.'

The widow Corvetto attended to nine jackets for Byron, and Trelawny's later elaboration of his tale—by which, without his benefaction, the shabby peer would have had nothing fit to land in—has a certain distasteful kind of pathos, showing as it does that even at eighty-five years of age, he was still daydreaming of lording it, by some means or other, over Byron.[3]

---

[1] 46877 Folio 183.   [2] Trelawny, *Letters*. 26/27 June 1823.

[3] Ibid. Letter to his gullible admirer, William Michael Rossetti, 14 June 1878, containing a circumstantial account—with dialogue—of giving Byron his jacket.

'Tita' (Battista Falcieri), Byron's gondolier and later
chasseur, in old age as a messenger at the Foreign Office,
c 1870

Byron's letter in Italian relating to assistance given to Lucas's
family, 24 November 1823

(The jacket is at Newstead Abbey. Since I wrote of it in my earlier work, its authenticity has been confirmed by letters in the South African Public Library. A boy of twelve, Charles A. Fairbridge, wrote to his parents in 1837 to say that George Gordon Fletcher, the younger son of Byron's valet, employed as carpenter by the family with which he (Charles) was staying at the Cape, constantly wore a blue jacket which had belonged to Byron, and that among other things of Byron's, he also had 'the most splendid jacket I have seen yet' which he kept in an old coffee sack. There follows an exact description of the garment. The boy obtained it, by gift or purchase, for himself, prevented the removal of the braid for trimming dresses and, in the 1860s, gave it to W. F. Webb, the next owner of the Abbey after Colonel Wildman.)[1]

It is strange that Byron, superstitious in many ways as he was, embarked on the 13th; and in fact he broke most of his usual habits from that day forward, even rising early. His suite consisted of Gamba, Trelawny, a highly recommended young Italian doctor, Francesco Bruno, and eight servants. These I think have never been fully identified before. They were Lega, with the well-filled money boxes, Fletcher with the clothes, pistols, swords (ten of them) and uniforms in all their complexity to look after, Vincenzo Papi and the new negro groom in charge of the horses (these too had trappings which filled a substantial inventory), Luigi Giro who valeted for Pietro but also acted as tailor to the company and whose wages of eight crowns a month Byron paid, the loyal and brave Tita of whom even Trelawny made an exception when he expressed his contempt for the Italians generally, Trelawny's man Croci, who of course was maintained by Byron, and Gaetano—that same nautical handyman, alias 'my Genoese mate', formerly employed on the *Bolivar* and re-employed, after the boat was laid up, on little jobs such as repairing a chess table. His wages were ten crowns a month. Like Papi, the coachman, he left a wife in Genoa who received a small allowance from Byron's banker Charles Barry.

The date fixed for departure turned out unlucky enough. The ship was becalmed and lay still. They slept aboard in readiness for the breeze, but there was barely enough to get them out of port next morning, the 14th, and they remained in sight of Genoa all day. Late at night a strong wind arose. 'We made head against it', writes Gamba, whose book was translated by Hobhouse, 'for three or four hours, but in the end the captain was obliged to steer back to the port of Genoa.' They had five horses,

[1] Information from Mrs Phillida Simons (née Brooke), great-granddaughter of Charles Fairbridge, whose library of thirteen thousand volumes with some of his correspondence is in Cape Town. George Gordon Fletcher appeared in bankruptcy proceedings at the Cape as 'carpenter and wheelwright'.

one of which was Trelawny's, and these in their terror kicked down their partitions and began to injure one another. Pietro, who was dreadfully seasick, says that those who were not in the same state helped Byron 'in his endeavour to prevent greater mischief'. Trelawny of course in his narrative copes with this catastrophe single-handed except for 'my black groom', while Byron, being advised by him to return to port, says 'Do as you like'. It is more credible that the captain, who was a very fine seaman though conspicuously fond of Jamaica rum, decided what to do with his ship.

Byron, whose spirits always rose in a storm at sea, remarked in the morning that he regarded the bad beginning as a good omen; but he grew melancholy while they waited on shore all day long for the repair of the damage. With what must have been a sense of anticlimax, he and Pietro went back to the villa, now occupied by Barry, and he expressed a wish to be alone for three or four hours.

It is impossible not to suppose that the absence of Teresa affected him. Her grief at their parting had been such that she had felt she was dying, and her father, whose exile had been revoked, had taken her, hysterical with misery, back to Romagna. Byron had counselled her to return to Count Guiccioli, who professed himself willing to forgive her, provided that relations with Byron were severed. And how it must have wounded her that her lover accepted that condition!

I do not think that a desire to bring the affair to an end formed any part of his motive in going to Greece but, while a liaison which broke all the rules of *serventismo* continued, it meant her exclusion from society as long as her husband or his wife lived; and flippantly as he expressed it in letters to close friends, between their lines we may read some real concern in his recognition that to remain with him was 'against her worldly interest in every way'.[1] But he was not less concerned to be bidding her goodbye, and he wrote asking her to believe that he would always love her, and promised to return. 'Where shall we be in a year?' he asked Pietro. It was in a year to the very day, Pietro reflected when he wrote his book, that he was 'carried to the tomb of his ancestors'.

'He dined alone on cheese and figs, returned to the city towards four o'clock, took a warm bath, and again went on board. In the evening we set sail, and a passage of five days carried us to Leghorn.' They stayed at Leghorn two days and Byron was busy on board collecting information and letters that would be useful on his mission, arranging further credits with his banker, Webb, and shipping a most curious assortment of goods from Henry Dunn:-

---

[1] Murray MS. To Hobhouse, 19 Apr. 1823.

	Fr[ancescon]i	Pauls	Crazie
9 Doz. Cyder	32	4	
3 ,, Soda powders	28	8	
1 Gross Shirt Buttons	1	8	
2 Blunder Busses	40		
2 Boxes Plate Powder		6	
Ream Brown Paper	1	2	6
2 Shaving Brushes	1		
Box Spermaceti Candles 40 lbs	18		
1 Pr Gloves		6	
Nails & Twine	1	4	4
Tallow Candles	1	5	
Sack of Bran	1	4	
Tinder		5	
Pumice, White Lead		4	
Tooth picks		2	
1 Doz. Tumblers	1	5	
Salt Petre		9	
Scourers & Sponge	1		
700 lbs Hay for Horses	4	5	
Swift's Works 19 Vols	48	3	
16 Horse Shoes	2	8	
16 lbs Honey	1	5	
50 bottles Cognac	25		
50 ,, Hollands	17	5	
Baskets &c		8	
6 Japan'd tumblers	1	5	
2 pr Spectacles	4		
6 Gun Brushes		9	
3 Setts Smyth's Tooth Brushes	5	4	
2 Boxes Ruspini Tooth Powder	4		
6 Bottles Arquebuzade [a lotion for healing wounds]	6		
2 ,, Blacking		8	
58 lbs [Gun] Powder	58		
Saddler's bill for Girths &c	6	4	
12 lbs Soap	1	2	
2 Needles			4
Bringing on board 18 Casks of Water	8		
Refilling Water Casks	1	6	4
6 lbs Pearl Tea	7	2	
6 loaves Sugar 50 lbs	8	7	4
Pr Boots Count Gamba	2	4	
Pd Consular Dues & Anchorage	19	9	2
Speaking trumpet	1		
Provisions as per annex'd Acct	12	2	

Dunn also had the linen Byron and Pietro had used on the ship launder-
ed, Captain Scott filled some requirements which are not listed, coach hire
and boat hire for several occasions were charged, and the whole bill, with
the addition of some things which had been ordered in advance—one of them
being a chart of Greece—came to upwards of five hundred francesconi,
the crowns in which our Pisa reckonings have been given. Byron had set

apart only a hundred and twenty for these needs,[1] but he had come prepared to spend the proceeds of all his economies, and much more, so long
as he could believe the money not squandered, and this he told Kinnaird
and Hobhouse again and again, pressing them to furnish him with funds.

It was at Leghorn that he took on board a young Scotsman to whom he
had promised a passage, James Hamilton Browne, who was thought to
have proved his sympathy with Greek aspirations by being obliged to
leave the service in the Ionian Islands, then governed from England,
because of his disregard for the principle of neutrality. He had actually
been dismissed for passing official information to an Opposition Member
of Parliament.[2] Nevertheless, he really was a devotee of the cause, and
his writings on Byron—a contribution to Stanhope's book in 1825 and
two long articles in *Blackwood's Magazine* in January and September
1834—have the stamp of authenticity. A close comparison will show how
much they were used, without acknowledgment, by Trelawny.

Two further passengers were glad to avail themselves of Byron's
hospitality, Greeks named Vitali and Schilizzi, one of whom gave him a
foretaste of the carelessness, the other of the trickiness, he was to meet
with very often in the months to come.

> His Lordship was within an ace of losing his life during one of the firing
> matches on board. Schilizzi inadvertantly discharged a pistol, the ball from
> which whizzed close past Lord Byron's temple. He betrayed no tremor, but
> taking the pistol out of Schilizzi's hand, pointed out to him the mechanism
> of the lock, and at the same time desired Gamba to take care that in future
> he should not be permitted to use any other pistols than those of Italian
> workmanship.[3]

The unthinking discharge of firearms was a peccadillo that was to
prove wasteful and trying at Missolonghi. Vitali's offence was more sordid.
He had a large trunk which, after some days at sea, gave off such a noxious
smell that Captain Scott ordered it to be brought on deck, threatening to
throw it overboard unless the owner claimed it. Vitali was compelled to admit it was his property, and the captain, who was a martinet, insisted on its
being opened. It turned out to contain a roasted pig which, in the heat of
late July, had decomposed. 'Vitali had perhaps thought he was to find his
own provisions', Hamilton Browne conjectured. But he had contrived also
to hide some cloth and other articles, intending to smuggle them to the
Islands, an opportunism which so infuriated the captain that he had to be
checked from sending these valuables over the side after the pork. Byron,
who had got on well enough with the man until then, turned against him

---

[1] *L.J.* To Barry, 24 July. Probably misdated, as they sailed from Leghorn on 23 July.
[2] St Clair.   [3] Browne, *Blackwood's*, Jan. 1834.

on seeing this attempt to take advantage and played a rather unkind joke on him.

> . . . It was insinuated to Scott that the Greek was addicted to certain horrible propensities too common in the Levant. The look of horror and aversion with which Scott then regarded the poor man was indescribable, swearing at the same time, and wondering how such a scoundrel could dare to look an honest man in the face. Scott could not speak a word of Italian, and the Greek, seeing him in this passion whenever he beheld him, could not comprehend the reason of it. . . .
>
> Lord Byron . . . was absolutely convulsed with laughter. Scott also attacked his Lordship expressing his surprise and concern that he could have thought of admitting so infamous a person into the ship. . . .[1]

Byron enjoyed the voyage, was in higher spirits than he had known for a long while, and bent on accustoming himself to hardships he thought a soldier might have to undergo. 'He was generally on deck', says Pietro, ' and as he never undressed to lie down, often rose at night.' His sleeping in his clothes seems odd in one so fastidious, but he was aboard a small and perilous sailing ship. Another departure from his normal practice was his shooting at live targets and in a way we would now think unsportsmanlike. With Trelawny, Browne tells us, he used occasionally to kill the ducks for the cabin dinner by shooting them in a wicker basket suspended from the main yard mast. Fortunately, they were both fine marksmen, capable of killing at first fire. Yet this activity is certainly one more sign of Byron's resolve to adapt himself to ways normally uncongenial to him.

His own diet was vegetarian except for a little fish. Browne says he dined alone at noon, Trelawny that 'every day at noon, he and I jumped overboard in defiance of sharks or weather'. On Browne's testimony, they did swim several times 'from the ship's side in calm weather', and there may have been sharks. But I have little faith in the story that Byron persuaded the cabin boy to bring him the captain's best waistcoat, and that Trelawny let loose all the geese and ducks, which took to the water while Byron and he jumped in after them, each with an arm through the sleeve-hole of the waistcoat, and followed by the dogs—the crew laughing at the fun and the captain raging. The anecdote sounds as fictitious as the name Trelawny gave Byron's Newfoundland—Neptune. Byron sometimes played practical jokes which were not of the most considerate, but his regard for discipline at sea would not have allowed him to mock a captain he liked in front of his crew.

He praised Scott warmly in his letters, and, when they parted at Cephalonia, where he continued to live on board the ship for some little

[1] Ibid.

time after landing, gave him an introduction to Hobhouse, in which he described him as having 'behaved very well':

> . . . He is a fine tough old tar, and has been a great amusement during our voyage, he is moreover brother to two of your constituents, and as such to be treated with all due respect, also some grog with which he regularly rounds off most hours of the four and twenty. He is a character I assure you, as you will perceive at a simple glance.[1]

Scott, for his part, admired Byron, and thought it regrettable that he was engaged on what he saw as a fool's errand, often giving him blunt counsel: '. . . Why, my Lord, with your fortune and fame, you ought to be sitting in the House of Lords, and defending the right side of the question, as your friends, Mr Hobhouse and Sir Francis Burdett are in the House of Commons, instead of roaming over the world.'[2]

The *Hercules* cast anchor at Argostoli, the chief port of Cephalonia, on August 3rd, and that day Lega began his first account in Spanish dollars and obols. The obol was equivalent to half a pre-1971 penny; but even half an obol, one farthing, had purchasing power. Lega, who must have rejoiced to see dry land for he hated sea travel, gave the Count three dollars, doubtless for casual tipping, and three more next day, and three again to his Lordship 'to treat the soldiers who assisted in disembarking the horses'.[3] These were men from the British garrison.

Byron's reason for remaining on the ship was to avoid embarrassing the authorities. However, this turned out to be needless punctilio: the Resident, Colonel Napier, his staff and the officers of the 8th Regiment, were all exceedingly glad to welcome him. The arrival of the celebrated author of *Don Juan* in the unexpected capacity of knight-errant was an event that stirred the greatest curiosity, and Byron did not disappoint it. A dozen years of fame, and perpetual reassurance of his ability to charm and fascinate, had given him the kind of authority that gathers about a successful performer in the theatre—a command of the audience not attainable even by the most talented beginner. It was at this stage of his life, as he approached the age of thirty-six, that everyone who reported an encounter with him spoke of his infectious liveliness, his affability, his easy, graceful manners, and his compassion. It is true that many commented with an air of disapproval on the openness of his communications —in Moore's words, 'that utter incapacity of retention which was one of his foibles'—but to hear the unguarded talk of an intensely amusing man of genius is seldom as embarrassing as, if cant is the fashion, we may like

---

[1] Murray MS. 11 Sept. 1823. Hobhouse was member for Westminster.
[2] Browne, 'Reminiscences' in Stanhope's book.　　　[3] 46877 Folio 10.

to make out. At any rate, the delight of being in his company was expressed again and again, and so many people took notes of what he said and did that sometimes he would surprise them at their jottings. 'This extraordinary person', wrote Stanhope, 'whom every body was as anxious to see, and to know, as if he had been Napoleon . . . used often to mention to me the kindness of this or that insignificant individual for having given him a good and friendly reception.'

But for all his apparent gaiety, Byron was under a strain which soon resulted in the first sign of a breakdown, the seriousness of which no one who was present recognized. While waiting for news from messengers he had dispatched to Corfu and Missolonghi—the Greek Committee in London having failed to supply the smallest amount of useful information —he decided to travel across Cephalonia to Ithaca, leaving the servants, except Tita and Fletcher, on board the *Hercules*, and accompanied by Pietro, Trelawny, Browne, and Dr Bruno. The return journey took a week and involved a good deal of physical hardship, long rides on muleback on very bad roads under a blazing sun, much walking and climbing difficult even for the others, sleeping in his cloak with the rest of the party in one cottage room—and a blow on the head from an overhanging branch on a steep mule track which literally stunned him.

During these adventures, recorded not only by Browne but by an observant and captivated newcomer in the unlikely shape of a London solicitor—one Thomas Smith who met him at the house of the British Governor, Knox—he kept his cheerful spirits flowing, and what Smith called 'glorious gin swizzle' flowed too, for when they had a water picnic, Tita produced a two-gallon jar of gin with a quart jug in which to mix it and some tumblers. Byron poured stiff drinks with grand panache and was very merry, but Smith had caught a glimpse of him that morning, leaving a rowing boat and trudging slowly up to the Governor's house looking 'like a man under sentence of death. . . . His person seemed shrunk, his face was pale, his eyes languid. . . . He was leaning upon a stick'. On joining the picnic party, however, he said nothing to indicate that he was unwell.

Perhaps, what with the voyage and his participation in the captain's grog, the stress of his situation, the constant presence day and night of strangers, and the effort of living up to his immense reputation, he was drinking somewhat too much, though none of the commentators says so; and indeed Trelawny explicitly states that he was abstemious in drink as in eating (but this was only to deny him an accomplishment then considered manly).

On the return journey, despite his previous painful experience of taking a long swim in scorching heat, and disregarding the pleas of Bruno, he did the same thing again. Immediately afterwards, they crossed to Cephalonia in an open boat, the sun still in full glare. On reaching St Euphemia, the small port opposite Ithaca, they were entertained at a feast given in Byron's honour, and he was unable to refuse the luxurious food that always played havoc with him. Following a long day, they went as night was falling to a remote monastery where sleeping quarters had been prepared for them. Unluckily, a number of monks met the party ceremoniously with torches, and the abbot made ready to declaim a formal address to the distinguished visitor. Byron's nerve suddenly gave way. He burst into imprecations, became incoherent with frenzied rage and was convulsed with a paroxysm, rushing wildly into the nearest room shouting that his head was burning, and demanding to be freed from 'this pestilential madman', the astounded abbot.

For once someone else's account of an event is more sensational than Trelawny's. Thomas Smith, whose convincing memoir of the occasion did not see the light until years after Trelawny had published his *Recollections*, tells how Dr Bruno pleaded for one of them to save his lordship's life by making him take some medicine. 'Trelawny at once proceeded to the room, but soon returned, saying that it would require ten such as he to hold his lordship for a minute, adding that Lord Byron would not leave an unbroken article in the room.'[1]

Smith himself then ventured and found Byron had barricaded the room with chairs and a table, and was standing half-undressed 'in a far corner like an animal at bay', uttering desperate cries for 'relief from this hell'. Although he had been getting on splendidly with Smith all day, he now tried to fling a chair at his head. Eventually it was Browne who pacified him, and he lay down to sleep on a mattress which was actually Smith's, while Smith spent the night 'on Lord Byron's beautiful and most commodious patent portmanteau bed'. Trelawny, not having seen what Smith wrote, missed a first-rate opportunity of describing Byron in the act of tearing up his clothes and bed linen, throwing chairs and breaking furniture, and was obliged to follow closely Browne's tamer narration, giving away how vaguely, as a sexagenarian, he recalled the incident by placing the monastery on the summit of a high mountain in Ithaca whereas it was on the famous hill of Samos in Cephalonia.

'On the following morning', says Smith, 'Lord Byron was all dejection and penitence.' And Browne tells that 'he could hardly give credit to his own frantic conduct, and was now disposed to be exceedingly courteous to the abbot',[2] unexpectedly attending a church service and leaving a sum to buy masses for the souls of his deceased friends. Pietro Gamba had

---

[1] Smith's story was printed for the first time in *Medora Leigh* edited by Charles Mackay, 1869.

[2] *Blackwood's*, Sept. 1834.

witnessed the disturbing scene, but he would not have been allowed by Hobhouse—who objected strenuously to all intimate disclosures—to say anything of it in his book, even if inclined, and he could not mention it to the despairing Teresa in his letters. It is not surprising that Pietro, young and eager as he was, should fail to see that his friend was unfit in health for the mission he had embarked on. The doctor felt some concern but held Byron in too much awe to be capable of influencing him, while Browne and Smith did not know him well enough to be aware that he had behaved in an entirely unprecedented manner, symptomatic of some incipient disorder. Trelawny at thirty might have had better judgment, but he was bent on a mission of his own for which he had to have Byron as sponsor. So there was no one except the servants and ship's captain to say to him 'Go back!'. Nor could he have done so without lowering himself in the eyes of friends who wanted him to erase by noble deeds the stigma of writing objectionable poems and associating with professed atheists and Cockney journalists.

On leaving Ithaca Byron had donated two hundred and fifty dollars to the Governor for the relief of refugees who had lost their possessions in Greece, and he took under his wing a family from Patras which, recently rich, was now destitute. He promised them somewhere to live in Cephalonia and gave them a monthly allowance for their keep. This act of charity was to have results that contributed nothing to his happiness.

On August 17th he returned with his suite to the *Hercules*, and was soon beleaguered by the representatives of jarring factions, while he himself was officially appointed principal agent of the Greek Committee in London—a body of maddening inefficiency but much greater potential than Committees supporting wars in foreign countries usually have, because of its ability, with the talismanic name of Byron, to aid the Greeks with what they esteemed more than all the panegyrics to their glorious cause that human lips or pens could utter—money. This was a need that Byron with his confirmed realism thoroughly understood and was willing to fill to the utmost of his personal capacity, but he did not want to line the pockets of mercenaries and intriguers.

He had been given no plan by the Committee, whose emissary, Blaquiere, after having urged the voyage on him, had come and gone without waiting to see him, a combination of discourtesy and ineptitude which annoyed him very much. There was thus an interim of about three weeks while he continued to live on board with his staff, for whom he provided, and substantial sums were also paid for the maintenance of the crew. A number of Lega's bills for the housekeeping have been preserved, showing that Captain Scott messed at Byron's table.

Expenses of catering for the Noble Lord, his suite, family, and the Captain of the ship:

	Dollars	Obols
7.02 lbs of kid's meat		57
16 bottles wine	1	12
16 loaves		48
13½ lbs grapes		19½
3 lbs figs		6
Herbs		2
	2	44½[1]

This would be one day's supply for fourteen to fifteen people, exclusive of the more durable commodities, such as tea, coffee, sugar and potatoes, which figure in the main ledger. Coffee was a luxury at one dollar twenty-five obols a pound, and tea nearly as dear at a dollar. The presence of Englishmen and Scots rapidly diminished the stock. Another day's catering is typified by:

	Dollars	Obols
17 lbs of meat		93½
Milk		8
Parsley and radishes		3
2 lbs tomatoes		4
14 loaves		42
16 bottles wine	1	12
19½ lbs grapes		29½
	2	92[2]

Byron did not share the meat, but had a store of *biscotto*, presumably ship's biscuit, which he took with cheese. Sometimes there was fresh fish, which he liked, and sometimes dried codfish. Once or twice there was an anchovy salad. Ox tongue was served several times, fruit always, which made up for the lack of vegetables in anything like the quantity consumed today. The dogs must have done well on the remnants of the meat supplied in such abundance. Additionally, Lega spent ten obols a day on their food.

In Pisa the disgruntled Mrs Hunt had enjoyed one gratifying discovery, an English laundress. No doubt it was equally satisfactory to Fletcher to make a similar find at Argostoli, and the reason was not mere insularity. Italian and Greek washerwomen were accustomed to scrub and beat the linen on stones in streams and rivers. Englishwomen used washtubs with hot water and soap. One of the last things Fletcher had done in Genoa was to spend eleven livres four soldi on making sure they

[1] 46877 Folio 94. Undated. Weights and measures were the same in the Islands ruled by Britain as in England.
[2] Ibid. Folio 92.

had a sufficiency of soap with them.[1] It must have been the friendly soldiers of the garrison who produced Mrs Hughes, the widow of one of their men. Sometimes she, or perhaps her daughter, wrote the laundry lists and sometimes Fletcher did them with his own distinctive spelling. Byron had been amused, passing through Ferrara in 1817, to see among the mementoes of Tasso correspondence about washing his shirts. Posterity is provided with still more intimate particulars relating to himself. Lega for some reason hoarded as fine a collection of washing lists as any poet ever left. Here are two for successive weeks in August, the second one written by Fletcher:

Lord Byron—Mrs Hughes Washing Acct
    6 shirts
  10 pocket Handkerchiefs
    6 pair Silk Stockings
    2 Waistcoats
    4 Pair Trowsers
    2 Night Caps

My Lord's Linning Aug. 24
    6 Shirts
    4 trowses   5 pr gaiters
    3 waistcoats 3 stockings
    3 pocket hank
    1 jacket

By doing up these fifty-five pieces Mrs Hughes earned four dollars six obols.[2] The washing bill for the whole 'family' was paid by Lega the same day but is not itemized. We may see, however, from one dated five days later, August 29th, a typical apportionment between the patron and his attendants. It is written by Lega:

	dollars	obols
2 lots for Milord at 1.83	3	66
1 ,, for Count Pietro Gamba	2	20
The surgeon (Bruno)		48
The Gamba servant (Giro)		72
The Treloni servant (Croci)		48
The Negro, head of the stables		48
Fletcher		94
The coachman (Papi)		54
Tita	1	60
Lega		44
	11	54[3]

[1] Ibid. Folio 9. On the same day, 15 July, two basins and a tin chamber pot were purchased, items evidently in short supply on board.
[2] Ibid. Folii 47 and 97.   [3] Ibid. Folio 95.

In point of cleanliness the secretary comes out rather badly, and it surprises us nowadays to see that the medical man was habitually less fastidious than the groom and the servant of 'Treloni' (Lega never got that name right). Fletcher would have had to be very neat, and there are many evidences that Tita was always well turned out. From those of higher rank more was naturally expected, if only because they possessed more. Even Trelawny, who was by no means over-scrupulous, prepared to pack eighteen shirts in the 'two very small saddle portmanteaus' which were all the luggage he took on the expedition.[1] Byron kept Mrs Hughes busy with bundles of washing every two or three days. Trousers, waistcoats, and gaiters, being nankeen, were changed almost daily, silk stockings as often as they were worn, shirts at the rate of more than one a day, but probably some were nightshirts, nightcaps about twice a week. Table napkins and cloths, both fine and 'common', with sheets, pillowslips, and towels, are entered too, but less often. The last laundry bill before Byron left the ship was written by Fletcher:

Lining [sic] of Ld Byron
    7 shirts
    4 Trowsers & Gaters $1\frac{1}{2}$
    3 Waistcoats
    9 p. Hank
    6 pr Silk Stockins
    1 dressing gown
    2 nt caps
    2 napkins
    7 Towels[2]

This came to three dollars eleven obols. Mrs Hughes continued to do the laundry-work after the move to quarters on shore, though it meant sending the linen to her in a cart: but when Byron heard her daughter was only fifteen, and pretty, he requested that she should not deliver the linen any more in case one of his all-male household should find the temptation too much.[3]

As August ran on, Captain Scott explained that he could not keep his ship any longer at risk in those waters, and Byron had no alternative but to live on the Island until he could get some clear picture of whom he

[1] Letter to Roberts, 26 June. Eighteen shirts or not, Trelawny's personal habits were always wanting in nicety. One of the servants who gave evidence in the divorce case in which he was co-respondent (1841) stated that she could generally tell if he had been in Mrs Goring's bed by the marks of dirty boots!
[2] 46877 Folio 133. 4 Sept. I do not know what the $1\frac{1}{2}$ stands for unless it means a pair of gaiters, and one odd gaiter. In another bill Fletcher enters '$8\frac{1}{2}$ pair of stackins'.
[3] Kennedy, p. 299.

should join and what he could do on the mainland. He took a house at Metaxata, a village with impressive scenery some miles from Argostoli. It must have been the smallest he ever occupied, having only four rooms, one of which was his bedroom and another the sole reception and living room. Pietro and Bruno may have shared a room, but how the servants were disposed of is hard to imagine. Cramped as the accommodation was, a great many mule-loads of goods were taken there. Cutlery and crockery were hurriedly purchased with several chamber pots and other necessaries, but the basic furniture must have been *in situ*. The rent was fifteen dollars a month.

On September 6th, Lega gave sixteen dollars to the first and second mates, five to someone called Neal, perhaps the ship's cook, and four each to the remaining members of the crew.[1] Byron would of course have made his parting gift to the captain personally; and he sent him to the brig before he sailed a huge quantity of grapes.

Scott carried with him to England a letter for Hobhouse[2] with Byron's statement of his position:

> On our arrival here early in August we found the opposite Coast blockaded by the Turkish fleet, all kinds of reports in circulation about divisions amongst the Greeks themselves,—the Greek fleet not out (and it is not out yet as far as I know),—Blaquiere gone home again, or at least on his way there—and no communications for me from the Morea or elsewhere. Under these circumstances, added to the disinclination of Capt. Scott (naturally enough) to risk his vessel among the blockaders or their vicinity without being insured for the full value of his bastimento, I resolved to remain here for a favourable opportunity of passing over, and also to collect if possible something like positive information. . . .
>
> The Turkish fleet has sailed leaving fifteen Algerine vessels to cruise in the Gulph.
>
> Mr Browne and Mr Trelawny are since then gone over in a boat to part of the Coast out of the blockade with letters from me to the Greek Government at Tripolitza, and to collect information. There is little risk for small boats, but it is otherwise with larger vessels which cannot slide in everywhere, as the Mussulmans are not very particular. Count Gamba, a young man about twenty-three, is here with me, and is very popular amongst the English, and is I assure you a fine fellow in all respects. . . .
>
> Great divisions and difficulties exist, and several foreigners have come away in disgust as usual,—it is at present my intention to remain *here* or *there* as long as I see a prospect of advantage to the cause, but I must not conceal from you and the Committee that the Greeks appear in more danger from their own divisions than from the attacks of the enemy.[3]

---

[1] 46877 Folio 13.   [2] A founder member of the Greek Committee.
[3] Murray MS. 11 Sept.

Byron was defensive about having Pietro with him, Hobhouse having disapproved much of the Gamba family for the way they had accepted Teresa's illicit lover.

Quite calculatingly, as his letters to Claire Clairmont and Leigh Hunt show, Trelawny had used Byron to provide the means for launching himself, once in Greece, upon exploits of his own.[1] He went off furnished by the unwitting leader of the expedition with money, a good pretext, and a companion who could speak both Italian and Greek, Hamilton Browne.

They hired a caique and landed at Pyrgos where their reception, frigid at first, changed when they made it known from whom they had come, for Byron's fame and the stories of his wealth—'exaggerated notwithstanding his efforts to undeceive them' says Pietro—had spread with extraordinary speed throughout Greece. Browne gives an excellent account of their journey, an enjoyable if somewhat hazardous sight-seeing tour. They went to Tripolitza and several other places, and came to rest on the Island of Hydra. Trelawny settled comfortably for some weeks as the guest of Orlando, a shipping merchant who was preparing—at a snail's pace—to go to London in connection with the vital war loan, accompanied by a compatriot Luriottis, and Browne made ready to sail with them.

Hydra was the place to which Mavrocordato, the head of the Legislative Council, had fled, threatened by the dangerous faction of Colocotronis. Anything but a romantic figure, to judge from his portrait, he was yet by far the most disinterested of the Greek leaders and the one with the best grasp of ideals that would appeal to Western sympathies. He had lived abroad and was of a cosmopolitan culture, whereas most, if not all, the chieftains were untravelled, unlettered men, barbaric in habits and pursuing personal aggrandisement and personal vendettas. He had been on very good terms with the Shelleys in Pisa, and was a man of breeding and polite, if diffident, manners. Trelawny took a vehement dislike to him. Numberless expressions of his pungent hatred were censored from his letters when published. His opposition was probably the consequence of his first having met Odysseus Andritzou, Mavrocordato's wily enemy. The most picturesque of the Klephts, Odysseus, whose cruelty, bravery, guile and cupidity, have been depicted by many historians of the Revolution, took the measure of Trelawny with remarkable astuteness, and though they had no language in common, managed somehow to cultivate and flatter him—the envoy of the Lord whose own fabled riches were to

---

[1] To Claire he wrote candidly that 'an unknown stranger without money &c would be ill received' in Greece, but that he would get there with Byron's means and under his auspices and would then shift for himself. (*Letters*, 27 June 1823.) He reminded Hunt that his decision to leave Byron had been made in Italy. (38523, 25 Oct. 1823.)

be augmented by a still greater shower of gold in the form of the loan from England.

By the time Byron's second instalment of money for Trelawny's needs had been sent, November 10th,[1] Odysseus already had him absolutely in thrall. He had become, instantaneously it seems, the object of hero worship in its most crude and immature shape, while his gullible admirer sent his friends in Italy rancorous denigrations of Byron, which are still embarrassing to read in the light of subsequent events, and letters of vainglorious posturing:

> . . . You will be anxious to hear of my intentions—amidst this hurley-burley—state of the Nation—after having attentively weighed the matter—I have decided on accompanying Ulysses [Odysseus] to Negropont to pass the winter there—their [sic] being excellent sport between Turk and woodcock shooting—I am to be a kind of Aidecamp. . . . the Gen! gives me as many men as I choose to command—and I am always with him—my equipments are all ready—two horses—two Zuliotes as servants—I am habited exactly like Ulysses—in red & gold vest with sheep-skin Capote—gun pistols sabre &c. red cap & a few dollars or dubloons—my early habits will be resumed—and nothing new—here dirt & privation—with mountain sleeping—are a good exchange for the parched desert—my locusts & camel's milk—[2]

This was written at Hydra, and though there may have been dirt— Trelawny boasts a good deal about it—there was no privation, nor did the gruelling winter campaign he described next day to Leigh Hunt[3] have any existence except in his vivid imagination. There was a lull in the fighting, and especially on or near that island.

Meanwhile, the siege of Byron, at Metaxata, by emissaries from every Greek leader or would-be leader, military, civil or religious, who wanted access to his cash, had become more intensive. He sent specimens of these overtures to Hobhouse, stating that he would not fail to 'take advantage of circumstances to serve the *Cause* if the patriots will permit me, but it must be *the Cause*, and not individuals or *parties* that I endeavour to benefit'. And he added a postscript: 'Remember me to D. K[innaird] from whom I have not heard, tell him, as usual to muster all my possible monies, as well for the present, as for the ensuing year, that I may take

---

[1] 46877. 11 Nov. Folio 20. The sum is not named. It was taken to Argostoli by Pietro and entrusted to one Gerasimo. On 20 Nov. there was a payment to a courier called Baccicino of a further eight crowns for Trelawny, too small a remittance to be sent to him wherever Byron believed him to be, so it may have been to settle some local account left unpaid. The same applies to the laundry bill of one dollar sixty obols from 'the old washerwoman of Argostoli for the washing of Signor Treloni', paid by Lega on 7 Nov. (Ibid. Folio 19.)

[2] To Mary Shelley, 24 Oct. 1823, quoted by Marchand from the Abinger Papers.

[3] An extract from his letter is given in Chapter XIII of *The Late Lord Byron*.

the field in force in case it should be proper or prospective of good that I should do so.'[1]

It has been assumed very often that Byron's prudent attempts to assess the situation before moving to the mainland were a rationalization of his reluctance to leave a place he found agreeable. What good he could have done by going to the seat of war a few weeks earlier I do not know, and, venturing an opinion that many must have held but few or none expressed, I think it a thousand pities that he did not remain in Cephalonia altogether and let us into the secret of what happened between *Don Juan* and 'her frolic Grace—Fitz-Fulke'. He could still have exercised considerable influence merely by providing and raising money and administering the loan: in fact, he might have prevented some of the disgraceful peculations which took place after his death both in England and in Greece itself; and we should have had several more cantos of our greatest comic epic.

Rationalization or not, despite some troubles at Metaxata—notably with forty Suliots he had taken into his pay, many of whom turned out to be mercenary impostors, not Suliots and in some cases not even Greeks— the sojourn at the village, as reflected in all dependable annals and in Lega's invoices, has about it a glow of something like serenity. Byron rose comparatively early and was at work by nine on his correspondence, Pietro often acting as secretary. (All Greeks of any education knew Italian, but how they translated Pietro's handwriting I cannot fathom, having suffered too much from it, even without their use of a different alphabet.) At eleven Byron would take his breakfast, a cup of tea. At noon he and Pietro would go for a long ride. They dined soon after three. Pietro says Byron ate only cheese and vegetables, but many other edibles were bought by Lega, who went to Argostoli almost daily in a cart to get provisions. Goose, capons, fish, eggs, ham, pigeons, quails, and woodcock, appear in the ledger, and, while in season, figs, melons, and grapes were plentiful.

Of course, much of this food must have been for Pietro, Bruno, and the others, but perhaps it was so surprising, in that age of heavy eating, for a man to restrict his appetite voluntarily, that there was a general tendency to exaggerate Byron's abstinence. Some observers did note that, when he dined out or had company and good things came to the table, he could not resist them. In less convivial circumstances, he stuck to his determination not to lose the lean proportions he had regained, a vanity that drew several disapproving comments from onlookers who did not dream how far in this he was in advance of his time.

After dinner, there might be pistol practice, his hand very accurate, though shaking. Then till seven he would usually retire to read in his

[1] Murray MS. 6 Oct.

room, Scott being his favourite. At odd hours and in the evenings, there
would be discussions with petitioners and advisers; sometimes the light-
hearted officers of the regiment might visit him, sometimes the earnest
Methodist, Dr Kennedy, who tried to convert him and, himself destined
to an early death, left a superb and convincing account of their conversations—to my mind the one most completely evocative of Byron's charm,
kindness, and candour. For a few genial days there was one of Augusta's
half-brothers on the maternal side, Lord Sydney Osborne, whom Byron
spoke of as 'clever and insouciant as ever'.[1] To the cottage too came the
young George Finlay, later to write an important history of Greek affairs
and valuable reminiscences of Byron, and that eccentric and doctrinaire
revolutionary, Col. the Hon. Leicester Stanhope, an ardent republican
who was one day to receive with humblest gratitude the title of Commander of the Royal Order of the Redeemer from King Otto of Greece—
Queen Victoria granting to her trusty and well-beloved subject, out of her
'Princely Grace and Special Favour', the right to accept the decoration.[2]

The simplicity of the mode of living was almost beyond understanding
today. Corn was carried to a water mill to be ground for flour, brooms
were made of twigs, fires lighted with flint and steel and a sparing use of
sulphur matches, not always procurable. Water was fetched from a well
and its visible impurities filtered. Candles and three or four tin lanterns
were the only illumination. A hundred goose quills at a time were bought
for writing. Local wine was delivered in a barrel.

Byron took pleasure in these unpretentious ways, recalling, however
delusively, his first travels when he and Hobhouse had been cut off for
long periods from the luxuries of urban life:

> I like this place [he told Kennedy] . . . and dislike to move. There are
> not, to be sure, many allurements here, neither from the commodiousness of
> the house nor the bleak view of the black mountain—there is no learned
> society—nor the presence of beautiful women; and yet for all that I would
> wish to remain, as I have found myself more comfortable, and my time
> passes more cheerfully than it has for a long time done.

Kennedy sensibly urged him to stay—'Your health and comfort
ought to be among the first objects of your consideration'—but he replied,
'I have pledged myself to the cause, and something is expected from me;
whether I can do any good I know not; but I cannot recede. . .'.

It is a mistaken view on the part of some commentators, contemporary or modern, that Byron found his confidence ebbing away when he

---

[1] Murray MS. 29 Oct.
[2] The honour was conferred in April 1836, the licence to accept it granted in May
1838 (Goulandris Papers).

came face to face with the prospect of having to prove himself a man capable of military leadership. On the contrary, he had always been most realistically aware that, while the Greeks would expect him to cut a soldierly figure, he could serve them best by money, moral support, and the reconciliation of mutually antagonistic factions. As early as September 14th, telling Hobhouse that Metaxa, the Commandant of Missolonghi, was pressing him to go there, he had said that he must hear first from the Tripolitza Government, adding: 'I have as little skill in fortifying a besieged town as "Honour hath skill in Surgery".'[1] On October 16th, (and indeed before leaving Italy) he had insisted that a military leader was wanted, and that if one were sent out, he would readily act under him,[2] and when he came to know Colonel Napier, who was retiring from the Governorship of Cephalonia, he was exceedingly eager that that distinguished soldier should be allowed, by some bending of army regulations, to assume command, giving him letters of introduction to Kinnaird[3] and John Bowring of the Greek Committee[4] with this end in view.

He was willing to 'take the field' in the sense of maintaining troops, and repeatedly asked for money—his own money—to do so; but he did not see himself as a Hotspur or King Hal and so had no occasion to feel incompetent in that line. The three helmets he had made for himself, Pietro, and Trelawny, with their classical or heraldic motifs, were merely symbolical. (They have been much derided, but were modest compared with most of the military headgear of the day, ornate as it was with horsetails, flowing plumage, and tall aigrettes. I doubt whether any of them were ever worn or intended to be worn except for ceremonial.)

He took advantage of the island interlude to order a suit of livery for his American groom and a new blue one for Tita, as well as a braided jacket for Pietro's servant, Giro. Availing himself of the services of an English tailor accustomed to work for the officers, Pietro himself had what must have been a splendid outfit made, adorned with several scores of olive-shaped silk buttons and a kind of trimming known as *spighetta* (ears of corn). For this Byron seems, very properly, to have paid. He also gave his faithful *aide* a pair of leather gloves when he bought one for himself.[5] A pair of pantaloons had to be bought too for Lega, who normally supplied his own, because Milord had riddled an existing pair with pistol shot![6] The explanation of so curious an accident has evaded me.

While building up all manner of preparations, from orders for yet

[1] Murray MS. Continuation of letter of 11 Sept.   [2] Ibid.
[3] Ibid. 10 Dec.   [4] *LJ.* 10 Dec. '*He* is *our* man to lead a regular force.'
[5] 46877, numerous entries, Folii 17 to 22. The tailor appears as Andrea Bon, but as Lega Italianized all foreign names, it may have been Andrew Bonn or Bunn.
[6] Ibid. Folio 24. 25 Dec. The cost was seven dollars thirty obols.

more toothbrushes and tooth powder to arrangements for importing the men and materials to make Congreve rockets, Byron's private charities continued as in Ravenna, Pisa, and Genoa, except that the sums were larger and must have gone still further, for the value of money in Greece was such that he wrote to Kinnaird:

> . . . A sum of trifling amount even for a Gentleman's *personal* expenses in *London*, or Paris, in Greece can arm and maintain hundreds of men. You may judge of this when I tell you that the four thousand pounds advanced by me, is likely to set a fleet and an army in motion for some months.[1]

The £4,000 had been produced at the request of the dilatory Greek Deputies—arrived at last from Hydra—to enable their navy, unpaid for months, to put to sea. These men, Luriottis and Orlando, Trelawny's recent host, had required a great deal of urging and pleading to embark for London on the business of the loan (and once there, they were to help themselves to a pretty liberal share of it), but Hamilton Browne, by his decision to accompany them, had had some influence in dislodging them. Byron had been just on the verge of leaving for Tripolitza. His stores were packed, his boats hired, and the servants who did not want to go forward with him were about to be repatriated to Italy:[2] but now there was a postponement, both for the quarantine of the party from Greece and for the negotiation of Byron's credits, which turned out difficult—the sum being an enormous one for the island bankers to supply in specie. (It was done by two very obliging merchant-bankers, Samuel Barff of Zante and John Hancock, Barff's partner in Cephalonia, although Byron had no account with them.)

> I was present [Finlay wrote] when he signed bills for the loan to the Greek Government of the 30,000 dollars for the fleet;—it took place in the health-office of Cephalonia. On his holding the bills in his hand, before giving them to Mr Hamilton Browne, who, with the Greek Deputies, was then in quarantine . . . I said, you may bid that money farewell, my Lord; you have taken the last look of it. He called out loudly, grasping the bills in his hand, 'Not if I can help it. I shall this very day write to Douglas Kinnaird, and request him to make them pay me with the very first proceeds of the loan, if they get one.'[3]

This is, I dare say, faithfully reported; it is the way Byron spoke in his self-created role of the man who was hard-headed about money, but

---

[1] Murray MS. 10 Dec.

[2] Those who went back were Vincenzo Papi and Gaetano, both married men, and Pietro's servant, Giro, which must have been unexpected in view of his new jacket.

[3] Finlay's Reminiscences in Stanhope's book.

it was not the way he acted. What he actually wrote to Kinnaird, taking one letter out of many, was:

> . . . Get together all means, and credit of mine we can, to face the war establishment, for it is 'in for a penny, in for a pound' and I must do all I can for the Ancients. . . . In short, if they can obtain a loan [from England], I am of opinion that matters will assume, and preserve a steady and favourable aspect for their independence.
>
> In the meantime I stand paymaster, and what not; and lucky it is that from the nature of the warfare, and of the country, the resources even of an individual can be of a partial and temporary service.[1]

One of the Victorian counsellors of commonsense—I think it was Smiles—wrote that a normally sober man who got drunk in public once a year would have a worse reputation for intemperance than one who privately went to bed half-drunk every night. By a similar superficiality of judgment, one who talks of loving money and hoarding it will be supposed a miser though he is quietly engaged in every kind of generous act, and so it was with Byron.

Hamilton Browne was one of those who took seriously badinage about avarice.

> With occasional liberality, Lord Byron certainly united a considerable degree of unnecessary parsimony, and those who had known him much longer than myself, stated that this habit was to be dated from the period of the increase of his fortune, arising from the large property which he had become entitled to at the demise of Lady Noel, his wife's mother.[2]

It is true that the love of money increases with increase of money, as Juvenal said, and probably a great many other people before and after him; but this 'large property', which caused various persons who wanted some of it to speak of Byron's parsimony, was never much more than a tantalizing mirage while he lived. Towards the end of 1823, a few months before he died, he wrote to Hobhouse that all he had received of it was £900 in two payments:[3] nor could he any longer count on earnings. Between his pledge to aid Greece, which he abundantly honoured, and the foolish debts of his youth from which he was still not wholly free, he could only keep up his individual charities by dint of personal economy.

Among his pensioners at Cephalonia were the family from Patras whom he had assisted on the visit to Ithaca. They had come to Argostoli

---

[1] Murray MS. 23 Dec.

[2] *Blackwood's*, Jan. 1834. Trelawny was the sole source at the time for tales of Bryon's parsimony.

[3] Murray MS. 6 Oct.

at his suggestion and he had found accommodation for them with a prosperous merchant, Corgialegno. The mother, in feeble health, had three
young daughters with her. Her two adolescent sons, whom Byron had not
seen, were in action in the Morea—then in the throes of civil war. The
demands on his funds from all sides were much more insistent and
clamorous than he could possibly have anticipated in the first few days
after landing, and by November he seems to have felt that Mme Chalandrutsanos and her daughters were throwing themselves too heavily on
his hands, and could have done a little more to help themselves: and he
wrote a fractious note on the back of an account for his expenditure:

> The Maiche [?] family will not receive from *this* day on more than six
> dollars a month to maintain the ailing mother—the girls if they are honest
> (and *I* at least know nothing to the contrary) may live in honest service,
> being young and capable—That family has already received in assistance
> from me (including fifty dollars paid for their debts in Ithaca) more than a
> *hundred and twenty* dollars in three months.
> The six dollars allotted to the mother must suffice for the time to come,
> being two dollars more than what is paid at the most for a good soldier—and
> that comprises also his family—a family more numerous than theirs.[1]

This was rather a harsh and capricious decision, the sort of thing he
was liable to do, as in the case of Allegra's posthumous expenses, when he
believed advantage was being taken of him. Part of the outlay for the first
week of November had been 'For goods supplied to Lord Byron at Argostoli comprising things for the Moreote family', and 'Clothes for that
family', two entries amounting to slightly under thirty-three dollars.[2]
Perhaps the beneficiaries had made some further request so soon after this
help that Byron resented it.

A week or so after his instructions should have been put into effect the
Chalandrutsanos boys, having heard of the English Lord's generosity,
made their way to Cephalonia and begged to be taken into his service.
One of them, Lukas, aged fifteen, could speak Italian. Byron was fully
occupied revising all his plans and preliminaries, having been urged to go,
not to Tripolitza as first arranged, but to Missolonghi, where Mavrocordato had now established himself, and at first he seems to have taken little
notice of these new applicants for his bounty. One of the brothers never
appears in the records—unless the payment of one Spanish dollar 'to a
young Suliot' (Lega called all Greeks Suliots) on December 9th refers to
him: but on December 22nd we find: 'To the Suliot Lucca [Lukas] for a
grammar book . . . 75 obols by order of Milord'. And next day: 'To Lucca
another grammar book . . . 68 obols'.[3]

---

[1] 46878 Folio 17. In Italian.   [2] Ibid. Folio 16. 3 Nov.   [3] 46877 Folio 23.

As Lukas could read and write, a refined accomplishment, Byron had a fancy that at Missolonghi he would study modern Greek with him; and perhaps the second book was bought to improve Lukas's Italian, which was not very good. In the thick of final preparations for joining the sole party which had any claim to call itself a government, Byron had agreed to let the boy go with him as a page.

In August they had taken on a Greek stableboy at the high wage of six dollars a month, more than the pay of a soldier as the letter last quoted shows, and just before leaving Cephalonia, they engaged another *marangone*, or, as Lega elsewhere called him, carpenter, at the same rate as the Genoese, Gaetano, whom he replaced (eight dollars);[1] but no wage for Lukas is shown in Lega's books. It is likely, however, that he received pocket money from Byron, and highly unlikely that the resolution to cut down the mother's allowance was persisted in. What the youth thought of his new patron is unknown to us from any direct evidence. That he often behaved in a petulant and intractable manner may be inferred from certain indirect clues. But in their last few days on the island, Byron's thoughts were all on his farewells, the details of his impending journey, and the courses he was to pursue.

As they left the village where he had lived through the last enjoyable days of his life, his steward paid the four months due in arrear to their landlord, Giorgio Decorò, and had two small panes of glass, broken by Dr Bruno, replaced. He gave twenty-five dollars to help the family of Drako, a Suliot officer, and two dollars on Milord's instructions to some needy soul whom he terms with irritation 'an old gossip of Metaxata'. He paid a porter forty obols to accompany his lordship to Argostoli with a box of money and a portfolio, and he received by express from Pietro a last minute consignment of goods from the stables which had been overlooked. He distributed money to Tita, Fletcher, and Milord himself, and paid twenty-five dollars for customs clearance of the twelve persons of several nations who arrived at the port bound for Missolonghi.[2] These were Byron and Fletcher—English; Pietro, Bruno, Lega, Tita, Croci, and the newly engaged Filippo Moscato—all Italians; Benjamin Lewis—American; Lukas and the stableboy, Giovanni (or Ioannis)—both Greeks, and a courier whose name is spelt Baccicino by Lega, but it was probably one of his transliterations of Greek.

Instead of accepting Mavrocordato's offer of transport, Byron had prudently hired two boats so as to sail under the neutral Ionian flag. Pietro and five of the suite embarked on a bombard, a large slow vessel

---

[1] 46877. *Marangone* is literally a Sardinian. I do not know how the term came to be applied to a nautical handyman.

[2] Ibid. Numerous entries.

which could take the horses and heavy luggage; and Byron with the remaining servants boarded a mistico, which was light and fast. Pietro had charge of most of the weapons, eight thousand dollars, and a package of Byron's war correspondence. Lega was to go on the bombard, but till the last hour he was busy sending provisions for men and horses on board both ships, a consignment of wine and beer invoiced at a little more than twenty dollars, bread, coffee, tea, rice, sugar, nine woodcocks for the table, eight drinking glasses, and enough fresh water for what they thought would be a very short voyage.[1] Some of these goods must have been obtained at Zante, where they made a stop so that Byron could raise yet more money from his newly acquired bankers, Barff and Hancock.

It was at Zante on December 30th that Lega laid in a stock of writing paper—two reams of the ordinary kind, one ream of the very large paper Byron favoured for composition, half a ream of small letter paper, and six quinterns of fine gilt-edged paper, presumably for formal communications to officials. He also procured smoking implements, it being the custom to offer pipes to visitors of dignity—for which purpose Byron early on had ordered a hundred quills to make mouthpieces, besides his hundred for pens.[2] Fifty-odd pounds of lead ball went on to the bombard, possibly for Pietro's sport, a useful one, the caterers' bills becoming noticeably smaller whenever he went shooting.

Still wishing to embroil the British authorities as little as he could, Byron declined an invitation to the house of the Resident, although Sir Frederick Stoven came out to see him in person. The two boats set sail again in the evening. With the illusion that they would be meeting at Missolonghi next day, the Greek crews sang patriotic songs till their voices faded away as the mistico shot ahead and then the passengers signalled to one another by firing pistols and carbines. The mistico, however, was to meet with perils that kept her at sea another six days, while Pietro's bombard, the name of which, as Italianized by Lega, was the *San Giorgio*, was captured within a few hours by the Turks.

The scenes that followed would have seemed far-fetched in a novel; for when the Captain, one Spiro Valsamacchi, had given himself up for lost and been taken on board the immense Turkish frigate of forty-eight guns, and Pietro had tied the fifty pounds of shot to the package of Byron's papers—which were then, unhappily, dropped overboard; when indeed the Turkish Captain, Zachiria Bey, had commanded, 'Cut off his head and sink the ship!' (' a trying moment', says Pietro), the Greek Valsamacchi suddenly recognized in him one whose life he had saved fifteen years before, at the risk of his own, from a shipwreck in the Black Sea. The

[1] Ibid.   [2] Ibid. Numerous entries.

Turk behaved in the handsomest manner, receiving Pietro, Lega, and three servants on his ship with the utmost courtesy and urbanity, says Lega,[1] not to speak of punch, coffee, and pipes of the finest tobacco: nevertheless, as his doings were observable by thirteen other ships of his own nation—the Turkish fleet, contrary to expectation, being out in force—he was compelled to make some show of acting according to protocol, and to escort the *San Giorgio* via Patras to the Castle of Morea for examination by the ruling Pasha, Yussuf.

Meanwhile, he treated the captives to what Lega describes as 'exquisite viands which almost overcame my usual sobriety, 15 or 16 dishes not counting the soup . . . and excellent punch in a vast bowl, from which we all three drank according to Turkish custom, and drained it many times. The Bey drank to our good voyage and we to his health. I and Gamba were served by two most polite young slaves . . .'. (The Greek captain was not at the feast because, feverish from the ordeal of the day, he had retired to bed.)

It was somewhat embarrassing that Pietro's hardly credible tale of being on the way to Calamo to join a friend on a hunting expedition was at odds with that of Captain Valsamacchi who, relying on Zachiria's clemency, had already admitted to being bound for Missolonghi, but the Bey, a chivalrous man, ignored the exasperation of an Italian interpreter who was hoping for booty, and managed to reconcile the conflicting stories: and it was guilefully arranged that Pietro should express astonishment, when he met the Pasha, at the Turkish captain's boldness in having come beyond the legitimate line of blockade to interfere with their voyage. Yussuf Pasha appreciated boldness in his captains; all the same the young Count was left hanging about in considerable anxiety for some days before the British Vice-Consul in that part of the world, an Ionian Greek, confirmed from his papers that he had a rendezvous with an Englishman at Calamo.

During this time Pietro had to keep up his pretence of being an impassioned sportsman who would go anywhere to shoot woodcock. He duly presented some to the Pasha, together with a first-rate map of Greece—perhaps the one Byron had bought from Henry Dunn before leaving Italy. To Zachiria he had already given a telescope, six bottles of rum, and twelve of beer. The Bey did much better than the Pasha, for he was partial to rum, but the Pasha did not know how to read a map.

---

[1] 46875. Letter of 13 Jan. 1824. Lega's account fills out many details omitted from Pietro's book. He was treated as one of the Captain's guests because Pietro always gave him the status of *maestro di casa* to a nobleman. Pietro was as much struck by the absence of amenities such as spoons and forks and the appallingly dirty quarters of a crew of more than five hundred (though the Bey's cabin was clean and comfortable) as by the hospitality.

Lega actually breaks almost into a staccato narrative to indicate these events in his ledger. The miracle was that his sole cash outlay was a tip of one dollar to a janissary!

It was a shock to the party from the bombard to find, when they ultimately reached Missolonghi, that Byron was not there. They had caught sight of the little mistico lurking under rocks called the Scrofes, while they sped reluctantly in the shadow of their captor, but, confident that none of the huge frigates could get into the crannies and shallows, they had rather optimistically assumed that Byron was safe. He for his part had seen the plight of the *San Giorgio* and feared she was lost with all the valuable persons and goods she carried. Built for speed, the mistico had been able to slip away after being hailed by a Turkish vessel in the dead of night. All on board had held their breath, even the dogs had curiously refrained from barking, and the Turks, in fear of a Greek fire-ship, had not chosen at that moment to risk the destruction of their own.

It was hazardous now to make for Missolonghi by sea, but they succeeded in reaching the small port of Dragomestri, and Byron got a letter off to Colonel Stanhope, who had joined Mavrocordato shortly before, saying that, if an escort of Suliots could be sent to guide them, they would try to come by an overland route; but the mountains were impassable. Finally, a Greek convoy brought them in on January 5th 1824, after they had been caught in a violent storm which drove them twice on the rocks.

> The sailors then, losing all hope of saving the vessel [writes Pietro], began to think of their own safety. But Lord Byron persuaded them to remain; and by his firmness and no small share of nautical skill, got them out of danger, and thus saved the vessel and several lives, with 25,000 dollars, the greater part in specie. . . .
>
> He had not pulled off his clothes since leaving Cephalonia; had slept upon the deck, and had purposely exposed himself to privations, which he thought would harden his constitution, and enable him to bear the fatigue of a campaign. . . . He swam for half an hour on the 1st of January.[1]

His greatest worry during these dangers was on behalf of his new page, first because Lukas himself was so frightened,[2] and then lest he should be taken by the Turks, who were reputed to have unmentionable ways of dealing with youthful prisoners; and in his otherwise calm and collected letter to Stanhope, he said he would rather cut the boy in pieces and him-

---

[1] Gamba. The reason for his hardihood was that he had not been able to wash for days and had 'to kill the fleas, and others'. (*LJ.* 13 Jan.)

[2] *LJ.* 2 Jan. 1824 to Hancock from Dragomestri, while waiting for a rescue: 'I disembarked the boy and another Greek, who were in the most terrible alarm—the boy, at least. . . .'

self too than have him captured.[1] During the long hours of the storm, he
had assured Lukas, who could not swim, that should the boat founder, he
would take him on his back; and from this time onwards his concern
became emotional. 'He naturally loved what he protected', he had written
years before of *Don Juan* and the child orphaned by the war. Lukas had an
instinct for exploiting that affection.

Pietro had had a splendid welcome at Missolonghi, but Byron was
received with nothing less than rapture. Through the combination of
their needs and his attributes, the fame of which had long preceded him,
Missolonghiots had built him up into a kind of messiah, and not only
Missolonghiots but, as Lega tells, 'all the French, Germans, English and
Italians who were there or came from the interior of the Morea to see
him, to revere him, and to intercede for something from him'.[2] With his
usual gift of showmanship, his 'star quality', he had somehow or other
managed, before landing in a Speziot boat, to don his scarlet uniform,[3]
and we may be sure he had shaved and groomed himself as best he could
for his reception. Yet it nearly overwhelmed him. A flotilla of small craft
came out to meet him while the waters reverberated with what Lega calls
a continuous '*rimbombo del cannone*' and with acclamations and cheers
of the entire population, as if he had been 'the father of all the Greeks. . . .
The whole day there was feasting and gaiety, amidst the noise of bands
and continuous discharge of muskets.'

But for all his joyful participation in reflected glory, Lega could not
but note that Missolonghi was an ugly and dreary place. Byron had been
there before. He and Hobhouse had spent two nights there on their Grand
Tour, and I here reprint, possibly for the first time, what Hobhouse
had written about it in his much under-valued book about their
travels:

> Messalonge is situated on the south-east side of the salt-marsh, or shallow,
> that extends between two and three miles into the land below Natolico, and six
> miles about beyond Messalonge itself, into the gulf of Lepanto. The breadth
> of the bay formed by these shallows, may be, in an oblique direction . . .
> about ten miles. At the extremity of the shallows, towards the deep water,
> for several miles in circuit, there are rows of stakes, and also, at intervals,
> some wicker huts raised on poles, forming, as it were, a line between the sea
> and the bay, and appearing to those sailing down the gulf like a double shore.

---

[1] Ibid. 31 Dec. 1823.   [2] 46875. Letter of 13 Jan. 1824.

[3] Not having seen any of the Zambelli Papers, which were not available, nor other
documents relating to Byron's extensive wardrobe, Harold Nicolson states that he had
borrowed this from Colonel Duffie at Cephalonia. What he had from Colonel Duffie
was a pelisse—a long overcoat, given to him, I imagine, because he had underestimated
the need he might have for really warm clothing in the bleak marshes where he was to
spend the winter.

Within this fence, there is a very valuable fishery, and many boats are stationed for that purpose in the marsh.

The port of Messalonge will not admit any vessel drawing more than three feet of water, nor is there sufficient water for those of more than five feet any where within the marsh. All vessels or boats, whether going in or out of the bay, are obliged, for want of depth, to pass close to a small fort, built on piles, where there is a cannon or two mounted, and where a Turkish guard resides, to see the passes of those who enter or leave the fishery. . . .

The inhabitants are partly Greeks, partly Turks, in number about five thousand. They subsist chiefly on the fishery. . . . None of them are very rich, but several possess about five thousand piastres per annum—a good income in that country. The houses are chiefly of wood, and two stories high. The bazar is furnished with some neat shops, and the streets are paved.

Leaving Missolonghi on November 23rd 1809 by water, Byron and Hobhouse had looked back at the rows of huts with stakes planted in front of them to break the force of the waves. '. . . They seemed the more wretched to us, as we passed them on a rainy day, and saw the waves washing over them with every gust of wind.' That sight was to become a dismally familiar one to Byron.

The reason why this remote, depressing, insalubrious spot had become the seat of Government was simply that small fort which, since Hobhouse described it, had been wrested from the Turks. The shallowness of the bay, the ease of controlling the shipping, had made it nearly invulnerable to an attack by water, while access through the mountain routes was practically impossible in winter.

Byron's reception must have been very gratifying and moving, but he was not allowed any time to savour it.

> After eight days of such fatigue, he had scarcely time to refresh himself, and converse with Mavrocordato, and his friends and countrymen, before he was assailed by the tumultuous visits of the primates and chiefs. These latter, not content with coming all together, each had a suite of twenty or thirty, and not unfrequently fifty soldiers. It was difficult to make them understand that he would fix certain hours to receive them. . . . Their visits began at seven o'clock [a.m.] and the greater part of them were without any object. This is one of the most insupportable annoyances to which a man of influence and consideration is exposed in the East.

So wrote Gamba; and Lega too, in his long and graphic letter, remarked that the petitioners arrived at all hours making no distinction between morning and evening. It was true, as Pietro said, that some came with feeble excuses or none, merely to gaze at him, but many were setting keen hope on his financial aid, and Byron realized with trepidation that, until the loan from England was in hand, the conduct of the war was literally dependent on how far he could stretch his personal resources and distinguish between genuine and factitious claims for his support.

The ground has been so well-covered by books easy to procure[1] that I shall concentrate on the figures, for the most part unpublished, in Lega's accounts. On January 10th, he paid Captain Valsamacchi the expenses of the voyage in the bombard, two hundred dollars, and fifty extra for gratuities, with reimbursements for some provisions which had come to upwards of fifteen; to the captain of the mistico thirty dollars for hire and twenty for tips, with a reimbursement of two dollars and sixty obols. Twelve dollars to the skipper of a boat 'in quarantine' may have been the gratuity to the sailors who brought Byron ashore at Missolonghi. Two to 'Vincenzo the Maltese' for half a month's wages is an item I cannot explain—unless he was engaged locally to lend a hand to Tita and Croci and the exhausted Fletcher (victim of a bad cold) with moving into the house in which Byron had to occupy what Pietro calls 'two wretched rooms' on the second floor with all his attendants except the stablemen, Stanhope having taken full possession of the first storey.

The landlord, Apostoli Capsali, a primate, charged twenty dollars a month for this dingy accommodation, and produced groceries and candles that first day for about thirteen more. The courier, Baccicino, who had probably delivered the letter to Stanhope from Dragomestri, recovered his expenses of some seven and a half dollars, and a man who brought his lordship the festive gift of a lamb was tipped one dollar.

From now on, except that the major units were still Spanish silver, Lega had to reckon in Turkish money—40 paras to the piastre, 10 piastres to the Spanish dollar. In his book, *Greece in 1823 and 1824*, Stanhope gives some idea of the purchasing power of this money:

Annual rent of a good house	500 to 700 piastres (50 to 70 dollars)
Cost of a horse fit for riding	150 to 200 ,,
A cow	100 ,,
A sheep	10 ,,
A goat	8 ,,
A male labourer	1½ piastres a day (less than a dollar for a 6-day week)
A female ,,	1 piastre a day
A boy	20 paras (half a piastre a day)
A manservant	20 piastres a month and maintenance
A woman servant	,, ,, ,, ,, ,, ,,

A turkey, 6 piastres, a goose, 4 piastres, a duck, 2 piastres, a chicken, half a piastre, eggs, half a piastre a dozen approximately.

[1] Notably Marchand's 3-volume and 1-volume biographies. Harold Nicolson's *Byron, The Last Journey* lacks particulars which were unknown or not thought important in 1924, when it was first published, but gives a persuasive picture of Byron's life at Missolonghi. William St Clair's *That Greece Might Still be Free* (1972) is a vista of the whole Greek War. In *The Late Lord Byron* I have devoted chapters to the antagonisms between members of his entourage, particularly Stanhope and Parry.

The food, which was much less varied than at Metaxata, cost two to three dollars a day for the whole suite, and of this, according to Pietro, Byron's share was only about one piastre, for he lived on almost nothing but bread, a little fish or cheese, and a few olives. This abstinence was sustained and meant, Pietro thought, to set the example of the leader not having better food than the troops; but it is also a possibility that the harassing difficulties by which he was surrounded, the lack of comfort and even warmth (there were no chimneys and so no fires in the living rooms), the endeavour to keep up his spirits in the face of waning hopes of unity among the people he had come to help, combined with the illness which had been sapping away his strength for months, had reduced his appetite and thrown him upon drink as a comforter—though it is fair to say we do not hear of this until he had been at Missolonghi some weeks. The indifference of his protégé, to whom even Pietro at twenty-three must have seemed forbiddingly mature, gave him a feeling of rejection which we know only from his final writings.

'Jan. 15th. Expenses on Milord's behalf, by his orders—ten dollars.' I fancy that was something for Lukas. Byron's pocket money is usually entered simply as 'Given to Milord', while other payments are always specified. On January 16th milk for Lukas is charged to the account, a rarity in Byron's household. On the 18th the really substantial sum of fifty-five dollars was paid for 'Lukas's expenses by order of Milord', and eleven dollars more for having a fascia made 'and for other things'.[1] On the 21st, we find 'To Lukas by order of Milord—twenty eight dollars'.[2] On the 25th, there is a similar entry of twenty dollars, and that alone was a soldier's pay for five months at nearly twice the rate the Government gave—when it was able to pay at all. The boy thus became thoroughly spoiled, and, evidently ignoring all the gifts he was receiving, demanded a regular salary and the privilege of taking tea like his Lordship instead of the milk which was now supplied to him daily. The comeback was swift and withering:

Feb. 2nd 1824

Tea is not a Greek beverage—therefore Master Lukas may drink Coffee instead—or water—or nothing.—

The pay of the said Lukas will be five dollars a month paid like the others of the household. He will eat with the Suliots—or where he pleases.

---

[1] 46877. The fascia may have been the swathed sash some Greeks wore.

[2] Ibid. The 21st, the day before Byron's thirty-sixth birthday, may have been the one on which he wrote his memorable and melancholy lyric beginning, "Tis time this heart should be unmoved/Since others it has ceased to move,/Yet though I cannot be beloved,/Still let me love'.

The lieutenant of Sr. Drako may eat with those of my house—others no—without at least that I know of it first.[1]

One of Lega's descendants who knew nothing of the situation endorsed this note, 'Directions to his Lordship Lord Byron's servants as to their eating and drinking whom he kept short as he did himself'. There was of course no question of 'keeping short' a boy accorded privileges enough to make all the others envious. He was being put in his place—only he did not stay there.

Concurrently, the ledger leads to an incident which reveals that aspect of Byron's character which must always command admiration.

	Dollars	Piastres	Paras
Jan 20th A cloak for the Turkish prisoner Mecmet [Mehmet] of Duligno	2	4	
,, 22nd Jacket, breeches, and shirt for the Turkish prisoner, Mecmet	4	0	20
,, 24th Tobacco and tinder for the prisoner		1	02
,, 28th Smoking tobacco for the Turkish prisoner[2]			32

These are the first of a long succession of Byron's humane acts to Turkish nationals, and they were done with great moral courage and at the risk of losing his popularity. The prisoner had been the only sailor who had not escaped when a Greek privateer had nearly captured his ship. Having fallen overboard, he had no recourse but to swim to the hostile vessel, which had taken him on board. No international body existed to frame a code for the treatment of prisoners, who were generally handled most ignominiously and brutally: but when Pietro wrote to the Governor of the town at Byron's request asking that Mehmet be taken off the ship, the favour could hardly be refused. That night, however, two of the Greek sailors came unheralded to demand 'their Turk'. They were blusteringly importunate, Byron angry and immovable, and the altercation resulted in his drawing a pistol and threatening to shoot unless they withdrew—which they did. The prisoner being left in his charge, Byron tried to inculcate ideas of a civilized attitude by the attentions Lega catalogued. Pietro tells us that he offered to send the man to neutral territory in the Ionian Islands but Mehmet was afraid to leave their protection.

On January 30th and 31st, we find entries of twenty dollars 'given to the 4 Turkish prisoners to send them to the Castle of the Morea', with bread, wine, cheese, and other food and also tobacco and tinder, and money for canoes to get them as far as the fort; an amount of about twenty-seven dollars in all. These four had been captured on another

[1] 46878 Folio 22. In Italian. The reading of the last few words is uncertain.
[2] 46877.

occasion, and it had occurred to Byron that by releasing and sending them back to Yussuf Pasha with a diplomatic letter, he might avert the cruelties which Greek prisoners not seldom suffered at the hands of the Turks. He was very happy to receive the Pasha's encouraging reply.

Such violations of custom naturally did not please everyone. The town in any case was seething with discontented and unruly soldiers whose pay was eight months in arrears, and who alarmed the civilians by the desperation of their sheer want. Byron was asked to take fifteen hundred of them into his service, but, with all the other calls upon his purse, was unwilling to be responsible for more than five hundred, and these he maintained and tried his best to discipline. The large sum he was known to have in his house—though it was rapidly being depleted and he had sent to Zante for more—placed him in some jeopardy from the wilder elements of the disorganized floating population, and he engaged five Suliots to guard his quarters, paying them each three dollars a month plus a special allowance of six paras a day and an extra dollar for the leader.[1] There were also sixteen picked Suliots under the command of Captain Drako, one of the more reliable men engaged in Cephalonia. All these counted themselves lucky, their pay being dependable.

The five hundred others became Pietro's soldiers, except for a company of thirty whom Byron placed under the fifteen-year-old Lukas. This was not quite so besotted an act as it may seem. In a day when good breeding, which Lukas had, constituted in itself a title to command, no one seems to have resented his promotion to officership nearly so much as that of William Parry, a highly capable man but not, except by nature, a gentleman. Out of liking for his character and respect for his ability, Byron, who had been appointed Commander-in-Chief, conferred the style of Major of the Artillery Brigade on Parry, though he had come out as an artificer sent by the London Committee to run a laboratory for making Congreve rockets and other weaponry. This abnegation of class distinction profoundly shocked Stanhope, himself an Earl's son, and gave such offence to Kinderman, one of the Prussian officers, that he could not brook the impropriety and departed. (Of all the foreigners who came to redeem Greece, the Germans were perhaps the touchiest, the least inclined to adapt their high-flown notions and rigid etiquette to the realities of life around them: but they were musical and Byron enjoyed their songs and their flute-playing, being partial, Pietro says, to German music.)

Parry, a former fire-master in the navy, who was making his way to Missolonghi by a long and difficult route, first appears obliquely in Lega's

[1] 46876 Folio 45. Their names in Lega's Italianized version were Giorgio Cilaga, Spiro Margari, Giorgio Darmani, Attanasio Savi, and Demetrio Canzopoulo. Later their number was increased to six.

books in the shape of payments to Sig.^{r} Ereschett (Lega's way of writing Hesketh) who had gone all the way to Cephalonia to warn him that the intermittent blockade by the Turks had been resumed and that he had better bring his valuable cargo to Dragomestri so that it could be fetched by boats able to negotiate the shallows. All the Europeans in Byron's brigade volunteered for the dangerous enterprise of passing the Turkish fleet by night, doubtless in another mistico. We cannot positively divorce their gallantry from the eagerness each of them must have felt to get away from Missolonghi if only for a few days. It had been raining so incessantly that the gates of the town were choked up with mud, and even the streets unfit for walking and the roads for riding.

Henry Hesketh, a somewhat pompous young Englishman who was one of Byron's two aides-de-camp, had the luck to be chosen for the exploit and to succeed; on his return he received eighty-three dollars, twenty-five being for the boat, eight for his expenses, and fifty for a gun Byron coveted.[1] Hopes ran high with the imminence of Parry's arrival, which had been preceded by many causes of concern.

One of these was the frequent contravention of Ionian neutrality by the Greeks. A privateer had recently taken an Ionian boat off Patras, and on January 26th, three British naval officers came in the *Alacrity*, a gunboat, to demand compensation. Byron was of the opinion that they were justified, but Mavrocordato argued that the infraction had been sanctioned by Greek tribunals and the prize was a fair one: in any case, they had no money to pay even as little as two hundred dollars, for which, after lengthy discussion in Byron's presence, Captain Yorke agreed to settle. No delay was to be granted. This was the sort of situation Byron could always handle dexterously. He took the officers to his own quarters, charmed them with his entertaining talk and warm hospitality, and, when they refused to accept restitution from him personally, secretly sent the money to Praides, the Secretary of the Government, so that it should appear to come from the Greeks; and honour was satisfied. After the entry of the two hundred dollars in Lega's book, we find slightly more than four for sending on to the *Alacrity* some bottles of gin, for the quality of which Byron apologized to the English captain in a note next day:

> . . . It is however the best that could be extracted from this Marsh. There has been no account sent in [the account had already been paid]—and the price must be in itself so very trifling that Ld B. begs Capt. Yorke will not think a moment on the subject as on some future occasion L.B. hopes to

[1] 46877 Folio 27. 5 Feb.

indemnify himself with interest from the Navy stores and more particularly
from those of Captain Yorke.[1]

While coping with a multitude of problems requiring diplomacy,
dignity, courage, and—invariably—money, Byron also had on his hands
the peculiar self-complacency and solemnity of 'the Typographical
Colonel', a dedicated disciple of Jeremy Bentham's political doctrines,
who imagined the Turks could be routed by printing newspapers, which
few Greeks could read, and founding schools on the Utilitarian principles
that Dickens was to satirize two generations later. Stanhope was the kind
of theorist who easily achieves importance on a committee by attention
to correctness of procedure and addiction to wrapping each subject in a
formula. A private conversation with him became like a committee
meeting. He was the very antithesis of Byron. 'The colonel could not
relish nor indeed understand Byron's pleasantry', Pietro ventured to
write, even with Stanhope on hand to read. '. . . The more his Lordship
laughed, the more serious the colonel became; and the discussion seldom
ended without a strong reproof. . . .'

Young Englishmen came and went, but Byron, confined in the same
house as Stanhope by rain and cold, was closeted with him evening
after evening, and the arrival of Parry, who turned up at last on February 7th, was a godsend. Parry was a humorous man, practical, earthy,
and somewhat bibulous; Stanhope was visionary, lofty, and strictly
temperate. Although to Byron Parry's presence was a comfort, his
advent was a keen disappointment considered as a contribution from
England towards victory. The longed-for cargo brought from Dragomestri
against all kinds of obstacles consisted, through no fault of Parry's, of
printing presses for the colonel's newspapers, and other items chosen, for
the most part, with that quaint idealism which characterizes committees
planning far from the places where actual work is to be done. They had
sent no coal, and armaments could not be manufactured without it; but
there was a plenitude of Greek testaments. Worse still, Parry had come
without the smallest supply of money, and soon, beside all his other
commitments, Byron was paying the accounts for him and the team of
eight mechanics he had brought with him.

	Dollars	Piastres	Paras
Feb. 15th To the English Captain Parry as account	116		
,, 19th To Sig.ʳ Parry as receipt	40		

[1] 46878 Folio 18. 27 Jan. The letter was never received, the ship having sailed. It
was as a consequence of their meeting that Surgeon Daniel Forrester, R.N. wrote one
of the very last accounts of Byron as he appeared at a brief but unforgettable
encounter—still most impressive in person and personality.

			Dollars	Piastres	Paras
Feb.	20th	To Capt. Parry, Col. Stanhope's account [Stanhope was always careful to recover from Byron every penny he felt entitled to claim]	50		
,,	21st	Sig.ᵣ Parry as receipt	60		
,,	28th	Sig. Parry as receipt	100		
Mar.	3rd	Captain Parry	222	7	
,,	13th	,, ,,	200		
Apr.	3rd	,, ,,	369	9	17
,,	6th	Work done by tailor approved by Captain Parry	10	7	
,,	12th	Captain Parry	250		
,,	17th	,, ,,	300[1]		

All these sums and more he gave with a good grace because, though helpless as to the manufacture of rockets, Parry was labouring to achieve some semblance of an Artillery Brigade and replenishing, so far as he could, the crumbling fortifications. After Byron's death, he certified that two more accounts were due amounting to more than three thousand two hundred dollars, and Lega settled them.[2] They were chiefly for running the Artillery Brigade. Byron at this period had literally been paying the whole expenses of the war in Western Greece and was constantly writing to his bankers for more money.

It was during the months of finding only frustration and pecuniary need wherever he turned that Byron had little Hatajè brought to his notice—a Turkish child of eight or nine whose mother, wife of one of Missolonghi's former leading citizens, was now obliged to work as an unpaid servant in the house where Julius Millingen, an English volunteer doctor, had a lodging. Her father, when Turkish males were massacred three years before, had fled to Yussuf Pasha; the rest of her family, with at least two brothers, had been killed. Byron must have seen her first on February 8th, when we find in Lega's book: 'To a Turkish woman with a little girl—two dollars':[3] and then an item for an errand of Tita's to buy sweets. Within a few days there is an entry of five dollars five piastres for 'An unhappy group of Turkish women, 11 persons including some children'. These were people who, Byron discovered, had been held in slavery since the beginning of the Revolution. There were also ten miserable men.

[1] 46877 and 46876. At the time of the last payment Byron was on his death-bed.
[2] Murray MSS. April 1824. Byron was also under the necessity of providing Parry with money from the day of his arrival, but as it must have come from his own purse, I do not know the sum. Though Parry was much disliked, no one has ever questioned his honesty.
[3] 46877.

His request to the Government to let him send them to their own countrymen was granted. He wrote to the British Consul at Prevesa, Mr Mayer, saying that one of his principal objects in coming to Greece had been to alleviate as much as possible the sufferings incidental to war— ('when the dictates of humanity are in question, I know no difference between Turks and Greeks')[1]—and he asked that the Governor of the town might see them to a place of safety and look upon them as a present, which the Ottoman commanders might be inspired to return if Greeks hereafter fell into their hands. The letter must have been sent the day when Lega paid:

		Dollars	Piastres	Paras
Feb. 17th	Provisions for 21 Turkish prisoners being sent to Prevesa	5	9	28
	For the same, assistance	21		
	To the dressmaker Gula of Janina, dresses for two Turkish women	8	2	34[2]

Most of the Turks were probably in threadbare clothes, and Byron had already ordered Fletcher to get one of them a dress—or dress material—some days before.[3] It cost a dollar, which was the price of ten sheep and adequate, I dare say, for respectable covering. The two by a named dressmaker must have been far superior, and we might think they were for Hatajè and her mother, but the recipients appear as '*due donne Turche*', and it would have been odd for Lega to call a small child a *donna*. She had been expected to leave with the party of fugitives, but the mother, learning that her husband, Hussein Aga, was at Patras not Prevesa, chose not to go. Byron was to see them often again.

He was very weak when the boatload of Turks left. Two nights before he had had a short but violent seizure, had been unable to walk or speak and his frame so convulsed that Parry and Tita with Hesketh had all been needed to hold him down. The pain had been so intense that he said if it had lasted a minute longer he was sure he must have died. Next day, when he was struggling to recuperate, the doctors, Millingen and Bruno, put eight leeches on his temples,[4] the flow of blood could hardly be staunched and he fainted.

Although the general opinion was that under-nourishment had been a factor in his illness, the doctors, true to their time, were convinced that further bleeding and a diet solely of chicken broth would restore him. Byron had loathed the idea of bleeding from childhood, when it had been ordered as the remedy for a fall from a tree! He had seen his nurse, the detested May Gray, being bled and had conceived such a horror of lancets

---

[1] *LJ.* Undated.   [2] Ibid.   [3] 3 Feb.
[4] Ibid. Lega entered the cost of the leeches as one piastre.

that he had threatened, if touched, to pull the doctor's nose and had been left alone.[1] Parry, though older than any other foreigner at Missolonghi, was the only person modern enough to see that, if Byron had got rid of his doctors, his life might have been saved.

The disturbances in the town had been rising to a crescendo, destroying all prospect of carrying out a carefully laid plan to take Lepanto, a conquest which would have been easy and yet a great stimulant to morale. The Suliots, always refractory, were perpetually engaged in strife, if not through incorrigible dissensions amongst themselves, then against the townspeople, and there were panics, injuries, and sometimes deaths. On February 19th, an affray took place in which a German officer, Sass, who had tried to repel an intruder in the Arsenal, met his end with three bullets in his head and his arm nearly severed. It was plain—it had been plain for weeks—that these fierce mountain soldiers were not an asset but a serious liability, and Byron, in accord with Stanhope for once, decided that either all the Suliots not in his personal service must leave the town or that the whole European contingent would withdraw. To get them to go, he had to give them a month's pay, and on February 22nd, Lega handed over to the Governor three thousand dollars of the money newly delivered from Zante to get rid of them,[2] a repetition on a much bigger and costlier scale of what had happened at Cephalonia.

At the same time, six of Parry's eight mechanics resolved to go back to England as fast as they could. They were frightened not only of further incidents such as the killing of Sass, but of accidental death through the Greek habit of discharging firearms in reckless high spirits. 'It was in vain', Pietro says with some naiveté, 'to tell them that the firing of ball was a daily occurrence—they would go.' Parry remained with only two assistants. They could not have been reassured by a pretty severe earthquake which happened that night followed by 'a general discharge of musketry throughout the town, according to a superstition of the Greeks on such occasions'.

On the 23rd, Dr Millingen came with an appeal for cash, and brought Hatajè and her mother. Byron gave Millingen twenty dollars, and six to the Turkish woman with her little girl.[3] Millingen, who is often inexact and inclined, like so many, to exaggerate his own part in the events he reports, says that Byron had 'immediately' wished to adopt Hatajè on first having her brought to him, and 'immediately'—he is fond of the word—ordered finer dresses to be made than those he (Millingen) had given them. The young doctor, whose salary for running a dispensary was not more than £20 a year augmented by what Byron subscribed, was

---

[1] Gordon, Pryse Lockhart.   [2] 46877 Folio 30.   [3] Ibid.

possibly alluding to those dresses from Gula of Janina, supplied on Byron's order. Lega's precise dates show that Byron's fondness for the child was not a thing of dramatic suddenness. It was after seeing her for the third or fourth time that he wrote to Augusta saying he had 'nearly decided' on adopting her.[1]

By March he was trying to make definite arrangements to have her brought up by Dr Kennedy of Argostoli and his wife. His benevolent plans were due perhaps to the memory of Allegra and the thought of his unknown daughter in England, who was about the same age and for whom he always felt a curiously pathetic longing. He bought the Turkish child, who was intelligent and beautiful, a red cap and two kerchiefs, one for the head and one to go round the waist, and later he presented her with an elaborate outfit which included a gold-braided headdress decorated with twenty-six gilded silver coins, a very handsome gift which cost more than forty dollars and caused intense jealousy.[2] When Byron heard that his favouritism was exciting ill-feeling towards the little Turk, he over-reacted in his customary way and ordered a yet more resplendent toilette for her—a gala dress Lega calls it—as well as a second everyday dress and two more kerchiefs, the dressmaker's bill coming to just under fifty dollars.[3] This caprice was offset the same week by his sending twenty-one more Turks to safety.[4]

Lukas meanwhile was not less extravagantly equipped than Hatajè, a bill for forty-five dollars being paid for him by Lega on March 21st,[5] while he ran up an account for nearly a thousand drachmas to buy such luxuries as gold-laced jackets and rich saddle-cloths and to have his pistols gilded.[6] Regaling so lavishly two young people he had rescued from abject poverty was certainly the only way of spending money which Byron could now find enjoyable. It may have been for them that he assented to a performance on Leap Year's Day of some 'masks', as Lega calls them, to whom he gave two dollars.[7]

The month of March began with Byron still in a low state. Light caused an uncomfortable sensation in his eyes, and, though four candles could not have been very brilliant, he had shades made for them.[8] He suffered from vertigo and attacks of apparently irrational apprehension.

---

[1] *LJ.* 23 Mar. 1824.   [2] 46876. 28 Mar. and 1 Apr.

[3] Ibid. 30 Apr. It was paid with the bill for some appurtenances of his coffin.

[4] Ibid. 3 Apr.   [5] Ibid.

[6] Murray MS. The bill was presented on the day of Byron's death. The drachma was a patriotic but premature revival of the ancient Greek name for a coin which was not actually revived till 1833. Probably in 1824 it was a synonym for a piastre.

[7] 46877. On 10 Apr. Byron contributed towards a gymnastic display which doubtless took place at the Arsenal. He was ill and did not go. (46876.)

[8] 46876, entered 16 and 18 Mar.

The rumour of his ill-health brought letters from Cephalonia strongly urging him to return there, but he would not leave the unlovable spot where it would be his task to administer the balm that would cure, as everyone imagined, the maladies that afflicted Greece—the vital loan from England. Unfortunately, the three British physicians of the garrison, led by the well-meaning Kennedy, wrote privately to Bruno urging him to persist in bleeding his illustrious patient, to which the inexperienced young man, not be be outdone in wisdom, replied that this was exactly what he intended to do.[1]

Byron strove to keep fit by riding, fencing, singlestick, and even joining in the drill for troops. He constantly took salt water baths, as at Pisa, and on every dry day he would go with Pietro by a monoxylo, the local type of canoe, to a place where they could manage some exercise on horseback. But in mid-March, heavy rains began again, and then, cooped up in the crowded house, he became querulous and would react unreasonably to small annoyances.

Stanhope by now had gone to Athens where he was planning to set up printing presses, to found a museum of antiquities, to start a Lancastrian school, to organize a Utilitarian society, and to impose universal suffrage. He wished for Englishmen to emigrate in large numbers to teach the Greeks how to live. His letters are so egregious in their total blindness to prevailing circumstances that, unless he had proudly published them himself, we should think they were written by a hostile parodist. Trelawny's idol, the robber chieftain Odysseus, was waiting for just such a one.

It is an extraordinary thing, showing a rare opacity of judgment, that Stanhope knew Odysseus had been a brigand and said so,[2] but was perfectly willing to believe, after one or two meetings with him and the eloquent Trelawny, that this former minion of Ali Pasha had no other object in life than to establish a free press, democratic government, equitable taxes, and the rule of law! He became almost as infatuated as Trelawny himself. I cannot put the case in a neater nutshell than Harold Nicolson's of 1924:

> It had not been very difficult perhaps for Odysseus to complete the conquest of Trelawny. The latter, it was obvious, was determined to play a leading part in Greece; it was obvious also that he was passionately jealous of Lord Byron. It was an easy thing to work upon these passions in order to detach Trelawny from the party of Mavrocordato. Colonel Stanhope was a more difficult, though far more glorious capture. It is to the credit of

[1] Kennedy.
[2] Stanhope. To Bowring, 11 Mar. 1824. 'The **General Odysseus** has been a mountain robber.'

Odysseus's diplomacy that he should have realised with remarkable rapidity the weak side of Colonel Stanhope. What Odysseus was after was Byron's money, and the London loan of which Byron and Stanhope would shortly be able to dispose. For such a prize it was worth while to bow the knee for a moment to the Phanar. [Mavrocordato was a Phanariot.] Meanwhile the important thing was to secure Lord Byron.

Both Stanhope and Trelawny implored him in most pressing terms to attend a conference Odysseus proposed to hold at Salona. Trelawny's letter pleaded the cause Byron had 'so gloriously and liberally aided',[1] a strain very different from that in which he wrote to Leigh Hunt about his miserliness and to Jane Williams about his 'imbecility'. Byron received the two communications on March 18th, but he had already heard of the projected congress some days before from George Finlay, who had arrived from Athens in the hope of persuading him to go there and also to send Odysseus arms and gunpowder.

At that time Finlay was a supporter of the Klepht, of whose nefarious ways he was, in maturer years, to write one of the most pungent denunciations. He came, it is hardly necessary to say, in want of money, and Lega paid him in all two hundred and fifty-four dollars on Byron's order;[2] but two hundred of these were for Trelawny. In crossing a swollen and rapidly flowing river on horseback, Finlay had lost his saddlebags which contained money he had received on Trelawny's behalf from the island bankers. After this setback, he remained for a while at Missolonghi, enjoying Byron's conversation each evening, much to the dissatisfaction of Parry; for Byron had not lost his capacity for inspiring an intense possessiveness in the members of his entourage.

Reluctantly he sent some gunpowder to Athens, but no other arms. He knew a good deal about Odysseus from Mavrocordato, and was not convinced that a congress at Salona under his auspices would be properly conducted. Nevertheless he undertook to attend, and only deferred his going on the day fixed, March 27th, because of flooded roads and rivers. His influence, partly through money in hand or to come, but also because of his sound sense and patently genuine disinterestedness, was perpetually increasing; and in the numerous chieftains and primates who visited or wrote to him he engendered a respect which has persisted as a tradition in the Greek people. He was offered the governor-generalship of the liberated parts of Greece but postponed acceptance until he could be sure the office would not be merely a nominal one. The freedom of Missolonghi was likewise conferred on him, only to be succeeded by new demands and new trials, and the departure for Salona had again to be put off lest he appear to be deserting the town when it most needed him.

---

[1] Stanhope. 6 Mar.   [2] 46876. 12 Mar., 1 Apr. and 8 Apr.

A contingent of soldiers from the chieftain Karaiskaki landed in boats, ostensibly demanding revenge for an injury inflicted by Missolonghiots on his nephew: but it was thought this was an excuse for discrediting Mavrocordato and promoting his own faction and that of Djavella, with whom he had entered into an alliance. Two primates were kidnapped, the fortress of the bay, the very key to the security of the city, was suddenly occupied by Suliots from Anatolico, and the Turkish fleet appeared in the offing. The local population was overcome with one of those contagious spasms of alarm which may so easily seize upon people who have been long in suspense; and Byron felt it was desirable for morale that he should show himself at the head of his brigade. It was a sensible decision and a brave one. For once that spring the day was fine, and this three-mile ride —himself and Pietro dressed undoubtedly in their best uniforms, Tita and the Negro also in uniform following them, and two groups of well-drilled soldiers all in white fustanellas acting as escort, their special skill being a running pace by which they kept up with the horses—this was a sight to put new heart into the citizens, who could not foresee that the next cortège to bring them from their houses would be the one that accompanied his coffin.

It was not the end of Byron's troubles or anyone else's at Missolonghi, but it did help to beget a spirit of resistance in the inhabitants. Byron gave swift and effective orders for the defence of the town with what weapons it had (two of them were the little cannons removed from the still un-paid-for *Bolivar*), and the mutiny subsided; the fort was evacuated, the kidnapped primates sent back from Anatolico, and Mavrocordato went there in person to place Karaiskaki under arrest.[1]

The two last letters Byron wrote, so far as is known, were both to bankers. The end of his life was bedevilled, as his youth had been, by having constantly to think about money: but then, along with great generosity, there had also been self-indulgence and waste. Now his course was one of self-abnegation and sacrifice—not reckless and spectacular to win praise but for the most part thoughtfully and prudently measured. At least he lived to know the loan had been raised—and died too soon to watch it being squandered.

The first instalment of the £800,000, much more than the whole annual revenue of Greece, was on its way—thirty thousand sovereigns in gold and fifty thousand Spanish silver dollars, which arrived at Zante six days after his death, in the ship that was to carry his corpse to England.

Of the illness that killed him the only eye-witness accounts we have were most regrettably written either with the total lack of medical know-

---

[1] He was exiled and took refuge in the mountains of Agrafa, but lived to fight the Turks and to be killed in action.

ledge, which was natural in Pietro and Fletcher, or else in the defensive spirit of the two principal doctors. (Parry, who clearly had intuition, is an exception, but unfortunately, he was not encouraged to be present.) Bruno and Millingen were so absolutely horrified that a patient of such renown should have succumbed in their hands, and at just the moment when his life was, in the sheerly material sense, of most value, that their anxiety to disclaim any accusation of incompetence coloured all they had to say. They scarcely stopped short of making Byron himself responsible for the fatality, stressing repeatedly his intemperance and wilful disobedience to their orders, which, if he had only followed them, would have saved him. Bruno in particular, being Byron's personal physician, was self-exonerating to the extent of falsehood.

His case history states that: 'On arriving at Missolonghi in the beginning of January', Byron considerably increased the quantity of spirits he drank, 'being induced thereto by the insinuations and persuasions of a certain captain, with whom he was in the habit of consorting every evening'.[1] This captain is shown by the context to be Parry, who never set eyes on Byron till February 7th! Parry is also blamed for tempting Byron to eat meat—and meat with strong 'heating condiments'—instead of remaining on the 'rigorous diet' Bruno had prescribed. That Byron did follow the diet is to be seen in Lega's incontrovertible entries for his Lordship's chicken broth as well as in the astonishment so often expressed by those who lived with him at the extreme sparsity of his regimen. If we clear Byron, on the strength of so many evidences, of the charge of overeating, we are entitled to doubt the excessive drinking too.

We may accept that he did try to cheer himself up by taking more drink than was good for him during his evenings with Parry until his seizure pulled him up, and in fact there is an item the night before it of seven and a half piastres spent on 'punch for Milord and company'. He himself admits in his journal that he had been 'not uniformly so temperate as I may generally affirm I was wont to be'.[2] But after February 15th he drank chiefly water—by no means the healthiest beverage at Missolonghi—until February 29th when a little wine was bought for him and two glasses.[3] It is more than a fortnight before wine appears again—seven bottles 'for the special use of Milord' at one dollar three piastres. This supply lasted a week. Then two dollars' worth of wine is entered,[4] and after that date—March 24th—no more. Parry is thus telling the strict truth as to the last two months when he says, 'He drank a very small quantity of wine or cider; but indulged in the use of no spirituous liquors'.

[1] Murray MS. Nicolson's translation.
[2] *LJ.* Journal written on 17 Feb., two days after the attack.
[3] 46877.   [4] 46876. 17 Mar.

Bruno further discredits himself when he writes: 'He insisted on abandoning the hot baths which I had prescribed for him, preferring to provoke perspiration by the game of singlestick . . . with the effect that his head became over-heated.' Here again we may turn to Lega's book, where payment after payment of about two piastres a time is entered for Milord's bath. 'Dr Bruno I believe to be a very good young man,' says Parry, 'but he was certainly inadequate to his situation.' Millingen, who was not called for the first three days, became hysterical, openly weeping as it grew more and more apparent that, despite the draining of his blood copiously with leeches and lancets, despite the application of blisters, the infliction of strong purgatives and repeated doses of antimony, a lingering and agonizing death was descending on the famous poet, the man of pre-eminent attractiveness, the hope of Greece.

Of Lega during those nine harrowing days we hear nothing directly. We know he was there because the household expenses go on and are dealt with, wages are paid, the stable is catered for—with Lukas's horse noted separately—and the books kept balanced weekly. On April 11th, the day when his patron was suffering from alternate cold and hot shiverings, with a pain that wandered over his body, Lega sent by his order a pair of slippers to the little Turkish girl.[1] They were meant, I assume, to complete the rich costume just given to her—and to atone, it may be, for scolding her on Finlay's suggestion because she had been 'pert and forward'.

It was on that date that Parry pleaded with him to go to Zante for 'a change of air and scene' and wrung from him 'an unwilling assent'. Boats, he says, were got ready for his conveyance, with Count Gamba, Hesketh, Bruno, Fletcher, and Tita, to the islands, and all arrangements for their departure completed by the 13th, when a hurricane came up making it impossible for ships to leave the port. There is not the slightest trace in the ledger of any plan to leave Missolonghi—unless some of the hundred and fifty dollars paid to Parry on April 12th were spent on prep-arations; but it is hard to believe that, if all was in train for the journey, not a single person would have mentioned it except Parry himself. I believe in this instance, he fell into the temptation of dramatizing his defeat by exaggerating in retrospect his nearness to victory. All Lega recorded was that on April 12th, Byron had his salt water bath and that, on the 13th, a clay carafe was purchased for his room, for with all the drugs Bruno was prescribing—besides antimony, castor oil, Epsom salts, hen-bane!—he had a torturing thirst.

On the 14th we find 'Sweet apples bought for Milord from the captain come from Ancona' and twice that day salt water was brought for a hot footbath.[2] On the 15th, his condition was recognized as grave. He was

[1] Ibid. [2] Ibid.

surrounded by people urging him to be bled and, on refusing, was given calomel and colocynth. He tried, as he had done the day before, to answer letters.

There is no hint anywhere of Lukas's presence, but at some time before the room became a scene of disorder and desolation such as Byron would not have wished him to see, he must have been admitted because, while fully conscious, Byron handed him the Government's receipt for the three thousand dollars he had spent on ridding the town of riotous Suliots, money which was to have been repaid when the funds from England arrived. This was intended to provide for Lukas's family. It was also known that he had let him have a bag of Maria Theresa crowns. There is even a question of Lukas's being given, or having helped himself to, a considerable sum of Italian and Spanish currency which was missing after his benefactor's death,[1] but Lega's account sheds no light on this because it was evidently not part of the money in his keeping. The sole service Lukas was able to perform was to fetch barley water for his Lordship, which cost about a dollar a time, on two occasions.[2] What he felt, a boy of fifteen completely cut off from all that was congenial to his age and condition, we can only speculate.

Whether in delirium or striving inarticulately to express himself, Byron constantly alluded to sums of money and in such a way as to leave little doubt that his mind was preoccupied with the future of his servants; but after the 16th, when the terrible process of repeated bleeding was added to all the other draconian remedies, he became incoherent.

Bruno supported by Millingen drew blood from his veins and temples as if it had been an alien fluid which must be got out of his system: and when two older doctors were at last called—Treiber, a German of the Artillery Brigade, and Vaya, a Greek who had attended Ali Pasha—and ventured to disapprove of the treatment, Bruno solemnly announced that, if the blood-letting were stopped, his Lordship was a doomed man. Temporarily, however, he yielded to their suggestions; a draught of cream of tartar and boracic was prepared, and Parry was sent for to get the patient to take bark (quinine). The ledger also shows that two drams of extract of tamarind, credited with having cooling and laxative properties, were brought. Laudanum and ether at least produced some fitful sleep.

Fletcher, who had become alarmed much sooner than the medical

[1] Pietro's letter to Hobhouse on the subject will be found in Chapter V of *The Late Lord Byron*. He angrily repudiated insinuations of a homosexual relationship between Byron and the boy.
[2] Ibid. 15 Apr. and 1 May, the second amount being among the posthumous expenses.

men, was ultimately successful in getting Lega to send a boat to Zante to fetch the English doctor Thomas, the Health Inspector in the islands, whose reputation stood high. The wind had subsided by the 18th sufficiently for a Captain Dragonotti to risk the voyage. A little bill for food to take with him was paid by Lega, and twenty dollars for the journey.[1] But Dr Thomas was absent and all the Greek captain could do was to leave messages for him.

That same day Pietro kept back a letter from the Archbishop Ignatius which contained the news that the Sultan of Turkey in full divan had formally proclaimed Lord Byron an enemy of the Sublime Porte. It was, I think, injudicious to withhold this declaration because, though nothing at this stage could have saved his ebbing life (excepting, possibly, blood transfusions, a technique as yet undreamed of), his mettlesome temperament, which had so often made him act with courage or with indiscretion, might have risen with a flicker of satisfaction to the challenge.

In the final hours another sailor arrived and was tipped two piastres for bringing him letters. Kinnaird and Hobhouse had written, to praise and encourage him, to tell him his financial affairs were in fine order, that his laurels were blooming, that the Greek Committee had passed a fervent vote of gratitude to him, and, ironically, that he was doing something worth living for.

Hobhouse had loved Byron devotedly from their early youth, but latterly with a nervous, possessive, paternalistic love which kept him on the *qui vive* lest his friend should fall in public esteem and again place his admirers on the defensive for him. He had seen the Greek expedition as a way of guiding the poet's erring footsteps on to a path loftier than the one they had been wont to take in the Italian years—that path of writings deemed seditious and subversive and of associations unfit for a nobleman to acknowledge. He had still had qualms in case the wayward creature should let him down. But since the road had led as far as Missolonghi, he could tell him proudly, 'I am in no fear now of your taking a sudden leave of the cause and the country. . . .'[2] But he was wrong. Byron was already gone.

'At quarter past six', Lega interrupted a tall column of figures to put on record, 'there passed from this to a better life the Noble Lord George Noel Byron at the age of 36 years, 2 months, and 27 days.'[3]

* * * * *

---

[1] Ibid. 18 Apr. and 24 Apr.
[2] Murray MS. 23 Feb.   [3] 46876. 19 Apr. 1824.

A Mourning Pendant

		Dollars	Piastres
Apr. 22nd	4 okes (about 10 lbs) of yellow wax candles on the occasion of the funeral procession of Milord's heart	7	2
23rd	3 okes of yellow wax candles to illuminate Milord's body in the house	5	1
24th	To the Captain of the boat Teodoro Cocoreba sent to Zante with letters for Corfu and London to announce Milord's death	25	
25th	To Giorgio Xacheri for white candles to distribute to the soldiers of the garrison	22	3
27th	Transport of sweet water to test the capacity of the coffin	1	24
28th	To Giovanni Papageopopolo for 40 okes of rectified spirits for embalming the body of the late Milord	36	
	To the barber to shave the defunct Milord and other services	1	
	To the tinsmith Giorgio for double-lining the coffin	10	
	To the joiner Filippo Moscato for the coffin	3	
29th	To Stamile Mavromatti for the materials for embalming	140	
30th	To Stavro Daguma for black cloth and linen for the funeral	28	5[1]

Twelve to fourteen persons sailed from Missolonghi for Zante at the beginning of May with the temporary coffin. Among them were Hatajè and her mother on their way to rejoin what was left of their family. 'I thought you slaves', said Hussein Aga, when he saw them in the rich dresses Byron had provided, 'and lo! you return to me decked like brides.'[2]

Lukas remained behind, trying no doubt to get the money he had been empowered to collect from the Government: but they could not afford to pay even the small expenses incurred in transporting the corpse and household stuff to the boat and sent Lega a bill for them. Lukas did not long outlive his patron.

Byron's body remained at the Lazaretto of Zante until May 25th, while a new series of expenses mounted up. But all those were as nothing to the cost of the actual funeral in England, for which the bill of the undertaker was £1101. 13s. 7d. 'He was buried like a nobleman since we could not bury him as a poet', Hobhouse wrote in bitterness at the stony rebuff from Westminster Abbey. All the sable hangings of the pulpit at Hucknall Torkard were stolen by souvenir hunters.

---

[1] 46876, selected entries. These items were paid for in arrear. The barber probably laid out the body. The tradition that a woman did so is erroneous. No women appear anywhere in Lega's Missolonghi accounts except those who received charity. Parry specifically remarks on the absence of women.

[2] Millingen.

Epilogue

The sorrow in Greece for Byron's death was profound, and it was not lessened by dreadful consternation, which no one felt more painfully than Lega Zambelli. That his employer had left no will had come upon him as a blow; and indeed it was so extraordinary a negligence on the part of a man whose consideration for his servants was notable that I am half-disposed to think he did make a will later than the old one which Hobhouse and Hanson proved, and that, unknown to Pietro and perhaps Byron himself, who may not have supervised the packing of documents, it was among those jettisoned when the bombard was captured. I incline the more to this opinion because Byron had raised the question of revising his will at the time of Shelley's obsequies, when mortality was naturally much in his mind, and he had asked the Rev. Thomas Hall of Leghorn quite explicitly to arrange for a notary to attend him with 'the necessary stamped papers'.[1]

We have no reason to suppose that, because Teresa refused to be a beneficiary, everyone else was to be left unprovided for.[2] There is also the salient point that Hobhouse and Kinnaird had long wanted him to get rid of his solicitor, and it seems to me that, though he could hardly do that while Hanson had in hand important outstanding matters such as the sale of Rochdale, he would certainly have taken the opportunity to appoint another co-executor for Hobhouse when planning whatever new dispositions he was thinking of in 1822. If I am right—and of course it is most hypothetical—his broken death-bed utterances about money must have related to what he wanted done for anyone not named among the legatees, chiefly Lukas.

However that may have been, Lega found himself in a miserable situation because he needed money badly for Fanny Silvestrini and his child by her, Aspasia, and had sent them all he could lay hands on, a hundred and thirty Maria Theresa crowns, to enable them to keep going in his absence. He knew that Fletcher, so long associated with the family,

---

[1] *LJ.* 14 Aug. 1822.

[2] In telling Kinnaird of Teresa's refusal, he said that he had therefore been obliged to leave the will 'as it was' (29 Oct. 1823). But this is an allusion to his preparations for departure from Italy, and the will to which he referred may have been one made, or revised, in August the year before.

could expect good treatment by the executors, and that probably they would do well for Tita, a favourite since 1818, but what could he, an altogether less conspicuous member of the household, count on? He wrote gloomily to Fanny:

> Greece is inconsolable and will weep long years on end for the loss of such a friend, father, and benefactor. His family, of which I am the head, is left orphaned. Nothing remains for them but the whole and sole hope of benefiting by the liberality of the heirs and relations, in which they place great confidence.[1]

Although he was a very bad and timid sailor, he had no alternative but to accompany the others to England. In any case, his services were essential. After the grim and elaborate posthumous proceedings in Missolonghi, there were all the local bills to be settled from the large sum he had in his possession and the receipts to be gathered for executors, the lengthy inventories to be made, and the two embarkations to be organized—both financially and physically—the first to Zante where the coffin and the accumulated goods of the deceased and his entourage had to be looked after during a period of quarantine, then to London, a voyage which took (counting the days the ship spent coming to the Docks from the Downs) from May 25th till July 5th. Oppressed with the sad and heavy responsibilities he shared with the even more stricken Pietro, he longed for Fanny and he longed for money.

But what was Lega's consternation compared with Mavrocordato's? There at Zante were the great coffers of gold and silver he and his supporters so urgently, so desperately, wanted to pay for ships, troops, fortifications, the wealth Lord Byron as chief agent of the Committee would undoubtedly have administered to the advantage of his Government; and now it was not only blocked by his lamentable death but the most self-seeking of the Klephts, Odysseus, had actually enlisted two troublesome Englishmen to dispossess him, the insufferable Stanhope and his sycophant, Trelawny.

Stanhope was, as has been said, an impassioned republican, and he had been afraid that, if Mavrocordato were confirmed in power, he would turn Greece into a monarchy. Trelawny played upon this fear and flattered Stanhope—he was a transparently vain man—with letter after letter artfully couched to make him feel he could now dispose of the loan so as to direct the course of Greek history along the lines his idol, Jeremy Bentham, would approve—which is to say, the lines Trelawny's idol, Odysseus, would find rewarding. When Stanhope published his book on

---

[1] 46875 Folio 25. 29 Apr.

the Greek War in 1825, he drastically censored Trelawny's correspondence which, taken together and in full, is a sustained endeavour to divert to the robber chieftain, who was on the verge of defection, any resources that might otherwise relieve Missolonghi.[1]

Trelawny had reached the 'mud isthmus', as he called it, a week after Byron's death and at once pursued two courses, in one of which he achieved remarkable success, while in the other he may be said to have over-reached himself. He wrote to Stanhope—as he was to write to many other people—establishing himself as Byron's closest companion, one who had lived with him 'in ships, boats, and in houses', unreserved with each other in their enduring intimacy.[2] When these statements came out in print, with their touching regrets for his beloved friend's frailties, they seemed incontrovertible. Concurrently, he proceeded with his enjoyable intrigues for the provocation and frustration of the Provisional Government, taking a cruel delight in Mavrocordato's predicament.

> I do really feel for Mavrocordato he had got himself so shacked [?shackled] by making promises, that he cannot fulfill, that his person is scarcely, indeed is not safe. for the Suliottes and others say if he does not put money in their purses they will have his head; nor do I think he can leave the town . . .
> Byron's death is a death blow to Mavrocordato, . . . [Tell my] sentiments on this head to Odyssea, tell him I am under [his] orders, ready on all points to obey him for I think I may say so without reservation, trusting he will not soil me by [any] dirty work.[3]

But there was plenty of 'dirty work' to be done for Odysseus, and Trelawny had already begun it. When he heard that the *Florida* had arrived at Zante with the hoard of money, he became frantic with anxiety in case any of it should go to Mavrocordato. He had been gloating over the threats of unpaid Suliots to storm Missolonghi and behead the Phanariot, the abuse showered on him by merchants whose claims he could not satisfy, the fears that beset him, enmeshed and, as Trelawny imagined, panic-stricken. 'I pitied him his writhings and shufflings. [They] did not serve him but like his entriguing friends left him in his dangers. The timely news from Zant has given him breathing [space].'[4]

---

[1] Goulandris Papers. The MS of Trelawny's first letter to Stanhope from Missolonghi is dated 26 Apr., the day of his arrival, not 28 as in Stanhope's book.

[2] By three times calling Ada Byron 'Ida', he showed—unless Byron spoke broad Cockney—how far from intimate their relations really were. Stanhope, or his editor Ryan, corrected the error.

[3] Goulandris Papers. 28 Apr. The words in square brackets are quite burned away. I have completed a few others where the meaning admits no doubt.

[4] Ibid. 1 May. As Stanhope, when publishing Trelawny's letters, omitted all such passages as I quote, his own side of the correspondence looks more innocuous than it really was.

Trelawny exerted all the pressure of his semi-literate but forceful prose to urge Stanhope to take such measures about the money 'frozen' at Zante as would confound Mavrocordato and provide Odysseus with 'a fair share'. Stanhope answered after consultation with the Klepht that they both entreated Trelawny himself to undertake this 'important mission'. Thus elevated, he had an excuse for going to Zante on the ship that carried Byron's coffin and accompanying the contingent from Missolonghi as if he were their leader. He lost no time, when among the cosmopolitan group who were gathered on the island, in representing himself as the chief mourner and dearest friend of the deceased, while yet, in his dexterous way, giving damaging accounts of him to journalists. He had naïvely hoped to have it all his own way in disseminating news and views about the great poet to the English press, and was enraged when he found that information was being collected by and from others besides himself.

> . . . Their is a mad Methodist (Kennedy) a Mad poet—of Corfu—and what is worse than all that mad borer (blockhead Blackquiere) all working like devils—to torture & make a prop for their crazy systems the fame & name of Byron —— The vain & shallow Italian Gamba, The Liston like old letcher Fletcher, with the lying Italian renegade priest Lega Gambelli [sic] (B.) secretary—Emperiss Bruno his Doctor—and the Prince of Charlatans Mavro are the sewers from which—the above said authors have extracted their materials to shed a baneful influence over the memory of the Noble Poet.[1]

Trelawny, however, could not resist Blaquiere's invitation to join the 'sewers'. The internal evidence that he produced the derogatory portions of the *Personal Character of Lord Byron* which appeared in the *London Magazine* in October leaves no room for question.[2] Apart from the very phrases he had used in private letters, the flattery of Stanhope at Byron's expense could have come from no one else available at the time. Stanhope himself also made an easily identifiable contribution to the article with a glowing panegyric on printing presses and 'societies for mutual instruction', and deprecation of Byron for having said, 'The Greeks must conquer first and then set about learning'.

Stanhope had believed that, as Byron's co-agent, he was empowered to administer the loan, and he arrived at Zante on May 12th determined to

---

[1] Ibid. Undated. Liston was a famous comedian. Bruno's name was Francesco or Francis. 'Emperiss' may be a mistake or is perhaps a mis-spelling of Empress. Trelawny was particularly fond of suggesting that anyone he disliked was homosexual. I do not know the identity of the mad poet of Corfu. Kennedy wrote an excellent book about Byron. Blaquiere was the member of the Greek Committee who had brought the first instalment of the loan.

[2] It was signed R.N., but with an admission that it was a compilation.

do so. Very fortunately for the Greeks, since he was much more concerned with giving them newspapers than liberating them from the Turks, the military authorities in England had become exasperated with his republican propaganda, and cancelled the long leave he had been granted, informing him that unless he prepared for return immediately, he would be 'visited with His Majesty's highest displeasure'. He had time to compose a few more Benthamite, and nearly Bedlamite, manifestos before nominally taking charge of Byron's body on its last journey. He was also able to do a very signal service for Odysseus.

Trelawny persuaded him to command the two remaining engineers, who had come from England with Parry (now ill at Zante), to take from Mavrocordato practically all the modern artillery Missolonghi possessed, together with cartridges, gunpowder, and the working tools of Parry's 'laboratory'.[1] Moreover, Stanhope paid Trelawny fifty dollars for his personal service in delivering the guns to Odysseus.[2] These munitions went, not to arm Greeks against Turks, but to fortify the cavern on Mount Parnassus where Odysseus placed Trelawny in charge of his considerable private treasure. To secure even more treasure, that eminent brigand made his devoted liegeman a member of his family by giving him in marriage his sister Terzitsa, aged twelve or thirteen.

'After Mavro had made every turn & shift possible to evade your order for the guns', Trelawny wrote triumphantly to Stanhope, 'I pressed so hard upon him as to force his compliance . . . . but why bore you with accounts of the paltry game this jugling Jew is playing[?]'.[3] He could not resist, in this series of machinating letters, quoting speeches of Iago's (which he knew because the Pisan circle had begun rehearsing a production of *Othello*); but in pitting himself so malignantly against Mavrocordato, he had, as I have hinted, gone too far. The Phanariot was a genuine patriot and had sacrificed his fortune to the cause, but it was not by guilelessness that he had survived all the plots and counterplots of Greeks and Turks.

When, after Stanhope's return to England, Odysseus made a unilateral peace with the Turks and was taken prisoner by the Greeks, his Cornish brother-in-law remained in the cavern it was his inglorious duty to guard —a comfortable cavern in itself furnished with all kinds of amenities, even to a set of the Waverley novels,[4] but not a pleasant abode for one who turned out to be blockaded there. It was when he was thus cornered that Mavrocordato, who had now acquired much of the money Trelawny had schemed to get, bribed two of his British companions to assassinate him. The attempt failed but he was severely wounded and had to be

[1] Stanhope. 18 May.   [2] Ibid. 2 June.
[3] Goulandris Papers. 28 May.   [4] St. Clair.

rescued by the intervention of apologetic relations, irritated Members of Parliament (chiefly John Cam Hobhouse), and ultimately an English man-of-war, the *Zebra*.

'While the Greeks have a piece of ground to fight for I shall be found on it', Trelawny had written to Stanhope in his heroic style,[1] but he ended his adventure in utter ignominy, having to be given a safe conduct to leave the country, while the family of Odysseus, now murdered by the Greeks he had betrayed, brought a lawsuit against him for money; and there was a discussion between General Sir Frederick Adam and Colonel Napier as to whether they could even let him land at Corfu. But restored at last to his native soil, he rose like a cork and sent rhetorical letters to the newspapers about the need to defend Missolonghi at all costs—which must have made Stanhope, after his removal of the artillery and also the Artillery Brigade, rather uncomfortable.

Stanhope, before the outcome of this folly became apparent, brought out a pompous and conceited book about his deeds in Greece. William Parry had vivid memories of what Byron had endured from Stanhope and hastened to publish a counterblast, giving a convincing account of the Missolonghi ordeal and exposing in a very brilliant manner the absurdities of Jeremy Bentham's theories applied to Greece in the conditions then prevailing. Stanhope, insensate with anger, enlisted Leigh Hunt's brother, the proprietor of *The Examiner*, to assist in crushing the impertinent plebeian. One of John Hunt's sons had intended to join the liberators and had embarked with Parry in the *Anne* as a volunteer; but, ostensibly through illness, more probably through dislike of Parry, he had turned back when the ship touched Malta. Hunt therefore had personal reasons for the onslaught he made on Parry's *Last Days of Lord Byron*, describing it as:

> the very contemptible production of a very contemptible fellow—one Parry lately a caulker, but now calling himself a Major. This extremely ignorant, boasting, bullying and drunken individual, it seems, while engaged in the cause of the Greeks, got introduced to Mr Bentham's table. . . . Taking advantage of this unexpected condescension, the worthless creature in question, in order we suppose to get up something that he thought would sell, has published various details (of no sort of interest whatever) respecting Mr Bentham's habits . . . designed to throw ridicule upon his excellent and enlightened host.

The indictment, clearly inspired by the intense animus the Hunt family had such an exceptional capacity for feeling, was reinforced by letters from Stanhope which *The Examiner* printed, full of scornful

---

[1] Goulandris Papers. Undated.

allusions to Parry's vulgar speech and low breeding, and most unseemly coming from an Earl's privileged son. To one of these there was a post-script by Hunt calling Parry 'a slanderer, a sot, a bully, and a poltroon', adding 'Who wrote the book to which he has affixed his name we cannot say; but he himself cannot write ten words of English'.[1]

These aspersions left Parry almost under a necessity to take a libel action. John Hunt was thoroughly accustomed to defend actions of all kinds and knew the ropes. He was quick to trace witnesses who would testify to the old firemaster's intemperate habits and incapacity to write a book. The case was heard before the Lord Chief Justice and a jury in June 1827. The defence pleaded justification, and tried to prove it by witnesses who stated that Parry was always tipsy, and would hold a brandy bottle to his lips, which was called 'drinking by word of mouth' (much laughter in court). Other witnesses, his former mates from Woolwich Dockyard, testified that he was no drunkard but a skilful engineer, a diligent workman, a decent and honest man.

The statement that he could not put together ten words of English had been ridiculously malicious. Byron refers on several occasions to Parry's writing of reports and letters, nor does he ever make a single criticism of the competence of this rough and uncultivated but highly intelligent man, toper though he might be. After having had Parry with him for more than seven weeks, he calls him 'a sort of hardworking Hercules', and pays this tribute, 'Capt. Parry is doing all that circumstances will permit in his department, and indeed in many others, for he does *all* that is done here'.[2] But Byron's letters were not produced in court, and Parry's publisher, Lacey, admitted that his materials had been put into the hands of an experienced and skilful author, Mr Thomas Hodgskin, who had welded them into a book.

There could not have been a better man for the job, Hodgskin being a lapsed follower of Bentham with first-hand knowledge of the arrogant iconoclasm with which so fanatical a disciple as Stanhope had tried to sweep away the customs and traditions of the Greeks. He also had a very fine ear for the kind of conversations Parry had held with Byron, which must have been most faithfully reported to him. As to the picture of Byron's day-to-day life at Missolonghi, so many of the facts he recounts can now be checked from other sources that the work still remains one on which every biographer may confidently draw. It is a remarkable instance of successful collaboration between a literary ghost and an unliterary but not unscrupulous narrator. Parry won his case and £50 damages, and that was no easy feat for a former dockyard labourer to

---

[1] 2 Apr. and 9 Apr. 1826.   [2] *LJ*. To Kinnaird, 30 Mar.

achieve in the 1820s, contending with aristocratic witnesses like Stanhope and learned witnesses like Bowring, and facing a jury of twelve middle-class citizens.[1]

Parry became insane and died in an asylum, and that has been held against him as though insanity were a fate reserved for the disreputable. That he was a heavy drinker is undeniable, but it is sad to relate that Lega and Fletcher were two of the witnesses who went into court to testify to his drunkenness. They had spent several weeks on the *Florida* with Stanhope when it made its mournful voyage from Zante, and it would have been difficult for two men of lowly rank to refuse to oblige a dictatorial gentleman who asked for their support.

Pietro would not have given it: he had always written kindly and courteously of Parry, had named him as one of the trustworthy people he had consulted about the disposition of things after Milord's death, and had told in his book how Byron, unable to speak, had taken Parry's hand and held it. But Pietro was not called upon for evidence one way or the other. 'A proper liberty boy', as Byron called him, he had gone back to Greece and died there two or three months before the case came on. Tita too was absent. He had renounced his comfortable employment with Mr Hobhouse to accompany his compatriot back to the Greek War—from which he emerged alive but destitute, to become the valet of young Mr Disraeli, who was never tired of hearing about his earlier master. Benjamin Lewis, the Negro groom, had succumbed to smallpox within about two months of landing in England after the long and melancholy journey on which he seems to have acted as cook.

That year, 1824, to which I now return, was a generally unlucky one, and especially for Lega. His sacrifice in going with Byron to Greece has never been recognized because his deep love for Fanny and his child has hitherto remained unrecorded. Fanny's health was bad at the time, and what money he could raise for her before leaving, he knew to be insufficient; but he had not had the courage to tell his patron of his worries because of Fanny's being *persona non grata*. Lega regarded Fanny as his wife and always directed his communications to 'L'Ornatissima Signora Fanny Silvestrini Lega Zambelli'. It was, and still is, a common custom in Italy for the maiden name to be retained with the husband's surname, and the only proof that he did not at some time marry her is that, when at Missolonghi, fearing he might never return, he made her an outright gift of all he had—that is, all the sums that were due to him if the lawyer could collect them—he did not then suffix his name to hers as on occa-

---

[1] My all too condensed description of the case is from *The Times*; my information about Hodgskin is from William St Clair, who first called my attention to this episode in Parry's history, which was unknown to me when I was writing about him previously.

sions of less legal significance. If he had been ordained, it may have been unlawful for him to contract a marriage, there being no civil ceremony allowed in Italy.

Lega was frank in telling her that he hoped something would be done for him with his Lordship's other dependants: he wrote her long descriptive letters and devised eager plans for seeing her again with their 'dilettissima Aspasia'. He had not heard from her for months and it was immensely disturbing, on arriving in London in July, to find no word awaiting him at Signor John Murray's. As week after week passed bringing him not a line, he ventured, halfway through September, to write to Countess Gritti in Venice to whose care he had transmitted the hundred and thirty crowns carried by Dr Thomas, the medical man who had received too late the call to attend Byron. He begged for news, but got none. By October 22nd, nearly frantic, he addressed Fanny herself a letter of deepest anxiety and tenderest reproach. Both she and the Countess, he thought, must be in the country, and yet he feared some fatality had overtaken her.

Then shutting out so painful an idea, he told her his news. The executors and Augusta Leigh had given him a year's pay together with thirty pounds for his homeward journey, a very disappointing sum as he considered, and he could only comfort himself with the thought of having spent five consecutive years in the faithful service of such a personage. Now he had taken a commodious house off Brunswick Square and was about to start the manufacture of Italian pasta in London. He had ordered the necessary utensils and expected to have everything in train by November. He looked forward to making a nice profit for 'the decorous support of my little family which is always before my eyes and engraved on my heart'. He begged Fanny to come to London with Aspasia in spring: she would suffer too much if she were to travel in winter. 'What a day of feasting and consolation it will be when it is given to me to press you both to my loving breast. . . . Oh, longed for day! After hearing from you I shall give you more definite instructions about managing these matters.'

It was at that point that Byron's chivalrous friend, Count Pietro, called on him. He had brought a letter which had arrived from his sister, Teresa Guiccioli at Rimeno. It contained, as Lega remembered them, these lines: 'Lega goes on writing to Fanny, but does he not know yet, poor thing, that she has been dead three months? Poor Lega.' In some dark hour when he was alone again, he rounded off his pathetic and now futile outpouring: 'Here the unlucky Lega broke off pen in hand at the dreadful news of his lost wife.'[1]

---

[1] The word is *compagna*, a term sometimes used referring to wives. I should translate it as 'mate' if that had not acquired connotations either of slang or soulfulness.

It is hard to envisage Italy and Greece as further away from England, by the measure of time, than New Zealand now is. Fanny had died on May 22nd. At that date no one could have known where to reach Lega, who was so unexpectedly at Zante waiting to sail to England, but at last letters began to arrive which told him of what had been going on without him—how Fanny had spent the final weeks of a long unspecified illness at her birthplace, Treviso, dying in debt and difficulty, the packet of his savings having come too late; how her sister Marietta, wife of Antonio de Rossi, an architect of some eminence, had become legal guardian of Aspasia, and how, since she could no longer defer joining her husband in St Petersburg where he was working on models of buildings by his great namesake, Carlo, other arrangements were hurriedly being made. It was not possible for Lega to participate in them except by undertaking responsibility for payments and agreeing to settle the accounts still due for Fanny's last weeks under the care of nuns and for nine months during which Aspasia had been maintained by her maternal grandmother and maiden aunt.

Lega longed for the child but his lawyer wrote advising him not to come back to Romagna. The clerical party had redoubled its vigilance, and Count Ruggiero Gamba, Teresa's father, had been sentenced to twenty years imprisonment for liberal activities. As a Carbonaro and an associate of that family through both Byron and Teresa, Lega was a marked man. It was doubtless his apprehension of this which caused him to remain in England in the unlikely profession of a macaroni maker. The executors thought him very grasping and clamorous. He seems not to have told them of the obstacles to his return home.

He corresponded frequently not only with Aspasia herself but with everyone concerned in caring for her, and he implored any acquaintance of his who was going to Venice, where she was in a boarding-school, to call on her. (They included Col. the Hon. Leicester Stanhope, and Mr and Mrs John Gisborne, whom Shelley at one time had found most congenial and at another 'odious and filthy animals'.)[1] A devoted but demanding parent, he made her write to him in French as well as Italian, corrected her grammar somewhat pedantically, paid for extras such as drawing and music which were really beyond his means, and gave her astute directions for keeping on the right side of Countess Gritti and other potential benefactors. At the same time, he tried to bring home to her the grief of losing her mother in a manner we should now think almost cruel, but it was felt

[1] Lega also gave the Gisbornes a letter of introduction to Count Guiccioli, temporarily reunited to Teresa, but they never turned up. 'The valorous colonel' too, after raising Aspasia's eager hope of seeing a hero, put off his visit. He was now (in 1827) President of the Greek Committee, and still given to lengthy discourses of a doctrinaire character.

in those days, and particularly by Latins, that to be acquainted with death was salutory to children. It was more than four years before Lega found any way of getting the little girl to London. Fanny's sister, Marietta, emerged occasionally from Russia, and on one of those trips managed to collect her niece and bring her, by way of Paris, to Cromer Street, where Lega lived and died.

There are so many adjectives of extravagant affection and praise in letters about 'the adorable Aspasia' that it may be assumed she was pre-possessing; her husband certainly thought so. She mixed, judging by the letters she kept, more with the Italian than the English community, especially the political exiles and revolutionaries, amongst them Mazzini with whom she was on cordial terms. Her father's pasta business had not succeeded, but in the course of years the tangled skein of his properties had been to some extent unravelled and the outstanding loans gradually repaid, so that he was no longer penurious. Aspasia also had property in Italy. It was at Treviso, inherited from her maternal relations. She was able to write in 1855: 'We do not know poverty.'

She had then been in possession of her father's papers eight years, but, like Lega himself, she was wholly ignored by biographers—perhaps because, as she came up in the world, she had no wish to advertise the nature of the links that would have made her recollections of value, or perhaps because the Victorians were little disposed to trouble themselves with research about Byron's Italian and Greek experiences. It was the phase of reaction, the 'gap in appreciation'.

As a tiny child, Aspasia had played with little Allegra; she could read in her inherited letters how they had sent each other love and kisses. She had been petted by the pretty and amiable Countess Guiccioli, and in 1850, a mature woman, had been graciously received by the rich Marquise de Boissy who was the same smiling person, remarried. She had almost certainly set eyes on Milord himself—a distant and sinister figure he would have been to her, who could make Papa nervous and who, she knew now if she had not known it then, had kept her mother at arm's length.

She had been only seven when Byron died, but she could surely have told many things about him, having been closely associated with the three men who had seen him daily for years on end, her father, her father's former partner, the valet Fletcher who, having lost his savings in the macaroni venture, had become a shabby and pitiful figure, and another Italian exile, Tita, the big, kindly, bearded compatriot, always the simplest and best-natured of creatures, who had become, as years went on, an India Office messenger.

Aspasia's only child, Clelia—so-named by Lega's wish—became an

American subject through marrying Anson Weekes, from Mattapoisett, Mass. In Italian style, she always called herself Mrs Lega-Weekes. On her mother's death the Zambelli Papers passed into her hands, and she applied herself earnestly to family history, giving it all what we might now term a build-up. With or without marriage lines for her grandparents—and perhaps she knew nothing on this topic—she chose to trace her descent legitimately through Fanny Silvestrini to the noble families of Soranzo and Cornaro (Catherine Cornaro was Queen of Cyprus). Such grandeurs must have compensated for her paternal ancestry, which was plebeian. Aspasia had married, very surprisingly, the son of that humble, nearly illiterate, and altogether penniless servant, William Fletcher.

Nobody has ever called Fletcher a gentleman's gentleman, nor is it to be supposed that he dreamed of gentility for his two sons. He had had little opportunity of bringing them up on any pattern of his own, having been dragged, protesting but not deserting, at his imperious master's heels even as far as the heart of awful Albania with its robber bands and total absence of English home comforts. The nearest thing he had had to a married life after the death of his first wife, Sally, was the brief season when his second, Ann Rood, had acted as Lady Byron's maid and given great offence by being unwilling to testify to that lady's wrongs and injuries—whereupon she had been denied a character.[1]

Ann lost her own child and who brought up Sally's two boys I cannot say. The younger one, George Gordon, emigrated to Cape Town in the 1830s, taking with him, as I have told, some of the clothes of his famous godfather.[2] Bankruptcy awaited him in the 1840s, and I can trace him no further. The elder son, William Frederick, was steady, aspiring, and idealistic. He wrote verses—of a naïve and anaemic kind, it is true— but it is odd to think of the son of the man whom Byron so often jocularly called 'the learned Fletcher' writing verses at all; and he drew simple pencil sketches such as we find in old autograph books. But he could also translate Italian and French, take down poems—especially Byron's—in very neat shorthand on an 18th-century system, and copy music for Aspasia's album with real skill. Perhaps because these accomplishments contributed nothing to his livelihood, perhaps because his courtship of Aspasia, still in her teens, was challenged by her father, he emigrated in about 1835 to Canada.

What he did there has not been revealed, but it is likely to have been manual work. From Quebec in 1836, he describes himself as having been employed for the best part of a week wheeling away snow in a barrow. A little later he sent 'three sovereigns and a half' to Lega. He made a will leaving anything of which he might die possessed to Aspasia, at the same

[1] Correspondence in the Lovelace Papers.   [2] See p. 375.

time desiring that his body might be 'anatomized' for the benefit of science, an unusual request at the time. Canada did not prove rewarding, and, still wrapped up in Aspasia, he set out for New Orleans, which was then anything but a salubrious spot. He failed to prosper there.

This worthy young man, a paladin of fidelity (he had been in love with Aspasia since she was twelve), was a member of one of the societies for Christian self-improvement which flourished in that epoch, and there seems to have been a transient plan for the 'Brotherhood', equipped with agricultural implements and sufficient provisions for six months, to form a remote, self-supporting community.[1] The friend who wrote proposing this and commiserating with him on his distresses in Louisiana, sympathized also with the suffering of his beloved Aspasia while parted from him and hoped in flowery terms that they would soon be reunited. It was not long before they were. William Frederick returned that same year, 1838, and overcame any parental resistance there may have been to the marriage.

We are bound to suspect resistance because Lega had very emphatically objected to being put on a footing with the servants, expressly naming Fletcher senior, when complaining of Byron's executors—although he had not minded using Fletcher's whole capital a few weeks later to help finance his business. (But it was a partnership that he never mentioned in his letters to Italy.) He had educated Aspasia as the daughter of a retired civic official rather than of a household steward, and he could reasonably have felt the alliance to be a come-down. Whatever his view of the attachment at first, he ultimately accepted it, and Aspasia wrote that they lived together in harmony. It is confirmed by one of several conjugal poems to her:

> Long may thy honoured father live
> To see his offspring blessed,
> Till hoary age his warning give
> That it is time to rest.

She describes her husband in the letter of 1855, already quoted, as a man of probity and honour, and the souvenirs of him that she kept suggest indeed a lovable and faithful if somewhat ineffectual character.

We can only speculate on what terms Fletcher the elder, a seedy and forlorn creature who had been in a debtors' prison, stood with his son's cultured wife. Destined to be the most renowned valet in English literary history, he spent his old age in such obscurity that imaginary deathbed gifts of (forged) letters from Byron were circulated while he was still alive!

[1] 46875 Folio 147. Letter signed W. H. Hunter.

Clelia, born in 1841, his sole grandchild—unless George Gordon had progeny in South Africa—was not proud of the connection, but she made the best of it by discovering that the Fletchers had a coat-of-arms with a hound rampant on the crest. It was not actually granted to her father, merely adopted by her from the family entitled to bear it. Having applied herself to tracing the pedigrees of Zambelli and Silvestrini, she rather touchingly called her house in Exeter 'Varnello' after the castle her other grandfather had, as she believed, forfeited.

Obituary notices when she died in 1924 contain no allusion to Lord Byron's valet but are expansive on the topic of his aristocratic secretary. The information was obviously supplied by her daughter, Ethel Lega-Weekes, likewise an only child, next and last private owner of the Zambelli Papers.

The cache was still entirely unbroached as far as writers on Byron were concerned, and those had now multiplied to a veritable international brigade. Possibly she had not enough Italian to look very deeply into the contents, for Lega had settled in England exactly a hundred years before, and after his death only her grandmother Aspasia, who had died in 1890, ever had occasion to use the language. Had she made any study of the documents, it is difficult to believe that certain biographical errors could have been so long unchallenged.

Some contemporary copies of Lega's correspondence found their way to the Public Library of Forlì, doubtless made because of the unhappy dispute between Lega and Byron's Ravenna banker, Pellegrino Ghigi, and they were used by Iris Origo in *The Last Attachment*, the earliest English book to devote any appreciable attention to Lega or to mention Fanny Silvestrini. The collection in the hands of Miss Lega-Weekes remained an unknown quantity until the year that book came out, 1949, which was also the year of her death at the age of eighty-eight. The British Museum acquired it from her estate, but even then, to sift and catalogue so large an assortment of letters and accounts, almost all foreign except for the Fletcher items, was a lengthy task. I was completely unaware of the existence of the papers—they were bound in 1963—when *The Late Lord Byron* was published in 1961.

The survival of such a hoard—the property of a family of very modest means—through revolutions, wars, far travel, great vicissitudes of social status, and double change of nationality, affords delightful hope of treasures still to be found and aspects of Byron's incomparably vivid life still to be illuminated.

Appendices

The Heirs to Byron's Fortune

Augusta had never been able to touch the capital secured by marriage settlement to Lady Byron for her life, but her sons, George, in the Army, and Frederic, in the Navy, must have borrowed on the reversion. Though they were not on speaking terms for twenty-five years, they resembled each other in improvident habits, and when their mother died were deep in debt. Her youngest son, Henry, about whom almost nothing is known, had an income of £50 a year. Byron's estate was in Chancery for many years after Lady Byron's death, and then passed to Ada Augusta Leigh, daughter of Augusta's younger son, Frederic, and (I presume) to Geraldine Leigh, George's child, the three brothers having meanwhile died.

Ada Augusta was a ward in Chancery when she married, in 1868, a 'Mr Stephenson of Cleevelands,[1] a man of fortune'. She is described by Captain Byron Drury, R.N., grandson of Byron's old headmaster, Dr Drury, and son of his friend, Henry Drury, and godson to Byron himself, as 'a considerable heiress' and 'very beautiful'.[2] Some of her fortune may have come to her through her mother, Mrs Frederic Leigh, but as Geraldine Leigh was also well off, Chancery cannot have swallowed up all of Byron's.

A bride of nineteen, Ada was given away by the Lord Chancellor, Lord Ellenborough, her guardian. Captain Byron Drury, who had known her father, was exceedingly anxious, in his own words, 'to rally round this wedding some connected with the great name of Byron', there being only Geraldine and their Aunt Emily, who, 'from an extreme nervous temperament' would not witness the marriage, though she consented to it. Captain Drury therefore begged John Murray III to go, and he did so. There is in the Murray MSS a charming letter from the bride thanking him for his wedding present.

Byron's Sexual Ambivalence

Sexual initiation by a nurse who was a religious hypocrite was a sad abuse of

---

[1] Probably J. G. Stephenson, later a Justice of the Peace, of The Cleevelands, Bishop's Cleeve, Cheltenham.
[2] Letters to John Murray III, Sept. 1868.

Byron's childhood which may have helped to engender his later general disrespect for women, but I do not agree with those authors who have supposed May Gray was able to indulge her depravity for long. Secrecy was so alien to his nature that he must soon have disburdened himself. He could not tell his mother, but he told the friendly Hanson and, in my opinion, at the first opportunity.

The evidence suggests that May Gray, disorientated on leaving Scotland, gave way to drinking habits and, when drunk, lost her control and self-respect. It is true Hobhouse says that Byron was nine and they did not leave Scotland till he was ten, but he was repeating what he heard from Hanson twenty-five years after Hanson had heard it from Byron in 1799.[1] I cannot see how, living at very close quarters with Mrs Byron in an Aberdeen apartment, the nurse would have been able to behave so iniquitously for any prolonged period. Nevertheless, however soon the little boy was, on his own appeal, extricated by her dismissal, the experience was plainly a significant one and possibly answerable in some degree for his dual sexuality, which several contemporary writers treat as out-and-out homosexuality.

Professor Marchand's summing-up on this topic is given on page 90 of his three-volume biography:

> There seems little doubt, if one considers dispassionately the total evidence now available, that a strong attraction to boys persisted in Byron from his Harrow days throughout his life. But there is no evidence that he felt guilt or shame about any of the friendships formed at Harrow. Hobhouse, however, who knew him from his Cambridge days, and who apparently was well aware of this tendency in Byron, wrote in the margin where Moore was glossing over the Harrow friendships with young favourites: 'M. knows nothing or will tell nothing of the principal cause & motive of all these boyish friend[ships].' Byron's attraction to women, however, did, on the whole, fulfill his emotional needs much more extensively and through longer periods of his life, though it was not necessarily stronger in individual instances. . . .
>
> These facts have long been known. Looked at without moral hysteria, they help to explain a great deal in Byron's character and his relations with both men and women.

This opinion I share, with the qualification that I think 'throughout his life' puts the matter too strongly. There were substantial periods when, except in the ordinary course of friendship, he was not interested in any male. Indeed, between his return from the Near East in July 1811 and (possibly) his phase of extreme licentiousness in Venice, chiefly in the winter of 1818–1819, all his known amours were heterosexual—and, what with those and his incessant work of composition, that there were unknown amours is unlikely. Again, from

[1] The fact was first published by Marchand from a note in Hobhouse's 1824 Journal.

his falling in love with Teresa Guiccioli in the spring of 1819 to his being powerfully attracted by the Greek boy, Lukas Chalandrutsanos, in about December 1823, no question arises of any deviation.

We cannot even be certain that he had homosexual adventures in Venice. Our information is based on nothing more solid than Shelley's remark in a letter to Peacock: 'He associates with wretches who seem almost to have lost the gait & physiognomy of man & who do not scruple to avow practices which are not only not named but I believe seldom even conceived in England.'[1]

This would be more significant if it did not follow immediately on a passage declaring that Italian women were 'perhaps the most contemptible of all who exist under the moon' (countesses smelling of garlic!) and that Byron had relations with the lowest of the low among them; while the letter begins with a statement that the spirit in which Canto IV of *Childe Harold* was written was 'if insane, the most wicked & mischievous insanity that was ever given forth'. In short, Shelley, whose feelings about Byron swung to and fro like a pendulum, was habitually intemperate when attacking anyone whose conduct was annoying him, and there was a struggle at this date between them because of Byron's attitude to Claire Clairmont. For all we know to the contrary, Byron, who had enjoyed the company of pugilists and jockeys in London and been delighted to have an escort of ex-robbers in Albania, entertained the 'wretches' with no more than his usual absorbing curiosity about every aspect of human character. Conversely he may have lapsed cynically into some form of sensual gratification with them. We are not sufficiently informed to come to a conclusion.

Whatever his inclinations at an earlier period may have been, I doubt if he had ever committed paederasty until he parted from Hobhouse at Zea in July 1810 and went back to Athens, installing himself soon after in a very unmonastic monastery with one abbot and half a dozen playful and acquiescent boys. Marchand quotes a letter from him to Hobhouse, October 4th 1810, in which, alluding to unrestrained indulgence with these and other youths until he was 'almost tired of them', he wrote, 'You know the monastery of Mendele, it was there I made myself master of the first'.[2]

As Byron and his particular Cambridge cronies, Hobhouse and Charles Skinner Matthews, were very well read and classically educated, they were all aware that there were parts of the world where sodomy was not, as in Great Britain, a capital crime, but an accepted practice, the corollary of the segregation of women; and there had clearly been discussions before the tour about this forbidden topic, especially with Matthews, for Byron daringly asked Hobhouse to tell 'the Citoyen' what he had been up to.[3] Hobhouse decided in the cen-

---

[1] Jones. 17 or 18 Dec. 1818.   [2] Murray MS.

[3] 'Citizen', after the French Revolution, was equivalent to 'Comrade' in Russia. Matthews, a Free Thinker, was probably teased by the others as a revolutionary. His letters show very decidedly homosexual leanings.

sorious air of England that it would be better not to reveal, even to their close friend, that deadly secret, and advised Byron to keep everything of the kind entirely to himself;[1] so it remained suppressed until he himself was unable to resist pencilling comments on the margins of Moore's biography, by way of scoring off the author.

That first of whom Byron made himself master—and the phrase implies what no serious student is likely to doubt, that his would be the active role— was apparently a youth whom he had met before Hobhouse's departure, and who, for a few months, played a part of some consequence, Nicolo Giraud, of French parentage but born in Greece, and fluent in Italian which Byron learned from him. Nicolo is one of the names in Byron's list of the monastery 'ragazzi', and he is mentioned to Hobhouse twice in words which show that the latter was acquainted with him. In one of these communications, written just before Byron moved to the monastery from the lodgings he had been occupying, where there had been three attractive girls to flirt with,[2] there is a hint that he and Nicolo were already lovers;[3] but of course there are degrees of homosexual practice and in speaking of 'the first' he may have meant the first fulfilling attainment.

It is not generally noted by those who reduce Byron's life almost wholly to sexual terms that his prolonged stay in Athens brought him in contact not only with sportive youths but with a large and intellectual circle of Englishmen, Danes, Germans, Frenchmen and Greeks, a high proportion of whom were, or were to become, distinguished as antiquarians, historians and classicists;[4] or, if it is noted, it is in order to insinuate some sexuality in the association. Byron has only to describe Dr Bronstedt of Copenhagen as 'a pretty philosopher as you'd wish to see' when writing to Francis Hodgson (who has never been suspected of anything worse than falling in love with a laundress), for some propagandist to quote the phrase as if a pretty philosopher meant an effeminate one.

As for Nicolo Giraud, I do not think he held a very important place among Byron's loves except inasmuch as he afforded him lively and useful companionship and a release from the inhibition he had been under with Edleston.

[1] Murray MS. 15 July 1811. Within three weeks Matthews was drowned.

[2] One of these was Teresa Macri, romantically immortalized by Byron on his previous visit as the Maid of Athens. She had two sisters, and he told his old schoolmaster, Henry Drury, now his friend, that he was 'dying with love' for all three. 'Teresa, Mariana, and Katinka are the names of these divinities.' (Trinity College Library, Cambridge. 3 May 1810.)

[3] He wrote to Hobhouse, 'You remember Nicolo at Athens, Lusieri's wife's brother. Give my *compliments* to Matthews, from whom I expect a congratulatory letter'. (*Correspondence*, 16 Aug. 1810.) This is a non sequitur unless we interpret it as an announcement that he had made the kind of conquest Matthews would approve. Looking back, Hobhouse considered that it had been Matthews who had encouraged Byron in debauchery. (Hobhouse *Journals*. 15 Jan. 1830.) Lusieri was the Italian artist who made numerous drawings of classical sculptures for Lord Elgin.

[4] This cosmopolitan society is described by Borst in *Lord Byron's First Pilgrimage*, and there is more about them in William St Clair's interesting biography of Lord Elgin.

Disguised or otherwise, his compelling passions always found utterance in his poetry. There is no trace of Nicolo in the verses he composed during their several months together. He acted, Byron said, as his Dragoman and Major Domo,[1] but he was much more than simply a catamite, as Byron showed by his parting gesture. He took him to Malta on his way home and placed him in a convent (the word was interchangeable with monastery), providing, hard up as he himself was, a sufficient sum for his education to be continued.

There are letters from a priest, Father Vincenzo Aquilina, undertaking that his pupil would learn English, arithmetic, fine handwriting and Italian—in which he needed perfecting.[2] Considering he spoke and wrote Greek proficiently, had French as his mother tongue, and that his writing was already good in both Greek and Roman characters, he seems to have been exceptionally intelligent. By this time, nearly a year after Byron's own sojourn in a convent, their relations had become those of patron and grateful, affectionate ward, recognized as such by his mother and family who sent respectful messages. It is amusing to find the boy of fifteen or sixteen telling the young man of twenty-three that he begs to remain under his protection and that he will be 'like your son and Your Excellency like my kindly father', giving many promises, such as sons give—or used to give—their fathers, always to respect his commands and, with the help of God, attend to his duties and prosecute his studies.

His writing, sometimes wholly in Greek and sometimes dropping into Greek for a sentimental postscript, shows that Byron had a good understanding of that language.

By October 1811 Nicolo was writing in halting English, and a month or two later, in fairly competent English:

My dear Lord,
    I have received your dear Letter by the hands of the two Albanians of the Marquess of Sligo, written by your Waiter Demetrio on the 6 of December 1811, so ordered by Your Excellency on which he writes that Your Excellency had received two letters of me and two from my Italian master and that if my letters were written in English they would have given you greater pleasure, but I remember very well that when you were in Malta, you told me not to write you until I could do it without mistakes, and for that reason I did not write to you in that Language then: but now that I can do it, I write you in English, and have also written you two other letters before this.
    He informs me that Your Excellency will come back to Malta in June, which gives me very great pleasure, and I shall begin now to pay more attention to my studies, that when you come you will find me as you wish.
        I remain your obliged and humble servant
                Nicola Giraud[3]

---

[1] Marchand, *Letters*. To Hobhouse, 26 Nov. 1810.   [2] Murray MS. 1 July 1811.
[3] Ibid. 18 Jan. 1812. Nicolo sometimes used an English signature, Nicholas, some-

The fact that Byron got his valet, Demetrio Zograffo (who had temporarily replaced Fletcher), to write instead of doing so himself, and that he had warned the boy that he 'would answer his letters very rarely for want of time',[1] shows clearly enough that nothing amatory remained on his side, although in the will —afterwards cancelled—that he drafted in August 1811, as a sequel to his dismal homecoming, he left him £7,000. Combined with his continued, though weakening, sense of responsibility, however, was the absence, through the deaths of so many of his friends, of anyone else conspicuously suitable to be a beneficiary. The surviving intimates with whom he was still in touch—not numerous—had, or could look forward to, private means.

He did not return to Malta, and neither did the accomplished Nicolo remain in the convent, albeit he was there longer than we might expect, well over a year. On December 12th 1812, not knowing that, by a startling transition, his patron had become the most lionized young man in London, he wrote:

> I must now inform you that I live no longer in the Convent because I once went with Mr Cockerell to the play and the head of the Convent would not permit me to remain in it, but one of the recommendations I had from Mr Lusieri, has taken care of me, and placed me in a Maltese family, with whom I live happy, without being among so many priests, who troubled my head every moment and taught me nothing.

He hoped he would see his Lordship very soon, assured him he was most assiduous in his studies, and sent the respects of his mother, Lusieri, and his family generally.

Byron did not reply either then or to later letters. When he had rejoined Western society, he had abandoned Eastern *mores*. After a period of intense depression, when all his anticipated delight in coming home with wondrous travellers' tales had been rudely shattered by calamities, he sought consolation among the women 'below stairs' at Newstead Abbey, one of whom was a pretty Welsh housemaid, Susan Vaughan, who injured his pride by an infidelity for which several other women, of much more exalted station, were to make recompense.

He began to meet famous men of letters, made his first speech in the House of Lords, published *Childe Harold* with dazzling success, became the 'curled darling' of the fashionable world, and was involved in a series of love affairs with society women too often recorded to need mention here.

He became enamoured with his half-sister, Augusta, or with the alluring danger of giving rein to so sinful a passion—and it is easy in the 1970s to forget

---

times his French one, Nicolas, and this would become Nicola. He never signed Nicolo, though it is the Italian form and he lived, for the most part, with Italians.

[1] Ibid. 12 Dec. 1812. Nicolo is quoting Byron.

that there used to be Byronians who would rather he had done murder—and from a complication of motives, among which was certainly the desire for escape and atonement, he married a quite egregiously priggish girl whose vanity of righteousness goaded him into boasting all sorts of obliquities, not sparing her such exploits as being in bed with two naked women at once,[1] and hinting pretty broadly at the sin which Englishmen, according to Shelley, did not name and scarcely even conceived, so we may imagine the stupendous horror with which it filled his wife. Almost insanely obtuse, he tried to persuade her that what were crimes in England were not so in other climates and conditions. This outraged her still more as she knew incontrovertibly, and explained in numerous documents, that there was one fixed morality at all times for all the human race. She thus remained immune from such hideous notions, an obstinacy which only rendered Byron more determined in his insistence:

> He laboured to convince me that Right & Wrong were merely Conventional, & varying with Locality & other circumstances—he clothed these sentiments in the most seductive language—appealing both to the Heart and Imagination. I must have been bewildered had I not firmly & simply believed in one Immutable Standard. . . . It would have required an abler logician than I was to expose the fallacy, when he stated such facts as that morality was one thing at Constantinople, another in London—& the requirements of the Divine Law different in the time of Abraham & of Christ.[2]

Byron was unable to persuade her, not only because of her Immutable Standard, but perhaps because he was not fully persuaded himself. He spoke with his reason, not from the depth of his inner conviction. In the East he had felt liberated, but back on English soil the idea that what he had been doing was criminal haunted him. Alluding to William Beckford, he had written in *Childe Harold* of 'th'unhallowed thirst of crime unnamed',[3] and though he very properly cancelled the stanza, seeing that from his own glass house, remote from England though it might be, he was in no position to throw stones, it expressed an authentic feeling.

Always fascinated by his own misdeeds, he was bent upon sharing that emotion with his wife, declaring 'I was a villain to marry you', and frequently accusing himself, although, in her own words:

[1] Lovelace Papers. Bathurst memorandum.

[2] Lovelace Papers. From an uncompleted Preface to her projected autobiography, dated March 1854. Designated 'Statement FF' by Lord Lovelace.

[3] Biographers of Beckford have supposed him not guilty of paederasty, but their books were written before the publication of his letters to the Chevalier Franchi, his friend, factotum, and sometimes procurer, in *Life at Fonthill 1807–1822*, skilfully translated and edited by Boyd Alexander (1957). Beckford lived to see the cancelled lines, and took a strong turn against Byron.

Lord Byron has never *expressly* declared himself guilty of any *specific* crime—but his insinuations to that effect have been much more convincing than the most direct assertion. [It is marvellously typical of Lady Byron to be more convinced by insinuations than by direct assertions. She herself was pastmistress of the insinuation as powerful as an assertion.]

At Halnaby he did several times declare that he was guilty of *some* heinous crime—which he said he would tell me when I had a child—for any woman might be bound by that tie.[1]

The only occasion she and Byron were at Halnaby together was on their honeymoon, so he lost no time in playing upon her preoccupation with sin.

She thought later on he had been corrupted at Harrow, and so did not allow the two grandsons she brought up to go to a public school; but though he may have added tales of schoolboy indecencies to the others with which he regaled her (more, sometimes, to assail her solemnity than to convert her, of that we may be fairly sure) there is nothing to suggest that his Harrow friendships were directed at any kind of physical consummation. His rejection of Lord Grey, Hobhouse's marginal note notwithstanding, was palpably spontaneous and his revulsion lasting.

Hobhouse would not have been pleased if he could have foreseen that his scribbled comments would one day be used to confirm the suspicions of Lady Byron, whom he detested. In *The Late Lord Byron*, I have explained in detail, and with documentary support, the state of mind in which he read Moore's biography. He was aggrieved to see so many proofs of Byron's affectionate intimacy with Moore, towards whom he had for years been as obstructive as possible. Moore's tactless statement that his company had grown to be 'a chain and a burden' on Byron during his first travels wounded him most painfully; and he took it out of both Moore and Byron, as it were, by observations which showed how much he could tell if he would. His remark about Lord Grey's effect on Byron's future morals[2] was an assumption founded on knowledge that Grey had made an advance, a tale that may have been told him with misleading flippancy. He had not met Byron before their Cambridge days, and his awareness of his friend's temptations may easily have made him, in his black mood, picture depravity where there had been none.

At Cambridge Byron had had a homosexual love and sought physical release in heterosexual relationships. 'I have not done an act *that would bring me under*

---

[1] Lovelace Papers. An early Statement, designated V by Lord Lovelace.

[2] See p. 77. Thanks to the kindness of the late Sir Harold Nicolson, the two quarto volumes, in which Hobhouse wrote his now famous comments, were in my possession for many months. No one who has not seen them can have any idea how light the pencillings are, some words having almost vanished from the pages. My belief is that Hobhouse, having relieved his irritation, meant to erase them. I greatly doubt whether he intended, in Byron's phrase, to paralyse posterity with them.

the power of the law', he told his wife, 'at least on this side of the water',[1] and even she, anxious as she was to amass damaging testimony against him, was satisfied that this was true. Homosexual practice would, of course, have brought him under the power of the law. In 1816, the very year in which she wrote down those words, a man who had committed sodomy was hanged for it, and it was reported in the press that, at his execution, 'the detestable nature of his crime appeared to avert, in the minds of the crowd, that sympathy usually shown to culprits undergoing the vengeance of the law'.[2] The jury had taken only ten minutes to invoke the death sentence.

That there was anything other than sheer God-defying turpitude which could predispose a male to feel drawn by an erotic stirring towards other males was scarcely credited, and those who were unfortunate enough to be born with that propensity had to disguise or overcome it as best they could. For Byron, adjustment was assuredly easier than for the out-and-out Uranian incapable of satisfaction with any member of the opposite sex. He was susceptible to women, exceptionally attractive to them and, to judge by their unwillingness to relinquish a sexual relationship once begun, more than adequate as a lover. He might have gone through life without awakening any doubt as to his whole-hearted masculinity if it had not been for that lust for tasting every kind of experience which made him eager to play with fire, and the belief in pre-destination to evil that may have been partly due to the Calvinist teachings of his nurse—herself so evil—and partly to his having read and reread in his highly impressionable childhood Dr John Moore's *Zeluco* and other such romances with anti-heroes.

Lady Byron said he always compared himself with Zeluco,[3] and he himself recorded, in the 'Additional Preface' to *Childe Harold*, that he had intended to develop that character as a poetical version of the one in the novel. Zeluco was dedicated to sin.

I am obliged to notice a theory which it has naturally been easy to popular-ize at a time when, for good or ill, there is a reaction against most of the codes of sexual morals which hitherto restrained modern Western man. This is that Byron lived in sodomitic intercourse with his wife, who was a 'not unwilling partner', that it was their 'marriage secret', and that her course of conduct after the separation was a series of manoeuvres to direct attention away from what she ultimately learned—having been ignorant of it before—would be con-sidered wickedness were it revealed. Moreover, that two anonymous porno-graphic poems, *Don Leon* and *Leon to Annabella*, were actually written by someone who had enjoyed Byron's confidence about his unnatural practices (for

---

[1] Lovelace Papers. 'Remarks on Lord B's Letter of Feb. 8th', Lady Byron's under-lining. Quoted in *The Late Lord Byron*.

[2] *The Public Ledger*, 24 Sept. 1816, quoted in *Life at Fonthill*.

[3] Lovelace Papers, a red leather octavo notebook inscribed '1817, Aug.'.

unnatural and also unlawful was their classification at the time); that this sympathetic listener was George Colman the Younger, whose leering jests thus record positive knowledge; that in 1818, when in Italy, Shelley was also told by Byron of his peculiar conjugal relations, and that in consequence he wrote *Julian and Maddalo* and introduced Byron as 'the Maniac' bewailing his remorse in a most odd manner; and that the hurried burning of the Memoirs after Byron's death was due to his widow's fear that they would contain the disclosure that would destroy her prized reputation for purity, while his friends dreaded that they would proclaim his guilt.

Now had Professor Wilson Knight contented himself with suggesting that Byron might have *tried* to commit what was called 'an enormity' with his wife —which was the most Lord Holland suggested to Hobhouse[1]—I should have had nothing to say. I have no idea what his behaviour in the bedroom might have been, and it cannot be ruled out that a man who was drinking heavily, and who had gone through a phase of practising sodomy with Eastern boys, would be capable of attempting a similar experience with a woman. But when it comes to representing Lady Byron as a consenting partner, too innocent to know what was being done to her, or too sensual to care; when we are asked to believe that the Leon poems are a genuine biographical source, and that Byron, who swore to his closest friend that he was guilty of 'no enormity', had already confessed a capital crime to the companion of an occasional drinking party and would avow the same thing again to a fellow-poet of notable high-mindedness, I feel compelled to speak, and not from guesswork.

I spent many a long day studying the documents known as the Lovelace Papers, from which Professor Wilson Knight could only give such extracts as had been published before 1956, the date of his book. I had a trunkful of the original MS in my house after the death of their owner, Lady Wentworth, and can fill in the omitted passages from which the Professor deduces his 'Evidence of Asterisks'—the sub-title of his book.[2] Sometimes dots were inserted by the various editors[3] to avoid irrelevance, sometimes because of the unmerciful long-windedness of Lady Byron and her circle, and sometimes because there were limits to what could be openly printed—in particular the passage about Byron's 'disgusting descriptions of his adulteries and indecencies with loose women, toying with more than one at the same time naked'. Sir John Fox was

---

[1] When Moore in his biography conjectured that the separation may have been due to Lady Byron's taking 'in sober seriousness' wild hints of 'undefined horrors', Hobhouse wrote in the margin, 'Something of this sort certainly unless as Lord Holland told me, he tried to —————— her'. The blank is Hobhouse's.

[2] *Lord Byron's Marriage.*

[3] Lord Lovelace, 1905; Lady Lovelace, 1921; Sir John C. Fox, 1924; Miss E. C. Mayne, 1929; André Maurois, 1930. The three last named worked from copies. Only the successive owners and myself had full and free access to the papers until 1960, when the last batch was passed over to Lord Lytton and they were used by Malcolm Elwin.

bound to omit that in 1924. But never was there a single passage excised which could conceivably be adduced as evidence of marital sodomy.

What is discernible in Lady Byron's numerous writings from an early age is precisely her lack of what we call innocence. She had been born an only child late in the life of her 18th-century parents, with whom she was very free-spoken, and who ministered with humility to her belief in her omniscience and right to pronounce judgment on others—whose vices she was much more disposed to observe than their virtues. The notion that she entered the marriage state, an intensively educated girl of nearly twenty-three, so uninformed that, to put it bluntly, she did not know one part of her anatomy from another, is perfectly ridiculous. Equally, the notion that she submitted *not* innocently but responsively to a perversion that was then a felony—and which would still, I fancy, repel any woman of delicacy—is totally at odds with her pride in being a paragon of morality, unswerving from one 'Immutable Standard'.

Those readers who wanted to believe what was congenial to their own proclivities, and those who merely skimmed over the tortuous arguments of the book, accepted its premises without pausing to consider on what convolutions of reasoning they were based, what rash assumptions, what quotations out of context, and what dependence on demonstrably bad witnesses.

Colonel Doyle's phrase about Lady Byron's 'too confiding disposition'[1] is cited at least five times as evidence that she had *said* too much, having naïvely told the 'marriage secret' to Mrs Clermont,[2] who was threatening (we have it on the authority of *Leon to Annabella*!) to disclose it unless she left her husband. One would think a professor of English literature would be sensible that 'too confiding' usually means *having*, not giving, too much confidence, and it is manifest even from so much of the correspondence as was in print that Doyle believed Lady Byron had been over-trustful in associating with Augusta Leigh when the latter was suspected of incest, because that might turn out an obstacle to denouncing her, should such a course be decided upon. Here is but one example of isolating a few words and interpreting them recklessly to fit the theory.

In like manner the question of burning Byron's Memoirs is dealt with. I have devoted a chapter of my previous book to explaining how this appalling act of literary vandalism came to be committed. Any investigation of openly published references would have revealed that Byron invited John Murray to show the Memoirs to whom he pleased,[3] and that Moore let so many people read

---

[1] Lovelace. 18 July 1816. Doyle and his mischief-making sister Selina were among the little regiment of Lady Byron's advisers.

[2] Mary Anne Clermont was a spinster. The courtesy title, Mrs, was given to most middle-aged or elderly unmarried women in respectable occupations (e.g. Mrs Hannah More). It would have been considered highly improper to discuss the secrets of the marriage bed with a maiden lady.

[3] *LJ.* 29 Oct. 1819.

them that he feared the original papers might 'become worn out by passing through so many hands'.[1] The names of upwards of twenty persons who read all or part of them are given, either in Moore's journals or other reliable documents, and the portion which contained the 'detailed account of my marriage and its consequences', was the one that had most readers. It is out of the question that Byron's widow or friends—or enemies—could suppose he would have confessed to being a sodomite, matrimonially or otherwise, in a document which, very plainly, as his letters show, was meant in some degree to vindicate him.[2]

Just as words must be set in their context to convey their proper meaning, so acts must be related to the context of their time. No one knew better than Byron that what he had done in Eastern Europe stood for sheer damnation in the West, and had he confessed to unspeakable erotic practices, repeated subsequently with an unwitting (or should I say half-witted?) bride who left him when she learned they had been doing wrong, the resulting scandal, as the pages were handed round, would have been explosive.

Professor Wilson Knight acknowledged in his Preface that he made no effort to see the Lovelace Papers. Had he done so, or indeed consulted other manuscript collections, he would have found that many of the passages he interprets by his 'faculty of "spatial analysis"' as intimations of unnatural marital union actually refer either to policies for dealing with Augusta Leigh, or else to Lady Byron's second but much less obsessive charge—not openly made but often canvassed—that of the Oriental iniquities about which, apart from his own broad hints, Caroline Lamb, breaking a tremendous oath of secrecy, had sensationally informed her.[3]

These were deemed, and clearly stated, to be 'worse crimes' than incest,[4] and it was they that provided Lady Byron with 'the *three words* that might annihilate him', as her congenial confidante, the Hon. Mrs Villiers, reminded her on September 20th 1816. Professor Wilson Knight reads into that phrase support of his case. I have quoted publicly that, in her reply to Mrs Villiers, Lady Byron said: 'I doubt if after all he *does* know that "*three* words from me would annihilate him"—though it would seem like madness he should not.'[5]

How could she write that if the crime, she and her friends believed she could fix upon him, was one he had committed with *her*? She went on, after pronouncing him blinded by pride, 'Having also made these disclosures

---

[1] Moore, Memoirs. 7 May 1820.

[2] E.g. 'You will perhaps say *why* write my life?—Alas! I say so too—but they who have traduced it—& blasted it—and branded me—should know that it is they—and not I —are the cause.' Byron to Lady Byron offering her perusal of the Memoirs, 31 Dec. 1819, quoted by Lovelace in *Astarte*.

[3] Lovelace Papers. Minutes of a Conversation between her and Lady Byron, 27 Mar. 1816. They are given in full in *The Late Lord Byron*.

[4] Ibid.   [5] Ibid. Villiers Correspondence. 26 Sept. 1816.

generally under the influence of strong & evil passions he is less likely to remember them distinctly'.

These disclosures! Why in the world should he need to *disclose* her own ineffable 'marriage secret' to her? And why, if she was at such pains to conceal having innocently compounded a felony that she made Augusta her scapegoat, did she then defeat her own ends by lifting the curtain on the awful truth to all those friends and counsellors who, according to the illuminations of 'spatial analysis', gave utterance to it again in various cryptic forms?

Seen by less occult lights, Byron's disclosures concerned his 'crimes' in Greece, and if he was not 'likely to remember them distinctly', it was because he had never made them distinctly, as she herself was constrained to acknowledge in the paper already quoted which, being for the guidance of her official advisers, was more circumspect than the sort of thing she told her friends.

After the Evidence of Asterisks, we have to consider the evidence of *Don Leon*. Unless it can be proved that this scurrilous composition and its companion piece were written by someone who was in Byron's confidence, the Professor's theory falls completely to the ground, because there is no evidence at all from anyone who was in his wife's confidence—no evidence, that is to say, of perverse intercourse, only a general charge of 'brutally indecent conduct and language', which her lawyer, Dr Lushington, stated to one of her trustees, in advanced old age, to be the chief cause of the separation.[1] I shall presently return to that.

If there is one shred, one slender filament of evidence, that George Colman received a confidence of any kind from Byron, the theorist has not condescended to reveal it. He has not even condescended to prove that the Leon poems were Colman's work! I do not share his overwhelming admiration of those monotonous imitations of the satires in heroic couplets which were already a nearly played-out form when Byron gave them a brief extension of life in *English Bards and Scotch Reviewers*; but it must be allowed that, if their mode was outworn, their lewdness was sustained and vigorous. *Don Leon*'s puns and double-entendres and lecherous Latin tags have a vitality that renders it, to say the least, unlikely that they were written by a dying man in his seventies. They contain topical allusions to events of the 1830s (Colman was born in 1762). The prurient footnotes are later still.

Professor Knight is not worried by anachronisms. He has ways of dealing with them. In *Don Leon*, for instance, there are certain lines about the victim of a homosexual scandal:

> Adieu to all his former well-earned fame.
> An exile to a foreign land he'll fly,
> Neglected live, and broken hearted die.

[1] Lovelace Papers. Bathurst Memorandum of a Conversation with Lushington on 27 Jan. 1870.

A note to the text tells us that the reference is to Grey Bennett who died abroad in June 1836. Colman himself died four months later, after a long painful illness. Mr Wilson Knight's explanation is that the line about Bennett's death is 'perfunctory' and may have been written while he was still alive! This really would have been carrying sympathetic premonition disconcertingly far. But even more naïve is the way we have it repeatedly pointed out to us that the verses contain biographical data which are true to the facts of Byron's life—thus giving the uninformed reader the impression that they must be by one who had enjoyed his confidence. Every single genuine fact of Byron's life that the versifier introduces had appeared in some book, chiefly Moore's biography, published in or before 1830, and the Leon 'masterpiece' was indisputably written after that year.

The only 'facts' not gleaned from Moore, or Byron's own printed works and other easily available sources, are quite inaccurate. Nicolo Giraud was not the son of a Greek who lived submissively with his father in Oriental style and was offered to Byron as a page. Edleston did not die before Byron went abroad on his Grand Tour, nor was *Childe Harold* addressed to his memory. The page, Robert Rushton, was in no way intimate with Byron in the latter's boyhood. There are many similar proofs of basic ignorance which would be amazing in one who had listened to the darkest deepest secrets of a young celebrity and carried them so ineffaceably in his memory that, long afterwards, he was identifying himself with him and addressing himself, in the guise of Byron, to Thomas Moore—for so *Don Leon* is framed. Moreover, Colman was a friend of Moore's and so, without revealing what he was about, could have avoided such factual errors. The internal evidence that Moore and the satirist were actually strangers is, to me at any rate, conclusive.

The theory that Byron confided in Colman hinges on Colman's being the writer of the *Leon* poems. Mr Wilson Knight leaves *that* theory unexplained except by bringing in another; namely, that Colman was the author of a still more odious work, *The Rodiad*—a 'serious satire on flogging' which, he says, was published in 1810, in itself not a very firm support on which to hang two satires about quite a different vice written more than twenty years later, and not containing any point of resemblance to their predecessor apart from rhymed couplets, puns, and what the Professor calls 'a strong prepossession . . . with the posterior areas of the human body'. He does not see fit to mention that *The Rodiad* is catalogued at the British Museum with this comment:

> The imprint is fictitious, the work having been published by J. J. Hotten about 1870, probably intended by the publisher to be regarded as the work of George Colman the Younger.

'George Coleman' (sic) appears on the title page with the imprimatur of 'Cadell & Murray, Fleet Street'. If Colman had dared to put his name to a work so eminently subject to prosecution, we may be assured he would not have misspelt it. Professor Knight is acquainted with 'Pisanus Fraxi' and the indices of prohibited books. One of them figures in his bibliography. But he omits to quote the following remark by that expert (H. S. Ashbee):

> The date 1810 is entirely false, as are the names of the author and publishers. The poem could not have been written earlier than 1820, because at p. 27, line 4, we find;
> I read his bill of 'penalties and pains;'
> and again at p. 61, line 3:
> Cut up with red-hot wire adulterous Queens,
> which evidently refer to the Queen Caroline scandal. . . . Nor was the poem written by either the elder or younger Colman . . . but by one of the clients of the notorious Sarah Potter. . . .

This person and her clientele are apparently described in the *Index Librorum Prohibitorum*, with which I need not concern myself. *The Rodiad* is emphatically not 'a satire'. Whether jocular or serious, a satire holds its subject up to reprobation or ridicule. From beginning to end, this is overt propaganda of the most repulsive kind for sexual pleasure achieved through the torture of unwilling victims, chiefly boys, by flogging. I do not propose to nauseate the reader with more than a comparatively mild extract. The schoolmaster gloats on the suffering he is about to inflict:

> Oh, hour that comes too late and goes too soon,
> My day's delight,—my flogging hour at noon;—
> When I count up the boys that stay behind,
> And class their bottoms in my cheerful mind!
> I whipped *him* yesterday, the *first*—to-day
> He's the *bonne bouche* with which to close the play,—
> For nothing charms the true schoolmaster more
> Than tickling up afresh the half-healed sore.

Professor Knight is able to detect in Colman's genuine and acknowledged works, his plays and comic poems, affinity with that pernicious rubbish and the laborious vehemence of *Don Leon*. I find his touch, on the contrary, deft and amusing, with ribaldry that is sometimes boisterous, sometimes coarse, but wholly without trace of neurosis or obsession. He has a gift of parody inconceivable in the heavy-handed pornographers responsible for *The Rodiad* and the Leon poems—which are themselves, I believe, by two different pens.[1]

---

[1] Professor Chew (*Byron in England*) was of the same opinion. He thought *Leon to Annabella* many years earlier than *Don Leon*. They are in different styles, and even give different accounts of the unnatural seduction: but his suggested date (1817 to 1818) is negated by costume evidence. There is an unintentionally ludicrous description of

It is beyond measure difficult to picture Byron in close friendship with the psychopath who was capable of writing *The Rodiad*—which ends with hopes that, in the next world, it might be his task 'to scourge the diabolic flesh,/For ever tortured and for ever fresh'. Physical sadism was a deviation towards which he never evinced the slightest leaning. When he had it in his power to follow the custom all too common in public schools of caning his fag and other younger boys, he refrained from it. He is known to have defended juniors at Harrow who were threatened with canings. He fought his equals with his fists, resolved to show he could hold his own though handicapped and, as an adult, he learned boxing, partly with a similar object and partly to keep down his weight. To be interested in 'the Fancy' was a cult of the day, and one which, in his case, did not outlast youth.

Professor Knight may have some recondite knowledge about Colman's sexual addictions—I mean, something that would *not* be catalogued as 'spurious' —but he does not share it with his readers. If the playwright and wit took delight in the infliction of pain, he must have concealed it socially. Byron, who claims no more than to have met him 'occasionally', praises him highly for his fun and geniality. He sets him in company with Sheridan. We have no word from any quarter that they were alone together for ten minutes.

The notion that Byron would confess to one of his men-of-the-world acquaintances that his wife had left him on account of his having seduced her into an act for which he could have been hanged on a gibbet is to lift him straight out of his time, and straight out of his character as well. He was rash and indiscreet, but not a shifty hypocrite denying to his friends, his lawyer and his readers matters he had unfolded to a mere convive.

As I explained in the Preface to *The Late Lord Byron*, I lost the notes I had made on the probable identity of the real author of *Don Leon* and was only able, as I said, to hint at it. Most readers missed the clues, amongst which were the wildly vitriolic style of the writer, the fact that he had gone to Newstead Abbey to try and purchase Byron's letters to his young page, Rushton, and his reference to himself, obliquely, in a letter to *The Times*, as one of those 'who conceived themselves to be his [Byron's] disciples' and professed the same opinions, an unusual turn of phrase if it simply meant he was an enthusiast of the poet's works. I had hoped not to have to return to a terrain of research most alien and disagreeable to me, but, finding Professor Knight persisted in his

---

Annabella undressing:
   . . . When, slipping to the tag, the bursting lace
   Has given you breath, and rumbling to their place
   The joyous entrails set your flanks at ease . . .
This could only apply to the removal of a tight corset, and no constriction of the 'entrails' was practised till tight-lacing was revived towards 1830.

doctrine even after I had published a letter from Mrs Clermont which alone should have demolished it,[1] and that he had propagated it so successfully that, in certain recent publications and reviews, it is treated as proved 'beyond a cavil', I have been obliged to resume the Indelicate Investigation.

While the chain of evidence lacks even one link, I will not give the name—a very obscure one—of the pornographer. I may fairly say, however, that I believe him to have been a man born fourteen years after Byron, who travelled both in the Far and Near East (as Colman never did), and apparently learned while in Greece—though only through echoes of old rumours—of the famous poet's attachment to Nicolo Giraud and his inclination to do what was criminal in England. The dates of his journeys show that he never could have encountered Byron in person; but he used him as the pivotal figure in his own sexual fantasies. He subscribed a sum much beyond his means towards the monument now in Trinity College Library, and carried possessiveness to the extent of pugnacious attacks on Byron's friends. His education had comprised both oriental and classical languages, and he had been an outstandingly gifted scholar; but by 1830, when he was twenty-eight, he was pensioned off from the Service which employed him because he had become mentally unhinged.

Thenceforward he lived, largely under his father's care, a life without visible occupation,[2] but—if my presumptions are right—intent on a private pastime in which some degree of derangement is distinctly observable. There is the obsession which gives rise to tedious and repetitive puns and scatological similes; there is also the want of any steady point of view so typical of the unbalanced. Sometimes he is vindicating sodomy ardently, almost devotionally, and sometimes he is representing it with every appearance of a desire to disgust.

It is not to be expected that any explicit record of being engaged in those salacious labours was kept by the author, but at any rate we have dates, characteristics and opportunities that fit, which is in no wise the case with Colman. The Graeco-Turkish local colour is brushed in with a realism quite beyond Colman's scope.

We now come to the 'brutal indecency' of Byron's conduct and language to his wife, which, naturally, Professor Knight called on for support. But if we

---

[1] 'He is sometimes charged with having done even worse things than is true', she wrote to Lady Byron about Feb. 18th 1816. (Lovelace Papers.) If he had committed 'an enormity', he *could* have done no worse, as Professor Knight himself acknowledges when he supposes Mrs Clermont threatened exposure of the horror unless the wife left her husband forthwith.

[2] In 1838 he rashly requested that his pension might be paid direct to him instead of to his father. This would have meant proving he was sane—in which case he was not entitled to a pension at all! He tried then to produce a certificate of his continued insanity, but was unable to do so, and his allowance was thereupon withdrawn. In 1839 he appealed to the Board to restore it, but they refused, and refused also to allow him to appear before them—a most suggestive fact seeing that this Company was noted for good treatment of its former employees.

take any broad selection of criticisms made in the press of the day about *Don Juan*, we find accusations of obscenity, blasphemy, brutality, coarseness and degraded immorality such as now would be applied only to what is called hard-core pornography. Happily we have the sparkling epic itself to set against those torrents of censure. We have also some examples of what the chief private witness in the case regarded as too shamefully indecent to be written down except in the obscurity of shorthand. One of them was Byron's teasing his sister with 'A[ugusta] I *know* you wear drawers'.[1] Another was that 'he would draw personal comparisons between us in the most vicious manner'.[2] Yet the comparisons could not have been very gross because she maintained in numerous statements that she only *suspected* his relations with his half-sister when she parted from him, and had he seriously overstepped the mark, her suspicion must have turned to certainty.

She took the trouble, as showing his abominable levity, to note for posterity that he had 'united Blasphemy with Indecency by jests about the Virgin Mary &c'[3]—a form of irreverence much commoner among non-Catholics than she realized. But even without allowing for her—and Lushington's—readiness to be shocked, and the limitless change in our moral standards, we must in justice perceive that a phrase like 'brutal indecency' carries a relative, not an absolute, weight. It is fantastic to deduce from it, or any similar vague charge, that Byron had violated his wife in a manner the more heinous because he had turned her (I am closely following the Professor's theory) into the partner of a form of union she was at first too innocent to resent.

As time went on, jealousy of Augusta, the gratification of having power over so vulnerable and tangible a victim, almost supplanted her sense of that other power she had at first been acutely conscious of possessing—to shatter what was left of Byron's reputation by announcing that he was a pervert. (So such men were called even in my own youth, when their tendency had become a mild joke rather than a fearful stigma—though, to be sure, there was the shadow of the prison house, which sometimes fell across the unfortunate.)

The abhorrence of homosexuality in thought or deed that was nearly universal when Lord Lovelace was compiling his books, placed a restriction on what he could impart from his grandmother's letters and written statements. After all, it was going very far to plead her cause by accusing his grandfather of incest, let alone still less condonable delinquency. But at any rate, though not honest with his readers, he scrupulously kept all the documents. He might tamper with the typed copies and omit important passages in *Astarte* but he left the originals intact.

Incest sufficed for Lord Lovelace, but not for Byron's wife, who wanted an

[1] Lovelace Papers, Narrative R. Drawers for women were a fashion recently introduced, and their use was still optional.
[2] Ibid. [3] Ibid. Statement U.

admiring audience to know the full extent of her martyrdom. Had she really been the silent sufferer she believed herself, by some very curious double-thinking process, to be, she could have justified her refusal to be reconciled to her husband without mentioning any sexual divagations at all. He had from the first behaved intolerably to her, neglected her, insulted her, lost his temper violently and often, got drunk repeatedly, been unfaithful to her with at least one actress (Professor Wilson Knight throws in the probability of actors too for good measure, though there was never a wisp of rumour to that effect), and treated her with crude inconsiderateness in pregnancy. She hated and distrusted all his friends, her household was disrupted by the consequences of his debts, and none of the privilege and prestige she must have expected in becoming the bride of a handsome, brilliant, sought-after man had accrued, because he seldom cared to go out with her. What more could she want to make her marriage unbearable?

She did want more. From earliest childhood, as she relates in her reminiscences, she had dwelt on scenes where, in imagination, she did noble deeds, such as visiting the sick in the midst of a pestilence, or going into dungeons with Howard, the penal reformer; and she cultivated susceptibilities that were morbid. The word is her own. She was always, she said, craving for excitement which, for a while, she got out of her system by what she calls 'theatrical pursuits', presumably plays acted for the family circle. The parts she felt the greatest pleasure in performing were those of Love and Revenge.[1] She never outgrew the habit of thinking theatrically and seeing herself as the heroine of dramas.

She cast herself in the role of one who is under heavenly protection against sin but able to extend sublime forgiveness to sinners; and, auspiciously, given the hunger to reform vice that her statements so often exhibit, she had two splendidly nefarious sinners to contend with. The frustrating circumstance was that nobody could applaud her struggle with the warped nature of Byron and guilt of Augusta unless she exposed what she claimed credit for concealing. She became incomparably adept at letting her friends guess at the dark mysteries of her sorrow and her generosity while persuading them that she was bravely pursuing a Policy of Silence. She also left copious autobiographical writings of a self-exalting kind, some of which were intended for ultimate publication. Here is a passage describing her matrimonial suffering and nobility:

> The Philosophy which regards Morality as wholly dependent on Circumstances—on Climate—on Tradition—was often plausibly advocated, and none can know how strong is the temptation to embrace it, but those who have loved the Erring and Unreformed!—The doctrine that would have exculpated *him* would have justified *me* in following the course dictated by my own

---

[1] Lovelace Papers. 'Auto-Description' written in the 1830s.

passionate devotedness. I can remember wishing it were right to give up all for one!—even to be a slave and a victim! But never did I yield to the weakness—I felt a responsibility for him as well as myself—and when my own interpretation of the natural law was clouded by my feelings, I referred to the *Revealed Will*—In this sense J. Christ may indeed be said to have been my Saviour! I found in his precepts the 'immutable morality' which the reason of man is often incapable of discerning. . . .[1]

We may either infer from this a general attempt by Byron to shake the rigid framework of the moral system by which she was always judging and condemning, or else a more than usually harrowing trial of her virtue, which, as I have already said, cannot be ruled out, but which seems absolutely to have passed from *his* mind; and that is why I have suggested that if it were so, he must have been drunk at the time. Had he recollected anything at all about a situation when she had been obliged to resist him with the sole aid of 'J. Christ' —a fairly frequent intervener in her affairs but one whose precepts would not have been very apposite in that particular dilemma—how could he write to her of 'the violence & outrageous latitude of accusation which has been indulged beyond all example and all excuse', or reproach her with having had his name 'as completely blasted as if it were branded on my forehead', and with 'the reports—which if once circulated not even falsehood—and their admitted and acknowledged falsehood can neutralize—which no contradiction can obliterate . . . ?'[2]

Was this nothing but the artful posing of one who was aware all the while of her ability to 'annihilate him'—not from hearsay but from her own incontrovertible knowledge?

Byron was, in my belief, like many men of extreme sensibility, born with a genuinely bisexual temperament. We might think this condition, whereby objects of love can be found in either sex according to propinquity, would be an enviable one—at least when passion can be fulfilled, which was no safe or easy matter in England. It seems, however, that bisexuality may be at times a less bearable state than homosexuality, since, whatever fulfilment is attained, the lover in some strange spirit of contradiction is liable to feel that he is being false to his nature; that is, unless there is attachment so devoted, so compelling, that it leaves no room for self-questioning.

Byron was not in love with his wife, nor had he been, after a few brief weeks, with Caroline Lamb, so there was, in each of these cases, a recoil from heterosexual desire, and it was this, I suggest, which produced hints, half-confessions, manifestations of guilt which were not, if they had but known it, because he had sinned with the youths in Athens or elsewhere, but because, loveless or nearly so, he supposed *then* that he was betraying the truth of his being. With more satisfying women, Augusta, Marianna Segati, Teresa

[1] Ibid.   [2] Lovelace Papers and Murray copies. 25 Mar. 1816.

Guiccioli, he did not behave in this provocative and mystifying manner, nor do I think he ever gave these and other mistresses the least reason to suspect him of any 'unhallowed thirst for crime unnamed'—though Augusta, needless to say, was enlightened by her sister-in-law.

The stereotype of homosexual characteristics is no longer acceptable, effeminacy, softness, archness, and so on; but there remain some indications which would still seem valid, and most of them were notably absent in Byron. He had no special relationship with his mother, except a bad one. He was strikingly non-aesthetic; he scarcely ever, for example, gave any sign of having noticed what the women about him—apart from exotic ones—were wearing, an all too heterosexual oversight. Nor, in immense contrast to Beckford, did he display much interest in the visual features of the rooms he occupied and houses he visited. (We may except a mild appreciation of sculpture.) He lacked masculine reserve, and there was a tang of humorous malice in his gossip in which we may detect a trace of 'queerness'. As a companion he had, when in a good mood, a cosiness—I can find no more adequate word—that could make any occasion memorably intimate, the cosiness that gives 'queer' men their agreeable sociability. On the other hand, he could be formidable in an essentially virile way, and as for his style in literature—what could be less epicene?

Having been greatly taken with girls at an age when most boys are despising them, and whole-heartedly infatuated with Mary Chaworth after reaching puberty, his sexual ambivalence must have taken him by surprise. Yet the announcement of plans to set up house with Edleston shows how little at first he suspected himself of abnormality.

> The kiss so guiltless and refined
> That love each warmer wish forebore—

that was really as far as he had gone, and how touchingly unByronic are the verses![1] It must have dawned on him slowly and dreadfully that the refined kiss, the pressure of hands, were less than he coveted. He was one of the accursed!

He went abroad and, becoming absorbed in whatever he saw, whomever he met, shook off for a while the fear of placing himself beyond the pale of manhood. He flirted happily enough with Spanish girls, one of whom cut off her long hair for him, and at Malta he charmed and was charmed by the fascinating Austrian, Constance Spencer-Smith. Women quarrelled over him.[2] He travelled for a year before, having got rid of his English companion, at last he got rid of English proscriptions.

---

[1] To Thyrza (Edleston).

[2] 'Lord Byron is, of course, very popular with the ladies, as he is very handsome, amusing, and generous; but his attentions to all and singular generally end . . . in *rixae femininae*.' Hobhouse, *Recollections*. 9 Sept. 1809.

He felt exhilarated by the freedom, but, returning to his country, he turned the other side of his Janus face—not a mask but a different reality—to the society about him. For all his pathetic efforts to convince his wife that what was wicked in Britain might not be so in Turkey, he was no reformer. He hated cant and pitted himself against it with all his courage and strength, but that was a battle he did not begin till he had exiled himself from the upper class English world. While he lived among English gentlemen, he fully accepted their strange sexual code—that one might seduce a servant girl or a seamstress but not another gentleman's daughter; that virginity in females, if they were young, was an attribute beautiful in itself and that the single woman who lost it no longer merited respect; that fidelity in marriage ought to be maintained long enough to guarantee that a husband's heir should be his own child; and that intercourse between men should be limited to conversation, conviviality, politics, and sport.

He came to terms with his odd, disquieting, disapproved self; it ceased to trouble him, ceased to demand expression. Venice, contrary to popular legend, was the scene of perpetual literary experiments and endeavours, relieved by amours, some lasting a night or two, some less transient, which were scarcely more than the equivalent of visits to a picturesque and amusing brothel. He became ashamed and was very glad, behind his cynical smile, to be rescued by a pretty girl of nineteen who could talk about Dante and Petrarch, and came of a good family, and positively refused money—which astounded him.

After four years of something like married life with her, more settled, despite difficulties, than any he had known, the delusive feeling that he should be a man of action combined with his genuine Philhellenism, and much discouragement from his friends about his work,[1] to send him to Greece. He took with him his Countess's agreeable brother, who was so little aware of any tendency in Byron to deviate that he thought it praiseworthy of him to assist a Greek widow without making any advances to her three good-looking daughters.[2] But there turned out also to be good-looking sons, one of whom, Lukas, entered his service as a page probably in December 1823,[3] and was taken by him to Missolonghi.

He had been celibate for five or six months and without any companion on whom he could lavish his natural flow of affection. And he was in the ambience

---

[1] 'I tried to break to him that he should write less and not think the world cared so very much about his writing or himself.' Hobhouse *Journals.* 20 Sept. 1822, quoted by Marchand. Byron was then writing the later cantos of *Don Juan.*

[2] Count Pietro Gamba to Hobhouse, 11 Aug. 1824. Murray MS. Quoted in *The Late Lord Byron.*

[3] The exact date of Lukas's appearance on the scene (at Cephalonia) is not established, but on 24 Nov. 1823, Byron wrote to his secretary about the 'ailing mother' and her daughters without mentioning any sons, and in a tone which shows that he felt he had done enough for the family and wished to reduce their allowance. (See p. 395.) After Lukas joined him he did the contrary, and gave him a considerable sum for them.

which brought a nostalgia for the liberty of his youth. Lukas thus easily captivated him, but now there was no liberty, not even privacy. He was surrounded from morning to night by suppliants, propagandists, unruly Suliots, factitious leaders and would-be leaders.

Had it been otherwise, Lukas would still have been unresponsive. Any emotional approach to him would have been rebuffed. This we know from Byron's three last unhappy poems—the ten stanzas completed on his thirty-sixth birthday:

> 'Tis time this heart should be unmoved
>   Since others it has ceased to move:
> Yet, though I cannot be beloved,
>   Still let me love!

Then the ten lines called 'Last Words on Greece' where he speaks of the 'maddening fascination' of the person he is addressing:

> I am a fool of passion, and a frown
>   Of thine to me is as an adder's eye.

And the final roughly sketched out verses, alluding to events very shortly before his death:

>   . . . And yet thou lovst me not
> And never wilt! Love dwells not in our will.
>   Nor can I blame thee, though it be my lot
> To strongly, wrongly, vainly love thee still.

Byron at fifteen had been utterly unable to impress Mary Chaworth, the first object of his passion after childhood; and Lukas at fifteen mutely rejected Byron, to him a middle-aged benefactor who could be counted on for money, and whose esteem gave him some prestige among his compatriots, but with whom conversation, either in his own halting Italian or his Lordship's imperfect Greek, must have been rather tedious. So the first and last loves of that most seductive of men had one unique feature in common—they were unrequited.

APPENDIX 3

The Hanson–Portsmouth Scandal

Elevation to the nobility was so enviable a destiny when 'democratic' was still a pejorative word that any father might be forgiven for going to considerable lengths to make his daughter a countess. Nobody knew better than John Hanson what the privileges were because his practice was essentially among the upper classes, but equally nobody knew better that the weak-minded Earl of Portsmouth was a most unpleasant person; for Hanson was the family solicitor and one of the trustees appointed in 1799 to superintend the Earl's property and prevent his weak-mindedness from impairing it. There was a younger brother, the Hon. Newton Fellowes, who was strong-minded, and determined not to see himself dispossessed as heir presumptive by the consequences of the sort of unsuitable match the Earl was likely to make. Therefore he (the Earl) was prudently married, when thirty-two years old, to the Hon. Grace Norton, Lord Grantley's daughter, a woman of forty-seven, who took him under a maternal wing. At the time of this arranged wedding, he was staying, in fact, at Hanson's house, and it was there and then that Byron, as a boy of eleven, met him.

As early as 1800 it was recognized that he was mentally unstable. He pinched and beat his servants: he also flogged animals unmercifully. (There was no legal means of protecting them.)[1] He had what was stated in Court to be 'an insane passion for attending funerals', and would insist on officiating as a mourner at the obsequies of 'low persons' whose families must have been very much surprised. He expressed hopes that sick acquaintances would die so that he could take part in the 'black jobs' afterwards, this being his name for his favourite entertainment. Once he put a rope round someone's neck, thinking no doubt to participate in the 'black job' that might follow.

And here I must pause to correct the usual interpretation of an anecdote often told about Byron to indicate the violence of his temper. In the Hansons' big conservatory, the 'Narrative' tells us:

> Lord P. took the Liberty of pulling Ld Byron's Ears in his usual rough way tho' in fun. There happened to be some large Shells laying [sic] near to Byron & he instantly seized one of them & threw it with all his might at the Earl. Fortunately it missed him and fractured a large pane of stained glass and it not only frightened Lord Portsmouth very much but every one else. . . . Mrs Hanson interfered and tried to pacify Ld Portsmouth by saying 'Lord B. did not do it intentionally my Lord', whilst Lord Byron kept reiterating he did do it intentionally and he would teach a fool of an Earl to pull another noble's lugs.[2]

Now Portsmouth's delight in inflicting pain, if notorious by 1800, was probably quite sufficiently established in the previous year to make 'his usual rough way' of pulling little boys' ears highly objectionable, and Byron's swift

[1] Lady Blessington was freely exercising her imagination when she made Byron say in one of their 'Conversations' of 1823 that he was only deterred from abusing some enemy 'much more severely by the fear of being indicted under the Act of Cruelty to Animals'. No such act existed until 1824. It was then called the Richard Martin Act.

[2] Murray MS. With slight adjustments of punctuation.

gesture of self-protection was natural and spirited. Moreover, in both the original MS and a contemporary copy, the word he used was '*lugs*', not 'ears' as always hitherto printed; and this northern colloquialism shows that the tone of his protest was partly facetious. If seriously reproaching one peer with misusing another, he would hardly have done so in the vernacular, and it seems to me evidence of much adroitness in so young a boy that, while firmly defending himself, he did so in a joking style so that they shook hands afterwards.

We can take the narrator literally when he speaks of the Earl's fright because it was brought out again and again by witnesses that, though brutal, he was peculiarly timorous, and would often cry like a child.

As the years went by, he grew more horribly crazy. Mere peccadilloes, like joining the bellringers at the Parish Church on his own estate, Hurstbourne Park, and making them share their pay with him, developed into atrocities. When his coachman, Charles Webb, lay with a broken leg which had been set, the Earl went into his room and broke it again, telling him it served him right. He liked to go to slaughter houses and, before the cattle were killed, would strike them with a stick or axe, saying 'Serve you right!'. He would interfere with waggoners at work so that he might beat their horses, and he would have his own horses bled to the extremest degree. He was obsessed by some repulsive notion relating to surgeons' lancets and women, and was altogether, as the judge summed him up, 'maliciously cruel to man and beast'.

Had it not been for his exalted station, he would, of course, have been confined. As it was, a man by the name of Coombe was engaged to watch over him and keep him, when possible, in check, which he did sometimes by threatening 'to tell Mr Hanson', and sometimes by pretending he would challenge him to a duel.

In November 1813 his elderly wife died. (Why she had ever consented to the union is incomprehensible except on the grounds that any marriage was thought better than none at forty-seven, and that becoming a countess and chatelaine of a great house was tempting even to a peer's daughter—and his nature had not yet fully revealed itself.) Here was an unrivalled opportunity for a 'black job', and he had two hearse drivers he knew personally brought from London. While the funeral procession was on its way, he ordered his own coachman, Webb, to whip one of these men. He also fined Webb half-a-crown for never having driven a hearse before.

Hanson was well aware of the infantile personality of a client who was almost his ward, and his children, now grown up, could not have been ignorant of it, even if they did not know the individual incidents which were ultimately to bring scores of witnesses to prove that he was mad. But, as the judge said, the unsoundness of his mind 'was of a mixed kind; it was not absolute idiotcy but mental weakness, and not constant insanity but a delusion showing itself in particular acts'. At school he had been backward and easily intimidated, and we may guess, from the dreadful turn his penchant was to take, that in consequence he had been subjected to much bullying. (As patron of a benevolent society which ran a charity school he had, without offering any reason whatever, ordered every pupil to be flogged, in the belief, perhaps, that he was getting his own back for suffering at the hands of boys.)

But his memory was very good, so he had been able to acquire just enough education, great pains being taken, to pass muster in society. When he was under the eye of those who had ascendancy over him—and Hanson was decidedly one of these—he would appear, not bright, yet not positively defective, 'but when freed from observation and constraint', the judge explained, 'he, like a child, behaved in a more unrestricted manner. He broke out when left to himself'.

Byron had seldom if ever seen him without Hanson—seldom seen him at all until the day of his wedding to Hanson's elder daughter, and was thus in no position to raise objection when the solicitor sent him a note one night asking him 'to give the bride away' to the Earl the following morning. Mary Ann was twenty-four, the dull-witted bridegroom forty-seven, but rank and money commonly brought about ill-assorted marriages, and it was more or less taken for granted in the most up-to-date circles that a wife might have her consolations later on. Besides, Hanson had baited the trap very skilfully for Byron by telling him that Lord Portsmouth's brother:

> Mr Newton Fellowes (with whom I have no personal acquaintance) was particularly desirous that Lord Portsmouth should marry some 'elderly woman' of his (Mr Fellowes') selection—that the title and family estate might thereby devolve on Mr F. or his children; but that Lord P. had expressed a dislike to old women and a desire to choose for himself.[1]

This is from the draft of Byron's affidavit some months after the wedding, when the bridegroom's brother had seemingly borne out all Hanson had said by attempting to get the union annulled. Any young man of twenty-six, flatteringly consulted by an experienced lawyer, would have been glad to assist in frustrating so selfish a design, and reluctant to oppose a match ostensibly so splendid. He could not have had any idea of what had been going on behind the scenes to furnish the Earl with a second wife little more than a dozen weeks after the death of the first.

Hanson had availed himself of his facilities as a trustee to order Coombe to bring his charge to London. They arrived on February 28th 1814, and Portsmouth was married one week later, Coombe having been got rid of. A settlement was drawn up a few days before the wedding without the knowledge of Hanson's co-trustees and was engrossed by a Chancery Lane writer who was not told any names but instructed to leave spaces for them. It was as advantageous

[1] Marchand, *Letters*.

to the bride as was possible considering how the bridegroom's fortune had been tied up. The trustees of this Deed were Hanson himself, a Mr Buckworth, who refrained from giving evidence, a barrister named Alder, later reputed to be the new Countess's lover and to have fathered her daughter, and Byron. The witnesses were not Hanson's normal associates or the clerks he employed but persons to whom such a document was unfamiliar.[1] His daughter took possession of it, and when the nullity suit was brought, it was necessary to apply to the Court of Chancery to get a sight of it.

Marriage licences in those days were obtained at short notice with the greatest ease. Hanson's eldest son, Charles, procured one on March 6th, causing the names to be left blank as he said it was required in haste. On the 7th, Lord Portsmouth arrived at the Hansons' Bloomsbury Square house where he had been every day that week to breakfast. Still wearing full mourning for his late wife, unshaven, and in a dirty shirt, he was hustled away from the servants, and we may be assured Byron did not set eyes on him till he was better groomed.

That same morning Charles went to the Parish Clerk of St George's, Bloomsbury, and told him a marriage was presently to take place, withholding the names till the licence had to be produced. Byron may—or must—have realized that the proceedings were clandestine, but it was to be expected that there would be no wish to alert Portsmouth's interfering relations. In a journal entry on the wedding day, he called Mary Ann 'a good girl', and nothing he wrote either there or to friends gives the least impression that he suspected the Earl of being out of his mind.

But in loyalty to Hanson, when it came to drafting his affidavit, he did not quote the exact words he had set down at the time but made a subtle difference. The journal says, 'Portsmouth responded as if he had got the whole by heart; and, if anything, was rather before the priest.' In the affidavit, this became: 'He seemed particularly attentive to the priest, and gave his responses audibly and very distinctly. I remarked this because in ordinary conversation, his Lordship has a hesitation in his speech.'[2]

It is likely enough that the bridegroom was well schooled beforehand in the responses. Byron records that, on the way to the Church, where the two walked together—the distance being short and the carriage full—Portsmouth told him 'he had been partial to Miss Hanson from her childhood . . .'. According to the coachman, he said after the ceremony, 'Charley, I've got a new wife', adding that he didn't know he was to have one when he went to breakfast at Mr

---

[1] I doubt very much whether Byron was party to this. Not once in his letters, including those to his future wife, when he was thinking he might be subpoenaed as a witness (Lovelace Papers), does he make a single allusion to being a trustee, either when he supposed the marriage an auspicious one or when he heard from his friends the revelations of 1823. In 1818 Douglas Kinnaird suggested to Byron that the Hansons, father and eldest son, had falsified documents.

[2] Marchand, *Letters*.

Hanson's, and that he didn't want the lady he had got, but her sister; 'and he subsequently made frequent declarations to the same effect'. Both these accounts may be accurate. Laura Hanson, the younger daughter, was, her brother said, 'cast in a beautiful mould'. Mary Ann, in Byron's opinion, was not even pretty.[1] It was not contested by either party in the lawsuit that the Earl's mind had been running on re-marriage ever since his wife's death. As he was poor at expressing himself, it may not have been understood by Byron that he was talking about the younger sister, and when he was presented at the altar with the elder one, he may have timidly decided—being, as the court adjudged, a puppet in the hands of the Hanson family—to make the best of it.

Byron drank their health in sherry and did not wait to see the couple off to the country. His testimony went a long way towards staving off the Hansons' disgrace for a few years. When Newton Fellowes first tried to get an annulment on the grounds of his brother's lunacy in 1814, Lord Chancellor Eldon's verdict was that he (Portsmouth) had known what he was doing.

This case, incidentally, did Byron's own marriage no good. Hanson was not impelled to hurry with *that* settlement, and he soon had the excuse of being in litigation on behalf of his daughter. Byron urged him in vain. The long delay made Miss Milbanke mistrustful and anxious, and she was forced into the humiliating position of repeatedly trying to speed up the preparations. Her mother felt affronted, while Byron himself had time for a cooling-off, and when at last the wedding took place, his mood was that of a man who has been cornered.

Meanwhile, the triumphant Lady Portsmouth was swiftly asserting her determination to put up with no nonsense from her partner. Her first move was to dismiss the servants who had been in the habit of indulging his fantasies even to the point of carrying logs on their shoulders and saying, 'Here, my Lord, is a black job', so that he could imagine he was walking after a coffin. New servants surrounded him who were taught not to regard him as their master. It was proved that, as early as May 1814, when they were in Worthing, she pushed him out of the carriage into the road and left him there. There is abundant evidence that, by 1815, she had taken to horsewhipping him severely while he was naked.

In that year, her lover, the barrister Alder—if lover he was—became a frequent visitor and inflicted various assaults on the Earl, knocking him down, whipping him, and generally keeping him subdued by the methods that were used to tame animals. Lord Portsmouth's 'Committee'—those who represented him in the later nullity proceedings—granted that his own disposition was vicious. The question at issue was—had the Hanson family taken advantage of his insanity to bring about the marriage?

[1] The Hanson Narrative and Byron's letter quoted later, 28 Mar. 1823.

Whether alone or with some support from outside, in 1817 Lord Portsmouth found his way to Acton, hoping to get a warrant against Alder, and he showed Sir Richard Birnie—presumably a magistrate—the wheals he bore from the lash. Sir Richard went to the house, where he was met by Lady Portsmouth who exclaimed in astonishment at his 'impudence' in entering the grounds. He seems to have retreated, baffled, and the cruelties continued, the victim being kept incommunicado and, in the word witnesses used, cowed.

In July 1822 he was taken to Edinburgh by his wife, with her sister, Laura Hanson, one of her brothers, and the bullying Alder. From there somehow or other the news reached his former brother-in-law, who had just succeeded to the Grantley peerage, of the condition he was in, and Newton Fellowes, accompanied by the one-time keeper, Coombe, hastened to Scotland and forcibly removed him. It was the end of Mary Ann's sadistic rule.

In January 1823 a writ was issued by the Chancery Court, and in February a Commission sat at the Freemasons' Tavern, where a jury spent seventeen days chiefly hearing evidence. Mr Commissioner Thrower, summing up at great length, called attention to Hanson's dereliction of duty in acting to further his daughter's marriage without the knowledge of his co-trustees, and the jury, after retiring for only an hour, returned an unanimous verdict that the bridegroom had been what was then termed a lunatic since 1809.

This annulled the marriage, a decree confirmed by the Lord Chancellor in August 1824. But Lady Portsmouth, now reduced again to Miss Hanson, had avoided ever having the citation served on her—probably by the obvious device of going abroad—so the annulment appears not to have been fully effectual.

Byron heard and read of the scandal and wrote about it from Genoa to a friend who was almost certainly Lady Hardy, explaining, in his usual compact style, how his name had been brought into the newspaper reports:

> Mr Hanson is my solicitor. I found him so when I was ten years old—at my uncle's death—and he was continued in the management of my legal business. He asked me, by a civil epistle, as an old acquaintance of his family, to be present at the marriage of Miss Hanson. I went very reluctantly, one misty morning (for I had been up at two balls all night), to witness the ceremony, which I could not very well refuse without affronting a man who had never offended me. I saw nothing particular in the marriage. Of course I could not know the preliminaries, except from what he said, not having been present at the wooing, nor after it; for I walked home, and they went into the country as soon as they had promised and vowed.
>
> Out of this simple fact I hear the *Débats de Paris* has quoted Miss H. as '*autrefois très liée avec le célèbre*,' etc etc. I am obliged to him for the celebrity, but beg leave to decline the liaison, which is untrue; my liaison was with the father, in the unsentimental shape of long lawyer's bills, through the medium of which I have had to pay him ten or twelve thousand pounds within these few years.

She was not pretty, and I suspect that the indefatigable Mr Alder was (like all her people) more attracted by her title than her charms. I regret very much that I was present at the prologue to the happy state of horse whipping and black jobs, etc. etc.; but I could not foresee that a man was to turn out mad, who had gone about the world for forty years, as competent to vote and walk at large; nor did he seem to me more insane than any other person going to be married.[1]

Every Byron scholar knows that he was inveterately, even ungallantly, truthful in speaking of his love affairs, and these observations seem to me to refute Newton Hanson's assertion that Byron had himself 'courted' Mary Ann for three or four years, and promised, since he could not marry her, to make her a countess: and equally Lady Byron's belief that he had not only seduced that young woman, but gleefully reminded her of it as he escorted her down the aisle.[2]

It is very credible that Hanson would have much preferred Byron as a son-in-law to the unattractive peer he secured, and that some of his many indulgences towards his younger client, as well as his readiness on every occasion to have him as a house guest, may not have been without an underlying motive; but Byron was steeped in debt before he reached his majority, while his successive emotional commitments, from Mary Chaworth onwards, must surely reduce the long 'courtship' to boy-and-girl banter while he was at Harrow, or still earlier. Newton Hanson, three years his junior, could only have based his belief on what his sister told him, and she—if the law did not err—was a notable liar.

As for Lady Byron's recollection, she may have taken seriously one of the little devilries with which he delighted to tease and scarify her, playing upon her tremendous preoccupation with evil (a trait evinced in a multitude of her papers, some written before she ever met him).

Byron did not live to know the full extent of the disrepute into which his solicitor fell. In 1825 the Court stated its determination that 'Mary Ann Hanson falsely calling herself Countess of Portsmouth' should respond to the citation of 1823 or be pronounced in contempt. This meant that in any part of the British Isles she could be committed to prison. Precisely why the nullity suit had to be tried all over again I confess myself unable to explain—the reason does not appear in the reports—but on February 23rd 1828 *The Times* announced that sixty-six witnesses had so far been examined, and there was a question of whether a sixty-seventh was acceptable, an ex-butler of Lord Portsmouth who could swear to having seen William Rowland Alder conducting himself in some unseemly way in the bedroom of the Earl and Countess. The

[1] *LJ.* 28 Mar. 1823.
[2] Hanson Papers. Quoted by Marchand. Lovelace Papers. Bathurst Memorandum.

last-named deponed that he had not left their service voluntarily, as claimed, but had been dismissed by her for bad behaviour and impertinence. His testimony was nevertheless admitted.

Mary Ann had forty-seven witnesses of her own, but neither her father nor any of her family came forward, which was detrimental to her cause. Counsel for Lord Portsmouth's 'Committee' made great play with their not daring to stand up to cross-examination.

Counsel on her side raised a rather neglected question—what was the Earl's state of mind at his earlier marriage? There was medical testimony from a Dr Jenner that it was the same in 1799 as in 1814, so that if he was sane then he was surely sane later? Even before his father's death, when he was still Lord Lymington, he had executed a Deed whereby provision was secured to the younger children of the family and had divested himself of the control of most of his property. It had remained operative through all these years, but would not have been valid any more than his marriage if his mind had been unsound when it had his assent.

This argument did not carry much weight. Nobody seems to have disputed —except Mary Ann—that his intellect had always been dull, and the judge agreed that the arrangements made for placing his affairs in the hands of trustees showed that he was being protected from the consequences of that; but he might be of feeble capacity yet not deranged. Besides, it was one thing— though this view remained unspoken—for a nobleman to be married to a fellow nobleman's daughter with the full approval of both families, and another for the daughter of a bourgeois to wed him secretly.

A point made by Mary Ann's defender, called the 'King's Advocate', was that the Earl and Countess had cohabited (there had been children) for eight years after their union had first been challenged and declared valid, and that it had been acknowledged by the Earl's family, members of which had visited them. That too made little impression: perhaps the particular members were insignificant ones, or perhaps their purpose was to see what was going on. He dealt with the Earl's repugnant practices and admitted they were 'unbecoming his station in life', but he called them 'perversions of taste', not proofs of insanity. Turning up unshaven and unkempt on one's wedding day was not a sign of being unhinged, because it might be one's ordinary mode of dress. This was not the kind of advocacy which did much for his client.

It told against Mary Ann that she had not attempted before to 'traverse' the verdict of 1823. Her counsel pleaded that the costs were a deterrent, and named £30,000 as the likely total in that Court alone. The judge thought that a gross exaggeration.

When Dr Stephen Lushington, who was acting for the Earl's party, came to his final address in May, he said he did not care whether adultery had taken place or not. 'Lord Portsmouth had stated the fact with disgusting details: if false, that statement was conclusive evidence of the unsoundness of his mind; if true it equally proved his imbecility since he had submitted to what no sane man would have endured.'

Dr Lushington had been Lady Byron's legal adviser in her Separation Proceedings, when Hanson had opposed him, and he had become one of her close friends and warmest sympathizers, and mortally antagonistic to Byron whom he had not met. The passion of his eloquence against the Hansons suggests that their connection with Byron lent vigour to his attack. He excused Lord Eldon for having sustained the validity of the marriage on the grounds that 'perjury was poured in upon him . . . by the contrivances of Hanson'—Byron's affidavit was possibly not the last thing in his thoughts—and he remarked that, as his Lordship was 'no more', he would say nothing upon the strange combination of such personages as he and Lord Portsmouth at the ceremony, by which he said a good deal. Lushington had certainly heard of Byron's supposed seduction of the bride because none of Lady Byron's large circle of confidants had been told so many of her husband's misdeeds—and that, again, is saying a good deal.

He represented forcibly that 'the degradation of a person who had abused the rank she had held, and the bastardization of her children, was a punishment most inadequate to her just deserts'.

His scarcely less eloquent coadjutor, Dr Pickard, pronounced the conduct of the so-called Lady Portsmouth and her family to be 'as disgraceful and atrocious as had ever disgraced humanity. . . . The punishment must, in a great measure, be left to the consciences of the parties, but the Court had the power to exact a *slight* retribution by giving costs against her who had been the agent of the grossest fraud ever practised in this or any other country'.

There are few who would have to rack their brains very hard to find other offences more heinous; and if Mary Ann had not stooped to such squalid depths to subjugate the unlucky madman, the fact of her manoeuvring him, with her father's and brother's aid, into an alliance that brought her rank and possessions would not seem much worse than many other kinds of opportunism. That Hanson had any idea of the depravity of her character is unlikely. He may even have reasoned himself into the belief that he was doing a good turn to both parties. In this, however, he had no support from his wife. A kind and motherly woman, Mrs Hanson was deeply shocked by the marriage, which she did not attend, and her son Newton blamed it for her death, which took place two weeks afterwards.

Because of his trusteeship, Hanson himself incurred special odium. The judge said that every part of the plan was his doing, and Lord Portsmouth used as a mere instrument. The wedding had been brought about by his conspiracy with his family to circumvent the Earl, over whom they had complete control, and who was clearly *non compos mentis*. The Court was bound in duty

and Lyon,[1] the animal firmly believed by all to be part-wolf, remained in effigy in their master's home, where they are still on view.

The stone parlour, which Susan Vaughan, the pretty housemaid, decorated on Byron's birthday, was a snug room with a hanging lamp, an 'excellent' wire and brass fender, brass fireguard and fire irons, a Kidderminster carpet, seven railed-back mahogany chairs and a matching elbow chair, all having loose seats with satin covers, a folding mahogany screen, a Pembroke table, a tea urn, two papier maché tea-trays, a small marble cistern, and the usual draped and lined curtains in French cotton. This room was used, at least on special occasions, by the servants instead of their immense hall which had little in it by the time the inventory was made but a flap table and two benches. Their meals seem to have been taken in the kitchen, where there were nine 'wainscot chairs' and a 'wainscot table', beside one of 'stout deal'.

I pass over the backstairs equipment generally, much of which would today be prized by collectors—polished steel fenders, fancy tea canisters, spice boxes, toast stands and cheese toasters, meat dish covers and pewter utensils, bottle trays and cheese trays from the butler's pantry. Some of the vessels belonging to the brewhouse were Gargantuan; a copper that held a hundred and forty gallons, numerous iron-bound hogsheads and half-hogsheads, and an iron pot to accommodate two hundred gallons.

The servants' rooms had good and plentiful bedding, rush-seated chairs, and dressing-tables of oak or deal. One wash-stand only appears for the maids (the men slept below), but there were two painted tin baths, one of which must surely have been for their use. Allowing that central heating, running main water, and refulgent artificial light, were as far beyond the aspirations of the master as of his attendants, there was clearly no want of comfort.

The auctioneer stated at the heading of his catalogue that the furniture was 'new within a few years'. Some of the things in the servants' quarters may have been banished relics of the 18th century, for instance the set of wainscot chairs and the wainscot table in the kitchen—where the words 'Waste not want not' were inscribed in large letters on the wall (a good deal before Byron's time, I should suppose). 'Wainscot' applied to furniture meant good oak. The lead statues of satyrs in the garden were inherited, and the little sailing boats on the lake are mentioned in the 1780s. But in general here was a huge quantity of the latest domestic appointments acquired by a youth of twenty who was at the same period preparing by every conceivable means to go abroad for years! Nothing shows more convincingly the mixture of self-will and uncertainty which resulted at so many stages of his life in his drifting on the stream of events that he appeared to be creating.

With his tremendous appetite for experience, he wanted to be a seasoned traveller, a man of as many adventures as the heroes he was to bring into vogue,

[1] Byron took another favourite dog called Lyon to Greece in 1823. See p. 364.

and yet to restore his ancestral home, so long impoverished, to the modern equivalent of its former glory so that he could play the convivial country nobleman; and he set about fulfilling both these incompatible ambitions regardless of the financial consequences. One thing the inventory, much condensed here, places beyond controversy: whatever the Newstead mansion may have been like during the few months that he spent there in boyhood, those later friends who wrote accounts of it which lay more emphasis on its aspects as a ruin than its up-to-date amenities were either indulging the taste of the day, when there was such a fondness for ruins that people were actually building them, or else making a contribution to the irresistible Byron legend.

The irony of ironies is to contemplate what all that lacquer, that mock bamboo, those Georgian pier glasses, that French chintz, those Pembroke tables, those scroll-ended couches, would fetch today at Sotheby's or Christie's. But unluckily many became mere lumber almost before they were paid for. The reason was given by an anonymous journalist, one of the few who had any knowledge of the resplendent embellishments which, as he put it, revealed 'more of the brilliant conception of the poet than of the sober calculations of common life'. Many rooms (he said, writing while Byron was in Greece):

> he had superbly furnished, but over which he had permitted so wretched a roof to remain, that in about half a dozen years the rain had visited his proudest chambers, the paper had rotted on the walls, and fell, in comfortless sheets, on the glowing carpets and canopies, upon beds of crimson and gold, clogging the wings of glittering eagles and destroying gorgeous coronets.[1]

This is certainly based on fact except as to the time when the depredations took place, which must have been after Lady Byron's 1818 visit when all was apparently in presentable order. It was a misfortune for Byron, since he was never to see Newstead Abbey again, that the advertised sale of 1815 was not held.

APPENDIX 6

Byron and his Young Servants

A gentleman could be very casual about getting a servant girl with child in the 18th and early 19th centuries, always provided he did not allow the offspring to become a burden on the parish—as was the case with the unlawfully begotten issue of the tenant farmer, Bowman. Parish children were treated most callously. Byron informed Hanson of his impending fatherhood in January and

[1] *The Mirror*, 24 Jan. 1824.

February 1809 (Marchand, Volume I, pp. 166 and 167) and he requested that £100 a year should be settled on the child and its mother. It will be remembered that he and his own mother had lived on £135 a year.

Whether the infant survived is not known. The rate of mortality was so high that its chance of death was about equal to its chance of life. He admitted to having had an illegitimate child in early youth (and it is utterly improbable from the context that he could have been referring to Medora Leigh); yet no payment at all that could apply to any such contingency seems traceable in the accounts, and clearly, when he got Lucy back to Newstead in 1811, no child accompanied her. She was sent away as relentlessly as Susan when Robert Rushton's dallyings with both came to light, and so far as I know disappeared from his thoughts as well as from his life after that episode—except that there is a rather sympathetic allusion to a seduced servant in the last completed canto of *Don Juan*, with an admission of his own lapse.

The two girls he classed as 'strumpets', while Rushton was practically exonerated. To us Rushton's conduct seems distasteful, but, besides the double sexual standard that almost nobody questioned, the youth was bound by ties of gratitude as well as by that subjection to benevolent despotism which Byron had the knack of imposing on his male servants (and which resulted at the end of his life in several of them accompanying him on his Greek expedition though it promised neither comfort nor safety).

In the confrontation between Byron and Rushton which Susan had so rashly brought about, the women were bound to lose. Not that I share the view of those recent writers who hold that Rushton was one whom Byron had 'corrupted'. The statement to that effect recorded so eagerly by Lady Byron after her interview with Lady Caroline Lamb[1] I consider to be merely a gambit in that mischievous woman's campaign to keep his wife from being reconciled to him. And we must not forget what a third-hand account it is—Lady Byron noting in her own words, always dramatic, what an even more dramatic character had told her of a conversation of two years before, in which Byron was obviously assuming the rôle of the anti-hero in a Gothic novel.

His tone to Rushton, or about him, is always that of a considerate master who feels himself in a position to be respected, and not as one who has forfeited any title to respect by committing what he called and deemed to be 'crime' with him. It is unreasonable to suppose he would have had an ulterior purpose in taking Rushton on his travels when he knew he was to be constantly accompanied by Hobhouse and served by Fletcher. He shipped the boy, then fifteen, back from Gibraltar with Joe Murray, deciding that the one was too old, the other too young, for further travel, and he wrote to his mother, 'Pray show the lad kindness, as he is my great favourite. I would have taken him on . . .'.

[1] The 'Minutes' of their meeting on 27 Mar. 1816, given in full in *The Late Lord Byron*.

Omitted in early publications are the words, 'but you *know boys* are not *safe* amongst the Turks',[1] which might allude either to their reputed habits of paederasty or even their propensity to make eunuchs of Frankish boys. Into that kind of protectiveness, it is tendentious to read ulterior motives.

Likewise I cannot find any significance in the nearness of Byron's bedroom at Newstead Abbey to Rushton's. In so large a house a manservant would have to be lodged at hand to be of any use, and Fletcher was a married man who lived—when he got the chance—with his wife. The exaggeration of Byron's homosexual activities is as distorting in its effects as the suppression of such matters used to be.

During his master's absence, Rushton had been at a boarding-school in Newark. We have seen how his time was occupied with heterosexual amours on his return. Byron kept him on as long as he could with old Joe Murray, but asked Hanson to find him some work as an assistant tithe-collector or a bailiff at Rochdale, saying he had a fair education and was well disposed.[2] The young man was no longer accompanying him as page, and his idleness was giving concern. At some date early in 1813, he got married, to whom I have not been able to learn. Byron himself had to enquire the name of his fiancée:

> If this *marriage* which is spoken of for you is at all advantageous I can have no objection—but I should suppose, after being in my service from your infancy, you will at least let me know the name of your *intended*, & her expectations. If at all respectable nothing can be better for your settlement in life, & a proper provision will be made for you—at all events let me hear something on the subject.[3]

That the wedding came to pass is shown by a complaint Mealey wrote to Hanson about 'young Rushton and his wife' taking possession of rooms in the Abbey in August 1913, when the estate had been sold. Byron, who was only awaiting completion by the purchaser to go abroad, was much relieved—Hanson having done nothing—when James Wedderburn Webster offered Rushton a place. 'Your taking him is no less a favour to me than him—and I trust he will behave well . . . honest I am sure he is, and I believe good-tempered and quiet. . . . Accounts and mensuration &c he ought to know, I believe he does.'[4]

Rushton duly went to Webster in Yorkshire a few weeks later, but he resumed his old service during Byron's marriage. When his wife left to return to her parents, it was Byron's intention to send him after her to Kirkby, but she asked her sister-in-law to prevent it, suspecting a form of espionage,[5] not at all the kind of plotting her husband really indulged in. Eventually he took Rushton

[1] Marchand, *Letters*. 11 to 15 Aug. 1809.   [2] Ibid. 22 Oct. 1812.
[3] Ibid. Vol 3, 24 Feb. 1813. Byron uses the word 'infancy' in its legal sense.
[4] Ibid. 12 Aug. 1813.   [5] *LJ*. 23 Jan. 1816.

with Fletcher to Geneva, but not on the further journey to Italy. Prothero states that he (Rushton) *then* entered the service of Webster. If this is not an error, it means that he went back to him. His first wife must have died, because in 1827 he married a Miss Bagnold. With her he set up a school in a village near Nottingham, but returned ultimately to the Newstead estate, where he died. He had three children. He is reported to have grumbled much that Byron had promised to provide for him and had not done so.

As for Lucy, she is said in Washington Irving's account of *Newstead Abbey*, published in 1835, to have married and taken over a public house at Warwick. His elderly and garrulous informant, a former servant named Nannie Smith, told him the girl had been to a fortune-teller who prophesied a high station in life for her, which so went to her head that she fancied she would become the lawful lady of the manor. For various reasons, including the fact that Byron had not even considered marrying her when she had been pregnant three years before the contretemps in 1812, I think Nannie—or Irving—may have been confusing Lucy with the giddy but by no means artless Susan.

APPENDIX 7

The Byron Liveries

Servants' liveries, for many years to come, were to do what gentlemen could no longer do in their own persons; and after a dinner party given at the Duke of Devonshire's, Hobhouse remarked in his diary that 'the guests looked very shabby in comparison with the attendants'.[1] Byron at nineteen was content with the established colours of his Newstead ancestors, claret coats and breeches with scarlet waistcoats and silver lace (which, it may be necessary to remind the modern reader, merely meant metallic braid). Their winter suits cost £4. 14s. each. In summer the groom had a claret greatcoat at £3, and in winter a drab cloth one at £3. 5s. Drab was then a brownish grey.

Before his master's coming-of-age, old Joe Murray was fitted out with 'a suit of best clothes' at £6. 15s. 6d. Perhaps it was the same in which he was painted in the portrait commissioned by Byron, reproduced in this book. Among the clothes for servitors supplied in 1809 and 1810 while Byron was abroad were two 'stout shooting coats' for the keeper, the self-same Billy Whitehead who was to explain that if the electors voted themselves to hell, they couldn't get Byron out of his chair in the House of Lords; and there was a suit of black for Murray. This was an outlay that Mrs Byron must have sanctioned, doubtless for the

[1] *Recollections.* 7th July 1827.

butler's use when waiting at table. She did not stint him; it cost £7. 8s. 6d., nearly as much as the mourning dress Byron ordered for himself after her death.[1] His whole staff then had to be furnished with black clothes at his charge, Spiro and Demetriou, the two Greek servants he had brought back from Athens, Fletcher, Rushton, Whitehead, and even the steward, Mealey, though he had high wages and a tavern out of which he did well. The cost, apart from all the funeral accessories was about £50. Three years later the tailors were asking somewhat brusquely for a remittance.[2]

All those items are from the account of a Nottingham firm, Green & Ibberson, but there is an overlapping one for servants' clothes only, with a London tailor, Thomas Edwards of 52 Conduit Street. It amounts to £175. 19s. 6d. and shows that Byron's taste for wearing sombre colours in his own person was now extended to his attendants. There was no more silver trimming. The groom, a man named Stroud, was fitted with three livery coats, a blue, a black, and a 'mixt' one, and corduroy breeches. He had a scarlet waistcoat with sleeves, and a fustian jacket and trousers, but these last must have been for stable work. The coachman, Everett, had two dark mixture great coats, which would certainly have had numerous capes, these having become traditional. He was supplied with breeches, velveteen or corduroy. There was a footman named Bayman who often wore black from head to foot and had 'a Corbo livery great coat'. This stood for *corbeau*—blue-black velvet or velveteen. He also had 'a blue coat complete' at five guineas, and two superfine brown coats at the same price, besides a number of waistcoats, trousers, and breeches, Florentine or cassimere.[3] 'Complete' may have meant 'with buttons'. Liveries had metal buttons with the crest or heraldic badge of the house.

The page who had temporarily taken Rushton's place, a youth named Evans, was provided with 'two mixt Florentine jackets' at £5. 10s., two matching waistcoats at £1 each, and three pairs of similar trousers at four guineas. Fletcher, like the footman, had three superfine coats, black, blue, and brown respectively at the same high cost, and an assortment of waistcoats; so it may be assumed that instead of the immediately recognizable liveries of his Cambridge days, Byron now had his servants differently dressed at different times or seasons, and like himself, in a subdued manner. This was in advance of the mode, for most noblemen's liveries were still spectacular.

[1] In *The Whole Art of Dress* by A Cavalry Officer, 1830, the following prices are given as average at a 'respectable' tailor's: Superfine dress coat—£4. Trousers—£2. 2s. Kerseymere waistcoat—£1. 1s., total for the whole suit £7. 3s. This amount could be reduced, wrote the author, to only £4. 8s. by buying the cloth oneself and going to a journeyman tailor. For various reasons, I think these prices would not have been much different during the Napoleonic War. Joe Murray's black suit is thus seen to be equal to that of a gentleman. Byron's mourning suit, delivered on August 8th 1811, cost about £8.

[2] These English accounts are all Murray MSS.

[3] Florentine in this instance is likely to be worsted. Cassimere was kerseymere, fine cloth.

APPENDIX 8

A Young Gentleman's Linen

Linen was not bought ready-to-wear any more than outer clothing. The valet usually obtained the materials and had them made up, so Byron's linen would have figured on Fletcher's accounts, few of which have been preserved. One or two bills for equipping him to go to Cambridge are, however, among the Murray MSS, and will be of interest for the prices and quantities required. In April and May 1805, when he was leaving Harrow, a draper called Cheetham, probably of Southwell, supplied:

26 yds Fine Irish linen	at 4s.	£5. 4s.
4¼ ,, British Muslin		17s.
2 lawn Handfs	3s. 8d.	7s. 4d.
2 ,, ,,	4s.	8s.
1 yd French Cambrick	11s.	11s.
27¾ yds Fine Irish linen	at 4s. 6d.	6. 4s. 10½d.
25 ,, ,, ,, ,,	3s. 10d.	4. 15s. 10d.
14 9/16 yds ,, ,, Muslin	at 5s.	3. 12s. 9½d.
5 yds French Cambrick	at 8s.	2.
4⅜ yds & ¼ Nail French Cambrick	at 18s.	3. 10s. 6d.
6 cotton [night] caps	at 2s.	12s.
3 Huckaback ,, ,,	at 3s. 3d.	9s. 9d.
8 doz. fine wire buttons	at 6d.	4s.

From another Southwell firm, James Wright, were ordered:

25 yds fine Irish linen	at 4s. 6d.	£5. 12s. 6d.
12 squares Cambrick	5s.	3.

The cambric squares would have been for neckcloths, the muslin for shirt frills. The buttons, tiny circlets of wire filled in with linen thread, were for shirts. The less expensive linen probably served for nightshirts. Nightcaps were considered indispensable: I believe they were not omitted from the wardrobe lists of Eton boys till the 1850s. The French cambric at the steep price of eleven, eight, or even eighteen shillings a yard may have been for shirt fronts to be 'worked'—i.e. embroidered. A Nail was only 2½ inches, so it must have been treated as precious.

Bed linen and towelling too had to be made up to order. Cheetham furnished a great many yards of Irish sheeting, Russia towelling, and diaper towelling (damask linen). There were ten tablecloths of various qualities, a dozen table napkins, and a dozen 'doilars', six at seven shillings and six at four. These were mats placed on the table when the cloth was removed for dessert. The number of napkins seems small in relation to the ten table cloths, but perhaps an additional dozen was made up from the diaper towelling.

The valet of that day, Frank Boyce, stole some of this generous trousseau.

APPENDIX 9

Eliza Francis

Though Byron was accustomed to require a consideration from the women who took his money, he was capable of waiving that claim in quite a delicate manner when he perceived that the recipient was guileless. Miss Francis, whose family fortunes were in disrepair, hoped to redeem them by bringing out a book of her poems—a notion which now seems rather droll, but even an unknown poet might find publication lucrative if energetic enough to secure a large number of good-natured purchasers who would pay for copies in advance. Having notified Byron of her intention, she was bold enough to go to his chambers in Albany to canvass his patronage.

Letters and visits from unknown ladies were to him a recurring trial, for their assurances of platonic motives invariably turned out to be self-deception, especially in that year, 1814, after both Thomas Phillips's portraits of him had been a magnet to viewers at the Royal Academy.[1] They came, these girls, excusing themselves touchingly or boringly for their breach of decorum in approaching a young bachelor, and were informed, in a general way, that he was not at home. This one persisted—they usually did—and was chillingly asked by the valet to state her business in writing. But when she was at last admitted, Byron behaved with captivating charm. She did not realize till she had left him that the piece of paper on which he had so nonchalantly written was a handsome cheque.

She must have been nice-looking and agreeable because he let her come to Albany several times and consented to read some of her poetry in manuscript although that was the kind of task he hated: and she was so rapturously in love with him that, at the age of nearly seventy-six, she poured out the story of those visits to another idolizing old lady, the Marquise de Boissy. It is wonderfully vivid and convincing, with dialogue so fresh and unfeigned that I cannot doubt it was based on a diary she kept at the time:

> As I stood with my head bent down, he lightly put aside some little curls which had escaped from my cap behind, and kissed my neck—this completely roused me and I struggled to free my hand, but then he clasped me to his bosom with an ardour which terrified me. . . .
>
> 'Let me go my Lord! you never behaved thus before,' I exclaimed.
>
> 'Well—but—but—you are not angry with me?' said he anxiously.

[1] The one Byron presented to John Murray and the one in Albanian dress (now in the British Embassy at Athens) which is much more impressive than the two small copies Phillips made.

'Oh! no—I am more angry with myself—let me go!' I said again, alarmed. 'Don't tremble, don't be frightened you are safe—with *me* you are safe,' said he impetuously, and throwing himself into an arm-chair he drew me towards him—for a moment I clung to him—I loved for the first time and this must be my final parting with this transcendant Being . . . he had drawn me down upon his knee, his arms were round my waist, and I could not escape. . . .[1]

She had already suffered a dreadful shock on his telling her, very properly, that he was engaged to be married ('My heart sank like lead in my bosom') and now she feared for her virtue because she imagined with great naïveté that he was in love with her. It is very obvious that she longed to surrender, but he contrived it so that she could depart treasuring both her honour and her exquisite temptation, and totally unaware that his contribution to her work, which she succeeded in publishing, was no small proportion of his disposable bank balance.

APPENDIX 10

Hoppner's Garbled Revelation

On September 6th 1820 Hoppner, with whom the Shelleys and Claire had been on the best of terms, wrote a letter to Byron in which, among other topics, he mentioned that he had tried to read Shelley's tragedy *The Cenci*, but was so revolted by it that he 'could make but little progress'.

If I had not the greatest reason to believe him one of the weakest or the most depraved of men, I could not have conceived that even he could have imagined such disgusting characters as Cenci & his accomplished daughter. . . . I hope for his sake that Clara and his Atheism have driven him out of his wits, as I am loath to believe him so thoroughly depraved as I must consider him if he has not this justification.[2]

Byron replied mildly and not very enquiringly:

I regret that you have such a bad opinion of Shiloh: you used to have a good one. Surely he has talent and honour but is crazy against religion and morality. . . . You seem lately to have got some notion against him.[3]

[1] Gamba Papers. There is a more extensive extract in Marchand, Vol. II. Teresa gives the account of the meeting, idealistically, in *Lord Byron*, calling Miss Francis 'Miss S'. She had married a Mr Smith.

[2] Murray MS.

[3] *LJ*. 10 Sept. The nickname Shiloh was a well understood joke between Shelley and Byron.

Hoppner seized the opportunity he had created, and wrote with that modest amount of encouragement to disclose a 'fearful secret' which it was necessary for Allegra's sake that Byron should know, 'as it will fortify you in the good resolution you have already taken never to trust her again to her mother's care'.[1] The story, here sifted down to its bare essentials, was that, without Mary Shelley's knowledge, and while showing brutal hatred of her, Claire and Shelley had had a child at Naples in 1818, and deposited it with the help of a bribed midwife, at the Foundling Hospital. The tale had been told to the Hoppners—with stress on Claire's ill treatment of Mary and endeavours to break up her marriage—by Elise Foggi, formerly nurse both to Shelley's children and Allegra, and now married to Paolo Foggi, an ex-servant who had been blackmailing Shelley—though that part of it was unknown to Hoppner.

Byron let some days pass and sent off a short letter saying:

> The Shiloh story is true no doubt, though Elise is but a sort of *Queen's Evidence*. You remember how eager she was to return to them, and then she goes away and abuses them. Of the facts, however, there can be little doubt; it is just like them.[2]

From this response it can hardly be inferred that Byron was gloating over the scandal. On the contrary, he obviously thought Elise ought to have kept it to herself, but, coming from such a quarter—a woman who had lived more than two years with the Shelleys and had been well-liked during that time—he gave it credit for truth. And that is what, until nearly the middle of this century, drove Shelley biographers almost to hysteria. 'He *believed* it!' they exclaimed to their readers outraged, forgetting that Byron had one inestimable advantage they had not themselves enjoyed—a close personal knowledge of both parties involved.

The discovery by the late Professor Newman Ivey White of the birth, baptism, and death records of a child registered by Shelley as his own in Naples,[3] made it impossible to deny after 1947 that the rumour, however distorted it might have been, was based on something more than the wicked invention of malignance. It also explained at last the puzzling remarks made by Shelley in letters to his confidants, the Gisbornes, about 'my poor Neapolitan' who had a teething fever, and his intention that she should come to them (i.e. to him and Mary) when she had recovered, and also his allusions to 'the rascal Paolo' (Foggi) who had been 'taking advantage of my situation in Naples in December 1818 to attempt to extort money by threatening to charge me with the most

[1] *Correspondence*. 16 Sept.
[2] Ibid. 1 Oct. 'Queen's Evidence' refers of course to the quality of the testimony at the trial of Queen Caroline in England.
[3] Birth 27 Dec. 1818; baptism as Elena Adelaide Shelley 27 Feb. 1819; death 9 June 1820.

horrible crimes', and his having to engage a lawyer, one del Rosso, to 'crush' this man. It accounted as well for his story to Medwin of a lady in Naples who had been in love with him and had died, the painful phase in his relations with his wife at this period, and later Claire's repeated meetings with the mischief-maker Elise, which are recorded in her diary with expressions of wretchedness and phrases she tried to obliterate, explicitly referring to the Naples scandal.

Whoever was the mother, it seems unlikely that she was, so she had good cause to be wretched. Mary, who had already had three pregnancies, could not have failed to notice that condition in an inmate of her home, and even if the delivery of the baby had been managed by stealth—not easy to achieve—the after effects, especially the rapid change in the mother's figure, would be apparent.

But so tenaciously did the ethereal, immaculate, and emasculated Shelley of legend haunt the imagination that White, though an honest biographer, could not bring himself to recognize the poet as the father he had claimed in official records to be, but contrived a theory of the utmost tortuousness, according to which Shelley adopted a newborn infant—probably at the Foundling Hospital—because he was lonely, Mary having lately grown cold to him, and because their little daughter, Clara, had recently died. How he thought to appease his loneliness by fostering a child whose existence he had to keep secret from his household, and who died at the age of eighteen months not with Shelley but still in Naples, we are not told: but the Professor postulates that he was gratifying a desire he had had since boyhood to adopt a little girl,[1] and that he hoped eventually to prevail on Mary to pass this one off as her own and keep up that pretence to their friends.

That a man of any sensibility at all could have planned to foist off on a bereaved mother (who still, however, had a child surviving) a foreign orphan about whom she had never been consulted is a most fantastic proposition, but Professor White admits that if Mary *was* consulted, she did not feel 'an obscure little Italian was a substitute for her own lost Clara'. Shelley's façade that he and his wife were the parents of Elena Adelaide was put up, he says, 'to secure the infant's position' because he was in fear of the Chancery Court in England. As the English Court had done its worst in depriving him of his children by his first marriage, we cannot envisage what more he feared from it; and the mystery becomes deeper when we know that he was living a conjugal life, and that, while the 'foundling' remained in the hospital, or wherever he had placed her, Mary conceived and before the end of 1819 had another child of her own.

'It was still possible to pretend that she had become a mother in the December of 1818'—so goes White's conjecture, but he thinks that by 1819 she was

---

[1] White says that Shelley, following this pattern, had tried and failed to persuade Byron to let him keep Allegra. This is simply contrary to the facts.

enlightened about the Naples infant and found the idea of adoption 'distasteful': and who can blame her? Besides the expected baby, she had her son William, and could not guess that in a few months he would be dead.

I have not gone into half the intricacies of this extraordinary hypothesis, which nevertheless has found favour with several writers who even now cannot credit Shelley with being a virile and highly susceptible young man (in early 1818 when Elena Adelaide was begotten he was twenty-five)—moreover a young man who had practised and preached free love, and written some of the most seductive incitements to it that were ever penned:

> The fountains mingle with the river,
>   And the rivers with the ocean,
> The winds of heaven mix for ever
>   With a sweet commotion;
> Nothing in the world is single;
>   All things by a law divine
> In one another's being mingle—
>   Why not I with thine? . . .
>
> And the sunlight clasps the earth,
>   And the moonbeams kiss the sea,
> What are all these kissings worth
>   If thou kiss not me?

This marvellously gifted interpreter of erotic emotion had practised adultery before, and, though he valued Mary and shrank from hurting her, he does not seem to have been incapable, under temptation, of practising it again. He begot two children by Harriet and five by Mary,[1] and it appears to me one of his more attractive features that he was not entirely given to Platonic rhapsodizing. The blackmailer, Paolo, though a scoundrel, could not have conjured so much anxiety and dismay out of thin air.

Trelawny is not a good witness, but he must have had something to go on when he told William Michael Rossetti, on March 11th 1870, before anything had been printed about Hoppner's scandal, that Shelley had attempted suicide in Naples;[2] nor is Medwin to be wholly discredited for the statement, in his revised biography, that Shelley had left that city in dread of arrest. The reason for that would surely be the threatened disclosure of his having falsified entries in official registers by naming his wife as the mother of a child that was not hers.

The best analysis of the elements of the tangled story was made by Ursula Orange in her paper, *Elise, Nursemaid to the Shelleys*.[3] Placing the evidences in a new light, she comes to the conclusion that Elise herself, whose wedding

---

[1] Three of Mary's died and one miscarried.
[2] *Athenaeum* 15 July 1882, 'Talks with Trelawny'.
[3] In the *Keats–Shelley Bulletin* 1955.

to Paolo had not yet taken place, was the mother of Shelley's extra-marital child. What Elise desperately needed was a husband. Paolo could be paid money to take on that rôle, but afterwards, being a rogue, he would want more; and so began what Mary called 'an infamous conspiracy against us'.[1] I cannot find this interpretation quite satisfying because I fail to see what motive Elise could have had for uttering a slander so perilous to herself. It might of course have begun merely to spite Shelley, whose relations with her (if any) had perhaps left her in a vindictive state of mind, jealous of Claire and sympathetic to Mary. She might have been drawn on by the gossip-thirsty Hoppners to tell more than she had intended and then cover up by rapid and careless invention: but whatever she said, and whether or not she herself was directly concerned in that 'fearful secret', it is beyond dispute now that she did not invent the whole of it.

Professor White believed Shelley innocent because of 'the tone of passionate trust and confidence in each other' which is manifest in the letters exchanged on that topic between him and Mary. This is inconsistent with his admission elsewhere, 'By their intensity of emotion, they have convinced all previous biographers that Elise Foggi's story was a complete fabrication. We now know that such was not the case.' Ursula Orange shows that Mary's letter of repudiation to Mrs Hoppner,[2] however impassioned its tone, has a considerable disingenuousness which no one troubled to observe when it was supposed that the infant in Naples was a figment of vile fancy, and that Byron had disgraced himself by believing in it.

Mary's principal red herring is 'Clare had no child—the rest must be false', which, we are now aware, does not follow. There are also certain phrases which the extremely slack punctuation of the period allowed to remain equivocal, and, I suspect, deliberately so. I offer them with two punctuation marks altered:

> I am perfectly convinced in my own mind that Shelley never had an improper connexion with Clare at the time specified in Elise's letter. The winter after we quitted Este, I suppose while she was with us, and that was at Naples, we lived in lodgings where I had momentary entrance into every room, and such a thing could not have passed unknown to me.

By placing a dash after 'Clare' and a comma after 'Elise's letter', one continuous statement, though a clumsy one, gives the impression of denying any 'connexion' at all between Shelley and Claire[3]—for Mary could not say straightforwardly, ' *There was no child* ', and so had to lean heavily on defending

[1] To Mrs Gisborne, 18 June 1820.
[2] From Pisa, 11 Aug. 1821. Published fully in *Correspondence*, and incorrectly, with significant omissions, by Dowden and some other Shelley biographers.
[3] Claire's relations with Shelley before his marriage to Mary are touched on in Chapter 10. She was known until 1816 as Jane (her baptismal name), Clara or Clare and added the i in Switzerland.

Claire. (Incidentally, no letter from Elise had been mentioned, but Mary may have imagined her communication was a written one.)

It is interesting to see from some parallel passages what Shelley made of Hoppner's letter to Byron, which he had before him when retailing its contents to Mary on the morning of August 7th 1821, while Byron was still in bed.

Hoppner: [writing of Claire when she was said by Elise to have found she was pregnant by Shelley]: I am uncharitable enough to believe that the quantity of medicine she then took was not for the purpose of restoring her health.

Shelley: She [Elise] then proceeds to say that Clare was with child by me— that I gave her the most violent medicines to procure abortion—

Hoppner: A Mid-wife was sent for, and the worthy pair . . . bribed the woman to carry it to the Pietà, where the child was taken half an hour after its birth . . .

Shelley: . . . that I immediately tore the child from her & sent it to the Foundling Hospital—I quote Mr Hoppner's words. . . .

Hoppner: During all the time of her confinement Mrs Shelley . . . was not allowed to approach her, and these beasts . . . have since increased in their hatred of her, behaving to her in the most brutal manner, and Clara doing everything she can to engage her husband to abandon her.

Shelley: In addition she says that both I & Clare treated *you* in the most shameful manner; that I neglected & beat you, & that Clare never let a day pass without offering you insults of the most violent kind, in which she was abetted by me.

When a melodramatic writer like Shelley exaggerates the statements of a scandalous writer like Hoppner, who is giving his own version of what he heard from an unscrupulous talker like Elise—who afterwards denies ever having said anything of the kind!—we can look for truth only in the unemotional archives of births, baptisms, and deaths; and even these may prove to be adulterated.

Mary herself was capable of fanciful elaboration.

You ought to have paused [she told Mrs Hoppner] before you tried to convince the father of her child [Byron] of such unheard-of atrocities on her part. If his generosity and knowledge of the world had not made him reject the slander with the ridicule it deserved what irretrievable mischief you would have occasioned her.

There is not a single word in Shelley's letter to Mary to indicate that Byron had received the slander with rejection and ridicule. It was a gratuitous flourish of her own, meant no doubt to flatter Byron, since she expressed a wish in her postscript that he should see what she had said, adding again for Mrs Hoppner's

benefit: 'He gave no credit to the tale.' Naturally such a blunder would call for a very tactful apologia on Byron's part when forwarding the vindication, which otherwise would make him look guilty not only of having broken a confidence, but of doing so most hypocritically.

Nevertheless, it would have been out of the question, as I have said, for him to join the Shelleys at Pisa if he had withheld a document about which Mary would have been on tenterhooks until she heard how it had been received. The assumption that he did so—often stated as a positive fact—leaves out of account what has been obvious ever since Newman White's Naples discovery; namely that the Hoppners, in returning Mary's feverish letter (how could they make a direct answer to her if they regarded her as the victim of a cruel deception by her husband?), would not have failed to provide some comments of their own, and of such a nature as to reveal that, whatever Claire's position might be, they could support the story of Shelley's illicit fatherhood with circumstantial detail. To save himself the bother of copying, Byron would forward that response to Shelley, now back in Pisa, and sooner or later it would meet destruction.

But there is an alternative possibility. The day after he wrote in such indignation to Mary, Shelley began another letter to her, still in a spirit of high resentment, and saying he would suppress Elise's slanders even if it meant the disagreeable necessity of prosecuting her: but he continued in a much pleasanter vein, describing his Ravenna sight-seeing in Byron's carriage, with some curious verdicts on the tomb of the Empress Galla Placidia, the 'rude mosaics', and other antiquities: 'It seems to have been one of the first effects of the Christian religion to destroy the power of producing beauty in art.'

Next day he resumes in excellent humour, talks most favourably of Byron, whom he believes on the way to becoming a virtuous man, praises *Don Juan* richly, and is generally, with slight reservations, euphoric.[1] A few more days pass and there comes Mary's vehement and distressed answer to his first letter, the answer he had asked her for—his exoneration. Does he receive it gratefully? By no means. There has been a complete change of mood.

> I do not wonder my dearest friend that you should have been moved with the infernal accusation of Elise—I was at first but I speedily regained the indifference which the opinion of any thing or any body except our own consciousness amply merits . . .

He says Lord Byron has engaged to send her communication to Mrs Hoppner, and after the casual remarks quoted elsewhere about his (Byron's) inability to keep a secret, and a broad hint that the Hoppners will have been equally incautious, he concludes, '*So much for nothing*',[2] and then proceeds to inform her in undisguised high spirits that Byron is coming to Pisa the moment they can get him a house, picturing the congenial circle they will make. He would prefer,

---

[1] Letter completed 10 Aug. 1821.   [2] My italics.

he says, to retire with her and their child to a solitary island, but the next best thing 'is to form for ourselves a society of our own class, as much as possible, in intellect, or in feelings'. Except for some vague lines at the end, of which the gist is that calumny has for its object depriving them of security and subsistence—evils from which he has already said Lord Byron will help to protect them—the matter of the Hoppners, Elise, and all that had driven him to appeal so pitifully to his wife less than two weeks before, provoking him to say it was hell to be part of this filthy world, is dropped into oblivion. Mary's gesture of loyalty carried to its most emotional pitch is dismissed with the barest acknowledgment.

I will suggest a reason. Byron was such a very snug, confidential companion that his friends spoke as well as listened. Shelley had told him many things, and perhaps even, during the long charmed nights together as Julian and Maddalo, the tale of Elena Adelaide and that still completely elusive being, her real mother. Certainly he disclosed his love for Emilia Viviani, the girl romantically immured in a convent and about to be thrust into marriage against her will. On returning to Pisa from that delightful fortnight, he wrote to say they were making 'a great fuss' there about: '. . . my intimacy with this lady. Pray do not mention anything of what I told you; as the whole truth is not known and Mary might be very much annoyed by it.'[1]

It was about this time that he borrowed for Emilia, if I am not in error, the sum of at least two hundred and twenty crowns which he repaid to Byron's secretary on January 29th 1822.[2] Between writing his first impetuous demand for redress on August 7th and reading Mary's fervent but undiplomatic reply to it on the 16th, he had been able to weigh the amount of truth there was in Hoppner's allegation against those parts of it that could be refuted, to remember that Mary's hot denial was not as frank and artless as it looked, and to reflect that it was a year since Hoppner had passed on Elise's revelation and it would be merely stirring up new trouble with her and her dangerous husband to give them the lie in every particular. Though in general not inclined to question his own righteousness, he may even have had some qualms of conscience about doing so. It would be easy then, after he had sealed the letter and while Byron was composing with some difficulty the explanation he must transmit with it, for Shelley to say in effect, 'On second thoughts, we might as well leave it, and Mary and I will find some way of dealing with it in Pisa'.

That way would be, after much discussion with Mary and Claire, to get Elise herself to make some kind of disavowal, and rather for Claire's sake than for Shelley's, since, once he had confessed to Mary—as he must have done when Paolo's scheme of extortion became intolerable—and in a Duchy where the laws of Naples were not operative, he could recover from the shock and rage of Hoppner's revelation. 'So much for nothing.' And that, whether I am right or

[1] *Correspondence.* 14 Sept. 1821.   [2] See p. 251 footnote.

not to shrink from condemning Mary Ann Hanson in the whole costs of the suit.[1]

These must have been enormous, for there were the expenses of a hundred and twenty-four witnesses to pay, not to speak of the two teams of eminent lawyers and all who ministered to them, and the massive accumulation of written documents. Whether Hanson contributed towards the settlement of the vast legal bills—or indeed whether they were ever entirely settled—I have not so far been able to ascertain: but there is correspondence to show that within a few years he was deep in financial troubles of his own.

Many years before, in 1807, he had been appointed Solicitor to the Stamp Office, the principal department of taxation, and in some way which it would take much research to unravel, he became very heavily indebted there. Government offices were then run in the most haphazard manner, salaries were paid irregularly, officials might disburse money from their own pockets with much confusion as to what they could or could not reclaim, and the scope for going wrong was almost unlimited—and not reduced by such procrastinating habits as those of Hanson. In 1835 the Treasury took action to recover just under £674, which he was obliged to pay into Court, and then a further sum of nearly £710 was judged to be in default.

Hanson put up a rather vague protest on the grounds that there had been disbursements on his part, that he had received an inadequate salary, and had no retirement pension. He wrote to Hobhouse, who had now succeeded to his father's baronetcy and had been a Cabinet Minister, asking him to use his influence in getting his debts remitted; otherwise, he was in danger of going to the Fleet Prison. 'I have no hesitation in telling you', he said, 'that from many unforeseen Family Causes my circumstances are very different to what they were and I have a huge family upon me.'[2]

Among the family were possibly his daughter's three children, now rendered illegitimate.[3] (One of them was named Byron.) What had happened to Mary Ann has never transpired from any source I have been able to examine; but it may be taken for granted she did not linger about the scenes where she had gloried in being a countess. As she must have been financially and socially ruined, it can only be conjectured that she found some obscure retreat, doubtless under a new name.

[1] This summary of the case has been taken from reports in *The Times*, the *Annual Register*, and other press sources. To condense the actual records of the Court of Arches would be a daunting task.

[2] Murray MS. 16 Nov. 1835.

[3] Dr Lushington told Hobhouse that Portsmouth was impotent. (Hobhouse, *Journals*. 14 May 1828.) If this was true, then Newton Fellowes's desire to have the marriage annulled is more than ever comprehensible. The Earl himself understood little about paternity: he thought the period of gestation was fifteen months. He lived until well on in his eighties, and was succeeded at last by his brother, who was in turn succeeded by his son.

Whatever was done about Hanson's debts to the Treasury, he grew poorer and poorer. His income from the Stamp Office, inadequate or not, had ceased. His practice as a solicitor could not have benefited from his having been publicly rebuked for betraying a trust. In 1838 he sent an importunate request to Hobhouse to lend him £4,000 until he could sell his country estate. He was being 'rigorously pressed', he said, and 'threatened with destruction'. His explanation was that he had engaged in farming for many years and had lost by it.[1] Hobhouse was the recipient of almost as many appeals for aid as Byron himself, and though Hanson was his co-executor, he had never been sufficiently intimate with him to feel any inclination to lend him so very substantial a sum.

In November 1839 Hanson wrote to him again telling him he had put his estate up for auction in lots, but the purchase would not be completed before the following midsummer, and meanwhile he had very urgent calls upon him which he needed £500 or £600 to meet.[2] Would Sir John send an early answer as to whether he would lend that money? Had Hobhouse done so, there would doubtless be an acknowledgment or some other record of the transaction among his papers. They remained, however, on an equable though distant footing because the still more deplorable financial situation of Augusta Leigh had to be coped with by both.

In March 1840 little over three months later, Hanson had a 'distress' in his house for between £300 and £400, which meant that his effects and even his home itself were liable to be sold up. He again approached Hobhouse, saying it was a sum he had never wanted for till now in the whole of his long life:

> . . . but from some Disappointments lately befalling me I have been placed
> in a condition of some Embarrassment though perfectly within the reach of
> Redemption if I could have time to get in my Funds. If Sir John you would
> be so kind as to assist me to the amount of £400 for six or eight months I
> might be able to sustain my position in that Station of Life I have maintained
> for upwards of fifty years. . . . I have myself in the course of my Life done
> many Acts of similar kindness and have never had reason to rue it.[3]

This would seem to be the last letter that Hobhouse preserved, if not the last he received from that quarter. Hanson by now was an old man and his many references to having been unable to leave his house for long periods indicate that his health was failing. We may gather from his increasing difficulties that none of his sons was in a position to aid him. He died in September 1841.

Through his mixture of negligence and complaisance, both carried to a culpable degree, he had done Byron much pecuniary injury. 'It is a great disadvantage to me to have such a solicitor', Byron himself wrote. 'However, he was made so when I was ten years old and I have no help for it.'[4] He transferred

---

[1] Murray MS. 12 Feb.   [2] Ibid. 30 Nov.
[3] Ibid. 8 Mar.   [4] Murray MS. 13 Sept. 1821.

as much of his business as he could to the hands of the recipient of this letter, the Hon. Douglas Kinnaird, who had his Power of Attorney. Considering his natural irascibility, he had been extraordinarily patient with delays and oversights of every kind and proportionately grateful when any affair was handled with speed and effectiveness.

As for Hanson, he remained devotedly attached to the memory of his rash and headstrong but illustrious client, and at one time contemplated writing a book about him—particularly, Hobhouse noted, about his life from eight to eighteen 'which he says was the most interesting of his existence'.[1] It is a great pity he did not work up the energy—or receive sufficient encouragement from Hobhouse—to do it, because he knew more about Byron's boyhood than anyone then living.

APPENDIX 4

'Old Joe Murray'

The Byrons' unvarying consideration for this aged and generally inactive retainer provides an interesting example of the patriarchal attitude which was widespread in the upper classes when servants were still part of the family. Mrs Byron might find him trying but she never suggested actually getting rid of him. Augusta too regarded him as a personal responsibility.

'Old Murray' was above sixty when Byron, aged ten, took him over with Newstead Abbey. Byron gives his age as seventy-four in 1811, which places the date of his birth at about 1737. He had entered the 5th Lord's service a year or two before the latter's trial in 1765 for killing his cousin and neighbour, William Chaworth, in a duel. Byron must have learned a great deal of what he knew about his forbears from him.

When Mrs Byron moved to Southwell, she found herself unable to keep a butler, but Augusta, though she feared even then, in 1804, that he was too old and infirm to go into new service, procured him a place with the Duchess of Leeds, her eldest half-brother's wife. He had shocked her by applying to Colonel Leigh, her fiancé, to ask the Prince of Wales 'to get him into some *City Charity*!'[2] After he was given notice by the Duchess in 1807, Byron, no matter how hard up he was himself, managed to find £20 a year for him, and, on resuming possession of the Abbey, wrote to Augusta: 'Joseph Murray is at the head of my household, poor honest fellow! I should be a great Brute, if I

---

[1] Hobhouse, *Journals*. 5 Jan. 1830.   [2] Murray MS. Letter to Hanson, 17 June.

had not provided for him in the manner most congenial to his own feelings, and to mine.'[1]

As long as Byron was owner, he was still butler at Newstead, and Moore records that while dining, with Murray standing behind his chair, he would pass a glass of wine over his shoulder to him. Though he was commonly referred to as 'poor old Murray', and seemed in those days of shorter life spans incredibly ancient, he recovered 'of a disease that would have killed a troop of horse, he promises to bear away the palm of longevity from Old Parr'.[2]

That his disposition was of the kindest is attested by his letters, in particular one pleading for Robert Rushton when the page, aged fifteen, was found to have been visiting a London brothel with Fletcher. Byron was enraged: having frequented brothels himself, he knew of the risks and squalors, which would be magnified in such haunts as the valet could afford. He dashed off an angry letter to his mother, and dispatched the boy back to Newstead with Fletcher, in disgrace, withdrawing his promise that Rushton should be taken abroad with him. On May 24th 1809 the old servant sat down and laboriously wrote:

My Lord,

      I Beg your Lordship will please to accept My humble duty. Am happy to hear you are well. Pray My Lord Excuse the liberty I take in giving you the Trouble of this which is only to say, how Sory I am that Robert offended your Lordship with his bad conduct as knowing how good your Lordship has been to him it reminds me of the Very Reason you gave for not Taking him with you before to Town, but Youth is easy to be Misled Where there is so great Temptation. I have not had the opportunity to speak to the Lad as yet upon it—I was Astonished when I was tould he was come home and Will[m]. with him but in the Very Moment next I was Rejoyc'd as thinking your Lordship was Coming—but poor boy the Moment he saw me his poor heart was Allmost broken and burst in a flood of Tears.

      My Lord I beg one Word further to say I have flattered myself very much with the thoughts of seeing you Once more before you left England you tould Me you might very probaly send for me up if you staid a Month in town—which I should be very happy if it suited your Lordship so to do.

      I am in duty bound

            Yours at command

                Jos[h]. Murray[3]

Of course Byron forgave the erring ones, and took Rushton, Fletcher and his aged butler as well on his first voyage. Murray was born to service and had no feeling that it was undignified to be so employed. He could end a letter without self-consciousness: 'My Lord I am in duty bound to Pray for your Lordships

---

[1] Marchand, *Letters*. 14 Dec. 1808.
[2] Ibid. Byron to Augusta, 30 Aug. 1811.   [3] Murray MS.

Goodness showd to me at All Times. . . . I remain Your Faithfull and Obedient Ser.ᵗ to command till Death.'[1]

In 1813, when Byron was contemplating fresh travels, James Wedderburn
Webster suggested taking both Murray and Rushton on at Aston Hall in Yorkshire. Byron replied that Rushton might do, but Murray, while 'honest and
faithful', was 'fearfully superannuated' and as he hadn't been in Webster's
family fifty years, Webster had no obligation to him.[2]

When the Abbey had been sold abortively to Thomas Claughton, it was Murray who packed up his master's portrait by Sanders, keeping it dry and 'in
great perfection' and who sealed up cases of letters including Mrs Byron's
japanned writing-desk, and sent him his 'best Oppera hat & Feather' and the
Turk's cap he had bought abroad, while Rushton and Fletcher's wife cleared
the contents of his dressing-room, except for the things he had worn for his
boxing practice. It must have been a profound grief for Murray, after half a
century's unremitting attachment to the family, to anticipate the passing of his
noble home into the hands of an unmannerly Lancashire lawyer; and he was
proportionately joyful when he heard the transaction was called off:

> My Lord pray give me leave to say I Never in all my Life was more Glad
> than to hear and to have the Pleasure of once more Seeing Your Lordship
> again at Newstead. . . . You may depend upon it my Lord I shall Never
> leave Newstead till I have your Lordships express orders to do so.[3]

Unhappily, those orders had eventually to be given. But after Byron became
domiciled abroad, he continued to insist that Hanson—ever neglectful—should
pay Murray both wages and board wages; and when he had got most of his
affairs into the hands of his much more punctual friends, Hobhouse and Kinnaird, he wrote to Hobhouse: '. . . By the way, *old Joe* must not be forgotten.
I give Carte blanche about him—*but let him above all have all possible* comforts
& requisites in any case.'[4]

Murray was then in his eighties. He died in 1820 and Byron was much
depressed by the news. He had been cherished as a piece of family history, and,
beyond that, his qualities of steadiness and good nature had won the lasting,
uncynical affection of an insecure little boy facing a new, intimidating world.

It must be added that, according to an old servant interviewed by Washington Irving,[5] although he 'made a most respectable appearance', being extremely
neat in his dress, nothing would stop Joe Murray from singing ribald and pro-
fane songs even in the most unsuitable company. Perhaps that was the reason
why he was dismissed by the Duchess of Leeds. He seems to have had a considerable repertoire, and this too may have awakened ideas in the mind of his young

[1] Ibid. 27 Feb. 1813.   [2] *LJ.* 2 Sept.   [3] Murray MS. 16 June 1814.
[4] Ibid. 27 May 1818.   [5] *Newstead Abbey*, 1835.

master—who went so far as to commission a portrait of him, which still hung in the mansion when Irving went there, and can be seen there to this day.

The Newstead Furniture

Contrary to the idea we vaguely receive from most books about Byron, the non-monastic part of his house during his adult years was not in a state of romantic decay, but the last word in smart furnishing, carried out chiefly in anglicized French Empire taste, to which the war then opposed no patriotic barrier. In fact, 'French' is repeatedly used as a commendation in the catalogue made in 1815 for an auction sale which was cancelled within two days of taking place. When Byron wrote to his mother that she could not object to his rendering his mansion 'habitable' (7 Oct. 1808), he was postponing the disclosure of what luxurious appointments he had ordered in anticipation of entertaining his friends with fashionable distinction. It is probable, however, that he left the choice of details to his principal supplier, the luckless Mr Brothers, for he himself had so little of the interior decorator in his composition that he hardly touches upon the appearance of the rooms in any of the great English houses he frequented, impressive though many must have been; while the literal description of Newstead Abbey—as Norman Abbey—in *Don Juan* is wholly confined to antiquarian features.

The modern ones, which had cost his mother and his local creditors a world of anxiety, had had the minimum of wear when he parted with Newstead. His wife never saw these transient household gods until she visited the Abbey after their separation, and he scarcely alludes to them.

The inventory that Farebrothers of Beaufort Buildings in the Strand printed for the intended sale of October 1815, which was to have taken three days, enables us to form a nearly exact estimate of what rooms in the house were used, however slightly, and what they contained. The accommodation consisted of drawing room, library, two dining rooms, breakfast parlour (or study), grand hall, stone parlour, servants' hall, housekeeper's room, footman's room, butler's pantry, kitchen, scullery, brew house, larder, beer cellar and wine cellars, long spacious galleries on the first floor, eight principal bedrooms, some with dressing-rooms, and, on the top floor, many sizeable attics.

Colonel Wildman, the eventual purchaser of the estate, kept Byron's bedroom more or less intact. Other furnishings too were in their place when the transaction was begun, because in the following year, 1818, Lady Byron wrote

that 'the apartments which he inhabited were in every respect the same—he might have walked in. They looked not deserted'. And she mentioned his fencing sword and singlesticks still standing on a table.[1] His bed, according to long-prevailing tradition, is the one he brought from Trinity College, and he must have meant to keep it. There are two coroneted beds in the catalogue, but neither corresponds to the one with the mock bamboo posts which may still be seen in his room. They were, judging by the descriptions, more sumptuous:

> Lot 131. A very superb (five feet six) double screwed FOUR-POST BED-STEAD, on French castors; the feet posts carved, and finished in burnished gold; rich pattern FURNITURE, lined with yellow; full green silk and yellow draperies, rich SILK French fringe, gilt cornice, surmounted by a carved coronet, lines, tassels, &c.

This bed had three mattresses, one filled with straw, one horsehair, and one of goose feathers, with bolster and two pillows, 'three *fine* and large blankets', and a Marseilles quilt (i.e. stiff, tightly woven cotton, figured). The curtains were not merely ornamental but kept out the perilous night air. The State Room bed was still grander:

> A superb LOFTY double screwed six-feet FOUR-POST BEDSTEAD, on French castors, the pillars japanned and richly gilt, with RICH CRIMSON furniture, folding VELVET and scarlet draperies and valence, with doom top, richly studded, surmounted by a Coronet, and the draperies richly fringed with scarlet and black French fringe, with tassels, &c. supported by carved Eagles, superbly gilt.[2]

Here there were four mattresses, straw, wool, horsehair, and finally 'very capital' goose feathers. Before the introduction of springs, layer upon layer of bedding was required to promote the slumbers of the gentry, and each four-poster had steps beside it like a mounting-block. In all the bedrooms the window curtains were *en suite* with the bed draperies and had elaborate pelmets beneath gilded cornices. The State Room material was crimson, and thickly fringed swags hung over 'a battle axe cornice'—appropriate for the 'doom top' of the bed. There was a scarlet and black carpet, six black and gold japanned

---

[1] Quoted by Mayne. Lady Byron had gone to the Abbey incognita and questioned the woman who showed her round, eliciting the information that Byron had been 'very loving' to his sister, and accepting with typical credulity the criticism that he had never given a thought to charity. The only female in attendance at the time is likely to have been Mrs Mealey.

[2] Several Victorian guide books call attention to a state bed (now gone) of much earlier type, surmounted by ostrich plumes and decorated with the finest French silk needlework centuries old. We hear nothing of this one during Byron's residence, though it was said to have had family associations and, with his respect for antiquity, I doubt if Byron would have displaced such an heirloom. It may have been installed by a subsequent owner and attributed by legend to the Byrons. The state bed provided by the poet was certainly in the Napoleonic style.

chairs with cushion seats in scarlet covers welted with black and studded, and a japanned and gilded dressing-table and chest-of-drawers with lion's head handles. It sounds rather a portentous room. As the best guest room, it was probably the one Augusta occupied.

The Chintz Room, the most fully furnished for residence, was perhaps Mrs Byron's. It was, judging by the size of the carpet, the largest. Besides a handsome double bed with green-lined draperies, two sets of bedsteps and two chamber cupboards—one for each side—it had a mahogany night table with drawers, 'an excellent mahogany dressing table', a chest of drawers on French feet, a full-length swing mirror, a hand mirror, a corner washstand, basin and ewer, and two 'soap glasses', an octagonal reading table, 'an elegant japanned cheffonier BOOKCASE, the under part enclosed with wire doors and yellow curtains, six neat japanned CHAIRS . . . en suite with the bed furniture', and a pair of coloured drawings in gold frames.

The bath tub and the airing horse belonged no doubt to the adjacent dressing room, and the brass bedstead numbered with the same series of lots may have been used by Mrs Byron's personal maid, Mrs Bye.

Off the Clock Gallery there were two bedrooms, each with a four-foot tent bedstead and cotton draperies, and a Pink Room with a 'very elegant' four-poster, having fringed and valanced pink hangings of French cotton. Four mock bamboo chairs seem to have strayed here out of Byron's bedroom, the rest of the copious furniture being mahogany. A field bedstead with full complement of mattresses, blankets, and quilt, had possibly been the one allotted to Rushton.

A guidebook of 1813, by an author whose visit was made in 1811 while Byron was in the house just after his mother's death,[1] mentions that what had once been the Singing Room for the practice of choristers had now been fitted up 'very handsomely' for a bath. There was no bathroom in the current sense, but every bedroom had its washstand with china set, and bidets in mahogany cases were supplied for all. It is not likely that, among all his modernizations, Byron had overlooked the opportunity of having a water closet—he was particularly keen on this invention—but it naturally has no place in the catalogue of furniture.

The great old refectory of Tudor and Stuart times had been used by Byron as an empty space for his fencing and other bodily exercises, but the inventory lists the contents of the Blue Dining Hall and the Abbey Dining Room. The second was curtained and upholstered in crimson and had a high fender, a fire guard, and polished fire irons, equipment lacking in the blue room, which I fancy was used only in summer. Here there was a pair of glazed bookcases eight feet high, with mahogany steps to reach the upper shelves, a

[1] The Nottinghamshire section of *The Beauties of England and Wales* by F. C. Laird, who tells us that Mrs Byron's personal things were still entirely untouched in her room when it was shown to him by Joe Murray.

green baize bordered carpet, and a 'very capital set of Mahogany DINING TABLES *on pillars* with lions' claw castors'. These could be joined to make one table seventeen feet long. It had fourteen 'fine English oak chairs, neatly ornamented', with stuffed seats and backs, finished in red and black velvet, and two ottomans in the same style as well as a matching couch. Lot 86 was 'a massy and truly elegant SIDEBOARD richly inlaid and ornamented', and Lot 87 'a superb CELLARET en suite'. A pair of bronze Grecian tripods supported the patent lamps on the sideboard.

Mrs Byron had kept fires going during her son's long absence lest the new wallpapers should be spoiled by damp. The Blue Dining Hall may have been so called because its paper hangings were of that colour. A table service of 'blue and white Roman pattern' seems to have been part of this scheme.

Byron's vinous dinners with his male cronies took place mostly in winter, and as Harness mentions the glow of crimson in the firelight,[1] the Abbey Dining Room was obviously the scene of these festivities. The main items were fourteen mahogany chairs with carved backs and upholstery of gilt-stamped leather, two similar ottomans and a sideboard en suite, six feet long, with carved legs, a first-rate solid mahogany two-flap dining-table, a richly gilded carved eagle on a scarlet and gold stand, a carved and gilt girandole for two lights (there were doubtless many table candlesticks), and a japanned scarlet and gold plate warmer—very necessary because the food had to be brought from some distance.

There was an abundance of plates, dishes, tureens, sauceboats, china fruit baskets, tea and coffee services, glass cruets, jugs, finger bowls, dessert plates, butter dishes, custard cups, and wine glasses and decanters, 'richly cut', and 'diamond cut'. The wine cellar still held about twenty dozen quart bottles of port, one dozen more which had been fourteen years in bottle, to be sold singly, four dozen of '*particularly* fine Bucellas' and twenty quarts of Priniac [? Preignac][2] also intended to be sold by the bottle, with thirty-four of white and six of red Hermitage, and twenty-four of 'very curious *old Madeira*', fifteen years in bottle. There are no spirits on the list: Byron must have kept his brandy, which he was drinking too freely during this period, at Piccadilly Terrace.

In the library the capacious bookcases were empty. What remained of his costly collection of books (he had been obliged to have a sale of them in 1813) was packed up or was in London, destined after he left England to be dispersed by creditors. Nothing could have suggested more comfort for a reader than the library tables, the 'sopha' upholstered in horsehair with attractively covered cushions and two little bolsters, the French window curtains lined with yellow —most fashionable of colours—the mahogany sideboard fitted with a cellaret,

---

[1] See p. 165.
[2] Bucellas is a Lisbon white wine in much favour at the date; Preignac one of the Sauternes usually listed with Barsac. Prignac, a claret, is a possible alternative.

the gilded flower stands, the fancy painted cups for chocolate, the shiny appurtenances of the fireplace, all reflected in 'a brilliant plate PIER GLASS' with a burnished gold frame.

Byron's admiration for Fox was shown in two likenesses of him, one marble, one a framed print which had been given him by Hobhouse. The most nostalgic of men, he had several coloured engravings of scenes at Harrow and of Cambridge colleges. The taste for sculpture, which always meant more to him than painting, was indicated by three busts, Milton, Cicero, and another whose identity baffled the cataloguer.

In both the library and the drawing-room there were fitted carpets with fringed hearth-rugs. The drawing-room had three window seats with cushions matching the French curtains, and a scroll-ended couch upholstered in the same fabric, as were the six lacquer and gilt armchairs and two library chairs: but a pair of ottomans with gilded ornaments were covered in black velvet. A wide triple mirror overmantel, a gold-framed pier glass, a pair of firescreens 'in imitation of old Japan', two glass lustres 'with spangle drops', and six paintings, three being seascapes and one an Annunciation declared in the inventory to be 'fine', were the chief adornments. A drawing, framed and glazed, of 'Mr Jackson the Boxer' may have been a souvenir from that admired mentor.

I believe the catalogue may have given the disused title, breakfast parlour, to what was really Byron's study, another room that Colonel Wildman kept for some years much as his predecessor had left it. The listed furniture is in no way appropriate for a breakfast room. The framework of the 'elegant sopha' was ornate with four carved eagles, and there were bronze eagles as candle-holders. Two ottomans mounted on gilt balls were upholstered in black velvet; either he or Mr Brothers had an enthusiasm for that sombre material. All this sounds ponderous, but the bright fireplace with a pier glass, another mirror in a carved and gilded frame with branches for candles, a china flower stand painted with landscapes, a cushioned window seat between graceful curtains, and a set of coloured prints entitled Rural Felicity, must have lightened the effect. A table with rising desk top, four lacquered chairs, some pictures of colleges and their founders, and two other tables, neither of them suitable for the service of a meal, combine to give the impression of a writing room. Byron, always a late riser, was no addict of hearty breakfasts.

The enormous Grand Hall I take to have been the first apartment the visitor entered. A flight of stone steps led up to it which Colonel Wildman removed, preferring to have the main entrance on a lower level. Four large octagonal lamps hanging on chains, a sideboard, a few chairs, some 56-foot lengths of floor covering, and 'a capital painting of a Wolf Dog'—these were all the items the Grand Hall boasted unless some were withheld from the projected sale; for example, the portrait of the Newfoundland Boatswain to whom Byron had erected a monument in the garden. In the event both Boatswain

wrong in my theory as to why Byron retained Mary's letter—if he did retain it—accounts for the meetings between Claire and Elise which were so numerous and so unhappy as late as the spring of 1822, and for Claire's writing, in 'miserable spirits', on March 10th that she had given 'the Naples commission' to Elise's husband, and again for the letter she sent to Mary on April 9th: 'I wish you would write me back what you wish Elise to say to you and what she is to say to Mad. Hoppner. I have tried in vain to compose it.'[1]

The outcome of all this pressure and possibly bribery—for what sort of 'commission' does one give to a detested conspirator and blackmailer?—was a letter from Elise to Mrs Hoppner saying she had never seen anything in the least reprehensible in the conduct of Mlle Clairmont, but evading altogether the topic of Shelley and the Foundling Hospital, and a barefaced sweeping disclaimer to Mary of ever having reported any 'horrors' at all about any of them.[2]

It is one of those ironies in which the converging stories of Byron and Shelley abound that, when the drama related by Hoppner found its way into print long after their deaths, it was Byron, thanks to the unusual discretion he had observed, who emerged as the villain of the piece with Shelley as the stainless Galahad he had wronged—wronged by a mean little act which has less plausibility than any other recorded of him.

APPENDIX 11

The Shelley Furniture

In the tale of his victimization by Byron, Hunt says the furniture provided for him was the 'plainest and cheapest' consistent with being 'good and respectable', and he might hardly have conceded those merits had he not been obliged to admit that 'it was chosen by Mr Shelley' and was similar to what Shelley used himself. This is the list of Shelley's furniture that Byron took over at a valuation:

	Crowns	Pauls
1 iron bed	60	
1 chest of drawers, cherry wood	9	
1 press of deal do. for hanging clothes	8	
1 nutwood table	8	
1 „ „ smaller	5	
1 work table	2	
1 sopha with horsehair	10	
1 settee	3	

[1] Letter quoted by Stocking.   [2] Both in *Correspondence.*

	Crowns	Pauls
1 sopha with cushions	8	
8 chairs with cushions	8	
6 cherry wood chairs	1	9
6 pieces of carpet	30	
1 filtering machine	3	
1 Argan lamp	3	
1 table carpet	1	
1 cherry wood table		6
	160	5[1]

A second list brings the total to the 221 crowns 4 pauls for which Mary signed a receipt:

	Crowns	Pauls
1 servant's bed	7	5
1 chest of nutwood drawers	9	
1 cherry wood table	1	5
1 writing table	8	
1 dozen nutwood chairs	6	6
6 cherry wood chairs	1	8
1 toilet looking-glass	2	5
1 sopha bed	24	
	60	9[2]

On this separate page we find in Mary's handwriting:

List of what I have sent to Casa Lanfranchi—but which I wish to be given into Hunt's care to be forwarded to me at Genoa.

The sopha bed at 24 crowns, the most expensive of these articles, was actually set apart and the price deducted from the reckoning, but not for some reason from the amount Byron paid. We should be wrong, however, to conclude it was the 'sopha' that he wished to keep, telling her it was not part of her furniture—'it was purchased by me at Pisa since you left it'—because that one, he said, was worth 'only about 12 pauls', a twentieth part of the price set on the other, which must have been a very good piece, bearing in mind that 'a sopha with cushions' was assessed at 8 crowns and a settee at 3, and that chairs could be had for little more than half a crown each. (The comparatively huge valuation of the iron bed, 60, can only be accounted for on the supposition that it was highly modern, and excellent of its kind.) 'I preferred retaining the purchased furniture', Byron wrote, 'but always intended that you should have as good or better in its place.' And then he made his famous remark about disliking 'any thing of Shelley's being within the same walls as Mrs Hunt's children . . . dirtier and more mischievous than Yahoos'.[3]

[1] 46878 Folio 9. In Mary's handwriting.   [2] Ibid. Folio 10.
[3] *LJ*. 6 Oct. 1822. It seems virtually certain, in view of Hunt's passionate defensiveness about his children when assailing Byron's memory, that Mary, during her alliance with him against Byron, repeated or showed him this unguarded but not unprovoked criticism.

Until I saw Mary's receipt, I thought Byron was behaving in a very high-handed manner, but then it became clear that 'the purchased furniture' he retained must have been that about which she had written her peremptory note after sending the items over to his house so that he could dispatch them to Genoa. Her dictating what he was to do with what was now his own property must have grated on him extremely, like her lecturing letters telling him how he ought to treat Hunt. There are several evidences that Mary's manners, like Claire's, were not those of a well-bred person. Their upbringing by such a woman as Mrs Godwin, vulgar in everyone's eyes, could not have instilled tact.

Selective Bibliography

N.B. This list does not include books or articles in periodicals which have been adequately identified in text or footnotes, except those to which reference has been made several times.[1] Sources of letters (other than Byron's own) which have been very frequently printed are given only when a recent editor has provided a fuller or more correct rendering than previous versions. Manuscript sources are named in footnotes throughout.

Biagi, Dr Guido, *The Last Days of Percy Bysshe Shelley*, New Details from Unpublished Documents. 1898

Blessington, Countess of, *The Idler in Italy*, 2 vols. 1839
Journal of the Conversations of Lord Byron. 1834

Broughton, The Rt. Hon. Lord. See Hobhouse

Byron, Lord, *The Poetical Works, Life and Letters*, edited by E. H. Coleridge and R. E. Prothero, 13 vols. (herein referred to as *Poetry* and *LJ*). 1898/1904

Clarke, Isabel C., *Shelley and Byron, A Tragic Friendship*. 1934

Cline, C. L., *Byron, Shelley and Their Pisan Circle*. 1952

Dallas, R. C., *Recollections of the Life of Lord Byron from the Year 1808 to the end of 1814*. 1824

Finlay, George, L. L. D., *History of the Greek Revolution*. 1861

Gamba, Count Peter, *A Narrative of Lord Byron's Last Journey to Greece*. 1825

Gordon, Pryse Lockhart, *Sketches from the Portfolio of a Sexagenarian*, New Monthly Magazine. 1829

Grylls, R. Glynn, *Claire Clairmont, Mother of Byron's Allegra*. 1939
Mary Shelley, A Biography. 1938

[Guiccioli, Countess] *My Recollections of Lord Byron*. 1869. Translated from the French by Hubert E. H. Jerningham, *La Vie de Lord Byron en Italie*, MS in the Biblioteca Classense, Ravenna, partly published.

Hobhouse, J. C., *A Journey through Albania and other Provinces of Turkey in Europe and Asia . . . during the Years 1809 and 1810*, 2 vols. 1812
Recollections of a Long Life, edited by his daughter Lady Dorchester, 6 vols. 1909/1911

Hunt, Leigh, *Lord Byron and Some of his Contemporaries*. 1828
The Correspondence of, edited by his eldest son, 2 vols. 1862

---

[1] A more comprehensive bibliography will be found in *The Late Lord Byron*. 1961.

Jeaffreson, John Cordy, *The Real Lord Byron*, 2 vols. 1883
Jones, Frederick L. (editor), *Mary Shelley's Journal*. 1947
   Maria Gisborne and Edward E. Williams, Shelley's Friends, Their Letters and Journals. 1951
   The Letters of Mary Shelley, 2 vols. 1944
   The Letters of Percy Bysshe Shelley, 2 vols. 1964
Kennedy, James, M. D., *Conversations on Religion with Lord Byron and others held in Cephalonia a Short Time Previous to His Lordship's Death*. 1830
Knight, G. Wilson, *Lord Byron's Marriage, The Evidence of Asterisks*. 1957
Lovelace, 2nd Earl of, *Astarte, A Fragment of the Truth Concerning George Gordon, Sixth Lord Byron*. 1905
Marchand, Leslie A., *Byron, A Biography*, 3 vols. 1957
Marchand, Leslie A. (editor), *In my Hot Youth*, Byron's Letters from 1798 to 1810, and *Famous in my Time*, Letters from 1810 to 1812 (herein both volumes are referred to as 'Marchand, *Letters*'). 1973
Mayne, Ethel C., *The Life and Letters of Anna Isabella Lady Byron*. 1929
Medwin, Thomas, *Journals of the Conversations of Lord Byron Noted during a Residence with his Lordship at Pisa in the Years 1821 and 1822*. 1824
   The Angler in Wales, or Days and Nights of a Sportsman (contains the account of Byron by Surgeon Daniel Forrester, R.N.), 2 vols. 1834
Millingen, Julius, *Memoirs of the Affairs of Greece*. 1831
Moore, Thomas, *Letters and Journals of Lord Byron with Notices of his Life*, 2 vols. 1830/1831
Murray, John (editor), *Lord Byron's Correspondence chiefly with Lady Melbourne, Mr Hobhouse, the Hon. Douglas Kinnaird, and P. B. Shelley*, 2 vols. (herein referred to as *Correspondence*). 1922
Nicolson, Harold, *Byron, The Last Journey*. 1924
Origo, Iris, *The Last Attachment*. 1949
Parry, William, *The Last Days of Lord Byron with His Lordship's Opinions on Various Subjects*, etc. 1825
Paston. See Quennell
Pratt, Willis W., *Byron at Southwell, The Making of A Poet*. 1948
Prothero, R. E., *The Childhood and Schooldays of Byron*, article in The Nineteenth Century. 1898
Quennell, Peter (editor), *Byron, A Self-Portrait*, 2 vols. 1950
   (with George Paston) '*To Lord Byron*', *Feminine Profiles based upon unpublished letters*. 1939
Rogers, Samuel, *Recollections and Table Talk*, edited by the Rev. Alexander Dyce. 1887
Romilly, S. H., *Letters to 'Ivy' from the First Earl of Dudley*. 1905
St Clair, William, *That Greece Might Still be Free*. 1972

Smiles, Samuel, L. L. D., *A Publisher and His Friends, Memoirs and Corres-pondence of the late John Murray*. 1891

Stanhope, The Hon. Col. Leicester, *Greece in 1823 and 1824, being a series of Letters and Other Documents on the Greek Revolution*. 1825

Symon, J. D., *Byron in Perspective*. 1924

Trelawny, Edward J., *Recollections of the Last Days of Shelley and Byron*. 1858
Records of Shelley, Byron and the Author. 1878
Letters, edited by H. Buxton Forman. 1910

White, Newman Ivey, *Shelley*, 2 vols. 1947

Spurious

Don Leon, A Poem by the Late Lord Byron . . . to which is added *Leon to Annabella* (apparently written in the 1830s, printed much later). No date

Index